The Ethnic Dimension
in American History

THE ETHNIC DIMENSION IN AMERICAN HISTORY

James Stuart Olson

Sam Houston State University

ST. MARTIN'S PRESS • New York

To my father and mother, and
To our Norwegian, Swedish, and English ancestors

Library of Congress Catalog Card Number: 78–65208
Copyright © 1979 by St. Martin's Press, Inc.
All Rights Reserved.
Manufactured in the United States of America.
32109
fedcba
For information, write St. Martin's Press, Inc.,
175 Fifth Avenue, New York, N. Y. 10010

Cover design by Jack McCurdy

Maps by Clarice Borio, New York City

cloth ISBN: 0-312-26611-1
paper ISBN: 0-312-26612-X

Preface

As a boy, I returned to California from a visit with my Norwegian and Swedish grandparents in Minnesota to discover that Jerry Pete, a Navajo boy, had moved next door. For the next ten years we were friends, even though I could never fathom the pull that the reservation in Arizona exerted on him and his family. My neighbor on the other side, Sammy Mester, was an Italian-American boy who attended the St. John Bosco parochial school. In my own elementary school the principal was Edward Beaubier, a descendant of French immigrants; and our family doctor was Zoltan Puskas, a tyrannical, Magyar-accented refugee from Hungary. George Beatag, a Rumanian-American, was my fifth-grade teacher, and I remember his proudly telling me that in all of America there was only one Beatag family. In high school my English teacher was Mitsue Maeda, who first told me of the Japanese-American relocation camps of World War II; and on the football and basketball teams I played with Dave Ronquillo and Ron Alvarez (Mexican-Americans), Sam Abajian (Armenian), Dean Chikami (Japanese), Michael James Patrick Clark (Irish), Tom Overholtzer (German), Mike Tortolini (Italian), and Dirk Bogaard (Dutch).

Eventually I married Judy Mehr (Swiss-American), and we lived for several years in Rocky Point, New York, a largely Italian colony on suburban Long Island. Among our friends and colleagues were Paul Bottino (northern Italian), Reed Johnson (Swedish), Herbert Zolot

(Russian Jew), Roberta Brown (English-Japanese-Polynesian), Eleanor Toon (Polynesian), Dirk Hooiman (Dutch), Olga Hooiman (Serb), Kaethe Paetz and Herbert Holtzer (German Jew), Joseph Marasco (Italian Jew), Wini Marasco (Japanese), and Heinz Phaff (German). In the history department at Sam Houston State University I have taught with scholars like Richard Yasko (Polish), James Hagerty (Irish), and Edward Chien (Chinese). Our students come from the Mexican-American barrios and black ghettos of Houston and Dallas; the German, Czech, Polish, and Cajun farming colonies of western Louisiana and eastern Texas; and the English and Scots-Irish neighborhoods of small southern towns. In the evenings my wife teaches English to Kiem Pham (Vietnamese), Emiliana Lopez (Ecuadorian), Etelvina Floyd (Panamanian), Samira Saqr (Egyptian), Maythe Al-Fohaid (Saudi Arabian), and Fatomeh-Aminian (Iranian).

What really is extraordinary about all this is that my odyssey with American pluralism is probably the rule rather than the exception. Most people who have lived in the United States for even a short period of time also have friends and acquaintances with a similar variety of ethnic backgrounds. And the American past, at virtually every turn in our history, profoundly reflects that pluralism, as will, no doubt, the American future.

For years I have taught the course "Ethnic Minorities in American History," but I was never able to find a text which exactly filled my needs. There has been no dearth of literature on American ethnic history; indeed, the topic has been a national obsession since the early 1960s, and the "Roots" and "Holocaust" television spectaculars in 1977 and 1978 clearly illustrated the continuing American fascination with the ethnic past. There are hundreds of volumes about individual ethnic groups; many others on such topics as abolition, riots, wars, relocations, laws, and social movements; and still others on immigration, religion, racism, nativism, and American culture. My teaching problem, however, was that no single text attempted a real synthesis. I wanted a book that not only described Afro-American, native American, Hispanic American, and European-American group life but also placed all of those accounts in the larger context of United States history. In *The Ethnic Dimension in American History* I have tried to fill that need.

Writing the book has been a formidable challenge. Problems of space and organization have been the most serious, and no single ethnic group has been given enough coverage to do it justice. But my purpose has not been to give comprehensive coverage to every ethnic group; such a project would fill libraries. Instead, I wanted to construct a reasonably complete picture of the major groups that have peopled America and show how their presence here has affected public policy. It will no doubt appear to many readers that I have given too much coverage to Indians, blacks, Hispanic Americans, and Asians (fourteen chapters) and too little to the white ethnic groups (eleven chapters). Actually, in terms of words, as much space has been devoted to white ethnics as to racial minorities. But given the size of the white majority, that may still seem too little. There was a reason for my decision. Since I wanted to survey the range of public debate through United States history, and because so much of that debate centered on the racial minorities, I decided to discuss blacks, Indians, Hispanic Americans, and Asian-Americans within each appropriate chronological period. The book is not just a history of American ethnic groups; it is also an ethnic history of American public life, and as such justifies expanded coverage of certain groups.

Several major assumptions governed my approach to the ethnic history of the United States. First, I am convinced, as many others are today, that the "melting pot" has not overtaken us and will not create an ethnically homogeneous society for many centuries. The forces of assimilation, of course, are as powerful today as ever before, but shifting coalitions of racial, ethnic, religious, and cultural values continue to create a pluralistic society. Second, I believe that the main sources of ethnicity are internal. Although discrimination and hostility from other groups may stimulate a sense of unity, the most powerful feelings of fidelity and security spring from the values and symbolic associations of the groups themselves. Internal perspectives, not external pressures, explain the continuity of group life in the United States. Finally, I believe that ethnicity is the central theme of American history, more important than the lack of an aristocracy, the existence of the frontier, the abundance of natural resources, the entrepreneurial impulses, or the isolated security behind two oceans. From the earliest confrontations between Europeans and native Americans in the 1600s to the United States Supreme Court's decision in the Bakke case, the pluralism of American society has shaped the course of public debate.

A number of people have helped me in the writing of this book, and I would like to express my appreciation to them. Many colleagues at Sam Houston State University read portions of the manuscript and offered suggestions that improved it. I am grateful especially to Lee Olm, David Anderson, John Payne, William Haynes, Thomas Camfield, Robert Shadle, Joseph Rowe, Gary Bell, Charles Frazier, and Barry Hayes. At St. Martin's Press, Bert Lummus and Carolyn Eggleston were especially helpful. I am deeply indebted to the hundreds of students who have passed through History 382 and provided invaluable insights into their own ethnic American histories. Finally, I am grateful to countless friends and strangers who have responded so graciously to my incessant questions about their surnames, family histories, and perspectives on American life.

James Stuart Olson
Huntsville, Texas

Contents

Part IV: CONFLICT AND CONTINUITY, 1945–PRESENT

Introduction: Ethnicity and Ethnic Relations in America

Because of their ethnic heritage and ideological values, Americans tend to think that the United States is more beset by ethnic conflicts than other countries. But ethnic politics in America is part of a global phenomenon. Today people everywhere are searching for identity and equality, and as "colored" people replace old deferences with new demands, white elites are witnessing an erosion of their traditional authority. The United States is clearly not the only country with ethnic problems.

What does set America apart is its ethnic diversity; a nation of minorities, it defies generalization. Within its boundaries nearly every major racial, religious, nationality, and language group on the planet has tried to achieve economic security and social order. Along with material plenty and economic success, ethnic pluralism is one of the organizing principles of American history and remains today a dominant theme in the way most Americans interpret their environment.

A precise definition of ethnicity is difficult because no set of characteristics is common to all groups; feelings of loyalty and community within groups rest on a variety of ties. In general, however, an ethnic group is a collection of people self-consciously united by physical similarities, cultural traditions, or common visions of the past and future. Skin color has been an especially powerful factor in the United States. Africans, native Americans (or Indians), Asians, and Hispanic Americans have often been segregated, excluded from wealth and power because of their darker skins. Blacks who three centuries ago came from African tribes with enormous differences in language and religion evolved into an ethnic community because of their common racial heritage and common destiny in America. Indians, Asians, and Hispanic Americans have also slowly acquired a self-conscious vision of mutual dependency within their communities.

Differences in nationality, religion, and language define group membership even more exactly. Europeans viewed native Americans as one group, but the Indian population consisted of hundreds of separate communities with completely different languages, religions, and customs, each tribe fired by an independent sense of destiny. The bonds of earth and soil, of region and locale, are central to community consciousness; people feel close to friends and neighbors, comfortable with others from their corner of the world. The region binding together immigrants to America was sometimes a country, as for the Irish; a province, as for the Germans and the Japanese; or even a village, as for the Italians and the Syrians. Language reinforces ethnicity. People sharing a verbal and gestural heritage communicate and resolve conflict more easily. Religion also unites people, sometimes even when they come from different backgrounds. The German, Galician, Russian, Hungarian, and Rumanian Jews immigrating to the United States all shared a historical and religious consciousness that was central to their ethnic identity.

In addition to customs, language, nationality, and religion, the immigration process itself contributed to the ethnic consciousness of European immigrants. In the peasant villages of the Old World life was closely circumscribed by personal relationships—in the family, church, and fields. People knew one another and felt secure. But that sense of community was lost in the migration to the industrial cities of the New World. Thus the pilgrimage helped create ethnicity. In the foods they ate, the holidays they celebrated, the way they raised families, and the subtle nuances of taste, morality, and religion, the immigrants found symbolic associations to preserve some of the way of life they had left behind.

Shared characteristics—whether of race, nationality, language, or religion—do not always produce ethnicity, however. Race was crucial in transforming African cultures into an organic whole in America, but it did not do the same for native Americans. Although Russian Jews and Russian Slavs, or the Irish and Scots-Irish, shared similar national origins, they never evolved into a cohesive ethnic community in America. The Irish and the English shared the same language but not the same sense of community; indeed, they were cultural enemies through much of American history. And although most Irish, Poles,

Czechs, Slovaks, Italians, Croatians, Slovenes, and Lithuanians were Roman Catholic, religion did not unite them ethnically. In short, shifting combinations of race, nationality, language, culture, and religion organized ethnic life in America, creating hundreds of culturally independent communities.

American Approaches to Ethnic Diversity

Over the years Americans have tried to cope with the heterogeneity of their society, seeking ways to fulfill egalitarian ideals while preventing ethnic conflict. The traditional and most rigid approach to diversity was "Anglo-conformity," the conviction that minorities should adopt the values of white Protestants. By rejecting and then forgetting their backgrounds, new immigrants and Indians would blend into the larger society and ethnic conflict would disappear. In the Dawes Act of 1887, for example, Congress tried to force native Americans to become small farmers by breaking up reservation land into small holdings. After World War I the "Americanization" movement sought to divest immigrants of their cultural heritage. Throughout the Southwest, teachers discouraged Mexican-American children from speaking Spanish in school. But minorities resented demands that they give up their ethnic identities. Had they done so, the surrender of language, religion, and culture would have left them naked in a strange environment, unable to interpret or adapt to their surroundings. A widely accepted ideology until 1945, Anglo-conformity with its implied derogation of other cultures has today fallen into disrepute.

A second view of cultural diversity was that America would act as a vast "melting pot" and a new culture would emerge from the amalgamation of minority groups. In 1909 the English playwright Israel Zangwill described the American melting pot:

> There she lies, the great melting pot—listen! can't you hear the roaring and the bubbling? There gapes her mouth—harbour where a thousand mammoth feeders come from the ends of the world to pour in their human freight. Ah, what a stirring and a seething—Celt and Latin, Slav and Teuton, Greek and Syrian, black and yellow . . .*

By embracing all groups and envisioning a new culture, the melting-pot ideology was more generous than Anglo-conformity, but its objectives were the same—cultural fusion and social stability.

But the melting pot produced no single culture shared by all Ameri-

*Israel Zangwill, *The Melting Pot* (New York, 1909), pp. 198–199.

cans. Indeed, it was naïve to think it ever would. For complete assimilation to have taken place, ethnic groups would have had to discard their cultural heritage, intermarry freely, lose their sense of national and religious peoplehood, and encounter no prejudice from other Americans. Obviously, assimilation stopped short of amalgamation, even though mass culture, mass education, economic prosperity, and geographic mobility have touched most people living in the United States. For immigrants, acculturation to American society (in the form of language, dress, transportation modes, holidays, use of the mass media, and consumerism) took place over several generations.

Frequently the first immigrants from a particular region experienced a period of culture shock when prejudice and the strangeness of American life threatened and confused them. To control their lives and deal with the new environment, they established their own schools, clubs, churches, newspapers, magazines, and fraternal societies, and largely confined their social life to those organizations. When the second generation adopted English and other American customs, ethnic organizations tried desperately to preserve Old World languages and loyalties. Intergenerational conflict in the immigrant communities was common, and native-born ethnics resented their parents' "parochial" attachment to the past as much as the parents disliked their children's "rebelliousness" and "disloyalty." The second generation's devotion to American customs often became exaggerated in response to their parents' conservatism. Then in the third and fourth generations major changes occurred: the Old World language was all but lost, membership in ethnic organizations was declining rapidly, acceptance of American ideas was becoming more complete, and many members of the group were acquiring middle- and upper-class status. Conflicts and fears about identity subsided and the descendents of the immigrants developed a comfortable interest in their heritage.

Although the pace of acculturation varied from group to group, it did set the stage for some forms of assimilation. At work, school, or in suburban neighborhoods the descendents of the immigrants established relationships with people from other ethnic backgrounds, and as these relationships developed over time, familial assimilation through intermarriage occurred more frequently. Over several generations of marital assimilation, forms of identificational assimilation based on groups much larger than the original immigrant groups appeared. Millions of Africans merged into a single Afro-American culture; Sicilians, Abruzzians, Calabrians, and Neapolitans evolved into Italian-Americans; Prussians, Bavarians, Hessians, and Palatinates became German-Americans; and Welsh, Scots, and English immigrants gradually formed an Anglo-American community.

Sociologists Ruby Jo Kennedy and Will Herberg believe that nationality mergers produced a triple melting pot of community identities based on Protestantism, Catholicism, and Judaism. Protestant immigrants from England, Germany, and Scandinavia have intermarried freely, and their descendents have lost touch with some of the more obvious expressions of their cultural heritage. This is especially true in the newer cities of the South and West, and in suburbs everywhere, where post–World War II migrations have blurred the ethnic distinctions so common in the East and Midwest. Jews from Germany, Russia, Poland, and Hungary merged into a self-conscious Jewish community. And among the Roman Catholic immigrants from Ireland, Germany, and eastern Europe, intermarriage has produced a large Roman Catholic group identity.

But distinctions based on race, religion, and class continue to sustain strong group identities. For blacks, Indians, Asians, and Hispanic Americans, there has been little marital assimilation, either with one another or with the larger European society. Discrimination based on color largely barred these people from most personal relationships with whites, so racial divisions remain the most visible separation in American society. Most Americans identify themselves in broad ethnic terms as whites, blacks, Indians, Asians, or Hispanic Americans. Within broad categories based on color, Americans also group themselves along religious lines. Millions of whites, proud of their Protestant, Catholic, or Jewish heritage, deliberately confine intimate relationships to members of their religious group. Asians and Indians may group themselves on the basis of Christian or non-Christian beliefs, and Hispanic Americans divide into Protestant and Catholic groups. And finally, within color and religious groupings, class divisions further retard assimilation. Sociologists are now, for example, describing a new "underclass" of desperately poor people alienated by extreme poverty from the rest of American society. Some Puerto Ricans in the South Bronx, some blacks on the South Side of Chicago, some Mexican-Americans in East Los Angeles, and some whites in Appalachia are so emotionally and culturally isolated that they feel affinities only for others in their racial, religious, and class status. Because of social ostracism, personal choice, or unconscious emotional needs, then, most Americans still claim membership in an ethnic community. The melting pot may be bubbling, but it is still a long way from creating an America of one race, one religion, and one culture. Pluralism, not complete assimilation, is the reality of life in the United States.

Recognition of that reality gave rise to the advocacy of cultural pluralism. Accepting each person's right to political and economic opportunity, cultural pluralists also uphold the right to affirm a special heritage. They exalt ethnic differences as the genius of American society, for although ethnic diversity guaranteed cultural conflict, it also prevented class conflict by dividing workers along ethnic lines and helped to stabilize American politics. Promoting equality and diversity, cultural pluralism is more tolerant than Anglo-conformity and more realistic than the melting pot.

Historians too are reconsidering ethnicity. For years most historians ignored ethnic minorities or treated them as troublesome, inferior people. According to many textbooks written before World War II, black people were happy, irresponsible children destined to serve white civilization. Either as noble savages or cruel beasts, native Americans were important only to measure the inevitability of white expansion. If blacks and Indians found a place in these textbooks, Mexican-Americans were invisible. Few scholars mentioned them. Finally, the immigrants from southern and eastern Europe were often dismissed as hopelessly backward though hardworking and colorful people. Until the 1940s, American history was primarily a history of white American Protestants.

But the history books changed as ethnic minorities pushed for equality after World War II. Some historians passionately condemned slavery, nativism (antiforeign sentiments), anti-Semitism, and anti-Catholicism. Even then, black people were usually significant only as the slaves of white racists; native Americans only as victims of the frontier juggernaut; or Slavs and Italians only as the butts of nativism. Ethnicity was still nothing more than a ghetto response to discrimination. Exaggerating the disruptive impact of the social environment on ethnic groups as well as the appeal of Anglo-American culture, historians focused on torment and conflict as the sources of ethnicity, ignoring cultural continuity with the Old World, the power of chain migrations, the intensity of religious nationalism, and competition among the immigrants themselves. They failed to see that ethnicity was as much a reconstitution of Old World visions of order and security as it was an accommodation to American society.

Recently this view too has been revised. Black society is studied as an independent, organic culture. Once seen as a morally disintegrating matriarchy, the black slave family is now believed to have been a relatively stable, two-parent institution. Historians are taking new interest in native American cultures as complex, tenacious ways of life. The whole field of Mexican-American history has opened up. And scholars are now revising old interpretations of migration, nationalism, ethnicity, and assimilation in European immigrant communities.

Cultural pluralism implies, of course, the indefinite survival of ethnic subcultures and their inevitable accompaniments—suspicion and prejudice. Prejudice is a state of mind in which a person negatively stereotypes the people of other groups, using his own background as the positive point of reference. And as long as prejudice exists, discrimination will continue as people act upon their emotional fears.

Forms of Discrimination

Discrimination assumes many forms. One form is verbal abuse. Some people may tell ethnic jokes; others repeat them maliciously. At its worst, verbal abuse is bitter and hateful. When Jackie Robinson first played with the Brooklyn Dodgers, he received intense abuse from fans and other players. In 1957, when the federal courts desegregated Central High School in Little Rock, Arkansas, black children encountered bitter verbal attacks as well as threats of violence. Verbal abuse also occurs when blacks use the terms "honkies" or "kikes."

Avoidance is another form of discrimination. Schoolchildren may consciously, or even unconsciously, segregate themselves at dances, games, and free periods. In restaurants and other public places Americans may congregate racially. The white flight to the suburbs is an example of avoidance; so are the antibusing protests in Detroit and Boston.

Discrimination can also involve unfair treatment of others, through either private or legal means. Segregation is formal discrimination, whether sanctioned by private custom or legal authority. Private restrictive practices are still common. Some private elementary and secondary schools in the South, for example, do not admit blacks, while fraternities, sororities, churches, clubs, and neighborhoods sometimes exclude certain ethnic groups. Restrictive practices go on in the labor market. Some minority groups have been relegated to menial, low-paying jobs. Even now black people are excluded from some of the most powerful construction unions. Federal courts are trying to decide where the right of one person to exclude others privately stops and where the right of the "others" to join begins. It will be a matter of controversy for years.

When the exclusion of certain groups is sanctioned by law, it is *de jure* segregation. From the 1880s through the early 1960s, southern blacks were subject to "Jim Crow" laws in schools, housing, hospitals, jobs, theaters, parks, restaurants, and transportation lines and depots. In the Southwest, Mexican-Americans were once unable to vote or hold public office because of restrictive laws. In the early 1900s Japanese-Americans were segregated in California schools, and during World War II they were confined in relocation camps. At one time or another most ethnic

groups have faced housing discrimination because of residential covenants and special zoning laws.

Although today *de jure* discrimination is dead, a more insidious form
of institutional discrimination involves admission and promotion pro-
cedures in government, business, and education. Admission and promotion in colleges, universities, medical schools, law schools, civil
service, and private corporations frequently depend on successful per-
formance on achievement tests. The tests, however, are usually written
by white middle-class scholars and are often culturally biased. People
from poor, rural, and non-English-speaking backgrounds cannot perform as well on the tests as middle-class whites. Although there is no
overt discrimination—every applicant is judged according to his or her
test score—the cumulative results favor whites. Since it is all but impossible to construct culture-free tests, other solutions to the problem have
been proposed, but they are extremely controversial. If, on the one
hand, admission and promotion quotas are established for minorities,
whites can legitimately claim that they are the victims of reverse discrimination. But if traditional criteria continue to be used, admission to
the top schools and the most lucrative and influential positions in
business and government will remain in the hands of middle-class
whites. Considering the debate over the end of *de jure* segregation in the
South, the controversy over institutional discrimination and affirmative
action promises to be even more prolonged.

Finally, discrimination can become violent. A Nazi group may van-
dalize a synagogue, or the Ku Klux Klan may burn a cross in the yard of a
black family. A Puerto Rican youth gang may wage "war" against a black
youth gang, while both groups may harass whites. An enraged mob may
join in a race riot over an alleged crime. Adolf Hitler's annihilation of 6
million Jews is the most destructive example of discrimination in recent
history. American history is free of outright large-scale genocide, except
perhaps in the warfare waged against native Americans in the
nineteenth century, when white attitudes at battles such as Sand Creek
and Wounded Knee came frighteningly close to a genocidal mania.

Sources of Prejudice

The intensity of prejudice depends on several conditions. In American
society color has been critically important. Northern Europeans (especially Protestants) have usually been readily accepted by the white
majority, and discrimination against them has been comparatively mild.
Discrimination against darker-skinned southern Europeans, such as the
Italians or the Greeks, has been more pronounced, as it has been for

Chinese, Japanese, and Filipino immigrants. And for the darkest-skinned people—blacks, some Puerto Ricans, native Americans, and Mexican-Americans—the road to success has been strewn with obstacles.

Cultural differences also contribute to prejudice. Presbyterians have been more tolerant of Baptists than of Catholics, and Protestants in general more tolerant of Christians than of Jews. Shared cultural values, such as language and religion, guarantee more tolerance. Spanish-speaking Puerto Ricans feel a greater affinity for Spanish-speaking Mexican-Americans than they do for English-speaking Anglos. It is not surprising that blacks, Indians, Hispanic Americans, and Asian-Americans have had more difficulty than other groups in dealing with whites in the United States.

Economic interests are another source of prejudice. Where one group is economically dependent upon exploiting a minority, prejudice will be more intense. Slavery is a good example. The southern economy before the Civil War depended on black slaves, and white planters opposed emancipation. Economic reality reinforced prejudice. Today, in the fruit and vegetable farms of California and southern Texas, the need for farm laborers has generated similar feelings about Mexican-Americans. The same was true for unskilled Chinese laborers in the nineteenth century and, to a lesser extent, for Scots-Irish indentured servants in the eighteenth century.

Economic mobility and job competition influence social tensions. In the textile factories of nineteenth-century New England, Irish and English workers bitterly resented Italians, Greeks, and Syrians because they depressed wages. Industrial workers hated black strikebreakers in the 1930s, and Mexican-American farm workers were alarmed at the immigration of Filipinos in the 1920s and 1930s. Today many whites resent federally mandated affirmative action programs.

Demography affects ethnic relations. If an ethnic group is small and scattered, prejudice is less intense. When 115,000 Vietnamese refugees settled widely across the country in 1975 and 1976, Americans expressed few misgivings. If, on the other hand, the ethnic group is large and concentrated, the sense of insecurity is much greater in the larger society. In antebellum South Carolina and Mississsippi, slaves outnumbered whites, and whites relied on harsh disciplinary codes to control them. Where whites outnumbered blacks, relations were more relaxed. Few people worried about Irish immigration before 1840; but when the potato famine brought millions of Irish Catholics, many Americans became concerned, a nativist movement developed.

Geographic mobility is just as important. When one group encroaches on the territory of another, confrontation is inevitable.

Native American history is one illustration; as white farmers moved west, Indian-white relations deteriorated. The migration of black families to northern cities during World War II led to several racial clashes, the most serious of which took place in Detroit. Today when black families move into an Irish neighborhood in south Boston or a Polish neighborhood in Chicago, it often precipitates a wave of resistance or home sales.

Finally, social problems intensify discrimination. Wars, depressions, or vast social upheavals create unusual tensions. Worried, fearful, and unable to solve their problems, people look for someone to blame, ultimately accusing innocent people. In Germany during the 1920s, Jews were blamed for inflation, unemployment, and national humiliation. Old Bostonian families blamed Irish Catholics for all sorts of problems during the 1840s, and many people made life miserable for German-Americans during World War I.

During the past twenty years, as minorities have protested poverty and discrimination, the United States has become the object of world criticism. And there is ample room for criticism. But the problem must also be placed in perspective. For three centuries literally hundreds of different racial, religious, and nationality groups have striven for success in American society. And that ethnic competition has occurred in a society in which egalitarianism is a national religion. Controversy is not at all surprising. Everyone expects equality and justice because the political culture of the first English immigrants demanded it. Everyone claims an equal right to "life, liberty, and the pursuit of happiness" and demands that the polity deliver on its promise. Considering America's unique mix of cultural pluralism and egalitarian philosophy, perhaps the nation has done rather well in dealing with the problems of ethnicity.

SUGGESTED READINGS

Ahlstrom, Sydney E. A *Religious History of the American People*. New Haven, Conn.: 1972.

Allport, Gordon W. *The Nature of Prejudice*. New York: 1958.

Dinnerstein, Leonard, and Reimers, David M. *Ethnic Americans: A History of Immigration and Assimilation*. New York: 1975.

Glazer, Nathan. "Liberty, Equality, Fraternity—and Ethnicity." *Daedalus*, 105 (Fall 1976), 115–127.

Gordon, Milton. *Assimilation in American Life: The Role of Race, Religion, and National Origins*. New York: 1964.

Gossett, Thomas F. *Race: The History of an Idea in America*. Dallas, Texas: 1963.

Greeley, Andrew M. *Ethnicity in the United States: A Preliminary Reconnaissance*. New York: 1974.

———. *Why Can't They Be Like Us: America's White Ethnic Groups*. New York: 1971.

Handlin, Oscar. *Race and Nationality in American Life*. Boston: 1957.

Higham, John. "The Immigrant in American History." In *Send These to Me: Jews and Other Immigrants in Urban America*. New York: 1975.

Kelley, Robert. "Ideology and Political Culture from Jefferson to Nixon." *American Historical Review*, 82 (June 1977), 531–562.

LaGumina, Salvatore J., and Cavaiolo, Frank J. *The Ethnic Dimension in American Society*. Boston: 1974.

Marty, Martin E. "Ethnicity: The Skeleton of Religion in America." *Church History*, 41 (March 1972), 5–21.

Nash, Gary B., and Weiss, Richard, eds. *The Great Fear: Race in the Mind of America*. New York: 1970.

Rischin, Moses. *Immigration and the American Tradition*. Indianapolis, Ind.: 1976.

Rose, Peter. *They and We: Racial and Ethnic Relations in the United States*. New York: 1964.

Seller, Maxine. *To Seek America: A History of Ethnic Life in the United States*. Englewood Cliffs, N.J.: 1977.

Smith, Timothy L. "Religious Denominations as Ethnic Communities: A Regional Case Study." *Church History*, 35 (June 1966), 523–543.

Sowell, Thomas. *Race and Economics*. New York: 1975.

Stein, Howard F., and Hill, Robert F. "The Limits of Ethnicity." *American Scholar*, 46 (Spring 1977), 181–192.

Wittke, Carl. *We Who Built America: The Saga of the Immigrant*. Cleveland: 1939.

Part I
COLONIAL
ORIGINS,
1607–1776

In the sixteenth century, political, economic, and religious upheavals were disrupting the lives of millions of people in western Europe. Nation-states were emerging in Spain, Portugal, France, and England as local monarchs extended their territorial authority; entrepreneurs were searching for lucrative business opportunities; and frustrated people were about to rebel against the Roman Catholic Church. The convergence of nationalism, the Commercial Revolution, and the Reformation would soon shake Europe to its foundation and send thousands of people across the Atlantic in a determined search for economic opportunity and religious security.

North America's first colonists had to cope not only with a harrowing ocean voyage and often hostile inhabitants, but also with their own religious rivalries and political expectations. Virginia had its "starving time"; the Plymouth colonists braved a horrible winter in flimsy wooden huts; and New England shuddered in fear during King Philip's War. Eventually the colonists adjusted to the environment, transforming scarcity into abundance and hope into confidence. On the shores of the New World, America played host to cultural pluralism, individual rights, and the beginnings of political nationalism; all three ideas were destined to become ideological standards for the world.

Cultural pluralism revolved around religious diversity. Compared with the rest of the world in the eighteenth century, British North

America seemed an island of toleration in a vast sea of bigotry—even though Congregationalists, Presbyterians, Anglicans, and Catholics were hardly known then for open-mindedness. Because America was settled by many groups, not just one, political loyalty was never identified with any one set of religious beliefs. There was, to be sure, a powerful Protestant spirit, but in the absence of a national church, American culture was nonsectarian. Love of country never implied love of a particular church.

Religious pluralism led slowly to toleration. Jews, Catholics, Friends (Quakers), Separatists, Congregationalists, Presbyterians, Baptists, Methodists, Dutch Reformed, Lutherans, and German Reformed all tried to save souls in colonial America, but no single group had an absolute majority. All were minorities, and to protect its own security each had to guarantee the security of others. Tolerance evolved slowly, even torturously. Virginia prohibited Jewish immigration in 1607; Governor Peter Stuyvesant of New Netherland imposed discriminatory taxes on Jewish merchants in the 1650s; and Pennsylvania tried to prevent Jews from voting in 1690. The Maryland Toleration Act of 1649, which promised freedom of worship for all Christians, was temporarily repealed in 1654. Massachusetts Puritans expelled Roger Williams and Anne Hutchinson for heresy in the 1630s and persecuted Quakers throughout the 1600s. Nor was any love lost between Anglicans and Scots-Irish Presbyterians in the South. Still, religious conflict slowly succumbed to the reality of life in America. Each denomination drifted toward toleration out of necessity, and crusades to win converts were largely voluntary affairs by the late 1700s. Freedom of religion was becoming a hallmark of American democracy.

As the colonists came to terms with diversity, they institutionalized the natural rights theory of the English philosopher John Locke—that governments were only temporary compacts protecting individual claims to life, liberty, and property. The colonists agreed with the English Whigs that power was evil, governments dangerous, and restrictions on political power absolutely necessary. Such basic American concepts as separation of powers, checks and balances, federalism, and a bill of rights would eventually circumscribe power and exalt the individual rather than state or church. Offering abundant land, economic opportunity, and geographic mobility, the New World reinforced individualism, and natural rights became the secular religion of America. The European colonists worshiped God in different ways but paid homage to themselves with remarkable consistency: they possessed "unalienable" rights, and the purpose of government was to sustain those rights.

Early American politics inaugurated the first successful colonial rebellion in modern history. By 1776 the colonists had concluded that England was fulfilling Locke's warnings about the dangers of concentrated political power. They believed that the British writs of assistance, the Sugar Act of 1764, the Stamp Act of 1765, the Townshend Acts of 1767, the Tea Act of 1773, and the Intolerable Acts of 1774 violated individual rights instead of protecting them. Parliament had thereby surrendered its legitimacy as a government of the colonies. The Declaration of Independence and later the Constitution formally established natural rights as a basis for governance. In the nineteenth and twentieth centuries, when colonial peoples rebelled all over the world — Latin Americans against Spain, Indonesians against the Netherlands, Algerians and Vietnamese against France, Indians against England, and Angolans against Portugal — the American Revolution was one of their models. As a goal of colonial societies everywhere, nationalism won a great victory in colonial America.

The colonial period, then, established three great ideas — freedom of religion and its implied respect for cultural pluralism, the natural rights philosophy, and political nationalism — as standards for American society. Nothing would test those standards more severely than racial, ethnic, and religious diversity. When nationalism unified Americans politically, ethnic pluralism divided them culturally. At the same time, the natural rights philosophy promised justice and equity to everyone. The tensions between political nationalism, cultural pluralism, and egalitarianism would be the central dynamic in United States history.

Chapter One

The First Americans

Although small bands of Europeans or Asians may have crossed the oceans to the Americas, most native Americans, scholars argue, descended from Siberian hunters who migrated to North America many thousands of years ago.

Sometime between 40,000 and 32,000 B.C., glaciers covered Canada and the northern United States with an ice sheet thousands of feet thick. These huge glaciers froze up millions of cubic miles of ocean water, dropping the worldwide sea level by hundreds of feet. As the sea retreated into glacial ice, the shallow ocean floor of the Bering Sea surfaced, leaving a land bridge (called Beringia) more than a thousand miles wide connecting eastern Asia with Alaska. Vegetation grew on what had once been the ocean floor, and animals from Siberia and Alaska slowly occupied the new land. Nomadic Siberian hunters followed the big game, and each season their villages moved farther east until, thousands of years later, the migration was complete. On several subsequent occasions warming trends melted enough ice to cover Beringia, temporarily separating the two continents. "Siberians" became "Americans" in a series of major migrations between 40,000 and 11,000 B.C..

Unable to drift deeper into the continent because of the ice sheets covering much of North America, the hunters remained in Alaska for generations. But during the warmer periods, when the Beringia land bridge narrowed or disappeared, the continental glaciers retreated down both sides of the Canadian Rockies and opened an ice-free corridor through the Yukon and Mackenzie river valleys. Thousands of small hunting bands moved south to what is now the United States in between the cold spells that sealed the corridor. Finally, around 11,000 B.C., the Ice Age ended, the glaciers melted, Beringia disappeared under three hundred feet of water, and the hunting groups in America were permanently separated from Siberia.

For the next fifteen thousand years native American hunters spread across the Western Hemisphere, from the Arctic Circle to the tip of South America, and from the Pacific to the Atlantic. Separate bands split repeatedly from one another, and as people in different regions adapted to the land and the varying climates, their ways of organizing life and looking at the world proliferated into hundreds of different cultures. Some tribes remained nomadic, dependent on the natural environment, while others learned to grow their own food and liberated themselves from the need to search for it constantly. This agricultural revolution led to more sedentary life styles, increases in food production and population, social and religious development, and more complex divisions of labor based on sex and status. Some of the agricultural communities developed elaborate social, economic, and political systems.

On the Eve of Colonization

Throughout United States history white people have stereotyped native Americans as "Noble Red Men," innocent children of nature, or fierce, bloodthirsty savages. But in fact, when European settlers first came to the New World, the native American communities had advanced far beyond their Siberian ancestors. Native American societies in 1500 A.D. ranged from the primitive foraging tribes of southern California to the advanced Aztec and Inca civilizations of Mexico and Peru. Although some historians and anthropologists believe the land may have supported several million people, most agree that on the eve of colonization there were only about a million Indians living in what is now the United States. They were divided into more than six hundred separate tribal groups speaking more than two hundred languages, and occupied seven major regions: the northeastern woodlands, the southeastern forests, the Great Plains, the Great Basin, the northern plateau, the southwestern desert, and the Pacific coast.

The tribes of the Northeast lived between the Mississippi River and the Atlantic coast, north of the Carolinas and the Ohio River Valley. In New England they included the Penobscots, Pennacooks, Pequots,

Narragansetts, Mohegans, Massachusetts, and Wampanoags. In the Hudson River Valley the Five Nations of the Iroquois Confederacy — composed of the Mohawks, Oneidas, Onondagas, Cayugas, Senecas, and later the Tuscaroras — reigned supreme. And between the Great Lakes and the Ohio River were the Eries, Conestogas, Sauk and Fox, Ottawas, Kickapoos, Shawnees, Chippewas, Peorias, Menominees, and Miamis. Except for the buffalo hunters of the Illinois plains and the nomadic foragers of the far north, they lived in settled agricultural villages and cultivated corn, squash, and beans in communal gardens. They lived in wigwams or bark houses separated by streets and surrounded by protective stockades, and hunted game for both food and clothing. Except for the highly centralized Iroquois Confederacy of New York and the Algonquian-based Illinois Confederacy, each tribe was independent.

The southeastern tribes lived between the Mississippi River and the Atlantic coast and south of the Ohio River Valley. They included the Cherokees of North Carolina and Tennessee; the Seminoles, Timucuas, and Calusas of Florida; and the Choctaws, Chickasaws, Creeks, and Alabamas on the Gulf Coast. Most were sedentary farmers who raised corn, beans, and tobacco; hunted small game; and gathered nuts, seeds, and wild rice. They lived in farming towns of mud-plaster homes.

A different native American society emerged on the arid short-grass plains of what are now the Dakotas, Montana, Wyoming, eastern Colorado, western Kansas, Oklahoma, and the Texas panhandle. The Blackfeet, Dakotas, Sioux, Crows, Cheyennes, Arapahos, Com-

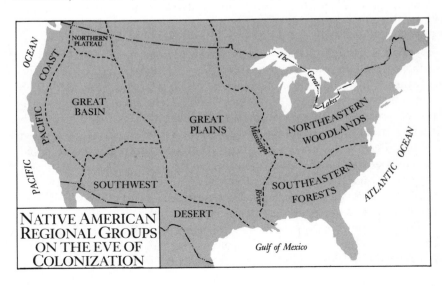

anches, Pawnees, and Kiowas were nomadic hunters whose social and economic life revolved around the buffalo herds. Bearing their portable tepees, they were constantly on the move. The buffalo provided them with meat, which they ate fresh or dried. Buffalo skins gave them their blankets, moccasins, clothes, and covering for their homes. Buffalo hair and tendons became thread and string for their bows. The buffalo stomach became a water bottle. Buffalo horns were used as cups and spoons. The hunters even turned the buffalo tongue into a hair brush and buffalo fat into hair oil. The sixteenth-century acquisition of the horse from the Spaniards vastly increased their range, improved the success of their hunts, and reinforced their nomadism.

For the Indians who lived in the Great Basin, the area between the Rocky Mountains and the Sierra Nevadas that includes present-day Utah, Nevada, southern Idaho, eastern Oregon, and eastern California, life was primitive. Water was precious, agriculture difficult, and the people extremely poor. Roving bands of Utes, Paiutes, Gosiutes, Monos, Panamints, Paviotsos, and Shoshones populated the region. With little agriculture there were no permanent villages, and small groups of extended families subsisted on small game, berries, roots, nuts, seeds, and insects. Here survival was problematical and prosperity unknown.

The plateau Indians—Flatheads, Spokanes, Yakimas, Nez Percés, Wallawallas, Chinooks, Modocs, and Klamaths—lived between the Rockies and the Cascade Mountains. The heavily wooded mountains and high plains of western Montana, Idaho, and eastern Washington were a generally nonagricultural environment. Most tribes hunted for small game, gathered berries and roots, and fished for the giant salmon. Relatively poor and politically decentralized, they lived in semipermanent villages along the major salmon rivers and streams.

Two cultures developed in the Southwest. One was made up of the Navajo tribe, which rose to power at the "four corners" junction of Utah, Arizona, New Mexico, and Colorado; and of the Apaches, who were dominant in southeastern Arizona and southwestern New Mexico. Both tribes were fierce, nomadic hunters who often raided neighboring settlements. They lived in tepees when moving through open country and in brush shelters in the mountains. The second culture was the sedentary, even urban societies of the Hopis, Zuñis, and Pueblos of Arizona and New Mexico. Despite dry weather they raised corn, squash, and beans; they also domesticated poultry, sheep, and cattle, wove cloth, and built towns of many-storied adobe dwellings into rocky hillsides. Labor was specialized, the social structure complex, and their cultures as sophisticated as that of any tribe in the United States.

Two more groups appeared on the Pacific coast. In southern California more than a hundred tribes—including the Yuroks, Salinas, Athapascans, Miwoks, and Chumosh—lived in nomadic villages and gathered acorns, seeds, shellfish, roots, and berries. Most were excellent artisans. In northern California, Oregon, and Washington another coastal culture included the Chinooks, Umpquas, Coos, and Tolowas. Though they were nonagricultural, an abundant supply of fish and game permitted the development of stable communities. They built gable-roofed plank homes and, unlike most other Indians, believed in private property.

Native American cultures had enormous variety. While the Plains Indians wore buffalo skins and the Basin Indians not much at all, the Pueblos were highly skilled weavers of blankets and clothing. The Plains and California Indians were nomadic, but the Iroquois and the Zunis lived in permanent, settled communities. Most northeastern, southeastern, and southwestern tribes raised corn and squash, while other tribes were hunters or gatherers. The Utes lived in primitive lean-tos and the Pueblos in multistoried buildings. Some Indians worshiped the "Master of Life"; others paid homage to ancestors, or animal spirits, or to the elements. Thus when the European settlers arrived, there were already hundreds of different ethnic groups in America.

Native Americans and Europeans: The Cultural Confrontation

The misunderstanding and persistent friction between New World natives and Old World immigrants grew out of competitive, mutually exclusive perspectives. In their approaches to life, death, and the earth, native Americans and Europeans were poles apart. To many Europeans the measure of a person was largely economic, a function of how much wealth had been accumulated. In many native American communities status was noneconomic, dependent upon courage and loyalty rather than on material possessions.

On attitudes towards the natural environment, the two peoples differed as well. White settlers mainly wanted to make a better living for themselves; they intended to use the wilderness, to convert nature into property, status, and security. The land was not sacred to them, and the earth had no transcendent meaning. But for native Americans the environment was holy, possessing a cosmic significance more important than its material riches. They viewed the earth as a gift of the gods which had to be protected and worshiped. Consequently the Indians lived in a symbiotic relationship with the environment, using resources without exhausting them. Chief Smohalla of the Wanapum tribe expressed this view of the environment when he said:

> God . . . commanded that the lands and fisheries should be common to all who lived upon them; that they were never to be marked off or divided, but that the people should enjoy the fruits that God planted in the land, and the animals that lived upon it, and the fishes in the water. God said he was the father and earth was the mother of mankind; that nature was the law; that the animals, and fish, and plants obeyed nature, and that man only was sinful.
>
> You ask me to plow the ground! Shall I take a knife and tear my mother's bosom? Then when I die she will not take me to her bosom to rest.
>
> You ask me to dig for stone! Shall I dig under her skin for her bones? Then when I die I cannot enter her body to be born again.
>
> You ask me to cut grass and make hay and sell it, and be rich like white men! But how dare I cut off my mother's hair?*

The use and ownership of land was the source of the most important environmental conflict between native Americans and Europeans. Impatient with native American economic values, whites considered Indian land-use methods inefficient, incapable of getting the most out of the soil. That fact alone, some believed, justified taking the land, peacefully if possible but violently if necessary.

In addition, the idea of private property was alien to most Indians; giving one man exclusive, perpetual control of land was as inconceivable to them as giving him the air or sky. The Reverend John Heckewelder, a Moravian minister, complained about an Indian's horses eating grass on his land. The Indian said:

> My friend, it seems you lay claim to the grass my horses have eaten, because you had enclosed it with a fence: now tell me, who caused the grass to grow? Can you make the grass grow? I think not, and nobody can except the great Manni-to. He it is who causes it to grow both for my horses and for yours! See, friend! The grass which grows out of the earth is common to all; the game in the woods is common to all. Say, did you never eat venison and bear's meat? . . . Well, and did you ever hear me or any other Indian complain about that? . . . Besides, if you will but consider, you will find that my horse did not eat all your grass.†

---

* *Fourteenth Annual Report of the Bureau of American Ethnology* (1896), pt. 2, p. 721.
† John Heckewelder, *Account of the History, Manners, and Customs of the Indian Nations, Who Once Inhabited Pennsylvania and the Neighboring States* (Philadelphia, 1819), p. 86.

This sketch of an Indian village in North Carolina, drawn by John White in 1590, reveals the compexity of native American society. (The Granger Collection)

This view was inconceivable to most of the settlers, and they began almost at once to displace the Indians, pushing them toward the vacant lands of the West.

The ethnocentrism of the Europeans also guaranteed conflict with native Americans. Convinced of their own religious and moral superiority, the Europeans approached native Americans from two different but equally destructive social perspectives. Some looked upon the Indians as savages requiring no more ethical consideration than the beasts of the field. By denying Indian humanity and creating negative stereotypes, they could rationalize the economic and military assaults on native American society. But other Europeans accepted the humanity, if not the cultural equality, of the Indians. Instead of annihilating them, these colonists wanted to transform native Americans into settled farmers who believed in private property and Christianity. Though more humane than the other point of view, this missionary impulse proved equally detrimental to native American society.

There were, of course, exceptions to the rule. In 1635 Roger Williams enraged the civil magistrates of Massachusetts by denying their Puritan authority and accusing them of violating native American rights. Insisting that the Indians owned the land and could keep or dispose of it at will, Williams went against the grain of European opinion, and the Boston magistrates expelled him from Massachusetts. A half-century later, in Pennsylvania, the Quakers tried to pursue an evenhanded policy toward native Americans. A persecuted people dedicated to nonviolence and the belief that all men and women were children of God, the Quakers wanted a colony in which everyone could live in harmony. They respected the Delaware Indians' right to the land and purchased it from them only after the most careful negotiations. Word spread, and in the 1690s and early 1700s the Tuscaroras, Shawnees, and Miamis all migrated to Pennsylvania. But as Scots-Irish Presbyterians, German Lutherans, and English Protestants pushed west and squatted on Indian land, traditional views triumphed in all the colonies.

Indian Resistance

Although the first years of colonial life were peaceful, the tranquility was short-lived. As soon as the Indians realized that more and more colonists would come to take more land, they began to resist. For years the Algonquian-speaking tribes of Virginia and North Carolina, linked together in a loose alliance under the leadership of Powhatan, had assisted the Jamestown settlers. Important cultural exchanges took place from the very beginning of the Chesapeake colonies. While Europeans excelled in transportation and the use of iron for tools and weapons, the Indians were far more advanced in regional geographic knowledge and economic adjustment to the land. The Powhatan tribes were quick to make use of English kettles, traps, fishhooks, needles, and guns, and they passed on to the English their knowledge of fishing; raising tobacco, corn, beans, squash, rice, and pumpkins; and using herbs and dyes.

In 1622 the peace was shattered. Powhaten had died in 1618 and a more aggressive relative, Opechancanough, had replaced him. During the next few years, as tobacco production became more profitable, the white population increased. Political relations changed dramatically. Feeling the enormous pressures of white civilization, the Indians began to fear it. On March 22, 1622, they attacked colonial settlements throughout Virginia, killing 347 people and destroying dozens of villages. More than a third of the white settlers died. Throughout 1622 and 1623 the English settlers pursued the Indians relentlessly, crushed the Powhatan Confederacy, and annihilated most of the native Americans who had participated in the uprising. Rather than trying to assimilate the remaining peaceful Indians, the colonists imposed a scorched-earth policy. Arbitrary treaties and forced land sales removed the Indians still living in the eastern counties.

Sporadic conflicts erupted throughout the next few decades, most notably in 1644, when Opechancanough himself rebelled, but Virginia would never again be threatened with extinction. After Opechancanough's rebellion the Virginians dealt with the Indians differently. Tired of wars and of native American resistance to English culture, the Virginians "reserved" land north of the York River as a permanent Indian homeland. For the next thirty years the reservation policy worked, and the two peoples even established a valuable fur trade. But it was only a temporary expedient. As the white population increased, pressure to open up the reservation land to settlement became increasingly strong. Convinced that the reservation policy was the only way to guarantee peace, Virginia Governor William Berkeley refused, but white settlers moved north anyway. Nathaniel Bacon, an English-born member of the colonial council, demanded the opening of reservation lands, greater militia protection for western settlers, and wars of extermination against the Indians. Berkeley still refused, and in 1676 Bacon took matters into his own hands. Marching against Jamestown, his supporters slaughtered peaceful Indians along the way and burned the colony's leading settlement. Bacon's Rebellion was over by 1677 and so was Indian resistance in Virginia. Divided politically and vastly outnumbered by Europeans, native Americans were weakened militarily; and by 1680, with a thousand Indians left out of an original population of more than thirty thousand, the clash of cultures was over in Virginia.

In New England the pattern of European land pressure, tribal rivalries, and ethnic conflict was repeated. With a proud sense of mission the Puritans had set out to build the kingdom of God in the New World. Squanto, a Pawtuxet Indian, had helped the Pilgrims in 1620, and for a few years the hatred of the Narragansetts, Wampanoags, and Pequots for one another prevented Indian resistance. When a smallpox epidemic wiped out thousands of native Americans in 1633 and 1634, the Puritans interpreted it as an act of God, proof that Christianity would triumph in the New World. But the Pequots were not convinced. They had moved into southern New England late in the 1500s and ever since the founding of Massachusetts and Connecticut, they had worried about Puritan expansion. Occasional acts of mutual brutality occurred between 1631 and 1636; but in 1637, when the Pequots allegedly killed several whites in Connecticut, the colonists retaliated with a vengeance. It was a bloody affair. Puritan armies drove to Long Island Sound, shooting and burning more than six hundred Pequots. By 1638 the Pequot tribe was nearly destroyed.

Some forty years later New England experienced one of the most savage racial conflicts in American history. Born in 1616 near what is now Warren, Rhode Island, King Philip became chief of the Wampanoag tribe in 1662. Resentful of white settlements, violations of land titles, and assaults on individual native Americans, he attacked on July 4, 1675. Joined by the Narragansetts, Nipmucs, and Penobscots, the Wampanoags eventually destroyed twenty New England towns and killed more than three thousand people. It was only a temporary victory, however, for in the battle of Great Swamp in December 1675, Philip saw a thousand of his warriors die. He too was killed late in 1676. By 1678 a colonial army had cleared southern New England of Indians, opening the area to white settlers.

In the South the conflict continued. Along the coastal plains of North Carolina, the Tuscaroras had lived peacefully for years, raising hemp, corn, and orchard fruits; but, despairing of white encroachment on their land, they killed 130 colonists in 1711. Two years later more than a thousand Tuscaroras were dead and another seven hundred sold into slavery in the West Indies. The Yamasees of South Carolina rebelled in 1715. Exploited in the fur trade and frightened of white immigration, they joined the Creeks, Catawbas, Appalachees, and Santees and killed more than four hundred colonists. Not until the Cherokees joined the whites in 1716 did the rebellion end. The Yamasees and Creeks retreated into the wilderness.

Tension between Indians and whites was intensified by Anglo-French rivalry. Both France and England wanted the Ohio Valley, and the Indians were caught in the middle. Except for the Iroquois, most Indians were loyal to the French because the French did not pose quite the threat of the English. French settlements in Canada were not nearly as large as the English colonies; and because the French were more interested in trade and commerce than in agriculture, they did not usually push the Indians off their land. The centralized authority of the Roman

Catholic Church and its interest in converting Indians guaranteed more humane treatment than that generally provided by English Protestants. It was only natural for the Indians to cast their lot with the French.

During the eighteenth century the French and English fought four colonial wars in North America: King William's War (1689–1697), Queen Anne's War (1702-1713), King George's War (1740-1748), and the French and Indian War (1754–1763). In each case the English and most of the Iroquois fought the French and other northeastern tribes. Not until 1763 did the French admit defeat and cede Canada. The Iroquois reaped the prestige and spoils of victory, but thousands of English, Scots-Irish, and German settlers began pouring across the Appalachians to take land from defeated "French-loving" Indians. Settlement pressures and unscrupulous land speculators angered the Indians, especially Pontiac, chief of the Ottawas. In 1763 he led the Ottawas, Delawares, Miamis, Kickapoos, and Shawnees against white settlements in the Ohio Valley. To mollify Pontiac and relieve the pressure on the western tribes, the British Parliament issued the Proclamation of 1763, prohibiting further white settlement in the region. After three more years of fighting, Pontiac signed a peace treaty with England. Except for some tribes in upstate New York and along the Gulf Coast, most of the Indians had been pushed from the Eastern Seaboard. Between 1766 and 1776 Indian relations improved with the British government and deteriorated with the colonists, and during the American Revolution most Indians would consider England their ally, again joining the loser in an international conflict.

The Indians had resisted the colonists almost from the beginning, but their resistance was doomed to failure. For one reason, the European population dwarfed them. Except for the first half of the seventeenth century, the Indians were always outnumbered. They might win some battles but they could never win the wars. Worse, they had no immunity to European diseases. Smallpox, influenza, scarlet fever, whooping cough, and diphtheria decimated Indian communities. Between 1607 and 1776 the European and African population in the British colonies grew to about 2.5 million people while the Indian population dropped from a million to about 600,000. Even when Indians had temporary superiority in numbers, intertribal rivalries—often exploited by the colonists—prevented the formation of effective, long-lasting confederacies. Finally, the westward shift of the white economy destroyed the Indians' habitat and upset the ecological balance of their communities. As the white population increased, the small game disappeared, the buffalo herds were slaughtered, and the land itself was denied them.

In spite of all this, native Americans continued to resist European civilization in many ways, and the presence of whites never resulted in acculturation. Historians and pulp writers have immortalized resistance, and in the colonial period the Powhatan tribal uprisings of 1622 and 1644, the Pequot War of 1637, King Philip's War of 1675, the Tuscarora War of 1711–1712, the Yamassee War of 1715, and Pontiac's Rebellion of 1763 symbolize the Indian refusal to accept white encroachments passively. Some tribes remained as cultural islands in the colonial society, usually confined to reservations; but even there, where white missionaries had unfettered opportunities to Europeanize the native Americans, they clung tenaciously to their own culture.

SUGGESTED READINGS

Chamberlain, J. E. *The Harrowing of Eden: White Attitudes Toward Native Americans*. New York: 1975.

Corkran, David H. *The Creek Frontier, 1540–1783*. Norman, Oklahoma: 1967.

Craven, Wesley Frank. *White, Red, and Black: The Seventeenth Century Virginian*. Charlottesville, Virginia: 1971.

Debo, Angie. *A History of the Indians of the United States*. Norman, Oklahoma: 1970.

Denevan, William. *Native Population of the Americas in 1492*. Madison, Wisconsin: 1976.

Farb, Peter. *Man's Rise to Civilization as Shown by the Indians of North America from Primeval Times to the Coming of the Industrial State*. New York: 1968.

Hagan, William T. *American Indians*. Chicago: 1961.

Jacobs, Wilburn R. *Dispossessing the American Indian: Indians and Whites on the Colonial Frontier*. New York: 1972.

Jennings, Francis. *The Invasion of America: Indians, Colonialism, and the Cant of Conquest*. Chapel Hill, N.C.: 1975.

Johnson, Richard R. "The Search for a Usable Indian: An Aspect of the Defense of Colonial New England." *Journal of American History*, 64 (December 1977), 623–651.

Josephy, Alvin M. *The Indian Heritage of America*. New York: 1968.

Lurie, Nancy O. "Indian Cultural Adjustment to European Civilization." James M. Smith, ed. *Seventeenth Century America*. Chapel Hill, N.C.: 1959.

McNickle, D'Arcy. *Native American Tribalisms*. New York: 1973.

Oswalt, Wendell H. *This Land Was Theirs: A Study of the North American Indian*. New York: 1966.

Sanders, William T. and Marino, Joseph P. *New World Prehistory: Archaeology of the American Indian*. New York: 1970.

Washburn, Wilcomb E. *The Indian in America*. New York: 1975.

Wise, Jennings C. *The Red Man in the New World Drama: A Politico-Legal Study with a Pageantry of American Indian History*. New York: 1971.

Chapter Two

The Europeans: Westward Expansion

The Europeans who moved to the New World were a special people, courageous enough to face an unknown wilderness, restless enough to leave the ties of home, and confident enough to believe they could succeed in such a daring enterprise. Some left Europe to escape poverty, jail, or persecution, and others to reform the world. Some wanted to save the souls of the Indians, and some sought challenge and adventure. Most came to America, however, for religious freedom and economic success; they intended to plant the kingdom of God and build a better life.

From the beginning, North America attracted different groups. In 1624 the Dutch West India Company established a trading post on the Hudson River in New York. Spanish and Portuguese (Sephardic) Jews, Belgian Protestants (Walloons), Puritans from Massachusetts, French Huguenots, and black Africans all lived in New Amsterdam before the English took over in 1664. The Swedish West India Company deposited Finns and Swedes along the Delaware River in 1638. A failure economically, New Sweden was annexed by New Netherland in 1655. After the Edict of Nantes—which had granted religious toleration to the Huguenots—was revoked in 1685, several thousand French Protestants immigrated to America. And after the union of Scotland and England in 1707, Lowland and Highland Scots began coming to the New World.

Early America was already a polyglot society, a cross-section of western Europe. But for all this diversity, three groups dominated the early migrations to British North America: English, German, and Scots and Scots-Irish settlers came in such large numbers that by 1776 they were the most visible and influential people in the thirteen colonies.

The English Settlers

The British colonies reflected the social, economic, and religious changes of seventeeth-century England. Since the early Middle Ages, English economic life had been remarkably stable, with farmers tilling the soil for landlords and closed trade and craft guilds controlling commerce in the towns. But the rise of a money economy and inflation created new social problems. Landlords increased rents to compensate for higher prices; and because commodity prices were not keeping pace with those of manufactured goods, tenant farmers were squeezed between their incomes and costs. Many began looking for new economic opportunities.

At the same time, the Commercial Revolution created a class of business entrepreneurs looking for profits. Highly successful in textiles, banking, and foreign trade, they reinvigorated economic life in England. During the 1500s they had accumulated excess capital; they anxiously sought new investments and were willing to assume great risks. Few ventures seemed riskier than colonization; but if the Spanish plunder of Aztec and Inca treasures was any indication, potential returns were immense. Their pursuit of wealth, along with the desires of more humble people for a better life, created a fascination with colonization. If the lower and middle classes were willing to settle abroad, the merchant capitalists would finance them.

England was also the scene of intense religious debate in the seventeenth century. Ever since the 1530s, when Henry VIII rejected Roman Catholicism, the Church of England had been a powerful institution. After 1558 church and state were a single entity, with religious and political loyalty different sides of the same coin. England was a spiritual battleground. Roman Catholics balked at Henry's break with Rome and the subsequent protestantization of the church by Edward VI and Elizabeth I, and the Quakers rejected all varieties of political, social, and religious authority. Zealous Anglicans persecuted both groups, and many Catholics and Quakers looked to America as an escape.

Puritanism was another powerful force. Committed to cleansing the social order of evil and corruption, Puritans rejected the hierarchical structure of the Church of England, repudiated free will for predestination, and believed in the inherent evil of man. That was the "Puritan dilemma," for while taking a dim view of human nature, they nonetheless felt called to perfect society. Eventually some Puritans decided that England was not ripe for purification and that perhaps in America a perfect community could be realized. Theirs was not an escape to America; the Puritans wanted to prove that a righteous community could succeed. It was an "errand into the wilderness."

Chesapeake Bay and New England

The first two European population centers were along the Atlantic coast, one at Chesapeake Bay and the other in New England. In 1607 a small band of settlers arrived at Chesapeake Bay, sailed thirty miles up the James River, and established Jamestown, the first successful English colony in America. Although some of the colonists hoped to convert the Indians, most had more secular interests in mind. Some dreamed of their own farms, while others planned to export valuable commodities to the mother country. Most of their hopes went unfulfilled until 1612, when John Rolfe "discovered" tobacco; after learning to improve the quality of the "noxious weed," the colonists made it the economic backbone of Virginia. By 1624, even though more than five thousand people had come to Virginia since 1607, only thirteen hundred were still there, the others dead or returned to England. Starvation, disease, and Indian hostility made life difficult; but through courage, tenacity, and luck, the remaining colonists survived.

Two hundred and fifty miles north, other English colonists founded Maryland. In 1632 Charles I granted George Calvert, the first Lord Baltimore, a huge tract of land between Virginia and Pennsylvania. A recent convert to Catholicism, Calvert sought a haven for his persecuted brethren and a fortune through land sales to incoming settlers. Religious idealism and economic enrichment were perfectly compatible for Baltimore. Maryland attracted both Protestant and Catholic farmers, artisans, and servants; and since the Catholics were a minority, the second Lord Baltimore drafted the Toleration Act of 1649, providing freedom of religion to all Christians to protect those of his faith. Tobacco plantations became central to the economy; at first they were worked by indentured servants from England, later by great numbers of slaves brought from Africa. By 1650 the two Chesapeake colonies were successful outposts of English civilization.

The New England colonies were established between 1620 and 1640. More concerned with religion than their Chesapeake neighbors, the New England immigrants were equally interested in succeeding economically. The northern colonies formally began in 1620, when the *Mayflower* unloaded a small group of English Separatists who founded

Plymouth Colony. The most radical of the Puritan sects, the Separatists believed that the Church of England was too hopelessly corrupt to be reformed, that Anglicanism was little more than Catholicism, and that only a complete break could restore true religion. Anglican persecution and their own intolerance for spiritual "deviations" explain their impulse to move constantly—to become "Pilgrims." Living first as nomads in England and Holland, they committed the ultimate act of separation by abandoning the Old World for America, where the kingdom of God would be free of "popish" distractions. Despite the hostile environment of the North Atlantic coast, they survived economically by farming and fur trading and emotionally by the absolute conviction of their righteousness.

The great Puritan migration commenced in 1629. Convinced of the terrible majesty of God and hoping for salvation, they wanted to establish the first sinless society in human history. Like the Separatists in Plymouth, the Congregationalists who founded Massachusetts Bay Colony believed in local church autonomy rather than authoritarian hierarchies, but unlike the Separatists they thought the Church of England could still be saved. Mainstream English reformers committed to social change, they left England to live where God's holy kingdom and the civil polity could be one. Boston, their "City on a Hill," would impress people back home and help reform Old World institutions. Between 1629 and 1640 more than twenty thousand people migrated to the "Bible Commonwealth" in Massachusetts, and they prospered from the very beginning, eventually absorbing Plymouth in 1691.

Three more New England colonies grew out of the first two. The Puritans had immigrated because they wanted religious freedom for themselves, not for anyone else. The Bible Commonwealth in Massachusetts was an oppressive coalition of church and state, an intolerable environment for free spirits. One such spirit, in the person of Thomas Hooker, led a group of settlers from Boston to the Connecticut River Valley, where they founded a new colony in 1636. At the same time, Roger Williams, expelled by Puritan leaders for criticizing church authority and whites' treatment of the Indians, established Providence Plantation—the colony of Rhode Island. And on the coast north of Boston, enterprising merchants and fishermen founded several fur and fishing villages in the 1630s. They were attached to Massachusetts until 1679, when they became the colony of New Hampshire.

New England was ethnically homogeneous, unlike American settlements that were to come. The people worked as small farmers, middle-class merchants, craftsmen, and fishermen. Unlike the commercial, cash-crop economy of Chesapeake Bay, New England built ships; exported fish, furs, timber, and rum; and shipped freight to England and the West Indies. Perhaps it was their intense religious faith that helped give New Englanders their remarkable optimism and sense of an American destiny.

The Middle Colonies

Between 1640 and 1660 the English Civil War discouraged colonization, and the composition of the Chesapeake and New England colonies remained essentially unchanged. But with the restoration of the monarchy in 1660, there was a new enthusiasm for colonization. During the next twenty-five years two new population centers developed in America, one between the Hudson and Delaware River Valleys and the other south of Virginia. By 1689 the British colonies had more than 210,000 people.

The English presence in the middle colonies began in 1664, when Charles II ceded to his brother, the Duke of York, a tract of land running from the Connecticut to the Delaware River Valley. This grant included New Netherland and New Sweden. Envious of the rich Dutch estates along the Hudson River and the deep harbor at New Amsterdam, the duke assembled a naval fleet during one of the Anglo-Dutch wars. It sailed into the colony, and the English peacefully assumed political control, renaming the area New York. A ready-made colony of ten thousand Puritans, Jews, blacks, Dutch, and Swedes, New York was the most ethnically diverse of the North American settlements.

Satisfied with his new possessions but worried about governing all of them, the Duke of York deeded the land south of New York to John Berkeley and George Carteret in 1664. They advertised for new colonists for their "Jersey" property, and the original Dutch, Swedish, and English settlers were soon joined by hundreds of Puritan families from New England. In 1674 Berkeley sold his share, known as West Jersey, to two Quakers; the Carteret family sold East Jersey to Quakers in 1681. By 1689 more than ten thousand people lived in the two Jerseys, and in 1702 England joined East and West Jersey into a single colony. New Jersey had an English majority of Anglicans, Puritans, and Quakers, and a minority of Finns, Swedes, Danes, Dutch, Germans, and French Huguenots.

The middle colonies expanded in 1681, when Charles II, to repay a debt to Admiral William Penn who had died, granted Penn's son, William, a tract of land west of the Delaware River. Several thousand settlers from New Sweden, New Netherland, and New England were already there, but Penn wanted to provide a refuge for persecuted

Edward Hicks' painting of William Penn's treaty with the Indians illustrates the careful, magnanimous approach the Quakers adopted in their relations with native Americans. (The Granger Collection)

Quakers. The Society of Friends, as they called themselves, were peculiar by seventeenth-century standards. By emphasizing the "Inner Light" between God and man, denying the legitimacy of political authority, and preaching pacifism, they invited hostility. There was little in William Penn's background to suggest that he would join this ridiculed and persecuted minority, but he had been a Quaker since he was a young man.

Born into the turbulent world of London in 1644, Penn came from a wealthy family. His father, a British naval hero, gave William a privileged, secure childhood. Penn attended Oxford, was a guest at the coronation of Charles II in 1661, and traveled extensively in France and Germany. He was tall, brilliant, handsome, and rich. Then, astonishingly, he seemed to throw his life away. Sometime in 1666 or 1667 Penn underwent a profound religious transformation, possibly precipitated by the London fire of 1666 or the great plague of 1665. Acquainted with several Quakers, he found the Inner Light and in 1667 was arrested for being a Quaker. Dumbfounded and enraged, his father begged William to renounce the new faith, but Penn refused. Between 1667 and 1681 he went to prison several times and became increasingly committed to the tenets of his faith.

William Penn guaranteed all the people of Pennsylvania religious freedom and humane treatment, and the colony attracted settlers from all over Europe and from other colonies. Only four years after he received his grant there were nine thousand colonists in Pennsylvania, and by 1700 there were more than twenty thousand. The Quakers brought to their new home a quiet faith in the dignity of all people, a repugnance for slavery, and a deep love for the human community.

The middle colonies were the breadbasket of the New World. With rich soil, good harbors, and navigable rivers, New York, New Jersey, Pennsylvania, and Delaware (which was under the executive control of Pennsylvania until 1776) produced wheat, rye, corn, and livestock— enough to feed themselves and export to New England, the South, and the West Indies. Economic prosperity and religious toleration were magnets that attracted Dutch, German, Scots, Irish, and English settlers as well as Quakers, Dunkers, Moravians, Puritans, Anabaptists, Schwenkfelders, Jews, Catholics, Lutherans, and German Reformed. They formed one of the eighteenth century's most cosmopolitan societies.

The Southern Colonies

Another population center developed along the Atlantic coast south of Virginia. In 1663 Charles II ceded land in the Carolinas to eight wealthy English proprietors, who planned to produce wine, silk, and olive oil. Not until 1670 did large numbers of people settle there. Many were frustrated English farmers from Barbados, where the introduction of slave labor had driven small sugar planters out of business. They settled in the southern reaches of the territory and established a plantation economy based on rice and indigo. Late in the seventeenth century settlers arrived from New York, New England, and the West Indies, but population growth was slow, and as late as 1700 only seven thousand people lived in southern Carolina.

Northern Carolina grew even more slowly. Without a good harbor, the colony was unable to fully develop the plantation system so characteristic of the South. Most settlers were poor tobacco farmers. Only about three thousand Europeans lived there when, in 1712, the crown separated the northern Albemarle region from the southern settlements, naming the two colonies North and South Carolina. During the seventeenth century the Carolinas were overwhelmingly English and Anglican, as ethnically homogeneous as New England.

Georgia was the last of the thirteen colonies. At the time England wanted a buffer colony protecting Virginia and the Carolinas from Spanish Florida. James Oglethorpe, an idealistic English general, was interested in establishing a refuge in America for poor people. Political and personal goals merged in 1732 when Georgia was chartered. Oglethorpe carefully screened prospective settlers and selected the "responsible poor"—hardworking men who, if some came from debtors' prisons, had been there through no fault of their own. As in the other southern colonies, the first settlers of Georgia were primarily English.

Common Bonds

The English colonists shared a perspective on life that transcended their differences. They were flexible, innovative, able to look beyond tradition and custom; America's characteristic optimism, transiency, and pragmatism originated with those first immigrants. In England many of them had deferentially accepted a rigid class structure as the natural order of things, but the American experience undermined that idea. It was the more easily undermined because the one social class that did not join the great migration was the English nobility. America lacked an aristocracy. Well-to-do landowners, political officials, merchants, and clergymen had usually risen from humbler circumstances, and their ties to the yeomanry were fresh. It was a fluid upper class, and poor people hoped to enter it themselves some day.

A belief in progress reinforced the expectations of the middle and lower classes. Many, perhaps a majority, of the colonists of the seventeenth and eighteenth centuries came as indentured servants. Because of labor shortages in most colonies, large landowners and merchants recruited workers by advertising the great opportunities of life in America. Prospective colonists mortgaged their futures, agreeing to work a certain number of years in return for passage to America, room and board, and severance pay after fulfilling their contract. Eventually they became the backbone of the large middle class. Since land was easy to acquire, most ended up as independent farmers, a status which would have been impossible for them in England. Others apprenticed themselves and ultimately became paid artisans. The middle class was always expanding, and the servant class was constantly changing as newer immigrants replaced liberated indentured servants. Membership in the lower class seemed a temporary station. Faith in upward mobility became part of the national ideology of a hardworking, confident people.

Only the middle colonies had large non-English minorities before 1689. Then the colonial population began to change, increasing tenfold by 1776. In the intervening years English immigration continued, but hundreds of thousands of other settlers arrived as well. Two new groups in particular, the Germans and Scots-Irish, immigrated during the eighteenth century, and along with the English became the foundation of American society.

The German Settlers

Between 1618 and 1648 the Thirty Years' War between the Catholic leaders of the Holy Roman Empire and the Protestant leaders of Germany, Denmark, and Sweden reduced much of Germany to misery, ravaging the countryside, destroying crops and livestock, and killing millions of people. From 1689 to 1713 the War of the League of Augsburg and then the War of the Spanish Succession brought more suffering to Germany. In addition, the small, decentralized German states of the seventeenth and eighteenth centuries were governed by princes who levied heavy taxes and periodically tried to expand their territory. Political instability deepened the frustrations that the wars of Europe had already bequeathed to Germany.

Germany also suffered from religious controversies: Catholics, Lutherans, German Reformed, Quakers, Dunkards, Moravians, and Mennonites were all struggling for survival or supremacy. Lutheranism was a German counterpart of Anglicanism. Authority-conscious and tied to the German elite, Lutherans believed in salvation by grace rather than works. The German Reformed Church was in many ways the counterpart of Puritanism. Its members too believed in predestination and argued that Lutheranism, though the creation of the Protestant Reformation, still resembled Roman Catholicism too closely. German pietists, such as Quakers, Dunkards, Moravians, and Mennonites, generally occupied the bottom of the social ladder, as did their Quaker brethren in England. They eschewed theological subleties and authority systems for a personal God with whom all men could communicate. Not surprisingly, they encountered the wrath of Catholics, Lutherans, and the Reformed, who looked upon them as threats to the social order.

Politics complicated religious life. If a Catholic prince suddenly took control of a Lutheran principality he might begin persecuting local Protestants. Lutherans might do the same in a Catholic state. It was no wonder many Germans yearned for the peace and stability they expected in the New World.

In the 1680s colonial agents advertised the fertile soil, political stability, and religious freedom of America. William Penn visited the Catholic Rhineland in 1682 and invited harassed pietists to come to Philadelphia. With Francis Pastorius as their agent, they purchased forty thousand acres outside Philadelphia and began immigrating in 1683. Known as Germantown, their community was the first German settlement in America. Thousands of German Quakers, Dunkards, Amish, Mennonites, Moravians, and Schwenkfelders soon followed. They came to America for religious freedom and, much to their joy, found it.

German immigration became a more complex affair in the eighteenth century. Between 1707 and 1709, after another French invasion and severe winters in the Palatinate, the trickle of German immigrants became a flood. Fifteen thousand German Lutherans came to London in 1708 and 1709, and from there most went on to settle in Pennsylvania and New Jersey. Nearly three thousand of them, under the leadership of Conrad Weisar, moved to the Mohawk Valley of New York and a thousand went down to North Carolina. During the 1720s another fifteen thousand Germans came to Philadelphia, followed by fifty thousand in the 1730s. In 1731, for example, Archbishop Firmian of Salzburg ordered all Protestants to leave the city, and more than thirty thousand people fled. Politics and economics, as well as religion, brought most of the eighteenth-century German immigrants to America.

During the early 1700s most Germans settled in southern New Jersey and eastern Pennsylvania. But as the valleys of the Delaware and the Susquehanna filled, land became more expensive, and new immigrants moved down the Appalachian front into the Cumberland Valley of Maryland and Virginia. There were a number of German settlements near Baltimore and Frederick, Maryland, by 1730, and in 1734 Robert Harper and a group of German immigrants founded Harpers Ferry in western Virginia. German settlers fanned throughout the Shenandoah Valley in the 1730s and by 1750 had reached the frontier of North Carolina, joining their compatriots who had settled there in 1709, and from there moved eastward to the Piedmont. Perhaps half the eighteenth-century German settlers went to the southern colonies, ending forever the English homogeneity of the South. By 1776 there were nearly 250,000 people of German descent concentrated in Pennsylvania and New Jersey and scattered through the western sections of Maryland, Virginia, North Carolina, South Carolina, Georgia, and upstate New York.

The Germans became a prosperous people whose stereotype of orderliness, cleanliness, and hard work is legendary. To this day southeastern Pennsylvania is known as "Dutch" country, since *Deutsch* was the German language and *Deutschland* their original home. With their large barns, neat houses, clean yards, flower gardens, well-built fences, and fine cattle, many of these German farms were models of thrift, efficiency, and profit. Although their native soil had been rich, feudal obligations, often requiring peasants to work several days each week for the landlord, had pressed hard on small farmers, and to support their families they had to extract everything the land could yield. It was no wonder they were such hard workers. As free farmers in America, with fine land and no landlords, no feudal obligations, no heavy taxes, they made their farms into the most productive in the New World. And because of their desire to be self-reliant, they preferred subsistence, self-supporting farming over the large commercial farms or plantations of the English and Scots-Irish, which were dependent on export markets.

The Germans settled in groups, kept to themselves, and did not assimilate easily. Because their homeland was divided into separate principalities, they lacked a national perspective, and their political loyalties remained locally oriented. Years of war had left them wary of strangers, and the petty princes of Germany had made them suspicious of politicians. The English saw them as reluctant to associate with non-Germans, remaining loyal to their language, churches, and communities.

For these reasons as well as economic ones, German immigration was not entirely welcome among the English majority. Germans constituted one-third of the Pennsylvania population by 1776, and even the enlightened Benjamin Franklin was afraid German customs might triumph there. In 1753 he remarked:

> Why should the Palatine Boors be suffered to swarm into our settlements, and by herding together, establish their language and manners, to the exclusion of ours? Why should Pennsylvania, founded by the English, become a colony of Aliens, who will shortly be so numerous as to Germanize us instead of our Anglifying them . . . ?*

English colonists required the Germans to take loyalty oaths to the king, and throughout the colonial wars suspected them, erroneously, of being pro-French. For the most part, however, the two groups kept their distance, and in the America of the 1700s that was still possible. In the future common bonds would link the two peoples. Both were white and sensed a community of interest against native Americans and blacks. Common physical characteristics would contribute greatly to assimilation in the nineteenth and twentieth centuries. As to religion, the German pietists respected the English Quakers in the middle colonies; and because the other eighteenth-century immigrants were generally Protestants, the Germans shared a heritage with them. Religious hostility between different Protestant sects was still intense, but in the future

---

* John Bigelow, ed., *The Complete Works of Benjamin Franklin* (New York, 1887–1888), II, pp. 297–298.

Protestantism would serve to bring them together. And in addition, after centuries of political repression, the Germans were cautious politically. They usually cooperated with local officials, which mitigated some of the insecurity and prejudice of the English settlers.

The Scots-Irish Settlers

Nearly three hundred thousand Scots-Irish left northern Ireland for the colonies in the eighteenth century. Their ancestors had departed from Scotland in the early seventeenth century and settled in Ulster, fought with the English against the Irish Catholics, and then established their own communities on the "Emerald Plantation."

Life in the sixteenth century had been difficult for these Scots. Except in the eastern Lowlands, near the English border, Scottish soil was thin and rocky, with marshes and lochs everywhere. Years of wasteful timber use had left much of the Lowlands a treeless, barren land where even the wild game had disappeared. Scotland was a feudal society; independent noblemen and town gentry manipulated tenant farmers, farm laborers, and poor workers, and before 1550 a constant state of war with England disrupted the lives of Lowland Scots. Finally, there was continual quasi-civil war between Lowlanders and Highlanders, for whom life was even more primitive and desolate. The Highland Scots survived in part by raiding and plundering the Lowlands.

Many Scots wanted to leave, and early in the seventeenth century an opportunity appeared. For centuries English kings had tried to subdue Ireland, but the Irish had resisted and the English had frequently abandoned the project. When James I assumed the English throne in 1603, he invited the generally Protestant Lowlanders to settle in Ulster, promising them low rents, long leases, and religious toleration. They jumped at the chance. Between 1610 and 1640 more than forty thousand Lowland Scots crossed the Irish Sea to colonize Ulster.

Other Lowlanders emigrated after 1660. Ever since the Reformation the Church of Scotland (Presbyterian) had dominated the Lowlands. The Scots were Calvinists who believed in God's decision to redeem a few and damn everyone else. They strongly objected to the regal ceremonies, clerical elitism, and hierarchical church governments of Catholicism and Anglicanism. In 1660, when Charles II forcibly created Anglican bishoprics in Scotland, the Lowlanders resisted violently. The "killing times" commenced. Thousands of Scots died and thousands more fled to Ulster, where Anglican landlords still promised toleration.

For the Scots as for the English, the major problem with Ireland was the Irish. After their defeat by English soldiers and settlement by the

Lowlanders, the embittered Ulstermen hid themselves in the woods and fought a guerilla war. The Scots were persistant, however, hardened by centuries of deprivation. That the natives were Roman Catholics only stiffened the Lowlanders' resolve; they turned the war into a religious crusade against the Irish "heathen." By 1650 more than six hundred thousand people were dead, most of them Catholics, and in the process the English and Scots had almost destroyed the Irish political and social order. Irish farmers had been pushed into tenancy on the worst land.

From the English settlers the Scots learned to drain the marshes, and by planting American potatoes they increased agricultural production enormously. Throughout the meadows of northern Ireland the Scots grazed sheep and built a prosperous textile industry. Dairy farms and cattle ranches flourished. Presbyterian ministers came with the settlers, and by 1680 the Lowlands had built a new life for themselves.

Unfortunately, they were too prosperous. As the Ulster economy matured, it competed with vested interests in England. Alarmed about shrinking markets and falling prices, English merchants and landowners persuaded Parliament to close England to Irish cattle and dairy products in the 1690s. English textile manufacturers lobbied until Parliament passed the Woolens Act, which eliminated foreign markets for Irish cloth by restricting exports to the British Isles. The textile industry in Ulster collapsed. More hardships were in store. Throughout the eighteenth century famines plagued Irish and Scots-Irish farmers alike; in the winter of 1740–1741 nearly five hundred thousand people starved to death. To recoup their financial losses, Anglican landlords began breaking Scottish land leases and raising rents. Tithes on the land, already offensive because they were destined for the Church of England, rose with the rents.

Persecution of the Scots made matters worse. The Test Act of 1673 required Presbyterians to pledge allegiance to the Church of England as a prerequisite for holding civil and military positions, teaching school, or attending college. All Presbyterians loyal to their consciences were denied access to power and influence in English society. And during the reign of Queen Anne, in the early eighteenth century, the Anglican Church began enforcing religious conformity throughout the British Isles. English officials refused to recognize Presbyterian marriages, and couples were often prosecuted for "living in sin" even though they had been married for years. The Scots-Irish were outraged.

As in Germany, a contingent of ship captains and real estate agents visited Ulster to promote emigration. The troubled Scots-Irish were ready listeners. If they could not pay their own way to America, the agents sent them as indentured servants, promising free land along the frontier once their contracts were fulfilled. To farm tenants working for absentee landlords, the prospect of land ownership was irresistible. The exodus began in 1717 and 1718.

The several thousand Scots-Irish who settled in New England were not welcomed by the Puritans. New England had no labor shortage and did not need new immigrants. The Puritans felt no affection for Presbyterians, and the latter bitterly resented having to attend the Congregational Church and support it financially. After 1720 the Scots avoided New England and headed for the middle colonies. Most disembarked in Philadelphia, where free farmers headed west while indentured servants remained behind to fill their contracts. The price of land in southeastern Pennsylvania soon pushed them into Maryland, Virginia, and the Carolinas. By 1730 the Cumberland and Shenandoah Valleys were filling with Scots-Irish farmers, and between 1730 and 1760 the Carolinas' population doubled as Lowlanders moved east from the mountains to settle the Piedmont. By 1776 the southern colonies were divided between the English settlements in the east and the Scots-Irish and German communities in the west.

Relationships between the Scots-Irish and the English and the Germans were complicated by geographical separation and cultural differences. Like the Germans, the Scots-Irish settled in separate communities, usually on the frontier, where they established their customs without resistance. Normal social intercourse between the Scots-Irish and the English did not often occur. That was fortunate. The Scots-Irish remembered Ulster and the Lowlands and had little affection for the English or their American cousins. And they were militantly Presbyterian. Wars against Ulster Catholics and Anglican discrimination against the Church of Scotland had only reinforced their religious commitment. Had they settled among Anglicans in the eastern cities rather than in the wilderness, there might have been more trouble between them.

Social tranquility, however, did not always make for good will. The English at first appreciated the Scots-Irish because their presence on the frontier was a protective buffer between native Americans and the eastern English communities, but soon they grew complacent, content for the Scots-Irish to struggle with the Indians. The Scots grew angry about eastern insensitivity—so closely related to the old country English feeling of superiority to the "uncivilized" Scots—and demanded assistance against the Indians. They felt shortchanged, convinced that eastern and English interests were disproportionately represented in the colonial governments. Insurgent political rebellions erupted in Scots-Irish communities. These were not, of course, purely ethnic rebellions, but because so many Scots-Irish participated, there were ethnic dimensions to them. In 1763 a group of Scots-Irish settlers known as the Paxton boys, terrified by Pontiac's Rebellion, slaughtered twenty peaceful Conestoga Indians in western Pennsylvania and then sent a delegation of angry frontiersmen to Philadelphia demanding military protection. They won more representation in the colonial assembly and consequently more protection. The "Regulator" movement in North Carolina consisted largely of Scots-Irish settlers resisting eastern tax collectors, land speculators, and politicians. The rebellion lasted only from 1767 to 1771, but relations between the two groups remained strained for years.

Scots-Irish and German relations were somewhat different. Because of language and religious barriers, the two communities were separate, even when they occupied neighboring valleys. While the Germans were politically cooperative, the Scots-Irish were politically independent and quick to rebel against what they saw as injustice, so much so that the English population considered them out of control. Still, the availability of land in America permitted separate communities, and the Germans and Scots-Irish shared little socially. Both, as westerners, had a political resentment toward easterners, even though the Germans were not as vocal about it as the Scots-Irish.

In spite or because of their stereotype of being pugnacious and stubborn, the Scots-Irish made lasting contributions to American society. Ever since the Reformation, when John Knox called for a literate clergy and Bible-reading congregations, the Presbyterians had revered education. Throughout the cultural wasteland of the frontier South and West, they established grammar schools to educate their children. Of the 207 colleges founded before the Civil War, the Presbyterians were responsible for at least forty-nine of them, including Hampden-Sydney College, Washington and Lee, Dickinson College, and Princeton. Their commitment to education merged with similar views by New England Puritans to generate the national belief in education as a natural right.

The Scots-Irish approach to religion helped shape the American character; for them, right and wrong should be clear, and it was the obligation of the righteous to guarantee social morality. People were responsible for their own behavior as well as that of their neighbors; tolerance for evil or compromise with it was unthinkable. They condemned Sabbath-breaking, card-playing, gambling, dancing, sexual licentiousness, and frivolity; and American culture would in many ways reflect that perspective. The Scots-Irish also contributed to the egalitarian philosophy. Their struggles against the English had left them keenly sensitive to individual rights, and life on the frontier had obliterated most social distinctions. Presbyterianism reinforced social democracy by criticizing the Catholic view that priestly power flowed from the hierarchy down to the people. The Scots-Irish argued that local congregations should elect representatives to general administrative convocations because power flowed naturally from the masses up through the hierarchy. It was only a short step from religious democracy to political democracy, and the Scots-Irish were among the first to take it.

The Growth of American Nationalism

Assimilation was retarded in colonial America because of language barriers, cultural diversity, social and geographical segregation, and political competition. Contact between the English, Scots-Irish, and Germans was limited. But there were common bonds. For most colonists the journey to the New World was a one-way trip; they would never go home again. Continued immigration infused the old culture with new vigor, but loyalty to the Old World slowly decayed. The passage of time and the birth of native generations weakened emotional ties to Europe. For English, German, or Scots-Irish descendants, the New World was home.

Economic reality gave them a common perspective as well. The availability of land created similar social structures in all the new communities of Europeans. Most Americans became small farmers with considerable independence of the ruling gentry. They owned land and enjoyed the security that accompanies property. Accepting what would later be called the Jeffersonian ideology of a nation of farmers and artisans, they saw themselves in democratic terms. Regardless of national origins, they were part of the middle class and shared an economic and social community of interest with one another. Economic interests often transcended ethnic differences, exerting similar effects on all the members of a class, regardless of ethnic origins. The new Americans had begun to sense a common destiny.

Finally, racial conflict and foreign enemies unified the European colonists. In the South all whites shared a racial unity transcending cultural differences, even though the English and Scots-Irish were much more willing to own slaves than the Germans. Throughout the colonies, especially on the frontier, fear of Indians brought Europeans together. The presence of the Spanish in Florida and the French in Canada did the same. In particular, the French and Indian War and the events leading up to the Revolution united many colonists. The French and Indian War was especially difficult for Germans and Scots-Irish living along the frontier. It posed a real dilemma for German-Americans. Since the 1680s the German Pietists, like the English Quakers, had tried to fulfill their ideals of Christian brotherhood by treating the Indians as equals. They had purchased land at a fair price and tried to avoid military confrontation. But the French and Indian War left them no choice but to fight. German communities in the Mohawk Valley, led by Captain Nicholas Herkimer and his German volunteers, defeated the Indians, in 1757 and 1758. Other German militiamen joined the Scots-Irish to defend the Pennsylvania frontier, and served under Colonel George Washington in Virginia. When forced to fight, the Germans did well, especially against a French enemy. In many ways the French and Indian threats forced Germans out of their isolation and into cooperation with Scots-Irish and English colonists.

The Scots-Irish also fought determinedly. As in Ulster, they had carved homes out of the wilderness, and this time they meant to keep them. They participated in every major engagement of the war, attacking the Indians or the French at every opportunity. In the process English-Americans developed a grudging respect for the courage and tenacity of the Scots-Irish.

The American Revolution also unified many colonists. The English-American community was deeply divided—ranging from the militancy of Lexington and Boston to the complacence of occupied Philadelphia—but Germans and Scots-Irish tended to be loyal to the revolutionary cause. Despite political isolation, the Germans harbored intense antiroyal sentiments and sympathized with colonial complaints about tyranny. As they took up arms against the British, the German volunteers sang:

> Englands Georgel Kaiser König
> Ist fur Gott und uns zu wenig.
>
> Old England's Georgie, emp'ror king
> For God and us is a trivial thing.

A number of Americans of German descent distinguished themselves in the Revolution. Several German regiments mustered in New York, Pennsylvania, and Maryland and won the praise of General Washington. Nicholas Herkimer was a militant proponent of American rights, leader of a New York Committee of Safety, and commander of four battalions of German-American soldiers. By delaying the British advance through New York in 1777, he contributed materially to the victory at Saratoga. He died in the campaign and remains today a martyred hero in German-American history. Johann Peter Muhlenberg served on a Virginia Committee of Correspondence and in the House of Burgesses, raised a cavalry regiment for George Washington, and rose to the rank of brigadier general.

Few Americans were more anti-English than the Scots-Irish. Except for considerable Tory sympathy in the Carolinas—based in part on the oath of loyalty to the crown that many had taken in order to emigrate— the Scots-Irish were ardent American patriots. Scots-Irish sentiments were so intense that some of the British thought the American Revolution was essentially a Presbyterian rebellion. In every colony, and in virtually every engagement from Saratoga in 1777 to Yorktown in 1781, the Scots were the backbone of the revolutionary forces. An anonymous New England Tory described the Scots-Irish as the "most God-provoking democrats on this side of hell." The Revolution gave the three largest groups of European-Americans a common cause, forced some political cooperation among them, and made them aware of their combined power. The beginnings of American nationalism were clear.

SUGGESTED READINGS

Ahlstrom, Sydney E. *A Religious History of the American People*. New Haven, Conn.: 1972.

Anderson, Charles. *White Protestant Americans: From National Origins to Religious Groups*. Englewood Cliffs, N.J.: 1970.

Bercovitch, Sacvan. *The Puritan Origins of the American Self*. New Haven, Conn.: 1977.

Boorstin, Daniel J. *The Americans: The Colonial Experience*. New York: 1958.

Bridenbaugh, Carl. *Vexed and Troubled Englishmen, 1590–1642*. New York: 1968.

Bushman, Richard. *From Puritan to Yankee: Character and Social Order in Connecticut, 1690–1765*. Cambridge, Mass.: 1967.

Craven, Wesley Frank. *The Colonies in Transition, 1660–1713*. New York: 1968.

———. *The Southern Colonies in the Seventeenth Century, 1607–1689*. New York: 1949.

———. *White, Red, and Black: The Seventeenth Century Virginian*. Charlottesville, Virginia: 1971.

DeJong, Gerald F. *The Dutch in America, 1609–1974*. New York: 1975.

Demos, John. *A Little Commonwealth: Family Life in Plymouth Colony*. New York: 1970.

Dickson, R. J. *Ulster Emigration to Colonial America, 1718–1775*. London: 1966.

Dunaway, Wayland F. *The Scotch-Irish of Colonial Pennsylvania*. Philadelphia: 1944.

Ford, Henry J. *The Scotch-Irish in America*. New York: 1915.

Gollin, Gillian L. *Moravians in Two Worlds: A Study of Changing Communities*. New York: 1967.

Graham, Ian C. *Colonists from Scotland: Emigration to North America, 1707–1783*. Ithaca, N.Y.: 1956.

Hall, David D. *The Faithful Shepherd: A History of the New England Ministry in the Seventeenth Century*. New York: 1972.

Hostetler, John A. *Amish Society*. Baltimore: 1963.

Laslett, Peter. *The World We Have Lost*. London: 1965.

Leyburn, James G. *The Scotch-Irish: A Social History*. Chapel Hill, N.C.: 1962.

Morgan, Edmund S. *Puritan Family*. New York: 1944.

Nash, Gary B. *Quakers and Politics, 1681–1726*. New York: 1968.

Notestein, Wallace. *The English People on the Eve of Colonization*. New York: 1954.

O'Connor, Richard. *The German-Americans*. Boston: 1968.

Parsons, William T. *The Pennsylvania Dutch*. Boston: 1976.

Redekop, Calvin W. *The Old Colony Mennonites*. Baltimore: 1969.

Rippley, LaVern. *The German Americans*. New York: 1976.

Sloan, Douglas. *The Scottish Enlightenment and the American College Ideal*. New York: 1971.

Smith, James M., ed. *Seventeenth Century America*. Chapel Hill, N.C.: 1959.

Vaughn, Alden W. *New England Frontier: Puritans and Indians, 1620–1675*. New York: 1975.

Wood, Ralph. *The Pennsylvania Germans*. Princeton, N.J.: 1942.

Chapter Three

Black People in Colonial America

The ancestral homeland of most black Americans is the rain forest of
West Africa, a broad stretch of land extending from the upper Guinea
coast to the Congo River basin. The grasslands of the northern Sudan
also furnished slaves to America. West Africa in 1500 was made up of a
bewildering variety of cultures ranging from the sophisticated, literate
Islamic nations of the northern Sudan to the nonliterate, agrarian states
of the southern rain forest. Most of the slaves brought to North America
were from the agricultural tribes of West Africa: the Ibos, Ewes,
Biafadas, Wolofs, Bambaras, Ibibios, Serers, and Aradas. Some came
from the large centralized states of Yoruba, Dahomey, Ashanti, Fulani,
Mandingo, and Hausa, and hundreds of slave expeditions invaded the
Islamic nations of the northern plains.

The northern Sudan was an early cradle of civilization comparable to
societies of the Near East and the Indus River Valley. By the fifteenth
century the kingdom of Songhay had risen to undisputed power in
sub-Sahara Africa under the leadership of Askia Mohammed I. Between
1493 and 1529 he transformed Songhay into one of the major empires of
the world, controlling much of West Africa south of the Sahara, from
the Atlantic coast in the west, through the Niger and Benue river basins,
to Lake Chad in the east. An orthodox Moslem, he ruled according to
the Koran. He codified the legal system, established a centralized bureaucracy to govern his kingdom, formed an effective banking and
credit system, and provided education from kindergarten through the

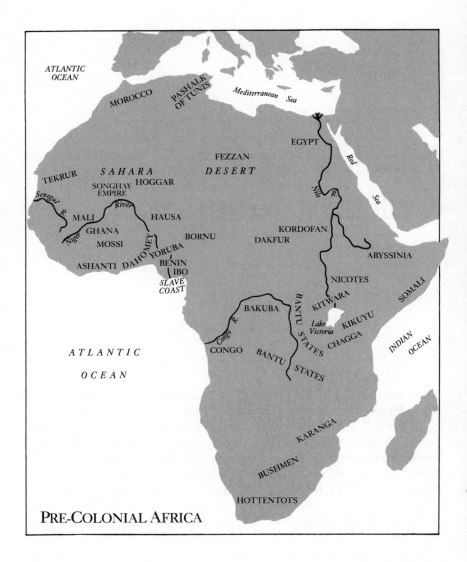

ATLANTIC
OCEAN

MOROCCO

PASHALK OF TUNIS

Mediterranean Sea

EGYPT

FEZZAN

SAHARA   DESERT

TEKRUR

SONGHAY EMPIRE   HOGGAR

Senegal R.

MALI

Niger River

GHANA

MOSSI

HAUSA

DAHOMEY

YORUBA

BENIN

IBO

SLAVE COAST

ASHANTI

BORNU

DAKFUR

KORDOFAN

Nile   R.

Red Sea

ABYSSINIA

NICOTES

KITWARA

BANTU STATES

Lake Victoria

KIKUYU

CHAGGA

SOMALI

INDIAN OCEAN

BAKUBA

Congo R.

CONGO

BANTU   STATES

ATLANTIC

OCEAN

KARANGA

BUSHMEN

HOTTENTOTS

PRE-COLONIAL AFRICA

University of Sankore at Timbuktu. He was an enlightened, literate
ruler.

Political power in Songhay rested on the royal family, whose authority
was not unlike that of the royal families in western Europe. Songhay's
economy was complex and specialized. Farmers raised sheep, cattle,
okra, sorghum, cotton, and a variety of garden crops. Artisans and
mechanics, organized into elaborate family craft guilds, manufactured
jewelry, tools, textiles, pottery, bronze castings, and farm implements.
Songhay miners produced copper, gold, bronze, and iron ore. A powerful merchant class, working the urban centers of Kumbi Kumbi, Timbuktu, Gao, and Kano, exported goods to Mediterranean nations. The
Songhay economy compared favorably with those in Europe during the

1500s, and the general population was as well off as the masses of western Europe. Songhay was also recognized in the sixteenth century as an intellectual center. Schools for young people could be found throughout the kingdom, and scholars from Africa and the Middle East gathered at the University of Sankore to study literature, languages, philosophy, law, medicine, and geography.

Though nonliterate and less sophisticated technically than Songhay, the smaller states of the coastal rain forest had advanced far beyond primitive nomadism. Yoruba, Ashanti, Dahomey, Mossi, and Hausa had a rich variety of cultural styles. Political authority usually rested in family networks which respected local prerogatives. The king was dominant, but his power was not absolute. In most cases the selection of a new monarch was made by an "electing family." Although the choice was limited to the immediate royal family, the electors did not have to choose the eldest son but could select the most capable male heir. Because the coronation of a new king required prior ratification by an "enthroning family," some community participation in politics was guaranteed. The king had to delegate authority to ministerial assistants drawn from the noble families; they performed many legislative and executive functions for him. Only rarely, as in Dahomey, did a king establish absolute centralized power.

The social structure was similarly decentralized; life revolved around the extended family. Kinship loyalties were strong, and individual identity was tied inextricably to family membership. As in most such societies, the problems of alienation and feelings of rootlessness were unknown. In a natural transition, people extended family ties into the next world, making ancestor worship an integral part of religion.

The economies of these states were generally stable. On coastal farms people raised yams, carrots, and potatoes; near the Sudanese grasslands they raised wheat and cotton. Others raised sheep and cattle, fished, and manufactured rugs, cloth, pottery, and iron tools. Private property was unknown to most Africans, so farmland was held in common and leased out on a temporary basis to families. The people were self-sufficient, labor was specialized, and their standard of living was well above that of primitive societies.

The people of West Africa lived productive lives. Their intense feelings of family loyalty and identification with the larger group made for a profound sense of community. Their political systems—whether in the kingdom of Songhay, the centralized despotism of Dahomey, or the village states of the coast—were generally stable. When Europeans moved into West Africa, they encountered highly developed societies whose political, social, and economic institutions were functioning reasonably well.

The Origins of Slavery

Slavery was both an economic and a social institution in America. With its fertile soil, long growing season, and navigable rivers, the South was ideal for a plantation economy. And with European demand for tobacco, rice, indigo, and cotton seemingly insatiable, commercial agriculture prevailed from the beginning. But commercial production of tobacco, rice, and cotton required a huge supply of cheap labor, and labor was scarce and costly. If southern farmers were to prosper, they needed workers who would not demand high wages, or be inclined to leave the plantation, or aspire to higher callings. It seemed impossible that free laborers would meet these requirements, particularly when most colonists worshiped the twin ideas of success and individual opportunity. Slave labor seemed to offer a solution.

True, there were white indentured servants, and plantation owners were not above exploiting them. But servants proved unsatisfactory. They were expensive. They sometimes escaped to the cities, where it was difficult to trace them. And they worked out their contracts in a few years and were free to go.

Nor was enslaving native Americans the answer. There were simply not enough of them. Only about 700,000 Indians were left by 1700, and not all of them were accustomed to a sedentary agricultural life. Nor, with their lack of immunity to European diseases, could the Indians survive contact with whites; epidemic death among native Americans was catastrophic. Finally, the Indians knew the land and could escape with relative ease. An economy based on slave labor required an abundant supply of easily recognizable people conditioned to settled agriculture and immune to European diseases. Americans turned to Africa.

The relationship between slavery and prejudice is complex. Some scholars believe slavery created prejudice—that debilitating involuntary servitude led to misconceptions about race and color. Others argue that slavery reinforced preexisting beliefs about racial inferiority. From their earliest contact with Africans in the sixteenth century, the English responded negatively, first with surprise and then suspicion; and long before plantations had created a demand for slaves, the English were prejudiced toward black people.

Color was important. For centuries Western society has instinctively attached meaning to various colors. Red, for example, suggests anger and green symbolizes envy. But the most powerful associations are those connected with black and white. Black has usually been linked with fear, evil, sin, death, and the unknown, and white with purity, chastity, light, spiritual essence, and truth. People still think of white as good and black as bad. A 1972 edition of Webster's New World Dictionary defines *black* as "totally without light; soiled; dirty; evil; wicked; harmful; disgraceful; sad; dismal; gloomy; without hope." Psychologists disagree about the emotional dynamics of color association. Some believe the aversion to blackness is tied to childhood fears of the dark—of loneliness and abandonment—while neo-Freudians argue that white people associate blackness with defecating, a repulsive act in Western society. In hindsight, perhaps these and other theories can be considered justifications rather than true explanations. Whatever the reasons, color is an element of racism.

But color association alone does not explain the origins of racism. Many Europeans fastened moral values to cultural differences. They examined African culture—homes, food, clothes, languages, and sexual practices—and decided that it was savage and primitive. They also disapproved of African religions. Sixteenth-century Protestantism left little room for toleration. To many Europeans, Africans were heathens, misguided children destined for hell. With its magic and mysticism, its worship of idols and ancestors, African religion seemed sacrilegious. Images of African heathenism reinforced white racism.

If the plantation created the need for involuntary servants, English racism turned American eyes to Africa as the source of slaves. That Africans were numerous, accustomed to settled agriculture, and relatively immune to European diseases made them even more likely candidates for slavery.

The Atlantic Slave Trade

The first African slaves were taken by the Portuguese in 1443. The Portuguese began the trans-Atlantic slave trade to supply their Brazilian sugar plantations. Late in the seventeenth century, after tobacco and sugar plantations were established in North America and the Caribbean, the English created the Royal African Company, ending the Portuguese and Dutch monopolies. From that time until its demise in the nineteenth century, the slave trade was dominated by the British.

There were three stages in the Atlantic slave trade. First, the slaves had to be captured, and European traders relied on other Africans to do this. Human bondage was nothing new to West Africa; for centuries West Africans had owned and traded slaves. But slavery was not a

African slaves, yoked in pairs, are forcemarched to the coast, where slave ships wait to take them to America. (The Granger Collection)

capitalist or a racist institution in West Africa. Most slaves were house servants who shared their master's race and whose opportunities for adoption or freedom were relatively good. Slavery was not the harsh, exploitive institution it became in the New World. And at first the slave trade was a casual affair; Africans sold their prisoners of war to the Europeans. By the eighteenth century, however, the trading had assumed economic importance and had become a major cause of war in Africa as coastal tribes competed to supply the New World plantations.

Moving captives from the interior to the coastal exchange posts was the second stage of the trade and was also handled by Africans. Along the way, slaves changed hands several times as African middlemen exacted their own profits. When they reached the coast, the Europeans bought them with rum, cotton cloth, guns, gunpowder, cowrie shells, brass rings, and pig iron.

After plying the African coast for several months acquiring cargo, the slave ship turned west and headed for America. This was the third stage—the "Middle Passage." Hundreds of slaves were crowded into the dark, damp holds of a slave ship for months at a time, with little or no exercise, subsistence diets, and no sanitary facilities. The mortality rate from flu, dysentery, pleurisy, pneumonia, and smallpox was devastating. Thousands died from "fixed melancholy," a form of mental depression so severe that the victims lost the will to live. Twenty percent of the Africans did not survive the voyage. Since perhaps 10 million slaves were taken from Africa to all the colonies in the Western Hemisphere between 1600 and 1800, it can be assumed that 2 million died in transit. It was, as one European trader recalled, "a dreadful business."

Slavery in Colonial America

Dutch merchants delivered the first Africans to Virginia in 1619. At that time Africans were legally indentured servants, and they were released after seven to ten years of work. Between 1619 and 1660, however, laws prohibiting interracial sex and the possession of firearms by black people began to appear in Virginia. The length of service for black servants was gradually increased, distinguishing them from white indentured servants. In 1661 the Virginia House of Burgesses called for lifetime servitude in certain cases and shortly thereafter declared that the children of lifetime servants inherited their parents' legal status. At first lifetime servitude was reserved for rebellious or criminal servants, but by 1700 it had become common throughout the country and meant hereditary servitude. Slave codes became more severe during the 1700s. Soon the law viewed slaves as property, people without civil liberties and subject to the absolute legal control of their masters.

Economic and social pressures hurt southern blacks. As tobacco, rice, and indigo plantations were developed, black indentured service seemed uneconomical. By requiring service for life, planters eliminated labor turnover and protected their investment. And as the black population increased, a sense of insecurity developed among whites. In the northern colonies, where black people numbered less than 5 percent of the population in 1750, there was little insecurity; but it was different in the South. Black people had comprised only 2 percent of the Virginia population in 1640, but they accounted for 31 percent in 1715 and over 40 percent in 1770. Similar situations prevailed in Maryland, the Carolinas, and Georgia. Whites feared the growth of the black population but believed it was economically necessary. Black indentured servitude was expensive and possibly dangerous. Black servants would someday be free, as would their children. Whites worried about the prospects of having thousands of free blacks living beyond the authority of the plantation. If all blacks were slaves, however, they could be controlled absolutely and, supposedly, would be less threatening to the white community. Not surprisingly, during the last half of the eighteenth century whites transformed black labor, replacing indentured servitude with lifetime hereditary slavery.

Deterioration in the treatment of slaves was especially severe in the South. In New England slavery was comparatively mild; slaves joined the Congregational Church, had their marriages recognized by the state, and received limited educations. To a lesser extent, New Jersey, Delaware, and Pennsylvania treated slaves liberally. In New York City, where blacks accounted for perhaps 15 percent of the population, racial tensions were more pronounced and the slave codes more severe. But for the middle colonies in general, with only 10 percent of the population black and the Quakers demanding humane treatment, race relations were better than in the South.

Changes in black status came just as the Africans were playing increasingly important roles in southern life. In the beginnings of colonial settlement, blacks and whites had to work closely together to survive. Since the climate and flora of West Africa resembled those of the South, blacks made conspicuous contributions to the economy. West Africans helped introduce rice cultivation to South Carolina, and Guinea corn was mixed with native Indian varieties. Experienced in animal husbandry, blacks were put in charge of the livestock. The use of gourds for drinking, grass and reeds for baskets and mats, and palmetto leaves for fans, brooms, and chairs all came from Africa. Familiar with swamps and marshes, Africans dominated fishing and passed on to Europeans their knowledge of temporarily poisoning rivers and streams with quicklime to catch fish. Europeans feared alligators, but Africans knew that, like the crocodiles back home, they could be used to protect livestock. Blacks also introduced the use of certain herbs and natural medicines to the colonies, dominated the fur trade as Indians disappeared, and served in the colonial militias well into the 1700s.

The basis of the southern economy, slavery provided whites with a degree of economic security; but at the same time it robbed them of their emotional security, troubling their consciences and disturbing their sleep. And yet, in an extraordinary paradox, slavery enabled white planters to join in the rhetoric of democracy; they could support civil rights for all whites, regardless of economic status, because Africans had come to occupy the bottom of the social ladder. With a readily exploitable slave caste, the whites could at least pay lip service to white democracy. Throughout southern history rich whites would manipulate the racial fears of poor whites, always holding out to them their elite social and political status as whites even though they were desperately poor. In this sense slavery permitted a plutocratic society to sustain a democratic ideology.

By the eighteenth century a distinct Afro-American culture had appeared. Many African traditions survived. Carrying infants by one arm with the child's legs straddling the mother's hips was an Old World custom, as was coiling, a method of sewing woolen trays. Special styles for braiding hair came from Africa, as did the wearing of head kerchiefs by black women. Except for isolated words (such as the West African "okay," which became "OK" to Americans) or the dialects of the most isolated Afro-American communities (such as the Sea Islanders of Georgia and South Carolina), few African words survived in America.

People from all over West Africa were thrown together in a melting pot which fused them ethnically. By the eighteenth and nineteenth centuries a fourth-generation Afro-American had little sense of tribal origins.

But although slaves spoke English, it was an English unique in pronunciation, grammar, and morphology. Some fusion with their native tongues occurred. Scholars speculate, for example, that the contemporary black phrase "dig the jive," meaning to understand what is going on, may be a combination of the Wolof term "deg," meaning to understand, and the English word "jibe." Black English also tended to eliminate predicate verbs, so that such statements as "He is fat" or "He is bad" became "He fat" or "He bad." Slave grammar neglected possessive constructions, saying "Jim hat" rather than "Jim's hat" or "George dog" rather than "George's dog," and it ignored gender pronouns and used "him" and "he" for both the masculine and the feminine. West African dialects had been similar to one another in structure, so in America the slaves used English words but placed them in a grammatical context which was both English and African in origin.

The West African roots of slave customs, family life, and religion are even clearer. In the black cultures of Guiana, Haiti, and Brazil, where slaves vastly outnumbered and rarely saw whites, African customs thrived; but in the United States, where whites outnumbered blacks and racial contacts were frequent, slaves adopted the outer forms of European social life but adapted its spirit to their own African and New World experiences. Threads of African secular culture survived in slave stories, games, dances, jokes, and folk beliefs and provided blacks with a rich verbal literature to express their joys and frustrations. Whites did not try to suppress that literature because it seemed trivial to them.

For years scholars believed that slave families were weak and matriarchal, but they disagreed about whether the source of the weakness was African society or the nature of slavery in America. But it is now accepted that if the native African family was polygamous and matriarchal, its American counterpart was monogamous and patriarchal. Most slave families consisted of two parents, most slave marriages were sound—when husband and wife were allowed to remain together—and most black children traced lineage through their fathers rather than their mothers. Still, the black family reflected its African origins. Although kinship systems were disrupted by the uprooting, blacks developed extended kinship ties in the United States. Elderly people were afforded a degree of respect unknown in white families; similarly, uncles, aunts, and cousins played more important roles in black than in white families. Under slavery the black family was a center of social life, not the debilitated institution many people have described.

The slaves adopted fundamental Protestantism, but they imbued it with an emotional spirit all their own. African musical rhythms and dances, voodooism and folk culture, and grave decorations survived in Afro-American culture; and since the idea of being possessed by a spirit was common in West Africa, the revivalistic flavor of fundamental Protestantism—with its handclapping, rhythmic body movements, public testimonies, and conscious presence of the Holy Ghost—appealed to the slaves. But while whites seemed preoccupied with guilt for sins, the slaves emphasized the redeeming features of salvation; while whites talked of eternal damnation, the slaves delighted in the story of the Jews' deliverance from bondage in Egypt. The result of both family mores and religious beliefs was a strong sense of group solidarity.

Despite their ability to rise above the dehumanizing effects of slavery, Afro-Americans were still embittered about their fate in the United States. Olaudah Equiano, an Ibo tribesman, expressed those feelings:

> Well may I say my life has been
> One scene of sorrow and of pain;
> From early days I griefs have known,
> And as I grew my griefs have grown.
>
> Dangers were always in my path,
> And fear of wrath and sometimes death;
> While pale dejection in me reign'd
> I often wept, my grief constrain'd.
>
> When taken from my native land,
> By an unjust and cruel hand,
> How did uncommon dread prevail!
> My sighs no more I could conceal.*

Slavery had profound effects upon the entire country, white people as well as blacks. In 1776, when the colonies rose up against England in defense of certain "unalienable" rights, more than 500,000 black Americans lived in bondage. Their plight would soon test the fabric of American values.

SUGGESTED READINGS

Bastide, Roger. *African Civilizations in the New World*. New York: 1971.
Craven, Wesley Frank. *White, Red, and Black: The Seventeenth Century Virginian*. Charlottesville, Virginia: 1971.

* Gustavus Vassa, *The Interesting Narrative of the Life of Olaudah Equiano, or Gustavus Vassa, The African* (London, 1794), p. 290.

Curtin, Philip D. *The Atlantic Slave Trade: A Census*. Madison, Wisconsin: 1969.

Davidson, Basil. *The African Genius*. Boston: 1969.

————. *Black Mother: The Years of the African Slave Trade*. Boston: 1961.

Davis, David Brion. *The Problem of Slavery in Western Culture*. Ithaca, N.Y.: 1966.

Degler, Carl N. *Neither Black Nor White: Slavery and Race Relations in Brazil and the United States*. New York: 1971.

Dillard, J. H. *Black English*. New York: 1972.

DuBois, W. E. B. *Black Folk: Then and Now*. New York: 1939.

Fage, J. D. *A History of West Africa*. London: 1969.

Foner, Philip S. *A History of Black Americans: From Africa to the Emergence of the Cotton Kingdom*. Westport, Conn.: 1975.

Forde, C. Daryll. *The Yoruba-Speaking Peoples of South-Western Nigeria*. London: 1951.

Forde, C. Daryll, and Jones, G. I. *The Ibo and Ibibio-Speaking Peoples of South-Eastern Nigeria*. London: 1950.

Franklin, John Hope. *From Slavery to Freedom: A History of Negro Americans*. New York: 1974.

Garrett, Romeo B. "African Survivals in American Culture." *Journal of Negro History*, 51 (October 1966), 239-245.

Gutman, Herbert. *The Black Family in Slavery and Freedom, 1750–1920*. New York: 1976.

Herskovits, Melville J. *Dahomey*. New York: 1938.

————. *The Myth of the Negro Past*. New York: 1941.

Jordan, Winthrop. *White Over Black: American Attitudes Toward the Negro, 1550–1812*. Chapel Hill, N.C.: 1968.

Levine, Lawrence W. *Black Culture and Black Consciousness: Afro-American Folk Thought from Slavery to Freedom*. New York: 1977.

Mannix, Daniel. *Black Cargoes: A History of the Atlantic Slave Trade*. New York: 1962.

Meier, August, and Rudwick, Elliott M. *From Plantation to Ghetto: An Interpretive History of American Negroes*. New York: 1970.

Morgan, Edmund S. *American Slavery, American Freedom: The Ordeal of Colonial Virginia*. New York: 1975.

Mullin, Gerald W. *Flight and Rebellion: Slave Resistance in Eighteenth Century Virginia*. New York: 1972.

Nash, Gary B. *Red, White, and Black: The Peoples of Early America*. Englewood Cliffs, N.J.: 1974.

Pope-Hennessy, James. *Sins of the Fathers: A Study of the Atlantic Slave Trade*. New York: 1968.

Rattray, Robert S. *The Ashanti*. Oxford, England: 1923.

Skinner, Elliott P. *The Mossi of Upper Volta*. Stanford, Cal.: 1964.

Wood, Peter H. *Black Majority: Negroes in Colonial South Carolina from 1670 Through the Stono Rebellion*. New York: 1974.

Summary

Ethnic America in 1776

As the historian Michael Kammen has written, colonial America was an "invertebrate" society of separate religious, ethnic, and racial groups lacking a "figurative spinal column." Economic individualism, abundant open spaces, and continuous immigration had created a pluralistic society. In 1776 perhaps 3 million people were living in what is now the continental United States. The 1.2 million people of English descent were the largest group. There were about 600,000 Afro-Americans, most of them slaves in the South, and 600,000 to 700,000 native Americans, by now living mainly in upstate New York, the Ohio Valley, the Southeast, and beyond the Mississippi River. The Scots-Irish and Germans, with 300,000 and 250,000 people respectively, were the other major ethnic groups in America. Finally, there were perhaps 200,000 French, Dutch, Belgian, Welsh, Scots, and Jewish settlers, most of them in the middle colonies.

The New England settlements were still ethnically homogeneous. After King Philip's War most native Americans had been driven into Canada and upstate New York or had died of European diseases; only 4,000 were left in New England. Without severe labor shortages, New England had only 16,000 blacks in a total population of about 700,000. The poor, rocky soil and Puritan intolerance of New England did not appeal to Scots-Irish or German immigrants. For all these reasons more than 97 percent of New Englanders were of English descent.

The middle colonies were more diverse. Although several thousand

Iroquois lived in western New York, the mid-Atlantic coast had been largely cleared of native Americans by 1776. Pennsylvania Quakers had cooperated with the Delaware Indians, but the pressure for land was so great that the Delawares had moved west of the Alleghenies. There were perhaps 60,000 blacks in the middle colonies out of a general population of nearly 700,000. Only in New York City, where 20,000 blacks lived, were race relations tense, and the slave codes especially harsh. But elsewhere in the middle colonies slavery was generally a dying institution, a victim of economic irrelevance and Quaker disapproval. Race relations in Pennsylvania and New Jersey were the most relaxed in North America. In eastern Pennsylvania more than 100,000 German settlers tended their fine farms, as did perhaps 25,000 more in upstate New York. Farther west, 75,000 Scots-Irish settlers were turning the frontier into farms. Along the Hudson River in New York, the Delaware River in New Jersey, and in New York City, several thousand Dutch colonists still retained the farms, estates, and businesses their ancestors had founded in the seventeenth century. The largest group, nearly 400,000 English colonists, led by the Quaker elite in Philadelphia and the Anglican elite in New York, controlled economic and political life in the middle colonies.

There were about 1,250,000 people in the southern colonies. As the number of plantations increased, most coastal Indians moved west, but there were still Cherokees, Choctaws, Chickasaws, and Creeks in the Southeast. Tidewater settlements had mixed populations, with black slaves outnumbering white owners in many areas. The result was a social paranoia that made life difficult for the 520,000 southern blacks. Farther west, particularly in the Piedmont and upper coastal plain, perhaps 110,000 German immigrants lived in farming communities, and in the back country approximately 200,000 Scots-Irish pioneers were pushing the wilderness westward.

Beyond the Alleghenies, English, German, and Scots-Irish settlers were opening up the Ohio Valley and the Southeast. As many as 100,000 Indians were still east of the Mississippi River, and west of it perhaps 550,000 more were living out their traditional lives oblivious to the European presence.

Despite more than a century of political and economic contact between the English, Germans, Scots-Irish, blacks, and Indians, they were still distinct ethnic communities in 1776. Although the French traveler John de Crèvecoeur wrote in 1782 that Americans were a "mixture of English, Scotch, Irish, French, Dutch, German, and Swedes," he was describing a mixture that did not exist as such. Some groups to be sure were no longer separate entities. The English settlements in Pennsylvania had absorbed New Sweden, and French

Huguenots were becoming part of wider communities everywhere. Nevertheless, most ethnic groups were not intermarrying or developing close social ties. On the eve of the Revolution, people were still divided by more than they shared.

Racial Divisions

The most basic division was racial. The history of North America differed dramatically from the Latin American experience. Ever since the Moorish invasions of Spain, Iberian society had interacted with nonwhite people, and by 1500 the Spaniards felt little ambivalence about miscegenation. Settlement patterns in Latin America led to even more mixing. During the early colonial period relatively few Spanish or Portuguese women migrated to America, so family life depended on the integration of Indian or African women into European households. The children of mixed marriages—mestizos (Indian-European) and mulattoes (African-European)—achieved a social status between that of upper-caste Europeans and lower-caste Africans or Indians. Spanish and Portuguese fathers openly claimed their mixed offspring.

But English America had no place for such mixing. Insulated from Africa and the European mainland, the English had had little contact with nonwhites, and their sixteenth-century meetings with Africans and Indians had been marked by fear and ambivalence. While sexual contacts between the races in Latin America were socially acceptable and necessary, such relationships in North America were seen as threats to the family and the social order. Although sexual contact frequently occurred between whites and blacks, it was a clandestine affair, disapproved of publicly and unsanctioned legally. Nor was there a mulatto class; such children were inevitably considered African.

For North American Europeans and native Americans, economic reality outweighed other considerations. In New England and the middle colonies the European and Indian communities met to make war or make money, but miscegenation was rare. Disease, war, and ecological change so thinned the ranks of native Americans that by 1776 there was little or no contact between most Europeans and Indians. Family life in the northern colonies was relatively stable, the sexes were numerically balanced, and sexual relations were racially contained. In the Carolinas and Georgia, however, until the sexual ratio balanced out later in the eighteenth century, European men often sought out Cherokee and Creek women. Still, these were exceptions; the two communities did not amalgamate. While most whites viewed Indians as primitive savages good only as military allies or fur trappers, the native Americans saw

Europeans as a selfish and destructive people. A mestizo class never emerged in the British colonies.

Sexual contact between Europeans and Africans in the South was a more complex affair because the two races lived together. Colonial officials began prohibiting interracial marriages in the seventeenth century; but if intermarriage was extremely rare, sexual liaisons were not. Mulatto children of white masters and black slave women appeared in every southern colony. Racial amalgamation did not imply assimilation, however, for legal status followed a matriarchal line. Children of white fathers and slave mothers were still slaves and legally defined as such. White fathers often freed their mulatto children, and these mulattoes made up the majority of free blacks. But fathers rarely claimed and raised mixed offspring, and interracial sexual relationships hardly ever created nuclear families. By forbidding interracial marriage but blinking at interracial sex, colonial officials conferred no special status on illegitimate mulattoes and increased the supply of slave labor.

Because of extreme declines in the native American population between 1607 and 1776, there was little opportunity for sexual contacts between Indians and Africans especially in New England, the middle colonies, and the Chesapeake colonies, where there were also few blacks. Runaway slaves often found refuge with Indian tribes; but only in South Carolina and Georgia, where the African and Indian populations were large, did the two communities coexist extensively. Creek, Choctaw, Cherokee, and Chickasaw Indians outnumbered Europeans in South Carolina and Georgia until well into the eighteenth century, as did African slaves. Frightened Europeans, worried about African-Indian conspiracies, prohibited blacks from traveling in Indian country, offered bounties to Indians for returning escaped slaves, and used black troops in the colonial militia to fight Indians. Even then, though, the Yamasees and Apalachees in Florida were known to harbor escaped slaves, and more often than not the slaves took Indian wives and disappeared into tribal society.

Ethnic Solidarity

The American environment provided Europeans with some common experiences. The vast open spaces, the labor shortage in many areas, and the absence of a state church or aristocracy provided Europeans with an unprecedented sense of freedom and opportunity. And because so many groups were living in the colonies, people simply had to give one another at least a grudging tolerance, even if only for the most personal reasons. Race united them against slaves and Indians; and foreign threats—the French in Canada, the Spanish in Florida, the Indians in the West, and finally the British Empire—also brought them together in the common defense. They gathered in local committees to protest British violations of their rights; they served in ethnic militia companies and then together in the colonial army; and after the Revolution they would come together in local politics. In the process, they associated with people from other backgrounds.

Still, for the most part each European ethnic group went its own way. In New England the Yankee culture of individual liberty, moralistic reform, technical ingenuity, and commercial acumen was already emerging; and throughout the colonies people of English descent felt superior to other ethnic groups. The English proprietors of Pennsylvania, for example, periodically wanted to restrict immigration from Germany and were dissuaded only because the colony's labor shortage was a more serious problem than its cultural diversity. They sponsored "charity schools" in German communities not only to teach reading, writing, and arithmetic but also to Anglicize the Germans. Though of necessity tolerant of other faiths, the English were nevertheless convinced that their Anglican, Congregational, or Baptist churches were the true vehicles for building the kingdom of God.

Of course, other groups felt the same way. The Swedish colonists in New Jersey and Pennsylvania burned trees to clear farmland, fertilized their land with the ashes, and built log cabin houses just as they had done in the Old World. They established Swedish Lutheran churches and parochial schools to preserve the old culture. But because the Swedes were so few and were surrounded by English, Dutch, and German settlers, they were unable to maintain a separate identity in colonial America.

The Dutch did better. In parts of New York City, up the Hudson River in New York State, and down the Delaware River in New Jersey, Dutch culture thrived. The steep-roofed wooden homes—with divided doors, built-in cupboards and cabinets, and blue-tiled fireplaces—were always near Dutch Reformed churches and Dutch parochial schools. The church was a community center and welfare association. Schools taught Dutch Calvinism and the Dutch language. In 1766 the Dutch built Queen's College (Rutgers University) to train the Dutch Reformed clergy in America. Because of their geographical concentration and their emphasis on the mother tongue, Dutch culture remained a powerful force in the middle colonies.

The Germans were another cultural island. Driven by memories of home, they had settled in heavily forested areas of rich limestone soil where they built their characteristically large homes surrounding a central fireplace and iron stove, large barns, and immaculate farms.

Conditioned to the Old World struggle to survive, they were thrifty, well-organized, provident, and efficient. Conditioned as well to political disaster and foreign invasions, they were suspicious of strangers and apparently apathetic about politics. German families were large, German women often worked in the fields, and because of powerful family and community loyalties, German children often settled near home after marrying. Only rarely did a German family move to another area in the South or West. German Lutheran, Reformed, and pietist churches dotted the German communities; and especially after the English had tried to convert them, the churches sponsored parochial schools to educate children in the language and faith of the Old World.

The Scots-Irish did not maintain the ethnic isolation of the Dutch or Germans. They too selected land that resembled their homeland, prizing river bottom land which was rich and not heavily wooded, preferably along the unsettled frontier where it could be bought cheaply. But neither family nor church could keep the ethnic community together for long. Scots-Irish kinship ties were weak, and families readily moved alone to distant places, leaving kin and friends behind. The Scots-Irish frequently held their farms for only a few years before selling and moving. And while they brought the Presbyterian Church to America, it could not unify them either, because the community was so scattered and the scholarly standards for its clergy so high. Although the Scots-Irish had by no means melted into oblivion by 1776, the fact that they were dispersed, spoke English, and were Protestants helped integrate them into the English community and set them apart from the Dutch and the Germans. Cultural assimilation was widespread by 1776, and more than half the Scots-Irish were intermarrying with other groups, usually to people of English descent.

In 1776, then, North America was a cultural kaleidoscope of three races and dozens of ethnic and religious groups. Assimilation, even among Europeans, did not occur. Not for another century would the cultural differences between the colonial Europeans disappear, and then only after massive new immigrations from the Old World.

SUGGESTED READINGS

Ahlstrom, Sydney A. *A Religious History of the American People*. New Haven, Conn.: 1972.

Bailyn, Bernard. *Ideological Origins of the American Revolution*. Cambridge, Mass.: 1967.

Bercovitch, Sacvan. *The Puritan Origins of the American Self.* New Haven, Conn.: 1977.

Boorstin, Daniel J. *The Americans: The Colonial Experience.* New York: 1958.

Chamberlain, J. E. *The Harrowing of Eden: White Attitudes Toward Native Americans.* New York: 1975.

Hartz, Louis. *The Liberal Tradition in America.* New York: 1955.

Heimert, Alan. *Religion and the American Mind from the Great Awakening to the Revolution.* Cambridge, Mass.: 1966.

Kammen, Michael. *People of Paradox: An Inquiry Concerning the Origins of American Civilization.* New York: 1972.

Kelley, Robert. "Ideology and Political Culture from Jefferson to Nixon." *American Historical Review*, 82 (June 1977), 531–562.

Kraus, Michael. *The Atlantic Civilization: Eighteenth Century Origins.* Ithaca, N.Y.: 1966.

MacLeod, Duncan J. *Slavery, Race, and the American Revolution.* London: 1974.

Main, Jackson T. *The Social Structure of Revolutionary America.* Princeton, N.J.: 1965.

Marty, Martin. *Righteous Empire: The Protestant Experience in America.* New York: 1970.

Nash, Gary B. *Red, White, and Black: The Peoples of Early America.* Englewood Cliffs, N.J.: 1974.

Potter, David M. *People of Plenty: Economic Abundance and the American Character.* New York: 1954.

Robbins, Caroline. *The Eighteenth Century Commonwealthman.* Cambridge, Mass.: 1959.

Schlesinger, Arthur Jr. "America: Experiment or Destiny?" *American Historical Review*, 82 (June 1977), 505–522.

Strout, Cushing. *The New Heavens and New Earth: Political Religion in America.* New York: 1975.

Wells, Robert V. *The Population of the British Colonies in America Before 1776.* Princeton, N.J.: 1975.

Part II
AMERICAN ADOLESCENCE, 1776–1890

If the eighteenth century gave America its cultural and political values, the nineteenth century tested them. Caught up in vast economic and social change, the young republic had to decide whether pluralism and liberty applied to all races as well as all religions. The community horizons of the early Protestant colonists were challenged by profound ethnic changes. In the eighteenth century, cultural conflict had largely involved white Protestants, and cultural pluralism had implied toleration for each Protestant denomination. But in the nineteenth century Catholic immigration from Ireland, Germany, and Quebec frightened Protestants, who had only recently learned to live with one another. At the same time whites had to decide whether blacks, native Americans, Mexican-Americans, and Chinese were entitled to freedom and equality. Americans would pass through the crucibles of cultural conflict and civil war searching for answers to those questions, and their basic values would emerge intact and expanded, ideologically more pervasive than they had been in 1776.

Economic changes created new subcultures in the United States. The transition from a mercantile and subsistence-farming economy to one based on industrial production, commercial farming, and resource extraction stimulated demand for land and labor, and millions of immigrants were drawn into that expanding economy. With jobs in the Northeast and land in the West, America seemed a beacon of opportunity, toleration, and freedom to small farmers and artisans in western Europe and southeastern China. Few social movements in modern history compare with the migration of 18 million people to the United States between 1820 and 1900. The Great Migration was like the eruption of a huge social volcano, and it transformed the human landscape throughout the Western world.

Although wars, revolutions, religious creeds, and political repression were important, economic unrest was the driving force behind emigration. The smallpox vaccine, the introduction of the American potato throughout Europe, and the absence of protracted war reduced mortality rates, and between 1815 and 1914 Europe's population increased dramatically. The German population, for example, grew from 24 to 68 million; the population of Sweden from 2.5 to 5.5 million; and that of Norway from 850,000 to 1.7 million. Europe's population jumped from 140 million in 1750 to more than 260 million in 1850, and to nearly 400 million by World War I. Farm sizes dwindled, and many younger sons and laborers had to give up hope of ever owning their own land. Even those with land were hard-pressed to improve their standard of living. As huge mechanized farms appeared in the United States and oceanic transportation improved, American wheat became competitive in European markets. World grain prices and the income of millions of small farmers declined. Except for the tragic potato blight in Ireland, these changes occurred little by little year after year. To supplement their incomes, European farmers had to find extra work in the winter. Many began traveling to cities—Bergen, Amsterdam, Christiania, Copenhagen, Hamburg, Bremen, Antwerp, Vienna, or Prague—to

TABLE I

IMMIGRATION FROM WESTERN EUROPE, 1820–1900

	1820s	1830s	1840s	1850s	1860s	1870s	1880s	1890s	Total
England	14,055	7,611	32,092	247,125	222,277	437,706	644,680	216,726	1,822,272
Scotland	2,912	2,667	3,712	38,331	38,769	87,564	149,869	44,188	368,012
Wales	170	185	1,261	6,319	4,313	6,631	12,640	10,557	42,076
Ireland	50,724	207,381	780,719	914,119	435,778	436,871	655,482	388,416	3,869,490
Canada	2,277	13,624	41,723	59,309	153,878	383,640	393,304	3,311	1,051,066
France	8,497	45,575	77,262	76,358	35,986	72,206	50,464	30,770	397,118
Germany	6,761	152,454	434,626	951,667	787,468	718,182	1,452,970	505,152	5,009,280
Belgium	27	22	5,074	4,738	6,734	7,221	20,177	18,167	62,160
Netherlands	1,078	1,412	8,251	10,789	9,102	16,541	53,701	26,758	127,632
Switzerland	3,226	4,821	4,644	25,011	23,286	28,293	81,988	31,179	202,448
Denmark	169	1,063	539	3,749	17,094	31,771	88,132	50,231	192,748
Sweden	91	1,201	13,903	20,931	37,667	115,922	391,776	226,266	794,665
Norway					71,631	95,323	176,586	95,015	451,647
TOTAL	89,987	438,016	1,403,806	2,358,446	1,843,983	2,437,871	4,171,769	1,646,736	14,390,614

SOURCE: *Annual Report*, U.S. Immigration and Naturalization Service, 1973.

look for jobs. Some became a migrant people long before they migrated to the United States.

Just as opportunities in agriculture were diminishing, changes in the industrial economy were eliminating other occupations. When cheap Canadian and American timber entered Europe in the nineteenth century, many jobs in the lumber industries of Sweden, Norway, Finland, and Germany disappeared. Shipbuilding in Canada and the United States eliminated more jobs in northern Europe. Factories gradually supplanted production of goods by independent artisans. Working longer hours for less money to compete with the mass-produced goods of American, English, and German factories, these independent artisans grew dissatisfied with the present and anxious about the future. After the 1870s millions of industrial workers immigrated to America looking for better jobs and higher wages in the Northeast and Midwest. Except for the Irish, immigrants were not generally the most impoverished people of Europe; chronically unemployed members of the proletariat and peasants working large estates usually did not emigrate. Both vision and resources were needed for such a drastic move. It was status-conscious workers and small farmers who traded Old World problems for New World opportunities.

Appetites whetted by the advertisements of railroads hungry for workers, steamship companies for passengers, and new states for settlers, they came from the British Isles, France, Germany, the Netherlands, Scandinavia, and China. The Irish left from Queenstown, in Cork Harbor, or crossed the Irish Sea on packet ships and departed from Liverpool; the Scots boarded immigrant vessels at Glasgow; the English and Welsh traveled by coach or rail to Liverpool and left from there; the Germans made their way to Antwerp, Bremen, or Hamburg; and the Scandinavians left first from Bergen, Christiania, or Göteborg for Liverpool, and from there sailed to America. Immigrant mortality rates in these sailing ships were extremely high. After weeks or months at sea in crowded holds, they landed in one of six places: the Maritime Provinces of Canada, Boston, New York, Philadelphia, Baltimore, or New Orleans. From Canada they traveled down the St. Lawrence to the Great Lakes or caught vessels to Boston; from the Atlantic ports most of them made rail, wagon, or steamboat connections to the interior; and from New Orleans they went up the Mississippi River and scattered out along its tributaries. The Chinese immigrants left from Canton, Hong Kong, and Macao, stopped over for a period in Hawaii, and sailed on to San Francisco.

Before 1890, most immigrants were white Protestants. Hardworking and literate, they scattered widely throughout the country, getting good jobs in the cities and building prosperous farms in the hinterland. Most

Americans welcomed them, and they in turn welcomed the religious toleration, political liberty, and economic opportunity they found in the United States. On the other hand, the immigration of Irish, German, and French-Canadian Catholics, as well as Chinese Buddhists, tested the American commitment to pluralism. Themselves affected by dislocations of industrialization and mobility—and without the traditional moorings of a powerful central government, a state church, or extended kinship systems—millions of Americans were afraid of the Catholic influx. Rumors of papal conspiracies and priestly orgies became common, as did discrimination against Catholics. Chinese immigrants ran into similar fears. Few Americans had any idea of how to incorporate these immigrants into the society.

While the Great Migration was generating cultural controversy, the westward movement was creating disputes involving Indians and Mexicans on the frontier. German, Scandinavian, English, and Scots-Irish farmers were moving into the Ohio Valley, the southeastern forests, and west of the Mississippi. In the Treaty of Paris ending the American Revolution, Britain ceded its land east of the Mississippi River, and in 1803 President Thomas Jefferson added the Louisiana Purchase. Spain sold Florida in 1819. Britain ceded all of Oregon below the forty-ninth parallel in 1846; and after the Mexican War the Treaty of Guadalupe Hidalgo gave Texas, New Mexico, Arizona, California, Nevada, Utah, and part of Colorado and Wyoming to the United States. The American empire now stretched from ocean to ocean. Native Americans pushed to the west and Mexicans whose ancestral homes were in the west had new difficulties. Both peoples faced the pressures of the immigration of tens of thousands of whites, and eventually both would lose their land. Their plight too would test the reality of freedom and equality in American life.

Finally, southern society confronted the natural rights philosophy. During the American Revolution the hypocrisy of fighting for freedom while ignoring slavery was clear, and first in New England and then throughout the North, slavery was attacked. Many southerners began defending it as a positive good that made possible an advanced stage of civilization for part of the population. There was little room for compromise, because the economic and social imperatives of slavery, the need to control a large black population, in order to make use of its involuntary labor, rendered natural rights irrelevant in most planters' minds. During the Missouri debates of 1819 and 1820, regarding the status of slavery in new states, the North and South became sharply divided over the question of slavery, and especially its expansion into the western territories. The Liberty party in 1840 and the Free-Soil party in 1848 campaigned to keep slavery out of the West, while southerners in the Democratic party wanted desperately to see slavery expand. The sectional crisis deepened in the 1850s and then exploded into civil war.

Meanwhile immigration was having significant effects in the northeast. One indication was the clandestine fraternities. In 1849 right-wing Protestants organized the Supreme Order of the Star Spangled Banner, a secret society complete with oaths, signs, and ceremonial garb. Described as Know-Nothings because of their refusal to talk about their activities, they called for immigration restriction, strict naturalization laws, discrimination against Catholics, and exclusion of Chinese. Renaming themselves the American party in 1854, they organized politically and did spectacularly well in areas where Irish Catholic immigrants were settling, taking control of the Massachusetts state government and winning local elections throughout the Northeast. Other shifts in political loyalty occurred. Throughout the nineteenth century, poor immigrants were drawn to the Democratic party—descended from Jefferson's Republican party—because of its cultural diversity and sympathy for working people. But because of the increasing numbers of Irish Catholics in the party during the 1850s, many immigrant Protestants, especially the British and Scandinavians, began looking for a new political vehicle.

They found it when the Republican party was formed in the 1850s. By supporting tariffs, a sound currency, a national bank, and internal improvements, the Republicans won the loyalty of conservative businessmen; by condemning slavery and opposing its expansion into the western territories, they were joined by abolitionists and Free-Soilers; by tacitly supporting stricter naturalization laws to keep new immigrants from voting, they gained the support of anti-Catholic nativists who feared foreigners; and by calling for free homesteads in the West, they won the support of English, Scandinavian, Dutch, and German farmers in the Midwest. The Republican party represented everything the South feared—abolition, free soil, a national bank, protective tariffs, and internal improvements, any or all of which might create an economic alliance between the North and the West. When the Republican candidate, Abraham Lincoln, won the election of 1860, the South panicked and seceded from the Union. The Civil War had begun.

For northerners the Civil War became a crusade against slavery, a reaffirmation of the American commitment to equality and toleration. The Emancipation Proclamation of 1863, the Thirteenth, Fourteenth, and Fifteenth amendments to the Constitution, and the Civil Rights Act of 1866 all extended political rights to black people. Cultural pluralism and the natural rights philosophy were sounding again, this time in a much broader context. Politics and society did not yet reflect those ideals: anti-Catholicism would rise again; native Americans and

Mexican-Americans were losing their land; the Chinese were about to be excluded permanently from the United States; and with the end of Reconstruction in 1876, Afro-Americans were consigned to a social and economic lower class for years to come. Still, American values had survived controversy and the most terrible war the world had seen. They were durable enough to remain a hope if not yet an all-embracing actuality.

Chapter Four

British Protestants and the Great Migration

During the Great Migration, the British Isles sent the largest number of immigrants to the United States; between 1783 and 1924 more than 8 million people emigrated from England, Scotland, Wales, and Ireland. More than 2 million British-Canadians crossed the border into America during the same period. These British Protestants made the most rapid adjustment to American society. Although the number of competing religious groups, the proud disdain for authority, the cult of the individual, and the national self-confidence bewildered many of them, they shared much with Americans.

Immigrants from the British Isles had, after all, peopled colonial America, and their religious values, cultural attitudes, and political institutions had become the ideological foundation of American society. Indeed, their beliefs in decentralized religious authority, individual liberty, hard work, and the dangers of concentrated power all had a place in the American political culture. Beyond that, those early colonists had generated the peculiarly American sense of mission and destiny that shaped United States history.

Anglo-America

By the nineteenth century a number of Anglo-American cultures had emerged out of the colonial migrations from England, Scotland, and northern Ireland. Most visible was the Yankee society of New England, an elitist group of people already proclaiming their special role in the religious, humanitarian, and cultural life of America. Central to the New England ethos was the idea of the chosen people which Puritan settlers had transplanted to America in the 1630s. Convinced of their own election by a transcendent God, they felt called to set an example of pure religion, good government, hard work, and a wholesome society for the rest of the world. This was their divine mission. Even in the eighteenth century, when the more rigid forms of Calvinism were deteriorating, that sense of mission still imbued New England religion.

Repudiating the notion of rigid predestination, the Congregationalist minister Jonathan Edwards set the stage for the Great Awakening in the 1730s; and in the 1740s, after George Whitfield's evangelical tour, the revivalist spirit spread throughout the American colonies. A Second Great Awakening occurred in the early nineteenth century, and these highly emotional religious experiences helped produce a host of nineteenth-century religious movements which emphasized the idea of the chosen people. Joseph Smith and Brigham Young, both born into New England Congregationalist families, led the Mormon Church in the 1830s and 1840s. William Miller, spiritual leader of Seventh Day Adventism, began his ministry in Portland, Maine, in 1840. Mary Baker Eddy, founder of Christian Science, was born to Congregationalist parents in New Hampshire in 1821. And Charles Taze Russell, early leader of the Jehovah's Witnesses, had left the Congregationalist Church in 1868. Although nineteenth-century Yankees were hardly tolerant of these new religions, New England had nevertheless given birth to them.

Yankee culture also initiated the major reform movements of the nineteenth century. William Ellery Channing helped transform Puritanism into Unitarianism, and by preaching the dignity and perfectibility of man, laid the foundation for the reform movements. George Ripley founded Brook Farm and John Humphrey Noyes the Oneida Community to demonstrate the virtues of utopian socialism; William Lloyd Garrison attacked the institution of slavery; Horace Mann started the public school movement in Massachusetts; Dorothea Dix campaigned for improvements in the treatment of the mentally ill. Susan B. Anthony and Elizabeth Cady Stanton led the movement for women's suffrage; Lyman Beecher and Justin Edwards worked tirelessly on behalf of prohibition; and William Ladd established the American Peace Society. In antebellum America, New England Yankees saw themselves as a moral aristocracy dedicated to equality and purity.

They also had a keen sense of their own history. Recalling the Sons of Liberty, the Boston Massacre, the Boston Tea Party, the battles of Lexington, Concord, and Bunker Hill, and the leadership of James Otis,

John Adams, Sam Adams, and John Hancock, the Yankees saw themselves as the cutting edge of the American Revolution, the real founders of the Republic. Groups like the Daughters of the American Revolution nurtured that vision. At the same time, Yankee prosperity justified the Puritan commitment to hard work and temporal success. Yankees put a premium on practicality and efficiency. In the technical ingenuity of men like Eli Whitney, Samuel Slater, and Paul Revere, and in the great commercial talents of the Amorys, Browns, Cabots, Lowells, and Russells, they saw proof of their election as leaders of the American destiny.

With that background of confidence and success, many New England Yankees devoted themselves to intellectual and cultural pursuits. Around an axis reaching from Yale in New Haven to Harvard in Cambridge, American literary culture produced the Transcendentalists Ralph Waldo Emerson, Henry David Thoreau, and Bronson Alcott; historians George Bancroft, Francis Parkman, Henry Adams, and Herbert Baxter Adams; novelists Harriet Beecher Stowe, Nathaniel Hawthorne, Herman Melville, and Henry James; and poets Henry Wadsworth Longfellow, John Greenleaf Whittier, and Emily Dickinson. In New England, Yankees believed, rested the center of American culture.

A completely different Anglo-American culture appeared in the planter aristocracy of the South. Resting on the labor of black slaves and poor whites, the planter class by the nineteenth century had constructed an elaborate collective ego. Deeply concerned about the drift of American development—industrialization, technological change, democratic egalitarianism, and business materialism—they chose to cultivate a different set of values based upon rural, aristocratic gentility. Planter society rested on two myths: that rich whites could trace their ethnic roots back to the "Cavalier" society of old England, and that they were somehow above the mercenary acquisitiveness of northern, Yankee businessmen. In reality they were usually neither patrician nor antibusiness; most of them came from the English and Scots lower and middle classes, and as planters they were businessmen who speculated in slaves, real estate, and commodity futures, seeking profits through commercial agriculture. The truth, of course, is hardly relevant, for these southerners came to believe in aristocratic origins and tradition, and their rhetoric expressed hostility to materialism, progress, cities, and social ambition. They looked down upon Yankee culture as crass and superficial, busy and unstable, hectic and unpredictable; on poor white southerners as a boorish lot of temperamental, uncivilized "trash"; and on black slaves as incompetent children unable to function on their own. Southern "Cavaliers" would consider marrying or mixing with none of these groups, and instead lived in a social world of their own, isolated and convinced of their moral superiority.

Closely related to planter society, though quite distinct from it, was the world of poor southern whites. Imbued with populistic resentments of concentrated wealth and power, they were nevertheless bound to the planter elite by shared convictions of white superiority, of the need for all whites, regardless of class, to maintain a solid front against blacks. Similar sentiments of white solidarity animated the southern middle class. Although Scots-Irish geographic mobility had made for a fluid society in the colonial South, the nineteenth century witnessed a settling down which created powerful localistic values—strong attachments to home and region. As a result of stable residential patterns in the rural and small-town South, extended family ties were more influential there than in other areas of Anglo-America. Finally, these white southerners shared the planter view of a society under siege, surrounded by a powerful and hostile Yankee culture. The abolition movement, the Civil War, and Reconstruction only reinforced that psychological posture during the nineteenth century.

A variant of this culture appeared in the southern Appalachian mountains by the nineteenth century. There, in the mountain hollows, thousands of people lived in isolation from the larger society. They nurtured a sense of individualism and family independence so profound that they could hardly conceive of membership in or loyalty to such corporate organizations as governments and schools. Respect and status revolved around economic and social autonomy. Mountain people were also highly traditionalist in their values; life was difficult and insecure, there was poverty and danger, and people developed a philosophical fatalism about the present and future, feeling little control over the course of their lives. They rarely complained or rebelled; their folk culture looked to the past rather than the future, and they were far removed from material progress and middle-class success.

The Search for a Better Life

Into this Anglo-American environment came the immigrants from England, Scotland, and Wales. The traditional lure of America survived in the British Isles, and glowing letters from other immigrants as well as American advertisements exaggerated the attraction. But unlike the colonial immigrants, these settlers were inspired less by social, political, and religious discontent than by economic motivations. Social and political conditions in Great Britain were better than during the tumultuous years of the seventeenth and eighteenth centuries. Some people, like the Mormon converts, left for religious reasons, but they were heading for the Utah Zion rather than escaping persecution in England;

In this cartoon, entitled "The Lure of American Wages," John Bull, symbolic of Great Britain, tries to restrain people from going to America while Uncle Sam, across the sea, invites them to immigrate. (The Granger Collection)

inspiration, not desperation, drove them to America. Except in Ireland, the religious atmosphere of nineteenth-century Britain was tolerant and calm; the sectarian controversies of the past had yielded to more worldly considerations. And because of the Reform Acts of 1832 and 1867, which had extended the franchise, democratic ideals were emerging. The English, Welsh, and Scots immigrants were not fleeing repression at home but were seeking their fortunes in America.

Nor were most coming to escape poverty. Some of the Welsh workers and Highland Scots farmers were poor, but most British Protestants had decided that opportunities for economic success were too limited at home. Most brought money with them to America; and because taxes, rents, and tithes were heavy in Britain, they expected the return on their capital to be higher in the United States. Writing home in 1818, one English immigrant said:

> I *own* here a far better estate than I *rented* in England, and am already more attached to the soil. . . . We are in a good country, are in no danger of perishing for want of society, and have abundant means of supplying every other want.*

---

* Quoted in Edith Abbott, *Historical Aspects of the Immigration Problem* (Chicago, 1926), p. 47.

By 1830 Great Britain was the most advanced industrial nation in the world, and perhaps half those immigrants were skilled workers. When the Industrial Revolution reached America, the traditional labor shortage became even more acute. The demand for skilled workers produced high wages, and skilled immigrants usually found work in their own crafts. Unlike most immigrants, whose residence determined occupation, British Protestants settled where their skills could best be employed. Theirs was a lateral, occupational move from one region in Britain to its economic counterpart in the United States. Cornish tin miners, for example, settled in New England not because it was the first place they landed but because hard-rock mining there resembled that at home.

For years textiles were the backbone of British industry. Processing cotton was mechanized by 1850, and huge mills replaced home and workshop production. Britain tried desperately to keep its industrial secrets, but the spread of technology to the United States was inevitable. In the 1790s textile factories appeared in New England, and soon hundreds of mills sprang up throughout the region. Because wages were much higher in America, tens of thousands of English and Scots mill hands, weavers, cloth printers, and spinners immigrated to New England, New York, and Philadelphia. So did woolen workers, carpet weavers, silk operatives, hosiery and linen workers, thread spinners, and lace-curtain workers. An English immigrant weaver wrote home in 1830:

> I hope brother William [and his family] will come all together, for they can get spinning here. I have just begun to work in a broad loom, and I think I shall get on with it. There is hundreds of factories here, both cotton and woollen, and some weavers wanted in the same shop with me. It is a very pleasant country. . . . Meat is very cheap, about two-pence half-penny per pound, and flour.*

By 1900 British textile workers had settled all along the East Coast.

Mining also supplied workers to the United States. British coal and iron ore miners came by the tens of thousands because their skills were in such demand. On both sides of the Atlantic the Industrial Revolution was based on coal because steamships, railroads, blast furnaces, forges, and factories needed energy. Colliers from South Wales poured into the anthracite fields of eastern Pennsylvania; Scots and English miners immigrated to the bituminous fields of western Pennsylvania, Maryland, West Virginia, and Ohio; and thousands of tin, copper, and iron ore miners from Cornwall went to various regions. In 1830 Cornish tin and copper mines were the most productive in the world, but wages were higher in the lead mines of Wisconsin and Colorado, the silver mines in

---

* Ibid., p. 77.

Nevada and Arizona, the tin mines in California and New Hampshire, the copper mines in Michigan and Utah, and the iron ore mines in Minnesota.

Heavy industry sent thousands more workers to America. As the furnaces and foundries of the United States boomed in the 1800s, demand for metal workers increased enormously; and iron and steel workers from Manchester and Sheffield, tin sheet-metal workers from South Wales, shipbuilders from southern England, machine-tool specialists from Birmingham, and skilled engineers from Yorkshire all immigrated in search of higher wages. Many ended up in the industrial towns of western New York, Pennsylvania, and Ohio.

Though not on the same scale as textiles, mining, and heavy industry, other British industries also contributed workers to America. Potters from Staffordshire moved to East Liverpool, Ohio, and Trenton, New Jersey, the two centers of pottery manufacturing. Skilled construction workers arrived. From the North Wales slate quarries came workers attracted to the slate quarries of eastern Pennsylvania. Scots granite workers moved to the New England granite deposits, and British masons, carpenters, and painters settled throughout the country. Life in America was good for them; they found good jobs and social acceptance.

Thousands of small leaseholders and farm laborers displaced by the rise of large-scale agriculture after the Napoleonic Wars joined the immigration to America. Most had gone into the cities to find factory jobs but had never lost the desire to become farmers again. The possibility of owning land in America was irresistible. Rural life in America came as a shock to them, however. There were often cold winters, hot summers, dust storms, droughts, and too many insects, as well as great distances and desperate loneliness. Nevertheless, they came by the thousands because property ownership made their hardships bearable.

More than seven hundred and fifty thousand British-Canadians immigrated between 1776 and 1900. Approximately ten thousand left Canada after the abortive rebellions of 1837 and 1838, when political radicals demanded popular sovereignty and the end of British rule. Nearly thirty thousand more left in the 1840s, when depression struck the timber and shipbuilding industries. Although thousands of skilled artisans left Canada for work in the factories and mines of America, most of the Canadian immigrants were farmers. When the Great Plains opened up after the Civil War, hundreds of thousands of farmers left Canada to take up land in the Dakotas, Iowa, Minnesota, and Nebraska. So great was the exodus that Canadian officials worried about depopulation, but they could not stop the flow. The border between the two countries was too long, too vague, and too unprotected. British-Canadian immigrants merged with the English Protestant community in the United States.

The English Immigrants

The English immigrants were readily accepted into American society, though the adjustment was not universally easy. Wages were high but so were prices, and many complained about the cost of living. Working conditions were more primitive than in England, and farming was different too. In England the land had long ago been cleared, but in America many of the English immigrants had to spend years clearing virgin land of trees, brush, and stumps. The work was tedious, backbreaking, and discouraging. Other complaints had to do with the loneliness of rural life in America, or the lack of stores, churches, schools, hospitals, banks, roads, and transportation. America was not an unmixed blessing.

But the advantages outweighed the disadvantages. The English were better off than other immigrants because they shared so much with the host society. In 1820 people of English descent were the largest group in the society, and most Americans felt comfortable with the English immigrants. Most of these immigrants were literate, and their command of the language enhanced acculturation. Yankee Americans respected their technical abilities, willingness to work hard, and commitment to success. Moreover, most of them joined Methodist, Baptist, Congregational, and Episcopalian churches. Not surprisingly, their absorption into the larger society was rapid. Language and industrial skills helped them get good jobs and supervisory positions while other immigrants often spent years at the bottom of the occupational ladder. English families were often smaller than those of other groups; and with fewer children to support parents were more likely to save money, enjoy material security, and promote education. Few stereotypes of English indigency ever developed. While often perceiving other immigrants as economic parasites, Americans looked upon the English as economic assets. Economically as well as socially, they moved directly into the mainstream of American life.

Their transition was made even easier by the fact that a transatlantic Anglo-American community existed in the minds of many Americans. People admired England, despite the bitter feelings aroused by the American Revolution and the War of 1812. Its industrial wealth was the envy of other nations and its Parliament a beacon for the oppressed. American liberals admired William Gladstone and the Liberal party, and conservatives held Benjamin Disraeli and the Conservatives in high regard. British literature and British universities were considered superior to their American counterparts; the children of wealthy Americans traveled to England for their educations; and Americans looked to England for models of municipal and industrial reform. In short, the United States functioned in a cultural framework that was largely British, and the English immigrants prospered because of that special relationship.

The English immigrants did not develop the ethnic culture so characteristic of other groups. There seemed no need. They were prosperous and socially accepted. They shared racial, religious, and cultural values with most Americans. British-American newspapers survived for a while, and British-Canadians held annual picnics to celebrate their origins, but these were tepid affairs when compared to those of the Welsh, Scots, Irish, Germans, and Scandinavians. The English settled widely throughout the country and were more evenly distributed than any other group. In the late nineteenth and early twentieth centuries nearly half the English immigrants married within their group, but only one in six of the second generation did. They were already at home with other Americans through their relationships at work and school. Assimilation through intermarriage completed the transition; intermarriage itself with other European Protestants did not immediately destroy ethnicity, but after several generations the vast majority of people of English descent came to define themselves as "Yankees," "Cavaliers," or "Old Americans."

The Welsh Immigrants

The Welsh shared a racial, religious, and national heritage with most Americans, but their language set them apart and led to a brief flowering of ethnic Welsh culture in the United States. Between 1820 and 1900, more than forty thousand people left Wales for America, and another fifty thousand Welsh came from England. Most were searching for good land or good jobs. More than 80 percent settled in Pennsylvania, Ohio, New York, Illinois, and Wisconsin, where they worked in slate quarries, coal mines, lead mines, and iron and steel mills, or took up land as farmers. Hardworking, literate Protestants, they too were readily accepted in America.

Unlike the English, however, the Welsh settled into ethnic enclaves. And wherever they settled, Protestant churches appeared offering services in Welsh. The Welsh Baptist Church, the Welsh Congregational Church, and the Welsh Presbyterian Church were all active, but the Welsh Methodist Church commanded the loyalties of most immigrants. The rise of Methodism had been a significant development in eighteenth-century England. Dissatisfied with Anglican formalism yet uncomfortable with the Calvinist emphasis on human depravity and predestination, John Wesley began preaching a different gospel to English and Welsh workers. He was convinced that neither Anglicanism nor Puritanism was meeting the spiritual needs of the lower classes, so he preached a salvation requiring only personal acceptance of a loving grace which Christ offered to everyone. Mankind was not depraved, everyone could be saved, and people in a state of grace could achieve spiritual perfection in this life. Wesley preached all over England and Wales and generated revivalist atmosphere wherever he went. He also established local societies in which people could discuss the Bible and "bear testimony."

Methodism spread rapidly throughout the working classes of England and Wales just as a series of economic crises were devastating the woolen industry south of Bristol, the industrial villages of Yorkshire, Lancashire, and the Midlands, and the mines of Cornwall and Wales. The evangelical emphasis on "sweet redemption" and disdain for theological disputes, clerical orders, and formal rites appealed to the working classes; Wesleyan societies which invited the participation of working people in church government gave them a stake in society; evangelistic revivalism provided poor people an outlet for the frustrations of toil and poverty; and the Wesleyan emphasis on achieving spiritual perfection inspired the working classes to labor constantly at improving their lives. Methodism conquered Wales and helped prevent social unrest in the British Isles. It was a conservative force that helped to abort the revolutionary pressures growing out of the Industrial Revolution. English and Welsh workers who came to America imbued with a sense of evangelical perfectionism blended well into the revivalistic atmosphere of nineteenth-century Protestant America.

Living together and worshiping in their own churches, the Welsh were a tight community and established other ethnic organizations to preserve Old World values. Founded in 1843, the Welsh Society of America was dedicated to preserving the Welsh language and culture, and the Ancient Britons Benevolent Society and Cambrian Mutual Aid Society assisted incoming immigrants. Throughout the Welsh communities the immigrants established the ubiquitous *Eisteddfod* to promote singing and choral competition as well as literary and cultural activities. A Welsh farmer in Kansas proudly wrote home in 1871:

> [It] is surprising to the Welsh in this country that so many of our nation stay at home rather than come here. I have now moved here to live and can describe the place better. I have not changed my opinion of this wonderful place. We expect to have an *eisteddfod* on 5 August, the subjects for competition being prose, poetry, etc. The choir is practicing for the occasion.[*]

[*] Alan Conway, ed., *The Welsh in America* (Minneapolis, 1961), p. 136.

Welsh America enjoyed a separate community spirit in the United States, but acculturation was rapid. With the second generation the Welsh church services began switching to English, and the Welsh language press, led by *Y Drych* in Milwaukee, gradually lost readers. In 1850 there were 29,868 people claiming Welsh heritage in the United States, and the number grew to 250,000 in 1920 when it began to decline. Although more than 50 percent of first-generation Welsh married within their group, the second and third generation began to move away from their home communities and intermarry with other ethnic groups—usually other white Protestants and more often than not the English. Small in number and generally conservative, they did not threaten American society; indeed, they flowed easily into the Anglo-Protestant mainstream. By the fourth generation Welsh culture was rapidly disappearing.

The Scots Immigrants

Similar forces worked on the Scots immigrants, but because they were divided into three separate peoples, acculturation and assimilation occurred at different rates. In the colonial period the Scots-Irish had far outnumbered other Scots, but between 1830 and 1924 the number of Scots immigrants increased dramatically. During the Great Migration more than seven hundred thousand came from the Lowlands and the Highlands, half before 1900 and half between 1900 and 1924. The Scots-Irish immigration continued as it had in the eighteenth century, with large numbers of the immigrants pouring into the South and West, mingling with the Scots-Irish and English communities, and then disappearing into the larger society.

Over the centuries Scotland was divided into the Lowlands and the Highlands. The Lowlands was south of a line running from Glasgow to Edinburgh and included a strip of land along the entire northeastern coast of the country. Scotland was first settled by Gaelic-speaking Celts from Ireland, but later, when Anglo-Saxons from southern England moved there, the Celts retreated north into the Highlands. By the eighteenth century the Lowlanders were largely English-speaking descendants of Anglo-Saxons while Highlanders were Gaelic-speaking descendants of Irish Celts. Most of the Scots immigrants of the nineteenth century settled in New York, Massachusetts, and Pennsylvania, but there were other concentrations in Ohio, Illinois, Michigan, and California.

Although both Lowlanders and Highlanders adjusted quickly to American life, there were differences in the pace of acculturation. As English-speaking Anglo-Saxon Protestants, the Lowlanders scattered throughout the Northeast, and after a few years it was difficult to locate many Lowland-Scot communities. Next to the English, they were the most readily accepted immigrant group in the United States. The Scots wanted to be accepted. One immigrant complained in 1866 that his brethren tried

> to smooth down the rough Doric of their northern tongue, and to lisp or sniffle out the natural speech with which the Creator has endowed them. They would just as soon have people believe that they had been born on this side of the Atlantic and that their grandfather had signed the Declaration of Independence as that they came direct from Drumclog with the parish minister's certificate that their luckie-daddy was ruling elder for forty years.*

They did organize charitable and literary societies, usually called St. Andrew's clubs, and tried to support a Scots-American press, but neither endeavor attracted more than a few. Scots sports such as curling and golf were transplanted. John Reid, a native of Dunfermline, founded the St. Andrew's Golf Club of New York in 1888, and the Grand National Curling Club introduced that sport to America. To be sure, they were proud to be Scots, and immigrants married Scots more than 40 percent of the time. Their children and grandchildren, however, did not, and by the third generation Lowlanders were disappearing into Anglo-American society.

Assimilation was more retarded for Highlanders. While the Lowlanders shared an Anglo-Saxon heritage with England and America, the Highlanders were descendants of Irish Celts, and many still spoke Gaelic. Nor was there any love between the Highlanders and the English, and some of that antipathy accompanied them to America. Highlands society had revolved for centuries around the power of isolated feudal clans. The clan chieftan was a tribal leader who leased land to blood-relative warriors in return for rent payments and military loyalty. Although the English conquest of Scotland had broken the political power of the clan chieftans by the eighteenth century, the social pull of clan loyalty and family obligation survived. Clan leaders, of course, lost their authority in America, but loyalty to the Highlander family was strong. Highlanders settled among other Highlanders, where Presbyterian churches could be established. They formed clan societies like the Clan Donald Society of America; they joined Caledonian clubs, the Sons of St. George, piper bands, Gaelic clubs, and in 1878 established the Order of Scottish Clans; they played bagpipes, wore kilts, celebrated Halloween and Hogmanay (New Year's Eve), enjoyed curling, and sponsored Highland games athletic contests.

* *Scottish-American Journal*, September 15, 1886.

But like the Welsh they soon filtered into the larger society through relationships at school and work and then intermarriage. Their white skin and Presbyterianism opened the society to them; they learned English and were caught up in the mass education and mass mobility of America; and, particularly after the fourth generation, they married outside the clan and merged into the Anglo-American culture.

Like the Scots-Irish, the Scots made a major contribution to American life. A dualism existed in Scottish culture. On the one hand there was the Calvinist asceticism of early Presbyterianism. The Scots clergyman John Knox, after visiting John Calvin in Geneva, returned to Scotland in 1559 and converted the nation to a belief in an awful, majestic God, the predestined election or damnation of every soul, and the presbyterian form of church government in which power flowed up from the congregation to the hierarchy. Because of English attempts to impose first Catholicism and then Anglicanism on the Scots, Presbyterianism became the national faith of Scotland, almost a test of citizenship. Being Presbyterian and being a Scot were almost synonymous. But equally embedded in the Scots mentality was the metaphysical tradition of the universities of Glasgow and Edinburgh, the spiritual homes of people such as the historian Thomas Carlyle, the economist Adam Smith, and the philosophers James Mill, Francis Hutcheson, and David Hume. Here was an analytical idealism which rejected dogma and tradition. Apparently contradictory, the dualism between religious loyalty and metaphysical intuition created the Presbyterian commitment to equity, individuality, intellectual virility, hard work, and success. The Scots immigrants carried those values to the United States in the nineteenth century and found ready acceptance for them by Anglo-Americans.

On another level Presbyterianism failed to hold the Scots-American community together. The Presbyterian Church was prone to schism because of its commitment to individualism and congregational independence. Since authority flowed from the bottom up, the Scots argued constantly over religion. In the colonial period the Scots-Irish had insisted that the American church was independent of the Church of Scotland, but Lowlanders disagreed. In the nineteenth century the "MacDonaldites" of Canada and Massachusetts claimed to be the true church; Alexander Campbell left the church and started the Disciples of Christ; and John Davie founded the Christian Catholic Apostolic Church in 1896. Constant schism and the fact that Highlanders, Lowlanders, and English settlers attended the Presbyterian Church prevented Presbyterianism from integrating Scots ethnic life.

Of all the immigrants to America the English, Scots, and Welsh made the most complete transition from Old World attitudes to the American value system revolving around competing loyalties to family, church, occupation, and income group. All of them enjoyed the color status conferred on whites and denied to blacks, Indians, Mexicans, and Asians. The English and Lowlanders spoke English, and the Welsh and Highlanders knew it as a second language. They had an Anglo-Saxon concern for fairness, success, and individuality. The English and Lowlanders benefited from the thinking of such men as Herbert Baxter Adams and William Graham Sumner, who were then attributing American success to the Anglo-Saxon heritage. Most of the British immigrants were also skilled workers, who were welcomed by the upper classes. And the immigrants were mostly Protestants; whether it was the Presbyterianism of the Scots, the Methodism of the English and Welsh, or the Anglicanism and Congregationalism of the English, their faiths were not alien to older Americans.

British-Americans went to college in record numbers, dominated membership in such professional groups as the American Bar Association and the American Medical Association, and disproportionately served in state legislatures, Congress, and the federal courts. In 1870 nearly 90 percent of corporate executives were of British descent, a number that would decline only to 65 percent in 1950. There were, to be sure, "swamp" Yankees—poor rural southerners of English descent— and an English blue-collar class of urban workers and miners who did not become rich or well-to-do, but in terms of political influence and occupational status, most British-Americans succeeded in their new homeland.

SUGGESTED READINGS

Amory, Cleveland. *The Proper Bostonians*. New York: 1947.

Anderson, Charles. *White Protestant Americans: From National Origins to Religious Groups*. Englewood Cliffs, N.J.: 1970.

Berthoff, Rowland. *British Immigrants in Industrial America, 1839–1900*. Totowa, N.J.: 1971.

Bushman, Richard. *From Puritan to Yankee: Character and Social Order in Connecticut, 1690–1765*. Cambridge, Mass.: 1967.

Conway, Alan. *The Welsh in America*. Minneapolis, Minn.: 1961.

Davis, Lawrence B. *Immigrants, Baptists, and the Protestant Mind in America*. Urbana, Ill.: 1973.

Dowie, J. Iverne, and Tredway, J. Thomas. *The Immigration of Ideas: Studies in the North Atlantic Community*. Rock Island, Ill.: 1968.

Eighmy, John Lee. *Churches in Cultural Captivity: A History of the Social Attitudes of Southern Baptists*. Knoxville, Tenn.: 1972.

Erickson, Charlotte. *Invisible Immigrants: The Adaptation of English and Scottish Immigrants in the Nineteenth Century.* Coral Gables, Fla.: 1972.

Esslinger, Dean R. *Immigrants and the City: Ethnicity and Mobility in a Nineteenth Century Midwestern Community.* New York: 1971.

Foster, Stephen. *Their Solitary Way: The Puritan Social Ethic in the First Century of Settlement in New England.* New Haven, Conn.: 1971.

Hansen, Marcus Lee. *The Mingling of the Canadian and American Peoples.* New York: 1940.

Hartmann, Edward George. *Americans from Wales.* Boston: 1967.

Hudson, Winthrop. *American Protestantism.* Chicago: 1961.

Huggins, Nathan I. *Protestants Against Poverty: Boston's Charities, 1870–1900.* Westport, Conn.: 1971.

Kelley, Robert. *The Transatlantic Persuasion: The Liberal-Democratic Mind in the Age of Gladstone.* New York: 1969.

Knights, Peter. *The Plain People of Boston.* Boston: 1971.

Lehmann, William C. *Scottish and Scotch-Irish Contributions to Early American Life and Culture.* Port Washington, N.Y.: 1978.

Marty, Martin. *Righteous Empire: The Protestant Experience in America.* New York: 1970.

Rowe, John. *The Hard Rock Men: Cornish Immigrants and the North American Mining Frontier.* New York: 1974.

Sennett, Richard. *Families Against the City: Middle Class Homes of Industrial Chicago, 1872–1890.* Chicago: 1970.

Shepperson, Wilbur S. *Emigration and Disenchantment: Portraits of Englishmen Repatriated from the United States.* Norman, Oklahoma: 1965.

Solomon, Barbara. *Ancestors and Immigrants: A Changing New England Tradition.* Cambridge, Mass.: 1956.

Taylor, A. M. *Expectations Westward: The Mormons and the Emigration of their British Converts in the Nineteenth Century.* Ithaca, N.Y.: 1966.

Thernstrom, Stephen. *Poverty and Progress. Social Mobility in a Nineteenth Century City.* Cambridge, Mass.: 1964.

Tindall, George B. *The Ethnic Southerners.* Baton Rouge, La.: 1975.

Tomisch, John. *A Genteel Endeavor: American Culture and Politics in the Gilded Age.* Stanford, Cal.: 1971.

Weller, Jack E. *Yesterday's People: Life in Contemporary Appalachia.* Lexington, Kentucky: 1965.

Woodward, C. Vann. "The Southern Ethic in a Puritan World." *William and Mary Quarterly,* 25 (July 1968), 343–370.

Chapter Five

The Irish Catholics in America

Thousands of years ago Nordic hunters crossed the land marshes of what is now the North Sea, reached England, and from there settled in Ireland. In the sixth century B.C. Celtic tribes swept out of western Europe and became the dominant culture in Brittany, Wales, the Scottish Highlands, and Ireland. British-born St. Patrick brought Christianity from Rome to Ireland in the fifth century A.D. (in legend he also drove all the snakes from the island); Bishop Palladius headed the first Irish bishopric in 431; and Roman Catholicism became a cultural foundation of Irish society. But an accident of geography directed the course of Irish history after 1169, when the Norman supporters of King Henry II of England invaded the island. Though culturally united by Celtic customs, the Gaelic language, and Roman Catholicism, Ireland before the Anglo invasions was politically decentralized into clan societies in which tribal chieftans controlled regional areas. Gaelic Ireland was divided into four general areas: Leinster, Munster, Connaught, and Ulster. The rich soil of Leinster made it especially attractive; and since Leinster also faced England across the Channel, the English settled there in Dublin, Meath, Louth, Westmeath, and Kildare counties. Known as the Pale, the area extended about forty miles inland from the coast, and English influence was pervasive. But it was only a bridgehead, and control of the Pale never implied control of Ireland.

From the Pale the English moved west and southwest into Connaught and Munster, but their control was not as strong there. Treacherous terrain isolated them from the Pale, and, outnumbered by native Irish,

they often married into local families. In 1366 England passed the
Statutes of Kilkenny, which forbade English settlers to adopt Irish
customs, but it was a losing proposition. Gaelic Ireland thrived in the
rural areas, and Anglo-Norman society had its only real foothold in the
larger towns. In Ulster, English influence hardly existed until the seventeenth century, when English landlords and Scots settlers took the land
from the Irish natives.

During the sixteenth century English monarchs extended their authority over Ireland, but beyond the Pale the island remained overwhelmingly Gaelic. After the English Reformation royal officials insisted that the Irish repudiate Catholicism as a test of loyalty. This
cultural imperialism succeeded in the Pale, where thousands of Catho-

lics reluctantly swore allegiance, but in Connaught and Munster the natives refused and in Ulster they resisted violently. What had once been a political struggle now became a religious and ethnic civil war between Anglo-Protestants and Irish Catholics.

Under such pressures Roman Catholicism became indelibly imprinted on Irish culture. It had always been a nationalistic faith, deeply mixed with older Celtic rites. Irish pilgrims walked barefoot up the rocky Croagh Patrick in County Mayo each July to celebrate St. Patrick's vanquishing of the snakes, but in July each year at that same rocky hill the ancient Celts had celebrated Lugnas, a festival in which the sun god Lug promised a bounteous harvest. On the eve of St. Martin's Day, Irish Catholics would kill a sheep or cock, sprinkle blood around their home, and trace out a bloody cross on the forehead of each family member to ward off evil spirits. Halloween was a mystical religious occasion for the Irish, the eve of the Samhain festival on November 1 that marked the end of the growing season and the beginning of the Celtic winter. It was a night of dread and ominous terror, for in the darkness the ghosts and spirits of the dead were thought to return to the real world; indeed, it was a night when the barriers between this world and the next broke down. Masks and costumes, acts of mischief, and jack-o'-lanterns distracted people from the fear of death. On March 17 they celebrated St. Patrick's Day and wore the green shamrock, national flower of Ireland, supposedly used by St. Patrick to explain the Holy Trinity to unbelievers. The three leaves and one stalk of the plant signified the three personages—Father, Son, and Holy Ghost—of the one God.

In Ireland, under centuries of Anglo-Protestant persecution, religion and nationality fused. Indeed, the Gaelic word *Sassenach* meant both "Protestant" and "English." England's attempt to Anglicize Ireland created an ideological dualism in Irish life: a deep, personal reverence for Roman Catholicism and a proud consciousness of Irish nationality. The Irish Catholic clergy were without vested interests or property to protect; like most of their parishioners they were poor, landless, and politically impotent. A siege mentality possessed both priests and peasants, and the Irish identified with the church as the central institution of their lives.

But the more Catholic Ireland became, the more England worried about it. Faced with a rival in Catholic Spain in the sixteenth century, and worried about Catholic Ireland on its western flank, England decided to Anglicize the entire island, not just the Pale. Queen Elizabeth awarded large plantations in Ireland to English landlords, who in turn invited Scots to settle there. The Scots fought ferociously against Catholic guerrillas, and between 1580 and 1690 Catholic ownership of the land declined from 95 to less than 15 percent. In the process the Catholic upper and middle classes were almost destroyed.

In England the fear of Catholicism as well as the new support for natural rights led to the Glorious Revolution; Catholic King James II was exiled to France, and Protestant William of Orange assumed the throne. Immediately after his flight from England, James II turned to Ireland, collected an army of French sympathizers and Irish Catholics, and summoned an anti-Protestant Irish Parliament. But in July 1690 William of Orange invaded Ireland and defeated the Catholic army at the Battle of the Boyne. He then dissolved the Parliament and chased James II back to France. Celebration of that victory, known as Orange Day, became a national holiday for the Anglo-Irish, a time when they chanted:

> To the Glorious, Pious and Immortal Memory of the great and good King William, who freed us from Pope and Popery, Knavery and Slavery, Brass Money and Wooden Shoes, and he who refuses this toast may be damned, crammed, and rammed down the Great Gun of Athlone.*

For Irish Catholics it was a call to battle.

Parliament magnified the crisis in the 1690s by abolishing civil rights for Catholics. Bishops were exiled, monastic orders prohibited, and foreign priests no longer permitted in Ireland. Catholics could not vote, hold public office or government jobs, teach school, own property, or carry weapons. England even prohibited the use of the Gaelic language throughout Ireland. Court proceedings had to be conducted in English; road and shop signs were in English; and school instruction had to be in English. English landlords controlled Ireland, and Catholics were a helpless lower caste. Hating all things Protestant and all things English, the Irish became united, and a strong Irish-Catholic identity emerged. An eighteenth-century Irish revolutionary song, "The Wearing of the Green," symbolized the discontent:

> O Patrick dear! and did you hear the news that's going round?
> The shamrock is by law forbid to grow on Irish ground.
>
> No more St. Patrick's day we'll keep—his color can't be seen,
> For there's a bloody law agen the wearing of the Green.
>
>   . . .
>
> I met with Napper Tandy, and he took me by the hand,
> Saying, "How is old Ireland and how does she stand?"
> She's the most distressful country that ever yet was seen
> They are hanging men and women for the wearing of the green.†

---

* Quoted in Edward M. Levine, *The Irish and Irish Politicians* (Notre Dame, Ind., 1966), p.29.
    † Quoted in Andrew M. Greeley, *That Most Distressful Nation: The Taming of the American Irish* (Chicago, 1972), p. xxv.

Savage economic problems also afflicted Ireland and precipitated the migration of 4 million Irish to the United States in the nineteenth century. During the Napoleonic Wars, European wheat production declined and prices rose, so Irish landlords put more land into wheat production and raised the rents of Catholic tenants. But when peace returned and European farming revived, prices collapsed and peasants were hard-pressed to pay the higher rents. With grain prices plummeting, landlords turned most acreage back to pasture in hope of recouping their losses by raising sheep. They evicted Catholic peasants by the thousands, and between 1815 and 1825 more than a hundred thousand of them came to America.

Nor did Ireland escape the enormous population increases that affected the rest of Europe. As a result, more and more people were crowded onto fewer and fewer leaseholds. Perhaps half the Irish lived on the edge of existence, in hovels and lean-tos, subsisting on milk and potatoes. Then came the Great Famine. Potatoes had become the staple because they flourished in poor soil, required little attention, and yielded enough per acre to feed a family. But they were also a risky crop because yield fluctuations could mean life or death for millions. Crop failures occurred in 1817, 1822, and the 1830s, but a fungus destroyed the entire crop in 1845. The blight continued in 1846 and 1847, bringing starvation to nearly a million people. In 1848 one of the largest of the perennial rebel movements, the Young Irelanders, was thoroughly defeated, and the cause of Irish separatism seemed doomed. For starving people evicted from the land that was their only hope of life, the future seemed across the Atlantic in America.

In a number of ways the typical Irish immigrants were a unique people. Most of them had little money and few skills to take to America, and even the more prosperous among them had only enough money to sustain them for a matter of weeks. Few Irish day laborers made the migration, so the movement was confined to small peasant farmers whose only economic skills consisted of primitive methods of raising potatoes and oats. Economic desperation characterized much of Irish life. But despite this poverty, the Irish possessed an ethnic culture which would serve them well in the United States. Theirs was a communal, "chain" migration to America in which whole families uprooted themselves; this transplanting of Irish villages from the Old World to the New made for an ethnic solidarity unknown among most other immigrants.

Immigration from the most Protestant and anglicized regions of Ulster and Leinster was quite limited, so most of the immigrants were Roman Catholics from Munster and Connaught, and their religion would bind them together in America. Because of the English elementary school program, probably half of the immigrants were literate and

This 1851 engraving shows the village priest blessing Irish emigrants who are leaving for America. (The Granger Collection)

most of them spoke English; and because of their political struggles against England, they were conditioned to Anglo politics and direct action. These immigrants heading for the United States were a highly politicized people.

Refugees of Disaster

Between 1820 and 1900 4 million Irish immigrants entered the United States—1,694,838 during the Great Famine years of the 1840s and 1850s. Ireland lost 3 million people to the famine and the famine migration in 1847-1855, and by the end of the century more Irish would be living in the United States than in Ireland. Poverty and the Atlantic trade routes left them along the Eastern Seaboard. Ireland had for years imported Canadian timber, and British shippers completed the round trip profitably by carrying immigrants back to the Maritime Provinces of Canada. Preferring the climate and economic opportunities in New England, they moved when they could to Massachusetts, Rhode Island, and Connecticut. Because Ireland also purchased cotton, wheat, flax-seed, potash, and naval stores from American producers, ships brought other immigrants to New York, Philadelphia, Baltimore, Charleston, and New Orleans.

The Irish were America's first ghetto people, the first to occupy large ethnic enclaves in the cities. Despite an agrarian background, they were ill suited for rural life in America. Farming in Ireland had been a primitive affair based on the potato, nothing like the large-scale, capital-intensive agriculture of the Midwest. After centuries of misery in Ireland, land had come to mean high rents, short leases, and capricious landlords. And in Ireland they had been a gregarious, close-knit people. Ireland was agrarian, to be sure, but far from sparsely populated. In 1830 8 million people were living on 26,000 square miles. There were more than three hundred people per square mile, compared to only around sixty-five in the United States today and around three hundred in India. People lived in sight of each other's houses, visited frequently, and watched their children play together. It was a village existence in even the most rural areas, with Catholic churches within walking distance, priests in every village, and religious holidays frequent. The Irish immigrants preferred cities because crowds meant friends, families, neighbors, and churches.

Urban life was also an emotional defense, security in a strange world. And it was especially important to those who came to the United States knowing little English. The Irish retained Old World loyalties to town, county, village, clan, and nation. Like that of the Germans, Italians, and Russian Jews, theirs was a "chain migration" of kinship and village systems which, under other circumstances, might have divided them into centrifugal subcommunities. But centuries of struggle with English Protestantism had imbued them with an intense sense of ethnic nationality. One immigrant wrote that his nationality was

> perhaps less of love . . . than of hate—less of filial affection to my country than of scornful impatience at the thought I had the misfortune . . . to be born in a country which suffered itself to be oppressed and humiliated by another. . . . And hatred being the thing I chiefly cherished and cultivated . . . I . . . hated . . . the British system . . . *

In many ways American Protestants intensified those feelings. American culture had a distinctly Anglo-Protestant flavor. To be sure, there were no tax-supported Protestant churches in the country by the 1840s, but Yankees controlled wealth and power in the United States. In New England especially, many Americans thought the Irish threatened Anglo-Saxon civilization. Irish immigration coincided with the democratic, antiauthoritarian worship of the common man popular during the era of President Andrew Jackson, and Roman Catholicism seemed contradictory because it gave authoritarian power to the pope. Some Yankees questioned Irish allegiance, doubting that they could become "true Americans" because dual loyalty to a religious monarchy and a liberal democracy seemed impossible.

Also present in most northeastern cities was a small but vocal minority

---

* Quoted in Lawrence McCaffrey, *The Irish Diaspora in America* (Bloomington, Ind.), p. 110.

of Anglo-Irish Protestant immigrants, descendants of the English settlers who had colonized Ireland in the sixteenth and seventeenth centuries. Known as Orangemen (after William of Orange's victory over Irish Catholics at the Battle of the Boyne), they were usually Episcopalians and Methodists after settling in America. Militantly anti-Catholic and anti-Democratic, they identified closely with Anglo-American Protestants. The immigrants transplanted their Old World rivalries to America. Conflicts between Anglo-Irish and Irish Catholic volunteer fire companies were frequent in Boston, New York, and Philadelphia, and in 1870 and 1871 ethnic competition erupted into open violence after Irish Protestants paraded through New York City on July 12 celebrating the Battle of the Boyne. Considering it an open affront to their history, Irish Catholics lined the parade route and taunted the marchers until a riot broke out and thirty-three people died.

Anti-Catholicism became a dominant social theme at mid-century. Newspapers, books, and pamphlets ridiculing Catholics became best sellers, and frightened Protestants avidly consumed the most sensational propaganda. *The Awful Disclosures of Maria Monk* (1836)— allegedly the confessions of a former nun, who described depraved priests, licentious nuns, and monastic orgies—was a piece of religious pornography that sold more than three hundred thousand copies before the Civil War. Many Americans were convinced that Irish Catholics were sexually irresponsible alcoholics subject to the dictates of Rome. Occasionally the anti-Catholicism turned violent. On Christmas Day, 1806, mobs in New York City disrupted Catholic religious services, and in August 1834 arsonists set fire to the Ursuline convent in Charlestown, Massachusetts. During the 1840s, when Catholics protested sectarian instruction in public schools and requested tax support for church schools, the parochial school issue caused considerable debate and exploded into the Philadelphia Riots of 1844, when priests and nuns were attacked, homes burned, and Catholic churches vandalized. In 1854 a mob destroyed the Irish ghetto in Lawrence, Massachusetts.

American Protestants also worried about Irish community organizations and the distinct ethnic culture represented in such newspapers as the *Gaelic-American*, the *Irish World*, and the *Irish Nation*. To assist incoming immigrants, the Irish formed the Irish Emigrant Society; and in every eastern city a number of volunteer firemen's groups, militia companies, and benevolent associations served the Irish community. The Irish also made enormous financial sacrifices to build Catholic parishes and parochial schools in their neighborhoods. With their devotion to the liberation of the old country, their religion, and their communities, they defied Anglo-American conformity. Many Americans resented such pride.

Poverty, crime, and unemployment in the Irish ghettos convinced some Americans that the Irish were an illiterate, brutish people incapable of improving themselves. Except for the most menial, low-paying jobs, many Americans preferred not to hire Irish workers at all. As always, much of the social prejudice had economic roots: the newest immigrants would work for the lowest pay, and were seen as a threat by other workers as well as by middle-class businessmen. Newspaper advertisements in New York and Boston during the 1840s and 1850s commonly asked for Protestant workers or stated flatly that "Irish need not apply."

Irish children were mistreated in public schools; but when their parents established parochial schools, some Americans were enraged. The Irish were poor but they could not get good jobs; they were illiterate but Americans did not want them educated in church schools.

For all these reasons large metropolitan areas like Boston, New York, Philadelphia, Cleveland, and Baltimore, as well as smaller cities like Springfield, Massachusetts, and Trenton, New Jersey, developed substantial Irish communities. In 1877 more than 80 percent of Irish workers were personal and domestic servants, porters, street cleaners, chimney sweeps, stevedores, longshoremen, hod carriers, ditch diggers, or highway and railroad builders. They could be found working the lead mines of Illinois; cleaning streets in Boston, New York, and Philadelphia; loading freight in port cities; digging the Erie and Chesapeake and Ohio canals; laying track on the transcontinental railroads; building houses in Chicago; working the rolling mills in Cleveland; breaking up rock quarries in New Hampshire; building ships in the Brooklyn and Philadelphia navy yards; or toiling in the New England textile mills. Some were farmers and businessmen, but most were poor workers in the cities.

From Poverty to Power

Still, the Irish eventually made a good life for themselves in the United States and came to enjoy a standard of living and influence that would have been unthinkable in the Old World. A fighting disposition was part of the Celtic heritage, and centuries of English rule had bred a spirit of resistance. The Irish who made it to America raised their children to have a sense of personal strength and encouraged participation in sports. The Irish game of hurling, a violent sport resembling field hockey, was one avenue for expressing strength and aggression, and Irish children easily made the transition to football in the United States. Because the squalor, disease, and poverty of the early ghettos in America engendered crime, Irish-American fathers taught their sons how to defend themselves. Indeed, being a good fighter was a measure of status in the Irish-American community, and it is no surprise that the first heavyweight boxing champions were Irish.

Occasionally the American Irish struck back at discrimination. During the Civil War the famous Draft Riots were provoked by conscription laws discriminating against poor people by allowing the rich to buy a replacement for $300. Although most of the Irish supported the Union during the war, there was opposition to the draft throughout the North, especially among the New York Irish, some of whom even termed the Civil War a "Protestant Republican war for black slaves." On July 11, 1863, when Republican officials and New York marshals began drawing the names of draftees, that hostility burst into violence. For nearly five days Irish mobs attacked blacks, Republicans, and rich "$300 boys," and set fire to dozens of buildings. More than a hundred people died before United States troops quelled the uprising. Later, in the anthracite coal fields of Pennsylvania, the Irish "Molly Maguires" allegedly killed nine people after being laid off by coal operators in the 1870s.

Such resistance was infrequent, however, and the Irish journey out of poverty was based on the strength of the family, urban politics, hard work, and a powerful sense of group identity. These sustained them in the first dreadful ghetto years. Poor, illiterate, and unaccustomed to urban life, the Irish suffered in the ghettos. Old mansions, stores, and warehouses were often converted into crowded tenements, and many Irish lived in lean-tos and shacks made of tar paper or wooden crates. In some urban areas, raw sewage flowed down the streets, there was a constant battle against rats and lice, and cholera and tuberculosis were common. Most jobs paid poorly, and many of the poor turned to crime and prostitution for surival. Yet the Irish family survived. In Ireland the father was always the head of the family, and he kept his role as the provider and decision maker in America. But mothers were emotionally dominant in the family because they were more often at home to influence and discipline the children and because the Irish believed strongly in the virtues of motherhood. The spirit of the Irish home was moralistic; children were expected to be respectful and obedient to church and family. Given the scarce resources of Irish families, emphasis on family cohesion and mutual cooperation was strong. In Ireland women had not been expected to work outside the home and farm, but in America it was acceptable. Children too could be called on to contribute to family resources. And kinship ties extended all the way through the father's relationships. Although a family's independence was a matter of great pride, people in need could call on paternal relatives for help and were expected to assist others when asked. Family ties were an important asset in coping with the American environment.

The political talents of the Irish also served them well. Arriving during the Jackson era, when property barriers to voting were collapsing, the Irish became a powerful voting bloc. Although they lacked industrial skills, they were equipped with centuries of experience in life-or-death political battles with the English. In Ireland mass and direct action politics had gone on for years; and slowly, between 1820 and 1880, the Irish constructed their famous American political machines, epitomized by Tammany Hall in the New York of the 1880s and the Richard Daley machine in twentieth-century Chicago. Working with ethnic and religious unity through local parishes and saloons, Irish politicians first became street captains, and later district and precinct leaders, aldermen, and state and national legislators. Using police, fire department, sanitation, and public-works jobs as patronage, they attracted the loyalty of voters economically dependent upon the political success of the machine. And by championing the workingman and the need to end poverty, Irish Catholic politicians became very influential in the Democratic party. In New York, Boston, Cleveland, Chicago, Pittsburgh, Baltimore, St. Louis, and New Orleans, Irish political machines were powerful, and power is easily translated into respectability.

Although often graft-ridden, Irish machine politics contradicted laissez-faire individualism by distributing food, fuel, and jobs to poor people in the cities. Skeptical about human nature, concerned with improvement rather than perfection, the Irish became the cornerstone of Democratic politics, which eventually became the New Deal of Franklin D. Roosevelt, the Fair Deal of Harry Truman, the New Frontier of John Kennedy, and the Great Society of Lyndon Johnson.

Through hard work and struggle the Irish soon defied stereotypes that tied them to poor ghettos. Second-generation Irish found skilled jobs in the construction industry and in factories; and although unskilled Irish workers had more difficulty finding skilled and white-collar jobs than Protestant workers, enough succeeded to make the possibility real. A small business and professional elite of grocers, dry goods dealers, real estate brokers, attorneys, physicians, and commission merchants also appeared and became the "lace-curtain" Irish, a socially respectable class in Victorian America. And all classes of Irish-Americans were highly mobile in the nineteenth century. They had an intense drive for property ownership, and they established ethnic savings and loan associations—with such names as Flanagan, Hibernia, Emerald, Erin, Shamrock, and St. Patrick—to help them buy or build homes. They were prudent and thrifty, put their savings into the banks, sent wives and children to work, and finally bought their own homes in more respectable neighborhoods. The ghetto survived, but a constant stream of new immigrants—many of them also Irish—filled the vacancies left by departing Irish workers and businessmen.

The new Irish immigrants were different from the old ones. During the Great Famine nearly half were illiterate; but after England introduced elementary education throughout Ireland, literacy rates increased rapidly. By 1900 more than 85 percent of the Irish immigrants could read and write English, and virtually all could speak it. And although the Irish economy was still retarded, the rural standard of living had improved somewhat since 1850. Death and emigration had reduced the population from 8 to less than 5 million people, the pressure on the land eased, and farms expanded in acreage. Though still poverty-stricken and unskilled technologically, these immigrants were better equipped to succeed in the United States. By 1900 the Irish were scattered throughout urban America.

The Irish succeeded in part because of the strengths they brought with them from the Old World, and they held on to their Old World identity. Throughout the nineteenth century they provided money and weapons to Irish revolutionaries fighting England, and just as frequently tried to use their leverage in the Democratic party to influence American foreign policy against England. Their nostalgia was strong. During the controversy with England over the Oregon territory in 1844–1846, the Irish clamored for war. American Fenians, a group of Irish-Americans dedicated to the liberation of Ireland, invaded Canada in 1866 hoping to weaken English power. Between 1914 and 1917 the Irish would lobby intensely to keep the United States out of World War I, and they would bitterly condemn President Woodrow Wilson when the United States finally joined England against Germany. And as late as the 1970s pacifists in Northern Ireland would be begging Irish-Americans to stop sending money to finance the violence between Catholics and Protestants. Old World politics were powerful ingredients in the New World ethnic nationalism of Irish America.

The Catholic Church solidified Irish-Americans, and when success came they did not desert it. By sheer force of numbers the Irish clergy controlled the Catholic hierarchy in America, and the bond between the Irish clergy and parishioners was very strong. The local parish church, in the center of the community, was surrounded by homes, apartments, taverns, stores, and shops. The priests knew all the families, directed their church activity, and comforted them. For a son to enter the priesthood was a great honor to an Irish-American family. People were active in the parish, attending weekly mass, parochial schools, catechism classes, and frequent confessions; serving as altar boys and abstaining from meat on Fridays and other worldly pleasures during

Lent; and faithfully contributing money for the construction and maintenance of parish institutions. A compact, relatively close community, the parish was the emotional heart of Irish-American life.

Catholicism in Ireland changed during the nineteenth century, and these changes were reflected in Irish Catholic life in the United States. Until the 1840s the Irish church was highly independent, more nationalist than worldly, more a function of Irish needs than of Roman demands. But after the famine the antinationalist Paul Cullen, appointed archbishop of Dublin in 1852, transformed the church by making parish priests loyal to their bishops and the bishops loyal to Rome. Authoritarian and legalistic, Irish Catholicism produced a morally austere people, while the effects of Anglo-Protestantism, especially its evangelical puritanism, were echoed in an emphasis on celibacy, chastity, and sexual morality, and on the evils of masturbation, homosexuality, birth control, and fornication. Thus post-1870 immigrants were more disciplined and morally conservative than their brethren of the famine years. Irish Catholicism would eventually have enormous consequences for the other Catholic immigrants who poured into America during the twentieth century. Militant, authoritarian, and puritanical, the American Catholic Church would have trouble absorbing the richly diverse, nationalistic traditions of eastern Europe. But for the Irish-Americans the new discipline had the virtue of helping to reassure many Americans that the Irish were not an unruly mob.

At the same time, patriotic enthusiasm swept through some American Catholic circles during and after the Civil War. Led by John Ireland, a chaplain in the Union army and then archbishop of St. Paul, Minnesota, Catholic patriotism extolled the virtues of an American democracy blessed by God. Ireland praised freedom of religion, began a modest dialogue with eastern Protestants, and even celebrated the public school system as the backbone of democracy. It became difficult for most Protestants to condemn the Catholic patriots, especially when they praised the American government and applauded the melting pot.

By 1924, when the National Origins Act finally restricted immigration from Ireland, Irish-Americans had become a powerful ethnic minority. Politically, they were—and still are—deeply ensconced in the urban machines of the Democratic party. Some of the most colorful figures in American politics have been Irish Catholics: "Honest" John Kelley, who took over Tammany Hall in the 1870s and 1880s; James Michael Curley, mayor of Boston in the 1920s; John, Robert, and Edward Kennedy; Mike Mansfield, Senate majority leader in the 1960s and 1970s; and even into the late 1970s, with Tip O'Neill, speaker of the House of Representatives; Hugh Carey, governor of New York; and Jerry Brown, governor of California. American Catholicism has seen men like John Ireland,

James Cardinal Gibbons, Richard Cardinal Cushing, James Cardinal McIntyre, and Dennis Cardinal Dougherty; American letters, such men as Eugene O'Neill, James Farrell, and F. Scott Fitzgerald. Paddy Ryan, John L. Sullivan, "Gentleman" Jim Corbett, and Jim Jeffries stand out in boxing; and Michael Kelly, John McGraw, Charles Comiskey, Mickey Cochrane, and John Doyle in baseball. Women too have made their contributions: New York City Police Commissioner Ellen O'Grady, social workers Margaret Gaffney and Mary Frances Clarke, labor organizer Mary Harris Jones, and authors Mary Deasy and Margaret Marchard. These were the Irish Catholics—a separate community with a powerful ethnic nationalism based on their Gaelic heritage, their resistance to the British Empire, their New World experiences, and their Roman Catholicism.

SUGGESTED READINGS

Abramson, Harold J. *Ethnic Diversity in Catholic America*. New York: 1973.

Adams, William F. *Ireland and Irish Emigration to the New World, from 1815 to the Famine*. New Haven, Conn.: 1932.

Alba, Richard D. "Social Assimilation Among American Catholic National Origins Groups." *American Sociological Review*, 41 (December 1976), 1030–1046.

Allswang, John M. *A House for All Peoples: Ethnic Politics in Chicago, 1890–1936*. Lexington, Kentucky: 1971.

Brown, Thomas B. *Irish-American Nationalism, 1870–1900*. Philadelphia: 1966.

Clark, Dennis. *The Irish in Philadelphia*. Philadelphia: 1973.

Cook, Adrian. *The Armies of the Streets: The New York City Draft Riots of 1863*. Lexington, Kentucky: 1974.

Dolan, Jay P. *The Immigrant Church: New York Irish and German Catholics, 1815–1865*. Baltimore: 1975.

Esslinger, Dean R. *Immigrants and the City: Ethnicity and Mobility in a Nineteenth Century Midwestern Community*. New York: 1975.

Farrell, James T. *Studs Lonigan*. New York: 1938.

Feldberg, Michael. *The Philadelphia Riots of 1844: A Study of Ethnic Conflict*. Westport, Conn.: 1975.

Glazer, Nathan, and Moynihan, Daniel P. *Beyond the Melting Pot: The Negroes, Puerto Ricans, Jews, Italians, and Irish of New York City*. Cambridge, Mass.: 1963.

Greeley, Andrew M. *The American Catholic: A Social Portrait*. New York: 1977.

———. *That Most Distressful Nation: The Taming of the American Irish*. Chicago: 1972.

Gutman, Herbert. *Work, Culture, and Society in Industrializing America*. New York: 1976.

Handlin, Oscar. *Boston's Immigrants, 1790–1865: A Study in Acculturation*. Cambridge, Mass.: 1941.

Kennedy, Robert E., Jr. *The Irish: Emigration, Marriage, and Fertility*. Berkeley, Cal.: 1973.

Knights, Peter R. *The Plain People of Boston*. Boston: 1971.

Levine, Edward M. *The Irish and Irish Politicians*. Notre Dame, Ind.: 1966.

MacDonagh, Oliver. "The Irish Famine Emigration to the United States." *Perspectives in American History*, 10 (1976), 357–446.

McCaffrey, Lawrence. *The Irish Diaspora in America*. Bloomington, Ind.: 1976.

Merwick, Donna. *Boston Priests, 1848–1910: A Study of Social and Intellectual Change*. Cambridge, Mass.: 1973.

Niehaus, Earl F. *The Irish in New Orleans, 1800–1860*. Baton Rouge, La.: 1965.

O'Connor, Richard. *The Irish: A Portrait of a People*. New York: 1971.

O'Grady, Joseph P. *How the Irish Became American*. New York: 1973.

Osofsky, Gilbert. "Abolitonists, Irish Immigrants, and the Dilemmas of Romantic Nationalism." *American Historical Review*, 80 (October 1975), 889–912.

Pessen, Edward. *Riches, Class and Power Before the Civil War*. New York: 1973.

Potter, George. *To the Golden Door: The Story of the Irish in Ireland and America*. Boston: 1960.

Quinn, David B. *The Elizabethans and the Irish*. New York: 1966.

Shannon, William V. *The American Irish*. New York: 1963.

Thernstrom, Stephen. *The Other Bostonians: Poverty and Progress in the American Metropolis, 1880–1970*. Cambridge, Mass.: 1973.

Wakin, Edward. *Enter the Irish-American*. New York: 1976.

Warner, Sam Bass. *Streetcar Suburbs: The Process of Growth in Boston, 1870–1900*. Cambridge, Mass.: 1962.

Wittke, Carl. *The Irish in America*. Baton Rouge, La.: 1956.

Chapter Six

Dutch and Deutsch: Immigration from Holland and Germany

From central Europe came a large bloc of immigrants in the nineteenth century. Although the Dutch and Germans shared a Teutonic heritage and similar languages, their national histories had led them in different political and religious directions. But as economic changes swept through central Europe in the 1800s, both the Dutch and German people experienced serious difficulties in supporting themselves, and millions turned to the United States for solutions to their problems.

The Dutch Immigrants

In the seventeenth century the Dutch empire stretched across the globe, from Newfoundland to West Africa to the East Indies, and in 1624 the Dutch West India Company planted a colony in North America. They purchased Manhattan Island from the Indians, named the settlement New Netherland, and extended the colony up the Hudson River in what is now New York State, down the Delaware River in New Jersey and Pennsylvania, and across the East River to Breuckelen (Brooklyn). Within forty years nearly ten thousand people lived in New Netherland.

But New Netherland never attracted enough settlers to remain independent of the surrounding English colonies. By 1664 more than fifty thousand Puritans were in New England and thousands of Anglicans were in Maryland and Virginia. Feudal Dutch patroonships along the

Hudson River discouraged immigrants from coming because few wanted to cross the Atlantic and become serfs in the New World. Conflict with the Indians also deterred settlement. Surrounded by English settlers interested in the port at New Amsterdam (New York City) and the rich estates on the Hudson, the colony was a ripe plum that fell to an English fleet in 1664. New Netherland became New York.

Thousands of Dutch still came to America. Some Dutch Quakers and Mennonites moved to Pennsylvania in the 1680s; Dutch Labadists, members of a utopian sect, settled in Maryland in the 1680s; and thousands of Dutch farmers came in the 1700s. By 1776 there were nearly a hundred thousand people of Dutch descent living in America, and from their original nucleus along the Hudson and Delaware rivers they settled throughout the Hudson Valley, the Mohawk Valley in upstate New York, the Passaic and Hackensack valleys of New Jersey, and in York, Bucks, and Adams counties in Pennsylvania. From there they moved out to western Pennsylvania and Kentucky.

They were a highly visible group in colonial America. Compact rural communities and poor communications kept Dutch culture intact. Virtually every Dutch community had its Dutch Reformed Church and parochial schools offering services and education in the native language. Most of the Dutch Reformed clergy serving in the United States were foreign-born, and they too helped preserve Dutch culture. Old World values were strong. In many parts of New Jersey and upstate New York, the Dutch often absorbed the English, Germans, or French Huguenots settling near them. Describing Bergen County, New Jersey, on the eve of the Revolution, an observer said:

> The men and women . . . spoke Jersey Dutch most of the time and English when they had to, just as many New Yorkers did. They listened to Dutch sermons on Sunday and gave their children Dutch names, and the women and children wore clothes having more than a hint of Holland in their style. Certainly no one could have confused the Dutch country in and around Hackensack with English settlements in middle Jersey or the Pennsylvania German settlements in the neighboring province to the south.*

The Great Migration sent nearly 250,000 Dutch immigrants to America, 128,000 between 1820 and 1900 and another 120,000 between 1900 and 1924. By 1840 King William I controlled the Dutch Reformed Church and closely supervised church meetings and the training of ministers. When "Seceders" protested, the government broke up their meetings, jailed ministers, and arrested parishioners. Whole congregations fled to America. Reverend Albertus van Raalte and fifty followers

---

* Quoted in Gerald F. DeJong, *The Dutch in America* (New York, 1975), p. 55.

settled near Grand Rapids, Michigan, in 1846, and in 1847 Reverend Pieter Zonne moved his congregation to Sheboygan County, Wisconsin, north of Milwaukee. Henry P. Scholte led another group to Iowa in 1847. During the 1840s thousands of Dutch dissenters came to the United States hoping to practice their religion without interference. But even more Dutch immigrants came because economic opportunities at home could not match those of the New World.

They followed the colonial Dutch to New York City and the Hudson Valley, and also settled in Michigan, Illinois, Wisconsin, and Iowa. Farms were small in Michigan, usually forty to eighty acres, and Dutch farmers raised hay, wheat, oats, corn, hogs, cattle, chickens, and truck crops. Adept at draining swamp land, they purchased "poor" land at low prices and were able to accumulate equity in a short period of time. They were also a careful, sober people uninterested in speculation, so they tended to remain in settled areas, not moving on to new farms every few years. The largest Dutch communities developed in Kalamazoo and Grand Rapids, Michigan, and after the Civil War the Dutch pushed out to southwestern Minnesota, the Dakotas, western Iowa, eastern Nebraska, Montana, and Washington because of the availability of cheap land.

Eventually a split developed between the descendants of New Netherland and the immigrants of the Great Migration. More liberal and relaxed after two centuries in America, the old Dutch and the Dutch Reformed Church seemed strange to the new immigrants. Offering Holy Communion to nonmembers, sending children to public schools, permitting members to join secret societies, and giving up Dutch language services, the Dutch Reformed Church seemed to have lost touch with its Calvinist roots. In 1857 some of the new immigrants founded the Christian Reformed Church. Conservative and strict in the Calvinist tradition, it insisted on services in the Dutch language and on Dutch parochial schools, and condemned worldly amusements, the participation of women in church services, membership in secret lodges, and any trace of an ecumenical spirit.

By 1900 there were two Dutch communities in the United States. In the East the descendants of New Netherland were in a state of advanced assimilation. English was their mother tongue; public schools educated their children; the Dutch Reformed Church attracted a wide variety of Protestants; and marriages to English and German Protestants were the rule. Across the whole range of social relationships they were mixing with other Americans.

But in the West the Christian Reformed Dutch held tenaciously to the Old World faith, speaking Dutch, attending church schools from kindergarten through Calvin College in Grand Rapids, and taking Dutch

Immigration to America could be a wrenching and frightening experience, as the faces of these Dutch immigrant children suggest. (Brown Brothers)

spouses more than 80 percent of the time. As Calvinists they were hardworking and ambitious, modest about their abilities, extremely pious, thrifty, and family oriented. Families prayed, read the scriptures, and attended church together. In 1912 Jacob Van der Zee argued that the Dutch immigrant

> prefers to throw in his lot with . . . fellow-countrymen, he conforms to a . . . social order based on Dutch stability . . . his Dutch neighbors have lived and worked within the confines of their settlement . . . nearly all are engaged and interested in the same occupations . . . their whole life is centered about their church. . . . Dutch national traits [are] intensified by constant accessions of fresh blood from the Netherlands . . . the Hollanders of Iowa . . . are still for the most part [an] unassimilated, clannish, though not entirely isolated, mass of foreigners who have necessarily acquired an American veneer from the environment created by the political and social ideas of America.*

They were also proud to be Dutch. The Netherlands had fought hard for its independence over the centuries, and most of the immigrants were literate and knew their Dutch history. In 1899, when the Boer War broke

* Jacob Van der Zee, *The Hollanders of Iowa* (Iowa City, 1912), p. 219.

out in South Africa, Dutch-Americans rallied to the support of the Dutch Afrikaners fighting to remain independent of the British Empire. Representatives of the Boer Republics traveled on speaking engagements throughout the Midwest, receiving money and even volunteers to fight the British.

The Dutch would contribute much to American history, not only in terms of the ambitiousness, cleanliness, and stability of their communities, but in people like presidents Martin Van Buren, Theodore Roosevelt, and Franklin D. Roosevelt; writers Herman Melville and Van Wyck Brooks; the inventor of the famous Norden bomb site during World War II, Carl Norden; and businessmen John Van Heusen and Cornelius Vanderbilt. The flavor of Dutch culture would survive in parts of New York City, in Sayville, Long Island, in Bergen County, New Jersey, and in Grand Rapids and Kalamazoo. The Dutch character was such that Dutch immigrants flowed naturally into an ideological mainstream prepared by English Puritans and Scots-Irish Presbyterians.

The German Immigrants

By 1820 colonial German society was rapidly acculturating in America, breaking out of the Old World patterns which had dominated it earlier. As late as 1790 German was the daily language of immigrant communities, and Germans married Germans nearly 90 percent of the time. But after 1800 church registers were frequently written in English, and regular English services were introduced. In 1820, at the Lutheran Church in Hagerstown, Maryland, 214 people attended the German service and 189 the English service. But by 1840 only 90 were attending the German services while 206 were going to the English meetings. Old-timers objected, but soon it became difficult to find a minister who could preach in both languages. The triumph of English was inevitable. And as English took over, the Lutheran and Reformed churches ceased to be purely German institutions and opened their doors to English, Welsh, Scots, and Scots-Irish settlers. But just as colonial German society seemed to be making the transition from acculturation to assimilation, the Great Migration began. Between 1820 and 1924 more than 5,700,000 people immigrated from Germany, perhaps 500,000 from Austria, 200,000 Germans from Alsace and Lorraine, 120,000 Russian-Germans from the Volga River and Black Sea coast, and more than 270,000 people from Switzerland. German culture revived immediately.

Before the 1880s the German community in the United States consisted primarily of religious dissenters, political refugees, and farmers. In 1805 Father George Rapp established a communist colony at Harmony,

Pennsylvania, just outside Pittsburgh, and in 1815 they moved to New Harmony, Indiana. In 1817 Joseph Baummler led 300 Germans to Zoar, Ohio, where their tiny community survived until 1898. After the Napoleonic Wars, several thousand German Mennonites settled in the Midwest. South of Cedar Rapids, Iowa, Christian Metz established the Amana colonies in 1842 for 800 German pietists; they held property in common, thrived economically, and founded the Amana Refrigeration Company, a successful manufacturer of electrical appliances. These colonies lasted well into the twentieth century.

In the early 1870s Germany—unified at last under Prussian dominance—began the *Kulturkampf*, "culture battle," annulling papal authority and abolishing Catholic orders and Catholic education. Some German Catholics emigrated to America. And after 1874 thousands of German Hutterites, an Anabaptist sect that had fled to Russia to escape persecution, came to the Dakotas, where even today they still speak German.

Political problems had inspired immigration even earlier. The Vienna Revolution of 1848 against the Hapsburg regime brought peasant and burgher uprisings which broke out in the states of Württemberg and Baden, engulfed the Rhineland Province, and spread into Prussia. Most of the radicals demanded popular sovereignty and liberal reform. On May 18, 1848, liberals and radicals convened the Frankfurt Parliament to draft a constitution for a united, democratic Germany, but bitter disagreements between the liberal bourgeoisie and radical intellectuals hurt the assembly. While they argued about the pace of change, whether to have a republic or a limited monarchy, and whether to create a unitary or federal government, the conservatives regained the initiative and suppressed the rebellion. Disappointed and in danger, perhaps five thousand of the rebellious "Forty-Eighters" came to the United States. Democratic, anticlerical, and intensely nationalistic, men like Carl Schurz, Edward Salomon, Jacob Muller, Gottlieb Kellman, Lorenz Brentano, Joseph Weydemeyer, and Heinrich Bornstein stimulated the revival of German ethnicity in America.

None was more illustrious than Carl Schurz. Born in 1829 at Liblar, Germany, he became active in liberal politics at the University of Bonn, and after the revolutions of 1848 he fled to London and then to Wisconsin. He joined the antislavery movement and played a major role in building the Republican party in Wisconsin. Appointed minister to Spain in 1860, he returned in 1862 as a brigadier general in the Union Army and served with distinction at Chancellorsville and Gettysburg. After the Civil War he was a United States Senator from Missouri, a leader of the liberal Republican uprising against President Ulysses S. Grant in 1872, Secretary of the Interior under Rutherford B. Hayes, president of the National Civil Service Reform League, and editor of several newspapers. He was perhaps the most influential German immigrant in American history.

Later in the century the unification of Germany sent more political dissidents to America. King William I of Prussia began universal military conscription in 1861, and to avoid the draft thousands of Prussian youths came to America. The king eventually summoned Otto von Bismarck, a political conservative dedicated to a united, Prussian-dominated Germany, and named him Minister-President of Prussia. Between 1862 and 1870 Bismarck created a North German Federation, annexed Bavaria and Württemberg, and in the Franco-Prussian War acquired most of Alsace and Lorraine. Thousands of Germans emigrated because of boundary instability and wars.

But for every German who immigrated to America for religious or political reasons, a hundred came for economic reasons. Like the rest of Europe, Germany experienced economic changes just when rumors about the United States were attracting interest all over the Continent. Population increases made life difficult for peasant families; American wheat depressed grain prices; periodic potato famines left thousands on the verge of starvation; factories centralized production and destroyed

GERMANY ON THE EVE OF WORLD WAR I

PROVINCES OF GERMANY
1 ANHALT
2 BRUNSWICK
3 HANOVER
4 LIPPE
5 MECKLENBURG-STRELITZ
6 OLDENBURG
7 PALATINATE
8 SCHLESWIG-HOLSTEIN
9 THURINGIAN STATES
10 WALDECK
11 WÜRTTEMBERG

jobs for many artisans; and skilled workers left country villages and crowded into Vienna, Berlin, Hamburg, Breslau, Munich, and Dresden. Food and labor riots erupted in Silesia, Saxony, Ulm, Bohemia, Berlin, and Stuttgart in the 1840s. From all over Germany workers headed for America: coal miners and heavy-metal workers left the Ruhr Valley; textile workers abandoned Saxony, Bavaria, Alsace, Lorraine, and Silesia; and glassworkers, cobblers, construction workers, leather workers, and cabinetmakers set out from Westphalia and Prussia. Describing Bavaria in the 1840s, a French journalist wrote:

> It is a lamentable sight when you are traveling on the Strasburg road, to see the long files of carts that you meet every mile, carrying poor wretches, who are about to cross the Atlantic. . . . There they go slowly along; their miserable tumbrils—drawn by such starved, drooping beasts, that your only wonder is, how can they possibly hope to reach Havre alive—piled with scanty boxes containing their few effects. . . . One might take it for a convoy of wounded, the relics of a battlefield, but for the rows of little white heads peeping from beneath the ragged hood.*

Not everyone was in such desperate circumstances, but for all of them the uprooting was a difficult experience.

Closely related to the Germans were the 270,000 Swiss who immigrated between 1820 and 1924. Although some were French- and Italian-Swiss, most were German-Swiss who, except for Mormons and Quakers, came to the United States for economic reasons. Industrialization was eliminating the jobs of rural craftsmen, and small farmers were leaving the land because they could not support their families on it. Most of the Swiss headed for Ohio, Illinois, Missouri, Wisconsin, New York, and Pennsylvania. After 1890, largely because of the immigration of the Italian-Swiss, California had the largest Swiss colony in the country. The German-Swiss maintained a distinct identity throughout the nineteenth century, but powerful forces linked them to the larger German-American community.

Finally, 120,000 Russian-Germans immigrated. After 1763 the tsars had invited German colonists to settle in Russia, promising them free land, free churches, and military exemptions. By 1860 there were more than 1.7 million Germans living along the Volga River and Black Sea coast, with other colonies in the Ukraine, Bessarabia, and Transcaucasia. In 1871, when the government decided to Russianize the Germans and force them into the Russian army, they headed for the United States. Accustomed to the vast wheat steppes of western Russia, they settled in North Dakota, South Dakota, Kansas, and Nebraska,

---

* Quoted in Richard O' Connor, *The German Americans* (Boston, 1968), p. 100.

bringing with them the hard Turkish red wheat they had planted in the Old World. Clannishly loyal to Lutheran, Reformed, Catholic, or pietistic churches and used to cultural isolation in a strange society, the Russian-Germans settled in more than sixteen hundred colonies across the northern plains and tenaciously resisted assimilation. Well into the 1940s their newspaper *Dakota Freie Presse* circulated throughout the Midwest, and their children married other Russian-Germans.

By the late nineteenth century, then, there was a German belt extending from northern Massachusetts to Maryland, through the Ohio River basin to the Great Lakes, and then on out to the northern plains. New York, Philadelphia, Boston, Charleston, Cleveland, and Chicago had large German communities, and the German immigrants landing in New Orleans sailed up the Mississippi River to Memphis, St. Louis, and Minneapolis, and up the Ohio River to Louisville, Cincinnati, and Pittsburgh. Most settled in Ohio, Illinois, Wisconsin, and Missouri, the great "German triangle" lying between Milwaukee, Cincinnati, and St. Louis. Smaller German communities could be found in virtually every other state, but especially in Minnesota, Iowa, North Dakota, South Dakota, Kansas, Nebraska, Texas, Colorado, California, Oregon, and Washington.

The German Culture

German culture at first revolved around religion, language, and agrarian folkways. The German immigrants were a spiritual-minded people whose faith in an omnipotent God was strong; their churches institutionalized that faith, controlled behavior, and ordered community life in rural areas. This was *Kirchendeutschen* —churches promoting German culture and tradition. Indeed, there was little need for other ethnic organizations because the churches played such a central role in community affairs. Life was hard in rural America, troubled by Indians, the vagaries of nature, and general privation. Making a living consumed most of the immigrants' energies, and whatever time or resources remained went to the churches.

The German immigrants were also united in their conviction that the German language and religion were inextricable, believing that German was the best vehicle for expressing spirituality. Language was the underpinning of German culture in America. When the public school movement began in the nineteenth century, German farmers resented the intrusion of the state into their lives, feeling that the responsibility for educating children rested with parents. They associated value with production, the making of concrete goods, and many looked upon higher learning and the professions as parasitic and wasteful. To them,

Yankee commercialism was rude speculation, making money not from genuine labor but from the gullibility or misfortune of others. Through Lutheran, Reformed, or pietistic church schools, parents made sure their children were not "Anglicized" into a life outside the community. Founded to teach reading, writing, and arithmetic, church schools preserved the German language and taught Biblical truth, safeguarding German faith and culture from the influence of public schools committed to Anglo-American industrial values.

Finally, German culture in the early nineteenth century rested on Old World agrarian folkways, on a belief in ruralism as a way of life, not just as a way of making a living. Less restless than the English and Scots-Irish, the German immigrants had always looked for the best soil, for places where they could establish self-reliant, permanent communities. In general, they were not inclined to purchase virgin land, clear it, and then sell it and move on. They placed great emphasis on having large patriarchal families and their grown children living close to home. Children would usually accept spouses selected for them by their parents. It was common for parents to help young couples acquire farms of their own in the community; and because of the prevailing social stability, money was often lent interest free on the security of a handshake. And as in the colonial period, Germans prefered family-size farms over plantations, intensive subsistence agriculture over commercialism, and free labor over slave labor. Roots, stability, and productivity were the values of rural German communities.

Even their farming methods reflected a conscious cultural style. They did not use slash-and-burn techniques to clear land, nor did they belt trees until they decayed and fell down. Instead, they cut the trees down and removed the stumps and underbrush to make the land fully productive right away. German farmers loved the land and introduced scientific improvements very early: to condition the soil they grew clovers and grasses and rotated crops on a four-year basis; and huge barns and grain feeding kept livestock healthy and strong. They also planted fruit orchards and flower gardens, and they insisted on well-constructed fences, straight furrows, enclosed storage areas for hay and harvested crops, and clean, well-kept yards. They were obsessed with almanacs because they believed successful farming was intimately associated with the behavior of heavenly bodies. To guarantee high yields, they planted grains with the waxing of the moon, beans when the horns of the moon were down, and onions when the horns were up; they picked apples only in the dark to prevent rotting and used cider for vinegar only during the astrological sign of the Lion. Both superstitious and scientific, generally stable and productive, these were the German farmers.

By the middle of the nineteenth century, however, rural folkways began to give way to the more secular interests of the immigrants who came exclusively for economic reasons and settled in dense rural areas or cities. *Kirchendeutschen* gave way to *Vereinsdeutschen*, German societies. New organizations fostering German traditions were formed: singing societies (*Sangerfeste*), militia companies, sharpshooting clubs, fraternal associations (Sons of Hermann, Order of the Harugari, Masons, and Oddfellows), social clubs, literary clubs, mutual aid societies, theaters, beer halls, orchestras, and debating groups. Mid-century Lutheran and Reformed immigrants no longer had their identities inextricably linked with the church. Community life for the German Catholics, of course, still revolved around the parish, but all the German immigrants were acquiring an identity as Germans that transcended older religious visions.

But the existence of a German culture did not preclude the appearance of a number of German subcultures in the United States. Indeed, of all the nineteenth-century immigrants, the German-speaking people were probably the least homogenous. Linguistic, ideological, ethnic, regional, and finally religious differences set them apart from one another as well as from other Americans. Although they spoke German, for example, there were differences of idiom and dialect. For a thousand years each separate German duchy or state had enjoyed its own dialect, and not until the Reformation did some language unity begin to emerge; even then there were dozens of dialects which were idiomatically distinct. The most fundamental difference was between such Low German dialects as Dutch, Flemish, Friesian, and Prussian prevailing from Belgium and the Netherlands through Westphalia and Hanover to Prussia, and the High German dialects of Alsace, Bavaria, Austria, and Switzerland. So while the Germans shared a linguistic heritage, it was by no means a monolithic one.

There were also major regional differences based upon ancient tribal origins and historical development. Swabian tribesmen had originally settled throughout southwest Germany in Alsace, Baden, Wurttemberg, and Switzerland. Bavarian tribesmen migrated to Bavaria, Austria, and Bohemia, and Franconians ended up in Austria. Upper Saxons made their way into Hanover and Brunswick; Lower Saxons into Saxony, Silesia, and Bohemia; and Thuringians into central Germany. Upper Saxons and Borussian Slavs mixed to become Prussians. When the Great Migration from Germany began, the immigrants came from Alsace, Lorraine, Baden, Bavaria, Wurttemberg, Switzerland, Austria, Westphalia, the Palatinate, Hanover, Hesse, Holstein, Schleswig, Saxony, Thuringia, Silesia, Prussia, Pomerania, Posen, Brandenburg, and Brunswick, all of which had been independent kingdoms or duchies with their own political and tribal histories. If the immigrants had been asked their nationality, they would probably have called themselves by their origins in one of the German states, not by the name of Germany, especially before 1871.

In addition to these linguistic, tribal, and regional differences, the German immigrants were distinct from one another in terms of ideology and worldview. The Forty-Eighters, for example, were liberal nationalists, deeply concerned with political philosophies and bitterly anticlerical; they blamed organized religion, Protestant but especially Roman Catholic, for the historic inability of Germany to unite. More devout Germans, of course, resented the Forty-Eighter hostility. On another ideological level, the northern Germans by the mid-nineteenth century had accepted a lifestyle known as *Gesellschaft*, an accommodation to the more formal, anonymous values of an industrial, corporate world, while south Germans still lived in a world of *Gemeinschaft*, of such traditional, preindustrial values as village ruralism, familialism, and personalism. So while north Germans viewed southerners as a hopelessly backward people, the south Germans viewed northerners as stiff and formal, too materialistic and out of touch with life's more important qualities.

But the most profound differences were religious. Ever since the Protestant Reformation, Germany had been the scene of *Kleinstaaterei*, of religious wars and dissension between Protestants, Catholics, and pietists. Between 1830 and 1865 most of the immigrants were Protestants, but after the Civil War more and more Catholics immigrated from southern and southwestern Germany until in the 1880s they constituted half of the incoming Germans. By contrast, most English, Scots, Welsh, and Scandinavian immigrants were Protestants and practically all the Irish were Catholics. Religion and nationality were closely integrated for them. But for the Germans, religious loyalties divided the community and retarded any sense of pan-German ethnicity.

German Protestants all shared certain basic values by linking the secular and the sacred, arguing that worldly institutions like the family, government, and business were ordained by God to promote the heavenly kingdom. The concept of the calling or vocation to serve in the world rather than make a monastic withdrawal imbued the mentality of the German Protestants, as did their belief that mere obedience to church law was not necessarily a measure of genuine spirituality. And virtually all of them believed that Roman Catholicism was evil and corrupt, and that the hand of God had orchestrated the Reformation in the sixteenth century.

But despite some similarities, German Protestantism evolved into a number of subcultures in the United States. German Reformed, Baptists, and Presbyterians, for example, adhered to John Calvin's decree of human depravity and predestination, believing that an omnipotent and inscrutable God determined the salvation of the elect. As long as German remained their mother tongue in America, the German Calvinists maintained a cultural isolation, but as the second and third generations adopted English, they acculturated religiously, closely collaborating with Anglo-American Baptists, Methodists, Congregationalists, and Presbyterians in the work of the Lord.

Perhaps the most visible German subcultures in the United States were those of the communitarian reformers and the Protestant pietists. George Rapp's colony at New Harmony, Indiana, and Joseph Baummler's settlement at Zoar, Ohio, for example, both cultivated an isolationist spirit as a means of creating their experimental, communitarian societies. The pietistic sects rejected all forms of religious authority and emphasized the "inner light" between God and man. Convinced the world was corrupt and sinful, the German pietists—such as the Hutterites in the Dakotas, the Amish in Pennsylvania, members of the Amana colonies in Iowa, or the Mennonites in their scattered settlements—deliberately separated themselves from other people, hoping that in the cultural isolation of tightly-knit communities they could preserve their language and faith. They too emerged as distinct ethnic communities in the United States.

Though less intense than the isolationism of the pietists, the ethnicity of the German Lutherans was strong and revolved around theology and cultural nationalism. They had replaced the authority of the pope with the immutable authority of the Bible and, especially the Missouri Synod Lutherans, believed that the Lutheran Church embodied the only true church on earth. Ecumenical movements were condemned as compromises with heresy, and parochial schools were used to transmit language and the faith to children. Reinforcing their theological isolation was a heightened sense of nationalism, especially among German Lutherans emigrating after 1871. As part of the German unification movement, the Prussian *Kulturkampf*, by repressing German Catholicism, had enabled many to equate Lutheranism with German nationalism, and they brought these feelings with them to the United States.

Finally, there was the separate world of the German Catholics. Many came from southern and southwestern Germany where High German was spoken and where the *Gemeinschaft* world of traditional family and personal values prevailed. That set them apart from northern and northwestern Germans, but religious differences were even more important. Generations of religious wars had created a profound cultural gap between Protestants and Catholics. In the nineteenth century

German Catholicism had enjoyed a spiritual renaissance in which the number of parishes as well as attendance at mass had increased, membership in religious confraternities had multiplied, and pride in Catholic culture had intensified. In the German Catholic parishes of America the renaissance continued.

The German Catholics' love of pageantry and ceremony contrasted with the Irish devotion to ascetic simplicity, and was expressed in elaborate and colorful processions, bands, choirs, orchestras, vocalists, and parades. In addition, the German Catholics enjoyed a number of parish societies. Some, like the Archconfraternity of the Holy Rosary, were devoted to the Virgin Mary or particular saints; others, like St. Raphael's, assisted incoming immigrants. The Jaegers and Henry Henning Guards were military societies originally established during the Know-Nothing era of the 1850s to protect parish property from mobs of nativists. The *Unterstutzung-Verein* were mutual aid societies formed in the parishes to help the sick and the poor, and in 1855 all the German Catholic mutual aid societies in the United States established the Central Verein. By the early twentieth century the Central Verein had become committed to social reform and was providing English language schools, settlement houses, health and life insurance, day care centers, employment agencies, and welfare programs for German Catholics. Like the Calvinists, pietists, and Lutherans, the German Catholics formed a distinct subculture in nineteenth century America.

The Rise of German Ethnic Nationalism

Still, despite all that divided them, the immigrants from Germany were able to acquire a proud ethnic nationalism in the nineteenth and early twentieth centuries. The hostility of Anglo-Americans helped create that ethnicity, but most incoming Germans were not thrust into a completely alien, hostile world. Most of the first German immigrants of the Great Migration settled in the Mohawk Valley of upstate New York, eastern Pennsylvania, or Maryland, where remnants of colonial German society still thrived. And after 1840 most went to the German belt and the German triangle. German-language newspapers, more than a hundred of them, were circulating by 1850; German clubs and societies had been founded; and German churches were available. German workers immigrating later in the century left German cities only to enter German-American communities where German culture flourished. Immigration was traumatic, but most Germans did not experience the total psychological disruption characteristic of culture shock.

Still, nativism helped define their ethnicity, if only because other Americans looked upon them as Germans, not as Prussians, Bavarians, or Swabians. Their exclusiveness and cultural peculiarities worried many Americans, who considered the Germans less frightening than the Irish but far more threatening than the English or Scandinavians. Many Germans were Catholics, and some Americans conjured up sinister German conspiracies to transform America into a papal outpost. Upper-class Whigs considered the Forty-Eighters a revolutionary underground, and others worried about the German attachment to Old World values.

Many cities outlawed German militia companies, gymnasiums, and shooting clubs, while others refused to charter German social and mutual aid societies. The Irish bore the brunt of Know-Nothing venom, but Germans and particularly German Catholics suffered as well. Anti-German disturbances erupted in St. Louis, New Orleans, Philadelphia, Cincinnati, Columbus, and Louisville in the 1850s, and in some cases homes, churches, schools, and businesses were vandalized. This anti-German paranoia would rise again during World War I. All this helped create a sense of unity among German immigrants.

But German-American values were even more important in building an ethnic nationalism. Some German immigrants possessed a keen national pride. Though few in number, the Forty-Eighters profoundly influenced the German masses entering America in the nineteenth century. They worshiped Germany, believing in the superiority of the German people, German education, and German destiny. To promote German patriotism, they transplanted "Turner" organizations to the United States. Founded by Friedrich Jahn in 1811, the Turner groups represented an incipient form of German nationalism, dedicated to patriotism, physical fitness, preparedness, and a free, united Germany. The Forty-Eighters supported the *Turnvereine* ("tournament" or "gymnastic") ideal, and Turner societies developed throughout German America. Even more important, the Forty-Eighters controlled the German-American press before the Civil War and constantly editorialized on the German destiny. During the Franco-Prussian War of 1870 those sentiments escalated into a chauvinistic support for the fatherland. Incoming Germans after 1850 rapidly acquired a sense of German nationalism because the Forty-Eighters—along with their Turner groups and newspapers—bombarded them with news of home and the preached future of a unified Germany. After Bismarck united Germany in the 1870s, more and more immigrants arrived with an awareness of their German nationality.

Language strengthened their sense of being German. A German Lutheran immigrant would have felt uncomfortable worshiping at a Norwegian Lutheran church or with an Anglican congregation, as would a Bavarian Catholic in an Irish parish. Like the colonial Germans, they believed their faith was best expressed in the language of the Old World. The Reverend Anton H. Walburg of Cincinnati decided that a

> foreigner who loses his nationality is in danger of losing his faith and character. When the German immigrant . . . seeks to throw aside his nationality . . . the first word he learns is generally a curse, and . . . like as the Indians . . . [he adopts] the vices rather than the virtues . . .*

In the Old World they had defined themselves only as Reformed, Lutheran, Catholic, or pietist, but in the United States they became German Reformed, German Lutherans, German pietists, or German Catholics. German-language services and German-speaking clergymen, both taken for granted in the Old World, became precious values in the New World, and they helped impose on the immigrants a special sense of being German. Although the transition to English was inevitable, the cultural struggle between the immigrant and native-born generations embedded into both personalities a pervasive sense of the German heritage.

Irish domination of the American church posed a special challenge for German Catholics. In Protestantism, authority was decentralized, and it was relatively simple to establish churches and recruit ministers. Religious initiative usually implied no theological disloyalty. But for Roman Catholics the "keys of the priesthood" rested in a hierarchy. Power flowed from the pope down through archbishops and bishops to parish priests and congregations. Hence in America Irish priests helped strengthen German Catholic ethnicity. Catholic dioceses quickly spread throughout the German triangle as hundreds of thousands of German Catholics settled in towns and cities where other German Catholics already lived. John Henni became the unofficial leader of German Catholicism when he became bishop of Milwaukee in 1844. After becoming archbishop of the German triangle, he insisted on having only German-speaking priests in the archdiocese, a policy that enraged the Irish clergy. In 1891 Cardinal Gibbons of Baltimore, an Irishman, preached:

> Woe to him who would breed dissention among the leaders of Israel by introducing the spirit of nationalism into the camps of the Lord! Brothers we are, whatever may be our nationality, and brothers we shall remain. . . . Let us glory in the title of American citizen. We owe all our allegiance to one country, and that country is America.†

---

* Quoted in La Vern J. Rippley, *The German Americans* (New York, 1976), p. 111.
† Ibid., p. 113.

Ethnic parishes were critically important to the German Catholics; for although these German immigrants came from diverse regional, class, and occupational backgrounds, they shared language and religion. The refrain "language saves the faith" became the watchword of German Catholics in the United States. English-speaking Catholic parishes were as dangerous to these immigrants as any of the American Protestant churches, because loss of the language implied loss of the faith. German Catholics did join some ethnic clubs and societies although the church specifically warned them to avoid contact with the fraternal lodges and the Turner groups, but the parish was the center of their social and spiritual lives, and its schools and societies protected them from the larger Protestant culture.

German Catholics thus established many ethnic parishes. Holy Trinity Parish, St. Peter's Parish, and St. Alphonsus Parish were serving German Catholics in Philadelphia by 1853, and in northern Ohio there were St. Stephen's and St. Vincent de Paul Parishes in Cleveland, St. Bernard Parish in Akron, and St. Joseph Parish in Lorain. Many Irish priests argued that language was irrelevant in a "world church." German Catholics claimed that the church hierarchy ought to reflect the nationality of parish members. The Irish then argued that although they had lost the use of the Gaelic language, it had not retarded their commitment to the Kingdom of God. Eventually the struggle went all the way to Rome, and the Irish retained control of the church hierarchy in the United States. Nonetheless, the Germans secured a powerful foothold. By 1910 there were more than two thousand parishes using German-language services, more than twenty-six hundred German-speaking priests, and twenty dioceses with more than fifty German-speaking priests each; and more than 95 percent of German Catholic parishes had parochial schools where German was taught. The language controversy played a major role in making the Catholic immigrants conscious of their German origins.

The language issue continued to agitate German Protestants and Catholics; by the 1880s and 1890s, as more and more German children attended public schools, states in the German triangle passed laws permitting academic subjects to be taught in German wherever there were heavy concentrations of German-Americans. After the unification of Germany in the 1870s and years of an increasing sense of ethnicity in the United States, the German-American community was proud of its origins, and the use of German in public schools no longer had only religious motives but was intended to preserve the whole range of German culture. Immigrants and their children were more aware of being German than they had ever been before emigrating.

This is not to say, of course, that German America was monolithically united. Old distinctions died slowly. The ethnocentric pride of being Prussian still survived in 1900; condescension of northern Germans to southern Germans persisted; and the anticlericalism of the Forty-Eighters had alienated them from German Catholics. Nor had the Swiss or Volga Germans melted into the larger German-American community. Still, they were more of an ethnic community after coming to the United States than before. Immigration was so large and so continuous, feeding hundreds of thousands of new immigrants into the German triangle, that it constantly reinforced German culture. The immigration of nearly one million Germans after 1945 would continue to inject new life into German-American culture. In Milwaukee, Cincinnati, St. Louis, or along East Eighty-sixth Street in New York City, as well as in places like Omaha, Nebraska, and Fredericksburg, Texas, one would be able to hear German spoken, purchase a newspaper and books in German, eat at a Hindenburg or Hofbrau cafe, or attend a Steuben parade, a Sangerfest, or a bock beer festival.

From Germans to German-Americans

The emergence of ethnicity and ethnic nationalism was a step toward assimilation, for as they transcended the parochial loyalties of the Old World the Germans' sense of interrelationships expanded considerably. A German melting pot operated in America. Lutherans from the Rhineland married Lutherans from Bavaria, or Catholics from Silesia married Catholics from Westphalia. The children and grandchildren of these mixed marriages saw themselves as German Lutherans or German Catholics, losing in one or two generations the old vision of being Bavarian or Prussian or Silesian. Russian-Germans, Swiss-Germans, Alsatians, and Germans frequently intermarried, and their German-speaking children melted into the larger German-American community. It brought Germans one step closer to a sense of an American national identity.

Because of the fluidity of the social structure, geographical mobility, and toleration of religious diversity in the United States, as well as the economic success of German-Americans, the immigrants could not help gradually becoming part of the larger society. With the arrival of each new generation the sense of being American became more pronounced. By 1900 the Prussian immigrant of 1880 and his children still felt intensely German, but descendants of colonial Germans who had emigrated out of western Maryland in 1790 possessed much weaker loyalties to German culture. Those same forces would work on the nineteenth-century immigrants as well.

Still, Germans remained loyal to one another. Among people of German descent living in Wisconsin in 1908, nearly 80 percent were marrying Germans, and the same was true for Nebraska Germans and Texas Germans. Assimilation and even acculturation remained retarded during the nineteenth century. Even then, however, subtle changes were occurring which would prepare the descendants of these immigrants for assimilation in the twentieth century. Just as the first generation acquired an ethnic nationalism, succeeding generations developed new role definitions based on residence, religion, politics, occupation, and income which would compete with nationality. By 1900 most German-Americans were living in cities. At first they congregated in ghettos, but they moved to the suburbs as soon as income permitted. New immigrants then replaced them in their downtown ghettos of Philadelphia or St. Louis or New York. In the suburbs upwardly mobile Germans lived near other Germans but were also surrounded by people of English, Irish, Welsh, Scots, or Scandinavian background. Their sense of community among suburban Germans broadened to include middle-class residents of their neighborhoods. Complete assimilation was still not common, for in most of those areas the Germans married among themselves more than 60 percent of the time. But acculturation was certainly underway.

When German Lutherans married Scandinavian Lutherans, their children—or at least their grandchildren or great-grandchildren—often reverted to an Old World tradition, considering themselves simply Lutherans again or perhaps white Lutherans. Political loyalties in the charged atmosphere of the nineteenth century were also important, and German-Americans, whether Republicans or Democrats, often identified themselves with a party. Occupational patterns were important too. A fourth-generation machine-tool specialist from Milwaukee would look upon his membership in the American Federation of Labor as an important part of his identity, perhaps as important as the fact that his great-grandfather had emigrated from the Rhineland in 1820. German culture was certainly intact in 1900, but the stage was set for important changes in the twentieth century.

The size of the German immigration and their economic success gave German-Americans a special place in United States history. In science the German luminaries include Charles Steinmetz, inventor of electric generators; and George Westinghouse, inventor of railroad air brakes. In big business John Jacob Astor controlled the fur trade in the early nineteenth century; Frederick Weyerhaeuser became the famous timber magnate; John D. Rockefeller founded the Standard Oil Company; Henry Villard was a famous financier; and Adolph Busch and

Adolph Coors were beer magnates. German-Americans have become influential politicians, from socialists like Eugene V. Debs, founder of the Socialist party; to liberals like Carl Schurz, John Peter Altgeld, governor of Illinois in the 1890s, and New York Senator Robert Wagner; to conservatives like former Senator Everett Dirksen of Illinois and anarchists like Johann Most. In virtually every area of human endeavor German-Americans have made important contributions. In other fields the list includes baseball players Honus Wagner, Babe Ruth, and Lou Gehrig; journalists Walter Lippmann and H.L. Mencken; author Clara Berens; cartoonist Thomas Nast; philosophers Paul Tillich, Eric Hoffer, and Reinhold and Richard Niebuhr; opera star Ernestine Rossler; entertainers Jack Parr, Lawrence Welk, Rod Steiger, and Oscar Hammerstein; and scholars Hans Rosenberg, Felix Gilbert, and Hajo Holborn.

SUGGESTED READINGS

Arndt, Karl J. R., and Olson, May E. *The German Language Press of the Americas, 1732–1968*. Pullach, Germany: 1973.

Billigmeier, Robert. *Americans from Germany: A Study in Cultural Diversity*. Belmont, Cal.: 1974.

Boxer, Charles R. *The Dutch Seaborne Empire*. New York: 1965.

Child, Clifton J. *The German Americans in Politics, 1914–1917*. Madison, Wisconsin: 1939.

Cole, Cyrenus. *I Remember, I Remember*. Iowa City, Iowa: 1936.

Colman, Barry. *The Catholic Church and German Americans*. Milwaukee, Wisconsin: 1953.

Condon, Thomas J. *New York Beginnings: The Commercial Origins of New Netherland*. New York: 1968.

Conzen, Kathleen. *Immigrant Milwaukee, 1836–1860*. Cambridge, Mass.: 1976.

Cunz, Dieter. *The Maryland Germans*. Princeton, N.J.: 1948.

DeJong, Gerald F. *The Dutch in America, 1609–1974*. New York: 1975.

Ellis, David M. *Landlords and Farmers in the Hudson-Mohawk Region, 1790–1850*. New York: 1967.

Faust, Albert. *The German Element in the United States*. New York: 1927.

Fleming, Donald, and Bailyn, Bernard, eds. *The Intellectual Migration, Europe and America, 1930–1960*. Cambridge, Mass.: 1969.

Frye, Alton. *Nazi Germany and the American Hemisphere, 1933–1941*. New Haven, Conn.: 1967.

Gilbert, Glenn, ed. *The German Language in America*. Austin, Texas: 1971.

Gleason, Philip. *The Conservative Reformers: German-American Catholics and the Social Order*. Notre Dame, Ind.: 1968.

Graebner, Alan. *Uncertain Saints: The Laity in the Lutheran Church–Missouri Synod, 1900–1970*. Westport, Conn.: 1975.

Hawgood, John A. *The Tragedy of German-America*. New York: 1970.

Hostetler, John. *Hutterite Society*. Baltimore: 1974.

Hyma, Albert. *Albertus C. Van Raalte and His Dutch Settlements in the United States*. Grand Rapids, Mich.: 1947.

Johnson, Hildegard. "Intermarriages Between German Pioneers and Other Nationalities in Minnesota in 1860 and 1870." *American Journal of Sociology*, 51 (January 1946), 299–304.

Johnston, William M. *The Austrian Mind: An Intellectual and Social History 1848–1938*. Berkeley, Cal.: 1972.

Jordan, Terry G. *German Seed in Texas Soil: Immigrant Farmers in Nineteenth-Century Texas*. Austin, Texas: 1966.

Kent, Donald P. *The Refugee Intellectual: The Americanization of the Immigrants of 1933–1941*. New York: 1953.

Korman, Gerd. *Industrialization, Immigrants, and Americanizers: The View from Milwaukee, 1866–1921*. Madison, Wisconsin: 1967.

Kromminga, D. H. *The Christian Reformed Tradition*. Grand Rapids, Mich.: 1943.

Lucas, Henry S. *Netherlands in America: Dutch Immigration to the United States and Canada, 1789–1950*. Ann Arbor, Mich.: 1955.

Luebke, Frederick C. *Bonds of Loyalty: German Americans and World War I*. Dekalb, Ill.: 1974.

––––––. *Immigrants and Politics: The Germans of Nebraska, 1880–1900*. Lincoln, Neb.: 1969.

Mulder, Arnold. *Americans from Holland*. Philadelphia: 1947.

Nelson, E. Clifford. *Lutheranism in North America, 1914–1970*. Minneapolis: 1972.

O'Connor, Richard. *The German-Americans*. New York: 1968.

O'Grady, Joseph P. *The Immigrants' Influence on Wilson's Peace Policies*. Lexington, Kentucky: 1967.

Peters, Victor. *All Things Common: The Hutterian Way of Life*. Minneapolis: 1965.

Raesly, Ellis. *Portrait of New Netherland*. New York: 1945.

Rothan, Emmet. *The German Catholic Immigrant in the United States, 1830–1860*. Washington, D.C.: 1946.

Sallet, Richard. *The Russian-German Settlements in the United States*. Fargo, N.D.: 1974.

Schelburt, Leo, ed. *New Glarus, 1845–1970: The Making of a Swiss American Town*. Glarus, Switzerland: 1970.

Singmaster, Elsie. *The Magic Mirror*. New York: 1934.

Walker, Mack. *Germany and the Emigration, 1816–1885*. Cambridge, Mass.: 1964.

Wittke, Carl. *The German Language Press in America*. Lexington, Kentucky: 1957.

––––––. *Refugees of Revolution: The German Forty-Eighters in America*. Philadelphia: 1952.

Wood, Ralph, ed. *The Pennsylvania Germans*. Princeton, N.J.: 1942.
Wust, Klaus. *The Virginia Germans*. Charlottesville, Virginia: 1969.
Zucker, A. E., ed. *The Forty-Eighters: Political Refugees of the German Revolution of 1848*. New York: 1950.
Zwaanstra, Henry. *Reformed Thought in a New World*. Kampen, New Netherlands: 1973.

Chapter Seven

The Scandinavian Presence in America

Next to the British and the Germans, the Scandinavians were the largest group of "old immigrants" coming to the United States. Between 1820 and 1924 more than 750,000 Norwegians came to America, 580,000 of them after 1880. The Swedish migration was larger: more than 1.2 million Swedes settled in America. Perhaps 320,000 Danes immigrated, as did 300,000 Finns. Together they developed the upper Mississippi Valley and made significant contributions to American culture.

There were important differences among the Scandinavians in terms of culture, language, and history, but in a number of ways they had a similar perspective on life, one born of circumstance as well as history. After centuries of scraping a living out of rocky soil in a cold climate, they possessed a stoicism about life and determination to hold out against its capriciousness. Theirs was a bittersweet attachment to their homeland. If stubborn is too harsh a word, the Scandinavians were dogged and tenacious, somewhat inflexible on moral questions and incredibly persevering on economic ones. Central to the Scandinavian character was a profound sense of honor. Above all else Scandinavians respected a contract or promise as a covenant and felt morally bound, not because of guilt but because of a highly developed conscience, to fulfill personal obligations. Honesty and reliability were the measure of personal worth, and this showed in Scandinavian attitudes toward work, dependability, thoroughness, and efficiency. Anything less than working at the peak of one's ability, and finishing a job satisfactorily and on time, brought dishonor. Thus the Scandinavians became some of the most reliable workers in America. The Scandinavians loved freedom, thrilled to the libertarian stories of ancient Viking warriors, and constantly preached the superiority of democracy over aristocracy. In America they would be most impressed with the lack of class distinctions.

The Scandinavians also tended to be a private people, careful about expressing their feelings, almost introverted and even morose in their dealings with others. Self-control was expected of men and women. For the Swedes, Danes, Norwegians, and Finns it was more important to be trusted than to be loved. Because they placed such value on dependability, emotional control, and predictability in personal behavior, they were also a conservative people deeply concerned with preserving traditional folkways. Out of all this came their vision of loyalty and trust, a clannishness based not so much on need as on fidelity.

The Scandinavian presence in America reaches back to Leif Ericson and the Vikings who explored "Vinland" in the eleventh century. In 1638 the Swedish West India Company placed five hundred Swedes and Finns on the banks of the Delaware River. Swedish Lutheran churches, Swedish-born ministers, and parochial schools tried to preserve tradition in New Sweden; but the colony was sparsely populated, new immigrants were too few, and the surrounding non-Swedish population was too large. New Netherland took over the colony in 1655; and when England conquered New Netherland in 1664, the Swedes and Finns lost their independence. On the eve of the Revolution there were nearly twenty thousand Swedes in America; but because they were vastly outnumbered by other Protestants, they were already learning English as their primary language, intermarrying widely into the general population, and disappearing as a self-conscious ethnic group.

Scandinavians and the Lutheran Church

Scandinavian culture revived with the Great Migration. During the first half of the nineteenth century, religious unrest swept through Scandinavia and inspired thousands of people to come to the United States. Since the Protestant Reformation Lutheranism had been the national faith in Norway, Sweden, Denmark, and Finland; and the Scandinavians were a profoundly religious people with strong pietistic inclinations. Family prayer, Bible and sermon reading, and hymn singing were as much the routine of the home as working, eating, and sleeping; and attendance at church provided a respite from the constant toil of farm life. In towns and villages throughout Scandinavia the Lutheran church was the largest, most prominent building; people gathered there for socials and services, to visit and gossip with friends and relatives as well as to commune with heaven. Children were taught obedience and fear of God, and parental admonitions to hold to their religious training helped build a sense of reverent respect for the church. When children were baptized on the first warm Sunday of spring, the whole community gathered in anticipation; similar feelings prevailed on Confirmation Sunday, when children renewed their baptismal covenants and took Holy Communion. In the church cemetery rested the bodies of family ancestors; some of the gravestones reached back six centuries. Religion and the church served as the psychological center of Scandinavian life in the nineteenth century.

Martin Luther had emphasized the belief that man's relationship with God was a personal responsibility and that salvation depended on a willingness to accept heavenly grace. Bureaucracies, ordinances, and religious authorities were all subordinated to that overwhelming personal responsibility. So the Scandinavians had faith in private judgments and a conviction that all people were equal before God. Consequently they felt no guilt in questioning a minister's decisions or even in debating the theological merits of confession, infant baptism, determinism, and freedom of choice. Characteristic of the Protestant spirit, the church as an institution of authority was less important than its role in bringing people closer to God.

But after three centuries state Lutheranism seemed to contradict the pietistic inclinations of Scandinavian spirituality. To many people the church seemed formalistic and conservative, more worried about protecting its position in the society than in truly building the kingdom of God. Local churches appeared too willing to acquiesce in the wishes of the wealthy and not concerned enough about the lives of humble people. Restlessness swept through the church. Quaker congregations began to grow and Mormon missionaries began having some success, especially in Denmark and Norway. But even more influential were the pietistic reform movements which appeared in the early nineteenth century. In Norway Hans Nielsen Hauge initiated a pietistic movement to purify the church of its formalistic overtones and bring it into the reach of common farming and working people, and Eric Janssen started a similar movement in the Swedish Lutheran Church. N. F. S. Grundtvig began the pietistic reform of the Danish Lutheran Church, and Lars L. Lastadius did the same in Finland. In each country tens of thousands of people were caught up in the movement to make religion more personal. The state churches felt threatened and began to harass the new converts.

In 1825 fifty Haugenists sailed in the ship *Restauration* from

Stavanger, Norway, and settled near Rochester, New York. After being tried and convicted of heresy, Eric Janssen led some of his followers to Bishop Hill, Michigan, in 1846. One Janssenist wrote home in 1847:

> And from this it follows that the light God has brought forth through Eric Janssen cannot be dimmed . . . we have opportunity here to edify each other in the most sacred faith . . . this country's laws are different from those of our fatherland. We are protected here by both the secular law and the secular power, and thus have the rights of citizenship which a true Christian could not enjoy in our fatherland.*

Thousands of other dissenters fled Scandinavia in the 1840s and 1850s to trade the oppressive atmosphere of state Lutheranism for the freer environment of the United States.

Immigration for Economic Gain

After the Civil War, however, most people immigrated for economic reasons. The Scandinavian soil was either too moist or too rocky; farmers were perpetually draining the land or removing the stones. The growing season was short, the winters bitterly cold and dark, and less than one acre in ten was arable. As the population grew and land became more difficult to acquire, many people wearied of life in rural mud homes, subsisting on potatoes and some meat in good times and rye bark or moss bread in bad times, and paying heavy mortgages. Later in the century, as American wheat, Canadian timber, and English and American manufactured goods flooded Scandinavian markets, and as the world shifted to steam-driven ships, Scandinavian peasants, lumberjacks, and shipbuilders in search of work moved to Christiania, Stockholm, Copenhagen, and Helsinki, and some then went on to America. Finland was not integrated into the Atlantic economy until the 1880s, but Finns began to emigrate then too. Finally, the Industrial Revolution, which reached Scandinavia in the 1870s, upset traditional systems of production and cut thousands of artisans loose from their moorings.

As steamship companies, railroads, and other immigrants littered Scandinavia with propaganda about America, the Great Migration began. When one emigrant returned home for a visit a Norwegian remarked:

*H. Arnold Barton, ed., *Letters from the Promised Land: Swedes in America, 1840-1914* (Minneapolis, 1973), pp. 40-41.

Whatever may have been the results of his visit . . . personally, they were of far-reaching importance to the emigration movement in western Norway. From near and far . . . people came . . . to talk with this experienced . . . man about life in New York or Illinois. . . . The "America fever" contracted in conference with Slogvig . . . was hard to shake off . . . when he prepared to go back to the United States in 1836 a large party was ready to go with him.*

Most of the Scandinavians were not destitute; but when the immigration fever caught hold of them, they became determined to find in America the security that was disappearing in Europe.

Until the 1880s most of the Scandinavian immigrants were farmers who settled in Michigan, Wisconsin, Illinois, Iowa, Minnesota, and the Dakotas. They carved out new lives on the great wheat fields of the northern prairies and forests where icy winters reminded them of home. Southern Wisconsin and northern Illinois contained more than 70 percent of the Norwegians in 1860, and from there they pressed into Minnesota, Iowa, and the Dakotas after the Civil War. During those first years they lived in sod houses or crude lean-tos, and braved blizzards, dust storms, humid summers, and locusts, but the rough shelters soon gave way to log cabins and then to more substantial wood-frame homes. One immigrant from Sweden warned that an immigrant would

have to suffer much in the beginning . . . and sacrifice much of what he is accustomed to in Europe. Without work, often with work that is hard and painful, he cannot hope to achieve success. I caution against all exaggerated hopes and golden air castles; cold reality will otherwise lame your arm and crush your courage; both must be fresh and alive . . . we do not regret our undertaking. We are living a free and independent life in one of the most beautiful valleys the world can offer . . .†

After 1880, when the best land was taken and most immigrants were workers, the Scandinavians increasingly settled in the cities. Large Scandinavian colonies appeared in New York, Buffalo, Cleveland, Chicago, Duluth, Minneapolis, Des Moines, and in dozens of smaller cities in the North. Along the Great Lakes Norwegian sailors were in great demand because of their maritime skills. Swedish painters, masons, machinists, carpenters, miners, and iron and steel workers filled the waiting industrial jobs, and next to the British they supplied more skilled workers to the American economy than any other immigrant

---

* Andreas Ueland, *Recollections of an Immigrant* (New York, 1929), p. 137.
† Barton, *Letters from the Promised Land*, p. 24.

This 1851 wood engraving depicts a party of Swedish immigrants heading west. (The Granger Collection)

group. Because of their unusually high educational level, the Danes secured white-collar positions as clerks and sales personnel. The Finns had few industrial skills and took the hardest jobs as miners, lumberjacks, stevedores, and laborers clearing farms. The largest Finnish settlement developed around the huge copper mines in Hancock, Michigan, and other Finns worked in the iron mountains of the Mesabi range in Minnesota and in the western gold, silver, and coal mines. In the Great Lakes port cities they loaded freight, and large Finnish settlements appeared in the New England mill towns, especially Worcester and Fitchburg, Massachusetts. By 1900 the Scandinavian community in the United States had both an urban and rural base.

Like so many other immigrants, the Scandinavians reconstructed Old World values in the New World setting. The rural pioneers arriving in the Midwest during the 1840s and 1850s were awed by the availability and fertility of land. In Scandinavia a farm of six acres had been a respectable holding, but in America the immigrants often acquired eighty to several hundred acres. Through pride, hard work, thrift, and fear of debt, they increased the values of their farms instead of trying to increase their size. Scandinavian farmers loved the land and believed that rural life preserved ethical values as well as family independence.

Scandinavian Ethnicity in America

At first Scandinavian ethnicity was centered in the Lutheran Church. The immigrants tried desperately to reconstitute the church just as it had been in the Old World. Church buildings were constructed at the highest point in the community so they could be seen from far away, if possible near the first graveyard so the dead could rest "in the shadow of the Lord's house." Meeting houses had a tower and bell and an altar facing east, covered with an altar cloth, candles, and a huge Bible. Ministers, often circuit riders in the early days, preached from a raised podium, and men and women sat on opposite sides of the chapel. The congregation sang the same hymns, repeated the same prayers, offered up the same confessions, and observed the same communion, baptism, confirmation, marriage, and burial rites as before.

But it was impossible for the Lutheran Church to play the same role in America that it had in Europe. The theological tensions inherent in Protestantism, contained in Scandinavia by the political power of the Lutheran Church, brought factionalism in the United States. Language was a major stumbling block; there was simply no way the Swedes, Norwegians, Danes, and Finns could worship together. Like the Germans, all four groups believed that language saves the faith. The Augustana Synod, for example, was formed in 1860; but in 1870 a Danish-Norwegian faction defected, and a few years later the Danes and Norwegians split into different synods. Soon there were Norwegian, Swedish, Danish, and Finnish Lutheran churches in the United States.

And just as frequently Norwegians fought Norwegians or Swedes fought Swedes over religion. The pietistic movement in Scandinavia had rejected rational formalism for a warmer, more personal faith that gave full reign to individual emotions. Immigrants naturally carried those feelings to America, and, free of the control of state Lutheranism, the Scandinavian churches disintegrated into many different units. In Scandinavia the state church had started all congregations, financed them, and appointed ministers. But in the United States the people of the community carried the major responsibility for incorporating a new church, supporting it financially, and recruiting a minister. With more control over the church, they were free to quarrel with policies or doctrines they disliked and always ready to bolt the congregation or the synod to create their own church.

Because of the strong pietistic tradition in Scandinavia and the puritanical overtones of American culture, immigrant congregations often struggled with issues of personal morality. A consensus condemned divorce because it dissolved a union sanctioned by God, and premarital sex was likewise forbidden. Old peasant mores had permitted premarital sexual unions between a betrothed couple because economic considerations often forced postponement of marriage. Few stigmas were attached to illegitimate pregnancy as long as the parents married later on. But in the New World the pietists, who triumphed in America, condemned premarital sex and ostracized those who engaged in it, especially the women. In the Old World consumption of alcohol had been common, but poverty usually confined it to special occasions and holidays. In America, where liquor was as plentiful as the money to purchase it, the custom became a vice. In the Scandinavian communities the pietists called for temperance, while other Lutherans defended the right to drink. The pietists also condemned dancing, social games, card playing, Sabbath breaking, and joining secret societies.

Such were the debates, and they led to fissures in the Scandinavian churches. The Augustana Synod represented Swedish Lutheranism, but it lost many groups, including the Evangelical Mission Covenant Church. Norwegian Lutheranism ranged from the pietist Haugenists to high church formalists, with many groups in between. Danish Lutheranism was divided between high church formalism and the Danish Evangelical Lutheranism. The Finns had the Finnish Lutheran Church, the Finnish Apostolic Lutheran Church, and the National Evangelical Lutheran Church. The individualistic, congregational autonomy so central to Protestantism prevented Scandinavian Lutheranism from consolidating immigrant ethnicity as Roman Catholicism did for the Irish and the French Canadians.

As a result, Scandinavian ethnicity in the United States soon expanded beyond the church. Home and family were basic values, and the immigrants appreciated America because the abundant land and non-rigid social structure permitted them to provide adequately for their families. Immigrant workers considered America superior to the Old World because they enjoyed a higher standard of living, manual labor was respected, there was a real possibility of moving into the middle and upper class without being stigmatized by lower-class origins, and families could be independent. In those families, the authority of the father went unquestioned; Scandinavian wives rarely defied his power, and children were expected to be obedient. Beyond the nuclear family, kinship loyalties were strong and required an older resident to board arriving relatives and help them find jobs. Repayment was not usually expected.

A number of ethnic organizations promoted group solidarity and Old World values. Like other groups Scandinavians established fraternal societies and mutual aid associations to provide a social outlet and help members through hard times. The Swedes had the Vasa Order, the Order of Vikings, the Order of Runeberg, and the International Order of Good Templars; the Norwegians formed the Sons of Norway; the Danes had the Danish Brotherhood; and the Finns established the Knights of Kaleva. Tens of thousands of Norwegians had immigrated in village chains, and once in the United States they revived those relationships in *bygdelag* societies, in which groups of immigrants were united by regional origins. Finns had the Finnish American Society, Finnish Halls, and the Finlandia Foundation. Swedish-Americans founded Augustana College, Kendall College, Adolphus College, and Bethany College; Norwegians had Concordia College, Luther College, and St. Olaf's College; and the Finns had Suomi College. During the Great Migration there were more than a thousand Swedish-American newspapers, more than three hundred Norwegian, three hundred Finnish, and one hundred Danish papers. All these institutions contained and expressed Scandinavian ethnicity in the United States.

Four Different Heritages

The Swedes, Norwegians, Danes, and Finns, however, had different levels of ethnicity and ethnic nationalism. Generally the Finns and Norwegians were more concerned about preserving Old World traditions, more dedicated to their own communities, and married compatriots more often than the Danes and Swedes. Those differences stemmed from their different cultures. In Denmark and southern Sweden small farms were mixed with large estates, all scattered around clustered village markets where peasants sold their produce and purchased goods from village artisans. These Scandinavians were commercial farmers functioning in a money economy. Because news, travelers, and goods from the outside world reached them through rail, steamship, and highway connections, the Danes and Swedes were more open and adaptable to social change, strangers, and new ideas.

But in Norway and Finland a rural society prevailed that enjoyed no central village existence. In the heavily wooded forests and mountains each valley had a separate identity complete with variations in food, dialect, clothing, and customs. Homesteads had to be largely self-sufficient, and the commercial production of surpluses was virtually nonexistent. From the nearby woods peasant farmers took the wood for building houses and warming them, carving shoes, and fashioning farm implements; from crude iron ore they made metal tools; from hides they cured their own leather; and from grain crops they distilled their own liquor. Extended families were close and so were neighbors throughout the valley; everyone knew everyone else. Less cosmopolitan than the Danish and Swedish peasants, as well as more isolated, they were suspicious of strangers, self-reliant, and more conservative about social change. In the United States the Norwegians and Finns held closely to people who spoke their language, worshiped in their churches, and joined their associations.

History contributed to immigrant ethnicity. Denmark had enjoyed a national history since the Middle Ages, and the Danish immigrants accepted nationality as a fact of life. And since 1523, when Sweden withdrew from the Kalmar Union with Denmark and Norway, Swedes too had had national independence. Consequently these people felt no need to defend their national identity in America.

It was markedly different, however, for the Norwegians and Finns. Sweden had lost Finland to Russia in 1809, and in the Treaty of Kiel of 1814 Denmark, which had sided with Napoleon in the European conflict, was forced to cede Norway to Sweden. Trapped in a semicolonial relationship with Sweden, nineteenth-century Norwegians had a strong national consciousness, and immigrants carried that consciousness to the New World. In 1849 a Norwegian immigrant wrote home:

> As American citizens who have tasted the joys of being free . . . and having in common with you the Norwegian temper, love of liberty, and warmth of heart, we would say to you who swell amid Norway's mountains: Show yourselves worthy sons of the north. Stand as a man for your liberties. Let freedom and equality be your demands, truth and the right your reliance, and the God of justice will give you victory. *

When Norway peacefully achieved independence from Sweden in 1905, Norwegian-Americans celebrated by forming the Nordmanns-Forbundet, to strengthen Norwegian freedom.

Finland had been part of Sweden from the twelfth through the eighteenth century, and the language of the state bureaucracy was Swedish. Swedes controlled politics and looked down upon the Finns as narrow-minded provincials. But Sweden ceded Finland to Russia during the Napoleonic Wars, and by the end of the nineteenth century the tsar was abolishing the Finnish army, drafting Finns into the Russian army, and trying to make Russian the official language of Finland. As a result of years of domination, nationalism pervaded Finland in the nineteenth century. Thus both the Norwegian and the Finnish immigrants arrived in the United States imbued with a sense of ethnic nationalism.

The Danes and to a lesser extent the Swedes did not resist acculturation and assimilation. In 1890, for example, when only 8 percent of the Danish population and 22 percent of the Swedish population could be considered the dominant group in certain upper midwest counties, nearly 60 percent of the Norwegians and 70 percent of the Finns were dominant in certain areas. The Norwegians and Finns showed a far stronger inclination to settle among their compatriots. While the Danes and Swedes enthusiastically supported the public school movement in Minnesota, Michigan, Iowa, and Wisconsin, the Norwegians and Finns

* Quoted in Theodore C. Blegen, *Land of their Choice* (Minneapolis, 1955), p. 203.

were more inclined to start parochial schools in conjunction with their Lutheran churches. And while half the male Danish immigrants and perhaps 30 percent of the Swedes married outside their nationality, only 20 percent of the Norwegians and less than 10 percent of the Finns did. In many counties in Minnesota, Wisconsin, Iowa, and the Dakotas, Norwegians held to the old ways, and well into the 1920s Norwegian was the spoken language in many public and parochial schools, churches, homes, and businesses, as Finnish was in many mining and textile towns.

Of all the Scandinavians, the Finns were the most exclusive and group oriented. The American environment interacted with Finnish clannishness to create a cultural tenacity unknown among other Scandinavians. Despite their Protestant traditions, many Americans—including some Scandinavian-Americans—were critical of the Finnish immigrants. Part of the problem was economic. Because Finnish industrialization and the integration of Finland into the Atlantic economy did not begin until late in the century, most Finns were unskilled workers and peasant farmers just when more and more German, Norwegian, Danish, Swedish, English, Scots, and Welsh immigrants were arriving with industrial skills. Many Americans considered the Finns a backward people and grouped them with the immigrants from southern and eastern Europe. And in the Midwest, other Scandinavians looked down on the Finns. The Swedes, Norwegians, and Danes were all descendants of ancient Nordic tribes and took pride in the legendary history of the Vikings. They were also able to understand one another's language. The Finns were descendants of ancient Magyar tribes which had emigrated out of central Asia, some to the Pannonian Plains of Hungary and others to Finland, and the Finnish language bore no resemblance to Swedish, Norwegian, or Danish. To other Scandinavians in America, the Finns were a rather primitive, culturally retarded people.

But even if older Americans and Scandinavian immigrants had welcomed the Finns, Finnish ethnicity would still have led to group isolation and solidarity. Language and cultural barriers, as well as an intense sense of nationalism, helped drive them together in the United States, but Finnish ethnicity also revolved around a strong impulse toward group integrity. Suspicious of others, Finns relied on Finns for help and security. Society was defined in terms of moral absolutes, usually on a class basis. For the Finns the economic world was divided between the *meikalainen* ("good working people") and the *herrat* ("bad aristocrats"), and the *herrat* would risk annihilation rather than surrender prerogatives to the *meikalainen*. Concluding that real mobility was impossible to achieve anywhere, some Finns withdrew to a rural environment, hoping there to work out their lives in peace. Others joined movements of American workers protesting capitalism. By 1912 they were the largest foreign-language group in the Socialist party (about 12 percent of its membership), and for a time in the 1920s the Finns made up nearly 40 percent of the American Communist party.

By 1900 there were four Scandinavian "islands" in the United States, and because immigration from Sweden, Norway, Denmark, and Finland was just reaching its peak, the forces of assimilation were still weak. Like the British and German Protestants, the Scandinavians—except for the Finns—were generally well received in America. They were literate, white, Protestant, and socially conservative, and older Americans did not fear Scandinavian culture. Nativistic criticisms focused much less on Swedes, Norwegians, and Danes than on the Irish and German immigrants. But the prevailing hospitality did little to destroy Scandinavian self-reliance and clannishness, and large-scale assimilation would not occur until well into the twentieth century.

SUGGESTED READINGS

Ahlstrom, Sydney. *A Religious History of America*. New Haven, Conn.: 1972.

Allswang, John M. *A House for All Peoples: Ethnic Politics in Chicago, 1890–1936*. Lexington, Kentucky: 1971.

Anderson, Arlow W. *The Norwegian Americans*. New York: 1975.

Anderson, Charles. *White Protestant Americans: From National Origins to Religious Groups*. Englewood Cliffs, N.J.: 1970.

Barton, H. Arnold, ed. *Letters from the Promised Land: Swedes in America, 1840–1914*. Minneapolis, Minn.: 1973.

Benson, Adolph B., and Hedin, Naboth. *Americans from Sweden*. Philadelphia: 1950.

Blegen, Theodore. *Land of Their Choice*. Minneapolis, Minn.: 1955.

———. *Norwegian Migration to America, 1825–1860*. Northfield, Minn.: 1931.

Capps, Finis Herbert. *From Isolationism to Involvement: The Swedish Immigrant Press in America, 1914–1945*. Chicago: 1966.

Choresman, Noel J. *Ethnic Influence on Urban Groups: The Danish Americans*. New York: 1973.

Dowie, J. Iverne, and Espelie, Ernest M. *The Swedish Immigrant Community in Transition*. Rock Island, Ill.: 1963.

Esslinger, Dean R. *Immigrants and the City: Ethnicity and Mobility in a Nineteenth-Century Midwestern Community*. New York: 1975.

Friis, Erik J., ed. *The Scandinavian Presence in North America*. New York: 1976.

Graebner, Alan. *Uncertain Saints: The Laity in the Lutheran Church–Missouri Synod, 1900–1970*. Westport, Conn.: 1975.

Hoglund, Arthur. *Finnish Immigrants in America, 1880–1920*. Madison, Wisc.: 1960.

Hvidt, Kristian. *Flight to America: The Social Background of 300,000 Danish Immigrants*. Copenhagen, Denmark: 1975.

Jalkanen, Ralph J. *The Finns in North America*. Lansing, Mich.: 1969.

Karni, Michael G., Kaups, Matti E., and Ollila, Douglas J., Jr. *The Finnish Experience in the Western Great Lakes Region*. Turku, Finland: 1975.

Knaplund, Paul. *Moorings Old and New*. Madison, Wisconsin: 1963.

Knudsen, Johanne. *The Danish-American Immigrant*. Des Moines, Iowa: 1950.

Kolehmainen, John I., and Hill, George. *Haven in the Woods: The Story of the Finns in Wisconsin*. Madison, Wisconsin: 1965.

Larson, Laurence M. *The Log Book of a Young Immigrant*. Northfield, Minn.: 1939.

Lindmark, Sture. *Swedish America, 1914–1932*. Uppsala, Sweden: 1971.

Lovoll, Odd Sverre. *A Folk Epic: The Bygdelag in America*. Boston: 1975.

Marty, Martin E. *Righteous Empire: The Protestant Experience in America*. New York: 1970.

Nelson, E. Clifford. *Lutheranism in North America*. Minneapolis, Minn.: 1972.

Nelson, Helge. *The Swedes and Swedish Settlements in North America*. Lund, Sweden: 1943.

Nyholm, Paul C. *The Americanization of the Danish Lutheran Churches in America*. Copenhagen, Denmark: 1963.

Riis, Jacob A. *The Making of an American*. New York: 1947.

Rolvaag, Ole E. *Giants in the Earth*. New York: 1927.

Runblom, Harald, and Norman, Hans, eds. *From Sweden to America: A History of the Migration*. Minneapolis, Minn.: 1976.

Skardal, Dorothy. *The Divided Heart: Scandinavian Immigrant Experience Through Literary Sources*. Lincoln, Neb.: 1974.

Stephen, George M. *The Religious Aspects of Swedish Immigration*. Minneapolis, Minn.: 1932.

Strandvold, Georg. *Danes Who Helped Build America*. New York: 1960.

Wefald, Jon. *A Voice of Protest: Norwegians in American Politics, 1890–1917*. Northfield, Minn.: 1971.

Chapter Eight

The French in America

In the seventeenth century France and England were competing ferociously for supremacy in North America. In 1534 Jacques Cartier had set out in search of Indian treasure and a water route to the Pacific Ocean, and after exploring the gulf of the St. Lawrence River he had established the French claim to Canada. For the next seventy years French fishermen worked the Grand Banks off Newfoundland catching codfish and seals, and French companies established temporary trading posts in what were to become the Maritime Provinces of Canada to purchase furs from the Indians. Then, at the beginning of the seventeenth century, both England and France established permanent colonies in the New World. Between 1603 and 1608 Samuel de Champlain placed several fur trading colonies in Acadia (Nova Scotia and New Brunswick) and along the St. Lawrence River in Quebec, and between 1607 and 1629 England was setting up permanent colonies in New England and near Chesapeake Bay. Both nations expanded their empires throughout the seventeenth century—the English moving down the Atlantic coast and the French toward the Great Lakes. After the voyages of Robert LaSalle down the Mississippi River in the 1680s, New France was a great colonial arc running from Newfoundland in the northeast, west along the St. Lawrence River to Lake Superior, and down the Mississippi River to the Gulf of Mexico.

But as the English colonies and New France expanded, the Ohio River Valley became a point of geopolitical contention. From the opening salvos of King William's War in 1689 to Napoleon's defeat at Waterloo in 1815, France and England struggled for world supremacy, and in North America hostilities revolved around the land and furs of the Ohio River watershed. They fought four colonial wars over it—King William's War, 1689–1697; Queen Anne's War, 1702–1713; King George's War, 1740–1748; and the French and Indian War, 1754–1763. England finally prevailed in 1763 when war-weary France ceded Canada in the Treaty of Paris. Caught in a financial squeeze and weary of administering his New World territories, Napoleon completed the work of the Treaty of Paris by selling Louisiana to the United States for $15 million in 1803. After nearly two centuries the Franco-American empire was gone.

That was not, however, the end of French culture in America. Over the centuries four separate waves of French immigrants came to the New World. Several thousand French Huguenots, fleeing religious persecution in France, relocated in America in the 1690s; more than seven thousand French Acadians were driven from Canada after 1755 and nearly two thousand of them settled in Louisiana; between 1820 and 1924 more than five hundred thousand people emigrated from France, although most of them were German-speaking immigrants from eastern France, Alsace, and Lorraine; and finally, perhaps four hundred thousand French-Canadians crossed the border to America before 1924. They became the nucleus of the Franco-American community.

The Huguenots

The Huguenots were Calvinist reformers, a tiny Protestant colony in Roman Catholic France. Like the Puritans in England, Presbyterians in Scotland, Walloons in Belgium, and Reformed congregations in Holland and Germany, they were mostly successful merchants and skilled artisans who found in Calvinism freedom from the restrictions of medieval life. The new spirit of the Reformation liberated them from the static, organic conservatism of medieval Catholicism; Huguenots enjoyed success without misgivings, prosperity without guilt. They were the most productive segment of the French population, an elite group responsible for much of the growth in the national economy. Out of personal sympathy for them as well as a sense of their importance to France, King Henry IV had granted them religious toleration in 1598 with the Edict of Nantes. They were, in effect, a "state within the state," with Huguenot military groups protecting Huguenot cities in southern and western France. They were a unique people, republicans in the age of absolutism, dissenters in a bastion of religious despotism.

Life became difficult for them in the seventeenth century. When Cardinal Richelieu took over the French bureaucracy in 1624, he was obsessed with centralizing the power of the monarchy. Huguenot independence bothered him, and although he still respected their religious freedom, he worked against their special status in France. Harassment and restrictive legislation continued throughout the century, and on October 18, 1685, King Louis XIV revoked the Edict of Nantes, setting off anti-Huguenot persecutions in much of the country. Protestant services were prohibited, Protestant books and Bibles burned, and Protestant chapels closed. Restrictions were placed on Huguenots becoming doctors, lawyers, teachers, or civil servants. Their property was confiscated, their ministers harassed, and their civil rights impaired. Remembering the terrors they had endured before the edict—especially the Massacre of St. Bartholomew in 1572—the Huguenots were enraged, and more than four hundred thousand left France in the 1690s. Most of them settled in Holland and England, but several thousand came to America.

They settled widely in colonial America, but especially in Massachusetts, New York, Pennsylvania, and South Carolina. Indeed, South Carolina was a center of Huguenot culture. Huguenot communities sprouted in Boston and New Oxford, Massachusetts; near Providence, Rhode Island; New York City, New Rochelle, and New Paltz in New York; Philadelphia, Pennsylvania; and Charleston, St. Thomas, St. Denis, and St. John, South Carolina. Although no more than fifteen thousand Huguenots ever lived in America during the seventeenth century, some of the most famous families in United States history—the Bayards, Marions, Du Ponts, Delanceys, Delanos, and Reveres—were of Huguenot descent.

There were reasons for such success. The Huguenots were Calvinists and adapted easily to the individualistic, success-oriented society developing in the British colonies. Like the New England Puritans, they prospered in commerce and craftsmanship. They also possessed a powerful sense of their own rights. The Edict of Nantes had granted them religious freedom and property rights; and when Louis XIV revoked those privileges, the Huguenots lost something they had enjoyed for nearly a century. With their strong convictions about rights, toleration, and property, the Huguenots found an ideological home in British North America. Americans welcomed the Huguenots, and some colonies actively recruited them.

Of all the non-English ethnic groups in early America, the Huguenots assimilated the most quickly and completely. As white Protestants who were successful and widely dispersed, they soon lost a separate identity.

Highly educated, ambitious, and skilled entrepreneurs, they appreciated the social climate of America, the economic opportunity, and the religious freedom. And Anglo-Americans appreciated them not only for their economic skills but as a Protestant people fleeing Roman Catholicism. Open acceptance encouraged assimilation. Learning English quickly, their children married Puritans in New England, Anglicans in New York and South Carolina, and Scots-Irish Presbyterians in the South and West. They did not, of course, disappear in a generation; their sense of self-esteem and personal worth was too well developed for that, and as late as the American Revolution recognizable Huguenot settlements still existed. But by the early nineteenth century French Huguenots hardly functioned as a self-conscious ethnic group.

The Acadians

The Acadians were the second wave of French-speaking immigrants. With roots in the beginning of New France, they are one of the oldest ethnic groups in North America. In 1603 King Henry IV of France had issued a large proprietary land grant to Pierre du Guast, who promptly established a fur trading post, commanded by Samuel de Chaplain, on the Bay of Fundy. The new colony of Acadia expanded around the main settlement of Port Royal. Acadians supported themselves by fishing, fur trading, and farming; but the cold, humid, and windy winters and mosquito-infested summers made life difficult and austere. Because immigration from Europe was small and population growth slow, at least when compared to the growth of the English colonies, strong village kinship systems developed throughout Acadia. The original families of the early seventeenth century became the Acadian clans of the eighteenth century. Roman Catholic in religion, Gallic in culture, and bound together in strong extended families, they were a distinct community in North America, imbued by a powerful emotional insularity.

Anglo-French rivalry eventually disrupted Acadian society. After Queen Anne's War ended in 1713, England acquired Acadia from France, and for the next forty years the Acadians preserved their culture in an Anglo-Protestant polity. It was an untenable position, living under English protection in an English colony but culturally loyal to France. England perceived the Acadians as potential traitors ready to rise and strike back in the name of French patriotism. When the Acadians refused to take a blanket loyalty oath to England at the outset of the French and Indian War, English politicians expelled them.

The exile began in 1755, when there were probably ten thousand

An artist's conception of the embarkation of the Acadians, who were herded onto ships with only the possessions they could carry. (Brown Brothers)

Acadians in Nova Scotia and another five thousand on Prince Edward and Cape Breton islands. To this day Cajuns (Acadians who settled in Louisiana) call the exile *Le Grand Dérangement*, the "Big Upheaval." Cramped into the dark holds of transport vessels, they were shipped out of Nova Scotia on a moment's notice with only the possessions they could carry. Men left for work one day only to return at dusk and find their families gone. Henry Wadsworth Longfellow's famous poem "Evangeline," itself now part of the Acadian heritage, was based on the life of Emmeline Labiche, an Acadian woman betrothed to Louis Arcenaux. They were separated during *Le Grand Dérangement*, but years later they found each other in St. Martinville, Louisiana. According to the story, he was already married and she lived out her life heartbroken.

For all the Acadians the voyages were terrifying. Passengers suffered from smallpox, scurvy, and starvation, as well as the loss of their families. More than 700 Acadians shipped to Philadelphia had to wait six weeks on board ship while the colonial assembly decided whether to let them land, and more than 230 died of smallpox during the delay. On December 10, 1755, two rickety ships, the *Violet* and the *Duke William*, sank off the Atlantic coast with 650 Acadian refugees. The *Cornwallis* left Nova Scotia with 450 Acadians, but only 210 survived the voyage to Charleston. The Acadians were dispersed throughout the Old and New Worlds, wherever anyone would take them in, with the largest colonies in Boston, New York, Philadelphia, and Charleston in America; Liverpool, Southampton, Falmouth, and Bristol in England; and Normandy, Brittany, Aunis, and Guienne in France.

Thirty years after the expulsion of the Acadians and more than twenty years after Spain had acquired Louisiana from France, the Spanish government recruited some sixteen hundred Acadians living in France to return to America, colonize the territory, and develop it economically. Seven expeditions deposited them in New Orleans in 1785, and from there they moved west to the bayous, rivers, swamps, and lakes of southern Louisiana. Loyal to their heritage, the Acadians became fishermen, fur trappers, and cattle, cane, and cotton farmers. (Earlier French colonists, in contrast, had tended to settle in New Orleans and along the Mississippi River as commercial farmers, merchants, craftsmen, and shop-owners.) In 1803, when President Thomas Jefferson completed the Louisiana Purchase, this was French Louisiana: the urban commercial elite in New Orleans and up the Mississippi River, and the rural Cajuns, as the Acadians came to be called, of the southwestern parishes. To this day, as the Cajuns trap the nutria and muskrat, gather shrimp, raise cattle, and grow rice, cotton, and cane, links to early Louisiana and Acadia remain strong.

Cajun society evolved on its own. The influx of English merchants, bankers, planters, and small farmers in the nineteenth century gradually overwhelmed the French-speaking people of northern and eastern Louisiana and New Orleans. And as they succumbed to English culture, retaining Catholicism but losing the French language and identity, the Cajuns became a linguistic and cultural island in southwestern Louisiana. From their early origins in France they had nurtured an independent spirit, and the powerful family clans of Acadia that were reinstituted in Louisiana helped reinforce their autonomy. Wronged historically and conscious of it, poor but independent, knitted into strong family networks, and isolated culturally and physically from the rest of the country, the Cajuns were deeply suspicious of outsiders, a separate people in nineteenth-century America.

By the 1970s there would be hundreds of thousands of Cajuns in Louisiana. When intermarriage occurred, the non-Cajun spouse would usually blend into Cajun society. Sugar cane, rice, shrimp, and fur festivals celebrating the benevolence of nature would still occur, and Cajun music and dancing would still thrive. The Council for the Development of French in Louisiana would promote the use of French in the state; all public schools would offer French at all grade levels; bilingual teachers would work in all Cajun schools; *Télévision-Louisiane* would broadcast in French to the Cajun community; Quebec would distribute French newspapers, magazines, and radio and television programs throughout southern Louisiana; and France would maintain a French Educational Mission there to teach French in the schools. Edwin Edwards would become the first Cajun governor in Louisiana history.

Suspicious and proud, still Gallic and intensely Roman Catholic, Cajun-America would continue to defy the melting pot, preferring instead the isolation of rural Louisiana.

The Great Migration from France

Between 1820 and 1924 more than 550,000 people immigrated from France; but until the Franco-Prussian War of 1870, when France ceded Alsace and Lorraine to Germany, most were German-speaking people leaving northeastern France for economic reasons. Perhaps only 200,000 French-speaking immigrants settled in America. Given the total population of France, that was a small number. Because of the French Revolution, France was more open socially and politically than the rest of Europe, and there was a maturity to French culture; people were more satisfied with their environment. The population of rural France remained relatively stable and the pressures for land that were so strong elsewhere did not cause serious trouble—in part because peasants divided and redivided their land through inheritance and did not practice primogeniture. Not even the Industrial Revolution could displace cottage industry and settled rural family life in nineteenth-century France.

In the years of the French Revolution and the Napolenic Wars, a few scattered French colonies developed in the United States. Royalists fleeing the French Revolution in 1794 founded Asylum, Pennsylvania, and other refugees settled in New York, Boston, and Philadelphia. Hoping to build wine and olive industries in the South, French immigrants organized the French Agricultural and Manufacturing Society in 1816 and built the town of Demopolis, Alabama. After the Revolution of 1848, perhaps twenty thousand French refugees came to America, and both royalists and radicals made their living teaching French, editing newspapers, and giving art, music, and dance lessons. Most of the nineteenth-century French immigrants, however, were neither royalists nor refugees but skilled workers and professionals. Settling into the major cities, they established ethnic cultural institutions similar to those of other immigrants. Fraternal and social organizations—like French benevolent societies, the Cercle Français, and the Societie Française de L'Amatie—appeared, as did French Catholic churches, military companies, political clubs, and cultural groups. French newspapers were common, such as New York *Franco Americaine* or *Courrier des Etats Unis*, the Philadelphia *Le Courrier de l'Amerique*, and the Charleston *Moniteur Français*.

In one sense French immigration was unique, for despite their Roman Catholicism the French encountered little hostility in America. It was partly demographic. French immigration averaged less than three thousand people each year; compared to the migrations from Ireland and Germany, it was inconsequential. At the same time, most of the French immigrants were craftsmen and professionals; Americans perceived them as economic assets. And in addition many Americans admired French culture. France had helped the colonies during the Revolution, and although many upper-class Federalists in the United States feared the French Revolution and resented Thomas Jefferson's love for France, most Americans shared his feelings. There was an affinity of political philosophy.

Many Americans of the 1800s seemed obsessed with things French. Inns and taverns became hotels, lunchrooms and saloons soon were cafés and restaurants, and cooks became chefs. French art salons, theaters, operas, conservatories, and dance schools were popular, and French became the second language of the American upper class. French finishing schools and tours of France were requirements for "sophisticated young ladies," as were French fashions and toiletries. French wines, liqueurs, pastries, breads, entrées, and soups became standard fare for wealthy Americans. Indeed, the American upper class, new and parochial, aped French culture and welcomed its proponents.

The French-Canadians

When England took Canada in 1763, there were about seventy thousand French citizens living there, most of them in Quebec. The two Canadas coexisted independently until 1840, with English Upper Canada and French Lower Canada functioning as a dual federation. The French-Canadians were a close-knit community, bound together by strong kinship ties, language, religion, and pride in the history of France. Four colonial wars with England had left them with an Anglophobia rivaling that of the Irish. Great Britain united Upper and Lower Canada in 1840, and the French lost control over their internal affairs, becoming a religious and political minority. English rule only intensified French ethnicity. When Britain made English the national language, the French converted their own language into a cultural symbol; and when the English made known their preference for Protestantism, French-Canadian Catholicism became a badge of faith and community. Quebec separatism today is only the latest episode in a long struggle for independence. This was French Canada: a conquered people devoted to the French language, Roman Catholicism, and ethnic nationalism.

But they too felt the same push-and-pull forces that influenced Europeans in the nineteenth century. Until industrialization began in the 1890s, economic life in Quebec was desperate. The land had become unable to sustain a growing population. Outmoded farming techniques were depleting the soil; and the old French inheritance system, which required subdivision of land among all children—and which was still working well in France—was reducing farms to small parcels unable to support a family. Speculators held the best land, and it was too expensive for small farmers. Other land was held by the British government and was unavailable for settlement. In upper Quebec, where some good land was still available there were few roads for shipment of goods to urban markets. Land in western Canada was open to settlement, but French-Canadians were reluctant to pioneer where Anglo-Protestants were too many and Catholic churches too few. Instead they looked southward.

The demand for labor in lumber yards, canals, railroads, mines, quarries, harbors, mills, and factories of the United States was enormous, and manufacturers sent recruiters to Quebec, Toronto, Montreal, and Ottawa looking for new workers. Before the Civil War most French-Canadian immigrants were itinerant workers intending to earn good wages, save money, and return home to rebuild the family farm and pay off debts. They formed few ethnic organizations, churches, or societies. But only 10 percent ever returned permanently to Canada; economic security south of the border made the exodus permanent. Whole villages were transplanted. Most French-Canadians settled in the mill towns of New England and replaced or displaced some of the Irish as unskilled workers. Others found work in the mines and steel mills of New York, Pennsylvania, and Ohio; the copper and lead mines of Upper Michigan; the automobile factories of Detroit; the mines and farms of Minnesota; and railroad labor gangs throughout the upper Midwest. By 1900 there were more than 500,000 French-Canadians in New England alone. That number would eventually grow to 1.25 million by 1945, out of a total New England population of 8 million. In upper New England they constituted more than 40 percent of the population. Another 400,000 French-Canadians would live in Michigan, 350,000 in New York, 300,000 in Illinois, and 125,000 in Minnesota—making them one of the more visible ethnic groups in the Northeast.

Like the Cajuns, the French-Canadians resisted assimilation. Nearly 180 years of conflict with English Protestants had sharply defined Gallic culture and Roman Catholicism, and supplied them with a strong sense of ethnic nationalism. What had happened in Quebec was the historical fusion of religion, language, and nationality. French was not simply the medium of culture to the French-Canadians; it was a mystical badge of ethnicity and the "defender of the faith." French-Canadians believed that the loss of their language implied loss of Catholicism. The center of cultural life had thus been the French-speaking parish and parochial schools; they were bastions of Gallicism and Catholicism where religion, society, and politics mixed. The French-Canadians made few distinctions between political citizenship in the state and religious citizenship in the church. The immigrants carried these feelings with them to the United States, and the proximity of Quebec, with its family ties and traditions, permitted them to return home frequently and maintain their culture.

Family life and religion were similarly inseparable in Quebec. French-Canadian families were always large, not only to encourage economic development but to fulfill procreation roles expected by the church. Elder males were ruling patriarchs, and extended families included those of married sons. Women and children played subservient roles. But even so the patriarch was subject to the rule of the parish priest. Since the parish was the center of social, religious, and political life and the priest had full authority there, French-Canadian fathers always consulted him about births, marriages, deaths, schools, and taxes. Higher education or migration from the local community was discouraged because either could create loyalties independent of parish life. Only economic desperation made migration to the United States acceptable, and even then the immigrants were expected to maintain a cultural separation.

The social climate of the United States further defined French-Canadian values. Americans welcomed craftsmen and professionals from France but worried about the French-Canadians. Poor and unskilled, ignorant of English, and concentrated into "Little Canadas," the French-Canadians were a conspicuous and growing minority in the nineteenth century. Their loyalty to Roman Catholicism and suspicion of public schools generated even more uneasiness. The nineteenth-century immigrants from France were often worldly and even rather secular about religion. But this was not true of the French-Canadians, and they encountered the wrath of Know-Nothing activists in the 1850s and the Yankee sensitivities of other antiforeign groups in the 1890s. As they competed with the Irish for jobs in the mills, businessmen frequently used them as strikebreakers. Irish workers resented them and fights were common.

There was religious competition as well. Like other immigrants, the French-Canadians wanted to worship in their own language, and the Irish Catholic hierarchy opposed them. French-Canadians resented Irish domination of the church, while the Irish clergy viewed French-Canadian priests as threats to their own power. Caught between the hostility of Anglo-Protestants and Irish Catholics, the French-Canadians established a separate ghetto culture in New England. Carrying their religious case to the Vatican, they gained their first ethnic parish in 1850, and by 1890 there were 86 French-Canadian parishes and 53 French-Canadian parochial schools, such as Notre-Dame des Canadiens, Saint Jean Baptiste, and Sacre-Coeur de Marie, and Précieux Sang. By 1945 there would be 320 Franco-American parishes, more than 250 parochial schools, and 30 hospitals and orphanages. Nearly a thousand French-speaking priests would minister to the pastoral needs of the French-Canadian population.

French-Candians would eventually establish more than 200 newspapers, such as *Le Messager* of Lewiston, Maine, and *L'Indépendent* of Fall River, Massachusetts, and such mutual aid societies and fraternal organizations as l'Union Saint-Jean-Baptiste d'Amerique, l'Association Canada-Americaine, l'Order des Chevaliers de Jacques Cartier, and les Francs-Tireurs. Separate and distinct, proud and hopeful, the French-Canadians were another cultural island in America, their children attending French-Canadian parishes and parochial schools and marrying one another, their loyalties to the language as powerful as ever, and their love for Quebec undiminished.

All this was Franco-America in the nineteenth century. The Huguenots had largely disappeared by the mid-1800s, victims of their Protestantism, urbanity, and economic prosperity. And the new immigrants arriving directly from France were readily accepted by an American society starved for French culture. The two main centers of French culture were in New England and Louisiana, where French-Canadians and the Cajun descendants of French-Canadians lived separate lives in homogeneous communities. Both were close-knit people bound together by an ethnic culture which fused language, religion, family, and politics.

SUGGESTED READINGS

Avery, Elizabeth H. *The Influence of French Immigration on the Political History of the United States.* New York: 1972.

Blumenthal, Henry. *American and French Culture, 1800–1900.* Baton Rouge, La.: 1975.

Byrne, William D. *History of the Catholic Church in the New England States.* Boston: 1899.

Chase, John. *Frenchmen, Desire, Good Children.* New Orleans: 1949.

Chopin, Kate. *Bayou Folk.* New York: 1894.

———. *A Night in Acadie.* New York: 1897.

Conrad, Glenn R., ed. *The Cajuns: Essays on Their History and Culture.* Lafayette, La.: 1978.

Dumarche, Jacques. *The Delusson Family.* New York: 1939.

———. *The Shadows of the Trees: The Story of the French Canadians in New*

England. Boston: 1943.

Dumont, Fernand. "The Systematic Study of the French-Canadian Total Society." In Marcel Rioux and Yves Martin, eds. *French-Canadian Society*. Vol. I. Toronto, Canada: 1965.

Eccles, W. J. *France in America*. New York: 1972.

Evans, Oliver. "Melting Pot in the Bayous." *American Heritage*, 15 (December 1963), 30–42.

Gilman, Malcolm B. *The Huguenot Migration in Europe and America: Its Cause and Effect*. Red Bank, N.J.: 1962.

Grayson, L. M., and Bliss, Michael, eds. *The Wretched of Canada*. Toronto, Canada: 1971.

Griffiths, Naomi. *The Acadians: Creation of a People*. New York: 1973.

Hirsch, Arthur H. *The Huguenots of Colonial South Carolina*. New York: 1928.

Hughes, Everett. *French Canada in Transition*. Chicago: 1943.

Jaenen, Cornelius J. *Friend and Foe: Aspects of French-American Cultural Conflict in the Sixteenth and Seventeenth Centuries*. New York: 1976.

John, Elizabeth A. H. *Storms Brewed in Other Men's Worlds: The Confrontation of the Indians, Spanish, and French in the Southwest, 1540–1795*. College Station, Texas: 1975.

Kane, Harnett. *The Bayous of Louisiana*. New York: 1943.

Lemaire, Herve-B. "Franco-American Efforts on Behalf of the French Language in New England." In Joshua A. Fishman et al., *Language Loyalty in the United States*. The Hague, Netherlands: 1966.

Lieberson, Stanley. *Language and Ethnic Relations in Canada*. New York: 1970.

McDermitt, John. *Frenchmen and French Ways in the Mississippi Valley*. Urbana, Ill.: 1969.

McInnis, Edgar. *Canada*. New York: 1947.

Miner, Horace. *St. Denis: A French-Canadian Parish*. Chicago: 1967

Podea, Iris. "Quebec to 'Little Canada': The Coming of the French Canadians to New England in the Nineteenth Century." *New England Quarterly*, 23 (Fall 1950), 365–384.

Porter, John. *The Vertical Mosaic: An Analysis of Social Class and Power in Canada*. Toronto, Canada: 1965.

Post, Lauren C. *Cajun Sketches*. Baton Rouge, La.: 1962.

Ramsey, Carolyn. *Cajuns on the Bayou*. New York: 1957.

Read, William A. *Louisiana French*. Baton Rouge, La.: 1963.

Sorrell, Richard S. "Franco-Americans in New England." *The Journal of Ethnic Studies*, 5 (Spring 1977), 90–94.

Theriault, George F. "The Franco-Americans of New England." In Mason Wade, ed. *Canadian Dualism*. Toronto, Canada: 1960.

Violette, Maurice. *The Franco Americans*. New York: 1976.

Wade, Mason. "The French Parish and *Survivance* in Nineteenth Century New England." *Catholic Historical Review*, 36 (July 1950), 163–178.

Winzerling, Oscar. *Acadian Odyssey*. Baton Rouge, La.: 1955.

Chapter Nine

Manifest Destiny and Native Americans

Between 1776 and 1830 the United States reassessed its Indian policy, replacing militance with more cautious, deliberate programs recognizing that native Americans had some rights to the land. Concerned during the Revolution about fighting Indians in the West and the English in the East, the government wanted Indians to resist British enticements and remain neutral. There were a number of isolated but serious confrontations, especially when British military officials encouraged the Indians to fight. Except for the Oneidas, Iroquois tribes were loyal to England, and on several occasions between 1777 and 1779 American troops invaded Iroquois territory; the invasion of General John Sullivan into upstate New York was perhaps the most successful of such missions. But generally the relationship between whites and Indians was tranquil; in a few instances the government even nullified the land claims of speculators. In 1777 and 1779 government officials repudiated attempts by speculators and white pioneers to settle on Indian lands in the Ohio Valley. The war had slowed the westward movement, and with fewer people crossing the mountains there were fewer confrontations; the government's policies seemed to be working.

Immediately after the Revolution, the government continued to be cautious in its policies toward the Indian tribes. American leaders hoped to avoid conflict with Indians in the West because it might divide westerners and easterners and threaten the young republic with political disintegration, especially if Britain and Spain tried to detach the western territories. American leaders therefore tried to some extent to conciliate the Indians. It was, of course, only a temporary lull in the tension, for as soon as the mass migration of whites across the Appalachians began again in earnest, the conflict over land would appear once more.

The hunger for land among white farmers was as insatiable as ever, and the government would have to respond by making way for those pioneers. The "backwardness" of native America was still used to justify taking land. A Baptist missionary journal argued in 1849 that the Indians were

> deficient in intellectual and moral culture. . . . They do not furnish their share to the advancement of society, and the prosperity and wealth of the world . . . their priests are ignorant and overbearing; their rulers are narrow and prejudiced; they have no properly instructed physicians, no schools . . . no hospitals . . . nor mutual aid associations. . . . There is nothing in their religious rites . . . but . . . that which is degrading and polluting.*

Such attitudes led inevitably to confrontation on the frontier. But at the same time, Europeans believed in Christian humanitarianism and the natural rights philosophy; missionaries as well as Jeffersonian idealists had to rationalize the taking of Indian land with their faith in natural rights. To these people assimilation seemed an ideal solution. Transforming native Americans into settled farmers who could support a family on only a few dozen acres of land would liberate millions of acres for white settlement, while upholding the natural rights philosophy. Another missionary society predicted in 1823:

> You may look forward to the period when the savage shall be converted into the citizen; when the hunter shall be transformed into the mechanic; when the farm, the work shop, the School-House, and the Church shall adorn every Indian village; when the fruits of Industry, good order, and sound morals, shall bless every Indian dwelling . . . red man and the white man shall everywhere be found, mingling in the same benevolent and friendly feelings, fellow citizens of the same civil and religious community, and fellow-heirs to a glorious inheritance in the kingdom of Immanuel.†

But this too would prove destructive to the Indians. Assimilationists wanted them to abandon their religious beliefs, the hunter-warrior ideal, tribal government, and communal ownership of the land—to exchange their culture for that of white society. Well into the twentieth century whites would pursue that dream.

---

* *Baptist Missionary Magazine*, April 1849, pp. 101–105.
† Quoted in Robert Berkhofer, *Salvation and the Savage* (Lexington, Kentucky, 1965), pp. 8–9.

After the Revolution the Indian tribes along the frontier were powerful, and the British agents still in the Ohio Valley could create trouble. Many Americans, wanting to placate the Indians, argued that Indian land claims were sovereign and could be nullified only with their consent. In 1784 Congress negotiated the Treaty of Fort Stanwix, which reestablished peace with the Iroquois, and in 1785 the federal government concluded a treaty with the Cherokees guaranteeing their land claims and inviting them to send a representative to Congress. Two years later Congress promised in the Northwest Ordinance to respect Indian rights in the Ohio Valley.

But these measures could not cope with the postwar wave of white settlers pouring across the Appalachians. By 1790 there were more than 35,000 settlers in Kentucky and nearly 75,000 in the Ohio Territory, and it was then that sporadic attacks on white settlements began. Whites demanded immediate assistance from the federal government, and President Washington dispatched troops to the Ohio Valley. There, on November 4, 1791, the Shawnees surprised the expedition, and in a pitched battle more than six hundred soldiers died, the worst single defeat United States forces were ever to suffer at the hands of native Americans. People roared for retribution. After three more years of periodic violence a military expedition led by General "Mad" Anthony Wayne defeated a large Shawnee force at the Battle of Fallen Timbers; the subsequent Treaty of Greenville of 1795 forced most of the Shawnees out of Ohio and into Indiana.

The Treaty of Greenville initiated a recurrent cycle in which the Indians, after resistance and military defeat, would surrender their land for guaranteed ownership of territory farther west. By 1810 there were 230,000 whites in Ohio, 406,000 in Kentucky, 260,000 in Tennessee, 25,000 in Indiana, 12,000 in Illinois, and 20,000 in Missouri. As white farmers cleared the forests, native Americans were hard-pressed to maintain their traditional lifestyles, and some rebelled. Tecumseh, a Shawnee war chief, and his brother, a religious leader called the Prophet, tried to unite the Great Lakes, Ohio Valley, and Gulf Coast tribes into a single military coalition. But the Indians could not overcome centuries of tribal conflict; some would temporarily bolt the alliance to support the government or to fight each other, and some even sold their land. Between 1811 and 1813 troops under William Henry Harrison, governor of the Indiana Territory, relentlessly pursued Tecumseh and the Prophet, defeating their forces at the Battle of Tippecanoe in 1811 and killing Tecumseh in 1813 at the Battle of the Thames. The end of the War of 1812 forced British officials out of the United States and weakened the Indians by depriving them of English support. After that, the northern tribes gradually yielded all their land east of the Mississippi River.

White idealists continued their crusade to remake native American culture. Throughout the early nineteenth century War Department agents introduced European culture into Indian villages, as did Protestant missionary groups like the Society of United Brethren for Propagating the Gospel Among the Heathen and the American Board of Foreign Missions. People like Isaac McCoy, John Heckewelder, and Stephen Riggs wanted the Indians to accept the superiority of individualism over tribal communism, Christianity over native religions, commercial farming over hunting and subsistence agriculture, and English over their own tongues. Missionary boarding schools like the Foreign Missionary School in Connecticut and the Choctaw Academy taught English, Christianity, Protestant views of morality, and European views of society and economics. Missionaries preached the same message to friendly tribes on the frontier, and envisioned native American villages where Indians worked their own farms and worshiped each Sunday at a community church. They hoped to reform native American society, not only to save Indian souls but to end the violence that was threatening Indian survival as well as white expansion.

But most Indians refused to oblige, believing that the Great Spirit had established two separate ways of life for the two peoples—had ordained each race to its own customs, land, languages, foods, and religions—and if people deviated from their own ways, the Great Spirit would bring the apocalypse. Furthermore, some argued, if God had wanted the Indians to be Christians, he would have given them the Bible years ago or would have sent Christ himself. In that the Indians cared about immortality and honorable behavior, they shared a broad perspective with the missionaries, but they wanted nothing of institutional Christianity. They still looked upon their tribal customs as more useful and humane than American individualism and found in their own culture the most sensible way of interpreting their environment. Christianity and European culture were alien.

Some native Americans did convert to Christianity, shed native dress for European clothes, attended mission schools, and tried to farm their own land. But once converted they were often outcast from their own tribes. The Chippewas ridiculed the converts as "praying Indians," and Sioux warriors often physically abused them. And no matter how sincere or pious, Christian Indians were not accepted by whites. Caught between two cultures, facing double discrimination, many returned to their tribe rather than endure a life of social ostracism. When tribes adopted the whites' faith but not white customs, their religions often became synthesized tribal and Christian beliefs. Many simply added God to an existing pantheon of deities or, like the Spokanes, mixed their medicine cermonies with Christian prayers.

Whether the Indians adopted or repudiated white customs, missionaries were realizing by the early 1830s that native American culture was tenaciously resilient and that most Indians had no intention of passively accepting European culture. Yet to white idealists Anglo conformity seemed the only way to stop the seemingly endless violence on the frontier. Eventually the removal policies of Andrew Jackson, the reservation policies, and even the allottment policies would be concerned in part with changing Indian society, not just for the sake of change but to guarantee native American survival.

If noble, the sentiments of white idealists were naïve. Even if the Indians had submitted to conversion, whites would still have wanted their land. By 1820, for example, there were hundreds of thousands of whites in Georgia, Alabama, and Mississippi. Much of the game on which Indians relied had disappeared, and Indian ways were difficult to maintain. Hoping to keep their land, some of the tribes tried to accommodate themselves to white society. In 1808 Cherokee leaders had formulated a legal code, and by 1821 the brilliant Cherokee Sequoyah had developed written characters for eighty-six Cherokee syllables. Most Cherokees then became literate. In 1828 the tribe began publishing its own newspaper; and books, Bibles, hymnals, and tracts circulated widely throughout Cherokee society. Missionaries established new schools in Cherokee communities, and Protestant churches made more converts than ever before. The Cherokees fenced their farms, built comfortable homes, sold livestock commercially, and established a political system based on a written constitution, democratic elections, jury trials, and a bicameral legislature. But it was all in vain; most whites were more interested in their land than in cultural accommodation. With cotton production booming in the 1820s, tens of thousands of whites poured into the southeastern states and territories, and the Five Civilized Tribes, of which the Cherokees were one, were forced westward. Cultural accommodation could not counter economic expansion.

The Trail of Tears, 1830–1860

Since 1789 Americans as distinguished as Thomas Jefferson, George Washington, and John C. Calhoun had been suggesting that the eastern tribes be evicted to lands across the Mississippi River. At first the proposal met opposition; but as white farmers pushed west, it gained acceptance, both among land speculators and white idealists interested in protecting the Indians. Materialism and humanitarianism again made common cause. When Andrew Jackson entered the White House in 1829, the proposal gained a powerful advocate. He had made his reputation fighting Indians in the Southwest, trying to drive them across the Mississippi River. When informed of Indian attacks on white settle-

Robert Lindneux's painting of "The Trail of Tears" migration that followed passage of the Indian Removal Act of 1830. (The Granger Collection)

ments, he would fly into uncontrollable rages. At the same time he was concerned about Indian survival and realized that as long as they remained in their traditional homelands, white assaults would continue. To open southeastern land for white settlement and to protect native Americans, President Jackson signed the Indian Removal Act in 1830.

In what is remembered as "The Trail of Tears," one hundred thousand Indians were transported to Oklahoma. The peaceful Choctaws of the Deep South were first to go, marching in the winter of 1831. Many died of hunger and disease along the way. The Creeks were moved four years later after massive white attacks on them in Georgia and Alabama. The United States Army supervised the removal of the Chickasaws in 1837. The Cherokees had fought removal in the federal courts, and the Supreme Court upheld their claims in 1832. Jackson refused to abide by the court decision. The Cherokees held out for several years, but in 1838 soldiers evicted them; four thousand died on the way west. Only the Seminoles resisted violently. Under Chief Osceola they waged a guerrilla war in the Florida Everglades between 1835 and 1842 that cost the government two thousand soldiers and $55 million. But they too were finally defeated and removed to Oklahoma in 1843.

Removal was equally relentless in the Ohio Valley. The Iroquois managed to stay in upstate New York, but since the defeat of Tecumseh in 1813 the fate of the other northern tribes had been sealed. The Ottawas, Potawatomis, Wyandots, Shawnees, Miamis, Kickapoos, Winnebagos, Delawares, Peorias, and the Sauk and the Fox had to leave. Only the Sauk and the Fox resisted. Under Chief Black Hawk they had been removed to Iowa in 1831, but they turned back a few months later. United States troops chased them across Illinois and Wisconsin and finally defeated them at the Battle of Bad Axe. Black Hawk wrote in his autobiography:

> On our way down, I surveyed the country that had cost us so much trouble, anxiety and blood . . . I reflected on the ingratitude of the whites, when I saw their fine houses, rich harvests, and everything desirable around them; and recollected that all this land had been ours, for which we and my people never received a dollar, and that the whites were not satisfied until they took our village and our grave-yards from us, and removed us across the Mississippi. *

The removal treaties guaranteed perpetual ownership of the new land to the Indians, but only a permanent end to the westward movement could have preserved Indian land tenure. By the 1850s white farmers were fighting Indians for control of the Oregon Territory; the gold rush and other expeditions were bringing the California Indians to the brink of extinction; Mormons were settling the Great Basin; miners, traders, and ranchers had invaded the lands of the southwestern tribes in New Mexico; and white pioneers in Kansas and Nebraska were already clamoring for removal of the "removed" tribes.

Since the Lewis and Clark expedition of 1804–1806, the Indians of the Pacific Northwest had encountered a few white explorers, fur trappers, and missionaries and had responded with curiosity and disdain. With the acquisition of the Oregon Territory in 1846, however, thousands of American farmers poured in. When a long winter killed much of the game and a measles epidemic devastated several tribes in 1847 and 1848, Cayuse Indians attacked the Protestant mission of Marcus and Narcissa Whitman, killing them both. In 1853, when a new territorial governor began placing various tribes on reservations to clear the way for a transcontinental railroad, the Yakimas revolted, and government troops did not subdue them until 1858. The Yakimas, Cayuses, Wallawallas, Nez Percés, Spokanes, and Palouses were all moved to reservations.

The gold rush of 1849 brought disaster to the nomadic California tribes. Massacres, epidemic diseases, and forced slave labor almost destroyed them entirely. Their population declined from more than 100,000 people in 1849 to less than 15,000 in 1860.

When Mormon settlers entered the Great Basin in 1847, the lives of the Utes, Paiutes, and Shoshones changed immediately. Persecution at the hands of fanatical Protestants had left the Mormons more tolerant of "others" than most whites. Also Mormon theology held native Americans in special esteem, seeing them as a remnant of the lost tribes of

* Donald Jackson, ed., *Autobiography of Black Hawk* (Urbana, 1955), pp. 164–165.

Israel whom God had led to the New World and had destined to become someday a mighty and noble civilization. Mormon treatment of the Indians was more careful and diplomatic than that of most other whites. But as Brigham Young established Mormon farming colonies in southern Utah, Nevada, California, Arizona, Wyoming, Idaho, and Canada, and thousands of non-Mormon settlers came to the Salt Lake Valley in the 1850s, the white population increased and Indians lost much of their land. Construction of the transcontinental railroad through Utah Territory nullified more Indian land claims. In the end the Utes, Paiutes, and Shoshones were confined to reservations in some of the least hospitable regions of the Great Basin.

In 1848, when the Senate ratified the Treaty of Guadalupe Hidalgo with Mexico, the United States took sovereignty over the southwestern Indians and their lands. Americans had traded with the Spanish and Indians in the Southwest for years, and during the 1840s more white settlers came to work the silver mines and establish cattle and sheep ranches. The Pueblo Indians rebelled at Taos, New Mexico, in 1847 and killed several whites, but the uprising was quickly crushed. After that the Hopis, Zuñis, and Pueblos remained passively cooperative. Kit Carson and several hundred American troops attacked Navajos who had been raiding isolated white settlements in 1864, and eventually the Indians were marched several hundred miles to a reservation in eastern New Mexico, where they remained for three years until the government transferred them back to Arizona. Except for the Apaches, the Indians of the Southwest were defeated by 1865.

In the 1850s the tribes "removed" to the Great Plains twenty years before faced new problems. As white settlers poured into Kansas and Nebraska, the pressures on Indian land intensified just as the gold rush and the opening of Oregon was increasing the pioneer traffic. New treaties pushed the Indians north and south of the pioneer trails. During the Civil War some members of the Five Civilized Tribes of the South, hoping to regain their land, sided with the Confederacy, but after the war victorious northerners gave some of the Indians' land in Oklahoma to white settlers. They were then confined to much smaller, poorer tracts of land scattered over the territory. By 1865 only the Plains Indians and a few isolated tribes in the Southwest and the northern plateau remained free, and their days were numbered.

The Final Conquest

Beginning in the 1860s three developments sealed the Indians' future. First, Congress passed the Homestead Act in 1862, and after the Civil War hundreds of thousands of white settlers took up 160-acre tracts of free land in the Dakotas, Montana, Wyoming, Colorado, western Kansas, western Nebraska, and Oklahoma. The mass migration imposed extraordinary pressures on the Plains Indians. Second, the completion of five transcontinental railroads, linking eastern manufacturers with western markets, made their situation worse because the roads sold parcels of their federal land grants to white farmers. The Union Pacific–Central Pacific line from Omaha to San Francisco was finished in 1869; farther north the Northern Pacific and the Great Northern railroads were completed in 1883 and 1893, passing through the Dakotas, Montana, Idaho, and Washington to link the Great Lakes with Puget Sound. And by 1884 two southern routes were completed. The Atchison, Topeka, and Santa Fe ran from eastern Kansas to Los Angeles and the Southern Pacific connected New Orleans with the West Coast. Third, at the same time the railroads were being built, the buffalo slaughter became large-scale. Some public officials encouraged the hunts, hoping they would destroy the Plains economy and make it easier to force the Indians onto reservations. It worked. By 1883 the southern herd was wiped out and only remnants of the northern herd were surviving in Canada. The economy of the Plains Indians was in ruins.

Conflict began along the major trade and migration routes, and later erupted wherever white settlers encroached on Indian land. Late in 1862, after repeated acts of fraud by traders and a massive increase in settlers along the Minnesota River, the Santee Sioux rebelled and killed several hundred whites. Panic spread throughout southern Minnesota and thousands of people fled. Soldiers eventually dispersed the Sioux, capturing more than four hundred and driving others into Canada and the western Dakotas.

The southern Cheyenne in eastern Colorado also reacted to white settlers. After several skirmishes with whites in 1864, they agreed to a negotiated peace and quietly moved to a temporary camp at Sand Creek, Colorado. There, on November 29, 1864, soldiers under the command of Colonel John M. Chivington brutally attacked the Indians. In an orgy of violence they murdered three hundred Cheyenne, sparing none, not even women and children. A general war spread throughout eastern Colorado and western Kansas as enraged Cheyennes, Sioux, and Arapahos avenged the Sand Creek massacre. Not until 1868, when Lieutenant Colonel George A. Custer's Seventh Cavalry defeated the southern Cheyenne, did calm return temporarily to the Great Plains.

The wars intensified in the 1870s. In Idaho, Oregon, and Washington, troops extinguished the final resistance of the plateau tribes. The Modocs went to the Oklahoma reservations in 1872, and a few years later the Flatheads and Bannocks moved to reservations in the Northwest. In 1877, after a dramatic attempt to escape to Canada, Chief

Joseph and the Nez Percés were captured in northern Montana. In his surrender message to the United States Army, Chief Joseph said with tragic eloquence:

> I am tired of fighting. Our chiefs are killed . . . the old men are dead. . . . It is cold and we have no blankets. The little children are freezing to death. My people . . . have no blankets, no food. . . . I want to have time to look for my children and see how many I can find. Maybe I shall find them among the dead. Hear me, my chiefs, I am tired; my heart is sick and sad. From where the sun now stands, I will fight no more forever.*

The remnants of the Nez Percé tribe went to Indian Territory in Oklahoma.

In the Southwest the city-dwelling tribes and the Navajos were defeated by the 1870s, but the Apaches resisted fiercely. Between 1862 and 1886 they carried on a successful guerrilla war against white settlements, and not until 1886, when Chief Geronimo of the Chiricahua Apaches surrendered, did peace come to Arizona and New Mexico. Geronimo was sent to prison and the Apaches to reservations, where they depended for survival on supplies from the Department of the Interior.

Hostilities resumed on the Plains in 1874, when the discovery of gold in the Black Hills of South Dakota brought thousands of white miners. Only six years earlier the Sioux had been given "eternal" control of the area, but under intense political pressure the federal government hedged on its promise and asked them to leave. They refused, and the Department of the Interior ordered them out of the Black Hills. Still they refused, and government troops under Custer, now a general, and General George Crook left for the Dakotas. In one of the most famous battles in American military history, a combined force of Cheyenne and Sioux warriors, led by Crazy Horse and Sitting Bull, killed Custer and more than two hundred of his men at the Little Big Horn River in 1876. Inspired by revenge, white troops drove Sitting Bull into Canada and the Oglala Sioux to a South Dakota reservation. After more hopeless fighting, Crazy Horse surrendered in 1877 and the northern Cheyennes were moved to the Indian Territory. In fury and desperation Morning Star and Little Wolf led them off the reservation the following year and tried to make it back to ancestral lands in Montana. The flight captured national attention and touched the hearts of many whites, but troops soon returned those who were left to Oklahoma.

The last vestige of Indian resistance disappeared after the murder of Sitting Bull in 1890. Born to the Hunkpapa Sioux in 1834, he was perhaps

---

* Quoted in Angie Debo, *A History of the Indians of the United States* (Norman, Okla., 1970), pp. 215–216.

the most renowned native American of the nineteenth century. He returned to the United States from Canada in 1881 after government agents offered him amnesty. Under house arrest at Fort Randall for two years, he later moved to Standing Rock, Dakota Territory, before spending a year on tour with Buffalo Bill's Wild West Show. By 1888 he was openly opposing any further Sioux land cessions, and after resisting arrest in 1890 he was shot to death by Indian police on the reservation. News of his murder spread quickly through the Dakota Territory, and at Wounded Knee Creek, South Dakota, an angry Sioux warrior killed an army officer. In the ensuing melée enraged soldiers killed more than a hundred and fifty Sioux men, women, and children. That tragedy formally closed a chapter in American history. After 1890, with the buffalo herds gone and white homesteads throughout the "Great American Desert," Indian resistance would have been totally suicidal. Stripped of their land, the native Americans finally gave up and headed for the reservations. The wars were over.

Life was different on the reservations. Instead of deferring to tribal leaders, native Americans found themselves subject to the authority of Interior Department agents. Traditional attitudes toward power, authority, and responsibility were expected to change completely. Reservation Indians had to surrender the hunter-warrior ideal and accept passive roles as dependent wards of the state. All this upset the emotional balance of families and communities. They also had to accept the constant presence of white idealists and missionaries bent on converting them to Christian civilization.

With their independence lost, their cosmic rationale gone, and their culture under siege, thousands of native Americans turned to alcoholism and peyotism. Despite laws against it, local Indian agents often supplied liquor as a pacifier, and Indians readily accepted it as an escape from reality. Other Indians turned to peyote hallucinations. A derivative of the cactus plant, peyote found a ready audience among the hopeless hunters of the Indian Territory because it gave its users spectacular dreams and a heightened sense of personal value. The peyote cult had come from Mexico to the Mescalero Apaches, who passed it on to the Kiowas, Caddos, and Comanches. Quanah Parker, who was a mixed-blood child of a Comanche chief and a white mother and had resisted white settlement until his surrender in 1875, became a leader of the peyote cult and gained great influence over reservation Indians. By the 1880s peyotism had spread to the Cheyennes, Shawnees, and Arapahos, and by 1900 to the Pawnees, Delawares, Osages, and Winnebagoes. In the early 1900s peyotism reached the Omahas, Utes, Crows, Menominees, Iowas, Sioux, and Shoshones, and in the 1920s and 1930s it spread to the Gosiutes, Paiutes, Blackfoot, Creeks,

Cherokees, Seminoles, and Chippewas. Eventually peyotism was institutionalized into the Native American Church, which was designed to bring peace to people living a life over which they had no control.

Reservation life also produced a burst of supernaturalism. Sometime between 1869 and 1872 a Paiute prophet named Wovoka claimed to have received a special revelation from the Great Spirit:

> When the sun died, I went up to heaven and saw God and all the people who had died a long time ago. God told me to come back and tell my people they must be good and love one another, and not fight, or steal, or lie. He gave me this dance to give to my people.*

The Ghost Dance religion spread throughout the plateau, the Great Basin, and on to the Great Plains. The ceremony consisted of four straight nights of physically exhausting dances, and the religion offered a spiritual explanation for the native American dilemma. As a Paiute Indian explained it:

> All Indians must dance, everywhere, keep on dancing. Pretty soon in next spring Big Man come. He bring back all game of every kind. The game be thick everywhere. All dead Indians come back and live again. They all be strong just like young men, be young again. Old blind Indians see again and get young and have fine time. When Old Man comes this way, then all the Indians go to mountains, high up away from whites. . . . Then while Indians way up high, big flood comes like water and all white people die . . . nobody but Indians everywhere and game all kinds thick. †

According to this theology, God had punished the Indians for their sins by sending whites to rape the land and slaughter the people. Soon, however, with Indian repentance complete and sins atoned for, God would destroy whites, resurrect the Indian dead, and restore the buffalo herds. Although details varied from tribe to tribe, the Ghost Dance looked for the day when the promises would come true, and in the meantime the Indians wore sacred undergarments to protect themselves from danger. Not until 1890, when the slaughter at Wounded Knee proved the Ghost Dance would not protect the Indians from the soldiers' bullets, did the religion begin to decline.

Finally, a new version of an old Indian religion called the Sun Dance appeared. Before the conquest several tribes had used the Sun Dance to bring successful hunts, shore up personal courage, and guarantee victory over enemies. Days of dancing, fasting, and self-mutilation —men

---

* James Mooney, *The Ghost Dance Religion and the Sioux Outbreak of 1890* (Chicago, 1965), p. 2.
† Ibid., p. 26

slicing open the skin of their chests, passing rawhide skewers through the cuts, tying the rawhide to poles, and stepping back forcefully until the skewers ripped through the skin—were supposed to bring peace with the Great Spirit and prosperity in the world. On the reservations the Sun Dance became extremely popular with the Utes, Shoshones, and Goshiutes of the Great Basin, and changed fundamentally in character to a redemptive, individual religion. By participating in the Sun Dance, avoiding alcohol and sexual infidelity, and living a thoughtful, considerate life, an Indian could transform his personality. Where the Ghost Dance promised changes in reality, the Sun Dance promised only the possibility of individual virility and understanding of reality, a oneness with the universe that white people could never achieve.

Alcoholism, peyotism, the Ghost Dance, and the Sun Dance were hardly the conversion that white idealists were after. Native Americans still had little to do with white culture and remained as hundreds of distinct ethnic groups in the United States.

SUGGESTED READINGS

Andrist, Ralph K. *The Long Death: The Last Days of the Plains Indians*. New York: 1964.

Anson, Bert. *The Miami Indians*. Norman, Oklahoma: 1970.

Berkhofer, Robert F. *Salvation and the Savage: An Analysis of Protestant Missions and American Indian Response, 1787–1862*. Lexington, Kentucky: 1965.

Brown, Dee. *Bury My Heart at Wounded Knee*. New York: 1970.

Brown, Mark H. *The Flight of the Nez Percé*. New York: 1967.

Cook, Sherburne F. *The Conflict Between the California Indians and White Civilization*. Berkeley, Cal.: 1976.

DeRosier, Arthur. *The Removal of the Choctaw Indians*. Knoxville, Tenn.: 1970.

Fahey, John. *The Flathead Indians*. Norman, Oklahoma: 1974.

Faulk, Odie B. *Crimson Desert: Indian Wars of the Southwest*. New York: 1974.

———. *The Geronimo Campaign*. New York: 1969.

Fehrenbach, T. R. *Comanches: The Destruction of a People*. New York: 1974.

Freeman, John F. "The Indian Convert: Theme and Variation." *Ethnohistory*, 12 (Spring 1965), 113–128.

Fritz, Henry E. *The Movement for Indian Assimilation, 1860–1890*. Philadelphia: 1963.

Gibson, Arrell M. *The Chickasaws*. Norman, Oklahoma: 1971.

Gunnerson, Dolores A. *The Jicarilla Apaches: A Study in Survival*. DeKalb, Ill.: 1974.

Heizer, Robert F., and Almquist, Alan J. *The Other Californians: Prejudice and Discrimination Under Spain, Mexico, and the United States to 1920*. Berkeley, Cal.: 1971.

Jorgensen, Joseph G. *The Sun Dance Religion: Power for the Powerless*. Chicago: 1972.

Joseph, Alvin M. *The Nez Percé Indians and the Opening of the Northwest*. New Haven, Conn.: 1965.

La Barre, Weston. *The Peyote Cult*. New York: 1975.

Lurie, Nancy Oestreich. "The World's Oldest On-Going Protest Demonstration: Native American Drinking Patterns." *Pacific Historical Review*, 40 (August 1971), 311–329.

McKnitt, Frank. *Navajo Wars*. Albuquerque, N.M.: 1972.

Metcalf, P. Richard. "Who Should Rule at Home: Native American Politics and Indian-White Relations." *Journal of American History*, 61 (December 1974), 651–677.

Mooney, James. *The Ghost Dance Religion and the Sioux Outbreak of 1890*. Chicago: 1965.

Olson, James C. *Red Cloud and the Sioux Problem*. Lincoln, Neb.: 1965.

Phillips, George H. *Chiefs and Challengers: Indian Resistance and Cooperation in Southern California*. Berkeley, Cal.: 1975.

Price, John A. "North American Indian Families." In Charles H. Mindel and Robert W. Habenstein, *Ethnic Families in America*. New York: 1976.

Prucha, Francis Paul. *American Indian Policy in Crisis: Christian Reformers and the Indian, 1865–1900*. Norman, Oklahoma: 1975.

_____. *The Sword of the Republic: The United States Army on the Frontier, 1783–1846*. New York: 1969.

Rogin, Michael Paul. *Fathers and Children: Andrew Jackson and the Subjugation of the American Indian*. New York: 1975.

Satz, Ronald. *American Indian Policy in the Jacksonian Era*. Lincoln, Neb.: 1975.

Sheehan, Bernard W. *Seeds of Extinction: Jeffersonian Philanthropy and the American Indian*. Chapel Hill, N.C.: 1973.

Strickland, Rennard. *Fire and the Spirits: Cherokee Law from Clan to Court*. Norman, Oklahoma: 1975.

Thrapp, Dan L. *The Conquest of Apacheria*. Norman, Oklahoma: 1967.

Trennert, Robert A. *Alternative to Extinction: Federal Indian Policy and the Beginnings of the Reservation System, 1846–1851*. Philadelphia: 1975.

Utley, Robert M. *Frontier Regulars: The United States Army and the Indian, 1866–1891*. New York: 1973.

Wallace, Anthony F. *The Death and Rebirth of the Seneca*. New York: 1970.

Washburn, Wilcomb E. *The Indian in America*. New York: 1975.

Wilkins, Thurman. *Cherokee Tragedy: The Story of the Ridge Family and the Decimation of a People*. New York: 1970.

Chapter Ten

Afro-Americans: From Slavery to Freedom

For Americans the first century of national life was tempestuous, marked by hope and despair, triumph and defeat, an era beginning with a burst of democratic euphoria and ending in 1877 after an agonizing civil war. Fundamentally the Civil War was an ideological and cultural crisis, an attempt to determine the real meaning of equality and freedom. Black people assumed a conspicuously public place in the national consciousness as the United States tried to carve out a philosophical place in Western civilization.

The American Revolution was more than a political separation from England; it also released a set of ideological forces that would ultimately lead to the Civil War. By 1776 the colonists were maturing politically, slowly becoming American nationals. From England they had inherited ideas of representative government, the evil nature of political power, and the unalienable rights of man, and when England violated those rights after 1763, the colonists became revolutionaries willing to resort to violence. By 1861 that spirit would ignite the Civil War.

Throughout the eighteenth century Philadelphia Quakers had denounced slavery because of their egalitarian theology. The antislavery movement was also strengthened by the Enlightenment emphasis on reason and natural rights which made legal justifications for slavery increasingly hollow. And evangelical Protestantism inspired a spirit of abolition in some northern circles by advocating charity toward all people. All these arguments had fallen on deaf ears until the Revolution.

But then the inconsistency of denouncing oppression while condoning slavery began to weigh heavily on the Founding Fathers. How could Americans criticize English oppression when 500,000 blacks were slaves? After 1776 Thomas Paine, Benjamin Franklin, Thomas Jefferson, James Otis, John Adams, Noah Webster, and John Jay all condemned slavery.

The military service of thousands of blacks during the Revoluation also pricked the conscience of America. Crispus Attucks, a runaway slave, was shot and killed during the Boston Massacre in 1770 and became the first American to die at the hands of British soldiers. Peter Salem and Salem Poore, both slaves freed to fight in the Continental Army, distinguished themselves at the Battle of Bunker Hill, as did Lemuel Haynes at the Battle of Ticonderoga and "Pompey" at the Battle of Stony Point. Manpower shortages forced state after state to free slaves who would volunteer to fight. Eventually more than five thousand blacks fought with colonial forces, participating in every major engagement from Lexington in 1775 to Yorktown in 1781. Their service further exposed the hypocrisy of slavery within a revolution.

Black People in the North

After the Revolution northern agriculture and industry became capital rather than labor intensive, relying on machines instead of people whenever possible. Because wheat, corn, and livestock farms as well as eastern factories did not depend on slave labor, the economic foundation of slavery crumbled. Nor was there a social rationale; the black population of the North was too small to threaten white society. There were only 75,000 blacks out of nearly 1.5 million northerners in 1776, and the ratio declined to only 250,000 blacks out of 20 million northerners in 1860. Not often frightened by the black minority, whites did not resist abolition; vested social and economic interests had little to lose from it.

For all these reasons a powerful movement arose in the North. Quakers organized the first antislavery society in 1775, and in 1780 Pennsylvania provided for the gradual abolition of slavery. Massachusetts abolished slavery by court order in 1783, and the next year Connecticut and Rhode Island passed general abolition laws. New York and New Jersey enacted similar laws in 1785 and 1786, and in 1787 the Northwest Ordinance prohibited slavery in the Ohio Valley. After fierce debate in 1787 the Constitutional Convention outlawed the importation of slaves after 1807. The American Revolution brought freedom from England and, for northern blacks, freedom from bondage.

Legal freedom, however, did not mean equality. In Ohio, Indiana, and Illinois white settlers from the South segregated free blacks whenever possible. White workers there feared economic competition from blacks, and black youths were often placed in long-term apprenticeships closely resembling slavery. Black adults could not serve on juries or vote, and immigration of blacks from other states was barred. Between 1807 and 1837 New Jersey, Connecticut, New York, Rhode Island, and Pennsylvania passed laws disfranchising blacks. And throughout the North black people were segregated in public facilities and widely discriminated against in the job market. The North was hardly the promised land.

Nevertheless, black people created meaningful lives for themselves. By 1860 there were more than 250,000 free blacks in the North; and although most were poor and restricted to menial jobs, several gained national recognition. Benjamin Banneker was a renowned astronomer and mathematician. Paul Cuffe, a black businessman from Massachusetts, became a wealthy shipbuilder and an advocate of black rights. Phillis Wheatley, Jupiter Hammon, and Gustavus Vassa were prominent black literary figures at the turn of the century. David Walker, a free black who had moved to Boston in 1829, wrote *Walker's Appeal*, which called on southern slaves to rise up against their masters. Robert Young, Theodore Wright, Sojourner Truth, Harriet Tubman, David Ruggles, and Charles Remond were all well-known black abolitionists.

Perhaps the most famous of all was Frederick Douglass. Born at Tuckahoe, Maryland, in 1817, Douglass escaped from slavery in 1838 and taught himself to read while working as a laborer. In 1841 he spoke at a meeting of the Massachusetts Antislavery Society, captivated the largely white audience, and immediately became one of the most popular abolitionists in the country. Writer, lecturer, and editor of the abolitionist *North Star*, Douglass went on to be active in Republican politics during the Civil War and, before his death in 1895, a Washington official and United States consul general to Haiti. His autobiography, published in 1845, was widely read.

Facing racial prejudice, Afro-Americans turn inward, relying on themselves for respect, recognition, and assistance. A number of early black organizations opposed slavery and campaigned for equal rights. The National Negro Convention, the American Moral Reform Society for Improving the Condition of Mankind, the General Colored Associations, the African Civilization Society, the American League of Colored Laborers, and the National Council of Colored People all demanded abolition and first-class citizenship for black people.

But the most important organizations in the black community were

Churches played a crucial role in Afro-American society. This engraving (1853) depicts a meeting in the African Methodist Church in Cincinnati, Ohio. (Culver Pictures, Inc.)

the fraternal, mutual aid societies and the churches. The African Union Society, the Free African Society, the Black Masons, and the Negro Oddfellows supplied medical, educational, and burial services to their members as well as a forum for recognizing achievements and resolving disputes. Even more important was the black church. Most blacks were Methodists or Baptists, probably because poor people generally joined those churches. But because of paternalism and forced segregation in white churches, black people began forming their own congregations late in the eighteenth century. In 1787, after being asked to occupy segregated pews at St. George's Methodist Church in Philadelphia, Richard Allen and Absolom Jones left and established the African Methodist Episcopal (AME) Church. In 1816 the independent AME churches in Pennsylvania, New Jersey, and Delaware joined into a national convocation and named Allen their bishop. Black Baptist churches also emerged in the North between 1805 and 1810. Independent of white influence, the black churches were influential forums where leadership could be developed and grievances freely expressed. In the process of selecting teachers, officers, ministers, and ecclesiastical representatives, black parishioners exercised a franchise power which the larger society denied them. The churches actively promoted educational and fraternal programs. Richard Allen, for example, played a leading role in the Free African Society and the Black Masons. Thus

when free blacks became active in their churches, they were also helping to build other social and economic institutions in their communities.
Even in our own time, the most influential black leaders—including
Martin Luther King, Jr. and Jesse Jackson—have come from the black
churches.

Black People in the South

The ideological revolution was stillborn in the South. A small but vocal
antislavery movement developed in the upper South during the Revolution, but it died out after 1800. To most white southerners abolition was
an ugly word. Slavery was still justified as providing cheap labor and a
means of controlling black workers.

Just as the economic need for slaves was disappearing in the North,
southern dependence on cheap labor was increasing. With their soil
exhausted and world markets glutted in the 1790s, tobacco farmers were
searching desperately for a more lucrative crop. The Industrial Revolution was stimulating demand for cotton, but the South could not fill it
because removing seeds from the fiber was too expensive. Eli Whitney
solved that problem in 1793 when he invented the cotton gin, a machine
which removed the seeds without destroying the cotton fiber, and
cotton quickly became the South's major cash crop. Production increased from 4,000 bales in 1790 to more than 5 million bales in 1860.
The southern plantation economy depended on having millions of black
slaves in the fields each day.

Southerners also opposed abolition for social reasons. By 1860 there
were 4 million blacks to only 7 million whites in the South. In Virginia,
Texas, and Arkansas, whites outnumbered blacks by three to one, but in
Mississippi and South Carolina blacks outnumbered whites. The population was divided almost equally in Louisiana, Alabama, Florida, and
Georgia. The size of the black population seemed ominous; whites were
obsessed with fears of slave uprisings, and only slavery gave them absolute control over black people. Emancipation was unthinkable.

Because the United States was in general a Protestant, capitalistic,
and states-rights society, there was no central authority—church or
state—to ameliorate the condition of slaves. Slave status imposed severe pressures on black people. The decisions of whites often invaded
the privacy of social and family life. Black men were not permitted full
decision-making power in their homes; black women had to work in the
fields even when their children were young and were sometimes
exploited sexually by white men; children had to go to work at an early
age; and family members could be sold separately at any time. Southern

states outlawed any education for slaves, hoping that illiteracy would keep them dependent on their white owners. Freedmen Bureau schools, established by the federal government during Reconstruction, provided most southern blacks with their first opportunity to learn to read and write.

Living conditions were primitive. At the age of ten or twelve, black children went to work in the fields and would perform backbreaking tasks all their lives unless they were among a tiny group of skilled workers or domestic servants. Typical food rations for field hands were four pounds of pork fat, a peck of corn meal, and a small amount of coffee and molasses each week; they usually had one dress or two shirts and one pair of trousers; and they lived in damp, small shanty homes in the "quarters." One slave song transcribed by Frederick Douglass pointed out the irony of slavery:

> We raise de wheat
> Dey gib us de corn;
> We bake de bread,
> Dey gib us de cruss;
> We sif de meal,
> Dey gib us de huss;
> We peel de meat,
> Dey gib us de skin;
> And dat's de way
> Dey takes us in.*

There were few rewards and few incentives.

But slave-owners had to provide a subsistence living for their property, if only to protect their own investment. Planters also had a vested interest in plantation stability because it boosted productivity; terribly unhappy slaves or slaves who hated an overseer were inefficient workers. Slaves resisted in many ways. To avoid field work, many convinced their masters that blacks were naturally lazy, clumsy, and irresponsible people from whom little could be expected. Other slaves injured farm animals, broke tools, and disabled wagons to postpone work. Some slaves even hurt themselves, inflicting wounds on their hands or legs, to avoid being overworked or sold. Feigning illness was common. Thousands of slaves also ran away, hoping to reach the North or Canada on the "underground railroad"—a group of whites and free blacks who assisted runaway slaves. And there were hundreds of slave rebellions. From the 1712 uprising in New York City, which killed nine whites, to Nat Turner's rebellion in 1831, which resulted in the death of sixty

---

* Frederick Douglass, *My Bondage and My Freedom* (New York, 1855), p. 253.

Virginia whites, discontented slaves often used violence to try to liberate themselves. Still, such rebellions were relatively rare; slave resistance was more often directed at ameliorating the conditions of slavery than at liberation.

Within the slave quarters, far from white society, was the world of Afro-America. "From sundown to sunup" a special slave culture appeared which eased the trauma of bondage, provided group solidarity and status, verbalized aggressions, and demonstrated love. The slaves' relationship with whites during the workday was secondary to their relationship with one another, and scholarly theories describing the slave personality only in terms of white society overlook the primary environment of the quarters. There blacks developed ethical and family values, positive self-images, and group unity. Recreation, religion, and family were the foundations of black society.

Leisure time permitted slaves to play social roles different from that of driven servants. In the evenings they gathered to visit and gossip, or to sing and dance; and on Sundays and holidays they hunted, fished, gambled, attended church, or had afternoon parties. Most excelled at something—racing, storytelling, singing, dancing, preaching, or teaching—and enjoyed prestige from such talents. Leisure activities offered a respite from the drudgery of the fields, a liberation from the emotional pressures of bondage.

Music was central to slaves' lives and accompanied daily activities— work, play, and church services. It was functional and improvisational, symbolically related to group solidarity and individual aspirations. In their songs the slaves retained the form and spirit of their African origins, fashioning expressive modes for dealing with the New World. Spirituals and secular songs helped them express anger or despair which whites would not have tolerated in speech. One slave song was:

> See these poor souls from Africa
> Transported to America;
> We are stolen, and sold in Georgia,
> Will you go along with me?
> We are stolen, and sold in Georgia,
> Come sound the jubilee!
>
> See wives and husbands sold apart,
> Their children's screams will break my heart—
> There's a better day a coming,
> Will you go along with me?
> There's a better day a coming,
> Go sound the jubilee!*

---

* W. W. Brown, *Narrative of William W. Brown, A Fugitive Slave* (Boston, 1847), p. 51.

Often whites had no idea what the lyrics of slave songs implied, but to blacks their meaning was quite clear.

Religion too liberated slaves from the white world and allowed them to express their deep feelings. Slave religion made few distinctions between the secular and the spiritual, between this life and the next, and symbolically carried slaves back in history to more glorious times and forward into a more benign future, linking them with the cosmos and assuring them that there was justice in the universe. Except for proud first-generation Africans tenaciously holding to the faiths of their fathers, most slaves converted to fundamentalist Protestantism, particularly that of the Baptists and Methodists because they sponsored the development of black clergies. Some white planters encouraged religion as a tool of social control, and white ministers preached bondage as the will of God. Patience, obedience, submission, gratitude—these were the themes of white-sponsored slave religion. Lunsford Lane, an escaped slave, recalled in 1848 that he had often heard white preachers tell slaves

> how good God was in bringing us over to this country from dark . . . Africa, and permitting us to listen to the sound of the gospel. . . . The first commandment . . . was to obey our masters, and the second was . . . to do as much work when they or the overseers were not watching us as when they were.*

But the slaves were not fooled, and they adapted Christianity to their own needs. In white churches they went through the motions of reverent attention, but they were rarely taken in by the joyless message of white preachers bent on molding them into submission. Instead they used white services to visit with friends and family from other farms or plantations, which they could rarely do at other times because the rigid pass laws confined them to their masters' property.

When permitted to worship on their own, the slaves reinterpreted Christianity and enjoyed an autonomy denied them everywhere else. Rejecting Calvinist notions of predestination, unworthiness, sin, and damnation as well as the Pauline doctrine of dutiful obedience, slave spirituals sang of redemption, glory, freedom, change, and justice. Black culture was not obsessed with guilt and depravity, and black preachers spoke of the spiritual equality of all people and God's uncompromising love for everyone. Threatened on all sides by a hostile environment, black slaves united the next world with this one and bound themselves into a single community, a "chosen people" loved by God. And this redemptive vision thrived in black America even though white society repeatedly tried to tell them that they were the lowliest of human beings. Slave religion allowed blacks to vent the frustrations of

* Lunsford Lane, *The Narrative of Lunsford Lane* (Boston, 1848), pp. 20–21.

bondage, united them in a sense of mission, and recognized them as individuals. Theirs was a spiritual world of deliverance, of Moses leading a special people out of bondage and Jesus saving them from a corrupt world.

Slave folk tales and beliefs in voodoo, magic, and the world of spirits reinforced the role of religion. African cultures had always assumed that all life had direction and that apparently random events were part of a larger cosmic plan, which could be divined by reading the appropriate "signs" in nature and human affairs. Man was part of a natural pantheon of life. All things had causes, and if one could figure them out they could be controlled. These ideas were not completely alien to Europeans either; beliefs in witchcraft, satanic influence, and magical healings were still widely held. Slaves used folk beliefs and folk medicine to heal the sick, and some folk practitioners were highly respected. Certain signs—an owl's screech, a black cat crossing one's path, the approach of a cross-eyed person—indicated bad luck ahead, which could be remedied by such devices as spitting, crossing fingers, turning pockets inside out, or turning shoes upside down on the porch. Dreams had great meaning. The world of magic and voodoo gave slaves a sense of power over their masters, for in the hexes, signs, and punishments of the supernatural they tried to control the behavior of whites and their own destiny. To blacks African folk culture offered a degree of power, a means of integrating life and transcending their enslavement.

Finally, in the slave family Afro-Americans found companionship, love, esteem, and sexual fulfillment—things the master-slave relationship denied them. Despite the breakup of families through the sale of slaves, white sexual exploitation of black women, and incursions on the authority of black parents, the family was the basic institution of slave society. Although antebellum slave society tolerated premarital sexual liaisons, adultery was strictly forbidden. Once two people had "jumped the broomstick," fidelity was expected. Typical slave households had two parents and were male dominated: the father exercised discipline and supplemented the family diet by hunting and fishing, and the mother was responsible for household duties and raising young children. That former slaves eagerly had their marriages legalized after the Civil War and searched the country over to reunite separated families confirms the loyalty of parents, children, and spouses.

Slavery and the Civil War

Since the colonial period economic interest and political philosophy had divided the North and the South. Committed to an agrarian economy and international export markets, the South had never seen the need for a national bank, high tariffs, internal improvements, or any other measures designed to stimulate industry. Most southern politicians preached laissez-faire, states' rights, and a strict interpretation of the Constitution to prevent preferential treatment of northern manufacturers. With a mixed economy of farming, commerce, and manufacturing, the North favored protective tariffs, a strong national bank, and federally financed internal improvements.

But when the issue of slavery was added to these differences, civil war erupted. Slavery was the structural foundation of southern society. It created a static caste system in the South, different from the more open class system of the North. And slavery went against the ideas of democracy, equality, and freedom. Some northerners attacked it as a moral evil, while many southerners defended it as a moral good, a way of preserving white culture and introducing black people to Christian civilization.

At first the national debate was limited. William Lloyd Garrison and Frederick Douglass called for the immediate abolition of slavery, but most northerners were unwilling to sanction such a radical disruption of southern life. Instead they opted for more gradual schemes. Formed in 1816, the American Colonization Society campaigned to resettle blacks in Africa, and before the Civil War the society sent several thousand blacks to Liberia. Most free blacks detested the idea, claiming the right of any other native-born American to dignity and equality *within* the United States. Other northerners wanted gradual abolition and compensation by the federal government to slaveholders for the loss of their property. The South would have none of it.

Most northerners realized that immediate abolition, gradual abolition, and colonization were naïve, unworkable approaches to the problem. They decided just to oppose the extension of slavery into the western territories, hoping to contain the "peculiar institution" in the Old South, where it might expire gradually. The Liberty party of 1840 and 1844, the Free-Soil party of 1848, and the Republican party—organized in 1854—committed themselves to that objective. But southerners believed that for slavery and the plantation system to survive they would have to have access to fresh soil in the West.

The sectional strife also reflected attitudes toward the composition of American society. A minority of northern whites opposed the expansion of slavery into the territories because they believed slavery was immoral and that any measures strengthening it were similarly evil. But they were joined by millions of others who opposed the expansion of slavery for economic reasons—free white workers could not compete financially with black slaves—or who disliked black people in general. Confining slavery to the South would guarantee free territories and a largely white society, where the entrepreneurial instincts of Yankee culture could flourish. Southern whites, convinced that containment of slavery was a first step toward its ultimate eradication, and terrified by the prospect of having 4 million free blacks in the South, insisted on the right to carry slaves into the territories, which the Dred Scott decision by the Supreme Court in 1857 permitted them to do. Southerners also realized that containment of slavery would guarantee the nationwide triumph of Yankee entrepreneurialism and its faith in technological change, material progress, and democratic egalitarianism. So in part the debate over free-soil politics was a cultural conflict between Yankee northerners and white southerners.

Between 1820 and 1860 every sectional crisis in the United States — the Missouri Compromise of 1820, the Mexican War of 1846, the Compromise of 1850, the Kansas-Nebraska Act of 1854, and the Dred Scott case of 1857 — involved slavery in the territories. When the Republican candidate, Abraham Lincoln, won the presidential election of 1860 on a platform of free soil, protective tariffs, a national bank, and internal improvements, white southerners felt threatened socially, economically, and philosophically. The South panicked and seceded from the Union.

The Civil War ultimately destroyed slavery and resolved, legally at least, the status of black people. At first Lincoln's objectives were narrowly defined. The Civil War had broken out, he thought, only because southerners had insisted on carrying their slaves to the West; the North was fighting to prevent that and bring the South back into the Union. Preservation of the Union, not abolition, was the central issue. Suspicious of radical social change, Lincoln opposed abolition in the early months of the war. When General John C. Frémont entered Missouri in 1861 and freed the slaves, Lincoln angrily rescinded the order, and the next year he nullified General David Hunter's abolition order in Georgia, South Carolina, and Florida.

But a number of pressures transformed the Civil War into a struggle to preserve the Union *and* liberate the slaves. First, most northerners, including the president himself, had anticipated a brief, conclusive war in which superior northern forces would overwhelm the Confederacy. But after staggering defeats at Bull Run and in the Shenandoah Valley in 1861 and 1862, a war of attrition developed. Lincoln hoped abolition might disrupt the southern economy by depriving the Confederacy of 4 million slaves.

Political and ideological concerns also pushed Lincoln toward emancipation. Republican abolitionists were steadily gaining strength by denouncing the hypocrisy of proclaiming democracy while condoning slavery. Radical Republicans including Thaddeus Stevens, Charles Sumner, Wendell Phillips, and Benjamin Wade insisted that Lincoln abolish slavery and were outraged when he nullified military abolition orders. Lincoln was in political trouble. Military defeats had dissipated his popularity, and a powerful wing of his own party was condemning his insensitivity to the plight of black people. If he was to be renominated in 1864, Lincoln had to revive his popularity and attract Radical support. Abolition might do it. By appearing as a moral crusader rather than just a political leader, Lincoln hoped to shore up his crumbling political fortunes.

But regaining Radical Republican support posed another dilemma. Abolition would please the Radicals, but if Lincoln freed the slaves he would sacrifice the support of Democrats loyal to the Union in Delaware, Maryland, Kentucky, and Missouri—slave-owners who had opposed secession. Abolition might win renomination, but it would just as surely cost Lincoln the general election. Some way of satisfying Radical Republicans without alienating loyal slave-owning Democrats had to be found. Lincoln slowly moved toward partial emancipation. In the spring of 1862 he supported congressional abolition of slavery in the District of Columbia and in the territories. Finally, on January 1, 1863, Lincoln issued the Emancipation Proclamation, liberating only the slaves in the rebellious states. The 400,000 slaves in loyal border states remained slaves. Lincoln thus gained Radical support without estranging border Democrats. And in another brilliant political maneuver he selected Andrew Johnson, a loyal Tennessee Democrat, as his running mate in the election of 1864. He then went on to reelection.

In April 1865 the Union armies trapped General Robert E. Lee's troops near Appomattox Court House in Virginia. The Confederacy was finished and Lee surrendered. The national nightmare was over. More than 600,000 young men and $15 billion had disappeared in the smoke of destruction; dreams were broken, faiths shattered, and lives wasted. The South was a pocked no man's land of untilled farms, broken machinery, gutted buildings, fresh graves, worthless money, and defeated people. Schools, banks, and businesses were closed; inflation was spiraling; and unemployment was on the rise. Only southern blacks were hopeful that a new age of liberty and equality was dawning.

Reconstruction

The status of black people in American society had become a national obsession. Were they to remain beasts of burden, slaves in everything but name, or were they to become full citizens protected by the Constitution?

Radical Republicans wanted to elevate the political status of southern blacks. Supporters of high tariffs, federal internal improvements, free homesteads in the West, and free soil, the Republicans had been unpopular in the South long before the war, but to keep control of the federal government, they had to construct a southern political base. Former slaves would be the new constituency; the party of Lincoln, of freedom, would become the party of equality. By giving blacks the right to vote and hold public office, the Republicans intended to preserve their ascendancy. Only then could they be sure that Congress would pass the tariffs and subsidies the business community needed. Northern businessmen were also looking to the South as an economic colony, a source of raw materials and a market for finished products. Interested in the coal, iron, tobacco, cotton, and railroad industries of the South, northern investors wanted southern state legislatures to be Republican and pro-business. And many former abolitionists, now active among the Radical Republicans, wanted freedom converted into civil rights for the former slaves. Politics, economics, and ideology all combined to create a movement for black political liberty.

Thus during the Reconstruction period, the late 1860s and 1870s, Radical Republicans insisted on political rights for 4 million blacks. In March 1865 Congress created the Freedmen's Bureau to help blacks make the transition to freedom. The bureau sent thousands of doctors, nurses, lawyers, social workers, teachers, and administrative agents into the South to provide emergency food, jobs, housing, medical care, and legal aid to former slaves. Many white southerners hated the bureau and called its agents "carpetbaggers," but the bureau played an invaluable role in the South. The Thirteenth Amendment, ratified in December 1865, extended the Emancipation Proclamation to the border states. Slavery was ended. Early in 1866 Congress passed the Civil Rights Act outlawing discrimination on the basis or race, and two years later the Fourteenth Amendment gave black people citizenship and prohibited states from interfering with their civil liberties. In 1870 the Fifteenth Amendment gave blacks the right to vote.

White southerners fought back. Some states elected former Confederate authorities to local and state offices. Mississippi refused to ratify the Thirteenth Amendment and was joined by Georgia, Texas, and Virginia in postponing ratification of the Fourteenth Amendment. State legislatures enacted "black codes" segregating blacks in schools and public facilities, prohibiting them from carrying firearms or changing jobs, imposing strict vagrancy and curfew regulations on them, and making it virtually impossible for them to enter the skilled trades or the professions. In July 1866, when several hundred blacks and Unionists held a rally in New Orleans to protest the Louisiana black code, state troops moved in and shot two hundred demonstrators, killing forty of them.

Organized in 1865, the Ku Klux Klan relied on shootings, lynchings, torture, and intimidation to terrorize southern blacks into political submission.

The presence of Union troups guaranteed Reconstruction. More than 700,000 black adult males received the right to vote in 1870, and along with the "carpetbaggers" (northerners living in the South) and "scalawags" (white southerners in the Republican party), they took over every southern government except Virginia's. Sixteen blacks, including Hiram Revels and Blanche Bruce of Mississippi, entered the United States Congress, and hundreds of others took seats in the legislatures of South Carolina, North Carolina, Louisiana, Mississippi, Alabama, Arkansas, and Florida. Yet blacks never dominated any state government, even though this period has been called "Black Reconstruction."

Reconstruction governments in the South have sometimes been criticized as corrupt and incompetent. There was some corruption, to be sure, but the Reconstruction legislatures built the South's first public school system, eliminated debt imprisonment and property requirements for voting, repaired war-destroyed public buildings and roads, rebuilt railroads, repealed the black codes, enacted homestead laws, and tried to end discrimination in public facilities. Southern state governments were responding to the needs of poor people as well as rich, black as well as white.

Reconstruction collapsed as soon as Union troops left the South; blacks did not have the economic independence to survive politically. Radical Republicans had worried about black economic status and had even considered breaking up the plantations and distributing land among black families. But the confiscation schemes never made it through Congress, probably because they so clearly represented an assault on private property. Although blacks had gained the right to vote, they were economically dependent on propertied whites. When the troops left, whites exploited that dependence.

Nor were Republicans as concerned in 1877 about southern blacks as they had been in 1865. Politically they felt more secure about the future because new states were entering the Union. Nevada had become a state in 1864, and Nebraska followed three years later. Colorado received statehood in 1876, and the Dakotas, Montana, Washington, Idaho, Wyoming, and Utah would soon apply. Republican members of Congress from the new states would more than make up for the loss of the black vote in the South. Removal of federal troops, disfranchisement of black Republicans, and the resurrection of the white aristocracy no longer seemed so potentially disastrous. Northern businessmen began to think their economic interests might best be served by white Democrats. The momentum for black political rights evaporated. By 1877 the federal government had withdrawn its troops and whites were back in power in the South. Reconstruction was over, and black voters would soon fall victim to poll taxes, literacy tests, and white primaries.

During Reconstruction southern blacks had to adjust to their new freedom, and most did so simply by struggling to create a stable family life based upon legal marriages, reunions, the purchase of land and education. When the Union armies entered the South, they had established "contraband" camps where escaped slaves could live. Although the camps were makeshift and run by white soldiers who were often openly racist, blacks used the camps enthusiastically to begin their new lives. At the Fortress Monroe, Craney Island, and City Point camps mass ceremonies were held to legalize slave marriages. Blacks longed for the sanctity and stability of family life which legal marriage held out for them. They also wanted desperately to find family members who had been sold away. One slave song proclaimed:

> I've got a wife, and she's got a baby
> Way up North in Lower Canady—
> Won't dey shout when dey see Ole Shady
> Comin', Comin',! Hail, mighty day.
> Den away, Den away, for I can't stay any longer:
> Hurrah, Hurrah! for I am going home.*

Black newspapers abounded with personal classified ads of people trying to locate loved ones. One reason black people wandered so widely throughout the South after emancipation was not because they were irresponsible or did not want to work but because they were searching for parents, spouses, and children. Family reunion was the first task of freedom. Next came land and education. Thousands sacrificed to acquire their own farms, despite opposition from local whites, and tens of thousands supported Freedmen's Bureau schools to help educate their children. Emancipation held out the hope of a normal life in the United States, and southern blacks were determined to have it.

SUGGESTED READINGS

Absug, Robert H. "The Black Family During Reconstruction." In Nathan Huggins, ed. *Key Issues in the Afro-American Experience*. New York: 1971.
Belz, Herman. *A New Birth of Freedom: The Republican Party and Freedmen Rights, 1861–1866*. Westport, Conn.: 1976.

* Frank Moore, ed., *The Rebellion Record*, 11 vols. (New York, 1862-1864), 8:63.

Berlin, Ira. *Slaves Without Masters: The Free Negro in the Antebellum South.* New York: 1975.

Berry, Mary F. *Military Necessity and Civil Rights: Black Citizenship and the Constitution.* New York: 1977.

Berwanger, Eugene H. *The Frontier Against Slavery.* Urbana, Ill.: 1967.

Blassingame, John W. *The Slave Community: Plantation Life in the Antebellum South.* New York: 1972.

Brown, W. W. *Life of William Wells Brown, a Fugitive Slave.* Boston: 1848.

Cox, Lawanda, and Cox, John H. "Negro Suffrage and Republican Politics: The Problem in Reconstruction Historiography." *Journal of Southern History*, 33 (August 1967), 303–330.

Davis, David Brion. *The Problem of Slavery in the Age of Revolution: 1770–1823.* Ithaca, N.Y.: 1975.

Dillard, J. L. *Black English.* New York: 1972.

Douglass, Frederick. *Life and Times of Frederick Douglass.* New York: 1941.

Elkins, Stanley. *Slavery: A Problem in American Intellectual and Institutional Life.* Chicago: 1959.

Fischer, Roger. "Racial Segregation in Antebellum New Orleans." *American Historical Review*, 74 (February 1969), 926–937.

Fogel, Robert W., and Engerman, Stanley L. *Time on the Cross: The Economics of American Negro Slavery.* Boston: 1974.

Frazier, E. Franklin. *The Negro Family in the United States.* Chicago: 1939.

Frederickson, George M. *The Black Image in the White Mind: The Debate on Afro American Character and Destiny, 1817–1914.* New York: 1971.

Genovese, Eugene. *The Political Economy of Slavery.* New York: 1965.

———. *Roll, Jordan, Roll: The World the Slaves Made.* New York: 1974.

———. *The World the Slaveowners Made.* New York: 1971.

Gerteis, Louis S. *From Contraband to Freedom: Federal Policy Toward Southern Blacks, 1861–1865.* Westport, Conn.: 1973.

Gutman, Herbert G. *The Black Family in Slavery and Freedom, 1750–1920.* New York: 1976.

———. *Work, Culture, and Society in Industrializing America.* New York: 1976.

Levine, Lawrence W. *Black Culture and Black Consciousness: Afro-American Folk Thought from Slavery to Freedom.* New York: 1977.

Litwack, Leon. *North of Slavery: The Negro in the Free States, 1790–1860.* Chicago: 1961.

MacLeod, Duncan J. *Slavery, Race, and the American Revolution.* London: 1974.

Matthews, Donald G. *Slavery and Methodism: A Chapter in American Morality, 1780–1845.* Princeton, N.J.: 1965.

Muraskin, William A. *Middle Class Blacks in a White Society: Prince Hall Freemasonry in America.* Berkeley, Cal.: 1975.

Northrup, Solomon. *Twelve Years a Slave.* New York: 1853.

Owens, Leslie Howard. *This Species of Property: Slave Life and Culture in the Old South.* New York: 1976.

Quarles, Benjamin. *Black Abolitionists.* New York: 1969.

Rawick, George P. *From Sundown to Sunup: The Making of the Black Community*. Westport, Conn.: 1972.

Rice, C. Duncan. *The Rise and Fall of Black Slavery*. Baton Rouge, La.: 1975.

Robinson, Donald L. *Slavery in the Structure of American Politics, 1765–1820*. New York: 1971.

Sernett, Milton C. *Black Religion and American Evangelism: White Protestants, Plantation Missions, and the Flowering of Negro Christianity, 1787–1865*. Metuchen, N.J.: 1975.

Smith, Elbert B. *The Death of Slavery: The United States, 1837–1865*. Chicago: 1967.

Stampp, Kenneth. *The Peculiar Institution: Slavery in the Antebellum South*. New York: 1956.

Williamson, Joel. *After Slavery: The Negro in South Carolina During Reconstruction, 1861–1877*. Chapel Hill, N.C.: 1965.

Yetman, Norman. *Life Under the Peculiar Institution*. New York: 1970.

Zilversmit, Arthur. *The First Emancipation: Abolition in the North*. Chicago: 1967.

Chapter Eleven

Cultural Fusion: Mexican-Americans, 1519–1848

Mexican-American history began when Siberian hunters slowly scattered across the Western Hemisphere; those who settled central Mexico developed one of the most advanced cultures in the New World. When Hernando Cortez entered Tenochtitlán, he came upon the last in a series of sophisticated Indian cultures in Mesoamerica. Mayan civilization was the first. Between 1500 B.C. and 700 A.D. the Mayans developed a sedentary life based on corn cultivation, twenty-five city states, an effective medium of exchange, a fine transportation network, good educational programs, and an excellent water delivery system. Using slash-and-burn methods they cleared the dense tropical jungle and raised surpluses of corn, beans, peppers, tomatoes, and squash.

The Mayan social structure was specialized into priest, noble, warrior, free farmer, and slave classes. Mayan achievements included a hieroglyphic writing system, use of the zero in mathematics, several accurate calendars, water reservoirs, causeways, temples, pyramids, roads, and astronomical observatories. The Mayans mined gold and silver, cut and polished precious gems, wove cotton into richly elaborate textiles, and created expressive pottery, murals, and mosaics. During the years of Mayan ascendancy Mesoamerica stood with the Near East, West Africa, and the Indus River Valley as a cradle of civilization.

Around 800 A.D., because of overpopulation, soil exhaustion, or both, Mayan cities declined, roads fell into disrepair, and tropical jungles reclaimed the corn fields. The Toltecs then rose to power. In architecture and metallurgy, if not in mathematics and science, they rivaled the Mayans, and their serpent god Quetzalcoatl was worshiped throughout Mexico and South America. Brilliant at its peak, Toltec civilization declined as quickly as it had developed. In the fourteenth century the Aztecs, coming from a region in northern Mexico (the fabled Aztlán), conquered the Toltecs, settled in the valleys, and built the city of Tenochtitlán. Eventually the Aztec empire had several urban centers and governed nearly 9 million people. The Aztecs flourished by clearing the land, irrigating the fields, terracing the hillsides, and constructing artificial islands in lakes. They raised corn, beans, tobacco, squash, tomatoes, potatoes, chili, and cotton; collected mangoes, papayas, and avocados; and domesticated dogs and turkeys. When Montezuma II assumed the throne in 1502, Aztec civilization was among the most advanced in the world.

The Spanish Origins

Spain was then one of the most dynamic nations in Europe. The marriage between Isabella of Castile and Ferdinand of Aragon in 1469 had created a national dynasty, and over the next twenty years they subdued the nobility and united Spain. After a final victory at Granada in 1492, they expelled the Moors from the Iberian peninsula, ending an ethnic, religious, and political crusade which had lasted for 800 years. They then looked beyond Spain to new opportunities for wealth and prestige.

During the 1400s Portugal controlled commerce along the African coast and Italians monopolized the Near East trade. Spain considered diplomacy and even war to break those cartels until geographers suggested circling the globe. Reach the East, they said, by sailing west. To assert its national glory, outdo the Portuguese, and destroy the Italian monopoly, Spain conducted worldwide explorations. Columbus discovered the Bahamas, Cuba, and Haiti in 1492, and in three subsequent voyages explored Central America and the northern coast of South America. In 1499 and 1500 Alonso de Ojeda, Juan de la Cosa, and Peralonso Niña went to northern Venezuela and the Gulf of Maracaibo, and in 1513 Vasco de Balboa discovered the Pacific Ocean and Juan Ponce de León entered Florida. In 1519 Ferdinand Magellan began the circumnavigation of the globe, and Hernando Cortez and seven hundred men invaded Mexico. Spanish guns and horses gave Cortez military advantages, and Indian belief in the return of a bearded white deliverer provided an awesome, if temporary, psychological advantage. The Aztecs' policy of exacting tribute and their practice of human sacrifice had left them with bitter enemies throughout Mexico. Cortez shrewdly exploited these enmities, using Aztec foes against Montezuma's forces. In two years Montezuma was dead and the Aztec empire crushed. Between 1521 and 1540 Spain extended its authority throughout central and southern Mexico.

Spanish Catholicism was a complex affair, reflecting the nationalism of the new monarchs, the missionary zeal of humble friars, and the fanatical commitment of the *Reconquista* (the reconquest of Spain from the Moors). Ferdinand and Isabella ordered the Spanish clergy to purify themselves and preach the gospel for the glory of God and Spain. Claiming divine authority in the New World, they hoped to convert Indians and glorify Spain.

The Spaniards also hoped to take Indian land and use their labor. The *encomienda* and the *hacienda* dominated the economic relationship between Spaniards and Indians. Technically the encomienda was a feudal covenant in which a Spaniard provided military protection and religious instruction to Indians in return for work. Encomienda Indians became an exploited lower class in Mexico, laboring on farms, ranches, sugar mills, construction projects, and mines. Catastrophic declines in the native population, however, destroyed the encomienda. Between 1519 and 1600 measles, smallpox, diphtheria, whooping cough, and influenza reduced the Indian population from approximately 25 million to about 1 million. With less labor to exploit, Spaniards shifted from a labor-intensive to a land-intensive economy, gradually taking abandoned Indian property. Haciendas, or landed estates, replaced the encomiendas in the seventeenth century. Native civilization deteriorated, with Indians living at subsistence levels, tied to the haciendas by economic dependence and debt peonage, and by force when necessary.

The class structure reflected ethnic divisions. At the top were white European families, divided into Spanish-born *peninsulares* and Mexican-born *criollos*. At the bottom were Indian and black slaves, peons, and encomienda laborers. In between were *mestizos* — offspring of Spanish and Indian parents. In the 1500s less than 10 percent of the colonists were women, so sexual contact between Spanish men and Indian women was common. The few mestizos born in wedlock were raised as Spaniards, part of the first criollo generation. Illegitimate mestizos remained in the Indian villages. They were ethnically distinct, neither Catholic nor Aztec, Spanish nor Indian. During the sixteenth century a mestizo middle class gradually emerged, caught between the white peak and the Indian base of the social structure. Mestizos eventually became the largest group in Mexico. Children of Spanish and mestizo parents were known as *castizos*, and functioned on the periphery of the upper class; mestizos married mestizos, enlarging the middle class; and other mestizos married Indians and stayed in the lower class.

In the towns and cities mestizos were domestic servants to criollos and peninsulares or unskilled dock and construction workers. Some became overseers on the haciendas, or cowboys, sheepherders, or miners. Others were artisans. Thousands more became soldiers, salesmen, and small businessmen. Not as rich as whites but not as poor as Indians, they were a unique consequence of the New World colonies—a new ethnic group.

The Borderlands: Expansion Northward

Late in the sixteenth century New Spain began expanding north and northwest. Catholic missionaries, mestizo soldiers, and Mexican-Indians carried out the borderlands colonization. Expeditions searched for gold, and conquest of local Indians became the first stage in the settlement process. Priests then moved in and established missions, taught Spanish and Catholicism to the Indians, and started farms. The final stage began when soldiers remained in the north after their tour of duty. To service them, artisans and merchants settled near the missions and *presidios* (military outposts). Upper-class criollo or peninsulare women did not migrate, so mestizos became dominant, in numbers at least.

What is now New Mexico became the first borderlands colony. Rumors of the fabulously wealthy "Seven Cities of Cibola" had circulated in New Spain since 1519, and when Cabeza de Vaca returned from his ill-fated expedition to Florida in 1536, he amplified the excitement by spreading stories of gold-laden Indian societies to the north. In 1539 Fray Marcos de Niza explored western New Mexico in search of the cities, and Francisco Coronado searched between 1540 and 1542. In 1581 several Franciscan friars began proselytizing the Indians in the north, and their labors continued well into the nineteenth century. Finally, geopolitical concerns inspired expansion. The Pacific voyages of Sir Francis Drake in the 1570s convinced Spain that England had located the legendary Northwest Passage; and to forestall any English presence in the area, New Spain sent colonists to New Mexico.

Dominican missionaries established the city of Santa Fe in 1609. When rich mineral deposits were not discovered, the missionary impulse became dominant. By 1680 New Mexico had more than twenty-five missions, encompassing nearly a hundred villages and seventy-five thousand Indians. But Chief Popé and the Pueblos slaughtered hundreds of colonists and captured Sante Fe in 1680, which retarded the development of New Mexico for decades. Not until 1692, after twelve years of bitter fighting, did the Spaniards reconquer New Mexico, and it was not until 1706 that they founded Albuquerque. More than a thousand colonists died in the Yaqui rebellion of 1740.

Because of the danger of Indian attacks, the colonists lived in villages along the major rivers where water and presidios supported life. A cultural symbiosis occurred there. Like the Indians, the *nuevos mexicanos* (Mexican settlers) cultivated corn, beans, squash, and chili, but they added cotton and fruit, which the Indians quickly adopted. From the Indians the Spanish learned about irrigation and in return taught the Indians to raise sheep. Spaniards built churches in the Indian communities, and the Indians learned to speak Spanish and worship Christ. Still, life was provincial in' New Mexico, and in 1800 there were only eight thousand Mexican settlers there—a well-to-do landowning class and an impoverished class of mestizo workers.

Present-day Arizona was settled more slowly because of the hostility of the Apaches and Navajos and the lack of water. The Jesuit priest Eusebio Francisco Kino led a missionary expedition deep into western Arizona in 1687. He worked closely with the Pima Indians and established a mission near Tucson after the turn of the century. The Arizona economy depended on subsistence agriculture and sheep grazing, and the people lived in fortified towns, but with only two thousand colonists the settlement remained underdeveloped throughout the Spanish colonial period.

Spanish colonization in what is now Texas began after the French explorations of the Jesuit Father Marquette and Louis Joliet in 1673 and of Sièur de La Salle in 1682 had opened the Mississippi River. To counter French influence, New Spain founded Nacogdoches in 1716 and San Antonio in 1718. Cattle and cotton became the bases of the Texas economy; and because of the weakness of local Indians, the colonists (known as *tejanos*) were more scattered than in New Mexico. A tense rivalry existed in Texas until 1763, when Spain took Louisiana from France. Without the French threat, Spain's desire to colonize Texas waned, and as late as 1800 only 3,500 Mexican settlers lived there.

The Spanish moved into California after hearing of Russian and English interest. José de Galvez, a royal official who visited Mexico in the 1760s, decided to colonize California and discourage England and Russia. The Franciscan priest Junipero Serra then left New Spain and founded San Diego in 1769. Franciscans had established twenty other missions by 1823, including Los Angeles, Santa Barbara, San Jose, and San Francisco. California's rich natural resources and temperate climate made it the most prosperous borderlands colony. With the avail-

An early Spanish mission in California. The Catholic church played a key role in the colonization of the borderlands. (Brown Brothers)

ability of good land and the Spanish inclination to make large land grants, the *ranchos* became powerful, independent economic units, much like the Mexican haciendas. Catholic missions and private ranchos dominated the California economy, producing corn, wheat, cotton, grapes, fruit, beans, hogs, sheep, and cattle. The *californio* upper class consisted of large landowners and the clergy; the *cholo* middle class of mestizo workers, soldiers, small farmers, and new settlers; and the lowest class of impoverished California Indians.

Borderlands society differed substantially from that of New Spain. A sparse population of only 25,000 people were living there in 1800, and the criollo and mestizo classes were quite small. In comparison, New Spain had over 3 million Europeans, as did the United States, and in both places Europeans vastly outnumbered native Americans. Compared to New Spain and the North Atlantic colonies, the borderlands were provincial, subsistence outposts of civilization.

The church was more dominant there than in New Spain. Lacking rich mines and encomiendas, the borderlands developed a subsistence economy under the control of the Catholic missions. The church was the primary educational institution as well. In California, New Mexico, and Texas the Indians spoke dozens of languages, and the priests were unable to master them all. Unlike the priests in Mexico, who had learned the Aztec dialects, borderlands friars had to teach Indians Spanish before theology, and their language instruction was as intense as their religious indoctrination.

The church was also the major agent of social change. Since the fifteenth century Spain had looked upon religious conversion as a civilizing force in the New World; but in the borderlands, native Americans appeared so "uncivilized," at least when compared to the Aztecs, that the "civilizing" role of the church assumed new importance. In California and Texas, where the Indians were nomadic, the mission congregated them in residential communities near the church, and they learned to raise crops and livestock, work in industry, speak Spanish, and become Christians.

From Spain to Mexico to the United States, 1810–1848

During the colonial period an immense social chasm developed between peninsulares and criollos. Resentment of peninsulare Spaniards was so intense in New Spain that Indians, criollos, and mestizos subordinated their own ethnic differences in a united assault on European imperialism.

Indians had always resented the power, insensitivity, and self-righteousness of the Spanish settlers. The Zacatecas led the Mixton Rebellion in 1541 and 1542, killing hundreds of colonists; food riots among the Indians led to the burning and looting of government buildings in Mexico City in 1624; the revolt of Popé in 1680 nearly destroyed New Mexico; the Indians in Nuevo León rebelled in 1704, as did the Yaquis of New Mexico in 1740; Mayans revolted in the Yucatán in 1761; and in 1802 the Mariano Rebellion broke out in Tepic province. When the general uprising against Spain began in 1810, Mexican-Indians participated enthusiastically.

Criollo resentment was both social and political. For centuries peninsulares had considered criollos crude and unsophisticated and denied them political power. Although criollos obtained land and succeeded commercially, economic power did not translate into social or political influence because peninsulares controlled most positions in the government, army, and clergy. Despite their numerical superiority, criollos felt powerless, and late in the 1700s they began forming insurgent groups and talking of political separation from Spain.

Mestizos too were weary of Spanish domination and yearned for important civil and religious positions. Peninsulares, they believed, had no real interest in Mexico beyond enhancing their political careers. Resentful of elites, some mestizos looked upon peninsulares as the backbone of an exploitive upper class; removal of Spanish authority might lead to male suffrage, separation of church and state, and full civil liberties. Some even hoped for an economic revolution that would break up the large estates and distribute them among the poor. Mestizo cooperation with criollos was expedient at best, since the criollos too were seen as part of the upper class, but mestizos were nevertheless willing to join forces against Spain.

In 1810 Father Miguel Hidalgo, the criollo son of a hacienda manager, led a revolt against Spain. As a parish priest in Dolores, Mexico, Hidalgo had grown close to the Indians and empathized with their plight. Frustrated at the gap between the rich and the poor and the arrogance of peninsulare rulers, Hidalgo led a march of fifty thousand people southward toward Mexico City. Along the way several criollo landowners were killed. Although Hidalgo's army reached the outskirts of the capital, Spanish troops defeated them; and because of the antirich sentiments of some of his supporters, he received no support from conservative criollos. In 1811 he was executed.

José María Morelos, an associate of Hidalgo, took up the revolutionary banner one year later. An uncompromisingly liberal mestizo, Morelos declared independence from Spain after taking military control of much of southern Mexico. He convened a congress which called for universal suffrage and the abolition of slavery, racial discrimination, and Indian tribute taxes. But like Hidalgo, Morelos angered criollos who worried more about revolution from below than repression from above, and Catholic prelates who sensed a threat to the church's vast property holdings. Without the support of criollos or the church, Morales was doomed, and in 1815 Spanish authorities captured and executed him.

An army revolt at Cádiz in 1820 precipitated a liberal revolution in Spain, and the new government abolished the Inquisition, took control of church tithes, outlawed ecclesiastical courts, granted civil liberties, ordered new elections to the Cortes (Spain's national legislature), and nationalized much church property. Conservative criollos and church leaders in Mexico awakened from their apathy, joined with the Indian and mestizo remnants of the older revolutionary movements, and called for independence from Spain. Augustine de Iturbide emerged as the criollo leader; his was a counterrevolution designed to preserve aristocratic privileges, and in 1821 he proclaimed Mexican independence. But Iturbide's coalition was too volatile: Indians and mestizos despised his conservatism. He wanted to stop the revolution after the expulsion of Spanish officials and had no desire to see it extend into economic affairs. In fact, Iturbide wanted to install a native monarchy. Facing intense liberal opposition, Iturbide resigned in 1823, and Guadalupe Victoria then came to power.

Rebellion was already brewing in the borderlands. Mexican liberals and conservatives had cooperated politically to destroy peninsulare dominance, but success exposed their differences. The conservatives were wealthy landowners, a political and social elite who believed in rule by the rich, the unity of church and state, and a strong central government. Liberals, mostly new businessmen and the lower classes, favored a weak federal government, strong provincial governments, separation of church and state, and extension of the suffrage. After Iturbide's resignation, the liberal government secularized the missions, nationalized church property, outlawed mandatory tithe paying, and suppressed ecclesiastical courts. These reforms spurred conservatives to depose the liberal government in 1834 and install Antonio López de Santa Anna. He weakened the provinces by abolishing their legislatures, restricting the powers of municipal governments, and ousting local officials. Upset about the loss of local power, provincial leaders in the borderlands began considering rebellion against Mexico.

Their restlessness coincided with Anglo-American expansion. Between 1820 and 1848 thousands of Americans settled in the Southwest. The Santa Fe trail opened in 1822, and the economic relationship between the borderlands and central Mexico changed dramatically; it was easier now to obtain goods from the United States than from central Mexico. Nuevos mexicanos began drawing closer to the United States. A similar situation developed in California during the 1820s and 1830s, when American settlers established farms in the rich central valleys and merchants and shippers crowded into San Francisco to profit from the Pacific trade. Mexico encouraged American immigration during the 1820s by giving large land grants in Texas to men such as Stephen Austin. There were more than twenty-five thousand Americans in eastern Texas by 1830. Some married into local families, but most looked down upon Mexicans as inferiors. American political loyalties flowed east to Washington, D. C., not south to Mexico City.

A coalition of discontented mestizos and Americans developed in all the borderland colonies. Texas was the first province to revolt against Mexico, and the rebellion there set in motion a chain reaction that eventually brought New Mexico and California into the United States. Attracted by the rich bottomlands of east Texas, thousands of settlers crossed the Louisiana border during the 1820s and started hundreds of cotton plantations. Mexican officials had encouraged the early settlers, but they became alarmed at the size of the immigration. To discourage American settlement, Mexico prohibited the importation of slaves into Texas and established customs houses and military presidios along the Texas-Louisiana border in 1830. But it was too late. After the conservative revolt of 1834 in Mexico City, Texans declared their independence. Despite an initial defeat at the Alamo mission in San Antonio in March 1836, a combined Texas army of Anglo-Americans and tejanos, under the command of Sam Houston, defeated Santa Anna at the Battle of

San Jacinto a month later. The subsequent Treaty of Velasco, which Santa Anna was forced to sign but Mexico never recognized, granted independence to Texas.

The Republic of Texas was not admitted to the Union for nine years, however, because many northern congressmen feared that five slave states might eventually emerge out of the area and give the south control of the Senate. But by 1845 the new expansionist Manifest Destiny ideology, which called for American sovereignty over the entire continent, had overcome all reluctance to accepting Texas. In 1845, in a joint session of Congress, the United States annexed the Lone Star Republic. Texas became the twenty-eighth state of the Union.

Mexico immediately severed diplomatic relations with the United States, but despite the breach between the two countries, late in 1845 President James K. Polk decided to try to purchase New Mexico and California. When Mexico bluntly refused, Polk ordered American troops into Texas south of the Nueces River hoping to create a military emergency. It was a pretext for acquiring the rest of the Southwest. After a brief clash between Mexican and American forces in a disputed area of southern Texas in May 1846, President Polk claimed that "Mexico . . . shed American blood upon American soil," and Congress declared war.

California and New Mexico became United States territories soon afterward. On the eve of the war a group of Anglo-American and Mexican leaders in California, upset about the conservative triumph in Mexico, declared independence and launched the Bear Flag Revolt. When American military forces entered California, the revolt merged with the larger conflict, becoming one theater in the war with Mexico. American businessmen in Santa Fe convinced nuevo mexicano colleagues that the province would be more prosperous under American control, and when General Stephen Kearny arrived in 1846 he met no resistance.

After months of bitter fighting, triumphant American troops entered Mexico City; and on February 2, 1848, the two nations signed the Treaty of Guadalupe Hidalgo. For $15 million the United States acquired California, Arizona, New Mexico, Nevada, Utah, and part of Colorado, and Mexico recognized American title to Texas. Manifest Destiny had triumphed.

Eighty thousand more people now lived in the United States. Concerned about the fate of Spanish-speaking mestizo Catholics in a white Protestant society, Mexican officials had inserted several guarantees into the Treaty of Guadalupe Hidalgo. Mexicans in the ceded territory had a year to decide their loyalties; if at the end of the year they had not declared their intentions, they would automatically receive United States citizenship. Only two thousand crossed the border; the others became Mexican-Americans. Article IX, as well as a statement of protocol issued later, guaranteed their civil liberties, religious freedom, and title to their property. Despite the guarantees, however, the Fourteenth Amendment was still twenty years in the future. Although the federal government had promised a great deal, it had little authority to enforce its will in the states. An ethnic and religious minority in the Southwest, Mexican-Americans would have difficulty enjoying their promised liberties.

SUGGESTED READINGS

Acuña, Rodolfo. *Occupied America: The Chicano Struggle Toward Liberation*. San Francisco: 1972.

Barker, Eugene C. *Mexico and Texas, 1821–1835*. New York: 1965.

Bolton, Herbert E. *Rim of Christendom*. New York: 1936.

———. *The Spanish Borderlands*. New Haven, Conn.: 1921.

Burland, C. A. *The Gods of Mexico*. New York: 1968.

Carter, Hodding. *Doomed Road of Empire*. New York: 1971.

Caso, Alfonso. *The Aztecs: People of the Sun*. Norman, Oklahoma: 1958.

Faulk, Odie B. *The Land of Many Frontiers*. New York: 1968.

Forbes, Jack. *Apache, Navaho, and Spaniard*. Norman, Oklahoma: 1960.

Gibson, Charles, *The Aztecs Under Spanish Rule*. New York: 1964.

———. *Spain in America*. New York: 1966.

Gladwin, Harold S. *A History of the Ancient Southwest*. Portland, Me.: 1957.

Grebler, L., Moore, J. W., and Gusman, R. S. *The Mexican American People*. New York: 1970.

Hallenbeck, Cleve. *Spanish Missions of the Old Southwest*. New York: 1926.

Hammond, George P. *The Treaty of Guadalupe Hidalgo, 1848*. Berkeley, Cal.: 1949.

Jones, Oakah L. *Pueblo Warriors and Spanish Conquest*. Norman, Oklahoma: 1966.

Lang, James. *Conquest and Commerce: Spain and England in the Americas*. New York: 1975.

Leon-Portilla, Miguel. *The Broken Spears*. Boston: 1962.

Lowrie, Samuel H. *Culture Conflict in Texas, 1821–1835*. New York: 1932.

Marshall, C. E. "The Birth of the Mestizo in New Spain." *Hispanic American Historical Review*, 19 (February-December 1939), 161–184.

Meier, Matt S., and Rivera, Feliciano. *The Chicanos: A History of Mexican Americans*. New York: 1972.

Meinig, Donald W. *Southwest: Three Peoples in Geographical Change, 1600–1970*. New York: 1971.

Moquin, Wayne. *A Documentary History of the Mexican Americans*. New York: 1971.

178 • American Adolescence, 1776–1890

Paz, Octavio. *The Labyrinth of Solitude*. New York: 1961.
Perrigo, Lynn. *The American Southwest*. New York: 1971.
Peterson, Frederick. *Ancient Mexico*. New York: 1959.
Price, Glenn W. *Origins of the War with Mexico: The Polk-Stockton Intrigue*. Austin, Texas: 1967.
Ramos, Samuel. *Profile of Man and Culture in Mexico*. Austin, Texas: 1962.
Riesenberg, Felix. *The Golden Road: The Story of California's Mission Trail*. New York: 1962.
Sanchez, George I. *Forgotten People: A Study of New Mexico*. Albuquerque, N.M.: 1940.
Simpson, Leslie B. *Many Mexicos*. Berkeley, Cal.: 1967.
Spicer, Edward H. *Cycles of Conquest: The Impact of Spain, Mexico, and the United States on the Indians of the Southwest, 1533–1960*. Tucson, Arizona: 1961.
Stoddard, Ellwyn R. *Mexican Americans*. New York: 1973.
Vaillant, George C. *The Aztecs of Mexico*. Garden City, N.Y.: 1962.

Chapter Twelve

Asia in America: The Chinese Immigrants

Emigration has long been a part of Chinese history. As early as the seventh century farmers looking for new land crossed the Taiwan Strait and settled on the island of Taiwan. During the Ming period (1368–1644) people from the coastal provinces of South China fanned out to the Philippines, Southeast Asia, and the East Indies. And as the New World opened, they went to Mexico, Brazil, Peru, and Canada. Eventually perhaps 10 million Chinese scattered throughout the world, and between the gold rush of 1849 and the Chinese Exclusion Act of 1882 nearly three hundred thousand, most of them from Kwangtung (Canton) Province in southeastern China, came to the United States. Ostracized socially, isolated culturally, and faithful to their values, the Chinese immigrants would have an extraordinary experience in the United States, one marked by pain as well as triumph.

Most of the nineteenth-century Chinese immigrants came from the Sunwui, Toishan, Hoiping, and Yanping districts of Kwangtung. Kwangtung is noted for hot monsoon summers and cool winters. With most of the soil arable. Kwangtung farmers raised rice on the wet, flat coastal plain, where seventy inches of rain fell annually. Sugar cane was an important cash crop, and so were mulberry leaves for the silk industry. Pears, organges, plums, mangoes, peaches, and pineapples grew in the mountains. Except for the cities of Canton (Kwangchow), Hong Kong, and Macao, Kwangtung was a rural, agrarian society where peasant families had tilled the land for millennia.

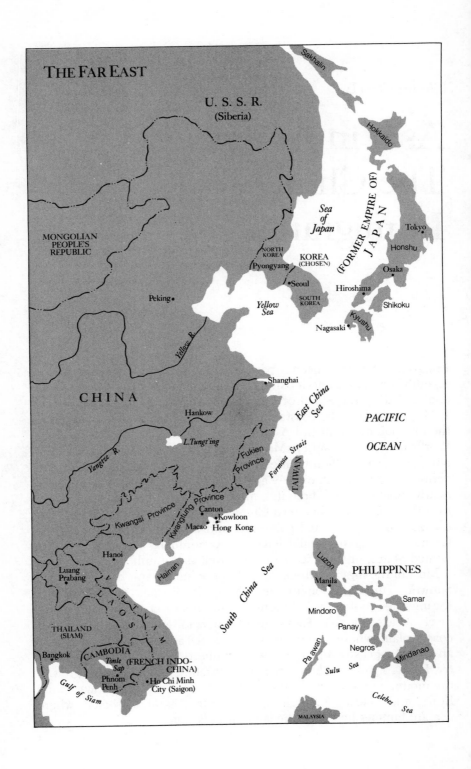

In spite of the land's fertility and its intensive use, life was a struggle. There were more than 400 million people in China in 1850, and population density along the coast averaged more than a thousand people per square mile. Agricultural techniques were primitive, and with only one-third of an acre to feed each person, production never satisfied demand. Even when the harvest was good, rice had to be imported. Frequent river flooding and periodic crop failures further beset peasant life.

There were ethnic problems as well. The Cantonese were natives of the Kwangtung delta who considered themselves superior to other groups. They controlled the economic and political machinery of the province. The Hakka (guest people) had immigrated from North China in the thirteenth century and were culturally and linguistically distinct from the Cantonese. They lived in separate villages, resented the patronizing attitudes of the Cantonese, and had competed with them for hundreds of years. Finally, there were the Tanka, chronically poor fishermen, smugglers, and ferrymen despised by Cantonese and Hakka alike. Social outcasts, the Tanka were prohibited from attending school or entering the civil service.

European imperialism created new problems. Since the seventeenth century, when Dutch merchants introduced opium to China, European traders had competed to supply the huge Asian demand for the drug. In the 1830s English merchants dominated the opium traffic, but Chinese officials wanted it to stop because they felt it was undermining the fiscal and moral base of China. When Chinese officials seized the English opium supplies at Canton in 1839, the British government sent military forces and occupied the city. After three years of intermittent conflict, the First Opium War ended when China signed the Treaty of Nanking. England imposed huge indemnities to pay for the war; took control of Hong Kong; and, on the principle of extraterritorialty, claimed the right to try all English criminals in China by British rather than Chinese law. It was a humiliating blow to Chinese pride.

The European presence disrupted traditional society. Christian missionaries preaching Jesus Christ and the church as a social institution challenged the Confucian emphasis on family authority. British textiles entered Kwangtung, ruined local producers, and vastly increased unemployment. Anglo-Chinese wars stimulated racial violence between the English and the native peasants. And the Taiping (Heavenly Peace) Rebellion in the 1850s devastated southeastern China. In one of the largest of China's many peasant revolts, Hung Hsiu-ch'üan, a Hakka student and a Protestant Christian convert, proclaimed himself the younger brother of Jesus Christ and led a mystical religious-military revolt against the Manchu authorities of Kwangsi Province, just north of

Kwangtung. Quickly spreading to Kwangtung, the rebellion turned into a general uprising of discontented scholars denied admission to the civil service (and thus consigned to a life of menial work); merchants resentful of taxes imposed by British officials; Cantonese residents suffering from economic disruptions; troubled peasants wanting land reform; democrats hoping to destroy political tyranny; and Hakkas planning to blunt the power of the Cantonese. It was a social catastrophe; the rebellion and its suppression completely destroyed the rural economy and killed more than 20 million people. Desperate peasants began looking beyond China for new opportunities.

But amidst all these upheavals the Chinese family continued to order peasant life. A basic institution of social control, the clan tied families together in village economies where property was held in common, graveyards administered, and ancestral halls maintained. Individuals subordinated their personal interests to the authority of the extended family, and kinship patterns of elder male dominance continued throughout life. Peasants were intensely loyal to the family: it supplied their reason for being. The disruptions of the mid-nineteenth century tested that loyalty, as peasant farmers became more and more hardpressed to support their families. In the end, family devotion pushed hundreds of thousands of peasants overseas.

Just as all these social and economic problems were developing in China, American merchants brought news of gold in California. Rumors spread, and the "Golden Mountain" and high wages in California seemed the answer to peasant troubles. The Chinese became sojourners, temporary immigrants who planned to work in America until they were fifty or sixty years old. Then they would return home bringing wealth and respect. During their years abroad, they hoped to make return visits to China several times, marry a woman selected by the clan, father many children, and help the family make ends meet. In America they would live frugally and send most of their money home to China. Emigration was not a turning away from their homeland but a defense of the family and the village, the only way to preserve the traditional order.

Chinese-American Society

By 1855 there were 20,000 Chinese immigrants in the United States, most of them in California. Of the 63,000 Chinese in America in 1870, more than 50,000 lived in California and nearly 10,000 in Idaho, Nevada, Oregon, and Washington. Ten years later there were 105,000 Chinese in America, 75,000 of them in California and 24,000 scattered throughout the western states. A few thousand Chinese immigrated to the Kingdom of Hawaii after the 1840s, and when the United States annexed Hawaii in 1898, they became Chinese-Americans.

Although a few Chinese merchants found work supervising American trade with Asia, most early Chinese came looking for gold and worked in the mines. But whenever they made a large strike, jealous white miners drove them off their claims. As mining became more expensive with the shift to hydraulic extraction, Chinese took jobs with the large mining companies. Thousands worked gold mines in Oregon, Idaho, and Montana; silver mines in Nevada and Arizona; and coal mines in Utah and Wyoming. Many Chinese were domestic servants, laundry workers, and restaurant owners; others were the backbone of the woolen, shoe and boot, and metal industries. After the Civil War the Central Pacific Railroad hired more than ten thousand Chinese workers to build the line from San Francisco to Utah. The Southern Pacific Railroad later employed them throughout the Southwest. Chinese could also be found building dams, levees, and irrigation systems in the San Joaquin and Sacramento River valleys. On the large wheat and fruit farms of California they were seasonal workers, the first generation of migratory laborers. Chinese truck gardeners and horticulturists were common in the West, and Chinese fishing villages dotted the Pacific coast, where they processed and sold salmon, sturgeon, halibut, bluefish, redfish, flounder, shrimp, and abalone.

Because the Chinese saw their move as temporary rather than permanent, they brought few women along—only one immigrant in twenty was female. It was not customary for a Chinese woman to leave her family, and the men believed they would soon be returning anyway. Theirs was a "bachelor society." Not surprisingly, because of the lack of women and because of their reasons for leaving home, the Chinese returned home far more frequently than European immigrants. But most conspicuous was the resiliency of their social structure—the central place afforded the family. The Chinese sense of identity was powerful. Family and kinship relations were far more personal and important than in European societies. In Kwangtung whole villages were often inhabited by one family. The patriarchal order was strong, and clans were the basic unit of the economy, society, and local government. Even in death, through ancestor worship, family lineage continued. Individuals, in terms of their origins and destiny, were indistinct from their family backgrounds.

Once in America the Chinese did everything possible to reconstruct familiar social and political institutions, not only to ease their adjustment to the New World but to maintain emotional ties to China. Traditional clans became important in America too. Because there were only 438 distinct family surnames in China, it was relatively easy for immigrants to identify their clan, and those who shared the same surname associated closely. Wei Bat Liu, an immigrant resident of San Francisco in 1913, remembered that

> all the cousins from the Liu family . . . had one big room . . . we slept in that room, cooked in that room, one room. Anybody who had a job had to sleep outside the room, because he could afford to rent space . . . for himself. Anybody who couldn't find work slept . . . in this room. At the end of the year, all the members would get together and figure out all the expenses . . . even the ones who didn't sleep were willing to pay . . .*

Leadership in China rested on village elders and the scholar-gentry; but since they did not migrate, the dominant figures in the immigrant communities were usually wealthy merchants. Stores were social centers for clan members as well as shelters for newcomers; merchants also offered charity to the old, the indigent, and the handicapped. Family elders in America served as proxy parents for new immigrants, and family associations provided guidance and discipline for the young. Clan ties directed settlement, and in the scattered colonies one or a few clans controlled local affairs. In San Francisco the Chan, Lee, and Wong families were dominant, as the Ong family was in Phoenix and the Chin family in Seattle. After World War II the Moi family rose to prominence in Chicago, and the Yee clan in Detroit and Cleveland.

Overlapping and transcending clan authority were *hui kuan* associations whose membership was determined by dialect and regional origins. Many different clans participated in each hui kuan, and these mutual aid societies played an important judicial role by mediating disputes between clans. In 1851 Cantonese immigrants in San Francisco formed the Sam Yup Company, a hui kuan association, and later in the year another group from Kwangtung established the See Yup Company. Chungsun immigrants formed the Yeong Wo Company and Hakka settlers the Yan Wo Company in 1852. The most powerful hui kuan association, the Ning Yeung Company, was formed in 1854, and in 1862 others organized the Hop Wo Company. Known as the Six Companies, these hui kuan functioned as a quasigovernment in Chinatown. They constructed large buildings to house their operations, and representatives of each company, after greeting new immigrants, would take them to the company's headquarters. During the immigrants' first weeks in America the companies found places for them to live, lent money, found jobs, cared for the sick, adjudicated disputes, and helped return

*Victor Nee and Brett deBarry, *Longtime Californin'* (New York, 1973), pp. 64–65.

the dead to China for burial. One immigrant recalled his greeting from the Six Companies upon arrival in San Francisco:

> One valuable lesson . . . which you will soon appreciate is that we must stick together . . . even though we are not kin. That is why we have formed . . . the Six Companies representing the six districts which most of us come from. . . . You will always find food and shelter here among us. . . . When you have earned money . . . you will pay dues into the company fund. This fund helps us to maintain the company headquarters and helps us set up an orderly system to take care of our own.*

In an age when public welfare was unknown, the Six Companies helped meet the social needs of Chinese immigrants.

Finally, there were the *tongs*. For more than a thousand years these secret associations had provided a form of social order independent of clan and hui kuan. Because of the tremendous loyalty expected in Chinese families, the country was atomized into hundreds of local elites lacking central direction. The Chinese could not unify because they were unable to transcend kinship, linguistic, and geographic differences. Secret societies, however, organized people without regard to these differences. People who failed civil service examinations joined tongs to get back at the government; angry tenants joined to punish landlords. During economic distress poor farmers, workers, and merchants joined to strike back at those who exploited them. In nineteenth-century China the tongs were a powerful social infrastructure—a clandestine linear system of political power organizing China along horizontal lines and helping to overcome family and language differences.

In America tong members chafed at the power of the merchant elite, whether clan or hui kuan leaders. The Suey Sing Tong repeatedly challenged the Wong family in San Francisco, and bloody battles between the On Yick Tong and the Yee clan were common. The secret societies were often involved in organized crime. In San Francisco's Chinatown the Hip Yee Tong, Chee Kung Tong, Wa Ting Tong, and On Leong Tong controlled gambling, prostitution, heroin, and opium traffic. Rival tongs fought wars to control illegal businesses, resisted bitterly when the Six Companies tried to stamp out crime, and at times violently confronted prominent clan leaders who opposed their activities. Where clans or hui kuan were weakly organized, tongs provided health care and life insurance, and welfare assistance to the sick, disabled, and unemployed. Along with the clans and hui kuan, the tongs

*Betty Lee Sung, *Mountain of Gold* (New York, 1967), pp. 24–25.

provided Chinese America with an invisible government based on district and family loyalty, fear, and piety.

The Chinese formed one of the most self-contained immigrant communities in America. Clans, hui kuan, and tongs exerted great authority, nearly as much as in China. At the same time, most Chinese lived in urban ghettos where they were physically as well as culturally isolated. Not permitted to naturalize, they could not vote and had little power in local politics. Without the need to court their votes, local politicians ignored them. As a result, the Chinese had extraordinary control over their own affairs; the clans, hui kuan, and tongs were the real political power in Chinatown. While other immigrants struggled to gain access to the political establishment, the Chinese lived in a social and political island.

The Anti-Chinese Crusade

As nonwhite, non-Christian, and non-Western immigrants, the Chinese frightened many Americans. Treated as "colored" people, they experienced the discrimination meted out to blacks, Indians, and Mexicans, and as a religious minority suffered the same indignities as German, Irish, and French-Canadian Catholics. And in addition, as non-Western people they seemed strange, different from all other immigrants. Despite the general decline of nativism during the Civil War, an anti-Chinese movement developed soon afterward.

In the early nineteenth century American traders and missionaries had passed on negative images of the Chinese. In addition to ridiculing Chinese tastes in food and music, Yankee traders living in China between 1780 and 1840 looked upon the Chinese as a backward people who were cruel, dishonest, immoral, and superstitious. And through sermons, books, magazines, and newspapers Protestant missionaries in China reinforced those images. To many Protestants the Buddhism, Taoism, and Confucianism of China were depraved religions and the Chinese faithful were heathens. Western society, with its emphasis on competitive individualism, embraced a monotheistic God and took an emotional, evangelical approach to religion, seeing human affairs as a struggle between good and evil. Coming from a communal, ascetic culture, the Chinese were polytheistic, accepting many gods and relying periodically on different ones for assistance; there were gods and goddesses of war, wealth, fertility, agriculture, and rain. The Chinese found devotion to one and only one God a particularly narrow-minded perspective. They were not at all in tune with sectarianism; instead they tolerated all faiths and were even able to accept the deities of other people. Ignored by most Chinese, the missionaries only became more convinced of "Oriental paganism." Finally, many missionaries spread pornographic rumors, saying that sexual licentiousness was widespread throughout the country.

During the Opium War Americans had sided with England and many rejoiced when China was defeated. The Taiping Rebellion reinforced the idea that the Chinese were uncivilized barbarians; so did the murder of Christian missionaries in Tientsin in 1870. These events in Asia served to increase American suspicions about the Chinese in the United States.

Nativism existed for economic reasons as well, especially among workers convinced that Chinese immigrants would depress wages and make jobs scarce. Businessmen, on the other hand, favored Chinese immigration as a source of cheap labor, and in 1868 business triumphed when Congress ratified the Burlingame Treaty, which permitted unrestricted immigration of Chinese laborers to work on the transcontinental railroad. But when the Union Pacific–Central Pacific Railroad was completed in 1869, ten thousand Chinese workers had to look for other jobs and competed directly with American workers. Many Americans believed all Chinese were "coolies," slave laborers controlled by contractors who had "shanghaied" them to the United States. To be sure, most Chinese did come under contract because they could not afford the passage, just as indentured servants had in the eighteenth century. But while many Chinese laborers who left Hong Kong and Macao for South America and the West Indies did work as slaves, contract workers in the United States were permitted complete freedom of movement as long as they paid monthly installments on their passage debt. Whenever there were wage cuts or unemployment, native workers held the Chinese responsible. Labor unions began demanding immigration restriction.

Social and cultural misgivings also surfaced. Many Americans believed stereotypes about Chinese proclivities for gambling, prostitution, and opium smoking, and the crowded, physically deteriorating conditions in San Francisco's Chinatown seemed a source of crime and unrest. The lack of Chinese women frightened people who believed Chinese men were sexually attracted to white women. The Chinese were believed to be spreading leprosy, venereal disease, and other illnesses. Finally, Chinese culture seemed strange. The immigrants believed China was the center of the earth, the highest expression of human civilization, and that Westerners were the barbarians. Not that they said so, but Americans were outraged anyway. They were also suspicious about the tongs, clans, and hui kuan that made the Chinese communities so autonomous. Most Americans viewed the Chinese as an alien group that would never assimilate. Demands for immigration restriction grew more intense.

Discrimination became more common. Between 1852 and 1860 several counties in northern California expelled Chinese miners; and as the mining frontier moved north into Oregon, Washington, and Idaho, similar measures were passed there as well. In the 1870s labor unions in California conducted anti-Chinese propaganda campaigns, and early in the 1880s the state legislature denied the use of California employment bureaus to the Chinese and prohibited them from working on dam, levee, or irrigation projects.

The Chinese encountered widespread social and civil discrimination. In 1854, for example, a white man was convicted of murder on the eyewitness testimony of a Chinese worker, but the California Supreme Court overturned the decision on the grounds that "Mongolians" could not testify against whites. After that it was difficult to prosecute whites for anti-Chinese violence, and the Chinese had no legal avenues to express grievances. California prohibited Chinese children from attending public schools in 1860; and although state courts later ordered "separate but equal" facilities, local school districts refused to build new schools for Chinese children. Harassment laws were common. One San Francisco law prohibited carrying baskets on long poles, a common practice in Chinatown, and in 1873 an ordinance required jailers to give short haircuts to all prisoners, cutting off the queues of Chinese men. Such laws resulted in second-class status for the Chinese in America.

Sporadic violence also occurred. On October 23, 1871, as Los Angeles police tried to end a feud about the status of a woman contractually bound as a worker to a hui kuan, two policemen were killed. Hearing the news, more than five hundred whites entered Chinatown, burned dozens of buildings, and lynched fifteen people. In 1876 a mob in Truckee, California, burned several Chinese homes and shot fleeing occupants. Ten months later vigilantes known as the Order of Caucasians murdered several Chinese in Chico, California. The 1877 riots in San Francisco destroyed thirty Chinese laundries. The worst race riot took place at Rock Springs, Wyoming, on September 2, 1885, when rampaging white miners murdered twenty-eight Chinese-Americans. Another riot occurred at Log Cabin, Oregon, in 1886. And individual muggings, beatings, and destruction of property were common.

As nativist fears mounted, the immigration restriction movement grew stronger. The Know-Nothing party called for an end to Chinese immigration, and in 1855 the California legislature passed a tax of fifty dollars for each Chinese worker brought into the state. Although difficult to enforce, the law's intent was clear. In 1870 California prohibited the immigration of Chinese women unless they could prove good char-

Anti-Chinese riots erupted in Denver, Colorado, in 1880. (Brown Brothers)

acter, and other western states passed similarly punitive laws to drive out the Chinese. Demands for exclusion were especially intense during the depression of the 1870s, when a lull in railroad construction brought thousands of unemployed Chinese workers back to California. The Workingmen's party demanded restriction of the Chinese. All this occurred just as immigration was swelling dramatically. More than 115,000 Chinese arrived on the West Coast in the 1870s, and another 50,000 came in 1881 and 1882. Under enormous pressure from western politicians and labor unions, Congress approved the Chinese Exclusion Act in 1882 prohibiting future immigration from China.

From then until 1943, when China was once again permitted to send immigrants, the Chinese-American population declined as tens of thousands returned to Kwangtung. And for those remaining in the United States, the melting pot did not exist; assimilation was impossible. Most Americans were too suspicious of the Chinese, and the immigrants lived in their own world anyway. Politically inactive, culturally distinct, and economically independent of the general economy, Chinese America was an isolated entity in the United States.

SUGGESTED READINGS

Barth, Gunther. *Bitter Strength: A History of the Chinese in the United States, 1850–1870.* Cambridge, Mass.: 1964.

Cattell, Stuart H. *Health, Welfare, and Social Organization in Chinatown.* New York: 1962.

Chen, Han-Seng. *Agrarian Problems in Southernmost China.* Shanghai, China: 1936.

Cheng, David Te-Chao. *Acculturation of the Chinese in the United States.* Hong Kong, China: 1949.

Ch'u, T'ung-tsu. *Law and Society in Traditional China.* Paris, France: 1961.

Chu, George. "Chinatowns in the Delta: The Chinese in the Sacramento–San Joaquin Delta, 1870–1960." *California Historical Society Quarterly,* 49 (Spring 1970), 21–38.

Coolidge, Mary Roberts. *Chinese Immigration.* New York: 1909.

Harrison, John H. *China Since 1800.* New York: 1967.

Hoyt, Edwin. *Asians in the West.* New York: 1974.

Hsu, Francis L. K. *Americans and Chinese.* New York: 1970.

———. *The Challenge of the American Dream: The Chinese in the United States.* Belmont, Cal.: 1971.

Hundley, Norris, ed. *The Asian American: The Historical Experience.* Santa Barbara, Cal.: 1976.

Kashima, Tetsuden. *Buddhism in America.* Westport, Conn.: 1977.

Kingston, Maxine Hong. *The Woman Warrior.* New York: 1976.

Kung, S. W. *The Chinese in American Life.* Westport, Conn.: 1962.

Lee, Rose Hum. *The Chinese in the United States.* Hong Kong, China: 1960.

Light, Ivan H. *Ethnic Enterprise in America: Business and Welfare Among Chinese, Japanese, and Blacks.* Berkeley, Cal.: 1972.

Lin, Hazel. *The Physician.* New York: 1951.

Lin, Yueh-hwa, *The Golden Wing: A Sociological Study of Chinese Familialism.* London: 1948.

Loewen, James. *The Mississippi Chinese: Between Black and White.* Cambridge, Mass.: 1971.

Lyman, Stanford M. *Chinese Americans.* New York: 1974.

———. "Conflict and the Web of Group Affiliation in San Francisco's Chinatown, 1850–1910." *Pacific Historical Review,* 43 (November 1974), 435–447.

McClellan, Robert. *The Heathen Chinese.* Athens, Oh.: 1971.

Melendy, H. Brett. *The Oriental Americans.* New York: 1972.

Miller, Stuart. *The Unwelcome Immigrant: The American Image of the Chinese, 1785–1882.* Berkeley, Cal.: 1969.

Nee, Victor G., and de Bary, Brett. *Longtime Californ'.* New York: 1973.

Olin, Spencer C., Jr. "European Immigrant and Oriental Alien: Acceptance and Rejection by the California Legislature of 1913." *Pacific Historical Review*, 35 (August 1966), 303–317.

Sandmeyer, Elmer. *The Anti-Chinese Movement in California*. Urbana, Ill.: 1973.

Saxton, Alexander. *The Indispensable Enemy: Labor and the Anti-Chinese Movement in California*. Berkeley, Cal.: 1973.

Sung, Betty Lee. *The Chinese in America*. New York: 1972.

———. *Mountain of Gold: The Story of the Chinese in America*. New York: 1967.

Wakeman, Frederick. *The Fall of Imperial China*. New York: 1975.

Summary

Ethnic America
in 1890

As the 1880s opened, American life seemed stable. People had resumed the normal business of life. After seventeen years of military conflict and political instability, the Civil War and Reconstruction were over. The Union was preserved, the states' rights philosophy defeated, and the noble experiment of black civil equality ended. Americans were taking up where they had left off in 1860, conquering the continent and transforming the environment into material wealth and security. Approximately 60 million people were living in the United States by 1890, and the end of one era and beginning of another would have enormous consequences for all of them, for the 23 million people of British descent as well as for the other European and racial minorities.

Afro-Americans were immediately affected by changes in the political and social climate. For thirty years they had been the focal point in the national debate over free soil, abolition, and equality. When the last federal troops left Florida, South Carolina, and Louisiana in 1877, there were approximately 7 million black people living in the United States, 85 percent of them still in the South. Black communities existed in most northern states, and thousands of black farmers and cowboys had moved west, but most Afro-Americans were still attached to the soil of the rural South. For fourteen years, between the Emancipation Proclamation of 1863 and the election of 1876, the Republican party had experimented with black equality, trying through the Fourteenth Amendment, the Fifteenth Amendment, and the civil rights laws of

1866 and 1875 to give blacks power at the ballot box. And as long as federal troops patrolled the South, the white descendants of the early English, Scots, Scots-Irish, and German settlers had put up with the reforms. But by 1877 northern Republicans had tired of their "southern strategy." New GOP votes were pouring in from the western states and the need for black votes was declining. Tired of the political instability generated by army troops and the Ku Klux Klan, and anxious to invest in the resources and labor of the South, northern businessmen had called for an end to the experiment. The troops left, conservative white "Dixiecrats" resumed their former positions of power, and black Republicanism was dead. With neither capital nor land, southern blacks were poor and dependent once again on the power of the white upper class. Jim Crow laws were already appearing.

Changes were also affecting native Americans. The advance of Christian missionaries, environmental change, disease, and hundreds of thousands of white settlers had devastated the Indian population. By 1890 there were only about 250,000 native Americans, most of them barely surviving on government reservations. Contemptuous of white values but unable to defend their traditional ways, some Indians were turning to pan-Indian spiritual movements to deal with their new lives. From the Great Basin the Sun Dance religion of the Utes and Shoshones was spreading into the rest of Indian America; the gospel of the Ghost Dance was still affecting Indians throughout the Plains; and from Mexico via the Mescalero Apaches the peyote cult was gaining thousands of native American converts.

On the West Coast, nativism had resulted in the Chinese Exclusion Act of 1882. Because of rumors from missionaries and traders traveling in China and fears of their own, local officials were passing harassment laws against the Chinese, and the Workingmen's party in California was demanding deportation. For their part, the Chinese were working hard on railroads, commercial farms, construction projects, factories, and in their own businesses, governing their own community while earning enough money to return to the "Celestial Kingdom," where their families would forever live in prosperity and honor, free of the poverty and pain of peasant life.

And throughout the Southwest nearly 300,000 Mexican-Americans were trying to keep hold of their land despite the influx of thousands of Anglo settlers. By 1890 the tejanos and californios were vastly outnumbered by Anglo farmers and were rapidly losing their land through fraudulent decisions by local judges, state legislatures, and public land commissions. In New Mexico the nuevos mexicanos still retained most of their land and a good deal of power in the territorial legislature, but large-scale Anglo immigration would soon develop, as it had earlier in

California and Texas. Mexican-Americans tried to save their land, but like native Americans, they would lose it, and like blacks, they would become a low-income laboring people.

Disfranchised and poor, these minorities were on the defensive. In the South people of British and German descent had wrested political power from black Republicans; on the Great Plains British, German, and Scandinavian farmers had pushed Indians onto reservations; in California English, German, and Irish workers had discriminated against the Chinese; and hundreds of thousands of white farmers, mostly of British and German descent, had acquired Mexican-American land.

Except in their attitudes toward nonwhites, there was little unanimity among white Europeans in the United States; they too were divided along ethnic lines in 1890. Scattered throughout urban American but concentrated in the Northeast were more than 6 million Irish Catholics. Still poor, ostracized socially because of their religion, and largely confined to poor housing downtown near the docks, warehouses, and railroad terminals or in peripheral shantytowns and "Paddy's Villages," they were a distinct ethnic community. Every major city had an Irish population, and the immigrants took great pride in being Irish and Roman Catholic. From the coal fields of Pennsylvania where the Molly Maguires had fought discrimination to the great railroad strikes of 1877, the Irish immigrants were working for a better standard of living. And from urban political machines they were about to strike back against Protestant assaults on their saloons, parochial schools, and Catholic charities.

Throughout rural and urban America there were more than 8 million people of German descent. A diverse group of Lutherans, Calvinists, Catholics, and pietists from various provinces in Germany, they had possessed neither nationalistic nor religious unity, but by 1890 they were nevertheless becoming more conscious of their German nationality. Mostly concentrated into rural villages and urban centers of the German belt and German triangle and linguistically isolated from the rest of America, they too constructed their own ethnic world and exhibited an overwhelming inclination, in the first generation at least, to marry other Germans.

The Norwegian, Swedish, Danish, Finnish, Dutch, Swiss, and French immigrants were too recent arrivals in 1890 to be threatened by assimilation. Of the 1.2 million Scandinavians living on the farms and in the towns of Michigan, Wisconsin, Illinois, Minnesota, Iowa, and the Dakotas, more than 900,000 of them and their children had arrived since 1870. Although many of the New York and New Jersey Dutch had deep roots in the colonial period, most of the 80,000 Dutch in Michigan and Wisconsin had come to America since 1870, as had 110,000 of the 200,000 Swiss settlers in the Midwest. And the French community in the United States—500,000 French-Canadians in New England and the Great Plains, 200,000 Cajuns in Louisiana, and 150,000 immigrants from France—was still separated by religion and language from the larger society.

For all these people the melting pot did not really exist in 1890. In schools, shops, and churches the Old World languages and customs were still flourishing; time and the passing of generations had not yet blurred the European past. Ethnic America in 1890 was still that—a nation of ethnic communities.

The most distinguishing feature of ethnic America in 1890 was the rise of the ethnic city. Rural, agrarian America was disappearing into the urban, industrial complex of the twentieth century. Cities were attracting all kinds of people with promises of jobs, freedom, anonymity, and excitement. It was an extraordinary time. New York City grew from 60,000 people in 1800 to more than a million in 1860, and cities like Buffalo, Chicago, Cleveland, and Cincinnati were doubling their populations every decade. But American cities were totally unprepared to absorb millions of new inhabitants. Housing, sanitation, transportation, water and utilities, and police and fire services were far from adequate; as a result, crime, disease, crowding, and vice were common. Entrepreneur landlords began building tenements and converting stables, cellars, sheds, and warehouses into multifamily housing. Even in smaller cities Irish and French-Canadian shantytowns appeared on the outskirts as the immigrants found work in the mills and factories. Poverty, unemployment, and sickness were a rude shock for the immigrants as well as for the more well-off Americans. Whether it was the Chinese in San Francisco, the Scandinavians in Minneapolis, the Germans in St. Louis, the Irish in New York, or the French-Canadians in Boston, urban life was new and strange to them.

In Holyoke, Massachusetts, for example, the Irish immigrants of the 1840s worked in the city's textile and industrial economy, and soon after settling they had established a Roman Catholic parish in what was once a center of English Congregationalism. Then in the late 1850s French-Canadians began moving in to take up jobs in the textile mills, and so did a few hundred German Lutherans. Soon there was a French Catholic parish in Holyoke as well as a German Lutheran church, and a Catholic hospital, orphanage, and parochial school. Similar patterns occurred in other mill towns—Lowell, Lawrence, Fall River. In larger cities ethnic diversity increased between 1776 and 1890. In Rochester, New York,

Irish Catholics had a parish in the 1820s; German Catholics, Lutherans, and Reformed in the 1830s; and a French-Canadian parish, a Reformed German-Jewish synagogue, and a Dutch Reformed church all came in the 1870s. In major metropolitan areas like Boston the massive influx of the Irish in the 1840s transformed the physical landscape. They were followed by other immigrants who crowded into downtown Boston near the piers, warehouses, markets, and factories while the English, Scots, and Germans fled for quieter suburbs in the West End, South End, and Charlestown. Eventually, as the street railways reached into every area of the city, prosperous immigrants or their children headed for better homes in the suburbs, leaving the downtown slums for poorer, newer immigrants to fill. In a few years they too would be moving toward the suburbs and replaced by southern and eastern Europeans, then by southern blacks in the 1920s, 1930s, and 1940s, and by Puerto Ricans after World War II. In 1890 most Americans were still living in a rural, agrarian world, but the outlines of the future were clearly drawn.

Assimilation among these people was almost nonexistent in 1890 because a third immigrant generation had not yet appeared. Except for the Irish, the mass migration from Europe did not begin until the 1850s, and not until after the Civil War did it reach flood-tide proportions. Immigrants and their children were tightly bound into their own ethnic families, churches, and associations, and social contact outside work and business was infrequent. Still, acculturation was well underway by 1890. Despite vigorous attempts to preserve Old World ways, the adoption of some dimensions of American culture was inevitable. For the second generation the use of English became the rule, and the Old World tongue became a relic used only in speaking to parents or grandparents. As historian Marcus Hansen has written, the second generation often worked at acquiring at least the appearance of American culture. They spoke English with relish, quickly shed Old World costumes for the utilitarian, mass-produced clothing of America, and celebrated such holidays as the Fourth of July and Thanksgiving with patriotic fervor. They were also affected by the ideological flavor of American life, and imbued with the American faith in progress, at least after the initial shock of migration and settlement had passed. They became enthusiastic supporters of Manifest Destiny, American democracy, and natural rights and popular sovereignty.

By 1890 the immigrants were also expanding their contacts with other white ethnic groups. They had long worked and done business with a wide variety of people, but their family and social contacts had been narrowly defined. That was slowly changing. As the immigrants made the transition to English, some contact with other groups occurred in the churches. When the German and Scandinavian churches switched to English-language services, some of the immigrants and their children began attending the Lutheran or pietist church closest to home. And as the public school movement spread throughout the country in the 1870s and 1880s, the Protestant ethnic parochial schools gradually disappeared and English, German, Scots, Danish, Norwegian, and Swedish children began attending the common school together. As the "streetcar suburbs" expanded out from the cities, the Germans, English, Irish, and Scandinavians fanned out to newer homes and apartments. Income, rather than just ethnic group, came to determine residential patterns, and people from different cultural backgrounds found themselves living together as neighbors. That too encouraged cultural assimilation and led to the full assimilation which would occur in the twentieth century.

Finally, political controversy helped integrate the immigrant communities into the larger society. Across the United States—from the Irish ghettos of the East to the German Catholic centers in the Midwest and the tiny Dutch Catholic settlements in Michigan—Roman Catholics supported the Democratic party in 1890. English Protestants, Welsh Methodists, Scandinavian Lutherans, Irish Protestants, and Dutch Reformed, on the other hand, were more likely to vote Republican. German pietists also voted Republican, while German Lutherans and Reformed broke the pattern by narrowly supporting the Democrats. In part, the ethnic cleavage in American politics had an economic base. The Whigs and Republicans had traditionally reflected the interests of business and commerce, and—in an economy just beginning to industrialize—those of skilled craftsmen who were still either small businessmen themselves or the elite of the labor force in mining and manufacturing. Generally, businessmen of British descent believed the Republican party would best promote their economic needs. And in the 1860s and 1870s, when most of the Dutch, German, and Scandinavian farmers poured into the Midwest, the Republican party had favored free land through the Homestead Act. So among businessmen, skilled workers, and northern farmers the Republican party enjoyed strong support.

But in 1890 cultural values were as effective a barometer of political behavior as economic interests. Ethnic groups supporting the Republican party were usually pietistic or evangelical in religion and more formal, ritualistic groups tended to support the Democrats; that is, the Baptists, Methodists, Presbyterians, Quakers, Scandinavian Lutherans, and Scandinavian and Dutch Calvinists in the North were often Republicans, while Roman Catholics and high church Lutherans were generally Democrats. Emphasizing formalism and priestly authority, the

Catholics and German Lutherans viewed the world skeptically, as if secular affairs really were distinct from religious ones and man could do little to purify the world of corruption or make it perfect. Instead of perfecting the world, they usually wanted to ameliorate some of society's worst conditions, particularly to ensure that people's standard of living was sufficient to make family and religious life fulfilling. The Irish poet John Boyle O'Reilly condemned poverty and class differences in his writings; the journalist Patrick Ford bitterly described urban poverty and unemployment in the pages of the *Irish World*; Henry George, author of *Progress and Poverty* (1879), proposed a "single tax" on all profits from the sale or rental of land; and Irish political machines freely distributed food, fuel, and jobs to poor people in the cities.

The evangelical Protestants, on the other hand, felt an intense need to purify the world of sin, to change people's minds and behavior. While the ritualists turned to the parish and parochial school to preserve their values, the evangelicals ultimately tried to legislate their morality. Because Catholics and conservative Lutherans would not abandon their saloons and parochial schools voluntarily, the evangelicals sought to force them to do so. To achieve their objectives, they turned to the Republican party, which in the middle of the nineteenth century had promoted strong government, free land, and abolition. Ritualists turned to the Democratic party for just the opposite reasons, because it opposed a strong central state and respected the prerogatives of local communities.

Throughout the nineteenth century evangelical Republicans advocated change while ritualistic Democrats supported tradition and stability. The Protestants opposed the parochial schools because they preserved Old World traditions and Catholic values, so they promoted public schools. The Catholics saw the public schools as "Protestant" schools: Protestant ministers served on school boards, Protestant prayers were repeated each morning, and the King James Bible was used for instruction. The Protestants supported prohibition as a means of purifying the world, but the ritualists viewed liquor as a harmless diversion and opposed the temperance movement. The Protestants supported Sabbath laws to close stores and taverns on Sunday, and the Catholics opposed them as unnecessary invasions of their privacy. So while the Protestants in the Republican party worked to create a homogeneous America free of sin, the Catholics and high church Lutherans in the Democratic party tried to create a stable world where family and religious values could flourish. After 1900, as industrialization continued its inexorable transformation of the social structure, economic issues would become more important, but in 1890 culture still shaped political loyalties and group relations in the United States.

SUGGESTED READINGS

Berthoff, Rowland. *An Unsettled People: Social Order and Disorder in American History*. New York: 1971.

Billington, Ray Allen. *The Protestant Crusade, 1800–1860*. New York: 1938.

———. *Westward Expansion: A History of the American Frontier*. New York: 1974.

Bruchey, Stuart. *The Roots of American Economic Growth, 1607–1861*. New York: 1965.

Buel, Richard, Jr. *Securing the Revolution: Ideology in American Politics, 1789–1815*. New York: 1972.

Cawelti, John G. *Apostles of the Self-Made Man: Changing Concepts of Success in America*. Chicago: 1965.

Chudacoff, Howard P. *The Evolution of American Urban Society*. Englewood Cliffs, N.J.: 1975.

Curran, Thomas. *Xenophobia and Immigration, 1820–1930*. Boston: 1975.

Davis, Lawrence B. *Immigrants, Baptists, and the Protestant Mind in America*. Urbana, Ill.: 1973.

Esslinger, Dean R. *Immigrants and the City: Ethnicity and Mobility in a Nineteenth-Century Midwestern Community*. New York: 1975.

Gutman, Herbert G. *Work, Culture, and Society in Industrializing America*. New York: 1976.

Hansen, Marcus Lee. *The Atlantic Migration, 1607–1860*. New York: 1940.

Jones, Maldwyn. *American Immigration*. Chicago: 1960.

———. *Destination America*. New York: 1976.

Kleppner, Paul. *The Cross of Culture: A Social Analysis of Midwestern Politics, 1850–1900*. New York: 1970.

Leonard, Ira M., and Parmet, Robert D. *American Nativism, 1830–1860*. New York: 1971.

Marty, Martin. *Righteous Crusade: The Protestant Experience in America*. New York: 1970.

Merk, Frederick. *Manifest Destiny and Mission in American Life: A Reinterpretation*. New York: 1963.

Nichols, Roy F. *The Disruption of American Democracy*. New York: 1948.

North, Douglass C. *The Economic Growth of the United States, 1790–1860*. New York: 1961.

Pessen, Edward. *Riches, Class, and Power Before the Civil War*. New York: 1973.

Potter, David. *The Impending Crisis, 1848–1861*. New York: 1976.

———. *People of Plenty: Economic Abundance and the American Character*. New York: 1954.

Potter, J. "The Growth of Population in America, 1700–1860." In D. V. Glass and D. E. C. Eversley, eds. *Population and History*. New York: 1965.

Rischin, Moses. "Beyond the Great Divide: Immigration and the Last Frontier." *Journal of American History*, 55 (June 1968), 42–53.

Schultz, Stanley K. *The Culture Factory: Boston Public Schools, 1789–1860*. New York: 1973.

Smith, Elwyn A., ed. *The Religion of the Republic*. New York: 1971.

Smith, Henry Nash. *Virgin Land: The American West as Symbol and Myth*. New York: 1950.

Somkin, Fred. *Unquiet Eagle: Memory and Desire in the Idea of American Freedom*. New York: 1971.

Taylor, Philip. *The Distant Magnet: European Emigration to the U.S.A.* London: 1971.

Thernstrom, Stephen. *Poverty and Progress: Social Mobility in a Nineteenth Century City*. Cambridge, Mass.: 1964.

Vecoli, Rudolph J. "European Americans: From Immigrants to Ethnics." In William H. Cartwright and Richard L. Watson, Jr., eds. *The Reinterpretation of American History and Culture*. Washington, D.C.: 1973.

Ward, David. *Cities and Immigrants: A Georgraphy of Change in Nineteenth Century America*. New York: 1971.

Warner, Sam Bass. *Streetcar Suburbs: The Process of Growth in Boston, 1870–1900*. Cambridge, Mass.: 1962.

Part III
AMERICA IN TRANSITION, 1877-1945

Between 1877 and 1945 the United States changed so much that all previous upheavals in American history seemed mild in comparison. Despite the Civil War, the westward movement, and 10 million immigrants, the United States in 1877 was still an isolated society of small farmers and small towns. Independent and relatively self-sufficient, most Americans lived in a world of "island communities," small clusters of people insulated in networks of personal relationships. They still looked out on the world through an individualistic lens and confidently believed that God viewed white Protestant America with special affection.

Seventy years later—after industrialization, the flight to the cities, the new immigration, two world wars, and the Great Depression— doubts had tarnished that confidence. America had become an even more ethnically complex society of white- and blue-collar workers living in crowded cities, and few people viewed reality through a single prism of individuality. Industrialization had created a vast national market of impersonal economic relationships, while the rise of the cities had brought an accompanying social anonymity. Individualism was giving way to organization and bureaucratic routine.

But some threads of history were intact, for Americans were still trying to make the ideals of 1776 succeed. Between 1877 and 1945

American pluralism became more intricate as new immigrants from eastern and southern Europe and Asia settled in the cities, and as blacks, Mexicans, and Indians began demanding their place in the sun. Once again Americans would have to decide whether egalitarianism applied to everyone regardless of race, religion, or national origins. Time and time again, from the rise of Jim Crow laws in the 1880s to the incarceration of Japanese-Americans in the 1940s, they would fail the test, but the ideological commitment survived. Most Americans tried to work out their dream amidst the traumas of war, economic collapse, and social change—to discover "America" and interpret its mission. Pluralism, equality, and nationalism, the ideological pantheon of the American Revolution, remained the vision of 1945.

The most fundamental transformation was economic, and changes in the production of goods brought monumental changes in social life. Ever since 1607 the American economy had been "exceptional," marked by a virgin continent, seemingly limitless resources, a labor shortage, and an entrepreneurial zeal unmatched in the Western world. The result was the greatest economic machine in history. As expanding networks of turnpikes, canals, and railroads created a national market, farmers mechanized commercial agriculture and large corporations shipped goods everywhere. Just as the rise of factories was drawing workers into the cities, the mechanization of agriculture was driving farmers off the land. Between 1877 and 1945 the United States ceased to be a country of farms and villages and became a nation of cities and factories, complete with an industrial proletariat and a bureaucratic middle class working for large corporations.

Public policy changed with industrialization. In the past Americans had viewed government as the greatest threat to individual liberty, and the Bill of Rights and the laissez-faire philosophy were originally designed to limit government interference in people's lives. But with the rise of giant corporations, people began to see private interests as the real threat to liberty. Once considered the enemy of freedom, the federal government now became the only force capable of dealing with corporate power. The Populist movement of the 1890s and the Progressive movement of the early 1900s worked to preserve competition and regulate the corporations, and in the 1930s the New Deal went on to underwrite economic investment, provide jobs, and supply social welfare. To offset corporate power, others organized countervailing interest groups. Doctors, dentists, lawyers, professors, and engineers formed professional associations. Skilled workers joined the Knights of Labor and the American Federation of Labor, and later on skilled and unskilled workers joined the Congress of Industrial Organizations. Farmers set up marketing cooperatives, federations, shipping associations, and trade groups. The reign of economic individualism was over, and only through interest groups could people hope to protect themselves.

The New Immigrants

If industrialization threatened individualism, the "new immigration" challenged cultural pluralism. Late in the nineteenth century, countries in southern and eastern Europe were integrated into the Atlantic economy just as industrialization was creating millions of jobs in the United States. Peasant life in Europe had remained unchanged for centuries. People yearned for stability and tradition, not for profit and change. At the center of their world was the family and the land. Land was the source of survival, status, and independence, and families possessed a temporary stewardship over it. Marriages were negotiated between families; spouses and children were expected to contribute to the family and the land, and to remain all their lives within reach of home and loved ones. Several families made up a village, and beyond that microcosm of family, farm, parish, and village lay an alien world of strangers. Life and destiny were local affairs, and governments, foreigners, and aristocracies were either malignant or irrelevant.

Economic changes upset that tranquillity, threatening land ownership and family security. Enormous population increases in Poland, Russia, Italy, Austria-Hungary, and the Balkans fragmented landholdings until it was difficult for peasants to support their families. Large landowners functioned as a social and political elite; and although serfdom was rapidly disappearing, most peasants were still tied to the large estates as tenants or owned tiny plots. In 1880, of the 1.7 million Polish peasants in Galicia, the average farmer owned less than six acres. Eighty percent of the Magyars in Hungary lived off agriculture, but half the peasant farmers owned less than five acres. Another 1.5 million were farm laborers or tenants. In some parts of Croatia and Serbia the average peasant holding was less than three acres.

Population increases were devastating. Serbia's population, for example, grew from 1.7 to 2.9 million between 1878 and 1910, and Russia's was expanding by a million people each year. Although population density was often lower than in western Europe, the number of people per acre of tilled land was much higher. In the Like-Krbava district of Croatia in 1880 nearly 270,000 people were trying to make a living on only 225,000 acres of arable land. Not only did peasants have difficulty supporting their families, but it was almost impossible for younger people to acquire land. One Polish peasant wrote to the Emigrants' Protective Association in Warsaw, asking it

> to advise me how I could migrate to America with my family . . . I intend to go also and buy there some land, for in Wolyn it is very dear—a desiatina costs as much as 500 roubles. What can I buy, when I have 5 boys and only 2,000 roubles? I could perhaps buy in Russia, but what is the use of it since there are no Catholic churches and my faith would get lost.*

Nineteenth-century Croatia was an agrarian society organized into *zadrugas*, communal villages where land was owned by kinship systems rather than by private individuals. Class distinctions blurred in the zadrugas, and the order and tempo of daily life were predictable. But population increases destroyed zadruga life; the village could not support all the people. Similar conditions developed throughout eastern Europe.

Technology also changed peasant life. Early in the nineteenth century cereal culture had spread throughout Bohemia, Moravia, Slovakia, out to the Pannonian Plain of Hungary, and into Poland, Lithuania, the Ukraine, Slovenia, and Croatia. But late in the century American wheat began depressing grain prices in eastern Europe. In some areas peasant income fell to only fifteen dollars a year. To compete with American producers, the larger commercial farms of eastern Europe converted to capital-intensive agriculture, increasing production and further depressing prices. With frightening consistency, peasant society deteriorated.

At the same time, alternative sources of income were being eliminated. For centuries industrial production had been a household affair. Peasants could supplement their incomes as artisans, and sons could remain close to home by apprenticing out as blacksmiths, coopers, cobblers, and carpenters. Industrialization changed all that by concentrating production in urban factories. Unable to compete with cheap, mass-produced factory goods, peasant craftsmen went on the road looking for work. Slovak and Rusin peasants (from the Transcarpathia region of modern Czechoslovakia) moved to the wheat fields of the Pannonian Plain in Hungary; Sicilians migrated seasonally into the northern provinces; Slovenes and Croatians moved to the factories of Trieste and Fiume; Magyar, Bohemian, Moravian, and Slovakian craftsmen traveled to Prague, Budapest, Vienna, and Graz. German-Poles went to the coal mines, iron mills, and leather tanneries of Upper Silesia, while Austrian-Poles drifted into the mines and mills of Bohemia and Silesia. Russian-Poles, Ruthenians, and Ukrainians took up jobs in

---

*W.I. Thomas and Florian Znaniecki, *The Polish Peasant in Europe and America* (Boston, 1918), pp. 27.

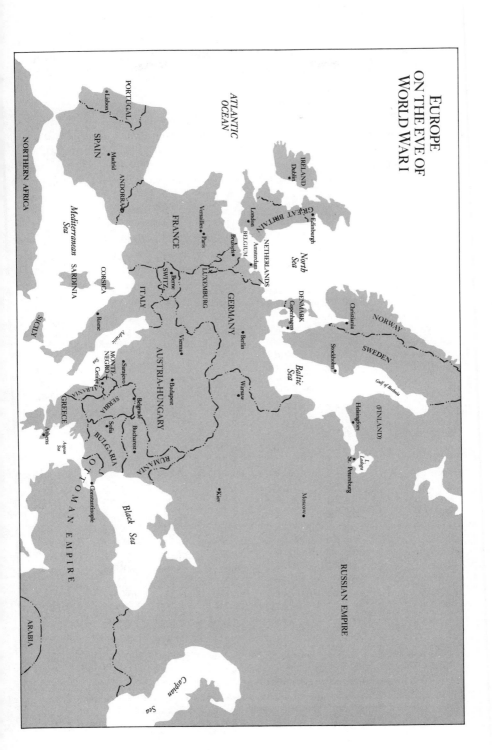

EUROPE
ON THE EVE OF
WORLD WAR I

ATLANTIC
OCEAN

NORTHERN AFRICA

PORTUGAL
•Lisbon

SPAIN
•Madrid

ANDORRA•

Mediterranean Sea

SARDINIA

CORSICA

SICILY

IRELAND
•Dublin

GREAT BRITAIN
•Edinburgh
London•

North Sea

NETHERLANDS
Amsterdam•
BELGIUM
Brussels•
LUXEMBURG

FRANCE
Versailles•
•Paris

SWITZ.
•Berne

ITALY
•Rome

Albania

MONTE-
NEGRO•
•Cettinje

ALBANIA

GREECE
Athens•

Aegean Sea

DENMARK
Copenhagen•

GERMANY
•Berlin

AUSTRIA-HUNGARY
•Vienna
•Budapest

Sarajevo•

SERBIA
Belgrade•

Sofia•
BULGARIA

RUMANIA
Bucharest•

•Warsaw

NORWAY

SWEDEN
Stockholm•

Christiania•

Baltic Sea

Gulf of Bothnia

(FINLAND)

Helsingfors•
St. Petersburg•
L. Ladoga

•Kiev

Moscow•

RUSSIAN EMPIRE

OTTOMAN EMPIRE
•Constantinople

Black Sea

ARABIA

Caspian Sea

the coal basins of Dabrowa, the textile mills of Lodz and Czestochowa, and the steel mills of Sosnowiec, Zgierz, and Tomaszow. Forced to stay away from home for months to make a living, peasants saw an opportunity to improve their lot in the United States.

Immigrants came not only from the regions characterized by large estates and landless peasants, but also from areas with a wide distribution of property or long leases on the land. Most peasant immigrants were independent people used to working land of their own, who found the discrepancy between need and income too great. Years of poverty

TABLE II
AMERICAN IMMIGRATION, 1890–1940

	1890s	1900s	1910s	1920s	1930s	Total
Austria-Hungary[1]	592,707	2,145,266	900,656	214,806	31,652	3,885,087
Denmark	50,231	65,285	41,983	32,430	2,559	192,488
Finland[2]			756	16,691	2,146	19,593
France	30,770	73,379	61,897	49,610	12,623	228,279
Germany	505,152	341,498	143,945	412,202	114,058	1,516,855
England	216,726	388,017	249,944	157,420	21,756	1,033,863
Scotland	44,188	120,469	78,357	159,781	6,887	409,682
Wales	10,557	17,464	13,107	13,012	735	54,875
Greece	15,979	167,519	184,201	51,084	9,119	427,902
Ireland	388,416	339,065	146,181	220,591	13,167	1,107,420
Italy	651,893	2,045,877	1,109,524	455,315	68,028	4,330,637
Netherlands	26,758	48,262	43,718	26,948	7,150	152,836
Norway	95,015	190,505	66,395	68,531	4,740	425,186
Poland[3]	96,720		4,813	227,734	17,026	346,293
Portugal	27,508	69,149	89,732	29,994	3,329	219,712
Rumania	12,750	53,008	13,311	67,646	3,871	150,586
Spain	8,731	27,935	68,611	28,958	3,258	137,493
Sweden	226,266	249,534	95,074	97,249	3,960	672,083
Switzerland	31,179	34,922	23,091	29,676	5,512	124,380
Russia	505,290	1,597,306	921,201	61,742	1,356	3,086,895
China	14,799	20,605	21,278	29,907	4,928	91,517
Japan	25,942	129,797	83,837	33,462	1,948	275,166
Turkey	30,425	157,369	134,066	33,824	1,065	356,749
Canada	3,311	179,226	742,185	924,515	108,527	1,957,764
Mexico		49,642	219,004	459,287	22,319	750,257
TOTAL	3,611,313	8,511,098	5,456,867	3,902,415	471,719	21,953,412

[1]Austria-Hungary includes Austrians, Hungarians, Galician Poles, Czechs, Slovaks, Rusins, Ukrainians, Slovenes, Croatians, and Serbians.

[2]Finland was part of Russia until after World War I.

[3]Poland was not really independent until after World War I, and Polish-speaking people were scattered throughout Austria-Hungary, Russia, and Germany.

SOURCE: *Annual Report*, U.S. Immigration and Naturalization Service, 1973.

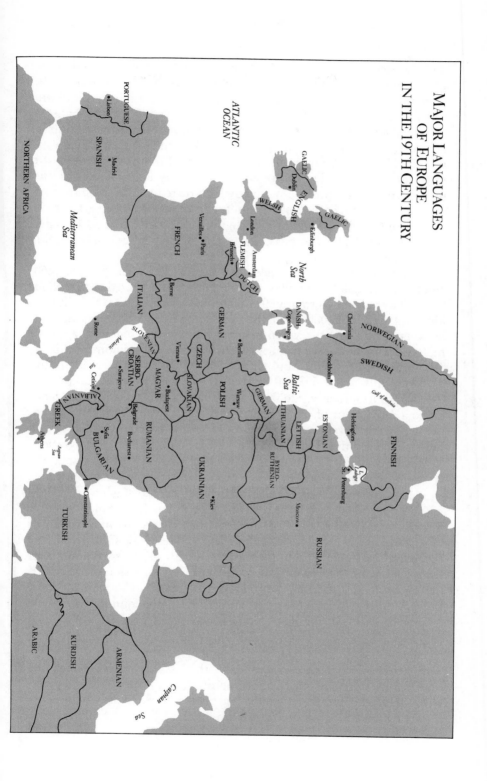

MAJOR LANGUAGES
OF EUROPE
IN THE 19TH CENTURY

NORTHERN AFRICA

PORTUGUESE
•Lisbon

SPANISH
Madrid•

ATLANTIC
OCEAN

Mediterranean
Sea

GAELIC
Dublin•
ENGLISH
WELSH
GAELIC
•Edinburgh

FRENCH
Versailles•Paris
Brussels•
FLEMISH
Amsterdam•
DUTCH

North
Sea

ITALIAN
Rome•
Rome•

SLOVENIAN
Adriatic

SERBO-
CROATIAN
Sarajevo•

ALBANIAN
Cettinje•

GREEK
Athens•

Aegean
Sea

Constantinople•

TURKISH

ARABIC

KURDISH

ARMENIAN

Caspian
Sea

GERMAN
Berlin•
Vienna•
CZECH
MAGYAR
Budapest•
SLOVAKIAN
POLISH
Warsaw•
GERMAN

DANISH
Copenhagen•

Baltic
Sea

Christiania•
NORWEGIAN

Stockholm•
SWEDISH

Gulf of Bothnia

LITHUANIAN
LETTISH
ESTONIAN

Helsingfors•
FINNISH

St. Petersburg•
L.
Ladoga

BYELO-
RUTHENIAN

RUMANIAN
Belgrade•
Sofia•
BULGARIAN
Bucharest•

UKRAINIAN
•Kiev

Moscow•

RUSSIAN

and the search for work made immigration palatable. Several young men from a village would usually set out together for America. Unencumbered with wives and children, and usually unskilled, they found work in the same mill, factory, or mine and lived in a boardinghouse with relatives or friends who had preceded them. A few came as contract laborers, and thousands of Italian, Greek, and Syrian workers were recruited or kidnaped by padrone labor bosses. Most came on their own however, and intended to live in America only long enough to save money and then return home to buy land or redeem the family mortgage. More than half the Italian immigrants returned home in the 1890s, and more than 500,000 Polish immigrants returned between 1900 and 1915. But gradually the peasants began staying longer and sending money back home to bring their families.

Immigration patterns changed dramatically. Between 1850 and 1860, when approximately 2.6 million people came to the United States, about 951,000 were from Germany, 914,000 from Ireland, 292,000 from Britain, and nearly 36,000 from the Netherlands and Scandinavia. But between 1900 and 1910, when nearly 8.8 million immigrated, approximately 2.2 million were from Austria-Hungary, 2.1 million from Italy, 1.6 million from Russia, and almost 308,000 from China, Japan, and Turkey. Only about 553,000 arrived from Holland and Scandinavia, 341,000 from Germany, 526,000 from Britain, and 340,000 from Ireland. Once a movement of white Protestants, the Great Migration had become a mass movement of Eastern Orthodox, Roman Catholics, and Jews from eastern and southern Europe. This was the new immigration.

Most immigrants left Europe as steerage passengers in transatlantic steamships. Walking, riding in wagons, or traveling in emigrant trains, they moved to coastal cities and lived in temporary steamship-sponsored villages until the vessels were ready to depart. The Jews, Poles, Czechs, Slovaks, and Lithuanians went to Bremen and Hamburg in Germany or to Antwerp and Le Havre; Scandinavians still left from Christiania and Göteborg for England, and then traveled with the British immigrants from Liverpool; the South Slavs and Greeks left from the Adriatic ports of Trieste and Fiume; and the Italians departed from Naples. All along the way, as they passed from district to district and country to country, they were checked, fumigated, and overcharged for food, drink, and passports. Short of money, confused, and wary of strangers, they boarded the ships and headed for America.

Steamships made the voyages safer than before, even though the immigrants were not much more comfortable. The old six-to-eight-week voyage of the colonial period had been reduced to only twelve days from Liverpool and twenty days from Trieste. The mortality rate fell dramatically. In 1907, when 1.2 million immigrants came to America, less than 250 died en route, as compared to 1847—admittedly the worst year—when Canadian officials discovered that 17,000 people of the 100,000 setting out for Canada had died at sea, in port cities, or in local hospitals. The voyage was also cheaper. At one point in 1911 an Italian laborer could sail from Naples to New York for fifteen dollars.

For most of the nineteenth century immigrant ships stopped at Staten Island, in New York Harbor, where state officials inspected people and quarantined the sick and insane. The ships would then dock on the Hudson or East rivers, the passengers would go through customs, and barges would carry them to Castle Garden, where a small hospital treated the sick and where the immigrants collected mail, bought rail or steamship tickets to the interior, exchanged money, and talked to employment agents. After 1892, when the federal government took control of immigration, the immigrants arrived at the new installation at Ellis Island. At Boston, Philadelphia, Baltimore, New Orleans, and San Francisco the receiving facilities were more primitive.

Most Jews and Italians stayed in New York City, while the Slavic Catholics and other eastern Europeans moved throughout the urban Northeast, taking unskilled jobs in mines, mills, and factories. Relatively few went into rural areas, because the best land was already taken and they would have been cut off from churches and compatriots.

After the Civil War white farmers began a trek to the cities that still continues today; poor blacks began leaving the South during World War I for jobs in northern factories; and millions of European peasants filled the cities after 1880. Urban American teemed with ethnic ghettos, jobs, and vitality. Eighty-five percent of Americans had lived in rural areas in 1877, but in 1945 more than 70 percent lived in the cities.

Industrialization, the rise of the cities, and the new immigration precipitated a series of cultural crises. By the 1890s the old faith in a political and economic system blessed by God no longer seemed so certain. In 1890 the Department of the Interior announced the closing of the frontier, and many Americans wondered where discontented people could go to release pent-up frustrations. The depression of 1893 left millions hungry and out of work; Jacob Coxey's army of the unemployed was marching on Washington; Eugene Debs and the American Railway Union had struck the Pullman Company; the Populists were up in arms in the South and West; and all this came in the wake of the Homestead Strike at the Carnegie Steel Works and the Haymarket Riot in Chicago. People feared revolution. And the cities—full of Catholics and Jews, strange languages, exotic foods, and crowded tenements— seemed breeding grounds for political and social unrest. An atmosphere of crisis—first in the 1890s and again during World War I, the 1920s, the Great Depression, and World War II—precipitated nativist fears throughout the country.

Nativism and Racism in America

These tensions first appeared just when racist theories were becoming popular. Many whites accepted implicitly the inferiority of blacks, native Americans, and Mexican-Americans, and late in the 1800s these theories reached fruition in Jim Crow laws, the reservation system and Dawes Act for the Indians, the acquisition of Mexican-American land, and even in the decision of the McKinley Administration to take possession of the Philippine Islands in 1898. Racism was a fact of life. But it gained new intellectual adherents in the 1870s, and some argued that there were fixed racial differences among white Europeans.

After Charles Darwin published his *Origin of Species* in 1859, social scientists like Herbert Spencer in England and William Graham Sumner in the United States began applying the theory of natural selection to human society. This was Social Darwinism, the belief that certain people were genetically more "fit" than others and destined for success. At the same time, historians George Bancroft and Herbert Baxter Adams, political scientists Francis Lieber and John W. Burgess, biologist Robert Knox, and classicist William F. Allen began promoting the theory of Teutonic origins, arguing that the Anglo-Saxon, Nordic, and Germanic peoples were the superior "race," responsible for free-enterprise capitalism, technology, and political liberty. They also claimed that Jews, Slavs, Italians, and Greeks, though racially "above" black and brown people, were markedly inferior to Germans, English, and Scandinavians in intellectual capacity, ambition, and social organization. A eugenics movement urging Anglo-Saxon, Nordic, and Germanic Protestants to marry among themselves and perpetuate their gene pool accompanied the racist propaganda. Written in 1916, Madison Grant's *The Passing of the Great Race* popularized those feelings:

> The cross between a white man and an Indian is an Indian; the cross between a white man and a Negro is a Negro; . . . and the cross between a . . . European and a Jew is a Jew . . . .
>
> The man of the old stock is being . . . driven off the streets of New York City by the swarms of Polish Jews. These immigrants adopt the language of the native American, they wear his clothes, they steal his name and they are beginning to take his women, but they seldom adopt his religion or understand his ideals . . . .

The Nordics are, all over the world, a race of soldiers, sailors, adventurers and explorers, but above all, of rulers, organizers and aristocrats in sharp contrast to . . . the Alpines. The Nordics are domineering, individualistic, self-reliant and jealous of their personal freedom both in political and religious systems, and as a result they are usually Protestants.*

Because of the new immigration, the white Protestants among the earlier immigrants now seemed much less ominous to most Americans. Except for the Norwegians, the "old immigration" had peaked in the 1880s, and second-generation British-, German-, Dutch-, and Scandinavian-Americans became more dominant in their communities. While their parents struggled to keep the old ways, the children were culturally assimilating at a rapid rate. As the public school movement permeated education after 1890, the children of the immigrants learned American history and spoke English fluently. Indeed, they preferred English, often to their parents' dismay. Some Anglicized their names, or gave their children first names more traditional in American society. The ethnic-language press for these white Protestants peaked around 1910 and then entered a long period of decline. And with each generation intermarriage became more common. Although British Protestants were by far the largest group in New England, they were intermarrying nearly half the time by 1910. Scandinavians were still marrying Scandinavians nearly 70 percent of the time in the upper Midwest, but in New Haven, Connecticut, for example, their in-marriage rate declined from more than 80 percent in 1900 to only 30 percent in 1930. In the German triangle Germans usually married among themselves, but in New York their in-marriage rate dropped from nearly 70 percent in 1900 to only 40 percent in 1939. When these people did intermarry, they selected white Protestants more than 90 percent of the time. All these changes reassured older Americans about the future of their culture. It was the "new immigrants," not the "old immigrants," who now seemed a threat.

Congress investigated the new immigration, and in 1907 issued the forty-one-volume report of the Dillingham Commission. Claiming the new immigrants were unskilled, illiterate, and transient males traveling without their families, the report confirmed some of the worst fears. To be sure, there were differences between the "old" and "new" immigrants. Most of the old immigrants were northern and western European Protestants while the new immigrants were generally southern and eastern European Jews and Catholics. Other distinctions were not so clear. Although the Italians and Slavs were frequently illiterate men immigrating on a temporary basis, the Jews, Syrians, and Armenians

*Quoted in Robert Kelley, *The Shaping of the American Past* (New York, 1976), p. 702.

were usually skilled, literate workers migrating with their families. Indeed, the English, German, and Scandinavian immigrants were more likely than they were to return home. Moreover, the Commission unfairly compared the immigrants of 1907 from eastern and southern Europe, where the Industrial Revolution had only just taken hold, with the 1907 immigrants from Britain, Germany, and Scandinavia, where industrialization had matured. Naturally, the two groups would differ in their level of skills. Back in the 1840s and 1850s, most of the "old" immigrants had also been unskilled peasant farmers. Most people, however, accepted the findings of the Dillingham Commission at face value.

As crisis after crisis struck between 1890 and 1945, nativist fears waxed and waned, erupting often enough to remind everyone that pluralism still challenged American ideals. In the 1890s rumors of international conspiracies of Jewish bankers or of the pope to take over America were spread by such groups as the American Protective Association, the American Super-Race Foundation, and the Daughters of the American Revolution. Discrimination against Jews and Catholics became common. In 1915 a Jew named Leo Frank was lynched in Georgia for allegedly murdering a young girl, and two months later the Ku Klux Klan began to grow again. It persecuted Jews and Catholics, as well as blacks, burning crosses on cathedrals and synagogues, and attacking priests, nuns, and rabbis. Klan membership rose to nearly 5 million by 1926. D. W. Griffith produced the epic film *Birth of a Nation*, which condemned Black Reconstruction and extolled the virtues of the Klan. When Al Smith, an Irish Catholic, ran for president in 1928 against the Republican Herbert Hoover, he stood no chance because of rural anti-Catholicism.

During World War I German-Americans experienced a variety of indignities, sometimes so severe that they lost their jobs or had to give them up and become recluses. Antiblack race riots broke out in dozens of cities during and after the war, the worst ones occurring in East St. Louis in 1917 and Chicago in 1919. After the war nativism intensified and led to the famous Red Scare, in which left-wing immigrants were harassed and deported, and to the Sacco and Vanzetti case of the 1920s, in which two Italian immigrants were executed in Massachusetts for supposedly committing an armed robbery and murder. Lynchings of blacks in the South were common before World War II. And during World War II, in addition to the relocation of 110,000 Japanese-Americans, more race riots against blacks and Mexican-Americans broke out; the most severe ones were in Detroit and Los Angeles in 1943.

The apparent crises, the periodic violence, and the vast changes occurring in the society worried many Americans, and they saw two solutions to the problem of cultural conflict. To eliminate it in the future, such groups as the Immigration Restriction League and the American Protective Association (both directed primarily by Yankee Protestants), along with allies in the Knights of Labor and the American Federation of Labor, began pressing Congress for immigration restriction. Despite the lobbying of German and Irish immigrant associations and business groups like the National Association of Manufacturers and the Chamber of Commerce (which hoped to keep wages low by increasing the supply of labor), Congress passed a long series of restrictive immigration laws, beginning in 1882 with the Chinese Exclusion Act and a law prohibiting the entry of convicts and the insane. Although contract labor had never been a major problem, Congress soothed labor interests by outlawing it in 1885. Polygamists, indigents, and people with contagious diseases were banned in 1891; epileptics, prostitutes, and anarchists in 1903; and the mentally retarded in 1907. Congress approved a literacy test for new immigrants in 1917. Finally, there was the National Origins Act in 1924. At first assigning each country an annual quota of 2 percent of its representation in the American population of 1890, the law after 1929 permitted each country a quota established according to its representation in the 1920 American population. Immigrants from the Western Hemisphere were exempted. After 1929, except for those from the Western Hemisphere, only 150,000 immigrants could enter the United States each year. The Great Migration was over.

But securing the future was not enough. Nativists also worried about the present, about "Americanizing" the immigrants. In a spirit of sympathy and tolerance such groups as the Young Men's Christian Association and the urban settlement houses (such as Hull House in Chicago) helped immigrants adjust to American life, but the nativist groups were more heavy-handed. While the Dawes Act and the federal government tried to turn the Indians into small-scale Christian farmers, nativist groups like the Daughters of the American Revolution and the American Legion demanded that immigrants adopt "American ways." After World War I the Americanization movement became a national crusade involving schools, churches, patriotic societies, civil groups, and chambers of commerce, all coordinated by the National Americanization Committee. They pressured immigrants to forget Old World languages, shed Old World customs, abandon parochial schools, and discard Old World political loyalties. Naïve as such campaigns were, they were still the dominant themes of the transitional decades. The American commitment to pluralism, equality, and nationalism would still survive in 1945, but only after being tested again.

Chapter Thirteen

From the Mediterranean: The Southern Europeans

The "new immigrants" from Spain, Portugal, and especially Italy seemed alien to many Americans, and the size of their migration made them look even more threatening. There had always been a few immigrants from the Mediterranean; more than thirty thousand people came from southern Europe before 1860, but compared to the 5 million western European immigrants, they were hardly noticed. And most of them were professionals, well-to-do merchants, skilled workers, or Catholic missionaries. Few were impoverished peasants. Another 5 million immigrants arrived between 1860 and 1880, but less than 2 percent were from Spain, Portugal, and Italy. Then, between 1880 and 1924, when nearly 20 million people came to the United States, more than 5 million were southern Europeans. Older Americans then became concerned.

The Portuguese and Spaniards

About 230,000 Portuguese came to America during the Great Migration, most settling in New England and northern California. A few thousand Portuguese Protestants left their homeland when Catholic persecution became intense, but most of the Portuguese immigrants came as economic conditions in Europe changed. In New England they worked in the fishing and cotton textile industries, and in California they became farmers and fishermen. By 1910 Portuguese communities could be found in Boston, Cambridge, Fall River, and Lowell, Massachusetts; Providence, Rhode Island; Hartford, Connecticut; New York City; and Oakland, California. Welcomed at first as hard workers, they soon fell victim to the anti-Catholic spirit of the 1890s, and their inclination to join labor unions angered many businessmen. Irish workers resented them because of job competition and declining wages.

During the same period nearly 140,000 Spaniards left Iberia for America. The Spanish heritage in the United States long predated them. Spanish place names, language, art, and architecture were central to southwestern culture and had been ever since the colonial period. But the golden age had come to an end. Spain had fallen on hard times by 1900. Since 1500 Spain had lived off its colonies, enjoying spectacular but superficial prosperity while neglecting real economic development. Spain lost its Central and South American colonies early in the 1800s, and after the Spanish-American War of 1898 it surrendered Cuba, Puerto Rico, Guam, and the Philippines. Impoverished financially, plagued by an arid climate, and burdened with much infertile soil, Spain declined economically and thousands of peasants headed to the United States. Many were Basques, an ethnic group in northern Spain who had long enjoyed their own language and cultural independence. They settled in Utah, Idaho, Oregon, Nevada, and California, and herded sheep where the Utes and Shoshones had once roamed. Northern Nevada and southwestern Idaho are still the home of thousands of Basque ranchers and herdsmen; summer Basque festivals are still popular; and Boise, Idaho, is still the center of Basque culture in the United States.

The Italians

Between 1880 and 1924, 4.5 million Italians came to America, and if the arrival of thousands of Iberians worried older Americans, millions of Italians from the Mezzogiorno (the six provinces of Abruzzi, Campania, Apulia, Basilicata, Calabria, and Sicily) generated a sense of shock. Until the 1880s Italians had immigrated quietly, but their numbers were few and most were artisans, businessmen, professionals, artists, and missionaries. With skills and money so desperately needed in the early American economy, they were considered assets. Father Eusebio Kino established twenty-four missions in the Southwest between 1698 and 1711, and Father Giuseppe Rosati constructed churches, convents, monasteries, seminaries, and orphanages throughout the Midwest. The scientist Filippo Mazzei came to Virginia in 1773 and worked for the colonies during the Revolution. Luigi Arditi wrote the first American opera; Giuseppe Ceracchi sculpted busts of famous American politicians in the 1790s; and Constantino Brumidi painted frescos in the rotunda of the United States Capitol. Perhaps ten thousand Italian merchants, plasterers, carpenters, cabinetmakers, stonecutters, and glass blowers lived in America in 1860.

Between 1850 and 1880 about eighty thousand people emigrated from northern Italy. For centuries northern Italians had considered themselves superior to southerners; more literate, closer to the rest of Europe, and more industrialized, northern Italy was more prosperous than the south, and lighter-skinned northerners looked down upon "colored" Sicilians. They left Italy to earn higher wages in the United States. By 1870 there were northern Italian colonies in Boston, New York, and Philadelphia. Their leader was G. F. Secchi de Casali, a journalist and the publisher of *L'Eco d'Italia*, the first Italian newspaper in America. Northern Italians established mutual aid societies to build libraries and schools, find jobs for new arrivals, and provide health and life insurance benefits. The Italian Mutual Aid Society of San Francisco was founded in 1858, and prominent New York Italians established the Society of Italian Unions and Fraternity in 1859. Although they experienced some hostility from worried Protestants and frightened Irish-Catholic workers, the northern Italians slowly merged into the American mainstream. Indeed, they were largely forgotten when southern Italians came in the 1890s.

From the Mezzogiorno to America

In the late nineteenth century southern Italy was undergoing a series of social traumas that would scatter its peasants across the globe. Italian padrone labor bosses had recruited teen-age Sicilians to come to work in America in the 1870s; but as life became more difficult between 1880 and 1910, the immigration movement achieved a momentum of its own, sustained by the letters and cash sent home to Italy from the first immigrants. Between 1890 and 1924 Italian immigrants sent more than $1 billion home to their families, and the money became so important to Italy's economy that the government established a postal remittance system to smooth its flow. American propaganda, emigration, and returning cash inspired hard-pressed *contadini*, or peasants, of southern Italy to come to the United States.

Until the 1860s Italy was divided into a number of small principalities and city states which had risen to world prominence during the Renaissance. Although Sardinia, the Papal States, and Sicily were independent of foreign control in 1850, Austria had Lombardy and Venetia while the Hapsburgs ruled Parma, Tuscany, and Modena. Inspired by the nationalism sweeping through Europe at mid-century, Italian patriots dreamed of the Renaissance, when Italian culture had defined Western civilization. Patriotic idealists like Giuseppe Mazzini, Camillo di Cavour, and Giuseppe Garibaldi knew the resurrection of Italian greatness depended upon political unification, and their *Risorgimento* began in the 1850s, when Sardinia, allied with France against Austria, united with northern Italy by conquering Parma, Lombardy, Tuscany, and Modena. Garibaldi's troops invaded southern Italy in 1861, conquered Naples and Sicily, and liberated the contadini from the despotic rule of Francis II. Acquiescing to the northerners, Garibaldi ceded the Kingdom of the Two Sicilies to Sardinia, and Victor Emmanuel became king of Italy. Five years later Prussia forced Austria to yield Venetia to Italy. Only the Papal States still existed on their own, and in 1870 they too joined the new nation. Modern Italy was born.

Unity did little to improve the lot of southern Italians, however, for everything south of Rome was neglected. The government financed land development programs or aided schools only in the north, and

former promises of land reform, particularly division of the great *latifundia* (landed estates), were quickly forgotten. Northern politicians taxed everything the contadini produced—wheat, olives, citrus, cows, mules, pigs, and poultry. When the contadini rebelled, at Naples in 1862 and Sicily in 1863, Sardinian armies suppressed the uprisings, and guerrilla war went on for decades.

Life had always been desperately hard for the contadini, and even a short drought or death of a farm animal spelled disaster. When economic change swept Europe in the nineteenth century, hundreds of thousands were pushed to the brink of starvation. Bumper citrus crops in California and Florida in the 1880s dealt a severe blow to Italian exports of lemons and oranges. The wine industry suffered a double blow between 1870 and 1900 when the plant disease phylloxera attacked the vineyards and France imposed heavy tariffs on Italian wines. Finally, between 1870 and 1910 cholera epidemics killed tens of thousands; volcanic eruptions from Vesuvius in 1906 and Etna in 1910 buried whole towns; and earthquakes rocked the peninsula every year. Several quakes hit Basilicata and Calabria in 1905, and three years later more than a hundred thousand people died when a tidal wave swept through Messina on the Sicilian coast.

In central Italy, Apulia, and the interior of Sicily, commercial agriculture prevailed, and landowners supplied capital and management to large tenant farms. The peasants who worked these farms were poor and landless and rarely able to emigrate. But in other regions peasants did own some land, and although they were poor too, they at least were independent and had enough resources to leave. When they were threatened by economic change, many went to America, not so much to abandon traditional ways as to preserve them. In the 1880s and 1890s, in fact, most of the southern Italian immigrants returned to Italy after a short stay in America. Their only intentions had been to find temporary work in the United States, live frugally and save money, and return home with the financial resources to buy land or redeem debts. Not until the early 1900s, when they saw that opportunities in America exceeded those in Italy, did they typically migrate with their families and stay in the United States.

Most Italians settled in urban centers from Boston to Norfolk, and another 15 percent in cities along the Great Lakes out to Chicago. Invariably they chose to live close to one another. If relatives were living in Lowell, Massachusetts, the immigrant would try to find them, live with them for a while, and take a job in a local textile mill where other family members worked. If the immigrant was the first of his family to come to America, he would usually seek out companions from his own region of Italy. This was the spirit of *campanilismo*, an extreme loyalty to the native *paese*, or village. In New York, for example, Mott Street between East Houston and Prince held Neapolitans, as did Mulberry Street. On the opposite side of Mott Street were the Basilicati. Calabrians settled Mott Street between Broome and Grand, Sicilians lived on Prince Street, and the Genoese were on Baxter Street. Italians even settled along village lines. In Chicago western Sicilians congregated together, with the immigrants from Altavilla on Larrabee Street; the people from Alimena and Shiusa Sclafani on Cambridge Street; those from Bagheria on Townsend Street; and the people from Sambuca-Zabut on Milton Street. When neither family nor neighbors could be found, the new immigrant settled with other southern Italians. Least desirable, of course, was living among strangers. Whether it was Mott and Mulberry streets in New York City, the West Side of Chicago, the North Beach of San Francisco, the North End of Boston, or North Broadway in Los Angeles, the southern Italians settled together. By 1900 there were Italian communities in every American city in the Northeast, with restaurants selling hard bread, wine, cheese, salami, and pasta; pushcarts and organ grinders; Columbus Day parades and religious *festas*; newspapers like *L'Italia* in Chicago or *L'Eco Italia* in New York; and tomatoes and garlic drying in back yards everywhere.

At first Italians filled the menial, unskilled jobs vacated by upwardly mobile northern and western Europeans. Like the Irish before them, the Italians worked for the railroads, carrying materials and laying track in the Far West. Italian communities sprang up in Omaha, Nebraska; Cheyenne, Wyoming; Santa Fe, New Mexico; and Great Falls, Montana—anywhere railroad construction was underway. Others worked in the quarries and mills of New England, and Italian settlements appeared in Boston, Providence, Hartford, Springfield, Lowell, and Fall River. Italian ghettos developed in the textile-factory towns of Newark, Trenton, Passaic, and Paterson, New Jersey. Italian men found jobs in coal mines, and "Little Italys" appeared in such diverse places as Huntingdon, West Virginia, and Price, Utah. In the great steel towns of Pittsburgh and Youngstown, Italian settlements were common, as well as in Detroit, where cars were assembled, and in Akron, where tires were manufactured. As migrant workers Italians helped harvest corn in Iowa, Nebraska, and Minnesota; wheat in Kansas and the Texas Panhandle; citrus fruits in California, Florida, and South Texas; sugar beets in Utah and Idaho, and sugar cane in Louisiana; vegetables in California and Arizona; and cotton in the South.

Some contadini bought land in rural America, and Italian farming communities appeared in Texas, Louisiana, Missouri, Arkansas, Wisconsin, and New Jersey. The famous Italian-Swiss vineyards in Sonoma County, California, and the Del Monte vegetable empire operated by

Marco Fontana became Italian agribusinesses. Italians were prominent throughout the garment districts, displaced Irish longshoremen along the wharves, and dominated musicians' unions in the East. Many established small shops, grocery and confectionery stores, restaurants, and pharmacies; others were coal dealers, ice cream and fruit vendors, and ragpickers. Italians, many of them skilled craftsmen, found jobs in the construction industry and became carpenters, plasterers, masons, cement workers, electricians, roofers, plumbers, and cabinetmakers.

Anti-Italian Reaction

Older Americans did not welcome the Italians. Calling them "black dagos" and "wops," many Americans considered them ignorant, inferior, and superstitious, lacking ambition and social taste. The size of the Italian migration alarmed them, as did Italian Catholicism and concentration in urban ghettos. Italian immigrants often became scapegoats for the problems of crime, slums, and poverty.

Rumors of organized crime circulated wherever Italians settled. In the 1890s the "Black Hand" conspiracy, imported from Italy, was supposedly responsible for the increase of crime in America. Some people blamed the "Mafia" for social problems in the 1920s and 1930s, and as late as the 1950s and 1960s people were worrying about the "Cosa Nostra." The relationship between crime and Italian immigration was complex, an outgrowth of life in America and the Mezzogiorno. For centuries Sicily and southern Italy had been overrun by Spanish, French, Italian, Austrian, and Turkish invaders, and disrespect for law, authority, and governments became central to Sicilian culture. Peasants lived in a hostile environment where personal security was the responsibility of the family. An Italian immigrant who came to America in 1907 recalled a day in Pittsburgh:

> We didn't know a word of English. Then we saw a policeman standing in the middle of the street. Back in the old country we used to run anytime we saw the police. This one was smiling and came over to us. He said something, but all we could say was "Pittsburgh." Then my brother, who was nervous and scared, took a piece of cigar out of his pocket and started looking for a match. Believe it or not, that policeman took out a match and lit my brother's cigar. Can you imagine that happening in Italy? They would just as soon clobber you . . . *

In western Sicily armed *mafiosi*, originally local strongmen hired to protect estates and collect rents from peasants, became a private gov-

---

*Quoted in Joseph Lopreato, *Italian-Americans* (New York, 1970), p. 39.

ernment of small groups controlling crime in different towns, villages, and cities. Few mafiosi migrated to the United States, but suspicion of authority and a tendency to resolve disputes outside the law accompanied many of the Italian immigrants.

There is a relationship between ethnicity and crime in American life, since crime was one route out of the slums. An analogy can be made to sports. The first generation of heavyweight champions—Paddy Ryan, John L. Sullivan, "Gentleman" Jim Corbett—were often Irish; after 1920 they gave way to Italians like Primo Carnera and then Rocky Marciano; and today Afro-Americans like Floyd Patterson, Sonny Liston, Joe Frazier, George Foreman, Muhammad Ali, and Leon Spinks dominate the sport. Similarly, the Irish were the first to dominate racketeering in the United States. Following its Calvinist impulses, Protestant America prohibited certain goods and services which they considered vices but which many people wanted. What legitimate businessmen could not supply illegitimate businessmen did supply, and gambling, liquor, and prostitution rackets—run largely by the Irish—came into being. But as the Irish created the Democratic machines, power and status came through politics and control of construction, public utilities, and the waterfront. For a time in the early twentieth century such Jews as Arnold Rothstein, Louis "Lepke" Buchalter, and Jacob Shapiro controlled gambling and labor racketeering in New York City.

Struggling to make a living in Little Italy, some Italian immigrants turned to crime, but it was more difficult in the United States than in Sicily. Except in densely populated New York City, extortion practices were not as lucrative. In every other city the concentration of Italian immigrants was not high enough; residential dispersion as well as the constant flow of new immigrants into the city and the flight of older immigrants to better neighborhoods prevented the stable colony life which made extortion threats meaningful. Still, some Italians displaced the Irish and used gambling, narcotics, liquor, and prostitution as avenues to success. During the 1920s they found in prohibition an unprecedented opportunity to market an illegal commodity, and on February 14, 1929, in what is known as the St. Valentine's Day massacre, Al Capone's Italian gang wiped out Dion O'Banion's (who had been murdered in 1926) Irish mob and took over the Chicago rackets. Later Italian racketeers branched out into loan-sharking, fencing stolen goods, and peddling narcotics. But there was never a nationwide crime conspiracy to take over America. When crime did exist in Italian America, it was family oriented, decentralized, and involved only a tiny segment of the population. Today, blacks, Puerto Ricans, and Mexican-Americans control some of the ghetto rackets in only the latest instance of what has become a tradition in American history.

Violence against Italian immigrants began as early as the 1870s. In 1874 four Italian strikebreakers were killed by union mine workers in Buena Vista, Pennsylvania, and in 1886 a mob in Vicksburg, Mississippi, lynched an Italian-American. When an Italian immigrant was murdered in Buffalo in 1888, the police summarily arrested 325 other Italians as suspects. The worst incident occurred in 1891. Since the mid-1880s New Orleans newspapers had speculated on the existence of a Black Hand conspiracy, and the Irish police chief of New Orleans, David Hennessey, had built a political reputation investigating Sicilian crime. In 1891 he was murdered, and an outraged public decided the Mafia was responsible. Nine Italians were arrested, but a jury acquitted six of them and declared mistrials for the others. An outraged mob entered the parish jail and lynched eleven Italian inmates, three of whom were Italian nationals. In 1899 a mob in Tallulah, Louisiana, murdered five Italian storekeepers because they had given black employees equal pay with whites. In 1914, after Italian miners had gone on strike in Colorado, the governor called in state troops, and in the ensuing melee three miners were shot and eight women and children burned to death. Other lynchings occurred in West Virginia in 1891 and 1906; Altoona, Pennsylvania, in 1894; Erwin, Massachusetts, in 1901; Marion, North Carolina, in 1906; Tampa, Florida, in 1910; Wilksville, Illinois, in 1914; and Johnson City, Illinois, in 1915. And in 1920 marauding people invaded the Italian neighborhood of West Frankfurt, Illinois, and systematically burned the community to the ground.

Anti-Italian sentiment reached its height in the Sacco and Vanzetti case of the 1920s. On April 15, 1920, a shoe company in South Braintree, Massachusetts, was robbed of $15,000 and two employees were killed. Two Italian immigrants, Nicola Sacco and Bartolomeo Vanzetti, were arrested and charged with the crime. A hostile judge instructed the jury to disregard eyewitness testimony that neither was anywhere near the scene of the crime. When the prosecution revealed that both men were under investigation by the Department of Justice for political radicalism, their fate was sealed. Both were convicted, and in 1927, despite serious doubt about their guilt, they died in the electric chair.

The Italian Commitment to Family and Village

Such treatment reinforced the isolationist strains of Italian culture, confirming the ancient maxims of the Mezzogiorno—that justice and the legal system were often contradictory, that the law was often an instrument of oppression, and that true security rested only in the family, *la famiglia*, and in the fellowship of friends and neighbors, the spirit of campanilismo. Italian-Americans were a proud, independent, and self-reliant people, committed to one another by blood and history.

An extended clan of relatives, the family was the purpose of existence, the marrow of the social system. All other institutions—political, economic, and religious—were of minor importance. Patriotism meant love for the family, and abiding by the law meant obedience to the rules of the family.

Centuries of invasions, of discrimination by northern Italians, and of exploitation by rich landlords had made southern Italians suspicious of strangers and the upper classes—the *signori*—and reinforced their commitment to family and the spirit of campanilismo. Even the Catholic church was suspect. In Sicily the church had been a major landowner, and after years of collecting tithes and rents from the contadini, the church had become part of the signori. Although the Italians were profoundly religious, their suspicions about the church prevented them from making the same institutional commitment the Irish, French-Canadians, and eastern Europeans made. Indeed, because of hostility from Irish Catholics, the church in the United States strengthened the Italian sense of distance from the larger culture. While many Protestants criticized the Italians for being Roman Catholic, many Catholics criticized them for being superstitious.

Italian Catholicism bore traces of Greek, Moslem, and Byzantine culture well into the twentieth century. For Italian peasants, life was not a series of random events. All events, blessings as well as catastrophes, had their origins in the world of spirits, and religion was a means of appeasing those spirits through rituals, prayers, and charms. Church doctrine and authority were not important to the peasants. Usually they considered the celibate, cassocked priests effeminate, an attribute hardly admired in a society placing so much emphasis on masculine virility. As the one person who could preside over baptisms, confirmations, marriages, burials, and exorcisms, the priest was essential to peasant religion; but as a moral leader who urged weekly attendance at mass, confession, and communion, he was often disregarded, especially by the men.

Peasant religion also reflected the paese view of the world. Italian Catholics believed strongly in *clientelismo*, the use of saints as intermediaries to God. Since God was a distant figure who could not concern himself with mundane affairs of the paese or famiglia, the peasants relied on saints—San Rocco, Santa Lucia, San Michele, San Gennaro, Santa Rita, San Biagio, and San Francesco di Paolo, to name a few—to intervene on behalf of the petitioner. Theirs was a cultist faith which also raised the Virgin Mary to the level of a deity. The sense of cosmic magic even transcended the power of the church, for most Italians believed in *malocchio*, the evil eye, as the source of disaster and disappointment. Malevolent spirits caused all sorts of problems, and could only be warded off through incantations, charms, and potions. Many southern Italians kept lucky charms and amulets to drive off evil spirits, and purchased wax statues of heads, hands, and feet to give to their favorite saints to cure physical ailments.

Once a year the Italians celebrated a *festa*, the day of their village patron saint. A party atmosphere imbued the entire community, and attendance at a high mass was exceptionally large. Money, candles, grain, or prizes were given to the church; elaborate afternoon processionals complete with brass bands, marching confraternities, and statues of the patron saint raised the festive mood and induced charismatic moods of weeping, tranced solemnity, and excited laughter; and feasts, dances, and fireworks were held in the evening. In the United States, because people from so many different villages were congregated in one area, there were several festas a year as each group sought to demonstrate the superiority of its patron saint. The festa was a patriotic act which bound the paese into an ethnic whole; the festival of Our Lady of Mount Carmel transformed New York's Little Italy each year and revived the links between the Old World and the New.

Many American Catholics were unable to tolerate the syncretic Catholicism of the Italian immigrants. The Irish viewed Italian Catholics as practically pagans. The cults of the saints, deification of the Madonna, beliefs in the evil eye and the world of spirits, and the emotionalism of the festas seemed sacrilegious to the Irish. An Irish Catholic later recalled his reaction to the Italian immigrants:

> These Italians were strange people, very strange to us . . . for God's sake, when they began to come to our church and made a market place of it, we were sure that they were the people whom the Lord chased from the temple. In those days we were quite sure, and even today I don't see how they have the nerve to call themselves Christians when they are not.*

The Irish were equally distressed about Italian apathy for the institutional church and their unwillingness to support it financially. Irish hostility only further alienated the Italians. An Italian living in East Harlem remembered:

> In 1886 the Italians in East Harlem lived within a radius of a quarter of a mile. There was one church to go to and that was what we used to call the "American Church" at East 115th Street. . . . In those days we Italians were allowed to worship only in the basement part of the Church, a fact which was not altogether to our liking. †

---

*Quoted in Marie Conistre, "Education in a Local Area: A Study of a Decade in the Life and Education of the Adult Italian Immigrant in East Harlem, New York" (unpublished Ph.D. dissertation, New York University, 1943), p. 273.

† Ibid., p. 273.

St. Rocco Day Festival in the Italian section of New York City around 1915.
(Brown Brothers)

Italian-language parishes appeared throughout the country, like Our Lady of Mount Carmel parish in East Harlem or Holy Rosary parish on East 121st Street in Cleveland, but the Italian impulse to establish them never matched the zeal of the Irish, French-Canadians, Germans, Poles, Czechs, Slovaks, Slovenes, Magyars, or Lithuanians. And finally, because parochial schools were so often controlled by Irish nuns and priests, Italian children usually attended public school. Not even the church competed with la famiglia or the village for the loyalties of the Italian immigrants. Only the family could be trusted; only the family deserved allegiance; and only the family guaranteed security.

Even Italian-American mutual aid societies had a Mezzogiorno flavor, for most of them provided employment, health, and death benefits for particular families and villagers. Italians rarely established community or national organizations. By 1924 every major American city had hundreds of Italian mutual aid societies, each governed by one or a few families from a village group. Despite their poverty, Italian immigrants rarely turned to Protestant philanthropies or social welfare agencies for assistance. Dependence on strangers brought dishonor to the family, exposing an inability or, worse, an unwillingness to care for one another. Honor, family, independence—these were the values of the Mezzogiorno.

If reverence for the family and the village translated into self-reliance, the Italian work ethic accounted for economic independence. Work, not necessarily prosperity, was the gauge of respectability. The indolent poor as well as the idle rich were despised in the Mezzogiorno and in the ghettos of America. Hard work, whether that of a common laborer or a famous surgeon, dignified people by sustaining the family. It trained people, disciplined them, prepared them for the vicissitudes of life. Idleness was a depravity, a sign of moral decay, because it made life difficult for the family and that was unpardonable. It was not surprising that the Great Depression of the 1930s was as much a moral crisis as an economic one in the Italian community.

Many Italian immigrants remained in blue-collar occupations even when opportunities for professional or corporate success began to materialize. First-generation contadini suspected higher education because it introduced young people to the outside world, created new allegiances, and might keep them from contributing economically to the family. A 1907 editorial in one Italian-American newspaper complained:

> The schools where the Italian language is taught are deserted. The Italian families falsify even the ages of their children in order to send them to the factories, instead of the schools, showing thus an avarice. . . . There is not a young Italian girl who knows to typewrite in both languages, and our men of affairs must employ Jewish girls or Americans for lack of Italians.*

Since education was a prerequisite to bureaucratic and professional success, many Italian-Americans cut themselves off from those livelihoods.

The contadini also avoided administrative work in corporations and bureaucracies because success there was a group rather than an individual matter and daily contact with *stranieri*, or strangers, was too common. They did take jobs with police and fire departments in the cities, but those local organizations had a Mezzogiorno flavor because so many Italians worked there. The corporate world offered no such compensations, however, and for most Italians its demands were excessive. Success required a realignment of loyalties from the family to the business, a step Italians were often unwilling to take. Nor did the contadini come to America with the compulsion to succeed. Life in the Mezzogiorno had too often destroyed their dreams, and stoicism permeated their view of life. For emotional stability they had often limited their ambitions. Finally, many Italians stayed in blue-collar jobs because work was synonymous with production. When the mason finished the wall, or the tailor the suit, he felt pleasure and satisfaction. Pride came from seeing the results of one's labor.

Some Italians did succeed in business. Amedeo Obici built the Planter Peanut Company from a pushcart; Marco Fontana established Del Monte Foods; Joseph DiGiorgio founded the DiGiorgio Fruit Corpora-

---

*Quoted in Thomas Kessner, *The Golden Door* (New York, 1977), p. 99.

tion; and Lee A. Iacocca first became president of Ford Motor Company and then of Chrysler Corporation in 1978. Corporate success was often a function of campanalismo. A. P. Giannini created the Bank of America chain in California and built it into one of the largest private banking systems in the world after discovering that most banks refused credit to Italian immigrants.

The Italian-American neighborhoods were cultural islands committed to *la via vecchia*—the old way—by tradition, love, and nostalgia. Mezzogiorno immigrants lived with other southern Italians not because of nativist hostility, however real it was, but because life was inextricably linked to the family and the village. The old way survived even while the cultural baggage of other immigrant groups was disappearing. To be sure, second- and third-generation Italian-Americans were torn between the old and new. Urban life, public education, and geographic mobility placed great pressures on the old way, but their loyalty to the family and the patterns of Italian life was powerful. In the second generation more than 80 percent of Italian men and nearly all Italian women married Italians, and even today Italian remains one of the strongest second languages in the United States. In the 1940s, when some Italians joined the exodus to the suburbs, they moved with the family in the spirit of campanilismo. Little Italys appeared on Long Island and in Westchester, New York, or in Wheaton and Silver Spring, Maryland. *La via vecchia* commanded an extraordinary loyalty.

SUGGESTED READINGS

Abramson, Harold J. *Ethnic Diversity in Catholic America*. New York: 1973.

Amfitheatrof, Erik. *The Children of Columbus: An Informal History of the Italians in the New World*. Boston: 1973.

Barton, Josef J. *Peasants and Strangers: Italians, Rumanians, and Slovaks in an American City, 1890–1950*. Cambridge, Mass.: 1975.

Barzini, Luigi. *The Italians*. New York: 1964.

Campisi, Paul J. "Ethnic Family Patterns: The Italian Family in the United States." *American Journal of Sociology*, 53 (May 1948), 443–449.

Carlyle, Margaret. *The Awakening of Southern Italy*. London: 1962.

Caroli, Betty B. *Italian Repatriation from the United States, 1900–1914*. New York: 1973.

Child, Irvin L. *Italian or American? The Second Generation in Conflict*. New Haven, Conn.: 1943.

DeConde, Alexander. *Half Bitter, Half Sweet: An Excursion into Italian American History*. New York: 1971.

Donato, Pietro Di. *Christ in Concrete*. New York: 1939.

_____ . *Three Circles of Light*. New York: 1960.

Douglas, William A., and Bilbao, John. *Amerikanauk: Basques in the New World*. Reno, Nev.: 1975.

Femminella, Francis X. "The Impact of Italian Migration and American Catholicism." *The American Catholic Sociological Review*, 22 (Fall 1961), 233–241.

Foerster, Robert. *Italian Emigration of Our Times*. New York: 1969.

Fumento, Rocco. *Tree of Dark Reflections*. New York: 1962.

Gallo, Patrick J. *Ethnic Alienation: The Italian American*. Cranbury, N.J.: 1974.

Gambino, Richard. *Blood of My Blood: The Dilemma of Italian Americans*. Garden City, N.Y.: 1975.

Gans, Herbert J. *The Urban Villagers: Group and Class in the Life of Italian Americans*. New York: 1962.

Glazer, Nathan, and Moynihan, Daniel P. *Beyond the Melting Pot: The Negroes, Puerto Ricans, Jews, Italians and Irish of New York City*. Cambridge, Mass.: 1963.

Greeley, Andrew M. *The American Catholic*. New York: 1977.

Iorizzo, Luciano, and Mondello, Salvatore. *The Italian Americans*. New York: 1971.

Juliani, Richard N. "The Origin and Development of the Italian Community in Philadelphia." In John Bodnar, ed. *The Ethnic Experience in Pennsylvania*. Lewisburg, Pa.: 1973.

LaGumina, Salvatore J., ed. *Ethnicity in American Political Life: The Italian American Experience*. New York: 1968.

Lopreato, Joseph. *Italian Americans*. New York: 1970.

_____ . *Peasants No More*. San Francisco: 1967.

Nelli, Humbert S. *The Business of Crime: Italians and Syndicate Crime in the United States*. New York: 1976.

_____ . *Italians in Chicago 1880–1930: A Study in Ethnic Mobility*. New York: 1970.

Puzo, Mario. *The Fortunate Pilgrim*. New York: 1964.

Rolle, Andrew. *The American Italians*. Belmont, Cal.: 1972.

Tomasi, Lydio F. *The Italian American Family: The Southern Italian Family's Process of Adjustment to an Urban America*. New York: 1972.

Tomasi, Silvano M., ed. *Perspectives in Italian Immigration and Ethnicity*. New York: 1977.

_____ . *Piety and Power: The Role of the Italian Parishes in the New York Metropolitan Area, 1880–1930*. New York: 1976.

Tomasi, Silvano M., and Engel, M. H. *The Italian Experience in the United States*. New York: 1971.

Valletta, Clement L. "The Settlement of Roseto: Worldview and Promise." In John Bodnar, ed. *The Ethnic Experience in Pennsylvania*. Lewisburg, Pa.: 1973.

Vecoli, Rudolph J. "Contadini in Chicago: A Critique of *The Uprooted*." *Journal of American History*, 51 (December 1964), 404–417.

_____ ."Cult and Occult in Italian-American Culture: The Persistence of a

Religious Heritage." In Randall Miller and Thomas D. Marzik. *Immigrants and Religion in Urban America*. Philadelphia: 1977.

––––––– . "Prelates and Peasants." *Journal of Social History*, 2 (Spring 1969), 217–268.

Winch, Robert F., Greer, Scott, and Blumberg, Rae L. "Ethnicity and Extended Familism in an Upper Middle Class Suburb." *American Sociological Review*, 32 (April 1967), 265–272.

Wolforth, Sandra. *The Portuguese in America*. Palo Alto, Cal.: 1978.

Chapter Fourteen

The Eastern European Catholics

Millions of Roman Catholics left Poland, Lithuania, Bohemia, Moravia, Slovakia, Hungary, Croatia, Slovenia, and the Ukraine for the economic bounty, political liberty, and religious freedom of the United States. Because of political rivalries and frequently changing national boundaries in eastern Europe, it is difficult to measure accurately the exact number of immigrants coming from that part of the world. The Poles were scattered through eastern Germany, western Russia, and northern Austria, and immigration officials often counted them as Germans, Austrians, or Russians. Still, perhaps 3 million Poles immigrated between 1877 and 1924. More than 200,000 Lithuanians left the northern Baltic coast and 400,000 Ukrainians moved from the Ukraine, but they too were often counted in the larger Russian migration. And from the Austro-Hungarian Empire came approximately 750,000 Magyars (Hungarians), 500,000 Czechs, 600,000 Slovaks, 225,000 Slovenes, 300,000 Croatians, and 600,000 Rusins.

The Slavic Peoples

The Slavs were a diverse group originating in central Asia who had slowly pushed into eastern Europe during the early Middle Ages. Around 400 A.D. they reached a frontier running from the Adriatic Sea to the Elbe River, but the Germans stalled further expansion west. Two hundred years later the Slavic fringe penetrated the Balkans. During the migration the Slavic communities developed into many political, religious, and linguistic groups. Eastern Slavs by 1850 consisted of perhaps 25 million Ukrainians, 4 million Lithuanians, and 40 million Byelorussians and Great Russian Slavs. About 11 million Poles and 7 million Czechs and Slovaks constituted the Western Slavs, and 3 million Bulgarians, 6 million Serbs and Croatians, and more than 1 million Slovenes made up the Southern Slavs.

The Slavs never united for the factors holding them together—common origins, hatred of the Germans, fear of the Turks—never overcame the political, geographic, religious, and linguistic forces dividing them. By 1840 pan-Slavic nationalism had emerged in central and eastern Europe. Slavic intellectuals attended pan-Slavic congresses at Prague in 1848 and Moscow in 1867; they talked of political unity, proclaimed the existence of Slavic culture, and extolled the superiority of Slavic values. But pan-Slavism foundered on Slavic nationalisms. Each Slavic group possessed its own history and cultural identity, and the Czechs, Slovaks, Poles, Rusins, Ukrainians, Slovenes, and Croatians were preoccupied with the Russians. They envisioned pan-Slavism as a loose confederation of independent subcultures, but the Russians had in mind an empire with the throne at Moscow. Other Slavs shuddered at the thought. Many Czechs used pan-Slavism as an anti-German ploy. Politics in Eastern Europe today reflects that historical tension. Although Russian domination certainly evolved from political and strategic realities in post–World War II Europe, it also represents the Russian version of pan-Slavism. Competing visions of Slavic nationalism divided the Slavs and retarded the development of Slavic ethnicity.

Nor did the Slavs enjoy territorial integrity. Western and Eastern Slavs were separated geographically from the Southern Slavs by German-Austrians, Hungarians, and Rumanians. Only the Russian Slavs had a nation state in 1877 and only the Russians, Poles, and Lithuanians had ever been independent in modern history. Ukrainians were under Russian domination. Poland was divided three ways: western Poles in West Prussia and Posen were controlled by Prussia; southern Poles in Galicia lived in Austria-Hungary; and eastern Poles were under Russian sovereignty. Czechs, Slovaks, Croatians, and Slovenes were in Austria-Hungary. And the Bulgarians were in the Ottoman Empire until the 1880s.

Religious allegiances also divided them. While the Poles, Czechs, Slovaks, Slovenes, Lithuanians, and Croatians were Catholic, the Russians, Bulgarians, and Serbians were Eastern Orthodox. Rusins and Ukrainians were "Greek Catholics" in Uniate churches that were loyal to Rome but retained a married clergy and insisted on Slavic rather than Latin liturgies. Finally, there were isolated pockets of Slavic Moslems throughout the Balkans.

Linguistic differences further undermined pan-Slavism. Although Slavic languages were Indo-European and shared similarities in morphology, syntax, and phonetics, major divisions had appeared in Slavic dialects and alphabets after the seventh century. By 1500 Slavs were using either Glagolitic, Cyrillic, or Latin alphabets, and individual Slavic groups were speaking separate dialects. The Serbs and Croatians, for example, could understand each other's spoken, but not written, words because the two alphabets were different.

Finally, group nationalisms would not permit Slavic unity. Poland and Lithuania had similar histories. Between 1386 and 1572 they had joined in a protective alliance. Both nations had enjoyed long periods of independence; both were overwhelmingly Roman Catholic; and both hated the Russians to the east and the Germans to the west. Each had lost its independence late in the eighteenth century, Lithuania falling to Russia and Poland being partitioned by Prussia, Austria, and Russia. Nationals in both countries remembered earlier glory and yearned for its return.

The Austro-Hungarian Empire was an unstable coalition of competing nationalities. The Hapsburgs had controlled central Europe since

PEOPLES OF
AUSTRIA-HUNGARY

the fifteenth century, but in the 1860s the monarchy finally gave way to more liberal ideologies. In 1867 Franz Joseph, Emperor of Austria and King of Hungary, approved a constitution for Austria that provided a bicameral legislature, and at the same time gave Hungary a separate constitution and parliament. Hungary still shared joint ministries of war, finance, and foreign affairs with Austria. This was the Dual Monarchy, a multinational, multilingual state of 50 million people.

Between 1848 and 1916 the rule of Franz Joseph held together a caldron of competing national, language, and religious groups. Twelve million Germans and Austrians suppressed the Czechs and Poles in Austria, while in Hungary 10 million Magyars suppressed the Slovaks, Serbs, Croatians, Slovenes, Rumanians, and Rusins. Denied the use of their language and ridiculed for their traditions, the Czechs yearned for independence. The Slovaks wanted independence or at least reunification with Czech Bohemia; the Serbs demanded a South Slav (Yugoslav) nation; and the Rusins wanted an independent nation in Transcarpathia. Not until the outbreak of World War I in 1914, the death of Franz Joseph in 1916, and the Treaty of Versailles in 1919 did these nationalistic impulses reach fruition in the separation of Austria and Hungary and the creation of Czechoslovakia, Poland, and Yugoslavia.

The Migration

While a small number of eastern Europeans came to the United States during the colonial and early national periods, no substantial immigration occurred. Thousands, however, came after the revolutions of 1848 and formed an elite group of politically aware intellectuals. And between the creation of the Dual Monarchy in 1867 and the disintegration of Austria-Hungary during World War I, more than 6 million eastern European Catholics settled in the United States.

After the invasion of Hungary in 1848 four thousand Hungarian political refugees fled to America. When he visited the United States, the revolutionary leader Louis Kossuth was the recipient of awards, banquets, salutes, parades, and audiences with famous Americans. Other political refugees were Franz Sigel, a colonel in Kossuth's Hungarian forces who eventually became chief of staff to General John Charles Frémont in the Union Army during the Civil War; Janos Xantos, who became a successful civil servant in the Department of the Interior; Anthony Vallas, later head of the New Orleans Academy of Science; Charles Tothvarady, founder of the first Hungarian newspaper in the United States; and Joseph Pulitzer, the father of "yellow journalism" and publisher of the *New York World*. Many Czechs, including

Vojta Naprstek, fled Bohemia in 1848 and settled in Milwaukee, where Naprstek published the liberal paper *Flug Blatter*.

Throughout the rest of the nineteenth century frustrated nationals left eastern Europe for the more enlightened political atmosphere of the United States. After 1860 Russian officials began persecuting Lithuanian nationalists, suppressing the Lithuanian language, and outlawing the use of the Latin alphabet. They also harassed Catholic priests. The Russians imposed similar controls in Poland and began confiscating church property. Bismarck pressured the Prussian and Posen Poles in the 1870s by outlawing the Polish language, taking control of parochial schools, and forcing Polish nobles to sell their estates to Germans. Thousands of these political refugees headed for the United States. Usually well-educated and intensely conscious of their nationalities, they settled in the Northeast and formed the nucleus of the eastern European urban communities. After them came millions of peasants fleeing economic problems.

Acquainted with industrial labor because of their wanderings in Europe, most of the peasants went to work in the mines, mills, and factories of the urban Northeast and Midwest. By 1920 substantial numbers of eastern Europeans were living in Massachusetts, New York, Ohio, Pennsylvania, Indiana, Illinois, Michigan, Wisconsin, and Minnesota. Although there were more than a thousand separate Polish and Lithuanian settlements in 1900, more than half the immigrants lived in Detroit, Milwaukee, Buffalo, Cleveland, and Pittsburgh, and the largest colonies were in Chicago. Chicago was also the center of Bohemian and Croatian culture. More than half the Slovaks, Rusins, and Ukrainians settled in Pennsylvania, and the major Slovenian colony was in Cleveland. "Little Hungary" could be found in every major northeastern city.

Less than 20 percent settled in rural areas. Because the Czechs were the first Slavic group to immigrate in large numbers, they established an agricultural base that set them apart from other Slavic immigrants. By 1877 there were eight thousand Czechs farming in Iowa, Nebraska, Wisconsin, and central Texas. The first Slovenes settled as homesteaders in Michigan, Minnesota, the Dakotas, and California, and founded their own town in Minnesota—Kraintown—named after Carniola, or Krain, a province of Austria. Polish farming communities could be found in Wisconsin, Minnesota, North Dakota, South Dakota, Nebraska, and Texas. But farming did not become the main livelihood of the Slavic and Magyar immigrants because the best land was either taken or too expensive. Nor did they want to be cut off from their Roman Catholic parishes.

They put up with menial, often dirty industrial jobs and tolerated life in crowded tenements at first because their migration was transitory.

Like the earliest immigrants from southern Italy, many eastern Europeans had no intention of staying in America. One Pole wrote to the Emigrants Protective Association in Warsaw that three

> of us have decided to go [to America]. We will leave our wives and children at home and perhaps we shall be able to earn some money and come back to our country. Many people among us go to America . . . they come back and everybody brings some money with him. Here it is very difficult to advance. I want to live, though poorly, yet decently, and to give my children some education at least . . . *

Living in a bachelor society without wives and children, and often traveling in groups and staying in the same boarding houses in American cities, they suffered poverty and discrimination, but, given their temporary intentions, they tolerated the abuse. Perhaps 500,000 Polish immigrants returned home between 1890 and 1924. Ultimately, eastern European immigrants decided that job and income opportunities were too good in America and too dismal at home, and they began bringing their wives and children with them. But they still lived in the cities, where they could hear Old World languages spoken, read of news from Europe, and worship in their churches. With their families here, they planted roots in America.

Ethnicity in America

Ethnicity among eastern European immigrants was in part a defensive reaction to American nativists who denounced them because of their peasant origins, poverty, and Roman Catholicism. Huddled into urban ghettos, the immigrants could insulate themselves from that ridicule. A Bohemian immigrant remembered:

> When I first came I thought I could not stand it . . . so many people would refer to the southern European class of people with great disdain. They seemed to look down upon Europeans from our land. I know that many have a serious misconception of class. Our peasant is a landholder, more nearly compared to the American farmer, and is far from the bottom of the social scale.†

For centuries the Anglo-Saxon, Teuton, and Latin peoples had looked down upon Slavs (and Magyars) as inferiors. Eastern European history

---

*Quoted in W. I. Thomas, and Florian Znaniecki, *The Polish Peasant in Europe and America* (Boston, 1918), p. 24.
†Quoted in William C. Smith, *Americans in the Making* (New York, 1970), p. 67.

Immigrants from eastern
Europe learn English in a
New York public school.
(Culver Pictures, Inc.)

has included a long Slavic quest to prove equality with western Europeans; and the immigrants, if only in subtle ways, carried a resentment of western paternalism with them to America. American snobbishness seemed an extension of European attitudes, and they felt more secure among other Slavs. They congregated in ethnic ghettos by choice, not just because of circumstance or American nativism. Prejudice against Catholic immigrants was common, but for the most part older Americans and the immigrants lived in separate worlds. Some contact occurred during work and commerce, but the two peoples functioned independently in family, social, and religious matters. Polite distance more accurately describes their relationship than constant hostility.

Adjustment was eased by the presence of earlier immigrants. Most Polish immigrants in the 1870s, for example, were literate, skilled workers and professionals coming from German Poland and understanding some German, so they often settled in established German or Czech Catholic communities. The first Lithuanian immigrants, most of whom also understood some German, did the same. Magyar, Czech, and Polish peasants, of course, were preceded by refugees of the 1848 revolutions from their own regions. For many their first contacts in America were familiar: when peasants began immigrating in large numbers after 1890, they moved into ethnic neighborhoods established earlier by Germans, German Poles, Lowland Lithuanians, Czechs, or Magyar refugees. Instead of experiencing total culture shock, they settled eventually into fluid, ethnic societies.

The closeness they felt for one another revolved around nationalism, land, family, and religion. Although peasants had little sense of nationalism, the educated, middle-class political refugees preceding them had well-developed national loyalties. They were to do for eastern Europeans what the Forty-Eighters had done for German-Americans. Since the partition of Poland in 1795, for example, Polish liberals had yearned for independence; and in 1831, 1846, 1848, and 1863 they had rebelled unsuccessfully against Prussia, Austria, and Russia. After each rebellion small streams of Polish exiles came to the United States and formed the nucleus of an American Polonia. They formed the Polish Committee and the American Committee for Polish Welfare in 1834, the Democratic Society of Polish Exiles in 1852, and the Polish National Alliance in 1880.

During the 1850s the Magyar refugees founded the mutual aid societies and ethnic newspapers so common to immigrant America. The Hungarian Sick Benefit Society, the New York Hungarian Association, and the Verhonay Fraternal Insurance Association were already in existence when the new immigrants arrived, as were such newspapers as the *Hungarian Exiles Journal*, *Hungarian America*, and the *American National Guard*. Few peasant immigrants had ever read newspapers before, but in the United States the ethnic press was a vital link with the Old World. The Czech Slavic Benevolent Society was formed in 1854 by nationalistic refugees of the Bohemian uprising in 1848. If ethnic politics based on an independent Poland or Bohemia or Hungary seemed remote to the peasant majority, they were real and immediate to the literate, politically conscious minority.

The Influence of National Histories

Early immigrants brought their national histories to America, and images of the past generated nationalism in the present. Educated Poles and Lithuanians were aware of their countries' former independence. Magyar history similarly united the Hungarian immigrants. In the tenth century German missionaries converted the Magyars to Roman Catholicism. Though periodically independent during the Middle Ages, Hungary suffered at the hands of many invaders. Hordes of Tartar tribesmen broke out of Asia and overran Hungary in the thirteenth century, and three centuries later the Ottoman Turks extended their empire all the way to the Carpathians. Magyar Catholics envisioned themselves as the last outpost of Christianity until the Ottoman Empire disintegrated in the nineteenth century. Soviet domination today, starkly symbolized by the brutal suppression of the 1956 uprising in Budapest, is only the most recent incident in a long history of occupation.

Despite a thousand years of political separation, the Czechs and Slovaks shared a vision of the future. They both belonged to the Western Slavic tribes, and until late in the ninth century were united under the Great Moravian Empire. They viewed life, death, and human affairs from the perspective of Slavic Catholicism. Not until 896, when the Magyars conquered Slovakia, did the Czechs and Slovaks part historical company: in Bohemia and Moravia the Czechs worked out their destiny against the surrounding Germans, while the Slovaks suffered under Magyar oppression. From the tenth century the Czechs had a great nation, the Kingdom of Bohemia, and struggled constantly to remain free of German control; but in 1620 the Hapsburgs incorporated Bohemia and Moravia into their jurisdiction, and until the twentieth century the Czechs had second-class status in a larger German society. Political power rested in Vienna, not Prague, and the people who controlled education, land, and urban wealth were German. Czech ethnicity was cut on the edge of German oppression.

The Slovaks suffered a similar fate when Magyars conquered Slovakia. Culturally tied to the Czechs, they looked to Prague rather than Budapest for leadership, even while they were under Magyar control. Without a past as an independent, organized state, the Slovaks at first possessed little sense of nationalism, but nine hundred years of Magyar rule gave them a political consciousness.

Of the Slavic cultures in southern Europe, the Yugoslavs of Slovenia, Croatia, and Serbia migrated to the United States in the largest numbers. Because the Serbs enjoyed national independence for a time and had fallen under Byzantine influence, their sense of ethnicity was closely linked to Eastern Christianity. The Croatians and Slovenes, on the other hand, never had national independence and were under the influence of Roman Catholicism.

South of Austria, surrounding the city of Trieste at the head of the Adriatic Sea, were the Slovenes, the western branch of the Southern Slavs. Numbering about 1.5 million people in 1900, they lived in Styria, Carinthia, Carniola, Istria, Gorizia, Gradisca, and in contiguous parts of Croatia, Hungary, and Italy. Bordered by the Austrian Alps in the north, the Slovenes occupied an area of strategic importance to the Germans because of its access to the Mediterranean. Slovenia fell under

German control in the eighth century, and like Bohemia became an educated, culturally sophisticated civilization. Overwhelmingly Roman Catholic, the Slovenes were a rural people. The major cities of Trieste and Maribor had large German populations while the countryside was occupied almost exclusively by Slovenian peasants. Although the nobility in Slovenia was usually German, a classic feudal society never developed because the mountainous terrain did not lend itself to large estates. But with German landlords in the country and a German business elite in the cities, Slovenian nationalism developed in counterpoint to German domination.

On the Adriatic coast, surrounded by Slovenia, Hungary, and Serbia, were the Roman Catholic Croatians. In the early Middle Ages Croatia had been independent, but in 1102 it fell under the rule of the Magyars. During the Napoleonic Wars France established the colony of Illyria, which included Croatia; and temporarily freed from Magyar rule, Croatian nationalism flowered. After Magyar authority was restored, the national movement continued. Croatian newspapers, reading rooms, literature, and schools developed. Thus the Slovenes and Croatians shared sentiments with the Czechs and Slovaks, they too suffered from German and Magyar oppression.

Finally, in the eastern reaches of the Hapsburg Empire, from Galicia and Bukovina in Austria to the Transcarpathian region of Hungary, Ruthenians slowly developed a sense of political nationalism. There were two separate groups: perhaps 60 percent were Rusins (Carpatho-Ruthenians) and the others were Ukrainians (Galician-Ruthenians). Both were Greek Catholics, lived in the eastern part of the Austro-Hungarian Empire or in western Russia, and had undergone long periods of foreign occupation. Related linguistically, their political histories were different. Dominated for a thousand years by the Magyars, the Rusins were hardly nationalistic; some felt close to the Russians, some to the Magyars, and some to the Ukrainians. The Ukrainians were different. During the Middle Ages Kiev and the Ukraine had been independent, and since the eighteenth century they had maintained a distinct vernacular and literature. Ukrainian nationalism was a product of hostility to Austrian control and fear of Russia. Ukrainians looked forward to the day when they would have neither Austrian nor Russian masters.

Land and Family

While the immigrant elites carried these histories to America and eventually imbued the peasant immigrants with an awareness of Old World politics, nationalism was only one dimension of eastern European ethnicity. Visions of land, family, religion, and community were more important. To Slavs in Europe the land was life and fertility, and they worked it not just to make a living but to define their place in the universe. The ownership of land brought social status and prestige. People farmed the land during the day and returned at night to compact villages where friends, family, and priests lived. Theirs was a life of mutual dependence and community support. Only when economic changes took the land, destroyed dreams of acquiring more, and undermined community life did Slavs look to America for new beginnings.

In America their love of property became a desire for home ownership. Despite low-paying jobs they saved money diligently, even while sending some back to their families in Europe. To concentrate capital and finance home construction, they established ethnic building and loan associations, such as the Pulaski Building and Loan Association of Chicago, and funneled money into them. Describing more than eighty Czech and Polish associations in 1904, an Illinois tax collector said:

> The industry, thrift and ambition to own a home prevalent to such a marked degree among the [Czech and Polish] classes, is responsible for the standing and splendid record of these institutions. The people, believing and trusting in them, deposit therein their savings and hundreds of homes have been and will continue to be acquired through the popular agency.[*]

After years of scrimping and saving to finance a home loan or purchase, eventually most eastern European immigrants owned their own homes in immigrant neighborhoods. Their yearning for property was fulfilled, and, more important, they were able to enjoy the village atmosphere of the Old World.

Within the New World communities the cement of the society was the peasant family. Status and reputation in the Old World were local affairs, confined to a village or at most an area containing several villages. Culturally and emotionally the Slavs lived in an isolated world. Individual independence was impossible because family networks were prerequisites to success. Daily life was public, society personal, and family reputations the standard gauges of respectability. Deviations from the norms compromised the family's good name. The Slavic family was a magnet which attracted the loyalty of generation after generation of children to the community.

Just before the migration, changes occurred in family life which prepared the immigrants for conditions in urban America. For centuries the nuclear family had been highly independent, and the rituals of

---

[*]Quoted in Victor Greene, *For God and Country: The Rise of Polish and Lithuanian Ethnic Consciousness in America* (Madison, Wis., 1975); p. 56.

baptism, confirmation, marriage, funeral, and name day had confirmed its central role. Such ritual occasions as Holy Week and Christmas provided symbolic links between the immediate family and the larger community. The social order was ceremonial and predictable. But the nineteenth-century consolidation of small estates and destruction of household industry placed peasants under the influence of impersonal economic forces and undermined family independence. People began to feel insecure and vulnerable, and turned to new institutions outside the family to sustain them. Slowly, kinship relations became more formal through marriage, dowries, foster parents, and godparents that bound several households together and increased the number of people upon whom families could rely. They also formed mutual aid associations to insure against sickness and death, support schools, organize trades, and promote political activity. Religious associations—to support feast days, shrines, and patron saints—multiplied, as did religious confraternities and sodalities. All these arrangements helped restore stability to family life—and they would continue to do so when the Slavs immigrated to America.

Building Churches and Parishes

Roman Catholicism was central to peasant ethnicity. Caught between the Eastern Orthodoxy of the Russians, the Islamic faith of the Turks, and European Protestantism, eastern European Catholicism was sharply defined and generated a spiritual as well as an institutional commitment to the church. Not as intense as French-Canadian or Irish Catholicism, both of which had struggled desperately against Anglo-Protestantism, eastern European Catholicism was still the major cultural force. It explained the mysteries of life, gave peasants a place in the universe, and served as the center of social and family life. Unlike Italian Catholics, who were suspicious of the organized church, the eastern Europeans cherished the church as an institution.

Like the German Catholics, they wanted to establish their own ethnic-language churches in America. The first eastern European immigrants worshiped in Irish or German Catholic parishes, but religion in an alien tongue hardly seemed religion to them. The village church and priest, the festivals, and the saints' days were too important, as the institutions through which peasants came to terms with their lives and deaths. In America they wanted to celebrate the same festivals, exalt the same patron saints, join the same confraternities and sodalities, and listen to the same priests, especially during confession, that they had had in the Old World. Only Czech or Slovak or Polish parishes with Czech or Slovak or Polish priests gave them ceremonial links to the past and spiritual continuity in the present. Polish parishes began appearing in the 1870s, and the largest, St. Stanislaus in Chicago, was founded in 1893. Eventually hundreds of Polish parishes emerged across the country. St. George's parish in Chicago became the largest Lithuanian congregation. The first Czech Catholic chapel, St. John Nepomuk, was dedicated in St. Louis in 1854, and by 1917 there were 270 Czech-speaking priests in 320 parishes and missions. Beginning in 1890, with the arrival of Father Karoly Boehn in Cleveland, the first Hungarian Catholic parish in the United States was established, and hundreds of others quickly appeared in other Magyar communities. Relatively few Croatian priests made the migration, and although there were many Croatian parishes across the country, including St. Jerome parish in Chicago, the immigrants from Croatia did not pursue ethnic-language churches with the passion of the Poles, Magyars, Lithuanians, Slovenes, Czechs, or Slovaks. Table III lists the development of ethnic parishes in Cleveland. By 1920, in every major city and many smaller cities in the Northeast, each nationality had its own Roman Catholic parish. All these East Europeans, but especially the Poles, would ecstatically celebrate the election of Karol Wojtyla, Cardinal Archbishop of Cracow, as Pope John Paul II in 1978.

TABLE III
NATIONALITY PARISHES IN THE DIOCESE OF CLEVELAND, OHIO

Polish
St. Stanislaus Parish, Cleveland (1873)
Sacred Heart of Jesus Parish, Cleveland (1888)
Assumption Parish, Grafton (1894)
Immaculate Heart of Mary Parish, Cleveland (1894)
Nativity of the Blessed Virgin Parish, Cleveland (1898)
St. John Cantius Parish, Cleveland (1898)
St. Barbara Parish, Cleveland (1905)
St. Hedwig Parish, Cleveland (1905)
St. Stanislaus Parish, Lorain (1908)
St. Hedwig Parish, Akron (1912)
SS Peter and Paul Parish, Cleveland (1927)

Slovak
SS Cyril and Methodius Parish, Cleveland (1902)
Nativity of the Blessed Virgin Parish, Cleveland (1903)
St. Wendelin Parish, Cleveland (1903)
Holy Trinity Parish, Lorain (1906)
St. Andrew Parish, Cleveland (1906)
St. John the Baptist Parish, Akron (1907)
Our Lady of Mercy Parish, Cleveland (1922)
St. Benedict Parish, Cleveland (1928)

Magyar
St. Ladislaus Parish, Lorain (1890)
St. Michael Parish, Lorain (1903)
St. Emeric Parish, Cleveland (1904)
Sacred Heart of Jesus Parish, Akron (1915)
St. Margaret Parish, Cleveland (1921)
St. Michael Parish, Cleveland (1925)

Ukrainian
SS Peter and Paul Parish, Cleveland (1910)
St. John the Baptist Parish, Lorain (1914)
Holy Ghost Parish, Akron (1915)
St. Mary Parish, Cleveland (1952)

Italian
Holy Rosary Parish, Cleveland (1892)
St. Rocco Parish, Cleveland (1922)
Holy Redeemer Parish, Cleveland (1924)
Our Lady of Mt. Carmel (West Side), Cleveland (1926)
St. Anthony Parish, Akron (1933)
Our Lady of Mt. Carmel (East Side), Cleveland (1936)

Lithuanian
St. George Parish, Cleveland (1901)
Our Lady of Perpetual Help Parish, Cleveland (1920)

Bohemian
St. Procop Parish, Cleveland (1872)
St. John Nepomucene Parish, Cleveland (1902)
Holy Family Parish, Cleveland (1911)

German
St. Stephen Parish, Cleveland (1869)
St. Joseph Parish, Cleveland (1896)

Slovenian
St. Vitas Parish, Cleveland (1893)
St. Lawrence Parish, Cleveland (1901)
SS Cyril and Methodius Parish, Lorain (1905)

Croatian
St. Paul Parish, Cleveland (1902)
St. Nicholas Parish, Cleveland (1902)
St. Vitas Parish, Lorain (1922)

The struggle to establish those parishes sharpened the ethnic identity even of apolitical peasants. In Europe parish and priest had been facts of life in every village; in America the immigrants had to take the initiative themselves in petitioning for an ethnic parish and making financial sacrifices to build it. In the process they became even more involved in religious affairs. They were irritated by the Irish control of the Roman Catholic hierarchy in the United States. Father Waclaw Kruszka claimed in 1924 that

> although the Irish form only about one-third of the Catholic population, of the hundred Catholic bishops in the United States, almost all are of Irish nationality . . . What the Poles . . . want is . . . to have bishops from any nationality, and not only from one exclusively. . . . The Irish . . . still present candidates of Irish extraction, to the exclusion of other nationalities, as if they alone had the monopoly of wisdom and sanctity . . .*

All the ethnic Catholics struggled for their own parishes, appointment of ethnic priests, and selection of ethnic bishops, and the religious controversies imbued people with a stronger sense of group identity.

Ethnic associations, which eastern Europeans had started in the Old World to broaden family networks, reflected their commitment to a Roman Catholic village perspective and acted to protect their values from the outside world. Church newspapers, parish societies, and parochial schools reconstructed the stable environment of preindustrial villages. More than 80 percent of these immigrants' children attended parish schools where Old World languages were used; and although the immigrants might move within the city or from one city to another, the need to attend the ethnic parish church, send children to parish schools, and participate in parish societies was overpowering. The Polish Roman Catholic Union, Lithuanian Roman Catholic Alliance, Czech Roman Catholic Central Union, Czech Roman Catholic Benevolent Union, Catholic Slovak Union, Slovak Catholic Federation, Croatian Catholic Union, Grand Carniolan Slovenian Catholic Union, Greek Catholic Union (Rusin), Ruthenian National Association (Ukrainian), and the American Hungarian Catholic Society supported parish societies to provide immigrants with life insurance, social events, and parochial schools. Parish newspapers—like the *Narod Polski* (Polish), *The New World* (Lithuanian), *Greek Catholic Messenger* (Rusin), *Svoboda* (Ukrainian), and the *Napredak* (Croatian)—kept the immigrants in touch with neighbors, friends, and the Old World. Cultural continuity and religious stability—promoted through the parish, parochial school, and parish society—supported the eastern European community in America, and the effort to sustain that subculture greatly sharpened ethnicity.

What clearly distinguished the Rusins and the Ukrainians from the

*Quoted in Joseph Wytrwal, *Poles in American History and Tradition* (Detroit, 1969), p. 269.

other Slavs was religion, for they were Eastern Rite Catholics, or Greek Catholics. During the Middle Ages the Orthodox church had expanded into eastern Europe, converting the Russians as well as the Ruthenians, and until the sixteenth century the Russian Orthodox church had governed both peoples. But late in the 1500s the Ruthenians broke away from Russian Orthodoxy and realigned themselves with Rome, though on their own terms. Preferring a married clergy and Slavic liturgies, they became "Eastern Catholics of the Byzantine Rite," Uniate groups loyal to the Vatican but equally committed to preserving symbolic differences with Rome. In America the Rusins and Ukrainians first worshiped with the Poles, Slovaks, and Hungarians because no Ruthenian parishes existed and no priests had immigrated from Galicia or Transcarpathia. Later they asked the Ukrainian Metropolitan of Galicia to send a Uniate priest, and in 1884 the Reverend John Volansky arrived in Pennsylvania and established the Ruthenian Uniate Church. Two years later he dedicated the St. Michael the Archangel Church in Shenandoah, Pennsylvania. By 1895 there were more than thirty Uniate priests in the United States, most of them Rusin because the Ukrainian migration did not become significant until after 1910.

Ruthenian-American history was laced with controversies which defined ethnicity. A key issue for the Rusins and Ukrainians was the attitude of the Irish hierarchy to the Uniate concept. Legalistic and committed to the church as one entity, the Irish abhorred the Ruthenian belief in a married clergy and Slavic rites. Under considerable pressure from the American hierarchy after 1890, Rome ordered Ruthenian priests to practice celibacy, urged Ruthenians wherever possible to join a Latin Rite church, and restricted the assignment of Ruthenian priests to the United States. The immigrants were furious, and the policy resulted in the excommunication of many Ruthenian priests and an exodus of thousands of Greek Catholics to the Russian Orthodox church.

Internal conflicts between Rusins and Ukrainians did as much to heighten ethnic identity as conflicts with the Irish. During the Great Migration Rusins had always outnumbered Ukrainians, and in 1910 most of the 140 parishes of the Ruthenian church were Rusin in composition. Although the Rusins and Ukrainians had cooperated at first, they were nevertheless two separate communities. When the Ruthenian church received its first bishop in 1907, it was the Reverend Stephen Ortynsky, a Ukrainian from Galicia. He enforced papal decrees against the Uniate philosophy, and the Rusin community, already piqued that he was not Rusin, denounced him until his death in 1916. Not until 1924 did the controversy subside, and then only after Rome appointed two Uniate bishops in America. The Ukrainian bishop was a Galician, the Reverend Constantine Bohachersky, and he headed the diocesan see at

Philadelphia; the Rusin bishop was the Reverend Basil Takach, a Transcarpathian, who headed an episcopal seat near Pittsburgh. The controversy was over.

In addition, the struggle between the American Catholic church and the eastern European immigrants helped pass on feelings of political nationalism from the educated elites to even the most apathetic peasants. The controversy involved control of the local parish. In the Old World the peasants had taken the parish for granted; it had always been there and its maintenance required little sacrifice. But in the United States the immigrants had to build their own chapels, schools, hospitals, and orphanages. For poor workers this required financial sacrifices, and as they transplanted their church and its institutions they developed a strong sense of lay power. To run the parish and parochial schools the priests had to delegate authority to parishioners, and that too gave the immigrants a sense of power in church affairs.

The Roman Catholic clergy insisted that Catholicism preempted ethnic nationalisms, that being Polish or Lithuanian or Slovak actually meant being Catholic. These "religionists" argued that the American church should exercise complete and direct control over all local parishes, including the nationality parishes. Claiming that Roman Catholicism was the only religion for "true Poles" or "true Czechs," they expressed these views through the national parish societies. On the opposing side was a small group of ethnic nationalists, descendants of the refugees of 1848, who yearned for the creation of independent nations in eastern Europe. Their ethnic consciousness extended beyond religion to embrace all nationals who shared their patriotism. They insisted that lay parishioners in the ethnic parishes control local church property, not the diocesan bishops. After all, it was the people who had sacrificed to build them. They formed such groups as the Polish National Alliance, the Lithuanian Alliance of America, the National Slovaks, Rumanians, and Serbs living there as minorities; when they Croatian Society, and the Slovenian National Benevolent Society.

When the Roman Catholic church would not turn over parish property to local Polish or Lithuanian leaders, for example, the nationalists left the church and established the Polish National Catholic Church and the Lithuanian National Catholic Church. Thousands defected to these independent churches, and Roman Catholic clergymen began to fear a general "reformation" in the United States. The church had already appointed ethnic bishops, such as Bishop Frederic Baraga for the Slovenes and Bishop John Henni for the Germans, and as a further compromise Pope Pius X named Paul Rhodes, a Pole, auxiliary bishop of Chicago. These appointments, added to those of the Ruthenian bishops in 1907 and 1924, placated the ethnic communities. With ethnic leaders now in control of diocesan politics, parish property also seemed to be in the control of the ethnic group itself. And the appointment of ethnic bishops reinforced a major principle of the nationalist argument: that Roman Catholics could also be ethnic nationalists—Poles, Czechs, Lithuanians, Slovaks, Slovenes, Croatians, Rusins, Hungarians, and Ukrainians.

Urban life in America also made eastern Europeans more aware of their individual heritages. Except for the Italian and Jewish neighborhoods of New York City, ethnic ghettos were not enclaves dominated by a single group. Instead, immigrants found themselves living with people from other backgrounds. Magyars, for example, had traditionally been the dominant group in Hungary and had always felt superior to the Slovaks, Rumanians, and Serbs living there as minorities; when they found ethnic Slavs near them in America, those feelings of superiority came to the surface immediately. Life in the Old World had also been rather homogeneous. Because peasants usually lived and worked only with people like themsleves, they were hardly conscious of an ethnic identity. But in the urban ghettos of the United States, the existence of dozens of other ethnic groups reinforced more particular feelings of community. Rudolph Vecoli, a historian of Italian-American descent, recently wrote:

> Ours was a mixed neighborhood. We lived among Germans, Irish, Hungarians, and Poles. I also attended an integrated school, not racially integrated, since there was only one Black family in the town, but including all ethnic and socio-economic groups, from the Yankees who lived in the big houses on the hill to the "Hunkies" and "Dagoes" from the valley. These contacts did not dilute our ethnic consciousness, rather they sharpened it. *

Old World Loyalties, New World Lives

More conscious of politics and ethnicity than ever before, the eastern European immigrants gradually acquired a strong sense of ethnic nationalism. By 1914 they were deeply concerned with events in Europe. The Polish National Alliance campaigned vigorously with the Wilson Administration during World War I to use American power at the peace conference to create a free Poland; and when Poland was reconstructed in 1918, American Poles celebrated. When German and Russian troops overran Poland in 1939, they protested vehemently; and as a powerful agent within the Democratic party they have insisted for

*Sallie TeSelle, ed., *The Rediscovery of Ethnicity* (New York, 1973), p. 121.

thirty-five years that Poland must someday be free of Soviet domination. From the Yalta Conference in 1945, when President Franklin D. Roosevelt asked Joseph Stalin to withdraw Russian troops after the war, to the election of 1976, when Jimmy Carter accused President Gerald Ford of being insensitive to Polish liberation, the Poles in the United States have influenced American foreign policy in eastern Europe.

Similarly, Magyar-Americans demanded a Hungary free from Austria in 1918, opposed Russian domination of Hungary after 1945, poured out sympathy to the victims of the Budapest rebellion in 1956, and protested President Carter's decision in 1977 to return the crown of St. Stephen, a thousand-year-old symbol of Hungarian independence, to the Communist government in Hungary. Czech- and Slovak-Americans, through their national organizations, played a critical role in persuading President Wilson to insist on the creation of an independent Czechoslovakia in 1918, and both groups denounced the Soviet takeover of Czechoslovakia in 1947 and the use of Russian military power to crush the liberalization movement in 1967. Croatian and Slovenian patriots in the United States wanted to see an independent Slovenia and Croatia carved out of the Austro-Hungarian Empire and accepted the establishment of Yugoslavia in 1918 as an effective compromise. The Rusins and Ukrainians campaigned in 1918 for national autonomy in Europe. Tired of a thousand years of Magyar domination of Transcarpathia, the Greek Catholic Union asked Wilson to place a clause in the Treaty of Versailles including Transcarpathia in Czechoslovakia. He complied. The Uniate clergy and Ruthenian National Alliance organized the Ukrainian National Alliance as early as 1916. Although they failed in their goal of creating an independent Ukraine, this campaign too forged stronger community bonds in the United States. Once bound to parochial villages, the eastern European peasants in America rediscovered their links to the fortunes of the Old World.

For all these immigrants the Old World values of land, village, and parish were translated into home, neighborhood, parish, and political nationalism in America. Social and geographic mobility seemed irrelevant to many of them; indeed, mobility was often the antithesis of order and continuity because it meant community disintegration. Corporate or professional success often implied movement out of the neighborhoods and parishes that meant so much to first-generation immigrants. Many peasants were also suspicious of intellectualism and discouraged higher education. As a result, the eastern European immigrants tended to remain in blue-collar occupations. More than 50 percent of first-generation Czechs and Slovaks moved into skilled jobs before their deaths, as did 80 percent of their children. This was typical of peasant immigrants from eastern Europe, who aspired to skilled, propertied, working-class status.

Their goals stood in contrast to prevailing Protestant values. For two centuries Americans had defined success in terms of social and geographic mobility and income. People who left their families and roots for new opportunities, new places, and new money were admired; those satisfied with their first homes and first jobs seemed to lack ambition and drive. But the eastern European Catholics had large families, acquired property in their original neighborhoods, and often maintained extended kinship ties. The local parish and parochial school filled all their social, religious, and educational needs. Being a school dropout and a blue-collar laborer carried no stigma as long as one worked and was independent, and staying in the same neighborhood among the same people was expected. Stable families, stable neighborhoods, religious loyalty, and hard work were the immigrant Catholic alternatives to the Protestant ethic in America.

SUGGESTED READINGS

Abramson, Harold J. *Ethnic Diversity in Catholic America*. New York: 1973.

Abucewicz, John A. *Fool's White*. Chicago: 1969.

Adamic, Louis. *Laughing in the Jungle*. New York: 1960.

Alba, Richard D. "Social Assimilation Among American Catholic National-Origins Groups." *American Sociological Review*, 41 (December 1976), 1030–1046.

Alilunas, Leo J., ed. *Lithuanians in the United States*. Palo Alto, Cal.: 1978.

Balch, Emily. *Our Slavic Fellow Citizens*. New York: 1969.

Bankowsky, Richard. *After Pentecost*. New York: 1961.

_____ . *The Glass Rose*. New York: 1958.

_____ . *On a Dark Night*. New York: 1964.

_____ . *The Pale Criminal*. New York: 1967.

Barton, Josef J. *Peasants and Strangers: Italians, Rumanians, and Slovaks in an American City, 1890–1950*. Cambridge, Mass.: 1975.

_____ . "Religion and Cultural Change in Czech Immigrant Communities, 1850–1920." In Randall M. Miller and Thomas D. Marzik. *Immigrants and Religion in Urban America*. Philadelphia: 1977.

Bell, Thomas. *Out of This Furnace*. New York: 1941.

Bodner, John. "The Formation of Ethnic Consciousness: Slavic Immigrants in Steelton." In John Bodnar, ed. *The Ethnic Experience in Pennsylvania*. Lewisburg, Pa.: 1973.

_____ . "Immigration and Modernization: The Case of Slavic Peasants in Industrial America." *Journal of Social History*, 10 (Fall 1976), 44–71.

_____ . "Materialism and Morality: Slavic-American Immigrants and Education, 1890—1940." *Journal of Ethnic Studies*, 3 (Winter 1976), 1–20.

Capek, Thomas. *The Czechs in America*. New York: 1969.

_____ . *The Czechoslovaks: The Bohemian Community of New York*. New York: 1921.

Dabrowski, Irene. "The Ethnic Factor and Neighborhood Stability: The Czechs in Soulard and South St. Louis." *Missouri Historical Society Bulletin*, 33 (January 1977), 87–93.

Davis, Jerome. *The Russians and Ruthenians in America*. New York: 1922.

Fox, Paul. *The Poles in America*. New York: 1970.

Galush, William J. "Faith and Fatherland: Dimensions of Polish-American Ethnoreligion, 1875–1975." In Randall M. Miller and Thomas D. Marzik. *Immigrants and Religion in Urban America*. Philadelphia: 1977.

Gazell, James A. "The High Noon of Chicago's Bohemias." *Journal of the Illinois State Historical Society*, 65 (Spring 1972), 54–68.

Govorchin, Gerald. *Americans from Yugoslavia*. Gainesville, Fla.: 1961.

Greeley, Andrew M. *The American Catholic*. New York: 1977.

Greene, Victor. *For God and Country: The Rise of Polish and Lithuanian Ethnic Consciousness in America*. Madison, Wisconsin: 1975.

_____ . *The Slavic Community on Strike: Immigrant Labor in Pennsylvania Anthracite*. Notre Dame, Ind.: 1968.

Halecki, Oscar. *Borderlands of Western Civilization: A History of East Central Europe*. New York: 1952.

Halich, Wasyl. *Ukrainians in the United States*. New York: 1970.

Kantowicz, Edward R. *Polish-American Politics in Chicago, 1888–1940*. Chicago: 1975.

Konnyu, Leslie. *Hungarians in the United States: An Immigration Study*. St. Louis: 1967.

Kowalik, Jan. *The Polish Press in America*. Palo Alto, Cal.: 1978.

Lengyel, Emil. *Americans from Hungary*. Philadelphia: 1948.

Lerski, Jersy J. *A Polish Chapter in Jacksonian America*. Madison, Wisconsin: 1958.

Morawska, Ewa T. *The Maintenance of Ethnicity: Case Study of the Polish-American Community of Greater Boston*. Palo Alto, Cal.: 1977.

Novak, Michael. *Naked I Leave*. New York: 1970.

O'Grady, Joseph P. *The Immigrants' Influence on Wilson's Peace Policies*. Lexington, Kentucky: 1967.

Pehotsky, Bessie. *The Slavic Immigrant Woman*. San Francisco: 1970.

Portal, Roger. *The Slavs*. London: 1969.

Procko, Bohdan P. "Pennsylvania: Focal Point of Ukrainian Immigration." In John Bodnar, ed. *The Ethnic Experience in Pennsylvania*. Lewisburg, Pa.: 1973.

Prpic, George J. *South Slavic Immigrants in America*. Boston: 1978.

_____ . *The Croatian Immigrants in America*. New York: 1976.

Rooney, Elizabeth. "Polish-Americans and Family Disorganization." *American Catholic Sociological Review*, 18 (March 1957), 47–63.

Sanders, James W. *The Education of an Urban Minority: Catholics in Chicago, 1833–1965*. New York: 1977.

Seton-Watson, Hugh. *The East European Revolution*. New York: 1956.

Stavrianos, L. S. *The Balkans Since 1453*. New York: 1958.

Stipanovich, Joseph. *The South Slavs in Utah*. Sarasota, Cal.: 1975.

Stolarik, M. Mark. "Immigration, Education, and the Social Mobility of Slovaks, 1870–1930." In Randall M. Miller and Thomas D. Marzik. *Immigrants and Religion in Urban America*. Philadelphia: 1977.

Thomas, W. I., and Znaniecki, Florian. *The Polish Peasant in Europe and America*. Boston: 1918.

Warzeski, Walter C. *Byzantine-Rite Rusins in Carpatho-Ruthenia and America*. Pittsburgh: 1971.

Weinberg, Daniel. "Ethnic Identity in Industrial Cleveland: The Hungarians, 1900–1920." *Ohio History*, 86 (Summer 1977), 171–186.

Wytrwal, Joseph A. *America's Polish Heritage*. Detroit: 1961.

———. *Poles in American History and Tradition*. Detroit: 1969.

Zivojinovic, Dragan R. *America, Italy, and the Birth of Yugoslavia, 1917–1919*. New York: 1973.

Zopata, Helen Z. *Polish Americans: Status Competition in an Ethnic Community*. Englewood Cliffs, N.J.: 1976.

Chapter Fifteen

The Orthodox Migrations

Between 1880 and 1924 many Orthodox people from eastern Europe, the Balkans, and the Near East decided for economic and religious reasons to come to America. More than 500,000 Russian and White Russian Slavs came from Russia; over 400,000 people came from Greece; about 200,000 from Syria and Serbia each; 150,000 from Rumania; 125,000 from Armenia; and 75,000 from Bulgaria. In some ways their experiences mirrored those of other Slavs and Magyars, but their ethnicity was unique and the pressures of American life operated somewhat differently on them.

Eastern Orthodoxy

Although the Russians, Greeks, Serbs, Bulgarians, Rumanians, Syrians, and Armenians were separate peoples, they were all loyal to the patriarch of Constantinople, the leader of Eastern Orthodox Christianity. The Orthodox church had been the religious arm of the Byzantine Empire since the fourth century. It was the state religion: the emperor selected the patriarch and the church was part of the political bureaucracy. Unlike the pope, who was expected to be independent of nationalism, the patriarch of Constantinople was clearly subordinate to the emperor. Church and state were one, and the state was supreme.

The schism between eastern and western Christianity began in the fourth century, when the popes began to call Rome the apostolic center of the church because St. Peter had given the keys of the kingdom to the bishop of Rome. All other bishoprics were secondary, since juridical authority flowed from the papacy through the priesthood; sovereignty resided in Rome. Emperor Theodosius of Constantinople, accustomed to controlling church and state, was unwilling to share power with anyone. In 381 he rejected papal claims and declared that there were two centers of Christianity; Roman Catholicism and Eastern Orthodoxy both represented God on earth.

Political relations between the two centers slowly deteriorated, and the split deepened during the iconoclastic controversy of the eighth century. Emperor Leo III of Constantinople, deciding Moslems were right in condemning images as superstitious idolatry, removed icons (painted or mosaic representations of Christ or a saint) from churches throughout the empire. Riots erupted immediately, troops crushed the rebellion, and Pope Gregory II bitterly condemned the decision. Not until 843 were the images restored, and by then the ill will between the two churches had become permanent. In 1054 the pope and the patriarch excommunicated each other, and the Fourth Crusade of 1204, when Catholic crusaders sacked Constantinople, completed the split.

Eastern Orthodoxy evolved into several independent exarchates and patriarchies. The reigning patriarch remained in Constantinople, but others appeared in Alexandria, Antioch, and Jerusalem. After the fall of Constantinople to the Ottoman Turks in 1453, the patriarch of the Russian Orthodox church assumed actual leadership, and several other independent exarchates emerged in Serbia, Bulgaria, Greece, Rumania, Syria, and Armenia, all with the power to consecrate priests and mediate ecclesiastical disputes. This was Orthodoxy—an autonomous association of the eastern patriarchies which recognized the patriarch of Constantinople as honorary leader.

Beyond the major controversy over power, other differences divided the two religions. Rome insisted on a celibate priesthood while the eastern churches permitted priests to marry. They also argued about the procession of the Holy Spirit; Catholics believed it went from the Father and the Son to man while Orthodox theologians claimed it came only from the Father. Other differences were cultural and demographic. Populations were relatively contiguous in the west, and Catholicism was comparatively homogeneous—the pope was the acknowledged head of the church and Latin was the liturgical language everywhere. But in the east, where ethnic groups were more isolated, religious pluralism developed, and in each region the church had its own liturgies, usually in the language understood by the congregation. In the west religion and nationality were distinct, but in the east the church was part of nationhood and the nation an expression of the church. The western dualism between church and state gave rise to the idea that all power did not rest in the state and that other segments of the society could criticize and even transcend the political establishment. But in the east a more authoritarian tradition developed; since the patriarch was an agent of the state, the church could play no role in criticizing national politics.

When the Slavic invasions weakened Byzantine control over the Balkans in the sixth century, missionaries from Rome and Constantinople proselytized there, converting the Slavic tribes; but as the Christian division became more pronounced, the churches competed for control of southeastern Europe. Much to the chagrin of the Catholics, Orthodox missionaries converted Serbs, Bulgarians, Greeks, and Rumanians. Each group formed its own national Orthodox church, reflecting the union of church and state, religion and nationality. After the Turkish invasions in the fifteenth and sixteenth centuries subjugated the Balkan peoples, the church became their sole expression of nationality. Orthodoxy was the only means of expressing ethnicity, nationalism, and religious loyalties.

By the nineteenth century population increases, industrialization, commercial agriculture, and competition from foreign goods were eroding peasant income in Orthodox countries. The silk industry in Syria, for example, was hard hit by the availability of cheaper Asian fabrics, made possible by the opening of the Suez Canal in 1869; and decisions by France and Russia to stop importing currants hurt Greek farmers. In various regions earthquakes and epidemics disrupted peasant life. The retreat of the Ottoman Empire in the nineteenth century inspired powerful independence movements in Greece, Serbia, Syria, Armenia, and Rumania, and rapid political changes had unsettling effects. Moreover, the Turks were persecuting Syrian and Armenian Christians. For all these reasons Orthodox peasants left the farms of eastern Europe, the Balkans, and the Near East for the United States.

They did not move into rural America because the only land not homesteaded was the dry acreage of the Southwest and the Great Basin. Agriculture there required capital and technology, and the peasants possessed neither. And for peasants who had lived in clustered villages of friends, neighbors, and churches, the rural west was a lonely place, a true "desert." It had neither the black earth of home nor the social networks that gave life its meaning. The immigrants settled instead in urban ghettos. Usually destitute, illiterate, and unskilled, they took jobs where they could find them, often dirty and menial work in coal mines, iron and steel mills, food-processing plants, and textile factories.

The Russian Slavs

At the beginning of the Christian era Russian Slavs lived in a broad arc extending from the Baltic coast in the north to the Black Sea in the south. They were primarily hunting and food-gathering tribes, and their economy remained somewhat retarded, especially compared to western Europe. Situated in a vast continental expanse lacking ports and contact with the outside world, Russia retained its peasant feudalism long after the Commercial Revolution had obliterated it in Europe. As late as the 1700s Russian peasants were practically slaves, the property of aristocratic landlords. Not until 1861, when Tsar Alexander II abolished serfdom and freed the peasants, did the social structure even begin to change.

Russian Slavs and White Russian Slavs (Byelorussians) were the largest Slavic group in nineteenth-century Europe, but relatively few came to America. Several hundred Russian colonists crossed the Bering Sea to Alaska in 1747 and settled on Kodiak Island. They survived by fishing, fur trading, and summer farming, and some of them gradually moved south until they reached the redwood forests of Sonoma County, California, in 1812. Their presence there helped precipitate the Monroe Doctrine, in which the United States in 1823 warned Europe against future colonization in the New World. Three diplomatic agreements formally brought the Russian settlers into the United States. The Treaty of 1846 with England placed Oregon and Washington in American hands; the Treaty of Guadalupe Hidalgo of 1848 did the same for California; and in 1867 the United States purchased Alaska from Russia for $7,200,000. Several thousand Russians then became Russian-Americans. Later in the century the main migration of 500,000 Russian Slavs to the United States began. More did not come because there was so much unoccupied land on the vast plains east of the Ural Mountains. While American farmers migrated west, Russian peasants were carrying out an eastward movement of their own.

For the Russians who did come to America the greatest shock was the realization that peasant agriculture would never again be the guiding theme of their lives. They would toil in the cities, producing industrial commodities rather than the fruits of the soil. For people accustomed to the rhythm of nature, it was a depressing prospect. In addition, many Americans treated them badly. Slavic customs seemed alien and the Russian language impossible. The Russian immigrants were often stereotyped as lazy and ignorant, even though they worked ten or more hours a day at their jobs, seven days a week, for perhaps two dollars a day. Although their poverty was only to be expected at first, some Americans held them personally responsible for it, as if it were due to a flaw in the Slavic character.

Cultural perspectives also set them apart. Russians had always had a passionate love for "Mother Russia," and it made them a cohesive people, willing to rely on one another for support. While Western values exalted the individual, Russian values had always subordinated individual interests to group concerns. Even the Russian communism of the twentieth century was to be fitted into the same cultural scheme. Moreover, from the thirteenth to the fifteenth century the catastrophe of the "Golden Horde" —the Mongol invaders—had left Russia with a fear of outsiders and an atmosphere of national emergency. Subsequent menacing threats by the Swedes and Lithuanians, by the French during the Napoleonic Wars, and, in the twentieth century, by the Germans during World Wars I and II reinforced those feelings. Russians were insular and trusted only other Russians.

Religion strengthened their sense of unity. For a thousand years the Russian Orthodox church had been the essence of Russian culture, the alter ego of Russian nationalism. For religion to survive institutionally in the United States, the Russian Slavs had to band together and form their own congregations; otherwise the patriarch in Moscow would not have sent priests or authorized the construction of chapels. It was not until 1792 that the first Russian Orthodox church was built on Kodiak Island, and not until 1872 that the headquarters of the church was established and a bishop placed in San Francisco. In a reinforcing cycle, ghetto settlements made possible the transplantation of the church, and the presence of the church strengthened the cohesiveness of the Russian community.

The Serbs and the Bulgarians

Slavs came to the Balkans in the sixth and seventh centuries and evolved into four groups: Slovenes, Croatians, Serbians, and Bulgarians. Two empires and two religions divided them, the Slovenes and Croatians becoming part of the Holy Roman Empire and the Serbs and Bulgarians falling under Byzantine and then Turkish influence. Slovenes and Croatians were Roman Catholics, while the Serbs and Bulgarians were Eastern Orthodox.

The Serbs lived south of the Danube River, west of Montenegro and Bosnia, and east of Bulgaria. Serbia had been part of the Ottoman Empire since the fourteenth century, but Turkish rule was relatively evenhanded. The peasants paid modest taxes and the Serbian Orthodox church functioned as a government, with the Turks appointing the patriarch but the church exercising sovereign legal and administrative powers. As the Ottoman Empire disintegrated between 1804 and 1830, the Serbs became independent.

Bulgaria too had been under Turkish rule since 1396, and the Bulgarian Orthodox church, though independent since 1767, was controlled by Greece. Greeks monopolized church offices; Greek liturgies were introduced into the mass; and Greek became the official language of the parochial schools. Bulgarian nationalism became in part a religious discontent at Greek domination of the church. Throughout the 1800s the Bulgarians insisted on the appointment of people from their own church to head all dioceses, and in 1870 the Turks created a separate Bulgarian exarchate, despite bitter protests from Greek authorities. Part of Bulgaria finally won independence in 1878, and the rest of the country in 1908.

Serbs and Bulgarians immigrated to America in significant numbers beginning in the 1880s. Political instability was partly responsible. After the Bulgarian uprising of 1876 preceding independence, the Turks wantonly slaughtered 15,000 Bulgarians in reprisal, and between 1885 and 1918—the later Bulgarian rebellions, the Balkan wars, and World War I—more Serbs and Bulgarians fled the political instability of the Old World. But even more important were the economic problems of overpopulation, declining farm prices, and artisan unemployment. Most of the Serbs and Bulgarians passed through New York City and settled in the industrial towns and cities of Pennsylvania, Ohio, western New York, Indiana, and Illinois, where they worked in mines, factories, and food processing plants. A large Serbian settlement rose in Pittsburgh; the headquarters of the Serbian Orthodox church was in Libertyville, Illinois; and Granite City and Chicago, Illinois, along with Pittsburgh, Pennsylvania, became home for thousands of Bulgarian-Americans.

As poor, unskilled peasants in a strange land, Serbs and Bulgarians experienced feelings of alienation. Stoyan Christowe, a Bulgarian immigrant, described them:

> Have I become an American? . . . I have done all I could. America will not accept me. I shall always be the adopted child, not the real son, of a mother I love more than the one that gave me birth . . . I once believed America demanded complete surrender from those who adopted it as their mother. I surrendered completely. Then I discovered that America wanted more—it wanted complete transformation, inward and outward. That is impossible in one generation. *

---

*Quoted in William C. Smith, *Americans in the Making* (New York, 1970), p. 231.

Most did not even want to surrender completely, preferring instead to reconstruct the environment of their Old World villages where they could attend their own church and speak their own language. Father Sebastian Daboric set up several Serbian Orthodox churches in the United States, the largest of which is St. Sara Cathedral in Milwaukee. Serbs and Bulgarians worked and saved to buy their own homes; newspapers such as *Unity* and *United Serbdom* kept them in touch with other immigrant communities and the Old World; and ethnic associations like the Serbian Orthodox Federation provided mutual aid and social outlets. Still, an identity crisis profoundly troubled Serbian and Bulgarian immigrants, as it did most of the Orthodox people in America.

The Rumanians

The non-Slavic Rumanians were descended from the Dacian tribes, and ever since the Romans conquered them in the second century Latin had been their language. Despite repeated conquests by Slavs, Hungarians, and Turks, their language retained its Latin vocabulary, syntax, and morphology. When the Roman Empire crumbled, Byzantine culture filled the vacuum. Western in language, the Rumanians became eastern in religion, and except for some Uniate Catholics in Transylvania, most people were Orthodox. Rumania fell to the Turks in the sixteenth century, but eventually achieved independence in 1859.

Rumanian immigrants took blue-collar jobs in the northeastern cities. Because they came in small migrations, they were geographically mobile, seldom remaining in their first city of settlement. While the Italian and Syrian immigrants came in major village clusters and transplanted their village loyalties to the United States, the Rumanians were committed to broader religious and national objectives, even though they still tried to recreate the social and ethnic atmosphere of the Old World. They began organizing Rumanian Orthodox parishes and parochial schools in 1902; Carpathian mutual benefit societies appeared shortly thereafter, as did Rumanian clubs, the Union of Rumanian Societies, and the Rumanian American Association.

They were successful economically. They moved more readily than other new immigrants, not only from place to place but from job to job. Most of the first generation went from unskilled to semiskilled and skilled jobs; the second generation retained that status and frequently moved into white-collar and professional positions. They were hardworking like other immigrants and acquired homes with a passion, but unlike many others, they limited family size. While most Slavic

A group of newly arrived immigrants from Rumania. (Brown Brothers)

families were large and parents urged their children to quit school early and go to work, Rumanian immigrants had fewer children, urged them to have good educations, and built a foundation for the success of the second generation. Nearly half their children finished high school and went on to some type of further education.

Success strained ethnicity. In the 1920s the rise of the second generation and the end of large-scale immigration weakened the hold of older ethnic organizations. Despite the establishment of evening and weekend Rumanian-language schools, singing societies, drama and debating clubs, and Rumanian libraries, the second and third generations lost touch with the Old World. As they moved about the country searching for better jobs, they broke with kinship systems and were often unable to find a Rumanian Orthodox church. Children attended public schools. Like the Serbs and Bulgarians, they frequently lacked institutional ways to express their identity in the United States. Sixty-five percent of the second generation and 90 percent of the third generation married non-Orthodox partners, usually Roman Catholics, and that too gave Rumanians membership in a broader community. By fostering education and by keeping their families small, they pushed their children toward middle-class status in America.

From the Near East: Armenians and Syrians

The Turks overran Constantinople in 1453, and the Ottoman Empire rose on the ruins of Byzantine civilization. South of the Black Sea and extending from the eastern Mediterranean to the Caspian Sea, Armenia had for a thousand years suffered repeated invasions by Persians, Russians, and Turks. Armenian Christians began feeling a religious nationalism in the nineteenth century, and Moslem rulers in Turkey worried about a possible secession from the empire. To discourage such a spirit, Abdul Hamid II slaughtered a million Armenian Christians between 1894 and 1915. Economic life was totally disrupted. During World War I, when Turkey sided with Germany, Armenian Christians allied with the Russians, and in retaliation the Turks murdered another million Christians. Nationalistic but not independent, the Armenians expressed their ethnicity through the Armenian Orthodox church, and their patriarch in Echmiadzin was a spiritual and patriotic leader. Searching for religious and political freedom, as well as economic security, more than 120,000 Armenian Christians came to the United States after the massacres of 1894.

They settled in New England, the mid-Atlantic states, and the Far West—especially Fresno, California. They worked in mines, smelters, and small trade shops; in textile, shoe, and wire factories; and were especially adept at oriental rug weaving. The Armenian Orthodox church moved with them to the United States; the Armenian General Benevolent Union helped new immigrants; the Armenian National Union campaigned for the liberation of Armenia from Turkish oppression; the Armenian Educational Association promoted vocational and professional education; and such newspapers as the *Hairenik* in New York City and the *Arekag* in Jersey City provided news of both the Old World and the New World settlements.

Perhaps 200,000 Syrians left the Ottoman Empire between 1877 and 1924, most from what became Lebanon in 1945. Most were members of the Syrian Orthodox church, and their faith was blended with ethnic nationalism. They yearned for independence from Turkey, and in the absence of a Syrian nation the Syrian Orthodox church symbolized Syrian patriotism. To discourage nationalism, the Turks had turned on them as on the Armenians, and had slaughtered thousands of people. One immigrant recalled:

> We had suffered from the Turks all our lives and had come to accept their methods of taking everything from us and giving us nothing in return but harsh words and more taxes. . . . For three days the men and women of the

village fought back. My husband shot and killed two of them and I was loading guns. They killed a good many of our neighbors before we fled . . . I was determined that if I ever got the chance to leave this place I would.*

The Syrians who escaped to America settled in the cities. The mill towns of New England and New Jersey, the automobile factories of Detroit, the steel centers of western Pennsylvania and eastern Ohio, and the garment districts of New York City all had Syrian workers. Independent and self-reliant, they became a blue-collar, lower-middle-class community. They had come to America with a talent for enterprise which went directly back to their great, ancient Aramaean heritage as commercialists in the Fertile Crescent. Thousands of Syrians worked as peddlers and salesmen, and tiny Syrian communities appeared in most major cities. After saving money and settling down, they often made the transition to shopkeepers, wholesalers, and department-store owners. (By the 1970s, Detroit would become the Arab capital of America with 150,000 Syrians living there.) These Syrians became a middle and upper-middle class in the United States.

In the Old World Syrian culture had revolved around the extended patriarchal family, the local village, and the church. Immigrants looked upon themselves not as Arabs but as Aleppo Melkites (Melkite Uniates from the Aleppo region), or Beirut Maronites (Maronite Uniates), or Zahleh Orthodox. Each family, village, and religion had a value of its own, and people felt comfortable only with their own family, neighbors, and parishioners. America provided them a larger consciousness. Since Melkites, Maronites, and Orthodox Syrians from many villages lived together in ethnic enclaves, many Americans lumped them together as Turks. The Arabic language united them, and village loyalties survived: the Damascus Club, the Aleppian Fraternity, the Becharre Welfare Society attested to the tenacity of community perspectives. But first-generation immigrants also began to see themselves as Syrian-Americans.

For thousands of years Syrians had feared "outsiders" and desperately wanted their children to marry people from their own villages. But in the United States, with small clusters of Syrians living in a sea of real "outsiders," Syrians in general became "insiders," suitable marriage partners for young people. A sense of being Syrian rather than being from a particular village developed among them. Finally, the Melkite and Maronite Syrians (Uniate Catholics) gradually accepted Roman Catholicism in the United States: Latin liturgies displaced the eastern rites in some parishes, and as Melkites and Maronites gained more in common religiously, Syrian ethnicity grew broader.

*Quoted in Philip M. and Joseph M. Kayal, *The Syrian-Lebanese in America* (New York, 1975), p. 62.

The Greeks

More than 400,000 Greeks came to America during the Great Migration; given the fact that Greece had only 2 million people in 1800, it was a major social upheaval. They came in three stages. During the 1820s and 1830s several hundred Greeks came to study in the United States at the urging of American Protestant missionaries. Then in the 1850s several Greek import-export firms opened in American cities, and a few employees brought their families with them. The major wave of Greek immigration, however, did not begin until the 1880s, when economic changes disrupted traditional ways of life.

Many of the new Greek immigrants went to work in the textile factories of New England; thousands of teen-agers, recruited by padrones, or labor bosses, worked as shoeshine boys; and others worked on railroad construction gangs. Those with entrepreneurial skills established restaurants, candy stores, flower shops, grocery stores, and ice cream parlors in Greco-American communities. Greek fishermen went after lobster in New England and sponges in Florida, and Greek peddlers sold their wares across the country. By 1924 there were more than a hundred separate Greek communities in cities throughout the United States.

The Greek immigrants may have abandoned Greece, but they did not turn their backs on Greek culture. Ethnocentrism, familialism, and religion were the three bases of Greek ethnicity and explain the rise of a ghetto culture in America. More so than most immigrants, educated Greeks were proud of their heritage, of Plato and Aristotle, the birth of democracy in the Greek city-states, and the courage and tenacity of the Spartans. They saw Greece as the cradle of Western civilization, and their repeated struggles for freedom against the Turks had reinforced national pride. During World War I more than 45,000 Greek-Americans returned to fight with Greece against the Turks. Family ties also kept them together. As in so many peasant societies, the extended family had for years been the mainstay of the social structure; and although kinship relations were disrupted by the migration, the need to continue them by mail or to persuade relatives to come to America helped sustain ethnic identity. Greek Orthodoxy was a final link to the Old World. Not only did the church represent God on earth, it was also the heart of anti-Moslem nationalism. Although most Greeks were more loyal to the spirit than the organization of Greek Orthodoxy, the church nevertheless helped support immigrant ethnicity. Beginning in 1922, with the establishment of the first archdiocese, the church eventually established more than 425 parishes in the United States.

The Greek immigrants established formal and informal organizations to govern life in the local communities. The *kinotitos*, a community council, supervised local churches and Greek-language schools, paid the salaries of priests and teachers, and resolved local disputes. More than a hundred Greek-language newspapers reported news from Greece and America. The Greeks also established *topikas*, societies based on regional origins and dedicated to debate, social intercourse, education, and health and life insurance programs. Founded in 1907, the Panhellenic Union recruited Greek-Americans to fight for Greece in case of another war with Turkey; the American Hellenic Educational Progressive Association asked Greek immigrants to take up American citizenship while preserving the Greek language, Orthodox church, and Hellenic culture. At the most informal level, Greeks established coffeehouses as recreational centers for drinking and card playing; employment offices where job information was exchanged; and political forums where Greek patriots, labor organizers, and priests could present their views.

Because of their cultural heritage, the Greeks became one of the most visible groups in America, even though their numbers were comparatively small. And because more than 260,000 Greeks have immigrated to the United States since 1924—225,000 of them since 1950—Greek culture has been continually replenished from the Old World. Even today first- and second-generation Greek-Americans account for a large segment of the Greco-American population.

Ethnic Orthodoxy in America

For all the Orthodox immigrants, religious nationalism withered in the New World environment, and in the process their sense of ethnicity weakened. Because of the great distances from their homelands, and also because of the intense political conflict in the Balkans, the mother churches of Europe gave little direction to their American branches. Orthodoxy had always been organized along authoritarian lines; power flowed down through church hierarchies to communicants. With neither Old World authority nor New World autonomy, the Orthodox churches were unable to resolve internal conflicts short of schism.

Within the Greek Orthodox church debates about monarchism versus democracy in Greece divided the immigrants into opposing factions. The Russian Orthodox church split into three groups, and the Ukrainians (thousands of whom had followed Father Alexis Toth's secession from Uniate Catholicism after the Irish clergy prohibited priests from marrying) divided into five different churches. The Russian Orthodox church was probably the best organized Orthodox group because of its early beginnings along the West Coast, but when a Serb or Rumanian worshiped there, it was just not the same as praising God in an ethnic-language parish. Rather than attend the services of another Orthodox group, many simply stopped going to church at all. Internal divisions and the problems of the Orthodox churches in America hastened acculturation.

America posed other problems. Orthodoxy had for centuries been identified with the history, culture, and language of a particular country, but in the religiously neutral atmosphere of the United States these dimensions of Orthodoxy lost their meaning. Confronted by a pluralistic society and a nonsectarian state, and undermined by geographical mobility, social mobility, and public education, the Orthodox churches lost their most critical function in the lives of members: they no longer served as the primary vehicle for ethnic nationalism. The Old World fusion of religion and ethnicity evaporated; Armenians, Syrians, Bulgarians, Russians, Greeks, Rumanians, and Serbians lost contact with the mother countries because the churches did not survive institutionally along Old World lines.

While Polish or Slovak immigrants worshiped in Polish or Slovak parishes, most Orthodox immigrants did not live close enough to their church to remain active. Instead of looking upon themselves as Orthodox within a particular nationality, they began identifying themselves, religiously at least, simply as Orthodox or even as Catholics. The creation of the Federation of Orthodox Churches in 1943 symbolized the expanding sense of religious community among the Orthodox immigrants and their children. Old World nationalisms were waning in the New World setting

The Armenians provide a good case study. The Armenian Orthodox church was synonymous with Armenian nationalism, for history and language had effectively isolated it from other groups. The Bible, liturgies, and literature had all been translated into Armenian, and, under Ottoman siege since the fifteenth century, Armenian culture and nationalism had come to center in the Orthodox church. When the immigrants came to America, the church followed them. One group of Armenian immigrants settled in Worcester, Massachusetts, to work in the wire mills and machine shops. They quickly formed an Armenian club and asked the Armenian patriarch in Constantinople to send a priest. Father Joseph Sarajian arrived in 1889 and founded the first Armenian Orthodox church, named it Surp Prgich, Church of Our Savior. The avowed purpose of the Armenian church, as it had been for centuries, was to preserve Armenian identity and prevent assimilation. But by 1910, despite the immigration of tens of thousands of Armenians, there were still only three Armenian Orthodox churches in the United States. Scattered widely into small colonies, Armenians had neither the money nor the people to sustain their own parishes. Many communities were lucky to receive even a yearly visit from an itinerant priest, who in a few days had to offer Holy Communion, perform several masses, and solemnize dozens of baptisms, births, marriages, and deaths. While the eastern European Catholics had immigrated in large numbers and concentrated themselves enough to support ethnic-language parishes, the Armenians were never able to summon the resources in their small communities. And ties with the Old World were tenuous. After the 1894 massacres the Armenian patriarch had left Constantinople for the more isolated Echmiadzin, but he was out of touch there, especially with the church in the United States. Repeated Turkish massacres, Russian seizures of church property, the Armeno-Tatar War of 1905, and then the terrors of World War I completely disrupted communication with the Old World. Only a dozen priests had come to America by 1910, and most of them were too old to build parishes from scratch.

Even more serious were the political squabbles that divided the Orthodox community. In Western history there had always been a separation of church and state; Roman Catholicism had thereby been able to keep itself insulated from some of the more devastating political controversies. In the realm of Eastern Orthodoxy, however, where church and state had fused, the church was expected to take political stands. That role proved destructive in America. Political parties had arisen in Armenia, and two in particular—the Armenian Revolutionary Federation (*Tashnags*) and the Armenian Constitutional Democratic party (*Ramgavars*)—gained adherents in the United States. One group urged revolutionary resistance to the Turks while the other promoted accommodation. Afraid of being attacked by the Turks, the Armenian Orthodox church condemned radicalism, but in the United States the conservative position enraged immigrants who had fled Turkish oppression. Riots and fights, sometimes in the chapels, erupted frequently. Tashnag and Ramgavar supporters competed for appointment as church trustees and demanded statements of support from the clergy. With trustees, priests, and church congregations constantly bickering over Old World politics, the church lost its status as a representative of the whole community.

Dispersed and divided, the Armenian Orthodox church could not withstand the secular environment of the United States. Without its traditional alliance with the state, and in competition with the rise of consumer values, the church began to lose its cultural and political authority. Church attendance declined severely, as did the cycle of religious festivals and observances. Some practices did continue, such as the long celebration of the mass, some two and a half hours each Sunday, and traditional Christmas and Easter services. Armenians also observed two annual mourning days in which they remembered the "Dead of Susan" of the 1894 Turkish massacres and the million Armenians killed in the 1915 massacres. But most of the saints' days, fast days, daily vespers and prayers, and the practices of kissing church walls and crossing oneself when nearing a sacred place disappeared. Once the only repository of ethnic nationalism, the Armenian Orthodox church gradually lost its hold on the immigrant community in the United States.

SUGGESTED READINGS

Arpee, Leon. A *History of Armenian Christianity*. New York: 1946.

Aswad, Barbara. *Arabic-Speaking Communities in American Cities*. New York: 1974.

Balch, Emily. *Our Slavic Fellow Citizens*. New York: 1969.

Bardis, Panos D. *The Future of the Greek Language in the United States*. Palo Alto, Cal.: 1976.

Barton, Josef J. *Peasants and Strangers: Italians, Slovaks, and Rumanians in an American City, 1890-1950*. Cambridge, Mass.: 1975.

Berger, Morroe. "America's Syrian Community." *Commentary*, 25 (April 1958), 314-323.

Cahnman, Werner. "Religion and Nationality." *American Journal of Sociology*, 49 (May 1944), 524-529.

Chervigny, Hector. *Russian America: The Great Alaskan Venture, 1741-1867*. New York: 1965.

Davis, Jerome. *The Russian Immigrants*. New York: 1922.

———. *The Russians and Ruthenians in America*. New York: 1922.

Govorchin, Gerald. *Americans from Yugoslavia*. Gainesville, Fla.: 1961.

Grigorieff, Dimitry. "The Historical Background of Orthodoxy in America." *St. Vladimir's Seminary Quarterly*, 5 (February 1961), 3-53.

Hagopian, Elaine, and Padan, Ann. *Arab-Americans: Studies in Assimilation*. Wilmette, Ill.: 1969.

Henry, Shiela. *Cultural Persistence and Socio-Economic Mobility: A Comparative Study of Assimilation Among Armenians and Japanese in Los Angeles*. Palo Alto, Cal.: 1978.

Hitti, Philip K. *The Syrians in America*. New York: 1924.

Housepian, Marjorie. *A Houseful of Love*. New York: 1957.

Katibah, Habeeb. *Arabic-Speaking Americans*. New York: 1946.

———. *The Story of Lebanon and Its Emigrants*. New York: 1968.

Kayal, Philip M., and Kayal, Joseph M. *The Syrian-Lebanese in America*. New York: 1975.

Kourvetaris, A. George. *First and Second Generation Greeks in Chicago*. Athens, Greece: 1971.

Lacko, Michael. "The Churches of the Eastern Rite in North America." *Unitas*, 16 (Summer 1964), 89–115.

Mahakian, Charles. *History of Armenians in California*. New York: 1935.

Minasian, Edward. "The Armenian Immigrant Tide." In Edward Minasian, ed. *Recent Studies in Modern Armenian History*. Cambridge, Mass.: 1972.

Mirak, Robert. "Armenian Emigration to the United States to 1915." *Journal of Armenian Studies*, 1 (Autumn 1975), 66–72.

———. "On New Soil: The Armenian Orthodox and Armenian Protestant Churches in the New World to 1915." In Randall M. Miller and Thomas D. Marzik. *Immigrants and Religion in Urban America*. Philadelphia: 1977.

Papanikolas, Helen. *Toil and Rage in a New Land: The Greek Immigrants in Utah*. Salt Lake City, Ut.: 1970.

Petrakis, Harry M. *Lion at My Heart*. New York: 1959.

Portal, Roger. *The Slavs*. London: 1969.

Pupin, Michael. *From Immigrant to Inventor*. New York: 1923.

Saloutos, Theodore. *The Greeks in the United States*. Cambridge, Mass.: 1964.

———. *They Remember America*. Berkeley, Cal.: 1956.

Seton-Watson, Hugh. *The East European Revolution*. New York: 1956.

Shadid, Michael. *Doctor for the People*. New York: 1939.

Smith, Hedrick. *The Russians*. New York: 1956.

Stavrianos, L. S. *The Balkans Since 1453*. New York: 1958.

Valaoras, Vasileos. *Hellenism of the United States*. Athens, Greece: 1937.

Vardoulakis, Mary. *Gold in the Streets*. New York: 1919.

Vartan, Malcolm. *The Armenians in America*. Boston: 1919.

Vlchos, Evangelos. *The Assimilation of the Greeks in the United States*. Athens, Greece: 1968.

Wakin, Edward. *The Lebanese and Syrians in America*. Chicago: 1974.

Wolff, Robert. *The Balkans in Our Time*. New York: 1967.

Chapter Sixteen

The Jews in America

Like the Quakers and the French Huguenots, the Jews left Europe in part to escape intense religious persecution, and, like the English immigrants, they made rapid progress economically, many of them rising to comfortable middle-class status after early years of extreme poverty. Like the Poles and Slovaks of the 1890s, the Jews were caught up in the disintegration of a peasant economy and underwent the same trauma of uprooting and acculturation. Like the Irish, Italians, Chinese, and eastern Europeans, they ended up in urban ghettos and experienced the pain of nativist rejection. Finally, like the Poles, Czechs, Lithuanians, Magyars, and Croatians, they developed a form of political nationalism: for Jews it was Zionism and Israel.

But the Jewish experience also had unique elements. No other group possessed their historical consciousness. For three thousand years they had looked upon themselves as children of Abraham, the chosen people of God. They had been enslaved in Egypt and later had suffered at the hands of Christians and Moslems; persecutions and pogroms had molded a collective Jewish ego. Only the Jews left ghettos in Europe for ghettos in America.

Nor did Jewish ethnicity involve territory. Polish-American ethnicity emerged out of Roman Catholicism and Poland; Greek identity out of Greek Orthodoxy and Hellenic Greece; and Russian ethnicity out of Russian Orthodoxy and the motherland. Jewish ethnicity rested solely on Judaism and Jewish history; political nationalism hardly existed among the first immigrants. But their theological, prophetic hopes for the ultimate gathering of Judah carried a dormant nationalism which would reach fruition in the creation of Israel after World War II.

The Sephardic and Ashkenazic Migrations, 1654–1776

The first Jewish immigrants came to America during the colonial period. They were Sephardim, Jews of Spanish and Portuguese origins, and Ashkenazim, Jews from central and eastern Europe. Both groups were fleeing from religious persecution.

Ever since Moslems from North Africa had conquered Spain in 711, Arabs and Jews there had accommodated each other as blood relatives (the Arabs as descendants of Ishmael and the Jews of Jacob, both descendants of Abraham). Between 900 and 1492, however, the Christian *Reconquista* (Reconquest) gradually drove the Moors back to Africa. After six centuries of war with "Islamic infidels," Spanish Catholics ruled with a vengeance. Holding Jews responsible for the death of Jesus, Spaniards persecuted them unmercifully, slaughtering three hundred Jews at Seville in 1391 and hundreds more at Toledo in 1449. Thousands of individual pogroms occurred during the Reconquista, and finally, after the expulsion of the Moors in 1492, Jews who refused to renounce Judaism were exiled. Many escaped exile by "confessing Christianity" but remained practicing Jews in secret. Of those who left, most went to North Africa and others scattered to Italy, Russia, Brazil, and the Dutch West Indies. But when Portugal conquered several of the Dutch colonies in 1654, the Jews fled, some to New Netherland. These Sephardic Jews spoke Ladino (Judeo-Spanish) rather than Spanish, generally had Spanish or Portuguese surnames, and, because of years of successful accommodations to the Moslems, were interested in success and even assimilation. Other Sephardic Jews followed in the 1700s.

Toward the end of the seventeenth century groups of Ashkenazic Jews came from central and eastern Europe. During the Crusades religious zeal led to intense persecution of European Jews. Pogroms continued during the Reformation and Counter Reformation. Jews were expelled from Lithuania in 1496; Pope Paul IV required all Jews to wear identifying symbols after 1555; thousands were slaughtered in Poland and the Ukraine in the 1640s and 1650s; and in 1648 Jews had to leave Hamburg and Vienna. Some came to America, and by 1776 there were nearly three thousand Jews in the colonies, half Sephardic and half Ashkenazic.

Compared to Europe, America was free and prosperous. An inconspicuous minority in a population of nearly 3 million people, the Jews inspired few fears. And in a society where more than 95 percent of the people lived in rural areas, the Jews settled in Boston, Newport, New York, Philadelphia, Baltimore, and Charleston. Few Americans even knew they were there. Jews also benefited from religious toleration. Calvinists had set the cultural tone in America, and they were fascinated with the "Hebrews." They read the Old Testament, studied the Hebrew language, and tried to convert the Jews. Though frustrated that more Jews did not convert, the Puritans did deflect anti-Semitic attitudes. Both people believed in decentralized congregations, despised Roman Catholicism, and dreamed of material success. Anti-Semitism was limited in colonial America, at least compared with persecution in Europe.

The early Jewish immigrants flourished in America. Often prohibited from owning land in Europe, they came from urban, commercial backgrounds and went into business as merchants, salesmen, peddlers, teamsters, and shippers helping transfer goods between eastern cities and the farms in the hinterland. In the labor-starved markets of colonial America Jewish artisans commanded high wages and often built their skills into small manufacturing concerns. As the economy matured after 1776, Jewish businesses began specializing in banking, commerce, insurance, securities, textiles, footwear, mining, warehousing, real estate, and construction. America was indeed the promised land.

The German Jews, 1830-1890

American Jewry changed with the immigration of German Jews in the nineteenth century. As late as 1830 there were still only 6,000 Jews in the United States, but the rapid influx of the Germans increased the number to 22,000 in 1850 and more than 250,000 in 1880. German Christians came to escape political and economic problems, but the Jews had strong religious reasons as well. Another wave of anti-Semitism swept through central Europe in the mid-1800s. Hundreds of Jews died in pogroms at Würzburg, Bamberg, Frankfurt, Darmstadt, Hamburg, and Danzig, and the homes and businesses of thousands were destroyed. To limit Jewish population, Germans established quotas on marriage licenses to Jews; and although industrialization was creating new jobs, Jews were forbidden to become apprentice trainees. Curfews, special taxes, and housing segregation were common. With little to lose, the German Jews joined the migration.

They settled in the cities with other Jews, even though they differed markedly from the Sephardic community. In addition to distinct dialects and rituals, the German Jews came from a Teutonic tradition and the Sephardic Jews from an Iberian, Mediterranean culture. Because the Sephardic Jews were already established and financially secure, class distinctions also divided the two groups. Still, assimilation soon occurred; sharing ethnicity as well as religion, they had much in common and slowly came together in the nineteenth century, the Sephardic Jews often disappearing into the much larger German-Jewish community.

German Jews also went into commerce and business. Immigration, industrialization, and the westward movement were creating unprecedented opportunities in merchandising and finance. A large, scattered population gave rise to enormous marketing problems. There was also a tremendous demand for investment capital. Some German Jews became skilled artisans and specialty farmers, but more than any other immigrant group the German Jews entered business and finance. Jewish peddlers trekked all over the country selling goods to housewives in the hinterland; eventually many of them established their own stores. Julius Rosenwald, a German Jew who started out as a peddler, purchased a small watchmaking company named Sears, Roebuck and transformed it into the most successful mail-order house in the world. Most of the famous department stores in the United States—including Saks Fifth Avenue, Bloomingdale's, Joske's, Sakowitz, Gimbels, Abraham & Straus, Macy's, Bamberger's, Goldblatt, Neiman-Marcus, and B. Altman's—began with those poor German-Jewish peddlers.

From this commercial elite came the great Jewish bankers. With excess capital from Jewish merchants and loans from Jewish financiers in Europe, Jewish bankers financed industrial projects throughout the country. Such famous banking houses as **Kuhn Loeb and Company, Goldman Sachs and Company, Lehman Brothers, Rothschild and Company, Bache and Company,** and **Guggenheim and Company** all had Jewish roots. With commercial skills finely honed in the past and living in an environment blessed with opportunity and freedom, German Jews succeeded far beyond their expectations. A perfect example was Henry Morgenthau. Born in Germany in 1856, he immigrated at the age of ten, became a lawyer in New York City, and eventually made a fortune from prudent real estate investments in Manhattan. In short order he became a multimillionaire and later served as ambassador to Turkey. His son, Henry Morgenthau, Jr., served as Secretary of the Treasury under President Franklin D. Roosevelt.

German Jews introduced Reform Judaism into the United States. In the eighteenth century, German Jewish intellectuals like Moses Mendelssohn introduced Western rationalism into traditional Judaism to prepare upwardly mobile Jews for life outside the ghetto. During the Enlightenment some Jewish intellectuals had grown impatient with traditional religion, and as free-thinking rationalists they drifted toward agnosticism, finding Judaism an inadequate tool for interpreting the modern world. In Europe, however, even the most agnostic Jew remained close to the security of the ghetto, by law if not by choice. But in America that social dimension of Judaism seemed less important. Middle-class Jews also yearned for social acceptance in America, not just toleration. Embarrassed by the traditions, flavor, and customs of Orthodox Judaism, they wanted to make the faith more relevant to life in nineteenth-century America. This was Reform Judaism.

Reform Judaism made changes in both the style and substance of Orthodox traditions. Instead of sexual segregation in synagogues, repeated Hebrew prayers, passionate recitations, and cantillation (chantings of scripture), the Reformers used a Protestant model, with hymns, instrumental music, sedate prayers, pews, choirs, sermons, and a subdued reverence. The Torah (scriptures) and Talmud (Jewish law) were translated into German and English. Reform Jews regarded the Torah and Talmud not as literal explanations of reality but as historical literature and religious symbols, and as a result they found strict Jewish law—such as multiple daily prayers, regular synagogue attendance, dietary rules, and complete cessation of week-day activities on the Sabbath—too restrictive. Thus they discarded much of the letter of the law and emphasized instead the ethical humanitarianism of Judaism. In some instances they changed their Sabbath observance from sundown Friday to sundown Saturday to the Christian Sunday.

Reform Jews also reinterpreted the whole concept of Zionism, the idea of setting up a Jewish national homeland in Palestine. While Orthodox Jews saw the exile from Palestine as a temporary condition awaiting messianic redemption, the Reformers saw it as a blessing, an opportunity to carry Judaism throughout the world. Instead of waiting for a literal, personal Messiah who would create a Jewish nation in Palestine, they yearned for a great leader who would bring peace and justice to all people. For them, America was Zion. Henry Morgenthau, Sr., once said: "We Jews of America have found America to be our Zion. Therefore I refuse to allow myself to be called a Zionist. I am an American."* This was the Americanization of German Jewry, an act of acculturation. Led by Issac Wise, Reform Judaism received its institutional base in 1889 with the creation of the Central Conference of American Rabbis.

But the Reform movement threatened Jewish ethnicity. Because of the relaxed social code, the attack on older ways, and the move toward liberal rationalism, the synagogue lost its rationale as a cultural foundation of the Jewish community. Resolution of congregational disputes was difficult because rabbis had neither the political nor the theological

---

*Quoted in Eric F. Goldman, *Rendezvous with Destiny* (New York, 1956), p. 142.

power to impose their will; congregations divided and subdivided until they became small autonomous units. Even Rabbi Wise's Central Conference could not stop the disintegration. Reform synagogues gradually resembled Protestant chapels in form as well as purpose—houses of weekly worship without the social, economic, and personal welfare functions so important to European Judaism.

New Jewish organizations, which had never existed in Europe because the rabbi and synagogue assumed temporal responsibilities, appeared in the United States. Jewish hospitals and orphanages were built in the 1860s; Bikur Cholim societies cared for the sick and indigent; Gemilath Chasodim served as mutual savings and loan banks; and B'nai B'rith functioned as a fraternal society. The synagogue was no longer central to Jewish life, and religious apathy eroded the commitment many German Jews felt to the faith of their fathers. Although rationalism seemed a more realistic way of interpreting the modern world, it separated Jews from their history. Only the arrival of the east European Jews would expose the weaknesses of Reform Judaism.

The East European Jews, 1881–1945

For centuries Ashkenazic Judaism had survived in eastern Europe as a communal people tied together by spiritual bonds, the Yiddish language, and a special sense of time and history. God and heaven were not myths or distant realities but part of everyday life. The Ashkenazim were intimate with God, sometimes even critical, because their conviction that they were the chosen people made them feel that God was bound to them in a holy covenant. All 613 of their elaborate commandments on how to slaughter ritual animals, what food to eat, how the Talmud was to be read, how to shatter the glass in a marriage ceremony, and so on reflected God's expectations of men, a divine arrangement for the chosen people. For east European Jews, the secular and spiritual worlds were one.

Although Hebrew was the language of prayer and the scriptures, Yiddish was the language of everyday affairs and reflected the scattering of Jews throughout much of central Europe and the Near East during the Middle Ages. Originally a Middle High German dialect written in Hebrew, Yiddish emerged between the ninth and twelfth centuries in Europe. Hebrew words peculiar to Jewish religion were added, and as most European Jews moved east out of Germany, a Slavic vocabulary was added as well. Traces of other European languages also found their way into Yiddish. Rich in idiomatic expressions, Yiddish was especially able to convey subtle nuances of personality and emotion. It was also an assimilative language for Jews. From the Pale of Settlement (an area of 386,000 square miles in Russia extending from the Baltic to the Black Sea where Jews were legally permitted to settle) and the Ukraine to Hungary, Poland, and Rumania, Yiddish united east European Jews into a single community.

Finally, east European Jews were caught up in a singular vision of time and history. Because they believed that the coming of the Messiah and their own redemption was imminent, they looked upon themselves as the central characters in the human drama. And having been so threatened for so long, they had an almost fanatical concern for the survival of Judaism, not only in the present but far into the future. The extension of the Jewish faith into that future—through ceremonial marriages, religious family life, and loyal communalism—was an ethnic compulsion. Survival of the group, of Judaism, was the marrow of social and cultural life.

Out of this world came millions of Jewish immigrants. Like the east European immigrants in general, the Jews suffered from the decline of the peasant economy, either directly or because people could no longer buy the goods and services they were selling. There were also population pressures: the Jewish population of the Pale increased from less than 1 million in 1800 to nearly 5 million in 1890. Chronic poverty set in. When Tsar Alexander II was assassinated in 1881, anti-Semitic fears ignited into vicious pogroms. It became the official policy of the Russian government and the Russian Orthodox church to rid the country of Jews, through conversion if possible or extermination if necessary. Pogroms erupted in Kiev, Odessa, Warsaw, and in countless smaller cities and towns. Government-sponsored propaganda increased; quotas on Jewish admissions to universities were imposed; and the May Laws of 1882 forbade Jews to purchase property, secure mortgages, conduct business on Sunday, or travel from town to town. When Russia lost the Pacific war to Japan in 1905, more pogroms broke out in Odessa, Bialystok, and Zhitomir. Similar persecutions occurred in Rumania and Austria-Hungary. Between 1881 and 1924 approximately 2,750,000 Jews left eastern Europe for the United States: nearly 2 million from Poland, Lithuania, and Russia; about 600,000 from Austria-Hungary; and perhaps 150,000 from Rumania.

These Jews were different from the other new immigrants. Driven from the Old World by bitter persecution as well as economic distress, they had no intention of ever returning; theirs was a communal, family migration, a collective movement of people ready to begin a new life in America. Just as important, they came from diverse backgrounds, from cities as well as from farming villages (shtetls), while most of the other new immigrants were peasants. Only 20 percent of the other new immigrants had occupational skills compared with nearly 70 percent of the Jews. They were suited for urban life in America, and only a tiny minority, like the *Am Olam* (Eternal People) group who tried to establish rural communes, settled outside the cities. During the centuries of their dispersion Jews had come to believe that "life is with people," that Jews had obligations to one another. They felt obliged to help other Jews, and as Jews moved into business other Jews were pulled along economically. Finally, they were more attuned than some groups to the idea of success, and had a long history of respect for learning. Many interpreted their own status according to the achievements of their children (as did many other immigrants). A Jewish immigrant in New York City wrote:

> I am a widow . . . with five children . . . I have a store and barely get along . . . I am obliged to employ a salesman . . . if I were to withdraw my son from high school I could dispense with the salesman, but my motherly love and duty . . . do not permit me . . . I must have his assistance to keep my business going . . . but at the same time I cannot . . . take him out of school . . . I lay great hopes on my child. *

The largest east European Jewish communities were in the northeastern cities, especially New York. By 1910 there were more than 500,000 Jews living in the Lower East Side of Manhattan, and smaller communities in Harlem, the East Bronx, Brownsville, Borough Park, and Brooklyn.

Extreme poverty characterized life in the *shtetl* (Jewish community) at first, particularly in the 1880s and 1890s. Manhattan's Lower East Side was then controlled by Irish and German immigrants who had arrived earlier; German and Irish youth gangs harassed the new Jewish immigrants at every opportunity. Housing was inadequate, and in tenements like "Big Flat" it was not uncommon to have a thousand people living on one acre of land. Congestion was intense, the noise unbearable, sanitation nonexistent, and the death rate well above the national average. Tens of thousands accepted the only work available—the crushing labor of garment district sweatshops. Whole families slaved at sewing and cutting machines in dingy tenement apartments yet barely eked out an existence. Indeed, because the industry was so competitive, wages actually declined in the 1880s from $12 to $7 a week. Those not in the sweatshops but without skills were out in the streets with peddlers' pushcarts. Economic success would soon come to many of these immigrants, but in the 1880s and 1890s they were suffering.

The first Jewish immigrants from eastern Europe experienced severe emotional problems in leaving the Old World, surviving the crowded steerage, and settling into the tenements of the Lower East Side. Unlike

*Quoted in Thomas Kessner, *The Golden Door* (New York, 1977), p. 97.

the Old World, America was a secular society. No longer could Judaism alone direct the political affairs of the Jewish community. In Europe, where Jews had suffered persecution, the suffering itself had been a communal experience transcending class lines, and no stigma followed the sufferers. But in the United States the suffering was an economic matter, and as such was an individual rather than a collective experience. Some Jews consequently found themselves cut off from traditional sources of psychological comfort. And out of the poverty and cultural chaos came previously unheard of problems, such as juvenile delinquency, prostitution, gambling, and crime. Arnold Rothstein became notorious as a gambler and fixer; Isaac Zucker as an arsonist; Harry Joblinski as a trainer of pickpockets; and Marm Mandelbaum as a fence. Family life was also troubled. It became common to hear of despondent fathers, emasculated by the poverty of ghetto life, who had abandoned their families; of people who had committed suicide; of children who refused to listen to their parents. It seemed impossible to transfer Old World stabilities to America.

But after 1900 conditions slowly began to improve. Crowding, noise, and unsanitary conditions still prevailed, but there was a new energy in the community as well. By the turn of the century the Jewish population on the Lower East Side had grown enormously, and Irish and German control of the area had declined. At the same time, Jewish organizations were more active on behalf of the arriving immigrants. Such German Jewish philanthropies as the United Hebrew Charities and the settlement houses of Lillian Wald and Jacob Schiff helped with housing, medical, and employment problems, while the Hebrew Immigrant Aid Society helped new settlers adjust to the United States. Between 1903 and 1910 thousands of *landsmanshaften* were formed in the Jewish communities. Lodge associations of people from the same villages or regions in Europe, the landsmanshaft provided a secular but nonideological outlet for the east European Jewish immigrants. Ordinary people found it a home away from home which provided health and death benefits, news of the Old World, and social association with peers.

After 1900 more Jewish intellectuals began arriving from Europe, and the cultural life of the community, especially through the Yiddish press and theater, quickened. Wages rose after the depression of 1893, and a small middle class of independent business people and storekeepers appeared. Synagogues, or *shuls*, had been established on a firm footing, and although not all the immigrants observed the daily attendance of the Old World, they celebrated Rosh Hashanah and Yom Kippur as periodic rituals to confirm their self-images as Jews. Physical conditions also improved. Streets were being paved; local housing codes were requiring improvements in the tenements; water and sewage systems

Jewish youth of the early 1900s wearing a *tallis* (prayer shawl), which is given to a Jewish boy when he is *bar mitzvah* at age thirteen. (Shames Family Archives/Black Star)

were becoming more reliable; and small parks, libraries, and theaters were being constructed. Life was slowly becoming more meaningful in the New World shtetl.

But in good times as well as bad, the Jews had not lost faith in the future, and that faith was buttressed by their ambition. The Jews had always had a high regard for education. Throughout history they had venerated learning, particularly Talmudic learning, for scholarship, just as much as service, worship, and righteousness, was the pathway to God. Those with learning enjoyed high status in the community and the right to sit along the eastern wall of the shul near the Holy Ark. For thousands of years the primary method of serving God had been studying the Torah.

In America the Jews quickly perceived education as the key to economic achievement, and the quest for secular knowledge became a passion. Samuel Gompers remembered immigrant cigarmakers working extra hard so one of their associates could read law, literature, and politics to them during the day; the Educational Alliance and People's Institute sponsored lectures attended by thousands each week; cafés throughout the Lower East Side bristled each day with debate and intellectual controversy; and people flocked to night schools sponsored by the Board of Education, the settlement houses, and the labor unions. Jews filled a disproportionate number of seats in the City College of New York; in less than a generation the shtetl was sprinkled with the offices of accountants, dentists, physicians, lawyers, and pharmacists. Although fear and resentment undoubtedly exaggerated his opinion, one civil official remarked in 1912:

> Nearly all of the 6,500 positions in the city government are awarded on the basis of competitive civil service examinations. As a result, the Jews are rapidly driving out the Irish, the Germans, and the native Americans. . . . The Jews study long and hard, and their examination papers are so immeasurably superior to the average offered by representatives of other races that they invariably secure preferred places . . . *

Similar observations were made by Yankee and German teachers in the public elementary and high schools of New York, Boston, and Philadelphia, where Jewish children consistently achieved at higher levels than other groups. Jews became one of the most upwardly mobile groups in America.

But they also encountered a nativist reaction. America in the 1890s was in the grip of self-doubt and fear, with people worrying about the depression of 1893, labor violence, and the Populist revolt. Some looking for scapegoats turned to the Jews. While Jews made up less than .5 percent of the American population in 1877, they would reach nearly 4 percent by 1920. Some people saw their increasing numbers as a dangerous omen for the future, especially in face of the migration of "bizarre" Orthodox Jews from east Europe. People were bewildered by women wearing ritual wigs and bearded, earlocked men wearing praying garments, by ritual slaughterhouses, and by Yiddish-speaking peddlers. Anti-Semitism increased in the 1890s and 1900s. In 1915 a Jewish businessman named Leo Frank was lynched in Georgia for the murder of a small girl even though there were serious doubts about his guilt. And throughout the country Jews were excluded from private clubs and schools, hotels, college fraternities, private universities, and certain residential neighborhoods.

American Jews Divided

Despite the bonds that held Jews together, profound differences existed in the community. After 1880 a split developed between the German and east European Jews in America. As anti-Semitism increased, the

*Quoted in Irving Howe, *World of Our Fathers* (New York, 1976), p. 166.

prosperous German Jews became concerned about discrimination in a nation which until then had been remarkably tolerant. On the premise that Americans discriminated against east European Jews only because of their numbers, poverty, and Old World ways, German Jews set out to change the east Europeans. In ghetto settlement houses they tried to Americanize the new immigrants, but their plan was hopelessly naïve. When they found that the new immigrants would not readily change their ways, German Jews then tried to separate themselves from their new associates. One Jewish writer recalled:

> We quit the Franklin Street [in Philadelphia] house in 1902. In that year almost every old family in the block moved away . . . A blight had hit the street in the form of a diaspora from the ghetto. With the arrival of the first few families, we . . . smiled tolerantly at their *scheitels* [ritual wigs worn by married women], their matted beards, and their Talmudized customs. We treated them distantly and with condescension, and a few of us hoped we might be able to freeze them out.*

The two communities grew apart, seriously divided by culture, class, religious practices, and Zionism.

Yiddish culture constituted an enormous difference between German and east European Jews. Interested in rapidly assimilating, the German Jews had quickly adopted English as their main language, so the Yiddish-speaking east European Jews seemed strange and incomprehensible to them. To many German Jews, Yiddish culture was the problem, so elimination of Yiddish became an important goal, one way of Americanizing their east European brethren. To speed that process, some famous German Jewish families, including the Marshalls, Guggenheims, Seligmans, and Bloomingdales, sponsored *Yidishe Velt* (Jewish World) in 1902, a Yiddish-language newspaper which advocated good citizenship, support for the Republican party, the virtues of Reform Judaism, use of the English language, Americanization, and gratitude to German Jewish philanthropies. East European Jews hated such condescending patronization and cultural imperialism and the newspaper failed, but it did provide an odd paradox—German Jews using Yiddish to support the destruction of Yiddish culture. German Jews were advocating Anglo conformity, and their efforts to "reform" east European Jews were just as offensive as Protestant attempts to convert them.

Class differences existed as well. Most east European Jews had been skilled craftsmen in the Old World and once in America they took factory jobs in sweatshops or did piece-work in their homes. More than

*Philip Goodman, *Franklin Street* (New York: 1942), pp. 3–4.

40 percent went to work making clothes, and by 1900 Jewish workers made more than 90 percent of the clothes produced in America. But they did so at a heavy price. Conditions in the sweatshops were oppressive and dehumanizing—crowded, hot, and dangerous. In the spring of 1911, at the Triangle Shirtwaist Company on the Lower East Side of Manhattan, a fire broke out and in less than twenty minutes killed 146 Jewish and Italian women workers. The working-class community was outraged. That German Jews often owned the sweatshops and let out the contracts only exacerbated class tensions.

To overcome low wages and degrading working conditions, Jewish workers began organizing labor unions. The United Hebrew Trades Union was founded in 1890, and by 1914 the International Ladies Garment Workers Union and the Amalgamated Clothing Workers dominated the clothing industry. Jewish workers controlled them. Strikes became common and desperate. Sidney Hillman was representative of the Jewish working class. Born in 1887 in Zagare, Lithuania, he attended the Slobodka Rabbinical Seminary and came to the United States in 1907. A worker in the needle trades at first and then active in labor politics, he became the first president of the Amalgamated Clothing Workers, a founder of the Congress of Industrial Organizations in 1935, and a political adviser to presidents Franklin D. Roosevelt and Harry Truman.

The Rise of Jewish Socialism

Jewish socialism reinforced class differences between eastern European and German Jews. Given the blue-collar character of the early east European Jewish community, ideas of class struggle and economic democracy appealed to some Jewish intellectuals. Men like Morris Hillquit, who had immigrated from Russia in 1886 and taken a law degree at New York University, accepted Marxist views of capital and labor, and decided that government ownership and worker control of production were the only means of redistributing wealth in the United States. Through their newspaper, the *Forward*, and such groups as the Workmen's Circle they supported socialist politicians throughout the country, especially in New York City. But German Jews hated socialism; they had too much to lose. Together, Jewish labor and Jewish socialism magnified class differences and precipitated more conflict between German and east European Jews.

Jewish radicalism played a critical role in helping the immigrants deal with life in America, and the Lower East Side seemed a likely place for the flourishing of radical politics. Jewish messianism, the faith in an ultimate redemption, could certainly be translated into a secular form, and the terrible conditions of the early slums encouraged the birth of new ideas. But at the same time, some Jews doubted the efficacy of Jewish politics, and many of the early socialists wanted Jews to abandon tradition for modern culture, to trade an ethnic perspective for an international working-class vision. They were so impolitic as to expect Jewish immigrants to give up religion for revolution. Not until the arrival of men like David Dubinsky and Sidney Hillman, people committed to Jewish culture and the Yiddish language as well as to economic democracy, did Jewish labor unions and socialist movements gain momentum and define political debate in the New World shtetl.

Even then the seeds of radical demise already existed; for while Jewish immigrants debated revolution, the vast majority of them also harbored deep middle-class yearnings for material comfort and security. Karl Marx predicted the ultimate abolition of the working class through the destruction of capital, but Jews abolished working-class status through upward mobility into the professions and private business. Jewish socialism was a lively but temporary phenomenon, a movement doomed to failure but one which politicized east European Jews and gave them the secular, worldly outlook needed to demand justice in the United States.

From Religious Factionalism to Zionism

Religious controversies also continued. After two generations in America the German Jews had accommodated themselves to the New World culture and in the Reform tradition had rejected older customs and theology. East European Jews found Reform Judaism repulsive, a denial of the faith and a rejection of their fathers, and they clung to the old Orthodox ways. But both sides were losing ground. Because Reform Judaism was so "Protestant," demanded so little of its communicants, and possessed no real commitment to Judaism, the children and grandchildren of German Jews found it meaningless. A minority already, Reform Jews were destined to have even less influence in the future. At the other extreme were millions of east European Jews trying to preserve Orthodoxy in secular America. What had been a key to survival in the hostile environment of eastern Europe was becoming a curious anachronism in the United States, as the children of the immigrants discarded the most visible dimensions of Orthodoxy. That faith too was threatened in America.

Out of the chasm between Orthodoxy and Reform, and the class divisions of German and east European Jews, came a cultural compromise known as Conservative Judaism. The moving forces behind it were Sabato Morais, founder of the Jewish Theological Seminary in

1886, and Solomon Schechter, head of the seminary after 1902, who tried to accommodate tradition with change and Jewish history with American reality. Conservatism preserved the vision of a chosen people, the direct relevance of the scriptures, the keeping of the Sabbath Day, and the observance of dietary laws, but it also adopted the quiet, reverent services of the Reformers as well as the mixed seating of women and men, congregational scripture readings, and the wearing of ordinary clothes. Loyal to tradition and Jewish ethnicity, the Conservatives accepted cosmetic changes in worship services, thereby appealing both to the middle-class mentality of the German Jews and to the more secular perspective of second-generation Orthodox children. The compromise worked. By 1920 Conservative Judaism had more active congregations than the Reform movement, and by 1945 more than the Orthodox branch.

The debate over Zionism also exposed differences between German and east European Jews. German Reform Jews had long since discarded the notion of any final gathering of "Israel" in the Holy Land. Assimilation in the United States, not the gathering of Israel in the Middle East, was their goal. But for east European Jews raised in the shtetl atmosphere of Yiddish culture and Orthodoxy, assimilation was unthinkable. Judaism was their world, their reason for being, their identity. For the Orthodox Jew the scattering of Israel was a curse, an aberration that would soon be remedied when the Messiah gathered them to Palestine. German Jews feared Zionism would retard the Americanization of the east Europeans, who supported it for precisely that reason—because it was the major thread in the fabric of Jewish identity. Zionism was the antithesis of assimilation because it predicted the indefinite survival of Jewish ethnicity.

Despite German misgivings, Zionism steadily gained ground in the United States. Zionist organizations appeared in the 1890s and won more and more followers between 1900 and 1945. Much of that success was due to the efforts of such German Jews as Louis Brandeis, Julian Mack, Felix Frankfurter, and other members of the American Jewish Committee. Just as Conservatism was a religious compromise between Orthodoxy and Reform, American Zionism became a middle ground between the organic cultural Zionism of east European Jews and the assimilationist spirit of German Jews. At first, Zionism aimed to resurrect Jewish culture as well as colonize Palestine, but the German Jews transformed Zionism into "Palestinianism." They supported Jewish settlement in Palestine but not the cultural demands that all Jews must settle there and resurrect Orthodoxy.

In many ways Jewish ethnicity underwent experiences similar to those of other immigrant groups. Like the Poles and Lithuanians, whose sense of nationalism increased in America, Jews enjoyed a rising sense of political nationalism in the Zionist movement. Like other immigrant nationalisms, Zionism was in part a product of intense controversies within the community over the future of ethnicity. During the 1920s the Jews too suffered from the Red Scare, the Ku Klux Klan, and the National Origins Act. External pressure helped define ethnicity for Jews just as it did for Catholic immigrants. But World War II had a greater influence on Jews than on other new immigrants.

Although the German invasion of Poland and the Soviet Union raised the ethnic consciousness of Russian-Americans and Polish-Americans, American Jews emerged from World War II with a vision of the Holocaust, Hitler's extermination of 6 million European Jews in such death camps as Auschwitz, Treblinka, and Maidanek. The Nazi onslaught represented anti-Semitism carried to the extreme of genocide. Prominent Jews like Albert Einstein, and Jews who would become prominent later like Henry Kissinger, had fled Germany in the 1930s. By 1942 American policy makers and Jewish organizations knew something horrible was happening to European Jewry, but the magnitude of the Holocaust was beyond belief to most American officials at the time. When President Franklin Roosevelt finally established the War Refugee Board in an attempt to rescue European Jews from Nazi persecution, it was already too late.

In 1945, with the liberation of the concentration camps, the enormity of the Holocaust became apparent. Hitler's Germany had practically annihilated European Jewry, leaving American Jews the dominant branch of the faith. In the wake of Nazi atrocities, the establishment of a Jewish state in Palestine seemed imperative to many Jews for the survival of world Jewry. Once a point of contention in the American Jewish community, Zionism had become more important than ever to Jewish identity. The Holocaust was the central experience in modern Jewish history, a tragedy which raised the consciousness of Jews everywhere. American Jews would enter the postwar era still divided by class and religious differences, still concerned about the secularizing effects of American life, but they were all committed to two ideals: the viability of the state of Israel and the notion, "Never again."

SUGGESTED READINGS

Baron, Salo. *The Russian Jew Under Tsars and Soviets.* New York: 1964.
Blau, Joseph. *Judaism in America: From Curiosity to Third Faith.* Chicago: 1976.
Cahan, Abraham. *The Rise of David Levinsky.* New York: 1917.

————— . *Yekl, A Tale of the New York Ghetto*. New York: 1896.

Cohen, Morris. *A Dreamer's Journey*. Boston: 1949.

Cohen, Naomi. *American Jews and the Zionist Idea*. New York: 1975.

Dawidowicz, Lucy. *The Golden Tradition*. New York: 1967.

Dinnerstein, Leonard. *The Leo Frank Case*. New York: 1968.

Dubnow, S. N. *History of the Jews in Russia and Poland*. Philadelphia: 1916–1920.

Feingold, Henry L. *Zion in America: The Jewish Experience from Colonial Times to the Present*. New York: 1974.

Friedman, Saul S. *No Haven for the Oppressed: United States Policy Toward Jewish Refugees*. Detroit: 1973.

Glazer, Nathan. *American Judaism*. Chicago: 1957.

Glazer, Nathan, and Moynihan, Daniel P. *Beyond the Melting Pot: The Negroes, Puerto Ricans, Jews, Italians, and Irish of New York City*. Cambridge, Mass.: 1963.

Goldman, Emma. *Living My Life*. New York: 1931.

Goren, Arthur A. *New York Jews and the Quest for Community: The Kehillah Experiment, 1908–1922*. New York: 1970.

Guttmann, Allen. *The Jewish Writer in America: Assimilation and the Crisis of Identity*. New York: 1971.

Heller, J. G. *Isaac Wise, His Life, Work and Thought*. New York: 1965.

Higham, John. *Send These to Me: Jews and Other Immigrants in Urban America*. New York: 1975.

Howe, Irving. *World of Our Fathers: The Journey of the East European Jews to America and the Life They Found and Made*. New York: 1976.

Howe, Irving, and Greenberg, Eliezer. *Voices from the Yiddish*. Ann Arbor, Mich.: 1972.

Hyamson, A. M. *The Sephardim of England: A History of the Spanish-Portuguese Jewish Community, 1492–1959*. London: 1952.

Jick, Leon. *The Americanization of the Synagogue, 1820–1870*. Hanover, N.H.: 1976.

Kessner, Thomas. *The Golden Door: Italian and Jewish Mobility in New York City, 1880–1915*. New York: 1977.

Kramer, Judith, and Leventman, Seymour. *Children of the Gilded Ghetto*. New Haven, Conn.: 1961.

Lavender, Abraham D. *A Coat of Many Colors: Jewish Subcommunities in the United States*. Westport, Conn.: 1977.

Marcus, Jacob R. *The Colonial American Jew: 1492–1776*. Detroit: 1970.

Minsky, Norman B. *Unorthodox Judaism*. Columbus, Oh.: 1977.

Philipson, D. *The Reform Movement in Judaism*. New York: 1931.

Poll, S. *The Hassidic Community in Williamsburg*. New York: 1962.

Rischin, Moses. *The Promised City: New York's Jews, 1870–1914*. Cambridge, Mass.: 1962.

Rose, Peter I., ed. *The Ghetto and Beyond: Essays on Jewish Life in America*. New York: 1969.

Shapiro, Yonathon. *Leadership of the American Zionist Organization*. Urbana, Ill.: 1971.

Stember, Charles. *Jews in the Mind of America*. New York: 1966.
Urofsky, Melvin. *American Zionism from Herzl to the Holocaust*. Garden City, N.Y.: 1975.
Whiteman, Maxwell. "Western Impact on East European Jews: A Philadelphia Fragment." In Randall M. Miller and Thomas D. Marzik. *Immigrants and Religion in Urban America*. Philadelphia: 1977.
Yezierska, Anzia. *Bread Givers*. New York: 1925.

Chapter Seventeen

The Assault on Tribalism: Native Americans

In 1876 the major crises of the previous century seemed over. The disruptive question of political sovereignty was resolved when the Civil War defeated the states' rights philosophy, and, at least on the surface, the Fourteenth and Fifteenth Amendments had enthroned racial equality as the natural right of all people. The melting-pot theory was gaining popularity. Mines were producing vast quantities of raw materials, and factories were transforming them into a glut of consumer and capital goods. Agricultural surpluses were flooding domestic markets, and western land was filling with settlers just as the railroads were creating a national market. The future seemed bright.

But one shadow still lurked from the past. It was the "Indian problem." Thousands of years of tribal autonomy, freedom of movement, and environmental harmony were coming to a tragic end. Native Americans were on the brink of annihilation—their land taken, their game gone, and their population dwindling rapidly. White people and their machines were everywhere. Between 1877 and 1890 the last vestiges of Indian resistance—the flight of the Nez Percé in Montana, the guerrilla wars of the Apaches in the Southwest, and the battles of the Plains Indians—were wiped out.

It was a terrible story, the stuff of which thousands of western novels and films have been made. Arapaho dancers by the 1880s were singing a plaintive refrain:

My Father, have pity on me!
I have nothing to eat,
I am dying of thirst—
Everything is gone.*

And it was gone. But images of military conquest should not be over-
done, even though it was frequent in the nineteenth century. It was
European civilization—with its large, fenced farms, towns and cities,
railroads, and diseases—that ultimately defeated native Americans.
One scholar estimates that between 1789 and 1890 "only" four thousand
Indians died by the sword, the rest succumbing to changes brought by
white society. As the buffalo disappeared, Indian men were deprived of
their economic importance; and Indian elders on the reservations lost
their decision-making authority to white agents. Restricted in their
movements, without independence or means of resistance, native
Americans were no longer able to struggle, violently at least, against
white society. Culturally, of course, they were no closer than ever to
accepting white values.

Anglo Conformity

As the Indian wars ended in the 1880s, a major reassessment of federal
policy was underway. Ever since 1607 the British and American governments had treated the tribes as independent nations, sovereign on
their own land, and Congress had negotiated diplomatic treaties to
resolve disputes. Some whites also believed in the ability of reservations
to protect the natives from white racism and to free surplus land for
development by whites. Virginia had established the first formal reservations in 1646, when the House of Burgesses set aside portions of York
County for the Pamunkey and Chickahominy Indians. Two hundred
years later, after President Jackson had pushed the woodlands Indians
across the Mississippi River, reservations seemed the only answer to the
"Indian problem." Sovereignty and reservations were the twin ideas
governing Indian policy before 1870.

Thousands of Americans, however, were concerned about the plight
of the Indians in 1877. The native American population had fallen from
600,000 in 1776 to less than 250,000, and smallpox, measles, mumps,
cholera, and syphilis were ravaging the reservations. Unaccustomed to
sedentary life, most Indians vegetated in their state of humiliating
dependency. The catastrophe was apparent to even the most casual

*Quoted in Ralph K. Andrist, *The Long Death: The Last Days of the Plains Indians* (New
York, 1964), p. 338.

observers. Although the federal government still recognized tribal autonomy, reservation life lacked the economic purpose so essential to social stability. Native Americans were wards of the state, dependent upon food shipments from the government for survival, and unscrupulous agents of the Department of the Interior worsened the situation by black-marketing supplies earmarked for the tribes.

In the 1870s and 1880s prominent whites, disturbed by the economic decline of native Americans and their turn toward the Sun Dance, Ghost Dance, and peyotism, questioned the wisdom of both sovereignty and reservations. In 1858 Bishop Henry Whipple of the Episcopal church had written A *Plea for the Indian*, which condemned the reservation system because of repeated white encroachments on the land. The Sand Creek massacre of 1864 had exposed the tragedy of military confrontation, and subsequent congressional hearings revealed the horrible conditions on most reservations. In 1868 Lydia Child wrote her *Appeal for the Indian*, and Peter Cooper founded the United States Indian Commission to bring an end to the frontier wars. The American Anti-Slavery Society changed its name to the Reform League in 1870 and took on the plight of native Americans as its new crusade. In 1881 Helen Hunt Jackson wrote her famous indictment of American Indian policy, A *Century of Dishonor*. Three years later her novel *Ramona* portrayed the tragic extinction of the California Indians. And in 1881 the Indian Rights Association came into existence to force changes in government policy. White liberals, even though paternalistic, were gaining influence.

But old approaches still survived. Reformers still wanted to divest Indians of their cultural heritage, introduce them to Christianity, teach them English, and prepare them to function in a white economy. Once the Indians had accepted Christ, learned to read and write, and decided to succeed economically, white hostitlity toward them, liberals confidently believed, would rapidly disappear. This was Anglo conformity in its purest, most naïve form, particularly since whites still coveted Indian land. Before American society would even begin to accept the Indians as anything but obstacles to progress, native Americans would have to yield all the land whites wanted. And even then, regardless of how Indians acted or what they believed, they would not be accepted as equals. Most liberals, however, were not conscious of the obstacles in their path; working through the federal government and Christian churches, they set about changing native Americans.

Congress began appropriating money for Indian education after the Civil War, and money also flowed in from white philanthropists and Christian churches. Enthusiastic missionaries descended on the reservations ready to teach and preach the gospel. Nonreservation boarding

Teachers and pupils at the government school on the Swinomish Reservation, La Conner, Washington, in 1907. Education was seen as a means of promoting Anglo conformity. (Culver Pictures, Inc.)

schools such as the Carlisle School in Pennsylvania, designed to remove Indian children from the tribal environment, sprouted across the country, and there missionaries taught Christianity, English, and various skills. Urging Indians to become commercial farmers, the Department of the Interior sent agriculture teachers, farm implements, and instruction books to the reservations. But the transformation never occurred. The Indians remained doggedly loyal to tribal ways. They preferred their own religious ceremonies to Christianity, and the once proud hunters viewed farming as demeaning "woman's work." Indian children, after graduating from the boarding schools, showed a marked propensity for returning to the reservations, even though they had learned valuable skills. Expecting eradication of native American society in a single generation, not through violence but through conversion, reformers were dumfounded at its tenacity.

Frustrated missionaries and government agents tried to prohibit the expression of Indian culture. In a nation where religious freedom was sacred, Congress authorized government agents on the reservations in 1884 to cooperate with local missionaries in suppressing Indian religions. They outlawed the Ghost Dance on the Sioux reservations and the Sun Dance on the Ute and Shoshone reservations. In New Mexico the Pueblo Indians could not continue their centuries-old initiation rites for the young, and the Arapahos in Wyoming had to give up their funeral ceremonies. Federal narcotics officers zealously tried to destroy the peyote culture. And on reservations everywhere, government agents punished Indian children for speaking native dialects and prohibited tribal dances, drumming, and body painting. Since the federal government was at this time trying to stamp out polygamy among Utah Mormons, reservation agents also dissolved plural marriages among the Indians, with little thought given to the plight of women deprived of their husbands. Some Indian agents even insisted that former warriors cut their hair short.

The reformers sincerely believed that cultural change would help the Indians. Trying to explain the continuing vitality of Indian culture, white reformers focused on government policy. Tribal sovereignty and reservation life, they decided, reinforced Indian culture. The real solution was to break up the tribes, distribute reservation land to individual Indian families, and turn the people into yeoman farmers. Only in the absence of tribal authority and social communion could native Americans be reasonably expected to shed their culture for white ways. What the reformers did not take into account was that although the reservation policy had been a failure, its original rationale had at least implied the existence of legal boundaries, acres of land confining the Indian but also restricting the access of whites. Even that legal implication was about to end. Once content to try to change the Indian outlook on heaven and hell, white reformers now wanted to destroy the native American tribal culture to save the Indians.

The Allotment Program

The idea of dissolving tribal lands and allotting small farms to individual Indians had had its advocates in the colonial period, but the first real allotment program came in 1839, when the federal government divided the lands of the Brotherton Indians in Wisconsin. Similar programs were later tried out on the Chippewas, Shawnees, Wyandots, Omahas, Ottawas, and Potawatomies. In each case the law provided that once the allotment process was complete, the Indians would become citizens of the United States. Convinced that allotment would protect the Indians from further white encroachments, white liberals in such groups as the Indian Rights Association and the Conference of the Friends of the Indians supported a national allotment program. Congress began moving on proposals to end tribal sovereignty in the 1870s, and in the 1880s the allotment programs finally triumphed.

In 1871 Congress stopped recognizing native American tribes as independent nations, and instead of negotiating with Indians the federal government began legislating for them and dealing only with heads of Indian families. Congress then directed its attention to the economy of native America, convinced that turning the Indians into farmers would be the best way of assimilating them. Thousands of Indians had tilled the land before the white conquest, but they had been communal farmers, producing just enough to meet their own needs. Commercial production of surpluses was alien to them, and for the nomadic hunters of the Great Plains, farming of any kind was degrading. Finally, there were enormous problems with agriculture in the West. On the dry, windy plains of the Midwest, in the semideserts of the Great Basin and the deserts of the Southwest, agricultural success depended upon capital and technological prowess. The Indians had neither, so most of their efforts at farming would be doomed to failure. Nevertheless, in 1875 Congress passed the Indian Homestead Act, which permitted individual Indians to take ownership of up to 160 acres.

Liberal reformers realized that few Indians would voluntarily leave their tribes for rural life. Benign, paternalistic coercion, they decided, would have to be employed. Carl Schurz, the German Forty-Eighter and Secretary of the Interior under President Grant, remarked in 1881:

> Stubborn maintenance of . . . large Indian reservations must eventually result in the destruction of the redmen . . . [it is necessary to] fit the Indians . . . for the habits and occupations of civilized life by work and education; to individualize them in the possession and appreciation of property by . . . giving them a fee simple title individually to the parcels of land they cultivate . . . and to obtain their consent . . . for a fair compensation, in such a manner that they no longer stand in the way of the development of the country as an obstacle, but form part of it and are benefited by it.*

An ominous note then sounded; land-hungry speculators began supporting the reform movement. If the reservations were broken up into individual holdings, it would be easier to purchase land from the Indians. The reservations totaled 138 million acres and were controlled by only 250,000 people. Even the most generous arithmetic showed that if every Indian received 160 acres, it would only amount to about 40 million acres. What was to become of the other 100 million? Greedy land lobbyists saw a windfall in the making. Senator Henry L. Dawes, a well-meaning but misguided reformer, introduced an allotment bill to Congress in 1879, and the ensuing debate raged for eight years. A few reformers realized that the bill might lead to the loss of even more land by Indians, but minority fears eventually succumbed to majority demands, and on February 8, 1887, the Dawes Severalty Act became law.

Under the law the president could allot tribal lands on the following basis: each adult Indian head of family received 160 acres; single adults and orphans got 80 acres; and single, unattached youths received 40

*Quoted in Robert Kelley, *The Shaping of the American Past* (New York, 1976), p. 500.

acres. Indians could choose their land, but if they failed to do so, the Department of the Interior would do it for them. To prevent them from selling their individual holdings, title to the property was placed in trust for twenty-five years. Indians accepting allotment and leaving their tribes were to be awarded American citizenship and come under the laws of the states they lived in. Finally, the act provided that surplus lands not allotted could be sold by the government to white settlers.

The prophets of doom proved correct; predictions that Indians would lose their land were tragically fulfilled. The most valuable land was first to go. Whites went after the rich grasslands of Kansas, Nebraska, and the Dakotas; the dense, black soil forests of Minnesota and Wisconsin; and the wealthy oil and natural gas lands in Texas and Oklahoma. In 1887, for example, the Sisseton Sioux of South Dakota owned 918,000 acres of rich virgin farm land on their reservation. But since there were only two thousand of them, allotment left more than 600,000 acres. In short order the Department of the Interior opened the surplus land to white farmers, who subsequently moved in among the Indians, thus wrecking any vestiges of tribal culture.

Similar events occurred all across the country. The Chippewas of Minnesota lost their rich timber lands; once each member had claimed his land, the government leased the rest to lumber corporations for exploitation. The Colville tribes of northeastern Washington lost their lands to cattlemen who fraudulently claimed mineral rights there. In Montana and Wyoming the Crows lost more than 2 million acres, and the Nez Percés had to cede communal grazing ranges in Idaho. In the Indian Territory the Cheyenne, Arapahos, and Kickapoos all had their lands allotted, and in the case of the Kickapoos, 200,000 surplus acres were sold for less than thirty cents an acre. In all, the native American tribes lost more than 60 million "surplus" acres under the allotment law.

Though exempted from the law, the Five Civilized Tribes also lost most of the land they owned in the Indian Territory. In their bitterness toward the federal government after the removals of the 1830s and 1840s, some had sided with the Confederacy during the Civil War, and in retaliation the government opened their land to white home-steaders in 1889. The subsequent discovery of oil in Oklahoma un-leashed new pressures on the land as excited wildcatters and large oil corporations, supported by corrupt county politicians, systematically took much of the remaining land from the Creeks, Cherokees, Choc-taws, Chickasaws, and Seminoles. Between 1887 and 1924 the land of the Five Civilized Tribes declined from approximately 30 million to less than 2 million acres.

Still the land hunger continued. In 1902 the federal government began voiding the twenty-five-year trust period originally designed to prevent the sale of allotted lands. The Dead Indian Land Act of 1902 permitted native Americans to sell land they had inherited from deceased relatives, and the Burke Act of 1906 authorized the secretary of the interior to declare Indian adults competent to manage their own affairs and sell their allotted lands. Between 1906 and 1917 the secretary cautiously issued competency patents to only 9,984 Indians, but then the pace quickened, and more than twenty thousand Indians received patents between 1919 and 1924. Greedy real estate salesmen, corrupt government agents, land speculators, and white merchants all began buying allotted land from Indians, usually at greatly deflated prices. The Sisseton Sioux lost another 200,000 acres, leaving them with little more than 100,000 of the 918,000 acres they had owned in 1887. Under the Burke Act more than 27 million acres were sold to whites by Indian farmers, and by 1924 native Americans held only 48 million of the 138 million acres they had owned in 1887, half of it arid and of marginal value.

White Atonement: The Indian Reorganization Act of 1934

In 1924 Congress passed the Indian Citizenship Act, conferring citizenship on Indians born in the United States. In one sense the law represented the final assault on tribalism. Assimilationists yearning to transform Indian culture hoped the law would distract Indians from their tribal loyalties. But in another sense the act inaugurated a new era. Conscious of what had happened to native Americans in the previous century, some whites believed citizenship was a first step in rectifying past wrongs, an admission that Indians had every right to expect equal treatment under the law. And despite three hundred years of mistreatment, native Americans had enlisted by the thousands during World War I to fight for the United States. Sympathetic whites demanded citizenship in recognition of that military service.

Conditions on the reservations inspired sympathy. Thousands of Indians had discovered that 160 acres in the arid West was insufficient to make a living, and as older native Americans died the inheritance of their children was even smaller. Four children, for example, received only forty acres each, and many nearly starved to death on such miserable holdings. Life was even more difficult for those who had sold land under the Burke Act. In a few months they had spent the cash, and left with neither money nor land, they drifted back to the reservations, destitute and again dependent on government welfare. By 1920 life on the reservations was scandalous, and the native American death rate—because of malnutrition, tuberculosis, trachoma, and dysentery—was more than twice the national average.

During the 1920s the entire allotment program and its Anglo conformity ideology collapsed under pressure from muckraking journalists, native American lobbyists, and white liberals. A new respect for tribalism and Indian religions appeared. Eager to expose corruption, muckraking journalists turned their attention to the plight of native Americans. Article after article in newspapers and magazines, and program after program on the radio and lecture circuits, described how the Dawes Act had plundered Indian land and destroyed Indian culture. Descriptions of the demise of Indian culture were premature, but the muckrackers did arouse public opinion.

Native Americans were also organizing to fight government policies, and young white liberals were joining them. Organized in 1911, the Society of American Indians—led by such educated Indians as Arthur Parker (Seneca), Sherman Coolidge (Arapaho), Charles Eastman (Santee Sioux), and Carlos Montezuma (Apache)—campaigned for Indian citizenship and denounced the Bureau of Indian Affairs. And in 1923 white liberals formed the American Indian Defense Association to oppose all future attempts to steal Indian land. Such resistance was timely, for the federal government was preparing its final assault on Indian land.

In the election of 1920 the Republican Warren G. Harding of Ohio became president, and in 1921 he appointed Albert Fall secretary of the interior. Sympathetic to land and timber interests, Fall selected none other than Charles H. Burke, author of the Burke Act, to be commissioner of Indian affairs. They quickly ruled that native Americans did not possess mineral rights on reservation land, and that oil and gas companies could petition the federal government for leasing options. At the same time they submitted the Omnibus Indian Act to Congress to pay native Americans cash for their remaining land. The government could then resell it and retire completely from Indian affairs. And finally, Senator Holm O. Bursum of New Mexico submitted a bill recognizing the land titles of white settlers who had illegally squatted on the Pueblo reservation. Had all three measures passed Congress, they would have taken most of the 48 million acres that Indians still owned.

Native Americans rallied immediately against the measures. Looking back to 1680, when they had revolted against Spanish oppression, the Pueblo tribes formed the All Pueblo Indian Council, enlisted the support of muckraking journalists, and carried their case to Congress and the American public, demanding rejection of the Bursum bill. A national uproar followed, and nervous congressmen, their ears to the ground politically, realized that a momentous shift in public opinion was underway. The results were immediate. The Osage Guardianship Act of 1925 reversed Fall's oil and gas leasing program and protected Osage land in Oklahoma. At the same time, Congress refused to act on the Omnibus Indian Act, thereby guaranteeing native Americans control of their remaining assets. In 1927 the Department of the Interior stopped issuing fee simple patents altogether, ending the Burke Act of 1906. And Senator Bursum's bill to take Pueblo land gave way to the Pueblo Lands Board Act of 1924, which established a government commission to mediate the dispute between Indians and whites in New Mexico. Whites retained title to the land, but not before Congress paid the Pueblos more than $1 million in compensation. It was a paltry sum compared to the value of the land, but it was the beginning of the end for allotment.

Other reformers concluded that only a return to tribal authority could save the Indians from extinction, and in 1926 such groups as the Committee of 100 and the Indian Rights Association persuaded Secretary of the Interior Hubert Work to investigate federal Indian policy. To make sure the Bureau of Indian Affairs did not prejudice the findings, Indian rights advocates asked the Brookings Institution to direct the investigation. Issued in 1928 and known as the Meriam Report, the study shocked the nation, confirming rumors of poverty and disease on the reservations and detailing the murders, physical intimidations, robberies, and legal chicaneries used to take Indian land under the Dawes Act. Although the Meriam Report held out hope for the eventual assimilation of Indians into American society, it argued that the process would have to be voluntary on Indian terms and at the Indians' pace. Until native Americans abandoned their own culture for white values, they would have to be able to enjoy community control through tribal authority, economic reconstruction, and freedom of religion.

In 1929 President Herbert Hoover appointed Ray Lyman Wilbur, the socially liberal president of Stanford University, secretary of the interior. Wilbur identified closely with native American problems, and named Charles Rhoads, head of the American Indian Defense Association, commissioner of Indian affairs. Rejecting the policy of placing Indian children in boarding schools far from home, Rhoads supported day schools near the reservations where children could learn useful vocations while remaining close to their families. It was a major change in the direction of federal Indian policy.

The Great Depression of the 1930s aggravated conditions on the reservations and made the findings of the Meriam Report even more urgent. Support for tribalism received strong encouragement when Franklin D. Roosevelt became president in 1933 and appointed John Collier commissioner of Indian affairs. A founder of the American Indian Defense Association, Collier opposed allotment and had argued for years that Indian culture must be preserved if native Americans were to survive. Despite protests from missionary groups, Collier set out to revive native American culture by introducing bilingual education in the schools; ending requirements that children living at federal boarding schools attend Protestant church services; encouraging traditional dances, crafts, and drumming; and diverting federal funds used for suppressing peyotism to other purposes. Finally, he campaigned for the Indian Reorganization Act, which Congress passed in 1934. Allotment was dead.

The Indian Reorganization Act restored tribal authority. Under the law each tribe could draft its own constitution and assume ownership of all reservation lands, and all unallotted surplus land reverted automatically to the tribe, as did Department of the Interior land withdrawn from Indian control for homesteading but never taken. The act encouraged the tribes to organize themselves into business corporations to manage reservation resources, and the federal government established a $10-million revolving fund to help Indians move toward self-sufficiency. Finally, the Act appropriated $2 million each year for the secretary of the interior to buy new land for the tribes. Fifty-eight tribes composed of 146,194 Indians approved the law, and thirteen tribes of 15,213 Indians opposed it. With such overwhelming support, the Indian Reorganization Act became the new bible for native American affairs.

If not completely successful, the act was encouraging. By 1945 ninety-five tribes had drafted constitutions and taken control of surplus reservation lands. More than seventy tribes had incorporated themselves and were developing reservation resources. The Department of the Interior spent more than $5 million purchasing 400,000 new acres of land, and several pieces of congressional legislation added another 900,000 acres. The department returned more than a million acres which had never been homesteaded and surrendered a million acres of public-domain grazing land. With their own funds Indians managed to buy 400,000 new acres, so that in all they recovered nearly 4 million acres of land they had lost under the Dawes Act. Most encouraging, the native American population decline, which had been unabated ever since the seventeenth century, reversed itself. After World War I a sustained period of growth began, and from its low of 220,000 people in 1910, the Indian population had grown to nearly 550,000 in 1945.

Tribal structures had been repaired, and the service of thousands of Indians in World War II had impressed the public, but serious problems remained. Although the Indians had recovered 4 million acres, they had lost 90 million acres since 1887, and much of what they recovered was land that whites had not wanted. Economic dependence on the federal government remained a fact of life on the reservations despite the lofty goals of the Indian Reorganization Act. Poverty, disease, and unemployment were far higher there than among other Americans. Compared with life in 1600 the conditions of 1945 were not good, but compared with 1920 times had changed, and the future was brighter for native Americans than it had been for many years.

SUGGESTED READINGS

For the effects of federal legislation during the late nineteenth- and early twentieth-centuries, please see the tribal histories listed in the Chapter 9 bibliography. Also see:

Cash, Joseph H., and Hoover, Herbert T. *To Be an Indian*. New York: 1971.
Cotroneo, Ross R., and Dozier, Jack. "A Time of Disintegration: The Coeur d'Alene and the Dawes Act." *Western Historical Quarterly*. 5 (October 1974), 405–419.
Debo, Angie. *A History of the Indians of the United States*. Norman, Oklahoma: 1970.
Eastman, Charles A. *From the Deep Woods to Civilization*. Boston: 1916.
———. *Indian Boyhood*. New York: 1902.
———. *The Indian Today: The Past and Future of the First American*. New York: 1915.
Hagan, William T. "Kiowas, Comanches, and Cattlemen, 1867–1906: A Case Study of the Failure of U.S. Reservation Policy." *Pacific Historical Review*, 40 (August 1971), 333–356.
Hertzberg, Hazel W. *The Search for an American Indian Identity: Modern Pan-Indian Movements*. Syracuse, N.Y.: 1971.
Kelly, Lawrence C. *The Navajo Indians and Federal Indian Policy, 1900–1935*. Tucson, Arizona: 1968.
Levy, Jerome E., and Kunitz, Stephen J. *Indian Drinking: Navajo Practices and Anglo American Theories*. New York: 1974.
Lurie, Nancy Oesterich. "The World's Oldest On-Going Protest Demonstration: Native American Drinking Patterns." *Pacific Historical Review*, 40 (August 1971), 311–332.
McNickle, D'Arcy. *Native American Tribalisms*. New York: 1973.
Meinig, Donald W. *Southwest: Three Peoples in Geographical Change*. New York: 1971.
Miner, H. Craig. *The Corporation and the Indian: Tribal Sovereignty and Industrial Civilization in Indian Territory, 1865–1907*. New York: 1976.
Otis, D. S. *The Dawes Act and the Allotment of Indian Lands*. Norman, Oklahoma: 1973.
Parman, Donald L. *The Navajos and the New Deal*. New Haven, Conn.: 1976.
Philip, Kenneth. "Albert B. Fall and the Protest from the Pueblos, 1921–1923." *Arizona and the West*, 12 (Autumn 1970), 237–254.
———. *John Collier's Crusade for Indian Reform, 1920–1954*. Tucson, Arizona: 1977.

Prucha, Francis Paul. *American Indian Policy in Crisis: Christian Reformers and the Indian, 1865–1900.* Norman, Oklahoma: 1975.

Szasz, Margaret. *Education and the American Indian: The Road to Self-Determination, 1928–1973.* Albuquerque, N.M.: 1974.

Washburn, Wilcomb E. *The Assault on Indian Tribalism: The General Allotment Law.* Philadelphia: 1975.

————. *The Indian in America.* New York: 1975.

Wilson, Raymond. "The Writings of Ohiyesa—Charles Alexander Eastman, M.D., Santee Sioux." *South Dakota History,* 6 (Winter 1975) 55–73.

Witt, Shirley Hill, and Steiner, Stan: *The Way: An Anthology of American Indian Literature.* New York: 1972.

Chapter Eighteen

Free at Last:
The Afro-Americans

The Civil War and Reconstruction had raised the hopes of black people, but dreams and even laws cannot immediately change the economic and social structure of a country. The economy of southern society had rested on slavery, and by themselves the Emancipation Proclamation and the Thirteenth, Fourteenth, and Fifteenth Amendments could not alter that reality. White southerners rapidly regained the power to enforce the roles they had assigned to blacks, and the imperatives of slavery, if not the institution itself, continued to assert themselves. Late in the nineteenth century whites tried to turn blacks once again into a controlled, exploited minority.

Black voting was the first target; as long as blacks voted, white politicians would have to treat them as a constituency, and such appeals would inevitably give the former slaves some power. Since the Fifteenth Amendment prohibited voting discrimination on the basis of race, whites had to use other methods to deprive blacks of the right to vote. Physical intimidation was common during the 1880s, as were threats by employers to fire blacks who tried to vote. Between 1877 and 1900 the South also adopted the poll tax, which required people to pay a fee before voting. The tax laws did not mention race and technically circumvented the Fourteenth and Fifteenth Amendments. The same was true of the literacy tests, which disfranchised citizens unable to read or answer complex legal questions. Because poll taxes and literacy tests discriminated against poor, illiterate whites as well as blacks, southern legislatures passed "grandfather clauses" declaring that those unable to pay poll taxes or pass literacy tests could vote if their grandfathers had been eligible to vote in 1860. Whites were thus exempt from the restrictions. And to keep educated, solvent blacks from the polls, the South created "white primaries." In primary elections to select candidates for office, Democratic party workers would not permit blacks to vote, and since the Republican party hardly existed in the South, the exclusion amounted to disfranchisement. Political parties rather than the state governments controlled primary elections, so the exclusion was not technically unconstitutional.

Disfranchisement was only a first step. For two hundred years the southern economy had relied on black labor, and after the Civil War whites still needed that labor. If blacks managed to gain economic self-sufficiency, they would be free of white control. So whites made sure black people stayed poor. Threats of physical injury kept blacks from applying for skilled jobs, joining trade unions, or buying their own farms. Some states passed laws prohibiting blacks from buying land or leasing it on a long-term basis. Most black workers ended up as tenant farmers, migratory laborers, sharecroppers, or domestic servants. Some whites demanded that black labor be replaced by white immigrants, and in the late nineteenth century thousands of white workers displaced black artisans, especially in such skilled, urban occupations as craftsmen, iron workers, trainmen, coopers, blacksmiths, tailors, and construction workers. Few whites replaced blacks in agriculture and heavy industry. It amounted to economic disfranchisement.

Debt peonage also appeared. Former slaves signed yearly labor contracts and borrowed food and commodities from local white merchants, planning to pay back the loans with the proceeds of the next harvest. But when settlement time came in the fall, they usually discovered their share of the crop would not pay the debt. They would borrow again to make it through the winter and spring, only to have the cycle repeat itself. Since they could never get ahead of the debt, and since farmers with debts could not leave the county, they were practically slaves again.

Finally, after emancipation many whites felt socially vulnerable. To restore the control they had once exercised over blacks, whites began enacting "Jim Crow" laws late in the 1880s, segregating blacks in theaters, buses, trains, streetcars, waiting rooms, schools, housing, hospitals, prisons, parks, amusements, toilets, restaurants, and at drinking fountains. The Supreme Court ratified the Jim Crow philosophy in the *Plessy v. Ferguson* decision of 1896, deciding that "separate but equal" public facilities were constitutional. Social ostracism now joined political oppression and economic discrimination.

Black People and Freedom

Active black resistance to white oppression began after the Civil War. During Reconstruction blacks in New Orleans, Charleston, and Louisville launched boycotts of city transportation lines when segregated horsecars were introduced, and after 1900 black transportation companies appeared in Norfolk, Chattanooga, and Nashville to meet the needs of black people refusing to ride segregated city lines. In 1899 black parents in East Orange, New Jersey, kept their children home from school after local officials began separating white and black students. Similar boycotts occurred in many Ohio schools in the 1920s. Even though most outlets for protest were closed to black people, they nevertheless tried to realize the freedom which the Civil War had promised. Ultimately they decided that political and economic organization would help them achieve the equality they so desperately wanted.

Fresh waves of antiblack violence made the need for organization even clearer. Between 1900 and 1917 more than eleven hundred blacks were lynched, and even then federal antilynching laws failed in Congress. After three companies of black soldiers were accused of rioting in Brownsville, Texas, in 1906, President Theodore Roosevelt discharged them without conducting a formal investigation. Between 1904 and 1908 race riots erupted in Statesboro and Atlanta, Georgia; Springfield, Illinois; Greensburg, Indiana; and Springfield, Ohio. During and after World War I there were more race riots, the worst in East St. Louis in 1917 and Chicago in 1919. Many blacks began realizing that their only hope lay in becoming economically and politically powerful in their own right. The idea of "black power" began to take form.

The rise of an educated black middle class reinforced the desire for equality. In the antebellum period southern blacks had relied on Afro-American culture to define values and supply emotional security. They had few alternatives: whites determined all their occupational and economic choices. Slaves yearned after the freedom, prosperity, and power whites enjoyed, but black culture still commanded their loyalty. Once they were freed, their opportunities had broadened. The Freedmen's Bureau set up more than four hundred elementary and secondary schools for black children in the South, and private philanthropists established Howard University, Hampton Institute, St. Augustine's College, Johnson C. Smith University, Atlanta University, Storer College, and Fisk University for black students. More than five thousand northern teachers descended on the South after the Civil War and taught ex-slaves that they were free, equal, and entitled to everything American democracy offered. Initially freedom had been the elusive goal of Afro-Americans, but contact with northern teachers made equality the new priority. Over the years, as business people, journalists, ministers, lawyers, teachers, physicians, nurses, and social workers came out of the black colleges, a self-conscious middle class appeared in the black community. Enjoying relative economic security, they constantly compared their segregation and discrimination with the egalitarian values of American culture.

All these changes came at a difficult time in American history. Early in the 1900s the Progressive movement was trying to solve the problems created by industrialization. Dedicated to political democracy and an end to corporate privilege, Progressives called for antitrust laws, railroad regulation, the use of the secret ballot in local as well as national elections, primary elections, women's rights, and conservation of natural resources. Most of them were not very sympathetic to black rights. President Woodrow Wilson, for example, acquiesced in the segregation of federal employees, and white primaries came to the South during the Progressive period.

Still, some white liberals felt that Progressive ideals of social justice applied to blacks, just as during the Revolution some northerners had seen the contradiction between slavery and the natural rights philosophy. Oswald Garrison Villard, grandson of the abolitionist William Lloyd Garrison, called for black civil rights; writers William Walling and William Dean Howells condemned racism; philosopher John Dewey protested Jim Crow laws; and social workers Jane Addams and Mary White Ovington demanded political and economic equality. These influential white liberals gave the civil rights movement respectability, convincing some whites that black equality was a compelling need instead of a revolutionary notion.

More important than white liberalism was the northern migration of southern blacks after 1914. Between 1870 and 1890 some 80,000 had moved out of the South, and 200,000 more left between 1890 and 1910. Compared to the influx of European immigrants, the black migration was inconsequential; Afro-Americans were still only a tiny minority in the cities. But that changed when the South was hit by an economic recession in 1914 and by the cotton-destroying boll weevil attacks in 1915. Thousands of jobs disappeared just as northern and midwestern industries were booming during World War I. Black people headed north by the thousands. Between 1910 and 1920 the black population of the North increased from 850,000 to 1.4 million people, and by 1930 to more than 2.3 million. Two million more left the South during the Great

Black soldiers returning home in 1919. Nearly 400,000 blacks served in the U.S. armed forces in World War I. (Culver Pictures, Inc.)

Depression and World War II, and black ghettos appeared in cities throughout the Northeast and Midwest.

Whites were frightened, and frequent race riots—as in East St. Louis in 1917, Chicago in 1919, and Detroit in 1943—were malignant responses to those fears. But despite white hostility black people now lived in their own communities without constant intervention by whites, and slowly but surely developed into a force to be reckoned with by white politicians. During the Great Depression urban blacks shifted from the Republican to the Democratic party. Most blacks voted for Franklin D. Roosevelt, and many northern Democrats began to support legislation blacks wanted. Afro-Americans had a new, if reluctant, ally.

The northern migrations produced a black renaissance that represented cultural separatism. Northern ghettos—with their black lawyers, teachers, ministers, doctors, nurses, social workers, and businesspeople—also produced black musicians, writers, and artists, all of them with a new determination. Their movement was centered in the "Harlem Renaissance." People like James Weldon Johnson, Claude McKay, Jean Turner, Countee Cullen, Langston Hughes, Richard Wright, Irving Miller, and Anne Spencer graphically portrayed the plight and promise of black people and protested discrimination. They revitalized African pride and treated black culture neither as a mirror of white culture nor as a pathological reaction to racism, but as a fulfilling if sometimes frustrating way of life. They became the moral spokesmen for the black community.

Both world wars also contributed to raising black consciousness. During World War I nearly 400,000 black men served in the armed forces, as did more than 1 million in World War II. Segregated though they generally were, they served with distinction, and when they returned home, they were less willing than before to accept second-class status. Hundreds of thousands had been overseas in less racist societies, where they had experienced a tolerance unknown in the United States. Their return to Jim Crow societies was a shock. And because both wars had stimulated black migration out of rural areas and the acquisition of good jobs and better pay, black people expected more. Raised expectations inevitably created more impatience with inequality.

Four Black Leaders

Several black leaders emerged in the late nineteenth and early twentieth centuries. Four men in particular—Booker T. Washington, W. E. B. Du Bois, Marcus Garvey, and A. Philip Randolph—symbolized the hopes of 10 million Afro-Americans. They took different approaches to the "American dilemma," but all four sought the same goal: the end of poverty and discrimination.

In the 1890s Booker T. Washington became the premier advocate of "black power," though he did not use the term. Born a slave in 1856, he went to Hampton Institute in 1872 and learned his lifelong philosophy: through hard work and industrial education black people could end the poverty of tenant farming and sharecropping. Washington believed that as long as southern blacks remained tied to someone else's land, they would always be poor and powerless, and only when they gained real economic skills would they become truly free. He assumed the presidency of Tuskegee Institute, in Alabama, in 1881 and built the school into a major center of vocational education. Washington came to national attention when he spoke at the Atlanta Exposition in 1895. Apparently uninterested in civil rights, he told black people to forget about social equality, accept segregation, and concentrate on material advancement and economic independence. White people, he insisted, could be allies as long as they did not feel threatened by social amalgamation:

We shall prosper in proportion as we learn to dignify and glorify common labour and put brains and skill into the common occupations of life. . . . It is at the bottom of life we must begin, and not at the top. . . . In all things that are purely social we can be as separate as the fingers, yet one as the hand in all things essential to mutual progress . . . agitation of questions of social equality is . . . folly . . . progress must be the result of severe and constant struggle rather than of artificial forcing . . .*

Privately Washington believed in civil rights, but he considered them subordinate to economics. His constituency was the poorest blacks of all, people locked into the rural poverty of the South, and he believed that for them economic survival took precedence over civil rights. Washington appealed to wealthy whites for funds to build black vocational schools, and concentrated on elevating the living standards of millions of poor people in the South. White people hailed him, presidents sought his advice on racial matters, and when he died in 1915 he was the most beloved black person in the United States.

But Washington was not universally popular among blacks. If for no other reason, antiblack violence had convinced many of them that whites would never willingly permit real black progress. William Edward Burghardt Du Bois became the spokesman for those who believed that blacks must work for their own civil as well as economic rights. Born in Massachusetts in 1868, Du Bois attended Fisk University and received a Ph.D. from Harvard in 1895. Later he taught history at the University of Pennsylvania. Calling for racial pride and group solidarity, Du Bois chastised Booker T. Washington for advocating a program that would forever keep blacks in an inferior social and political position. Instead of accepting discrimination, black people should openly demand equality. Instead of confining themselves to vocational education, the "talented tenth" of the black population should study law, medicine, and public administration. Only then could they end racism and discrimination. Separation meant subordination, and Du Bois wanted no part of it.

To implement his philosophy, Du Bois invited a group of northern blacks to Niagara Falls, Canada, in 1905, and they formed the Niagara Movement to fight discrimination and urge young blacks to enter the professions. Five years later a group of white liberals led by Oswald Garrison Villard gave him their support, and Du Bois joined them and other black activists in forming the National Association for the Advancement of Colored People. Through legal action in state and federal courts, the NAACP hoped to overturn Jim Crow and enfranchise black

*Robert C. Twombly, ed., *Blacks in White America Since 1865* (New York, 1971), pp. 79–81.

people. Much of the misunderstanding between Washington and Du Bois can be traced to their different constituencies, Washington representing the rural southern poor for whom higher education seemed infinitely remote and Du Bois representing in part a more economically secure middle class able to take action to achieve equality.

The third major black figure of the early twentieth century was Marcus Garvey, a West Indian immigrant. Between 1890 and 1930 more than 350,000 West Indian blacks immigrated to the United States, most of them from the British West Indies, Haiti, the Dominican Republic, and Cuba. They settled primarily in the northeastern cities, especially New York, and worked at a number of different occupations. Although they faced the same prejudice that affected Afro-Americans, they kept their distance from other blacks because of cultural differences. Coming mostly from British backgrounds, they spoke standard English and shared middle-class traditions with other Americans. Most were Episcopalian or Roman Catholic, status conscious and upwardly mobile, and competitive. West Indians became prominent in the needle trades and clothing workers' unions; were the elite in the cigar-making industry of New York; and by the 1930s most of New York's black doctors, dentists, lawyers, and businesspeople were of West Indian descent. Like the Chinese *hui kuan*, West Indian rotating credit associations helped immigrant entrepreneurs get a financial start. Coming from predominantly black cultures in the West Indies, they were generally a proud and secure people.

Marcus Garvey was one of them, and he based his theories on pan-Africanism. A Jamaican, he came to the United States, settled in Harlem, and founded the Universal Negro Improvement Association (UNIA) in 1916. Protesting white imperialism in Africa and discrimination in America, he asked black people to look to Africa for strength, telling them that the world could not ignore 400 million people. Garvey exalted everything black, urging his followers to be proud of their color, physical characteristics, and heritage. By 1920 there were branch offices of the UNIA in Boston, Philadelphia, Pittsburgh, Cleveland, and Chicago claiming a total membership of more than 1 million people. Garvey had become a national figure.

For Garvey the ultimate salvation of black America depended upon resurrecting the African background and creating a broad base of economic power. The UNIA established a network of businesses to implement his ideas, including the Black Star Shipping Line, the Black Cross Navigation and Trading Company, the Negro Factories Corporation, the African Legion, and the Black Cross Nurses. As far as Garvey was concerned, whites would always be prejudiced, and blacks would have to build their own economic civilization. Convicted in 1923 of using the federal mails fraudulently, he was imprisoned at the federal correctional facility in Atlanta for two years and then deported to Jamaica. Deprived of his leadership, the UNIA slowly disappeared, but its record of black pride and pan-Africanism remained a powerful element in black social thought.

The last great pre-World War II black leader was A. Philip Randolph. Publisher of the radical New York *Messenger* in the 1920s, Randolph questioned the theories of Washington, Du Bois, and Garvey. He criticized Washington for acquiescing in segregation, and yet accused Du Bois of being too concerned with the black upper class, oblivious to the economic suffering of the masses, and too willing to court white liberals. Garvey, he thought, was a curious oddity who would do little to improve the lives of most American blacks. Randolph was also suspicious of social movements composed of blacks and whites because he feared the coalitions offered only subordinate positions to blacks. He concentrated on black workers and argued that only through labor unions would they exert any real power. He organized the National Association for the Promotion of Labor Unions Among Negroes in 1920, and five years later created the American Negro Labor Congress. In 1925 he also formed the Brotherhood of Sleeping Car Porters and Maids, and after twelve years of struggle the railroads finally recognized the union.

When World War II broke out in Europe, Randolph was enraged over job discrimination in American defense plants. He demanded equality in defense industries; and when the Roosevelt administration ignored him, he turned to mass action and threatened to lead a hundred thousand black workers in a march on Washington to promote his demands. In response Roosevelt issued Executive Order 8802 on June 25, 1941, creating the Fair Employment Practices Commission (FEPC) and outlawing discrimination in defense industries. Compliance with the order was mixed, and the FEPC went out of existence at the end of World War II, but the commission was an important victory in black history.

Despite the efforts of Washington, Du Bois, Garvey, and Randolph, racial equality was still a distant goal in 1945. There had, however, been some notable accomplishments. In 1925 the New York Citizens' League for Fair Play boycotted white-owned businesses in Harlem until black workers were hired. In 1928 Oscar DePriest of Illinois became the first black to enter Congress since Reconstruction, and Arthur Mitchell followed him in 1936. In 1930, after Republican President Herbert Hoover nominated the racist John J. Parker to the Supreme Court, the NAACP lobbied so powerfully against the nomination that the Senate refused to confirm him. And throughout the 1930s the NAACP blocked the executions of the "Scottsboro boys," nine black youths falsely accused of raping two white prostitutes in Alabama. The Congress of Industrial Organizations—which included such unions as the United Mine Workers, Amalgamated Clothing Workers, and International Ladies Garment Workers—accepted black workers as full, equal members during the 1930s, and the NAACP worked closely with the CIO in strikes against the steel, automobile, rubber, and packinghouse industries. A. Philip Randolph had been right: black workers in the CIO unions benefited from their union membership, eventually enjoying higher wages, shorter hours, and better working conditions because of it.

To increase black support in the Democratic party, Franklin Roosevelt appointed several black leaders to advisory positions in his administration. Edgar Brown and Mary McLeod Bethune worked as advisers on black affairs for the National Youth Administration and the Civilian Conservation Corps. Robert C. Weaver was a racial adviser in the Department of the Interior, and Robert L. Vann served as assistant to the attorney general. During World War II the government integrated army officer candidate schools and hundreds of infantry units in Europe.

Black Culture in America

Beneath this increasingly visible world of black organizations was the cultural world of black people as a whole. Some historians concluded that because there was so little resistance to slavery and discrimination, blacks must have internalized white descriptions of Afro-American inferiority, that they had no group consciousness, and were an "infantilized" people who passively accepted a subordinate role in America. Black society was pictured as docile, obsequious, and immature. But Afro-American culture after slavery was much like it had been during slavery—positive, fulfilling, and spontaneous—and blacks were well equipped to deal wth American society.

The desire to acculturate to white values had never taken root during slavery because the advantages of white society were so out of reach. Freedom, however, had quickly given birth to visions of equality, and some blacks assumed that by conforming to white expectations they might be able to achieve their dreams immediately. The Jim Crow system even intensified those attitudes, making it seem even more imperative to adapt to white culture. All the northern white teachers in the South after the Civil War confirmed those hopes and told blacks that by discarding black English for standard English, emotional religion for a more subdued Protestantism, and traditional games, dances, and stories for white activities, they would accelerate their acceptance into white society.

Some blacks, especially educated people, became embarrassed by black English and adopted white phrases, accents, and grammatical constructions. In churches the old slave spirituals gave way to standard Protestant hymns, and shouting, dancing, and hand clapping became less common. Even the traditional slave story of the "trickster" declined. In West Africa trickster tales had often involved "Anansi the spider," but in America it was frequently "Brer Rabbit" who outwitted the aggressive foxes, bears, and wolves; won contests and games; escaped from one tight situation after another; and constantly came out on top at the expense of the rich, the powerful, or the aristocratic. After emancipation, although trickster tales continued to serve as vicarious experiences in success and power for poor blacks, they were no longer as common as they were before the Civil War, and largely died out among the black middle class. Some blacks even began using skin-bleaching cream, hair dye, and hair-straightening lotions to appear more "white."

But like native Americans, blacks let acculturation proceed only to a certain point and eventually developed a dualistic way of dealing with reality. Many blacks were essentially bilingual, able to speak two languages. When they were with whites, they spoke a more standard English, but when they were with family, friends, and neighbors, they reverted to black English. Although slave spirituals had declined, they were gradually replaced by the gospel sounds of people like Mahalia Jackson. To be sure, gospel singing was different from the spirituals. The gospel hymns were usually performed by a soloist for a church audience, rather than sung by the congregation; and while the spirituals had been spontaneously created and passed from generation to generation, the gospels were professionally composed and produced. Still, the gospels were links with the Afro-American past: performances had a communal flavor and were always accompanied by shouts of "Hallelujah" and "Amen"; and singers were physically active and rhythmic, their bodies swaying with music.

The same dualism was reflected in the rise of blues music. Promoted by people like "Big" Bill Broonzy and "Jelly Roll" Morton, the blues tradition reflected the individualistic ethos of modern America; each song was little more than the experiences, fears, and hopes of the individual performer. And yet, with its emphasis on improvisation, polyrhythmic routines, and calls and responses, the blues retained communal ties to antebellum black America and West Africa. Even the instrumental jazz music of Louis Armstrong, which emerged early in the twentieth century, confirmed the black sense of freedom, spontaneity, and communal power. Black music was clearly different from the more standardized white music of the time.

Finally, black people still had their own heroes. Although the black middle class attending Presbyterian or Episcopal churches may have been ill at ease about black English, folk religion, gospel songs, the blues, and jazz, and may have held up prominent whites as role models, most Afro-Americans still looked to other blacks as psychological surrogates. The most common heroes—one of whom was portrayed in Alex Haley's book and film about his ancestor, Kunta Kinte—were slaves or Reconstruction blacks, those who had escaped; resisted or outwitted masters, overseers, or the Ku Klux Klan; or helped others beat or resist the system. Blacks in the twentieth century also had their bandit heroes, people like Aaron Harris or Staggerlee whose violence and aggressive independence of all standards pained and outraged white society.

Joe Louis's defeat of James J. Braddock for the heavyweight championship on June 22, 1937, made him a hero in the black community because he had overwhelmed the white world playing by white rules. His quiet, well-mannered domination of heavyweight boxing sustained that heroic status through the 1940s. Decades earlier Jack Johnson had also become a black hero after defeating Tommy Burns for the heavyweight championship in 1908, but his status in the black community had been raised even more by his willingness to flout the conventions of white society by living flamboyantly and ridiculing white values. Joe Louis and Jack Johnson had different styles, one aimed at cooperative success and the other at rebellious success, but both thrilled the black masses with their victories. Afro-America, if somewhat more attuned to white society under freedom than it had been under slavery, was still a distinct society in the United States.

The great irony of Afro-American history, of course, was that blacks were in many ways the most "American" of any people in the United States. Their families had lived here as long as those of any other immigrant group; their labor had helped build the American economy since colonial times; and their yearnings for freedom and equality had been prolonged and intense. And yet they had encountered the worst discrimination of all; the color line was carefully drawn, hindering their progress and keeping them from assimilation.

SUGGESTED READINGS

Bullock, Henry Allen. *A History of Negro Education in the South: From 1619 to the Present*. Cambridge, Mass.: 1967.

Cantor, Milton, ed. *Black Labor in America*. Westport, Conn.: 1970.

Cooper, Wayne. *The Passion of Claude McKay.* New York: 1973.

Dalfiume, Richard M. "The Forgotten Years of the Negro Revolution." *Journal of American History*, 55 (June 1968), 90–106.

Daniel, Pete. *The Shadow of Slavery: Peonage in the South, 1901–1969.* Urbana, Ill.: 1972.

Ellison, Ralph. *Invisible Man.* New York: 1952.

Finkle, Lee. "The Conservative Aims of Militant Rhetoric: Black Protest During World War II." *Journal of American History*, 60 (December 1973), 692–713.

Foner, Philip S. *Organized Labor and the Black Worker, 1619–1973.* New York: 1974.

Frederickson, George M. *The Black Image in the White Mind: The Debate on Afro American Character and Destiny, 1817–1914.* New York: 1971.

Fullinwider, S. P. *The Mind and Mood of Black America.* Homewood, Ill.: 1969.

Gatewood, Willard B. *Black Americans and the White Man's Burden, 1898–1903.* Urbana, Ill.: 1975.

Glazer, Nathan, and Moynihan, Daniel P. *Beyond the Melting Pot: The Negroes, Puerto Ricans, Jews, Italians, and Irish of New York City.* Cambridge, Mass.: 1963.

Gordon, Rita W. "The Change in the Political Alignment of Chicago's Negroes During the New Deal." *Journal of American History*, 56 (December 1969), 584–603.

Gutman, Herbert. *The Black Family in Slavery and Freedom, 1750–1920.* New York: 1977.

Harlan, Louis R. *Booker T. Washington: The Making of a Black Leader, 1856–1901.* New York: 1972.

Hendricks, Glenn. *The Dominican Diaspora: From the Dominican Republic to New York City, Villages in Transition.* New York: 1974.

Henri, Florette. *Black Migration: Movement North, 1900–1920.* Garden City, N.Y.: 1975.

Huggins, Nathan. *Harlem Renaissance.* New York: 1971.

Katzman, David M. *Before the Ghetto: Black Detroit in the Nineteenth Century.* Urbana, Ill.: 1973.

Kirby, Jack T. *Darkness at the Dawning: Race and Reform in the Progressive South.* New York: 1972.

Kusmer, Kenneth L. *A Ghetto Takes Shape: Black Cleveland, 1870–1930.* Urbana, Ill.: 1976.

Latham, Frank. *The Rise and Fall of Jim Crow, 1865–1964.* New York: 1969.

Levine, Lawrence. *Black Culture and Black Consciousness: Afro American Folk Thought from Slavery to Freedom.* New York: 1977.

McKay, Claude. *A Long Way from Home.* New York: 1937.

Meier, August, and Rudwick, Elliott. "The Boycott Movement Against Jim Crow Streetcars in the South, 1900–1906." *Journal of American History*, 55 (March 1969), 756–775.

Newby, I. A. *Black Carolinians.* Columbia, S.C.: 1973.

Osofsky, Gilbert. *Harlem: The Making of a Ghetto, 1890–1930.* New York: 1966.

Pleck, Elizabeth H. "The Two-Parent Household: Black Family Structure in Late Nineteenth Century Boston." *Journal of Social History*, 8 (Fall 1972), 333–356.

Rabinowitz, Howard N. "From Exclusion to Segregation: Southern Race Relations, 1865–1890." *Journal of American History*, 63 (September 1976), 325–350.
Redkey, Edwin S. *Black Exodus: Black Nationalist and Back-to-Africa Movements, 1890–1910.* New Haven, Conn.: 1969.
Reid, Ira deA. *The Negro Immigrant: His Background Characteristics and Social Adjustment, 1899–1937.* New York: 1939.
Spear, Allan H. *Black Chicago: The Making of a Ghetto, 1890–1920.* Chicago: 1967.
Tindall, George A. *The Emergence of the New South, 1913–1945.* New York: 1967.
———. *The Ethnic Southerners.* Baton Rouge, La.: 1975.
Tuttle, William M., Jr. *Race Riot: Chicago in the Red Summer of 1919.* New York: 1970.
Weisbord, Robert G. *Ebony Kinship: Africa, Africans, and the Afro-American.* Westport, Conn.: 1973.
Weiss, Nancy J. *The National Urban League, 1910–1940.* New York: 1974.
Wharton, Vernon. *The Negro in Mississippi, 1865–1890.* Chapel Hill, N.C.: 1947.
Wolters, Raymond. *Negroes in the Great Depression.* Westport, Conn.: 1970.
Woodward, C. Vann. *The Strange Career of Jim Crow.* New York: 1965.
Wright, Richard. *Black Boy.* New York: 1945.

Chapter Nineteen

Land and Labor: The Mexican-Americans

With the stroke of a pen the United States had acquired more than a million square miles of land and 78,000 new citizens in 1848. Manifest Destiny and the lightning victories of the Mexican War led most Americans to see it all as the will of God, but it was a different story in Mexico. The proud young nation had lost nearly half its territory, for which it received only $15 million, and saw the war as a humiliation by the "colossus of the North." As for Mexican-Americans, they became a "colored," Spanish-speaking, Catholic minority in a white, English-speaking, Protestant society.

Mexican-Americans and the Land, 1848–1900

California

Except for 3,000 whites, California in 1848 was a social pyramid of more than 110,000 people. At the top was the Mexican (*californio*) elite, a small aristocracy of 1,000 people who controlled more than 15 million acres of land and the best positions in the government. In the middle was a *cholo* class of 10,000 mestizo artisans, soldiers, *vaqueros* (ranch hands), and small farmers. And at the bottom were 100,000 California Indians. Even before the discovery of gold, people had considered California a bonanza of lumber-filled forests, rich soil, mineral wealth, good rivers, excellent harbors, and one of the world's most temperate climates. The californios (elite and cholo classes) were among the 78,000 Mexicans who became United States citizens in 1848. Despite the presence of American military forces, they were a majority and still owned 15 million acres of land.

All that changed, however, when the gold rush raised the white population to more than 80,000 people, most of whom settled in northern California. The californios were an instant minority, and although a few entered the territorial assembly and constitutional convention of 1849, they were hard-pressed by the American influx. Despite their protests the assembly passed the Foreign Miners' Tax law prohibiting Chinese and californios from the mine fields. At the same time white vigilantes attacked californio miners and drove them from the gold fields. White terrorists lynched twenty californio miners in Sonora, California, in 1849 and burned the homes of hundreds of others. Californio society was facing Manifest Destiny.

As the gold fields played out and prospecting gave way to corporate mining, the "forty-niners" who had not struck it rich turned to farming. But the best acreage was already in the hands of the californios, especially the wealthiest two hundred families, and their titles were guaranteed by the Treaty of Guadalupe Hidalgo. Poor whites began squatting on californio land to support themselves and protested to Congress and the state legislature when the californios tried to remove them. Congress then passed the Land Act of 1851.

The Land Act created a Board of Land Commissioners to resolve confusing land titles, but it was hopelessly biased in favor of the squatters. White Americans controlled the board, hearings were conducted in English, and the obligation to prove title rested on californio owners rather than on the squatters. That alone encouraged thousands of whites to invade the ranchos. Between 1852 and 1856 the board received 813 title cases and rejected 175 californio claims, freeing more than 3 million acres for white homesteading. If the squatters appealed the decisions upholding californio titles, the cases entered federal courts, where the average litigation took seventeen years. Court costs and attorney fees imposed enormous financial burdens on hundreds of California landowners. Salvador Vallejo, a rancher in Napa, spent a decade and nearly $100,000 clearing his title; in the process he had to mortgage his land and sell much of his livestock to meet legal expenses. Hundreds of other californios had similar experiences, and even after clearing title many were short of capital and had to sell anyway.

Mobs of armed squatters often completed the process. After rioters burned his crops and slaughtered his herds, Salvador Vallejo finally sold his Napa ranch; another rancher, Domingo Peralta, was held hostage by a vigilante army until he sold out. Dishonest lawyers sometimes defrauded Spanish-speaking clients into signing English-language documents that forfeited title to their land. In addition, economic changes hurt californio landowners. Heavily in debt to banks for loans used to pay court costs, many californios went under economically when the Sonora and Texas cattle drives of the 1850s glutted beef markets and depressed cattle prices to less than a dollar a head. The severe California droughts of the 1860s ruined hundreds of other landowners who had survived everything else. By 1880 Mexican-Americans had lost their land, and during the 1850s and 1860s people with Spanish surnames gradually disappeared from the state legislature.

Many protested, none more vocally than Francisco Ramirez, editor of *El Clamor Publico* in Los Angeles. He denounced the Board of Land Commissioners in editorial after editorial, proclaiming that "we are Native California Americans born on the soil and we can exclaim with the Poet, this is 'OUR OWN, OUR NATIVE LAND.'" Other forms of protest were more violent, exposing the fine line between revolutionaries and bandits. In California bandit-heroes emerged as social prototypes of revolution. Juan Flores, for example, escaped from San Quentin prison in 1851 and led fifty Mexican-Americans in a minor rebellion. Joaquín Murieta terrorized Anglos in Calaveras County in the early 1850s. Tiburcio Vásquez also escaped from San Quentin several times and attacked and robbed Anglo settlements in the 1860s and 1870s. All three men became folk heroes to californios. Stereotypes of Mexican-Americans quickly moved beyond paternalistic images of "lazy Latins" to pictures of criminally irresponsible people with no respect for law.

In southern California the ethnic accommodation was more peaceful. Because of the absence of gold and lack of water, southern California attracted few white settlers, and immigration from Mexico provided californios with a majority until 1880. Although whites controlled business in Los Angeles and San Diego as well as most state government offices, californios participated in local politics. Juan Sepúlveda served as Los Angeles *alcalde* (mayor), and Antonio Coronel was superintendent of schools there. But that participation ended in 1876, when the Southern Pacific Railroad finally linked Los Angeles with the rest of the United States. Thousands of white settlers poured into southern California and by 1890 outnumbered Mexican-Americans by ten to one. The cycle of land litigation, fraud, and forced sales repeated itself.

New Mexico

Ethnic relations in New Mexico also had relatively tranquil beginnings. According to most historians, the conquest of New Mexico in 1846 was a bloodless affair; *nuevos mexicanos* welcomed American soldiers. Nuevo mexicano society rested on a small group of wealthy businessmen and landowners (*ricos*) living in Santa Fe and Albuquerque and a larger class of perhaps fifty thousand *peon* workers. When General Stephen Kearny's troops arrived, the ricos welcomed them because they were desperate to keep their property. Aware of American prejudice against "greasers" (Mexicans), the ricos defined themselves as "Spanish Americans," European descendants of the original conquistadores rather than the mestizo progeny of Spaniards and Indians. It was, of course, a fantasy; most ricos as well as peons were of mestizo descent, but the ricos nurtured the myth of "pure" origins and hoped whites would distinguish between them and the others. Fear, not enthusiasm, inspired cooperation.

Hispanic culture remained dominant in New Mexico for twenty-five years. Since Juan de Oñate established Chamita in 1598, the nuevo mexicano elite had functioned in a stable, well-organized society; and the lack of major mineral discoveries until the 1880s saved them from the massive American immigration that overwhelmed californios in the 1850s. The nuevos mexicanos outnumbered whites and would continue to do so until well into the twentieth century. And between 1850 and 1890 there was little conflict over land titles because transfers were based on legal sales. Individuals with Spanish surnames functioned in the territorial legislature; and when New Mexico became a state in 1912, the nuevos mexicanos obtained constitutional guarantees of their right to vote and hold public office. State law also required sessions of the state legislature to be conducted in English and Spanish. Miguel Antonio Otero served three terms in the territorial House of Representatives, and in 1897 President William McKinley appointed Otero's son the first nuevo mexicano governor of the territory.

But troubles had already begun for the nuevos mexicanos in the 1870s. Completion of the southern transcontinental railroads in the 1870s linked New Mexico with the national market and stimulated booms in mining, cattle, cotton, and timber. Pacification of the Apaches in the 1880s brought the political stability necessary for economic investment. White settlers began immigrating. The silver, coal, and copper mines of southeastern New Mexico expanded, as did the gold mines near Taos; ranchers moved cattle to the eastern grasslands; timber interests bought property and leases in northwestern New Mexico and began cutting off all the timber, destroying game and pastures; and on the northeastern plains bordering the Texas Panhandle southern farmers transplanted cotton culture. The new settlers wanted exclusive control of the land they were using, and schemes to get it led to a repetition of the California experience. Pressures on the land increased in 1891, when Congress created several national forests in New Mexico. Millions of acres of land formerly used as communal grazing property were suddenly closed to nuevo mexicano sheep and cattle herds.

Led by the Santa Fe Ring, whites gradually took control of much nuevo mexicano land between 1860 and 1890. A small political clique of white bankers, merchants, and lawyers allied to twenty wealthy nuevo mexicano families, the ring controlled the territorial legislature and courts. It manipulated the law and imposed heavy property taxes on nuevo mexicano land. When Mexican-Americans could not pay the taxes, their land was auctioned, and ring members purchased it at bargain prices. And by charging nuevo mexicano landowners exorbitantly high interest rates, ring bankers forced defaults and foreclosures. As owners of railroad stock, ring members indirectly gained control of still more land when Congress and the territorial legislature made land grants to the railroads. In all, the Santa Fe Ring acquired several million acres of land from the original nuevo mexicano owners.

White immigration and vigorous lobbying in Washington produced more land fraud when Congress created the Court of Private Land Claims for New Mexico, Colorado, and Arizona in 1891. Like the Board of Land Commissioners in California, the Court of Private Land Claims put the burden of proof on the nuevo mexicano owners. But land titles were extremely difficult to prove in New Mexico. The Pueblo uprising of 1680 had destroyed records of the earliest land grants; retreating Mexican soldiers had carried other records away in 1846; and the state archives had burned in 1892. With little evidence to support their claims, the nuevo mexicano landowners were helpless, and in thirteen years of hearings the Court of Private Land Claims upheld their titles in only 75 of 301 cases. Whites took the uncleared grants. Even though an elite group of nuevo mexicano landowners were able to keep their property, most land fell into the hands of white Americans.

As white authority increased, so did the hostility between the two communities. Just after the arrival of American troops in 1846, Diego Archuleta and Father Antonio José Martínez conspired unsuccessfully with the Taos Indians to expel the invaders. One month later several nuevos mexicanos assassinated territorial governor Charles Bent and killed twenty other white landowners. As in California, the bandit-hero emerged in New Mexico; Sostenes L'Archeveque, in retaliation for the murder of his father in Santa Fe, killed twenty-three whites and became a folk hero to the nuevo mexicano masses. Nuevo mexicano vigilante organizations like Las Gorras Blancas (The White Caps) and La Mano Negra (The Black Hand) periodically raided white settlements in the 1880s and 1890s, cutting fences, slaughtering cattle, and destroying railroad property. One night in 1885 Las Gorras Blancas destroyed nine thousand ties along three miles of track of the Atchison, Topeka, and Santa Fe Railroad.

Still, the situation in New Mexico was not as severe as in California, where Mexican-Americans had become totally powerless in state affairs. Because of the large numbers of nuevos mexicanos and their population superiority throughout the nineteenth century, the generally peaceful transition to American rule in 1846, and the survival of the elite nuevo mexicano families in the Santa Fe Ring, ethnic relations in New Mexico were more relaxed than in Texas or California. Throughout the twentieth century, from Congressman Dennis Chavez in the 1930s to Senator Joseph Montoya and Governor Jerry Apodaca in the 1970s, people with Spanish surnames have been influential in New Mexican politics. Racism and discrimination occurred, to be sure, but not on the same scale as in Texas and California.

Texas

Race relations were the most violent in Texas, where antagonisms were deep and bitter. Ethnic relations there grew out of the 1836 revolt, when Texans seceded from Mexico. Conflict was common along the border for ten years before the Mexican War. Most Texans were southern Protestants, intensely prejudiced against "colored" *tejanos*. As early as 1840 they outnumbered tejanos by ten to one and twenty years later by sixteen to one. Tejano political activity was discouraged at all levels, and the Texas Rangers (state police) enforced the unwritten rule.

In the Rio Grande Valley, where the tejano population was most heavily concentrated, conflict over land was widespread. Unlike California and New Mexico, where the Spanish government had made vague land grants during the colonial period, Texas had well-defined property boundaries. There was no need for a public land commission to clear titles. Improving standards of living in the industrialized nations, as well as the rise of railroads and steamships, greatly increased world demand for beef in the 1870s and 1880s; sheep raising increased too, fed by the textile revolution and railroad links with eastern markets; and a boom in cotton production came in the 1880s. The white desire for grazing and farming land increased enormously.

A mad scramble ensued. The state legislature and local townships imposed heavy taxes on tejano land, and banks charged high interest rates, forcing many Mexican-Americans to default. Foreclosures followed. In Hidalgo County land was auctioned at a penny an acre after tejano owners failed to pay their taxes. Judicial fraud also occurred. After dozens of poor white settlers illegally squatted on the land of Francisco Cavazos, in Brownsville, Charles Stillman, a white settler, purchased their claims. When Cavazos appealed in the courts, Stillman offered him $33,000 for the land, perhaps 15 percent of its real value. Fearful of mounting court costs, Cavazos agreed to sell and the deeds were signed. But Stillman then refused to pay, and Cavazos lost his land and received nothing.

Some whites used intimidation to acquire land. Historians believe that the Texas Rangers may have killed nearly five thousand Mexican-Americans during the nineteenth century. To be sure, the Texas frontier was a violent place and criminals abounded, but in hundreds of cases the Rangers simply helped whites "dislodge" tejanos from the land. Richard King was one of the Texas "Robber Barons" who used the Rangers by having them uphold his often fraudulent land claims. The son of poor Irish immigrants, he moved to south Texas and founded the King Ranch. In 1852 he bought the fifteen-thousand-acre Santa Gertrudis Grant for two cents an acre, and as president of the Stock Raisers Association of Western Texas he increased his holdings to more than six hundred thousand acres. Similar events occurred throughout south Texas, and by 1880 only two of the wealthiest three hundred landowners in the state were tejanos. The transfer of land was complete.

As in California and New Mexico, the Mexican-Americans resisted. The Cart War of 1857 broke out when white teamsters began ambushing Mexican-American freight trains and murdering drivers. The tejanos responded in kind. Twenty years later the El Paso Salt War erupted over access to the Guadalupe salt mines. Hoping to corner the supply, a few whites killed some tejanos trying to get to the salt, and the war went on for six months, until federal troops arrived. Once again the bandit-hero, this time in the figure of Juan Cortina, emerged. During the 1850s Cortina raided several towns and killed whites who had mistreated tejanos. After federal troops drove him across the border, Cortina became a hero to Mexicans on both sides of the Rio Grande. Eventually he became governor of the state of Tamaulipas. Cortina, however, was more of a revolutionary than a bandit. From Cameron County in south Texas he said in 1859:

> Mexicans! My part is taken; the voice of revelation whispers to me that to me is entrusted the work of breaking the chains of your slavery, and that the Lord will enable me, with powerful arm, to fight against our enemies . . . to the improvement of the unhappy condition of those Mexican residents . . . exterminating their tyrants, to which end those which compose it are ready to shed their blood and suffer the death of martyrs. *

The Mexican-American Community in 1900

By 1900 Mexican-Americans were becoming almost a colonial people. The appearance of huge commercial farms with heavy investment in machinery, fertilizers, and irrigation systems gradually priced

---

* U.S. Congress, House of Representatives, House Executive Document No. 52, *Difficulties on the Southwestern Frontier*, 36th Cong., 1st Sess., 1861, p. 81.

Mexican-American farmers out of business. Unable to compete, they had to sell their land and became laborers. Whites dominated politics throughout the region, and in some areas, especially south Texas, Mexican-Americans faced the poll taxes and literacy tests that had already disfranchised southern blacks. Whites segregated Mexican-American children in schools and discouraged the use of Spanish. The Treaty of Guadalupe Hidalgo was being turned upside down.

Yankee immigration, racial discrimination, and the decline of the hacienda ranchos imposed severe strains on the Mexican-American family. Traditional family life had revolved around extended kinship ties wherein children and young adults, even after marriage, deferred to the discipline and leadership of their parents. Respect for elders and family solidarity were highly valued, and the authority of the father was unquestioned. But nineteenth century changes in society and the economy brought on a decline in the extended family. The demise of the old rancho system undermined the agrarian values which had sustained the paternalistic extended family. Between 1850 and 1880 in Los Angeles, for example, the number of californio families headed by women rose dramatically until more than one-third were matriarchal. The number of common law marriages and consensual unions similarly increased. Both phenomena played central roles in the transition from extended to nuclear family life, but in the process the family became less able to cope with economic modernization. Now a suppressed ethnic minority in a secular, industrializing society, Mexican-Americans saw an erosion in parental authority, discipline, and the financial resources which extended families could muster; nor could the Catholic church or the old *hacendado* (hacienda owner) sustain their moral authority. The Mexican-American community was ill-prepared for the American vision of progress and modernization.

North from Mexico, 1900–1945

Before 1900 the Mexican-American population never exceeded three hundred thousand, but between 1900 and 1930 more than 1.5 million people left Mexico for the United States. Porfirio Díaz had taken over the Mexican government in 1876 and ruled with an iron hand for thirty-four years. Openly sympathetic with large landowners, foreign investors, and upper-class criollos, he encouraged investment, helped the rich acquire more land, and discriminated against mestizos and Indians. As hacienda owners and foreigners grew richer, the masses became poorer. Their standard of living further declined as the population grew from 9 to 15 million.

A revolutionary upheaval destroyed the Díaz government in 1910, and until 1920 Mexico suffered from widespread instability and economic disruption. Francisco Madero assumed power in 1911, but his refusal to return hacienda lands to the Indians led Emiliano Zapata and his guerrilla warriors to begin assassinating hacienda owners and attacking the Madero government. Madero was killed in 1913 and Victoriano Huerta took over; but after two years of fighting with Venustiano Carranza, Pancho Villa, Emiliano Zapata, and Alvaro Obregón, Huerta went into exile and was replaced by Carranza. When Carranza was assassinated in 1920, Obregón took over and the bloodshed diminished, but during the chaos more than a million Mexicans had died.

At the same time, economic growth in the United States was attracting immigrant workers. Because of irrigation and fertilizers, farm acreage in the West had increased three times and irrigated land from 60,000 to nearly 1.5 million acres between 1870 and 1900. Cotton production in west Texas, the Salt River Valley of Arizona, and the San Joaquin Valley of California boomed; so did sugar beet production in Utah, Idaho, and Colorado; and vegetable and citrus production in south Texas and the Imperial Valley of California. Meanwhile, the Chinese Exclusion Act was passed in 1882, and the so-called Gentlemen's Agreement limited immigration from Japan in 1907. Demand for farm laborers was rising just as the pool of workers was shrinking, and American growers sent labor bosses to Baja California, Sonora, and Tamaulipas to recruit Mexican workers.

Industrial development also stimulated demand for workers. The Southern Pacific and Santa Fe railroads recruited Mexicans to complete trunk lines in the Southwest. When World War I broke out in Europe, the international demand for United States foodstuffs soared, and tens of thousands of new acres were brought into production. More Mexicans immigrated. And when the United States entered the war in 1917, thousands of Mexican-Americans took jobs in the North: in coal, lead, tin, and iron mines; steel and sheet-metal plants; automobile, rubber, and glass factories; electric utilities and oil refineries; and packing houses and food-processing plants. There were Mexican-American *barrios* (ghettos) in Denver, Detroit, St. Louis, Chicago, and Pittsburgh as well as in El Paso, San Antonio, Albuquerque, Tucson, Phoenix, San Diego, and Los Angeles. As Mexican-Americans left their jobs in the Southwest, new Mexican immigrants moved in to fill them. The trend continued in the 1920s, especially after Congress passed the National Origins Act in 1924 limiting immigration from Asia and Europe. Immigration fell off drastically during the Great Depression, but picked up again when World War II improved the domestic economy.

Most immigrants left northern Mexico for south Texas and California, and they left behind a powerful folk culture which had governed their lives. Many came from a hacienda background as *peones*, people with no land or power who labored for the hacendado. Status competition in such a neo-feudalistic society was largely unknown because changes in status seemed impossible. As a result, the Mexican peasants exhibited a greater concern for the present than for the future, stability rather than change, political acquiescence rather than rebellion, and traditional stations in life rather than social mobility. After many generations in such a setting, they were more interested in perseverance than conquest, in survival rather than triumph. Theirs was a small, culturally isolated society where people were accustomed to homogeneity rather than diversity. People lived within an emotionally secure world of patriarchal, extended families where all daily acquaintances were familiar. Consequently, they highly valued personalism, even to the point of applying human attributes to animals and nature. And finally, they were not inclined to make fine distinctions between the sacred and secular worlds, but instead viewed the two as one—religion, magic, folk medicine, work, life, and death were all part of one holistic existence. It is not surprising that when they were suddenly thrust into the American world of urban anonymity, rapid social and technological change, democratic mobility, and secular competitiveness, they experienced a long period of confusion and alienation.

The barrios of the Southwest became internal colonies for the Mexican immigrants, the place where they lived out their lives and made their accommodation to white society. Very rapidly they adopted the utilitarian items of American culture, such as wooden and metal toilets, metal kitchen utensils, sewing and washing machines, automobiles, radios, bathtubs, sinks, metal stoves, and refrigerators. Language in the barrio reflected the acculturation process as well. Although public schools were dedicated to the elimination of Spanish, several border languages developed, like Calo in California and Texmex in south Texas, which were part English and part Spanish. English words were adapted to Spanish syntax, and the result was a vocabulary containing such terms as *el troque* (truck), *la ganga* (gang), *loncherias* (lunch counters), *huachale* (watch it), *pushele* (push it), and *parquiarse* (park the car). In the barrios the immigrants could relax amidst the smells of corn tortillas, beans, fried rice, and peppers; the sounds of traditional folk songs like "La Cautiva Marcelina" or "El Vaquero Nicolas"; and the noise of children playing *la pelota* (ball) or *el coyotito* (little coyote). Like the first Little Italys, shtetls, Chinatowns, and Paddy's villages, the barrios were a unique combination of economic poverty and emotional comfort, one more cultural island in ethnic America.

Whites in the Southwest tried desperately to Americanize the Mexican immigrants. The Southwest needed unskilled laborers for its rail-

Political turmoil at home and employment opportunities in the United States caused large numbers of Mexicans to cross the border after 1900. (Culver Pictures, Inc.)

roads, mines, ranches, and factories; but as Mexicans arrived to fill that demand, whites began to fear for the future of their culture. Viewing Mexican culture as an anachronism unsuited for industrial society, business, educational, and social groups attempted to acculturate Mexican immigrants. Individual employers, trade associations, and chambers of commerce tried to convince Mexican laborers to work gratefully at low wages without complaint, to come to work on religious holidays, to show up on time every day, and to remain on the same job for as long as possible. Public schools forced Mexican children to abandon Spanish for English, inculcated consumer culture and American patriotism, urged young men into vocational rather than academic studies, and through homemaking classes encouraged young women to discard Mexican foods and clothing for American ways. And Protestant missionary societies proselytized the immigrants, hoping to divest them of their Catholicism, extended family life, use of alcohol, and folk culture.

Mexican-Americans had always faced discrimination in American society, and some, like Juan Cortina and Joaquín Murieta, had always resisted; but it was not until the twentieth century that organized Mexican-American groups began demanding equality. It was the tejano, californio, and nuevo mexicano natives who first worked for change. Mexican immigrants arriving after 1900 seemed more apathetic, partly because they had little inclination to conform to American society. Like the French-Canadians, they were close to the mother country, returned home frequently to visit friends and relatives, and repeatedly renewed their cultural roots. Many viewed their sojourn in the United States as a temporary means of supporting their families back in Mexico.

At the same time they were a mestizo people who for centuries had encountered poverty and discrimination at the hands of the Spanish upper class. Lower-class status was all they had ever known, and unlike the californios, nuevos mexicanos, and tejanos, who had known prosperity and hated losing it, they had never enjoyed comfort and security. The treatment they received from white growers in the Southwest was not much different from the treatment meted out by hacienda owners in Mexico. By 1945 there was only one descendant of a tejano, nuevo mexicano, or californio for every ten Mexican-Americans of immigrant heritage. And for all the poverty and discriminatin first-generation immigrants found in the United States, it was still better than the chaos they had left behind. Not until their children and grandchildren reached adulthood after 1945 would *Chicanismo*, a movement for cultural pride and political activism, really begin. Chicanos would inherit few recollections of Mexican suffering but would share the bitterness of californios, nuevos mexicanos, and tejanos.

The Beginnings of a Mexican-American Political Movement

In the late 1930s and early 1940s the *pachuco* culture emerged in the barrios of the Southwest. Caught in a cultural squeeze between Mexico and America, Mexican-American teen-agers formed gang clubs in their blocks and neighborhoods. Carrying such neighborhood names as the White Fence Gang and the Happy Valley Gang, the clubs served as outlets for the frustration and social needs of young people living in the barrios. Members tattoed emblems on their left hands, spent their time together, wore flamboyantly styled "zoot suits," spoke Calo or Texmex, and asserted territorial rights in their neighborhoods. Wars between rival gangs were common. Through their clothing, tattoos, and barrio language, and their attitude of sullen rebellion, they flaunted their cultural differences with the larger society. Indeed, they were different. Unlike their immigrant parents, the pachucos had attended public schools and had been exposed to white values. But instead of assimilating, they insisted on maintaining their own values; pachuco culture was an instinctive rebellion, a stubborn assertion of personal and ethnic identity. *Pachuquismo* was exaggerated and aggressive, and by flaunting the values of American society, the pachucos established contact with a culture that was rejecting them. Notoriety established them as anti-heroes.

By representing pure liberty and disorder, rebellion and the forbidden, pachuquismo seemed erotic and dangerous to those Americans conditioned to expect smiling obsequiousness from Mexican-Americans. That fear erupted into the "zoot suit" riots in June 1943 when hundreds of white sailors entered Los Angeles barrios and assaulted Mexican-American youths wearing zoot suits. Police ignored the attackers and the local press treated the incident as if Mexican-American gangs had precipitated it. The fracas went on for several days, until military police sent the sailors back to their ships and canceled all shore leave.

Middle-class Mexican-Americans faced special problems of their own, for while a relative prosperity separated them from lower-class immigrants, Mexican culture isolated them from the surrounding white society. Like middle-class blacks or German Jews, they wanted to be accepted in American society, even to the point, for some, of assimilation. Worried about white attitudes, many of them still adhered to the idea of being "Spanish-American," denying their origins in a mestizo culture. They hated pachuquismo for fear it would invite the wrath of Anglo-conformists and make life difficult for all Mexican-Americans. Border languages like Calo and Texmex embarrassed them as being culturally inferior, poor English as well as poor Spanish. And cloistered in neat homes and apartments, they were alienated by the sights and sounds of the barrios, by the poverty and folk culture.

Politically, the middle class concentrated on civil rights problems. More secure economically, they saw discrimination rather than poverty as the immediate problem, and in the 1920s they organized to deal with it. Established in 1927, the League of United Latin American Citizens (LULAC) advocated higher education as the "way out of the barrio" and called for an end to discrimination. In the 1930s the Congress of Spanish Speaking Peoples also emphasized education and denounced discrimination. Then, in the 1940s, these civil rights groups rallied to the support of the defendants in the Díaz murder trial. In 1942 José Díaz was found dead in the Sleepy Lagoon barrio of Los Angeles. Police arrested twenty-two members of a pachuco gang, and a grand jury indicted them for assault and murder. During the trial the prosecutor and judge repeatedly declared that Mexican-Americans were cruel and violent, Communist-inspired, and had probably murdered the boy. In January 1943 three of the young men were convicted of first-degree murder, nine of second-degree murder, and five of assault, while five were acquitted. Mexican-American organizations formed the Sleepy Lagoon Defense Committee and campaigned against the convictions. Nearly twenty months later a federal appeals court reversed the convictions on the grounds that the judge had been biased and that there had been no evidence linking the boys to the crime. It was an important victory for Mexican-American civil rights groups.

Unlike the middle class, Mexican-American workers found their economic plight more compelling than discrimination, arguing that the right to enter a restaurant was meaningless without the money to pay the bill. Union organization seemed especially promising. Such agribusinesses as the Newhall-Saugus Land Company and the Di Giorgio Fruit Corporation were powerful, but perishable crops made them vulnerable to labor disruptions. Even a brief strike could be disastrous. For just these reasons growers were determined opponents of unionization; they fought to keep the farm labor force as large and mobile as possible in order to keep wages down, overcome work stoppages, and prevent the growth of unions. American unions lobbied to restrict Mexican immigration, while the farm bloc, sugar companies, mining concerns, and southwestern railroads lobbied for open borders. Before World War II business prevailed over labor in the national debate, and Mexico was exempted from the National Origins Act of 1924.

As difficult as union activity was, some workers organized. Sugar beet workers in California struck in 1903 and won the right to deal with growers directly rather than through labor contractors. Mexican-American railroad and factory workers in Los Angeles struck for higher wages several times. In 1915 copper workers walked out in Arizona to protest higher wages paid to whites. The cantaloupe workers struck in the Imperial Valley in 1928, as did the pecan workers in San Antonio in 1938. The Confederation of Mexican Workers Unions was established in 1927, and the Cannery and Agricultural Workers Union followed in 1931. Before their strike in 1938 the San Antonio laborers established the Pecan Shelling Workers Union to represent them. Most of these unions failed, but foreshadowed the 1960s, when Cesar Chavez would successfully organize farm laborers.

By 1945 the Mexican-American community had changed. Those eighty thousand californios, nuevos mexicanos, and tejanos of 1848 had become more than 3 million people of mestizo descent. Most of the original inhabitants had lost their land, and along with millions of immigrants from Mexico they found themselves without much power or respect in American society. Poverty and discrimination were serious problems, and there were differences in the community based on class and generation values. But at the same time powerful bonds of language, religin, culture, and family united Mexican-Americans. Resentment about past discrimination was accumulating across class and generation lines, and Mexican-Americans were beginning to organize cultural, political, and economic interest groups. Like so many other groups in American society, they too would soon be demanding equality.

SUGGESTED READINGS

Acuña, Rodolfo. *Occupied America: The Chicano's Struggle Toward Liberation*. San Francisco: 1972.

Alvarez, Rodolfo. "The Psycho-Historical and Socioeconomic Development of the Chicano Community in the United States." *Social Science Quarterly*, 53 (March 1973), 920–942.

Beck, Warren A. *New Mexico*. Norman, Oklahoma: 1962.

Blawis, Patricia Bell. *Tijerina and the Land Grants*. New York: 1971.

Camarillo, Albert M. "Chicano Urban History: A Study of Compton's Barrio, 1936–1970." *Aztlan*, 2 (Fall 1971), 79–106.

Cassavantes, Edward. *A New Look at the Attributes of the Mexican American*. Albuquerque, N.M.: 1969.

del Castillo, R. Griswold. "La Familia Chicano: Social Changes in the Chicano Family of Los Angeles, 1850–1880. *Journal of Ethnic Studies*, 5 (Spring 1975), 41–54.

Clendening, Clarence C. *Blood on the Border*. New York: 1969.

Cockcroft, James D. *Intellectual Precursors of the Mexican Revolution*. Austin, Texas: 1969.

Craig, Richard P. *The Bracero Program: Interest Groups and Foreign Policy*. Austin, Texas: 1971.

Cumberland, Charles C. *Mexico: The Struggle for Modernity*. New York: 1968.

Galarza, Ernesto. *Barrio Boy*. Notre Dame, Ind.: 1971.

———. *Merchants of Labor: The Mexican Barcero Story*. San Jose, Cal.: 1965.

———. *Spiders in the House and Workers in the Field*. Notre Dame, Ind.: 1970.

Garcia, Mario T. "Americanization and the Mexican Immigrant, 1880–1930." *Journal of Ethnic Studies*, 6 (Summer 1978), 19–34.

Garza, Roberto. *Contemporary Chicano Theater*. Notre Dame, Ind.: 1976.

Gonzalez, Nancy. *The Spanish-Americans of New Mexico: A Heritage of Pride*. Albuquerque, N.M.: 1967.

Grebler, Leo, Moore, Joan W., and Guzman, Ralph. *The Mexican American People*. New York: 1970.

Hahn, Harlan H. *People and Politics in Urban Society*. Beverly Hills, Cal.: 1972.

Heizer, Robert F., and Almquist, Alan F. *The Other Californians: Prejudice and Discrimination Under Spain, Mexico, and the United States to 1920*. Berkeley, Cal.: 1971.

Hernandez, Luis. *Aztlan: The Southwest and Its Peoples*. Rochelle Park, N.J.: 1975.

Hoffman, Abraham. *Unwanted Mexican Americans in the Great Depression: Repatriation Pressures, 1929–1939*. Tucson, Arizona: 1974.
Humphrey, Norman D. "The Cultural Background of the Mexican Immigrant." *Rural Sociology*, 13 (Spring 1948), 239–255.
Keleher, William A. *Turmoil in New Mexico, 1846–1868*. Santa Fe, N.M.: 1952.
Lamar, Howard R. *The Far Southwest, 1846–1912: A Territorial History*. New York: 1970.
Lamb, Ruth. *Mexican Americans: Sons of the Southwest*. Claremont, Cal.: 1970.
Lea, Tom. *The King Ranch*. Boston: 1957.
McWilliams, Carey. *Factories in the Fields: The Story of Migratory Farm Labor in California*. Boston: 1939.
———. *North from Mexico: The Spanish-Speaking People of the United States*. New York: 1949.
Meier, Matt S., and Rivera, Feliciano. *The Chicanos: A History of the Mexican Americans*. New York: 1972.
Meinig, Donald W. *Southwest: Three Peoples in Geographical Change*. New York: 1971.
Moore, Joan W. et al.*Homeboys: Gangs, Drugs, and Prison in the Barrios of Los Angeles*. Philadelphia: 1978.
———. *Mexican Americans*. Englewood, Cliffs, N.J.: 1976.
Moore, Joan et al. *Homeboys: Gangs, Drugs, and Prison in the Barrios of Los Angeles*. (Philadelphia: 1978).
Pitt, Leonard. *The Decline of the Californios: A Social History of Spanish-Speaking Californians, 1848–1890*. Berkeley, Cal.: 1966.
Poggie, John J. *Between Two Cultures: The Life of an American Mexican*. Tucson, Arizona: 1973.
Reisler, Mark. *By the Sweat of Their Brow: Mexican Immigrant Labor in the United States, 1900–1940*. Westport, Conn.: 1976.
Rolle, Andrew F. *California: A History*. New York: 1963.
Samora, Julian. *Los Mojados: The Wetback Story*. Notre Dame, Ind.: 1971.
Sanchez, George I. *Forgotten People: The Story of New Mexicans*. Albuquerque, N.M.: 1940.
Servin, Manuel. *The Mexican Americans: An Awakening Minority*. Glencoe, Ill.: 1970.
———. "The Pre-World War II Mexican American: An Interpretation." *California Historical Society Quarterly*, 35 (Fall 1966), 325–338.
Taylor, Paul S. *An American Mexican Frontier: Nueces County, Texas*. Chapel Hill, N.C.: 1934.
Wagoner, Jay J. *Arizona Territory*. Tucson, Arizona: 1970.
Webb, Walter Prescott. *The Texas Rangers*. Austin, Texas: 1965.
Weber, David. *Foreigners in Their Native Land: Historical Roots of the Mexican American*. Albuquerque, N.M.: 1973.

Chapter Twenty

From East Asia: The Japanese Immigrants

The second wave of Asian migration began in 1868, when Japanese workers crossed the Pacific to take up homes in Hawaii and the North American mainland, and by 1924 there were more than 275,000 Japanese in the United States. Although they came in the wake of the anti-Chinese agitation, most Americans welcomed them at first. Japan was becoming a major industrial power; and American politicians, aware of Japan's new strength in the Pacific, were concerned about the treatment given the Japanese immigrants. Equally important, the Japanese-American community seemed less sexually threatening than the Chinese: Chinese men had outnumbered women by nearly twenty to one, but the ratio was much smaller for the Japanese. Finally, most of the Japanese immigrants were literate, and that impressed Americans. Unfortunately, their toleration would be short-lived.

The Island Kingdom

On July 8, 1853, Commodore Matthew C. Perry of the United States Navy sailed four ships into Tokyo Harbor, ending the self-imposed isolation that had marked Japanese history since the 1600s. Japan was a rural, agrarian nation of about 150,000 square miles concentrated on the islands of Hokkaido, Shikoku, Honshu, and Kyushu. When the reign of the Tokugawa shoguns (military rulers) began in 1603, Japan was a feudal society of 18 million people. It had had considerable contact with the West and the Japanese were concerned about European aggressiveness. In 1638 the shoguns turned the Island Kingdom into a cocoon, expelling foreigners, prohibiting emigration, and calling all overseas Japanese home. During the two centuries the Tokugawas ruled Japan, the standard of living rose modestly and the population increased to about 30 million. Tokugawa Japan seemed cut off from time, a feudal nation still living in the Middle Ages.

At the top of the social pyramid were the shoguns. The old imperial family (of which present-day Emperor Hirohito is a descendant) lived in opulent obscurity at the palace in Kyoto, but it had long since been stripped of power. The shoguns presided directly over one-fourth of the country, getting richer on rice tributes from peasants, and indirectly governed the rest of Japan through the *daimyo*, a class of feudal lords who payed tribute to the shoguns in return for the right to exact tribute of their own. The *samurai* were a warrior class tied by feudal obligation to the daimyo, but during the peaceful Tokugawa reign they lost much of their military usefulness and often performed bureaucratic functions. At the base of the pyramid were merchants, artisans, and peasants.

Concepts of place and conformity were strong in Japan because the Japanese believed power flowed from above. Peasants eked out a living on less than an acre of land but rarely protested their fate. Precise codes of social conformity governed individual behavior, and spontaneous deviance was unthinkable. The Japanese strongly discouraged aggressive behavior and contentiousness. The ability to compromise and resolve disputes privately was an intimate part of social morality. While American society would produce hundreds of thousands of lawyers trained to solve disputes through political agencies, Japan had little need for so many attorneys. Criminal behavior was limited by social conformity, and civil lawsuits were rare because of a widespread desire to avoid controversy and conflict.

Religion reinforced the social order. Although Shinto, Buddhism, and Confucianism were the three main religions of Japan, history had witnessed a great divergence in theology and ritual between various sects of each faith, and all three religions had at one time or another borrowed from one another.

Shinto, the oldest religion in Japan, combined a pantheistic worship of nature with deification of the emperor. The emperor was the living *kami*, the eternal authority who guarded the temporal fortunes of ordinary people, and Shintoism demanded duty to the nation and devotion to the interests of the community. The basic unity of all people with all of nature was similarly essential to the Shinto faith. So while Shintoism underwrote Japanese nationalism, it reinforced the prevailing social code by emphasizing duty, honor, and suppression of individual needs to community interests.

Buddhism, which came to Japan from Korea and China in the sixth century, filled a void in Shinto by furnishing a vision of eternal life. While the Shinto *kami* governed earthly affairs, the Buddhist deities controlled the world of the dead. Consistent with Japanese values, Buddhism offered not a conscious individual immortality but a promise that through self-denial and personal righteousness the soul would merge after death with Nirvana, a divine freedom from pain and sorrow. Still, Buddhism was less concerned with morality than with existence, less worried about good and evil or innocence and guilt than about the cosmic nature of human life.

It was Confucianism, also introduced from China in the sixth century, which supplied the Japanese with their vision of morality. Confucianism emphasized worship of the family and ancestors and imposed on all people the obligation of accepting their station in life. Personal honor depended on social complacency; one had to behave in accordance with the expectations of society, and the essence of personal behavior was obedience, submissiveness, and peaceful acquiescence in the social hierarchy. Filial piety and acceptance of authority were central tenets of Confucianism. Thus all three Japanese religions sustained the prevailing social code. Religion was eclectic, and many Japanese claimed to be simultaneously Shintoist, Buddhist, and Confucianist. Duty, obedience, and personal subordination—these were the standards of society.

Veneration of the family was deeply embedded in the culture, with the extended family the basic legal entity. Property ownership resided in the clan, and when branch families were begun, they still owed deference and service to the stem family. Nuclear families were looked upon as economic devices, means of transferring property from one generation to another. An economic bond between two clans, marriage was never undertaken on romantic whim but was carefully arranged to serve both families. The Japanese honored family name, and each individual was duty bound to respect the *ie* (house). Indeed, absolute obedience was the norm for all adults. The internal bonds of the Japanese family had little to do with romantic love, which the Japanese found to be temporary and unpredictable, but with the eternal social and economic interests of the clan. And the pull of family values was so strong that other political and corporate institutions in the society reflected similar attitudes. The now famous loyalty of Japanese workers to private corporations is an excellent illustration of those values. Rebellion only shamed the family, so loyalty and discipline ran through the entire fabric of Japanese society.

Internal changes and external pressures stimulated a modest wave of emigration in the 1800s. A series of earthquakes, fires, floods, and tidal waves struck Japan early in the century, but a more important stimulus was the disintegration of feudalism. For years the shoguns had looked down upon the *chonin* (merchants) as parasites; but as agricultural production increased and people moved to the cities, the rise of a money economy enriched the chonin. Dependent upon rice tributes for their income, the daimyo and samurai needed the chonin to convert the rice into money, so a coalition of the three classes emerged.

The merchant princes of Osaka and Kyoto hated restrictions on foreign travel and international commerce. Fortunes were to be made in foreign trade, and they insisted on reopening Japan to the world. Perry's visit exacerbated tensions already existing; the shoguns yielded in 1854 and Japan joined the world economy. But foreign manufactured goods soon brought trade deficits and inflation. The daimyo and samurai, their incomes fixed in rice payments, lost purchasing power and increased demands on the peasants. Everyone blamed the Tokugawas; and, joining forces in 1868, the daimyo, samurai, chonin, and peasants deposed the shogunate and restored the emperor to at least symbolic power. This was the Meiji Restoration.

During the next fifty years Japan changed from a feudal kingdom to a modern power. But daimyo and samurai still demanded tribute from peasants and inflation also hurt them. The new government began assessing taxes on the value of land rather than on the size of the harvest. In the past peasants had been liable only for a percentage of profits, but after 1873 they paid a fixed tax regardless of income. Between 1873 and 1900 hundreds of thousands of Japanese farmers lost their land because of tax delinquency. Recognizing the need for some relief, the Meiji government legalized emigration, and from the rural prefectures of Hiroshima and Yamaguchi on Honshu and Kumamoto Prefecture on Kyushu, thousands of peasants began leaving their homeland, first for Hawaii and then for the American mainland.

First Stop: Hawaii

Although historians still debate Polynesian origins, it now seems clear that Polynesia was occupied early in the Christian era, and from Samoa or Tonga to Fiji, and then to Tahiti, the Polynesians sailed to Hawaii around 750 A.D. Governed by a royal family, worshiping the gods of ancestors, animals, and the elements, the Hawaiians grew to more than 250,000 people by 1750. The English explorer and naval captain James Cook ended their isolation in 1778, and throughout the nineteenth century Europeans and Americans colonized the islands. Christian missionaries, intent on ending idolatry and sin, poured in. American settlers also came, seized land from the natives, and created vast sugarcane plantations. In 1893 the planter-missionary elite deposed Queen Liliuokalani and established the Republic of Hawaii. Five years later the United States annexed the islands. While liberal reformers, unscrupulous speculators, and well-meaning settlers were destroying native Hawaiian society, the conquest of the islands continued. Unable to resist European diseases, the Hawaiian population declined to 100,000 people in 1840 and 35,000 in 1890.

As the native population declined, the need for labor increased, and in 1850 sugar planters began importing workers from China. By 1890 there were 12,000 Chinese in Hawaii. Japanese workers also immigrated and eventually became Hawaii's largest ethnic group. Later, after Hawaii and the Philippines became United States territories in 1898, Filipino migration to the sugarcane fields began. Although racial and ethnic tolerance developed in the nineteenth century, cultural life in Hawaii remained pluralistic and intermarriage was relatively rare. In 1941 there were approximately 80,000 Europeans, 160,000 Japanese, 70,000 Filipinos, 30,000 Chinese, and 25,000 Hawaiians, with a mixed population of only 20,000 Hawaiian-Europeans and 18,000 Asian-Hawaiians.

The Issei, first-generation Japanese immigrants, who settled in Hawaii were a blend of the old and the new. Because Japan had modernized so recently, feudal remnants still survived in a reverence for the past, for roots, tradition, and family. But the Issei also had the desire for financial betterment so characteristic of industrial societies. Memories of the past and visions of the future provided them with the ambition to succeed in an industrial economy and the cohesiveness to survive in a racially mixed society.

Hawaii began recruiting Japanese workers in the 1860s, and after the Meiji Restoration a few hundred people immigrated. Then, when Japan began to permit freer emigration in 1886, many more Japanese made the move to Hawaii. Maintaining a unique interest in the fate of its people, Japan contracted with Hawaii to send workers only as long as Hawaii paid full passage for them and their families, helped settle them, and guaranteed free housing, medical care, a minimum wage, and a maximum ten-hour work day. Between 1886 and 1894 nearly 30,000 Japanese workers settled there. When the United States annexed Hawaii in 1898, the Issei became Japanese-Americans.

From Japan and Hawaii to the Mainland

The first Japanese settlement on the mainland was the Wakamatsu Colony, near Sacramento, California. Arriving in 1869, they planned to produce silk and raise tangerines, grapes, and tea, but in a few years drought, poverty, and internal bickering destroyed the settlement. Except for a few hundred students attending American universities in the 1870s, these were the only Japanese immigrants before 1882. But after Congress passed the Chinese Exclusion Act, demand for farm laborers increased dramatically, and Japan's decision to permit emigration helped fill the demand. More than 25,000 Japanese farmers immigrated in the 1890s, and thousands more came to the mainland from Hawaii. In the next decade 129,000 Issei immigrated, as did another 125,000 between 1910 and 1924.

Most Issei went into farming, and by 1910 nearly 35,000 were working on commercial citrus, grape, vegetable, hops, and sugar beet farms. At first they were poor, seasonal field hands moving from farm to farm, but they were ambitious, and through contract labor succeeded in raising their wages and improving their standard of living. By underbidding competitors, Japanese labor gangs monopolized the farm labor market in California, but as harvest approached they often threatened to strike. Rather than worry about the labor supply, many growers chose to lease their land to Issei tenants. Avoiding the commodities whites raised— wheat, citrus, walnuts, and livestock—the Issei concentrated on beans, celery, peppers, cauliflower, strawberries, tomatoes, lettuce, onions, watermelons, carrots, spinach, and flowers. Soon they dominated the truck-crop industry along the West Coast. They saved money, bought land, and became independent farmers. In 1900 there were only thirty-nine Issei farms, totaling 4,700 acres, but by 1920 there were five thousand Issei farms with more than 460,000 acres. In Japan the average farm had been only one acre, but in America a typical farm was forty acres, and by any standard of the Old World that meant success.

Aside from farming, employment opportunities were limited. The skilled trades were not open because of union hostility; discrimination by colleges eliminated professional careers; and federal laws against Issei citizenship closed the civil service. The Japanese had to rely on unskilled jobs and their own resources. More than 10,000 worked as section hands on the Southern Pacific, Central Pacific, and Great Northern railroads; 3,000 labored in the lumber mills of northern California, Oregon, and Washington; perhaps 2,500 worked in the coal mines and smelting plants of Utah, Nevada, and Colorado; nearly 5,000 had jobs in fish

Japanese workers on a Texas rice seed farm around 1910. (Brown Brothers)

canneries and food-processing plants along the Pacific coast; nearly 10,000 were domestic servants by 1940; and 5,000 Japanese went into gardening, landscaping, and horticulture, and came to dominate the industry. The Issei ran cafes, restaurants, laundries, cleaners, produce stands, grocery stores, dry goods shops, barber shops, and newsstands; collectively these establishments employed more Japanese-Americans than any other field except agriculture.

The Anti-Japanese Crusade, 1900–1940

In the American environment Japanese culture underwent several changes which were natural consequences of acculturation. Most Issei were Buddhists, and they brought with them the Tendai, Zen, Shingon, Nichiren, Jodo, and Shin denominations. But rather than confining themselves exclusively to religious activities, the Buddhist temples in America set up English-language schools, sponsored scout troops, and organized self-help groups. Unlike their counterparts in Japan, Buddhist priests in America often became preachers too, offering sermons every Sunday. Buddhist Sunday Schools were complete with hymn books, blackboards, pictures, magazines, and school and national flags. Like Reform Judaism, the Buddhist temples took on the external trappings of American Protestantism. Conversion was another form of acculturation. While the vast majority of Issei were Buddhists, nearly half of the Nisei (second-generation, American-born Japanese) were Christians and most Sansei (third generation) and Yonsei (fourth generation) were

Christian. But even then, the Japanese Buddhists and Christians in the United States still preached the Buddhist-Confucian ethics of filial piety, obedience, and reverence for authority.

But the acculturation was not extensive enough to prevent the development of a virulent, anti-Japanese nativism along the West Coast. Issei immigration went relatively unnoticed during the 1890s. Too many people were worrying about Catholics and Jews to be concerned about a few thousand Japanese. But as the pace of Issei immigration quickened, many Americans began lumping the Japanese and the Chinese together, seeing both groups as strange "aliens" who would never be assimilated. Since Japan was a rising military power, some saw the Issei as agents preparing an invasion of America. An exclusion movement gathered force, led by California and its labor unions. After Japan defeated Russia in the war of 1904–1905, immigration increased; and the Japanese Exclusion League, a group of prominent California politicians and labor leaders, along with the American Federation of Labor, called for an end to Japanese immigration. The state legislature supported the demand.

A diplomatic crisis developed after the San Francisco earthquake of 1906 destroyed school buildings. To guarantee a place for white children, the board of education ruled that Asian students would have to attend makeshift, segregated schools. The Japanese government immediately protested, demanding equal treatment for its emigrants, and rumors of war flashed on both sides of the Pacific. President Theodore Roosevelt wanted to defuse the controversy but knew he had no authority to interfere in California affairs. Realizing that the school crisis was only a symptom of a deeper problem, he worked out the "Gentlemen's Agreement" with Japan in 1907 and 1908. Japan promised to restrict future emigration to nonworkers and the wives of Issei already in the United States if the federal government would work for the equal treatment of Japanese in America. Roosevelt then persuaded the San Francisco board of education to permit English-speaking Nisei to attend public schools with white children. The crisis was over—for the moment.

Immigration from Japan slowed after the Gentlemen's Agreement but never ceased completely. Yearning for a normal family life, the Issei began writing home asking single women to immigrate. To get around the Gentlemen's Agreement, they exchanged pictures and married these women by correspondence; the "picture brides" received passports and came to America. California nativism revived, and some towns began refusing to license Japanese businesses. Calls for total exclusion became more intense.

As more and more Issei bought their own land, white farmers began worrying about filling their labor needs. The California State Grange and the California Farm Bureau Federation campaigned for laws to restrict independent Japanese farms, and in 1913 the state legislature passed the Alien Land Act prohibiting those ineligible for citizenship from purchasing land. Since federal law prevented Asians from becoming naturalized citizens, the Issei could no longer buy land. Six other states passed similar laws between 1917 and 1923, and the Supreme Court upheld their constitutionality in 1923. Japanese agricultural holdings declined to 300,000 acres in 1925 and 221,000 acres in 1940.

After World War I the exclusionists succeeded. Immigrants founded such organizations as the Japanese Association of America and the American Loyalty League to promote their interests, but they had no political strength since Issei could not vote and Nisei citizens were too young to vote in the 1920s. White politicians had nothing to lose by ignoring them and everything to gain by supporting nativists. The American Legion, the Japanese Exclusion League, and the Native Sons of the Golden West all joined the clamor, and the National Origins Act of 1924 ended immigration from Japan.

External hostility bound the Japanese together, but group cohesiveness had existed long before they arrived in the United States. Most Japanese immigrants came from eleven prefectures in southern Japan, where they had belonged to *kenjinkai* associations based on prefectural origins. Each prefecture had its own dialect and personality, and the members of each kenjinkai felt a sense of obligation to one another and a need to marry within the group. They brought the kenjinkai to America, and the ken sponsored social activities, published newspapers, offered legal assistance, and served as employment agencies. When ten thousand Japanese were left homeless after the San Francisco earthquake, the kenjinkai took over and few Issei had to accept public welfare. The ken looked after their people the same way during the Great Depression. In rural areas the Issei settled in small villages or *buraku*, and members of each buraku met to conduct Buddhist or Shinto ceremonies and discuss community problems.

Because skilled jobs were closed to them and California farmers were pushing them off the land, the Issei began to move to towns and cities. White banks would not make loans to the Issei, so the kenjinkai sponsored *ko*, *tanomishi*, and *mujin*—rotating credit associations providing investment capital to members. The kenjinkai also directed the economic and demographic development of the Issei community. Since employed Issei were socially and morally obligated to locate jobs for others in their ken, ken members congregated in the same occupations and same areas. The Issei of San Francisco and Oakland, for example, were from the Hiroshima ken, and in Seattle most of the restaurateurs were from the Ehine ken. Competition arose, so the Issei founded trade guilds to set prices, regulate markets, and sustain one another during times of sickness or recession. By 1940 the Japanese-American economy was self-contained; nearly 40 percent of all Issei were self-employed, and the majority were independent of the larger economy.

The Issei also founded the Japanese Association of America. A coalition of kenjinkai, the association provided English-language instruction, translation services, legal aid, employment advice, and maternal and child care. It also campaigned for Issei citizenship. Because the Meiji government had promoted education, most Issei were literate; they encouraged their children to learn English and established part-time Japanese-language schools to preserve their cultural heritage. Buddhist and Shinto temples bound Japanese-Americans together as well. Amidst widespread discrimination the buraku, tanomishi, kenjinkai, trade guilds, Japanese Association, and religious temples provided strength and security to the immigrants and their families. Loyalty to family and ken, the great social ethos of Japan, became the lifeblood of the Issei in America.

The Internment Camps, 1941–1945

Immigration restriction in 1924 eased nativist suspicions. The Nisei-based Japanese American Citizens League campaigned against alien land laws and for Issei citizenship in the 1920s without raising nativist ire, but after 1930 the old fears revived. When Japan invaded Manchuria in 1931, and four months later attacked Shanghai, white antagonism immediately reignited. The Committee of One Thousand, a group of prominent southern California citizens, boycotted Japanese-American businesses, and the American Legion warned about war with Japan. Rumors circulated that Issei farmers were poisoning their products, and that thousands of Issei and Nisei engaged in secret military training. By 1937, after Japan had taken Nanking, Peking, and Tientsin, and its planes had destroyed the United States gunboat *Panay* in the Yangstze River, the American mood turned even angrier. Hollywood discontinued the once popular "Mr. Moto" films, and many Americans came to believe that Issei and Nisei wanted to destroy the United States. The stage was set for a social and constitutional nightmare.

The nightmare began on December 7, 1941, when Japan bombed Pearl Harbor, the naval base in Hawaii. Americans were shocked, and Californians felt especially vulnerable, not only because of their geographical proximity to Hawaii and Japan but because more than 90 percent of the 125,000 Japanese on the mainland lived there. Japanese victories at Guam, Wake Island, Hong Kong, Singapore, Sumatra, Borneo, Bataan, and Corregidor in the first few months of the war aggravated those fears. Rumors of an imminent invasion appeared frequently in the press, and stories of Issei and Nisei sabotage circulated freely. The Chamber of Commerce, the American Legion, the Veterans of Foreign Wars, and the remnants of the Japanese Exclusion League demanded the arrest of all Japanese aliens.

Hoping to expose sabotage, the Federal Bureau of Investigation began investigating Japanese-Americans and in a few months arrested nearly two thousand people of Japanese descent, including Issei and Nisei businessmen, leaders of the Japanese Association and the Japanese Citizens League, Shinto and Buddhist priests, editors of Japanese publications, and teachers in Japanese-language schools. Only one man was convicted, and his crime was forgetting to register an importing firm as a business agent for the Japanese government. The others were released, much to the distress of the general population, and calls for incarceration of all Japanese-Americans became more intense. An editorial in the *San Francisco Chronicle* in January 1942 said the Japanese should be moved

> to a point deep in the interior. I don't mean a nice part of the interior, either. Herd 'em in the badlands. Let 'em be pinched, hurt, hungry, and dead up against it. . . . If making one million [sic] innocent Japanese uncomfortable would prevent one scheming Japanese from costing the life of one American boy, then let the million innocents suffer . . . let us have no patience with the enemy, or with anyone whose veins carry his blood.*

Tensions mounted early in 1942, and many people blindly concluded that all Japanese-Americans were threats to the national security. General John DeWitt, army commander of the western defense area, called for the evacuation of the Japanese from the coast. State and federal officials worked out the details, and on February 19, 1942, President Franklin D. Roosevelt signed an executive order calling for the relocation of 40,000 Issei and 70,000 Nisei living in California, Oregon, Washington, and southern Arizona. Because the 15,000 other Japanese-Americans on the mainland were widely scattered, they were not affected by the order. The 157,000 Japanese living in Hawaii were vital to the local economy, and even though there were demands for their removal, they were never relocated.

Although thousands of German and Italian aliens were arrested by the FBI, no general evacuation occurred, for while the Japanese were

---

*Quoted in Dennis Ogawa, *From Japs to Japanese: An Evolution of Japanese-American Stereotypes* (Berkeley, 1971), p. 20.

Asians, the Germans and Italians were white. They were also Christian and European, whereas the Japanese were Shintoists and Buddhists from a totally different culture. Nor were the German and Italian populations densely concentrated as the Japanese were. Besides, most Americans in 1942 looked upon the war in Europe as a distant threat; the Germans and Italians had not attacked American territory. The war with Japan seemed closer and more ominous on the West Coast.

Late in March 1942 army troops took the first group of Japanese-Americans from their homes in Los Angeles and moved them to an assembly center in Owen Valley, California. By May more than 100,000 Japanese-Americans were living in sixteen temporary assembly centers. They lost their homes, farms, and businesses in the evacuation. Federal officials offered to help them in protecting their property, but only if the evacuees agreed to sign documents waiving any government liability if monetary losses occurred. Most Japanese-Americans were understandably suspicious, and tried to store their valuables or sell them immediately. Because of the time factor, tremendous financial losses were incurred as homes, farms, and businesses were liquidated on short notice. Contemporary historians estimate that more than $400 million in property losses occurred among Japanese-Americans during World War II. After the war, a series of unfavorable federal court decisions as well as complicated legal procedures made it extremely difficult for Japanese-Americans to recover more than 10 percent of their losses.

The War Relocation Authority (WRA) administered the detention program, and between March and October 1942 it constructed ten concentration camps in California, Arkansas, Idaho, Wyoming, Colorado, Utah, and Arizona. By November all 110,000 Japanese-Americans had left the assembly centers for permanent homes in the camps. They had no idea how long they would be confined there nor what the circumstances of their incarceration would be.

Respectful of authority, most Japanese-Americans accepted their fate quietly, going peacefully to the assembly centers and the camps. Rebelliousness was out of character. Still, some did resist. At the Santa Anita assembly center in California a riot broke out after the Japanese heard rumors that WRA authorities were confiscating Japanese property for personal use. At the Mansazar assembly center and the Poston relocation camp mass protest demonstrations against crowded, dehumanizing conditions occurred late in 1942. The most militant Japanese were sent to the camp at Tule Lake, California, where security and discipline were strict. But generally the evacuation process was an orderly, if humiliating and frustrating, experience for Japanese-Americans.

The relocation centers resembled minimum-security prisons where the bare necessities of life were provided. At each center hundreds of wood-frame tar-paper barracks housed the evacuees. Divided into four 20 x 25 foot rooms, each barrack housed four families or thirty people. Community mess halls and latrines met basic physical needs, and schools and hospitals were added later. Barbed-wire fences surrounded each center, and military police patrolled the perimeter. Within each center the evacuees were permitted some self-government. Several barracks had a block leader and an elected block council responsible to a WRA administrator. They maintained records, kept count of evacuees, planned cultural events, and carried grievances to the WRA. Buddhist and Christian churches flourished at each camp, but because of its emperor worship Shinto was suppressed. Camp authorities permitted inmates to publish newspapers in both English and Japanese.

Still, life was difficult. Most of the camps were in barren desert areas; the poorly insulated buildings were stifling in summer and cold and drafty in winter. Family life, because of the barracks and community mess halls, was strained and privacy severely limited. Mine Okubo, a Nisei, later recalled:

> There was a lack of privacy everywhere. The incomplete partitions in the stalls and the barracks made a single symphony of yours and your neighbors' loves, hates, and joys. One had to get used to snores, baby-crying, family troubles, and even to the jitterbugs. . . . The flush toilets were always out of commission. . . . Many of the women could not get used to the community toilets. They sought privacy by pinning up curtains and setting up boards. . . . The sewage system was poor, and the stench from the stagnant sewage was terrible. . . .
>
> We lined up for mail, for checks, for meals, for showers, for laundry tubs, for toilets, for clinic service, for movies. We lined up for everything.*

Problems erupted between Christians and Buddhists; Shintoists felt frustrated; rural and urban Japanese competed for influence; and geographic divisions between people from various western states emerged. The most serious rift was between the Issei and the Nisei. Issei parents felt deprived of authority, especially after the WRA gave the most responsible positions in camp government to Nisei citizens. Financially ruined and politically powerless, the Issei experienced identity crises and the old family structures weakened. During the loyalty-oath controversy in 1943, when men of draft age were asked to declare allegiance to the United States, most Nisei agreed but many Issei refused. The debate intensified the generation gap.

*Quoted in William Petersen, *Japanese Americans: Oppression and Success* (New York, 1971), pp. 70–71.

Despite the penal atmosphere of the camps, some resettlement began even before the last evacuees had reached the centers. Sponsored by denominational colleges, four thousand Nisei left the camps to attend school in the East and Midwest. Agricultural laborers worked seasonally in the fields, and after receiving security clearances some moved to the East. Nearly eighteen thousand Nisei served in the army, a few in nonsegregated units but most with the 100th Infantry Battalion and the 442nd Regimental Combat Team, which served in Europe but were not trusted to fight in the Pacific. In Italy and France the 442nd sustained nearly ten thousand casualties, and—with 3,600 Purple Hearts, 810 Bronze Stars, 550 Oak Leaf Clusters, 342 Silver Stars, 123 divisional citations, 47 Distinguished Service Crosses, 17 Legions of Merit, 7 Presidential Unit citations, and 1 Congressional Medal of Honor— became the most decorated military unit in World War II. In one of the most painful scenes in American history, Issei parents, still in the relocation camps, were awarded posthumous Purple Hearts for their dead sons.

Of those Nisei serving in the 442nd Combat Team, Daniel K. Inouye became one of the most influential. Born in Honolulu in 1924, he was a premedical student at the University of Hawaii before the war. A volunteer soldier, he was wounded in the stomach in Italy, and later during a charge up a ridge received wounds that resulted in the amputation of one arm. After the war Inouye became more and more concerned about Republican control of Hawaii politics, and along with a group of Democratic insurgents formed a coalition that came to dominate the territorial and later the state government. He became Hawaii's first member of the House of Representatives after statehood was granted in 1959, and has served in the United States Senate since 1963, the only senator of Japanese descent until S. I. Hayakawa, former president of San Francisco State University, joined him in 1976.

Such political successes, however, were still in the future in 1945. Dissolution of the camps was the first priority, and as victory over Japan became more certain, Japanese-Americans seemed less threatening. In July 1942 Mitsuye Endo, a Nisei from Sacramento, filed a writ of habeas corpus, arguing that the WRA had no right to detain her. On December 18, 1944, after nearly two and a half years of litigation, the court unanimously decided that as a civilian agency the WRA had no constitutional authority to incarcerate loyal, law-abiding citizens. Two weeks later General Henry C. Pratt of the western defense area ordered the camps closed, and by December 1945, except for some pro-Japan sympathizers awaiting deportation, the Japanese-Americans were released. The ordeal was finally over.

SUGGESTED READINGS

Auesaki, Masaharu. *Religious Life of the Japanese People: Its Present Status and Historical Background*. Tokyo, Japan: 1938.

Bailey, Thomas. "California, Japan, and the Alien Land Legislation of 1913." *Pacific Historical Review*, 1 (February 1932), 36–59.

Bosworth, Allan R. *America's Concentration Camps*. New York: 1967.

Broom, Leonard, and Reimer, Ruth. *Removal and Return: The Japanese American Family in World War II*. Berkeley, Cal.: 1956.

Conroy, Hilary. *The Japanese Frontier in Hawaii, 1868–1898*. Berkeley, Cal.: 1953.

Conroy, Hilary, and Miyakaka, T. Scott. *East Across the Pacific: Historical and Sociological Studies of Japanese Immigration and Assimilation*. Santa Barbara, Cal.: 1972.

Daniels, Roger. *Concentration Camps USA: Japanese-Americans and World War II*. New York: 1971.

———. *The Politics of Prejudice: The Anti-Japanese Movement in California and the Struggle for Japanese Exclusion*. Berkeley, Cal.: 1962.

Henry, Sheila E. *Cultural Persistence and Socio-Economic Mobility: A Comparative Study of Assimilation Among Armenians and Japanese in Los Angeles*. Palo Alto, Cla.: 1978.

Hosokawa, Bill. *Nisei: The Quiet Americans*. New York: 1969.

Hundley, Norris, ed. *The Asian-American: The Historical Experience*. Santa Barbara, Cal.: 1976.

Iwata, Masakuzu. "The Japanese Immigrants in California Agriculture." *Agricultural History*, 36 (February 1962), 25–37.

Kashima, Tetsuden. *Buddhism in America*. Westport, Conn.: 1977.

Kitano, Harry H. L. "Japanese-Americans: The Develoment of a Middleman Minority." *Pacific Historical Review*, 43 (November 1974), 500–519.

———. *The Japanese-Americans: Evolution of a Subculture*. Englewood Cliffs, N.J.: 1976.

Kitigawa, Daisuke. *Issei and Nisei: The Internment Years*. New York: 1967.

Light, Ivan. *Ethnic Enterprise in America: Business and Welfare Among Chinese, Japanese, and Blacks*. Berkeley, Cal.: 1972.

Melendy, H. Brett. *The Oriental Americans*. New York: 1972.

Modell, John. "Class or Ethnic Solidarity: The Japanese American Company Union." *Pacific Historical Review*, 38 (May 1969), 193–207.

———. *The Economics and Politics of Racial Accomodation: The Japanese of Los Angeles, 1900–1942*. Urbana, Ill.: 1977.

———. "The Japanese-American Family: A Perspective for Future Investigations." *Pacific Historical Review*, 37 (February 1968), 67–81.

———. ed. *The Kikuchi Diary: Chronicle from an American Concentration Camp: The Tanforan Journals of Charles Kikuchi*. Urbana, Ill.: 1973.

Myer, Dillon S. *Uprooted American: The Japanese-American and the War Relocation Authority During World War II.* Tucson, Arizona: 1971.

Nakane, Chie. *Japanese Society.* Berkeley, Cal.: 1970.

Nordyke, Eleanor C. *The Peopling of Hawaii.* New York: 1977.

Ogawa, Dennis. *From Japs to Japanese: An Evolution of Japanese-American Stereotypes.* Berkeley, Cal.: 1971.

Okubo, Mine. *Citizen 13660.* New York: 1946.

Petersen, William. *Japanese-Americans.* New York: 1971.

Smith, Bradford. *Americans from Japan.* Philadelphia: 1948.

Spicer, Edward H. et al. *Impounded People.* Tucson, Arizona: 1969.

Sue, S., and Kitano, Harry L. "Asian American Stereotypes." *Journal of Social Issues,* 29 (February 1973), 83–98.

Tenbroek, J., Barnhart, E. N., and Matson, F. W. *Prejudice, War, and the Constitution.* Berkeley, Cal.: 1970.

Summary

Ethnic America
in 1945

By 1945 Americans were looking back on the 1800s with nostalgia, as if those years had been especially stable. Industrialization and urbanization, the fluctuations of the business cycle and the Great Depression, two devastating world wars, and immigration had transformed America from an isolated agrarian society to an industrial world power. The United States had also become the most heterogeneous society in the world. Of more than 150 million people, perhaps 110 million consciously sensed membership in an ethnic community, either as foreign-born immigrants or their descendants. Although each ethnic group had people in virtually every social class and a wide variety of jobs, occupational patterns had emerged.

Seven million blacks living in the rural South of 1877 had become more than 16 million in the South and in the cities of the North and West, from Harlem in New York to Watts in Los Angeles. Most of them worked as small or tenant farmers, farm laborers, sharecroppers, factory operatives, and domestics. The Mexican-American community, especially after the Revolution of 1911, had expanded from 300,000 to 3 million people, and they too were still living in the rural Southwest and urban barrios. After the Indian Reorganization Act of 1934 nearly 550,000 native Americans were living on government reservations, economically dependent on but culturally free of white society. Finally, more than 550,000 Asian-Americans were primarily on the West Coast and in Hawaii: 200,000 Chinese and 240,000 Japanese worked as farmers, service employees, and independent entrepreneurs, while approximately 125,000 Filipinos worked on large commercial farms.

The world of the "old immigrants" had also changed by 1945. More than 25 million people still claimed a British heritage, as English, Scots, Welsh, or Scots-Irish, and they were scattered throughout the country as skilled workers, successful farmers, white-collar employees in government and business, corporate managers, and educated professionals. With an urban and rural base still centered in the German triangle, the German-American community numbered nearly 20 million people. Throughout urban American but especially in the Northeast and Midwest, more than 13 million Irish Catholics worked in skilled blue-collar jobs or as civil servants in state and city government. In the mill towns of New England, the rural villages of southwestern Louisiana, and in some well-to-do neighborhoods in New Orleans, perhaps 4 million people still looked to France or French Canada for their cultural roots. In the upper Midwest more than 6 million Scandinavians worked as skilled laborers, businesspeople, farmers, and white-collar workers. And in New York, Michigan, and Wisconsin, approximately 750,000 people of Dutch descent retained their group identity.

The most drastic change since 1877 had been the arrival of the southern and eastern Europeans. Numbering only 250,000 Germans in 1877, the Jewish community consisted of nearly 5 million people in 1945. An urban people, they lived in the Northeast, especially in New York City, where they were skilled workers in the needle trades, independent entrepreneurs, educated professionals, entertainers, and intellectuals. More than 9 million Slavic immigrants and their descendants—Poles, Czechs, Slovaks, Rusins, Ukrainians, Croatians, Serbians, Slovenes, Russians, Bulgarians, and Lithuanians—lived in the industrial cities and worked in mines, mills, factories, and railroads. By 1945 they had purchased homes in their own neighborhoods, established Catholic and Orthodox parishes, and moved into skilled trades. More than 500,000 Greeks took pride in their heritage and worked in small businesses and skilled crafts, while more than 200,000 Rumanians had become skilled and educated white-collar workers. Approximately 6 million Italian-Americans, largely a working-class community, lived in the urban North and East, as did nearly 1 million Magyars. These were the "new immigrants."

The Security of the Ghettos

American cities were collections of ghetto communities inhabited by European and Asian immigrants, southern blacks, and Mexican-Americans. The ghettos had two dimensions, cultural and residential, and what had characterized the Irish and German settlements in 1877 became norms for the Italians, Poles, blacks, Rusins, Ukrainians, Czechs, Slovaks, Croatians, Serbians, Slovenes, Magyars, Chinese, Japanese, Greeks, Mexicans, and Russians by 1945. The ghettos were neither pathological expressions of fear nor walled, escape-proof communities. Ethnic groups lived there in part because of the emotional security they offered. Havens rather than prisons, the ghettos eased the adjustment to American life.

In the ghettos—the Polonias, Paddy's Villages, Chinatowns, Little Tokyos, Little Syrias, or Little Italys—the immigrants could hear their own language and live near friends and relatives. On New York's Lower East Side, the Italians were divided into Genoese, Calabrians, Abruzzians, and Sicilians, for example, while the Jews clustered along Galician, Rumanian, Hungarian, Russian, or German lines. Germans had divided themselves according to their origins in Prussia, the Palatinate, Bavaria, Württemberg, Swabia, Darmstadt, Schleswig-Holstein, or the Weser Valley. After several years the regional clusters within national groups broke down, but they were important in the beginning, comforting to immigrants in a strange land.

Informal institutions of all kinds also reassured them. The buildings and shops of the ghettos had the flavor of home. In Milwaukee the hotels served ethnic clienteles: the Cross Keys (English), the Caledonian (Scottish), the Lakes of Killarney (Irish), and the Zum Deutschen Haus (German). Italian immigrants on Mulberry Street in New York noticed the cheeses and sausages and pasta in the stores, the opera posters, or the ubiquitous pictures of the Madonna; Greeks, Syrians, and Armenians frequented such coffeehouses as the Acropolis, the Parthenon, or the Beirut House; Jews sat in cafés along Hester Street and talked business or debated religion and politics; Germans in St. Louis or Cincinnati had their beer gardens, bowling alleys, and shooting galleries; Japanese and Chinese could purchase the fish and vegetables they prized in the shops of Little Tokyo in Los Angeles or Chinatown in San Francisco; Irish and Slavic Catholics used local taverns as gathering places; and young Mexican-Americans in the barrios walked the streets in their zoot suits. Boardinghouses sheltered new immigrants from the same country; neighborhood youth gangs—the Irish Bowery Boys in New York, the Mexican Pachuco gangs in Los Angeles, the Italian Forty-Two gang in Chicago, the Chinese tong societies in San Francisco—taught young people how to survive in urban America; and baseball and football teams organized along ethnic lines competed for neighborhood and city championships.

The ghettos celebrated ethnic holidays: St. Patrick's Day for the Irish; Cinco de Mayo for Mexican-Americans; *Volks und Schutzenfest* for the Germans; Passover for the Jews; New Year or the Festival of the Dead for the Chinese; Mardi Gras for the Cajuns; Independence Day or St. Basil's Day for the Greeks; Midsummer for the Scandinavians; St. Ignatius Day for the Basques. Ethnic theaters produced plays depicting the problems of immigrant life or the great classics of Shakespeare, Goethe, and Schiller. Uptown Jews as well as the poorest sweatshop workers crowded each night into the Yiddish theaters of the Lower East Side; Chinese workers sat through six-hour segments presented over several weeks until a single long play was completed; Italians by the thousands laughed and cried at the experiences of the comedy character Farfariello. These neighborhoods, hotels, stores, cafés, coffeehouses, bowling alleys, boardinghouses, gangs, holidays, and theaters were the emotional fabric of the ghettos.

More formal ethnic institutions met community needs as well. Fraternal lodges, among the most common, provided a peaceful setting for social activities as well as health, life, and burial insurance. Some of the lodges—*bydelag* societies for the Norwegians, the *landsmanschaften* for the Jews, the *kenjinkai* for the Japanese, the *hui kuan* for the Chinese, and the *topikas* for the Greeks—were based on regional origins in the Old World. Other groups, like the Sons of Norway, the Vasa Order, the Knights of Kaleva, or the Sons of St. George, were simply based on national origins. To help new immigrants settle, find jobs, or bury family members, thousands of mutual aid societies were established, including such groups as the Six Companies of Chinatown, the Ukrainian National Association, the Sons of Italy, and the Hungarian Sick Benefit Association. For economic assistance to start a business or purchase a home, the immigrants founded various financial institutions, including the Chinese *hui kuan*, Japanese *tanomishi*, Finnish food cooperatives, and Jewish, Polish, German, Irish, Hungarian, Czech, and Slovakian building and loan associations. And finally, ethnic ghettos sustained the churches so important to immigrant ethnicity: Presbyterian, Episcopal, Methodist, and Baptist; English Congregational, Dutch, Belgian, and German Reformed; German, Danish, Swedish, Norwegian, and Finnish Lutheran; Irish, German, Czech, Slovak, Croatian, Slovenian, Polish and Lithuanian Catholic; Melkite, Maronite, Rusin, and Ukrainian Uniates; Reformed, Conservative, and Orthodox Jew; Russian, Greek, Serb, Rumanian, Bulgarian, Armenian, and Syrian Orthodox; and Buddhist, Shinto, and Confucian. Parochial schools, parish societies, and denominational colleges completed the institutional framework of immigrant religion in the United States.

The ethnic press further helped immigrants adjust to America. Most had been illiterate peasants in the Old World, but they took up reading with a passion as the only way of keeping in touch with distant friends and relatives and getting news of the old country, as well as protecting themselves from exploitation in America. And because many European languages had traditionally been suppressed—such as Finnish by the Swedes and Russians, Polish by the Germans, Ukrainian by the Russians, or Bulgarian by the Greeks—the ethnic press offered a perfect medium for pent-up literary energies. In 1920 there were more than a thousand ethnic newspapers offering news of Old World politics and harvests, ghetto events, editorials, advice columns, and advertisements. The most prominent ethnic newspapers were the *Pittsburgh Courier* and the *Chicago Defender* for blacks; *Y Drych* for the Welsh; the *Scottish American Journal*, the *Irish World* and the *Gaelic American*; the *Dakota Freie Presse* for the Russian-Germans; the *Staats-Zeitung* for the Germans; the *Skandinaven* for the Swedes; the *Nordlyset* for the Norwegians; the *Amerikan Uutiset* for the Finns; the *Japanese American News*; the *Desteaptate Romane* for the Rumanians; the *Daily Forward* and the *Freiheit* for the Jews; *Il Progresso Italo Americano*; the *Zenske Listy* for the Czechs; the *Russkoye Slovo* for the Russians; the *Svoboda* for the Ukrainians; the *Franco Americaine* for the French; *L'Independent* for the French-Canadians; the *Hungarian America*; the *Narod Polski* for the Poles; the *New World* for the Lithuanians; the *Greek Catholic Messenger* for the Rusins; the *Napredek* for the Croatians; the *United Serbdom*; and the *Hairenik* for the Armenians. Some ethnic newspapers had circulations in the hundreds of thousands and others in the dozens, but all promoted ethnicity and aided adjustment to the New World.

Ethnic nationalisms and Old World events bound the immigrants into self-conscious communities. Many organized gymnastic and athletic groups to promote physical training, love for America, and a patriotic concern for the Old World. The German *turnvereine*, the Scandinavian *turners*, the Czech *sokols*, and the Polish *falcons* stimulated ethnic nationalism in the United States. More formal organizations—such as the Fenian Society for the Irish, the *Nordmanns-Forbundet* for the Norwegians, *l'Union Saint-Jean-Baptiste d'Amerique* for the French-Canadians, the Polish National Alliance, the Lithuanian Alliance of America, the National Slovak Society, the Czech-Slavonic Benevolent Society, and the National Croatian Society—promoted national unification or liberation abroad, or both. Dutch-Americans assisted the Boers in their war with the English in 1899, and the Irish repeatedly tried to influence American foreign policy against the English. During World War I Polish-Americans lobbied with the Wilson Administration for the creation of an independent Poland; Czechs and Slovaks for Czechoslovakia; Serbs, Croats, and Slovenes for Yugoslavia; the Rusins for incorporation of Transcarpathia into Czechoslovakia; Ukrainians for an independent Ukraine; and Magyars for the separation of Hungary and

Austria. Irish-Americans campaigned to keep America out of World War I and some hoped for a German victory that would liberate Ireland; many German-Americans were also isolationist at that time. Nazi aggression in the 1930s and 1940s raised the political consciousness of those descended from Poles, Lithuanians, Czechs, Slovaks, Croats, Serbs, Slovenes, Greeks, Russians, Norwegians, Danes, Dutch, Belgians, French, Jews, and the British, for they worried about the survival of ancestral homelands. Old World politics in 1945 were still contributing to ethnicity in America.

Finally, the fact that the residential ghetto was not a fixed, static, and closed neighborhood reinforced ethnicity. Except for a few massive concentrations of immigrants—the Jews and Italians of New York, the Irish of Boston and New York, the Poles of Chicago, or the Chinese of San Francisco—the ghettos were mixed neighborhoods. In most cities the "stranger next door" was very real. In the mill towns of New England the Irish, Italians, Portuguese, and French-Canadians worked together in the factories and lived within a few blocks of one another; the same was true of the Slavs, Italians, and Irish in the Pennsylvania mines; of the Italians, Slovaks, and Rumanians in the Cleveland steel mills; of the Jews, Syrians, and Italians in the New York needle trades; and of the Poles, Irish, Lithuanians, Germans, Czechs, and Italians in Chicago. Churches, synagogues, businesses, public schools, parochial schools, and ethnic societies were concentrated spatially, and people were able to see clearly the differences between their own and other ethnic communities. Not until World War II, with the continued migration of southern blacks to northern cities, did large, ethnically homogeneous ghettos appear throughout the country.

Ethnic Mobility

Just as ghetto boundaries were diverse and vague, ghetto populations were fluid. The idea of a stable population, with the same people spending their whole lives trapped in urban ghettos, inadequately explains urban life in America. Poor urban immigrants were just as mobile as earlier nineteenth-century farmers, but instead of moving from farm to farm they moved from city to city or neighborhood to neighborhood. In preindustrial pedestrian cities the rich had lived downtown, close to the seats of political, religious, and economic power, while the poor were near the warehouses and railroad terminals where they worked. But as factories appeared downtown and streetcars, subways, and elevated trains crisscrossed the city and reached outside its limits, the rich relocated in the suburbs. The poor filled the vacuum, often turning the large single-family homes of the rich into multifamily tenements. But even then immigrants did not live out their lives in one neighborhood. As quickly as they could save enough money, they purchased homes in the outskirts of the city or in the suburbs and traveled downtown to work. Although the Irish, Italian, German, Slavic, and Jewish neighborhoods survived in the cities, they were rarely occupied by the same people for more than a few years. New immigrants from Europe would crowd into the same tenements while older immigrants and their children moved to nicer neighborhoods. English, German, Scandinavian, Rumanian, and Jewish (except those in New York City) immigrants moved most quickly out of the original settlements, while the Italians, Slavs, Hungarians, and Greeks followed them at a slower pace.

By 1945 blacks were filling up the old immigrant neighborhoods as the most recent arrivals to the cities. Surrounding the black ghettos were rings of housing districts based on income. Except perhaps in New York, where ghetto populations were more stable, the pattern of mixed ethnic neighborhoods was repeating itself. Depending on their incomes, the immigrants and their children lived near people with different backgrounds, "strangers next door," as they had done in the urban ghettos. Because of their high incomes, the British, Scandinavians, Germans, and Jews lived in the most distant suburbs; the Italians, Irish, Hungarians, and Slavs occupied the newer housing districts in the cities; and the blacks and remaining immigrant poor came into the urban core. Alive with an extraordinary mix of people, the ethnic ghettos between 1877 and 1945 were transit stations from which people moved to more permanent neighborhoods.

The Shaping of New Identities

By 1945 ethnic America was more complex than ever before, and the melting pot still an elusive dream. Acculturation, however, was rapidly increasing, largely because of the decline of immigration after 1924. Because of restrictions imposed by the National Origins Act of 1924 as well as the Great Depression, which dimmed the attraction of America, immigration had dropped drastically between 1931 and 1940. During those ten years 3,563 people came from Austria; 7,861 from Hungary; 4,817 from Belgium; 938 from Bulgaria; 14,393 from Czechoslovakia; 2,559 from Denmark; 2,146 from Finland; 12,643 from France; 114,058 from Germany; 21,756 from England; 6,887 from Scotland; 735 from Wales; 9,119 from Greece; 13,167 from Ireland; 68,028 from Italy; 2,201 from Lithuania; 7,150 from the Netherlands; 4,740 from Norway; 17,026 from Poland; 3,329 from Portugal; 3,871 from Rumania; 3,258 from Spain; 3,960 from Sweden; 5,512 from Switzerland; 1,356 from Russia; 5,835 from Yugoslavia; 4,928 from China; and 1,948 from Japan. Compared with the more than 4 million immigrants of the 1920s, the decline was dramatic.

As immigration waned, so did ethnic institutions. The foreign-language press lost ground: between 1920 and 1945 the number of German-language publications dropped from three hundred to seventy; *Skandinaven*, the oldest Scandinavian newspaper, stopped publication in 1940; and between 1940 and 1945 more than two hundred other ethnic-language newspapers failed. Active membership in the ethnic associations began to decline as well. In the German Catholic Central Verein, membership dropped from 125,000 in 1917 to 85,000 in 1935 to less than 40,000 in 1945, and the Norwegian Nordmanns-Furbundet suffered severe losses in membership. The whole range of ethnic theaters, language schools, political organizations, and lodges began to serve an older clientele, as the second generation accustomed themselves to American values and new immigrants stopped entering the country.

Some of the changes were deceptive. For the Germans, Hungarians, Czechs, and Poles arriving after 1890, the presence of tiny colonies of German, Magyar, Czech, and Polish refugees of 1848 raised their political consciousness and helped make them more aware of ethnicity. Also, many peasant immigrants exchanged their parochial perspectives of the past for broader, national outlooks. At first, for example, the German, Galician, Rumanian, Hungarian, and Russian Jews had settled into separate neighborhoods, but by 1945 they were intermarrying. Similar mergers affected other groups. Slowly but surely German, Austrian, and Russian Poles melted together, as did Neapolitan, Abruzzian, Calabrian, and Sicilian Italians; Banatan and Bukowinian Rumanians; Bohemian and Moravian Czechs; Prussian, Bavarian, and Palatinate Germans; and Alleppian, Zahleh, and Beirut Syrians. In the process organizations based on regional origins declined: the Jewish landsmanschaften, Japanese kenjinkai, Norwegian bydelags, Chinese hui kuan, and Greek topikas. The process occurred at different rates among different groups, with the Italians retaining regional loyalties for the longest period of time, but for everyone the parochial mentality of the Old World gradually died out. Although on the surface national identities seemed to intensify, immigrants were actually developing a broader sense of community and settling into the larger society.

The immigrants were also acquiring new identities based upon occupation and political affiliation. When Syrian, Jewish, and Italian workers in the neddle trades suffered from poverty and inhumane working conditions, they were drawn together by an *esprit de corps* that transcended ethnic lines. Although only their relationships at work were affected, the immigrants did feel membership in a group larger than their ethnic community. In the International Ladies Garment Workers Union or the Amalgamated Clothing Workers Union, immigrant members sensed a kinship based on class. The same was true of the Irish, Italian, and Slavic immigrants of Pennsylvania and Ohio who joined the United Mine Workers and the Steel Workers Union, and of the Syrians, Greeks, Italians, and Slavs in the United Automobile Workers Union. By urging members to learn English, become citizens, organize economically, and vote, the unions stimulated the transition from purely cultural to economic interests.

American politics was another acculturating force. In 1877 political divisions had often been cultural, between the western European pietists—Norwegian, Swedish, Dutch, Welsh, and German sectarians and British Baptists and Methodists—who usually voted Republican, and the ritualists of the conservative churches—Irish and German Catholics and liturgical German Lutherans—who usually voted Democratic. The great exception was the South, which had become solidly Democratic despite the Protestant loyalties of its white population. Between 1877 and 1945 such issues as anti-Catholicism, anti-Semitism, nativism, prohibition, and parochial schools had reinforced the prevailing cultural bias. Except for the South, the Republican party still reflected the interests of native Protestants and the Democratic party those of newer immigrants and Catholics.

But industrialization had introduced an economic cleavage to American politics, with people from upper-income, business backgrounds usually voting Republican and lower-income, working-class people supporting the Democrats. The Great Depression of the 1930s widened the economic cleavage. Working-class people—whether Welsh miners, Polish steel workers, Swedish butchers, or Italian construction workers—came into the Democratic party. Blacks and Mexican-Americans also voted Democratic. In Minnesota, for example, the Scandinavian voters, who had always been solidly Republican, slowly began showing more support for the Farmer-Labor ticket, which represented workers and small farmers. All these working-class people, including blacks by 1936, became part of the New Deal coalition that elected Franklin D. Roosevelt (1932, 1936, 1940, 1944), Harry S. Truman (1948), John F. Kennedy (1960), Lyndon B. Johnson (1964), and Jimmy Carter (1976) to the White House and kept Congress a Democratic club for years. In 1928 Chicago Democrats sent Oscar DePriest, a black, to Congress, and the voters of Harlem sent Adam Clayton Powell in 1944. Dennis Chavez, a Mexican-American, became the United States senator from New Mexico in 1935; Lucien J. Maciora, a Ukrainian, became a congressman from Connecticut in 1941; John Blatnik, president of the Minnesota American-Yugoslav Association, was elected to Congress in 1946; Frank Lausche, a Slovenian-American, became governor of Ohio in 1944; Anton Cermak, a Czech, was mayor of Chicago in 1931; and John Pastore, an Italian-American, was elected governor of Rhode Island in 1945. The ethnic communities were acquiring political identities.

In addition to being of English descent, an Anglo-American living in Worcester, Massachusetts, in 1945 might also have looked upon himself as a physician, a Yankee, a Republican, and a member of the upper class. A Chicago Pole might have also identified himself as a butcher, a Democrat, a member of the Packinghouse Workers Organizing Committee, and a worker. A German-American in Milwaukee could consider his job as a machinist, his membership in the AFL, or his Democratic loyalties more important badges of personal identity than the fact that his great-great-grandfather had immigrated from the Rhineland in 1844.

Social and economic developments accelerated acculturation. World War I and World War II both generated American loyalty crusades; unquestioning allegiance and service in the armed forces helped blur surviving Old World loyalties. The two world wars also stimulated unprecedented movement across the country. A young Polish marine, stationed at Camp Pendleton near Oceanside, California, might not be able to locate a Polish Catholic parish or a Polish chaplain and would have to be satisfied with a nonethnic parish. The same would be true of a Minnesota Swede in Seattle. Cut off from the traditional centers of ethnic culture, people became more acculturated to other values. This process was helped along by the rise of mass culture. Radio, movies, and the syndicated press undermined ethnic culture and acclimated Americans to similar tastes and styles. Jewish entertainers like Al Jolson, Eddie Cantor, Jack Benny, George Burns, and Groucho Marx began to reach broader audiences, as did Irish performers like James Cagney, Bing Crosby, and George M. Cohan, and Italians like Frank Sinatra, Perry Como, and Tony Bennett. Under the impact of mass culture, English became the language of the entire society and dialects began to disappear. Finally the Great Depression exacerbated class tensions and intensified feelings of community based on occupation and income.

The pace of acculturation varied from group to group and place to place. Among French-Canadians and Mexican-Americans, the use of the old language survived because of the proximity of the mother country, but for Serbs or Slovenes the Old World was gone forever and English the only language for survival in the United States. German Jews rapidly acculturated because they wanted so much to assimilate, while Orthodox Jews resisted acculturation and only accepted Conservative Judaism as a compromise with American reality. Polish Catholic ethnicity survived because of the Poles' ability to create ethnic institutions in the large urban ghettos, but the Orthodox ethnicity of the Rumanians and Bulgarians weakened because they were so dispersed.

If acculturation was well advanced, full assimilation was still a long way off. True, more than 40 million Americans, primarily the descendants of the colonial and early-nineteenth-century immigrants, possessed such diverse, multiethnic backgrounds and complex social and economic roles that they no longer identified themselves as members of a particular ethnic community. After five generations of intermarriage—among the Norwegians, Finns, Danes, Swedes, Germans, Dutch, and British in the Midwest; or among the the English, Scots, Scots-Irish, and Germans of New England, the mid-Atlantic states, and the South—many had lost touch with their roots. Indeed, one primary American identity was that of being white and Protestant. Another was that of being white and Catholic, for when the Poles, Czechs, Lithuanians, or Irish married into other ethnic groups, they chose Catholics nearly 90 percent of the time in the first and even the second generation. These perspectives, however, were in the minority in 1945. Most whites still had a distinctly ethnic outlook on the world.

The racial minorities, of course, had not even begun to assimilate. They had acculturated to some extent—opting for the clothes or cars or homes of other Americans when opportunity permitted—but for all intents and purposes, the black, Asian, Mexican, and native American communities were sealed off from the larger society. Native Americans were still confined to reservations and many retained the cultural integrity they had possessed in 1607. Japanese- and Chinese-Americans were edgy in 1945 because of the relocation camps. Although the Chinese had escaped them, they realized only too clearly that anti-Asian racism could hurt them at any time. Filipino- and Mexican-Americans still lived in extreme poverty as migrant workers and factory laborers and continued to face racial hostility. And black people, now split into a rural base in the South and an urban one in the North, still maintained a structural and cultural separation from the larger society. These 20 million people were nowhere near being absorbed into America's legendary melting pot.

SUGGESTED READINGS

Abbott, Edith. *Historical Aspects of the Immigration Problem*. Chicago: 1926.

Abramson, Harold J. *Ethnic Diversity in Catholic America*. New York: 1973.

Alba, Richard D. "Social Assimilation Among American Catholic National-Origins Groups." *American Sociological Review*, 41 (December 1976), 1030–1046.

Allswang, John M. *A House for All Peoples: Ethnic Politics in Chicago, 1890–1936*. Lexington, Kentucky: 1971.

Appel, John J. *The New Immigration*. New York: 1971.

Asbury, Herbert. *The Gangs of New York*. New York: 1927.

Baltzell, E. Digby. *The Protestant Establishment*. New York: 1964.

Berthoff, Rowland. *An Unsettled People: Social Order and Disorder in American History*. New York: 1971.

Boorstin, Daniel J. *The Americans: The Democratic Experience*. New York: 1973.

Carlson, Robert. *The Quest for Conformity: Americanization Through Education*. New York: 1975.

Chalmers, David M. *Hooded Americanism: The First Century of the Ku Klux Klan*. New York: 1965.

Chudacoff, Howard P. *The Evolution of American Urban Society*. Englewood Cliffs, N.J.: 1975.

Curran, Thomas J. *Xenophobia and Immigration, 1820–1930*. Boston: 1975.

Davis, Allen F., and Haller, Mark H. *The Peoples of Philadelphia: A History of Ethnic Groups and Lower Class Life, 1790–1940*. Philadelphia: 1973.

Divine, Robert. *American Immigration Policy, 1924–1950*. New York: 1957.

Erickson, Charlotte. *American Industry and the European Immigrant*. New York: 1957.

Esslinger, Dean R. *Immigrants and the City: Ethnicity and Mobility in a Nineteenth Century Midwestern Community*. New York: 1971.

Fishman, Joshua, and Nahirny, Vladimir. *Language Loyalty in the Schools*. New York: 1966.

Furniss, Norman F. *The Fundamentalist Controversy, 1918–1931*. New York: 1954.

Gans, Herbert. *The Urban Villagers*. New York: 1962.

Gossett, Thomas F. *Race: The History of an Idea in America*. Dallas, Texas: 1963.

Grant, Madison. *The Passing of the Great Race*. New York: 1916.

Greeley, Andrew M. *The American Catholic*. New York: 1977.

Handlin, Oscar. *The Uprooted*. Boston: 1951.

Harney, Robert F., and Troper, Harold. *Immigrants: A Portrait of the Urban Experience, 1890–1930*. Toronto, Canada: 1975.

Hays, Samuel P. *The Response to Industrialism, 1885–1914*. Chicago: 1957.

Higham, John. *Send These to Me: Jews and Other Immigrants in Urban America*. New York: 1975.

———— . *Strangers in the Land: Patterns of American Nativism, 1860–1925.* New York: 1965.

Hutchinson, Richard. *Immigrants and Their Children, 1850–1950.* New York: 1976.

Jackson, Kenneth T. *The Ku Klux Klan in the City, 1915–1930.* New York: 1967.

Kantowicz, Edward R. *Polish-American Politics in Chicago, 1888–1940.* Chicago: 1975.

Kinzer, Donald L. *An Episode in Anti-Catholicism: The American Protective Association.* Seattle, Wash.: 1964.

Kirschner, Don S. *City and Country: Rural Responses to Urbanization in the 1920s.* New York: 1970.

Korman, Gerd. *Industrialization, Immigrants, and Americanizers: The View from Milwaukee, 1866–1921.* New York: 1967.

Krug, Mark. *The Melting of the Ethnics: Education of the Immigrants, 1880–1914.* New York: 1976.

Leuchtenburg, William E. *Franklin D. Roosevelt and the New Deal, 1932–1940.* New York: 1963.

———— . *The Perils of Prosperity, 1918–1932.* Chicago: 1958.

Lieberson, Stanley. *Ethnic Patterns in American Cities.* New York: 1962.

Lifson, David. *The Yiddish Theater in America.* New York: 1965.

Linkh, Richard M. *American Catholicism and European Immigrants.* New York: 1975.

Litt, Edgar. *Ethnic Politics in America: Beyond Pluralism.* Glenview, Ill.: 1970.

McBride, Paul. *Culture Clash: Immigrants and Reformers, 1880–1920.* New York: 1975.

Meyer, Donald. *The Protestant Search for Political Realsim, 1919–1941.* New York: 1960.

Miller, Sally M. *The Radical Immigrant.* Boston: 1974.

Naeseth, Henriette. *The Swedish Theater of Chicago, 1868–1950.* Chicago: 1951.

Osofsky, Gilbert. "The Enduring Ghetto." *Journal of American History,* 55 (September 1968), 243–255.

Park, Robert E. *The Immigrant Press and Its Control.* New York: 1971.

Pitkin, Thomas M. *Keepers of the Gate: A History of Ellis Island.* New York: 1975.

Polenberg, Richard. *War and Society: The United States, 1941–1945.* New York: 1972.

Quandt, Jean B. *From the Small Town to the Great Community.* New York: 1970.

Smith, Daniel M. *The Great Departure: The United States in World War I, 1914–1920.* New York: 1965.

Soltes, Mordecai. *The Yiddish Press.* New York: 1925.

Suttles, Gordon. *The Social Order of the Slum: Ethnicity and Territory in the Inner City.* New York: 1968.

Taylor, Philip. *The Distant Magnet: European Emigration to the U.S.A.* London: 1971.

Thernstrom, Stephen. *The Other Bostonians: Poverty and Progress in the American Metropolis, 1880–1970.* Cambridge, Mass.: 1973.

Tindall, George B. *The Emergence of the New South, 1913–1945.* New York: 1967.

Ward, David. *Cities and Immigrants: A Geography of Change in Nineteenth Century America.* New York: 1971.

Warner, Sam Bass. *Streetcar Suburbs: The Process of Growth in Boston, 1870–1900.* Cambridge, Mass.: 1962.

Weston, Rubin F. *Racism in U.S. Imperialism: The Influence of Racial Assumptions on American Foreign Policy, 1893–1946.* New York: 1972.

Wiebe, Robert. *The Search for Order, 1877–1920.* New York: 1968.

Wilson, R. Jack. *In Quest of Community: Social Philosophy in the United States, 1860–1920.* New York: 1968.

Wyman, David S. *Paper Walls: America and the Refugee Crisis, 1938–1941.* Amherst, Mass.: 1968.

Part IV
CONFLICT AND
CONTINUITY,
1945-PRESENT

Ever since 1607 Americans have tried to define their identity and find a place for everyone, but the Great Migration, the "unmeltable" racial minorities, and the continuing movement of people has worked against simple identities, standards, and communities. The texture of American life has changed dramatically since the seventeenth century. Industrialization, urbanization, the rise of big government, and the triumph of business values created the wealthiest, most powerful nation on earth. But beneath the surface old questions are still unanswered, old values still unfulfilled. Tensions among cultural pluralism, individual rights, and political nationalisms, the dominant themes in the eighteenth and nineteenth centuries, still pull at the social fabric, testing the American experiment.

After World War II such tensions became severe. No longer satisfied with the rhetoric of equality, racial minorities began insisting that the society and its values come together. Afraid of losing cloistered security, many whites responded by demanding the preservation of their own exclusivities. The consequence was a political debate over culture and ethnicity which would set the tone for modern American history.

Postwar America seemed an unlikely place for conflict. Social and economic changes were blurring old cultures and creating new communities; mass education was producing an educated people freer of prejudice than ever before; and the image of Adolf Hitler still reminded people of racism's potential destructiveness. Anti-Catholicism, a consistent theme of American history since the 1840s, was waning, enough that Americans elected a Catholic president in 1960 and gave Pope Paul VI a tumultuous welcome to New York City in 1965. Anti-Semitism eased as housing and resorts became equally available to Jews and colleges eliminated quotas on Jewish admissions. Mass production, a national market, and the mass media had integrated the country into an economic community of consumers dedicated to growth; and as always, geographical mobility continued to shape the American experience. In the new growth areas of the South and West, and in the suburbs circling every metropolitan area, white Americans lived in small homes and garden apartments and were isolated from the urban cultural centers of the East and Midwest. The prosperity of the 1940s, 1950s, and early 1960s eased ethnic conflict and produced a more tranquil social climate. Changing immigration patterns helped to lessen nativist tensions. Once about 10 percent of the total population each decade, immigration declined to less than 2 percent in the 1970s.

Americans felt more generous toward new immigrants. In December 1945 President Harry Truman admitted 40,000 World War II refugees, and the War Bride Act of 1946 permitted 120,000 foreign-born wives and children of American GIs to enter the United States. The Displaced Persons Act of 1948, though discriminating against Jewish refugees until its amendment in 1950, admitted more homeless Europeans, as did the Refugee Relief Act of 1953. Germans came throughout the 1950s, Chinese after the Maoist revolution of 1949, Magyars after the Hungarian rebellion of 1956, Cubans after the victory of Fidel Castro in 1959, and Vietnamese after the fall of the Saigon government in 1975.

Although the McCarran-Walter Act of 1952 retained the quota system, it had ended the prohibition against Asian immigration. Then the Immigration and Nationality Act of 1965 ended the forty-year-old system of ethnic quotas based on national origins. The United States would permit a total of 170,000 people from the Eastern hemisphere to immigrate each year on a first-come, first-served basis, except that no more than 20,000 people could come from any one country. Preferences went to refugees, those with family members already in the United States, and professional and skilled workers. The act also, for the first time in United States history, limited immigration from the Western hemisphere to 120,000 people per year, and they were allowed to enter on a first-come, first-serve basis without categorical preference or limits from any given country. The 1976 amendment to the act extended the preference system and 20,000-people-per-country limit to immigrants from the Western hemisphere, and it exempted Cuban refugees from the annual Western hemisphere quota. Under these various laws, more than 11 million people legally immigrated between 1945 and 1979.

But if one set of forces was obliterating cultural differences, other forces were strongly affecting the racial minorities. When Rosa Parks refused to step to the back of a bus in Montgomery, Alabama, in 1955, she unleashed the hopes of Afro-Americans and precipitated a major political and social controversy. World War II had already tested American values. Setting themselves up as the standard for equality and justice, Americans had made the war against Nazi Germany a holy crusade to cleanse the world of racism and spread the gospel of pluralism and freedom. From the beginning of the Cold War to President Jimmy Carter's controversial commitment to international human rights, the United States promoted individual liberty and tried to make America an ensign to the world.

But standard-bearers invite scrutiny, and just as politicians were broadcasting American virtues abroad, blacks, Indians, Asians, and Hispanic Americans were taking a closer look at reality. Just out of the relocation camps or back home from the war in Europe, Nisei and Sansei Americans were especially familiar with discrimination, as were poor blacks in the rural South and urban North, native Americans on the reservations, and Mexican-Americans in the barrios. Poverty and discrimination were still very real to them, and after 1945 these minority groups felt that it was time for all Americans to enjoy the equality their citizenship promised. The civil rights movement reflected a broad consensus about American values. It called not for the destruction of the society but for political action to achieve the American promise. To be sure, times were better for most people than ever before, but progress is relative, and minority groups wanted the ideal and the real to be closer still.

Because of their numbers, dispersion across the country, and power in the Democratic party, black people became the cutting edge in the civil rights movement. Beginning with the Montgomery bus boycott of Martin Luther King in 1955, Afro-Americans built on a foundation laid earlier by W. E. B. Du Bois and the NAACP. Through civil disobedience and the direct political action of marches, boycotts, and litigation, they sought to end the discrimination which had plagued them since 1619. Joined by politically conscious Mexicans, Indians, Puerto Ricans, and Asian-Americans, as well as white liberals, the movement achieved the Civil Rights Acts of 1964 and 1968 and the Voting Rights Act of 1965.

Federal laws, however, do not necessarily change reality, and millions of poor people still suffered from poverty. Urban rebellions erupted in black, Puerto Rican, and Mexican-American communities throughout the 1960s. Political activitists decided to move beyond civil rights to the economic sphere. They succeeded in getting the War on Poverty from the Johnson Administration in 1965, and having conquered *de jure* racism, turned to the *de facto* institutional racism permeating the society. Tired of poverty and unemployment, they demanded economic equality and equal access to labor unions, law and medical schools, political parties, government agencies, and corporations, insisting that America guarantee equality in the present and compensate for injustices in the past.

Changes in the society and the economy are often more disruptive than changes in the law. In the 1970s, when economic problems in the United States became more intense, many Americans became increasingly concerned about the volume of illegal immigration. While 11 million people immigrated legally between 1945 and 1979, perhaps another 20 million had come illegally. Totaling more than 30 million people, that migration appeared to be among the largest in American history. Older fears of job competition, declining wages, and unemployment reasserted themselves, and resentment toward foreigners, especially Mexican laborers, became more severe. People accused them of taking jobs from other Americans, filling the welfare rolls, and burdening the schools with children.

Federal attempts to institutionalize equality further exacerbated people's feelings. When the federal courts and the Department of Health, Education, and Welfare ordered school districts to integrate—which sometimes required busing children to city schools—graduate schools to admit minority students, and labor unions and corporations to accept members of all races into the same seniority lines, a backlash set in. The 1970s was the decade of "Roots," of the search for ancestral origins, and whites too were reaching back for their origins as a means of identifying themselves in a mass, secular society. More important, the revolution in demands by the racial minorities threatened the position of whites in the society. Many whites objected to the busing of black children into suburban schools, but even more were upset about having their children bused into distant ghetto schools. With few positions available in medical, dental, and law schools, white students resented quota systems reserving several openings for minorities. And white workers feared the loss of seniority to minority workers employed by government mandate. By the late 1970s not only were blacks, Mexicans, Indians, Asians, and Puerto Ricans pressing the struggle for pluralism and equality, but white people were showing themselves quite unwilling to let that movement undermine their own security.

The ethnic controversies of the 1960s and 1970s were played out against a background of war, dissent, and economic stress. Ever since John Winthrop and the Puritans had settled in Boston, Americans had possessed a special sense of mission. In the beginning that mission had been to build the kingdom of God on earth; in the nineteenth century it had been to conquer the continent; and in the twentieth century it became a mission to export American values abroad. But the underlying philosophy in all three periods contained the same basic assumptions: that American democracy was the best political system; that free-enterprise capitalism was the most effective economic system; and that God had destined both someday to govern the world.

The traumas of the 1970s revolved in part around the demise of these assumptions. The corruption of the Nixon Administration showed the world that the American government was less than perfect, while inflation and recession exposed weaknesses in the economy. Forty million "colored" Americans were decrying poverty and discrimination. And finally, the war in Vietnam, the most unpopular war in United States history, had soured domestic and world opinion about the virtues of American democracy and capitalism. Americans were frightened in the 1970s, riddled with misgivings about the future, and social debates were infected with that malaise.

Chapter Twenty-One

Black Power: The Afro-Americans

When World War II ended, black people joined other Americans in celebrating peace. After four years of sacrifice and death the country was anxious for tranquillity and the more mundane pursuits of life. But although blacks were escaping the more overt racism of the South for better jobs in northern factories, life there was hardly carefree; they had traded *de jure* for *de facto* segregation. In housing, schools, jobs, and public facilities they found themselves separated from the white community, still victims of prejudice and discrimination. By 1945 race riots had become common, the worst ones in Philadelphia and East St. Louis in 1917; Chicago and Washington, D.C., in 1919; and Detroit and Los Angeles in 1943. Slum housing, unemployment, crime, poor schools, inadequate city services, and poverty characterized ghetto life. Concentrated in urban islands rather than rural villages, blacks were more visible than ever before.

But ghetto life had also strengthened them. For the first time black people were functioning in an environment largely free of whites. The Harlem Renaissance of the 1920s had fueled the new confidence, and the words of author and educator James Weldon Johnson, W. E. B. Du Bois, the writer Claude McKay, the poet Countee Cullen, and the novelist and poet Langston Hughes built an ideological foundation upon which Martin Luther King, Jr., Elijah Muhammad, Malcolm X, Stokely Carmichael, Whitney Young, and Jesse Jackson would later construct the civil rights movement. Urban life had also provided blacks with political power they had not enjoyed since Reconstruction. The urban machines of the Democratic party needed black votes, and the mass-production unions of the CIO needed their support. Blacks were becoming the most loyal Democrats in the country. A black professional and white-collar class had also emerged to serve the economic, medical, legal, and educational needs of the community. West Indian immigrants especially helped this middle class accumulate property, status, and power. Just as inexorably, blacks became less patient with social segregation and began demanding access to government jobs, professional schools, transportation facilities, theaters, parks, restaurants, and recreational facilities, wanting nothing less than the end of both *de facto* (in fact, real) and *de jure* (by law) discrimination.

The Supreme Court and the End of Jim Crow

In 1945, as never before, blacks were ready for changes. Of all the approaches of the past, the NAACP had been the most successful. Thurgood Marshall, leader of the NAACP Legal Defense Fund, had always argued in the federal courts that racial discrimination was unconstitutional, a violation of the First, Fifth, Fourteenth, and Fifteenth amendments. And under chief justices Harlan Stone (1941–1946), Fred M. Vinson (1946–1953), and Earl Warren (1953–1969), the Supreme Court proved surprisingly consistent in condemning segregation. Between 1941 and 1964 the court invalidated virtually every form of *de jure* segregation.

The *Plessy* v. *Ferguson* decision of 1896 had upheld "separate but equal" facilities, but after 1940 the whole constitutional edifice of Jim Crow collapsed. In *Mitchell* v. *United States* (1941) the court declared that the denial of a Pullman berth to a black traveler violated the Interstate Commerce Act, and in *Morgan* v. *Virginia* (1946) the court prohibited segregation in public buses crossing state lines. Subsequent decisions invalidated racial segregation in other interstate transportation as well. With *Shelley* v. *Kraemer* and *Hard* v. *Hodge* in 1948, the court also prohibited restrictive covenants excluding blacks from housing developments. Other court orders integrated parks, theaters, and private businesses operating on public property, and in 1964, in *Mc-Laughlin* v. *Florida*, the court outlawed a Florida statute prohibiting interracial sexual relations. Finally, in an assault on political discrimination, the court declared that white primaries (*Smith* v. *Allwright*, 1944) and literacy tests (*Schnell* v. *Davis*, 1949) were violations of the Fifteenth Amendment.

But if these court decisions irritated white southerners, desegregation of the schools enraged them and led to "massive resistance" in the 1950s and 1960s. Arguing that "separate but equal" was inherently discriminatory and unconstitutional, the Supreme Court dismantled the central institution of Jim Crow. The outline of the future had appeared in 1938 when the court declared, in *Missouri rel. Gaines* v. *Canada*, that by refusing to admit a black student to the state law school Missouri had violated the equal protection clause of the Fourteenth Amendment. After World War II the NAACP continued to set its sights on higher education, and in *Sweatt* v. *Painter* (1950) the Supreme Court decided that a separate law school for Texas blacks was unconstitutional. Shortly thereafter, in *McLaurin* v. *Oklahoma State Regents* (1950), the court outlawed University of Oklahoma regulations segregating a black graduate student to special desks and tables. Then, in *Brown* v. *Board of Education* (1954), the court unanimously declared that *de jure* segregation of schools, by imposing inferior status on black children, denied them equal protection of the law. In one stroke the court had destroyed the legal foundation of *de jure* segregation.

While the Supreme Court was taking on Jim Crow, urban blacks were flexing their new political muscle in the Democratic party. In such cities as Chicago, Detroit, New York, Cleveland, and Philadelphia, they often held the balance of power. Their demands for equality received firm support from sympathetic Jews and ethnic Catholics, who had so often been the victims of discrimination themselves. Franklin Roosevelt and the New Deal had periodically expressed concern for the economic condition of black people, and the first fruits of black power had appeared in 1941 when Roosevelt created the Fair Employment Practices Commission (FEPC) to stop discrimination in defense industries. Facing a close election in 1948, President Harry Truman appointed a Commission on Civil Rights and called for a permanent federal Civil Rights Commission, a federal antilynching law, prohibition of the poll tax, and a comprehensive civil rights bill. By executive order he integrated the armed forces between 1948 and 1950. At the Democratic National Convention in 1948 Truman won the nomination, but his civil rights measures had exposed an Achilles heel in the Democratic party: the split between southern whites and northern blacks erupted when Strom Thurmond of South Carolina led a "Dixiecrat" rebellion from the convention. Truman surprised everyone by defeating Thurmond as well as the Republican Thomas Dewey of New York, and black voters provided him the margin of victory, as they would later do for John Kennedy in 1960 and Jimmy Carter in 1976.

But white resistance threatened all the achievements. After the *Brown* v. *Board of Education* decision, when resistance to integration spread throughout the South, the desegregation movement stalled. At first whites tried an outdated constitutional ploy, "interposition," which supposedly nullified federal court decisions in individual states. The Civil War had long since resolved that question, and the Supreme Court quickly overturned all interposition laws. Southerners then tried to gerrymander school districts, offer tuition support of private white schools, and cut funding to integrated public schools. Finally, when all else failed, a number of southern governors tried to block integration. After federal courts had ordered Little Rock, Arkansas, to integrate its all-white high school in 1957, Governor Orval Faubus called out the Arkansas National Guard to prevent black students from entering the school. President Eisenhower had to send United States troops to enforce the court order. Governor Ross Barnett of Mississippi used state police to keep James Meredith out of the state university in 1962, and white mobs rampaged through the campus until President Kennedy sent in federal troops. A year later Governor George Wallace blocked the registrar's door at the University of Alabama to keep two blacks from registering, but he too yielded at President Kennedy's insistence.

For black people massive resistance was terribly frustrating, especially after the exhilaration they had felt when Truman integrated the armed services and the Supreme Court destroyed Jim Crow. By 1960 less than 1 percent of southern schools were integrated, and segregation was still widespread in other areas because court orders were not being enforced. In Congress southerners were filibustering civil rights measures; and when civil rights acts did emerge in 1957 and 1960, they were very weak, giving the federal government authority to condemn segregation and investigate voter fraud but little else. Black people had expected much more. Southern life had changed little despite the laws and court decisions.

Tired of delays and impatient for change, some blacks began considering more direct action. They even resented traditional black organizations. Upper class in its values and closely allied with white liberals, the NAACP and National Urban League were beginning to seem timid and conservative, too willing to accept a "glacial" pace of change.

The Civil Disobedience Movement

The shift in black attitudes had already begun, modestly enough, in the most unlikely of places, a commuter bus in Montgomery, Alabama. One day in 1955 Rosa Parks, tired after a long day of work, sat down on a city bus and refused to move to the back, where blacks were traditionally confined. Her decision set off a chain reaction in which Montgomery blacks boycotted city buses and pushed the system toward bankruptcy, demanding integration and more black bus drivers. The leader of the boycott, a young minister named Martin Luther King, Jr., rocketed to national prominence as the boycotts spread to other southern cities. In retaliation, white groups like the Ku Klux Klan, the National Association for the Advancement of White People, and White Citizens' Councils tried to boycott blacks and, in some cases, even assaulted them in their homes. Several blacks were murdered in Mississippi, South Carolina, Alabama, and Georgia.

On February 1, 1960, black students from the Negro Agricultural and Technical College at Greensboro, North Carolina, entered several department stores and demanded service at lunch counters. When denied service because they were black, they refused to leave and the "sit-in" movement began. It quickly spread across the country; white and black students "sat in" in "white sections" of restaurants, theaters, bars, libraries, parks, beaches, and rest-rooms, all in defiance of segregation statutes. Martin Luther King, Jr., became the unofficial leader of the movement, using nonviolent civil disobedience to startle whites into accepting social change. For King,

> nonviolence . . . does not seek to defeat or humiliate the opponent, but to win his friendship and understanding. The nonviolent resister must often express his protest through noncooperation or boycotts, but he realizes that these are not ends themselves; they are merely means to awaken a sense of moral shame in the opponent. The end is . . . the creation of the beloved community . . . *

Jailed in Atlanta for a department store sit-in in 1960, King was released after John Kennedy, then the Democratic nominee for president, intervened with local authorities. The significance of the event was not lost on black people; they turned out in record numbers and helped to elect Kennedy.

In May 1961 the Congress of Racial Equality organized black and white "freedom riders" to go into the South to see if interstate transportation facilities had been integrated; white mobs attacked the demonstrators and federal troops had to be called in. The Southern Christian Leadership Conference (SCLC) and the Student Nonviolent Coordinating Committee (SNCC) sent thousands of freedom riders into the South until the Interstate Commerce Commission ruled that all terminals serving interstate carriers had to be integrated.

The pressure mounted in 1962 and 1963, especially after Martin Luther King, Jr., took his crusade to Birmingham, Alabama. Celebrating

*Quoted in Robert C. Twombly, ed., *Blacks in White America since 1865* (New York, 1971), p. 387.

the centennial of the Emancipation Proclamation, his SCLC marched in favor of equal employment opportunities, integration of public facilities, and enforcement of court-ordered desegregation formulas. Birmingham police used tear gas and guard dogs against the demonstrators while millions of Americans watched on television. When Medgar Evers, director of the Mississippi NAACP, was assassinated in June 1963, civil rights demonstrations erupted all over the South. Most Americans were convinced that black people had rarely been afforded the freedom and equality guaranteed by the Constitution. Sensitive to that problem and looking to the election of 1964, when he would again need the black vote, President Kennedy submitted a civil rights bill to Congress in 1963 calling for integration of all public facilities, even those privately owned, and the withholding of federal money from segregated institutions.

Southern opposition was fierce, but a string of events, tragic and ennobling, brought history and black demands together. In August 1963 nearly 250,000 people, led by the NAACP, SNCC, SCLC, American Jewish Congress, National Council of Churches, American Friends Service Committee, and the AFL-CIO, gathered at the Lincoln Memorial to support the bill, and Martin Luther King, Jr., gave his famous "I Have a Dream" speech. One month later, when a black church in Birmingham was bombed on Sunday morning and four children died, white sympathies were touched and support for the civil rights bill grew stronger. Finally, in November 1963 John Kennedy was murdered in Dallas, Texas, and his successor, Lyndon Johnson, pushed the civil rights bill as a legacy to the fallen leader, a sign of his own liberalism, and a redemption of his home state. After a Senate cloture ended the filibuster in June 1964, the Civil Rights Act became law. It outlawed discrimination in voting, education, and public accommodations; established the Equal Employment Opportunity Commission; permitted the federal government to freeze funds to state and local agencies not complying with the law; and provided funds to the Department of Health, Education, and Welfare to speed desegregation of the schools.

The rhetoric over the Civil Rights Act of 1964, the pain and struggle to see it through Congress, and the rejoicing over its passage raised people's expectations. Some blacks expected the act to make a difference right away, and when life did not change, they became frustrated. Some decided, as others had done when "massive resistance" began in the South, that more vigorous steps would have to be taken to reshape America.

The Civil Rights Act of 1964 did not put an end to segregation, but even had it done so, it had little to offer the black ghettos. As whites fled to the suburbs, businesses were relocating outside the city, making it more difficult for blacks to find work. At the same time the whole

Martin Luther King, Jr., leading the 1965 Selma-Montgomery civil rights march. (Dan Budnik/Woodfin Camp)

American economy was shifting from a manufacturing to a service base; blue-collar jobs were steadily decreasing as white-collar ones became more plentiful. But white-collar jobs required educational and technical skills, and large numbers of underprivileged blacks were unable to qualify. While earlier immigrants had used unskilled urban jobs as the bootstrap out of the ghettos, blacks no longer had those choices. They were trapped in a changing economy and a deteriorating physical environment, and their poverty became endemic and permanent, passing from one generation to the next. In 1970 more than one in three black families functioned below the poverty line, and the median black income was only about 60 percent that of whites. Unemployment was twice as high as for white workers, and joblessness for black teen-agers reached more than 40 percent in some cities during the 1970s. A terribly poor black "underclass" emerged, made up of people who had never had jobs or lived in decent homes. In the face of such debilitating economic problems, the end of formal segregation no longer took first place. For people worrying about how to pay their rent, utility, and food bills, whether or not their community was integrated was less important than how to support themselves.

In addition to focusing on economic problems, black activists began looking at the *de facto* segregation of the North. For years many Americans had assumed racism was a southern problem, but in terms of housing, jobs, and schools, black people were just as segregated in the North, even if the law had nothing to do with it. Combined with ghetto poverty, *de facto* segregation seemed even more insidious than *de jure* segregation, for by 1970 most black people in the United States were in segregated communities often deprived of normal city services, living in dilapidated slum housing, attending poorly financed schools, and looking fruitlessly for jobs. Many Afro-American leaders decided that *de facto* segregation would have to go the way of *de jure* segregation.

Black leaders also worried about unconscious, institutional racism. To many people it became increasingly clear that as long as blacks were trapped in poor neighborhoods and deficient schools, they would be unable to compete successfully with middle-class whites for jobs and status. Corporations, government agencies, and universities all based admission and promotion on competitive examinations which underprivileged people or those from different cultural backgrounds had more difficulty in passing. Some attempt to reverse such subtle but insidious forms of discrimination had to be made.

In the South, despite the Civil Rights Act of 1964, whites were still resisting federal mandates, harassing blacks and making it difficult for them to vote. An atmosphere of violence—after the assassinations of John Kennedy in 1963, Malcolm X in 1965, Martin Luther King, Jr., in 1968, and Robert Kennedy in 1968—gripped the nation. The Ku Klux Klan was gaining members, and as SNCC and the SCLC escalated voter registration drives, abrasive confrontations were inevitable. In July 1964, a month after the Civil Rights Act was passed, a black teacher on duty with the army reserve in Georgia was murdered, and a few weeks later three civil rights workers in Mississippi were killed while under arrest for an alleged traffic violation. During the summer of 1964 more than fifty black homes were bombed and burned, and early in 1965 two more civil rights workers were murdered in Selma, Alabama. One month later Martin Luther King, Jr., and fifty thousand civil rights demonstrators marched in Selma to protest the violence, and that evening angry whites shot and killed another civil rights worker. President Lyndon Johnson and Congress responded to the violence by passing the Voting Rights Act of 1965, permitting representatives of the Department of Justice to register voters in the South.

The Black Power Movement

The shift to "black power" appeared in two guises, one spontaneous and emotional, the other deliberate and ideological. In August 1965 the Watts ghetto of Los Angeles exploded when thousands of blacks rioted after a young black was arrested for reckless driving. White businesses were looted, snipers fired at police, and before it was over, thirty-four people were dead, more than a thousand wounded, and over $40 million worth of property destroyed. There was another racial rebellion in Newark, New Jersey, in 1967, and in the summer of 1967 Detroit was engulfed in a major conflagration, with angry blacks turning on police and white-owned businesses. The assassination of Martin Luther King, Jr., in April 1968 caused racial uprisings in many cities; and nine years later, when an electrical failure darkened New York City for a night, thousands of unemployed blacks and Puerto Ricans engaged in an orgy of looting. In every instance the eruptions were unpremeditated rebellions, illegal to be sure, against the frustrations of ghetto life. White America was outraged and frightened by the insurgency; but as they condemned the violence, whites also scrutinized the racial crisis as never before.

The ideological rise of black power came to the surface in 1966, even though signs of the philosophy had appeared earlier. After a lifetime of scholarly writing and support of black political activism, W. E. B. Du Bois finally despaired of changing America and joined the Communist party. The Black Muslims, founded by Elijah Muhammad in 1930, rose to national prominence in the 1960s. Preaching the ultimate doom of "devil" whites and the triumph of blacks, the Muslims took up where Marcus Garvey had left off, calling for black pride, black enterprise, and a separate black state. They also called on black people to think less about being nonviolent and more about returning violence for violence. In 1959 Robert Williams, an NAACP leader in North Carolina, was dismissed from the NAACP for advocating violence in self-defense; escaping to Cuba after allegedly kidnaping an elderly white couple, he became leader of the Revolutionary Action Movement (RAM).

But all these groups were relatively obscure until James Meredith, a black, decided to prove in 1966 that he could march to Jackson, Mississippi, during voter registration week without harassment. One day into the march, he was wounded by a shotgun blast, and civil rights leaders from all over the country descended on Mississippi to complete the "freedom march." But while Martin Luther King, Jr., still spoke of nonviolent civil disobedience, Stokely Carmichael, the young leader of SNCC, startled the nation by ridiculing nonviolence and crying out for black power. On the other side of the country, Eldridge Cleaver and Bobby Seale established the Black Panthers in Oakland, California, and called for black control of the urban ghettos.

Despite the rhetoric of black power and the fear it sent through white America, it meant different things to different people. To whites the slogan was incendiary, somehow implying that the social order was about to undergo revolutionary change. To the Congress of Racial

Equality (CORE) black power meant direct political action through the Democratic party, the mobilization of black votes in the South. The Black Panthers and SNCC viewed it as community control; they demanded black police and black firemen in black neighborhoods, black teachers and principals in black schools, and black-owned businesses to serve the black market. And to some radical groups—including the Black Panthers, RAM, The Republic of New Africa, and SNCC—black power implied the use of retaliatory violence to end poverty and discrimination.

Although the rhetoric of black power alienated many moderate blacks, the new movement inspired a more open spirit among all black people. In May 1968 Ralph Abernathy led the SCLC in a march on Washington, D.C., and at their "Resurrection City," between the Lincoln Memorial and the Washington Monument, they dramatized poverty in America. The Reverend Jesse Jackson, working out of Chicago in the 1970s, carried his People United to Save Humanity program throughout the country demanding black control of the ghettos. Whitney Young and then Vernon Jordan of the National Urban League turned from mild, solicitous attitudes toward white businessmen to more heated demands for funds and federal job assistance. The Black Economic Development Conference in 1969 demanded "reparations" from white churches to atone for past sins against the black community. Black moderates may have rejected the militant rhetoric of black power, but they could not help being affected by its spirit.

Led by the NAACP, the black community set its sights on the end of *de facto* discrimination. The Civil Rights Act of 1968 had eliminated many forms of housing discrimination, but black leaders concluded that if school integration were to wait for integrated neighborhoods, it would probably never happen. They believed that busing children was the only way to overcome segregation in schools and second-class education for black children. And to deal with black economic problems, the NAACP, CORE, National Urban League, SCLC, SNCC, and other black organizations demanded economic assistance and job training for educationally disadvantaged and low-income blacks, and "affirmative action" admissions, hirings, and promotions of black people by business, government, and universities. Congress passed the antipoverty program in 1965 to assist lower-class blacks and other poor people, and in the 1970s the Equal Employment Opportunity Commission ordered government agencies, corporations, and universities to establish hiring, promotion, and admission policies favoring blacks until the racial mix in American institutions, from the lowest service positions through the administrative hierarchy, reflected the racial composition of the whole society.

Black Pride: The Common Denominator

By the late 1970s there were several Afro-American worlds in the United States. For the black lower class in the ghettos there was poverty, crime, and unemployment, but there was also a subculture of energy and survival, a world with its own sights, sounds, and values. From Harlem to Watts, the ghettos abounded with the smells of barbecued and deep-fried food, soul music from bars and pool halls, the swagger of teen-agers, the talk of groups of men on street corners, and the sounds of black English. Black people felt comfortable there. Among the ghetto underclass, abject poverty and hopelessness encouraged gambling, alcoholism, narcotics addiction, sexual promiscuity, and pathological violence. But for the rest of the lower class there was the fulfilling world of the church and lodge, the status given to deacons, ushers, Sunday School teachers, gospel singers, preachers, and fraternal officers. These blacks respected stability and family values, yearned for economic advancement, and felt emotionally secure among other blacks.

The black middle class, people who had good jobs and lived in the "gilded" ghettos, looked down upon the emotional religions and ghetto English of lower-class blacks. They desperately wanted civil rights and decent schools for their children, and were torn between their desire for acceptance by whites and their pride in being black. At the same time that they favored de facto integration, they worried about the dilution of black values. Finally, there was the black upper class, well-to-do businesspeople and professionals who lived in a world of Greek fraternities and sororities, alumni associations, professional groups, and civic, social, and business clubs. No longer tainted with feelings of inferiority, they resented the fact that upper-class white society remained unprepared to accept them.

Despite class differences, the black community was still united by race, if only on an emotional level. The career of Muhammad Ali serves to illustrate those feelings. When he took the heavyweight championship from Sonny Liston in 1964, Ali at once electrified black audiences and became a folk hero. At first his appeal was much like that of Joe Louis or Floyd Patterson; by defeating white people at their own game, he brought status to the black community. But shortly after the Liston fight Ali announced his conversion to the Black Muslim faith of Elijah Muhammad, implicitly suggesting that American whites were depraved and doomed. In that instant he took upon himself the mantle of Jack Johnson, the earlier black champion who had flouted the conventions of white society. In 1967 Ali refused induction into the U.S. Army on religious grounds; denied conscientious objector status, he was indicted, convicted, and sentenced to five years in prison. Stripped of his title, he still defied militarism and white values. After the Supreme Court overturned his conviction, Ali fought again, this time taunting such black opponents as Joe Frazier, Floyd Patterson, and George Foreman as "Uncle Toms." Ali defeated Foreman and regained the title, which he both lost to and regained from Leon Spinks in 1978. Proud and rebellious, yet successful and generous, for many people Muhammad Ali symbolized the hopes of black Americans in the 1970s.

SUGGESTED READINGS

Baldwin, James. *The Fire Next Time*. New York: 1963.

———. *Nobody Knows My Name*. New York: 1960.

———. *Notes of a Native Son*. New York: 1955.

Bartley, Numan V. *The Rise of Massive Resistance: Race and Politics in the South During the 1950s*. Baton Rouge, La.: 1969.

Bennett, Lerone, Jr. *Confrontation: Black and White*. Baltimore: 1965.

Bernard, Jessie. *Marriage and Family Among Negroes*. Englewood Cliffs, N.J.: 1966.

Billingsley, Andrew. *Black Families in White America*. Englewood Cliffs, N.J.: 1968.

Brimmer, Andrew F. "The Black Revolution and the Economic Future of Negroes in the United States." *American Scholar*, 38 (Autumn 1969), 629–643.

Bullock, Henry Allen. *A History of Negro Education in the South*. Cambridge, Mass.: 1967.

Cleaver, Eldridge, *Soul on Ice*. New York: 1970.

Daniel, Pete. *The Shadow of Slavery: Peonage in the South, 1901–1969*. Urbana, Ill.: 1972.

Foner, Philip S. *Organized Labor and the Black Worker, 1619–1973*. New York: 1974.

Fullinwider, S. P. *The Mind and Mood of Black America*. Homewood, Ill.: 1969.

Garrow, David J. *Protest at Selma: Martin Luther King, Jr. and the Voting Rights Act of 1965*. New Haven, Conn.: 1978.

Glazer, Nathan, and Moynihan, Daniel P. *Beyond the Melting Pot: The Negroes, Puerto Ricans, Jews, Italians, and Irish of New York City*. Cambridge, Mass.: 1963.

Gutman, Herbert. *The Black Family in Slavery and Freedom, 1750–1925*. New York: 1976.

Handlin, Oscar. *The Newcomers: Negroes and Puerto Ricans in a Changing Metropolis*. Cambridge, Mass.: 1959.

Harrell, David E. *White Sects and Black Men in the Recent South*. Nashville, Tenn.: 1971.

Kousser, J. Morgan. *The Shaping of Southern Politics*. New York: 1974.

Kronus, Sidney J. *The Black Middle Class*. Columbus, Oh.: 1971.

Lawson, Steven F. *Black Ballots: Voting Rights in the South, 1944–1969*. New York: 1976.

Levine, Lawrence. *Black Culture and Black Consciousness: Afro American Folk Thought from Slavery to Freedom*. New York: 1977.

Light, Ivan. *Ethnic Enterprise in America: Business and Welfare Among Chinese, Japanese, and Blacks*. Berkeley, Cal.: 1972.

Lincoln, C. Eric. *The Black Muslims in America*. Boston: 1973.

McMillen, Neil R. *The Citizens' Council: Organized Resistance to the Second Reconstruction, 1954–1964*. Urbana, Ill.: 1971.

Meier, August, and Rudwick, Elliott T. *From Plantation to Ghetto*. New York: 1970.

Moore, LeRoy Jr. "The Spiritual: Soul of Black Religion." *Church History*, 40 (March 1971), 79–81.

Nelsen, Hart M., and Nelsen, Anne. *The Black Church in the Sixties*. Lexington, Kentucky: 1975.

Newby, I. A. *Black Carolinians*. Columbia, S.C.: 1973.

Nolen, Claude H. *The Negro's Image in the South: The Anatomy of White Supremacy*. Lexington, Kentucky: 1967.

Pinkney, Alphonso. *Black Americans*. Englewood Cliffs, N.J.: 1969.

Rainwater, Lee. "The Crucible of Identity: The Negro Lower-Class Family." *Daedalus*, 95 (Winter 1966), 172–216.

Salamon, Lester M. "Leadership and Modernization: The Emerging Black Political Elite in the American South." *Journal of Politics*. 35 (August 1973), 615–646.

Waskow, Arthur I. *From Race Riot to Sit-In, 1919 and the 1960s*. Garden City, N.Y.: 1966.

Weisbord, Robert. *Bittersweet Encounter: The Afro-American and the American Jew*. Westport, Conn.: 1970.

_____ . *Ebony Kinship: African, Africans, and the Afro-American*. Westport, Conn.: 1973.

Williams, Robert F. *Negroes with Guns*. New York: 1962.

Wright, Nathan, Jr. *Black Power and Urban Unrest*. New York: 1967.

X, Malcolm. *The Autobiography of Malcolm X*. New York: 1964.

Zinn, Howard. *SNCC: The New Abolitionists*. Boston: 1964.

Chapter Twenty-Two

Hispanic Americans in the United States

From 78,000 people in 1848, the Hispanic American community has grown to more than 18 million people today, and Mexicans, Cubans, and Puerto Ricans continue to immigrate. Including illegal aliens, there may be 15 million people of Mexican descent living in the United States, most of them in California, Arizona, New Mexico, Colorado, and Texas. The Puerto Rican population is expanding because Puerto Rico, a commonwealth partner of the United States, is exempt from immigration laws. There are more than 2 million Puerto Ricans in America, most of them in northeastern ghettos, especially New York City. Cuba has sent a stream of refugees until today there are about 1 million Cubans living in Miami and the Southeast.

Despite major differences in customs and history, the Cubans, Puerto Ricans, and Mexicans share a common perception of life. Although Puerto Ricans and Cubans claim a more racially diverse heritage than Mexicans, all three groups have some cultural fusion of Spanish and native American values, a "Hispanic" heritage. From the voyages of Columbus to the Spanish-American War of 1898, Puerto Rico and Cuba were colonies of Spain, as Mexico was from the arrival of Cortez in 1519 to the end of the revolution in 1821. From the Spanish the Hispanics inherited a spiritual individualism that saw the soul as the most important ingredient of character; and a romantic individualism that, in the tradition of Don Quixote, emphasized honor, self-respect, integrity, and personal self-expression. From native Americans they acquired a trust for one another, a spiritual communalism, a comfort with the rhythms of nature. The Hispanics judged people according to their inner value, not their political or economic status.

In the United States individualism was a matter of competing for social and economic power, of fulfilling oneself, but Latin individualism rested more on pride in the uniqueness of each human spirit, attended by an implicit trust of one's *compadres*. Organizations and groups, bureaucracies and systems, were suspect and commanded no loyalty in Hispanic American society. Puerto Ricans in New York City, for example, often preferred shopping at a local *bodega*, a small grocery shop, even though bodega prices were considerably higher than those at supermarkets. Out of that personalism and spiritual individualism came *machismo*, or personal courage and masculine confidence, fortitude in the presence of crisis. While many Americans were primrily interested in success in the material world, the Hispanics were equally concerned with defining the spiritual world and their place in it.

Finally, the Hispanics shared a Roman Catholic heritage, one quite different from the Catholicism of the Irish, Germans, Slavs, or French-Canadians. Hispanics viewed religion more as a community than a church. Their faith was another form of personal individualism and community membership, not an obedience to specific ordinances. Like the Italians, they perceived religion in this world and the next as a set of personal relationships to the saints, the Virgin, and the Lord. And with or without the church, Latin spirituality thrived. Indeed, they could be bitterly hostile to the church without feeling disloyal to the faith. Individual spirituality, not bureaucratic or organizational loyalty, was their religion.

The Cuban Immigrants

Ever since the Spanish-American War of 1898, Americans had felt close to Cuba. Washington had recognized the dictatorship of Fulgencio Batista, who came to power in 1934, only because he was anti-Communist and protected American investments. But there were two Cubas under his reign, the glittering gaiety of Havana and the grinding poverty of the American-owned sugar plantations. Batista lived off the Cuban people as a parasite, and his oppressive policies began to disturb many Americans. Then Fidel Castro led a guerrilla uprising, and in 1958 the Eisenhower Administration embargoed arms shipments to Batista. Castro's popularity became hero worship in Cuba, and Batista's government, built so precariously on "Yankee" capital and a tiny Cuban upper class, collapsed in 1959. Castro assumed power.

He soon shocked everyone by announcing he was a Communist. Nationalizing American property, executing or imprisoning major

Batista supporters, and redistributing land among the peasants, he enraged the United States and exhilarated most of the Cuban masses. Hoping to force Castro into submission by economic action, Washington stopped the importation of Cuban sugar and embargoed exports to the island. The Soviet Union then began to fill the vacuum. Although the peasants continued to revere Castro, discontent spread among independent farmers, small businessmen, and corporate employers frightened by socialism. Immigration to the United States increased dramatically. Some came on authorized refugee airlifts from Havana and others sailed the ninety miles to Florida in motorboats and dinghys. By 1979 more than 700,000 Cubans had settled in the United States, and the Cuban-American population had reached more than a million.

Today nearly one-third of the city of Miami is Cuban, and "Little Havanas" have sprouted all over Florida. The Cuban Refugee Emergency Center on Biscayne Boulevard in Miami greets new immigrants and helps settle them while the English Center of the Cuban Refugee Program helps them overcome language problems. Along West Flagler and Southwest Eighth Street, block after block of cafeterias, *farmacias*, *panaderias* (bakeries), *mueblerias* (furniture stores), and bodegas serve Cuban consumers. Indeed, coming mostly from middle-class backgrounds, the Cuban émigrés possess a strong entrepreneurial spirit. In Miami alone there are more than ten thousand independent Cuban businessmen, and perhaps twenty thousand throughout Florida. There is a Latin Chamber of Commerce, a Cuban Rotary Club, a Cuban Lions Club, and a Cuban Kiwanis Club. Most construction in Miami now involves Cuban contractors; service workers in tourist businesses are largely Cuban; and the Miami garment district depends on Cuban seamstresses. Four Cuban-owned radio stations broadcast to the Cuban community; dozens of Spanish-language newspapers, including *Diario Las Americas* of Miami, circulate throughout Florida; and Cuban bars, theaters, schools, and clubs thrive in the Little Havanas.

Although Cuban-Americans share Catholicism and Spanish with Puerto Ricans and Mexican-Americans, they differ in many ways. While the Puerto Ricans and Mexicans originally came for economic reasons and view their contemporary problems in social and economic terms, the Cubans immigrated for political reasons and have been successful economically. Puerto Rican and Mexican-American activists criticize American society, but the Cubans are unashamedly patriotic, grateful to the United States for their freedom. And while Puerto Ricans and Mexican-Americans can return to the old country, the Cubans are cut off by political barriers, and their love for the island is a deep, nostalgic yearning fired by hatred of Fidel Castro.

Cuban-American ethnicity, therefore, is a function of political nationalism as well as language and personalism. Fiercely anti-Communist and pro-American, Cuban activism revolves around foreign-policy issues as well as cultural ones. Since the first refugees filtered into the United States in 1959, Cuban groups have worked to overthrow Castro, and during the Cold War of the 1960s the United States government supported them. Soon after Castro announced that he was a Communist, the Central Intelligence Agency began training a Cuban refugee army in Guatemala. In 1961 the CIA-trained forces landed at the Bay of Pigs, but Castro's soldiers, joined by civilians, crushed them on the beaches. The "invasion" was a fiasco. World opinion condemned the United States, but Cuban-Americans were still determined to overthrow the Castro regime. Throughout the 1970s radical groups like Alpha 66 ran guns to Cuba, launched hit-and-run attacks on the island, and engineered repeated acts of sabotage against Castro. Their love for "their" Cuba still strong, and their commitment to what they consider its liberation undimmed, Cuban-Americans, like an earlier generation of Irish-Americans, are today a united, self-conscious ethnic community bound by blood and birth to the mother country and by recent history to the United States.

Puerto Rican Americans

After the Spanish-American War, Puerto Rico became an American possession. There were about 1,500 Puerto Ricans in the continental United States by 1910 and more than 50,000 by 1930, but after World War II the migration became much larger. There were approximately 900,000 Puerto Ricans on the mainland in 1960, nearly 1.4 million in 1970, and about 2 million by 1979. With only 3,400 square miles of territory, a population of more than 3 million by 1977, and most capital controlled by United States corporations, Puerto Rico had severe economic problems. Because the economy revolved around sugar, tobacco, and coffee production, much employment was only seasonal. With jobs available on the mainland, air fare to New York City less than $50, and no immigration restrictions, the United States seemed the answer. Thousands went first as contract laborers working commercial farms from Florida to Massachusetts, but nearly all the Puerto Ricans ultimately settled in the cities, especially New York's urban ghettos in the Bronx, the South Bronx, the Lower East Side, Spanish Harlem, and the Williamsburg section of Brooklyn. By 1970 many school districts in New York City had a sizable Puerto Rican population, and there were other colonies throughout major northeastern cities.

The immigrants brought a uniquely syncretic heritage with them.

Because of their Hispanic culture, they placed great value on the uniqueness of human nature, seeing a special quality to life regardless of race, religion, or class. Compassion and empathy, for them, were the most important parts of human character. But after more than sixty years of United States rule in Puerto Rico, they had acquired some Anglo-American attitudes about politics—an emphasis on political equality, individual freedom, and the rule of law. This view of society, to be sure, was still in its infancy in the Puerto Rican value system, but it had appeared nevertheless. Theirs was a dual heritage, at once a love of compassionate emotionalism and at the same time a growing respect for utilitarian pragmatism.

Still, the immigrants had problems. Especially troubling was their lack of a firm ethnic identity. The United States granted Puerto Ricans citizenship in 1917 and the right to elect their own governor in 1947, but Puerto Rican politics always revolved around the question of independence versus commonwealth status (granted in 1952) or statehood. In 1978 elections a plurality of Puerto Ricans expressed support for statehood. But the political debate retarded nationalism. The immigrants' displacement from an agrarian society into North American cities and the disruption of family and kinship networks so important to Hispanic society further eroded their sense of identity.

Color also challenged Puerto Rican ethnicity and divided the community. At home race had hardly been an issue; for centuries whites, blacks, mestizos, and mulattoes had mingled socially. But on the mainland a racial wedge split the community for the first time, with white Puerto Ricans aligning themselves with white Americans rather than with black Puerto Ricans, and black Puerto Ricans emphasizing their Spanish language to distinguish themselves from American blacks. In the 1960s and 1970s, when the civil rights movement gained momentum, white Puerto Ricans could not sympathize with calls for integration and cared little about *de facto* segregation.

The more educated Puerto Ricans opened bodegas, *botanicas* (stores selling herbs and spiritual medicines), cafés, restaurants, bars, and travel agencies, but these ethnic businesses could not maintain the community economically. Well into the 1970s nearly half the Puerto Rican families in the continental United States had poverty-level incomes, and nearly 40 percent were receiving welfare assistance. Less than 10 percent in 1970 were employed in professional, technical, and management positions.

Several problems explain Puerto Rican poverty on the mainland. Discrimination was real, but there were other reasons as well. One was the welfare system. Although it helped the Puerto Ricans at first by providing a minimal level of assistance, it also prevented them from developing the mutual aid spirit of earlier immigrants. There was no Puerto Rican equivalent of the Chinese hui kuan, the Japanese kenjin-kai, the Finnish cooperatives, or ethnic building and loan associations. Open housing laws and welfare housing assistance dispersed the population throughout the cities, weakening the immigrants' potential political strength. Their Hispanic bias against bureaucracies further retarded efforts to form ethnic institutions to fight poverty. And because the Irish controlled the Catholic church and they and other groups dominated the labor unions in New York City, Puerto Ricans had little access to the institutions that affected their lives.

Their language and cultural values also hurt them economically. Most Puerto Ricans did not speak English, but because of their Hispanic pride they chose not to speak English at all rather than speak it poorly. Reading levels and educational attainments were far below the national average. The American emphasis on personal achievement and competition in an impersonal economic world was alien to Puerto Ricans; they had little desire to embark on such a struggle, and American society judged them accordingly. The Puerto Rican love of children and large families, a fact of life on the island, became an economic handicap on the mainland, exacerbated by the lack of extended kinship networks to help them out. And to cope with life on the mainland, people had to be able to deal with large organizations and bureaucracies—social service agencies, health clinics, government bureaus, educational institutions, and the like—but the Puerto Rican suspicion of impersonal relationships made them shy away from such encounters. And finally, most Puerto Ricans entered the cities just as job opportunities were shifting to the suburbs and employment required education and technical skills; they found only minimum-wage service jobs that would never lift them above the poverty line. Most Puerto Ricans joined the "working poor," people with jobs that do not generate enough income for a minimum standard of living.

Not until the 1960s did Puerto Ricans begin organizing in their own interests. Following other poor people, many joined the Democratic party, and in New York Puerto Rican voters made Herman Badillo their most successful politician. Born in Puerto Rico in 1929, Badillo migrated to New York City in 1941, and after working odd jobs graduated from City College and then the Brooklyn Law School. In 1965 Puerto Ricans elected him borough president of the Bronx, and in 1970 sent him to the United States House of Representatives. New York labor unions and Democratic politicians mounted campaigns to register Puerto Rican voters, but because of population dispersal and the Hispanic alienation from organizations, getting out the vote continued to be a major challenge.

Some Puerto Rican groups concentrated on education as the way out of the ghetto. In 1961 the Puerto Rican Forum established Aspira to help young Puerto Ricans go to college. Aware that young people needed positive images, the Forum, Aspira, and the Conference on Puerto Rican Education became the most active groups in the Puerto Rican community. The Puerto Rican Legal Defense and Education Fund, a largely middle-class organization, promoted higher education and fought discrimination. Other Puerto Rican leaders promoted bilingualism and demanded bilingual teachers in schools, special programs to preserve the Spanish language, courses in Puerto Rican history and culture, and community participation in education. Arguing that the school system was top-heavy with Anglos and Jews, groups like the United Bronx Parents called for community control of schools, Puerto Rican administrators and teachers in predominantly Puerto Rican schools, and Puerto Rican paraprofessionals. Jewish and Anglo educators felt threatened, fearing the loss of their jobs or lack of promotions in favor of Puerto Ricans, and decentralization met bitter opposition from the New York United Federation of Teachers.

Other Puerto Ricans opted for economic action. The Puerto Rican Merchants Association encouraged small businesses, and the Puerto Rican Civil Service Employees Association promoted the interests of Puerto Rican government workers. Under the War on Poverty program begun in 1965, the federal government funded a Puerto Rican Community Development Project which sponsored drug treatment, summer jobs, job training, and school tutoring programs. Puerto Rican workers joined labor unions and eventually constituted a major segment of the International Ladies Garment Workers Union. A number of welfare rights groups demanded greater funding, fairer treatment of recipients, and more advertisements of benefits. The East Harlem Tenants Council organized for lower rents, safer apartments, and better maintenance from landlords. Puerto Rican social workers formed the Puerto Rican Family Institute to assist families coming to the mainland, and after securing funds from the Council Against Poverty in 1965, the institute began marriage, employment, and family counseling.

Some Puerto Ricans turned to militancy. The Free Puerto Rico Now group and the National Committee for the Freedom of Puerto Rican Nationalist Prisoners advocated the use of violence to achieve Puerto Rican independence and "occupied" the Statue of Liberty in 1977 to dramatize their demands. During the 1960s the National Committee for Puerto Rican Civil Rights demonstrated for civil rights, affirmative action in the hiring of Puerto Rican teachers, policemen, and firemen, and Puerto Rican studies programs in schools. They also protested the City University of New York's decision in 1975 to charge tuition. The

Young Lords, a militant group of Puerto Rican students formed in the 1960s, demanded Puerto Rican studies programs in the city colleges, community control of community institutions, and an end to police brutality.

The Mexican-Americans

In 1979 Mexican-Americans were the largest foreign-language group in the United States; because of their ability to visit their homeland and the constant flow of new immigrants, group identity remained strong.

The need for farm workers in the United States grew dramatically after the end of European immigration, the flight to the cities, and World War II job opportunities. To meet that demand, the United States established the *bracero* (work hands) program in 1942, and by 1964 more than 5 million Mexican braceros had worked seasonally in the Southwest, most of them on commercial farms and railroads. By American standards they were poorly paid, but they welcomed the chance to send money home to their families. After more than twenty years of lobbying between commercial farmers and labor unions, Congress finally gave in to the unions and terminated the bracero program in 1965.

Abolition only increased the flow of *mojados* (undocumented Mexican aliens) because Mexican workers formerly admitted under the bracero program contacted their previous employers and went to work illegally. Since 1942 Mexicans not included in the bracero program had crossed the border anyway, only to become the most exploited workers of all. Afraid of immigration authorities, they could not complain about job conditions; and employers, free of government-mandated wage, housing, and transportation standards, actually preferred them. When the Immigration and Nationality Act of 1965 imposed a quota of 120,000 immigrants from the Western Hemisphere each year, the number of illegal aliens increased again. And the amendment to the law in 1976 gave Mexico a quota of only 20,000 immigrants per year. Under these laws the number of legal Mexican aliens declined and illegal immigration increased.

But federal legislation was only a minor factor influencing the flow of undocumented aliens; traditional push-pull forces were responsible for the Mexican migration. Population growth in Mexico has been staggering, rising from an annual rate of 2.1 percent in 1940 to more than 3.5 percent in 1970. With a total population of 65 million today, more than 2 million people are added to the work force each year. But the labor market has been unable to absorb them. Industrial development and agricultural mechanization are breaking up the traditional hacienda society, and millions of farm laborers have been displaced from the land. In 1940 more than 65 percent of the Mexican work force was engaged in agriculture, but that declined to less than 50 percent in 1974. Unemployment rates climbed above 30 percent in the late 1970s. In the meantime, more than 15 million new acres of irrigated land were put into production in the American Southwest, and along with industrialization there, the need for unskilled laborers increased greatly. With wages in the United States three to four times as much as Mexican wages for equivalent jobs, millions of farm laborers crossed the border.

The undocumented aliens constituted a rather homogeneous social group once in the United States. Most of them came from either Baja California or the densely populated, economically depressed western mesas of central Mexico, and they usually left behind rural villages rather than urban centers. They were generally Spanish-speaking mestizos, for Indians and upper- or middle-class criollos rarely emigrated. And for the most part, they came to the United States in search of low-skill labor occupations as a means of supporting family members back home.

Until the 1970s the illegal migrations did not create a sense of national crisis; labor unions in the 1950s protested the presence of undocumented Mexican aliens, but the general prosperity of the 1950s and 1960s, as well as the full economy of the Vietnam War years, produced a labor shortage and an unemployment rate, by 1966, of only 4 percent. But in the 1970s, as both unemployment and inflation rates reached frightening proportions, the national sense of alarm over the aliens was magnified. Many Americans argued that illegal aliens exacerbated unemployment and underemployment problems, depressed wage levels, and overburdened the welfare and educational systems. From Operation Wetback in 1954, when the Immigration and Naturalization Service deported more than a million mojados, to President Jimmy Carter's grant of amnesty to long-term resident aliens in 1977, the federal government has grappled unsuccessfully with the issue. Between 1945 and 1978 border patrols apprehended more than 15 million undocumented Mexican aliens, but perhaps that many more made the crossing successfully. The Mexican government generally ignores the problem because the migration serves as a safety valve to lower-class frustration in Mexico and as a source of hard currency to offset trade deficits with the United States. And when the Immigration and Naturalization Service decided to construct a six-mile fence along the border between El Paso, Texas, and Juarez, Mexico, the illegal migration became a cultural issue as well because Mexican-American activists termed the proposal a "racist measure."

But the illegal migrants infused Mexican-American culture with old traditions, perpetuated ethnic characteristics, and retarded acculturation. By the late 1970s Mexican-Americans were one of the most self-conscious, visible ethnic communities in the United States. More than 90 percent of Mexican-Americans—citizens, legal alien residents, and undocumented aliens—still lived in the Southwest, and 85 percent of them were in California and Texas. And most Mexican-Americans in California lived in the Los Angeles area while those in Texas resided in the lower Rio Grande Valley. In Colorado and New Mexico perhaps one-third of the Mexican-Americans lived in rural areas, but in California more than 90 percent were urbanized. And by 1970 16 percent of Mexican-Americans were foreign-born; 29 percent were second generation; and 55 percent were third generation or older.

Until recent years, several subcommunities existed in the Southwest. The Hispanic people of New Mexico gradually came to refer to themselves as "Spanish-Americans," and although they too were a mestizo rather than European group, they had retained a good deal of Spanish folk culture. When the United States took over in 1848, most of the Spanish-speaking people of the Southwest lived in New Mexico, and because twentieth-century migration from Mexico to New Mexico was minimal, they did retain certain archaic speech patterns, folk songs, and religious art forms which were Iberian in nature. By "Spanish-American" they meant a native-born person of Spanish (European) descent, free of mixed or Indian parentage, and they also maintained feelings of superiority toward other Mexican-Americans, whom they considered to be poor, uneducated, and "Mexican."

In California and Texas, where so many millions of twentieth-century Mexican immigrants settled, the forms of self-identity were different. The violence and siege mentality prevailing for so long in Texas between the white majority and tejano minority made for a more tense situation. Throughout the nineteenth century the latter referred to themselves as "tejanos" or "Mexicans"; but after the massive immigration from Mexico began in 1910, the term "Latin Americans" became more common as a means of distinguishing themselves from the immigrants. In California also there was a division between the californio natives and the Mexican immigrants. Hoping to avoid white discrimination, the californios separated themselves from the new immigrants and began using the term "Spanish" in the early twentieth century.

Thus for reasons of nativity and class, a number of Hispanic subcommunities had appeared in the Southwest by the 1950s: the more prosperous and established "Spanish-Americans" of New Mexico, "Latin-Americans" of Texas, and "Spanish" of California; the "pachuco" culture of the urban barrios, where native-born Mexican-Americans found themselves caught between American and Hispanic value systems; the rural society of native-born Mexican-Americans in parts of New Mexico and southern Colorado; and the lower-class Mexican culture of the legal and illegal immigrants living in Texas and California.

But other factors united them and helped build a sense of Mexican-American identity, especially after World War II. As a mestizo people despised for generations in Mexico by white *peninsulares* (Spaniards born in Spain) and *criollos* (Spaniards born in Mexico), they felt a community spirit when faced with similar treatment by whites in the United States. At the same time, many Mexican-Americans held similar prejudices against blacks, and were caught in the unique position of being a lower class separated from blacks by race and culture and from white Americans by race, culture, and income. As with blacks, Indians, Puerto Ricans, and Asians, the color line in America served to isolate Mexican-Americans from whites while uniting them to one another.

Religion also bound them together, though not so much in an institutional sense. Allied with the white elite, the Catholic church had been a conservative force in Mexico, controlling vast amounts of land while peasants starved. Many mestizo farmers had come to view the institutional church as an adversary, and since the 1830s they had periodically attacked church property and driven priests into the cities. The Mexican immigrants came from that part of Mexico where parochial schools were few, finances weak, religious instruction sporadic, and attendance at mass irregular. In the United States they still viewed the church suspiciously, not only because of past hostilities but because of the legalistic, organizational stamp of the Irish hierarchy. By insisting on English instruction and citizenship training, the church in the early twentieth century became an Americanizing force, and Mexican parishioners maintained their polite distance. In 1890, for example, in the Tucson, Arizona, diocese there was only one priest to minister to a parish containing more than a thousand people spread out over 7,000 square miles. Though loyal spiritually to the Savior and the saints, and definitely Roman Catholic in a village and cultural sense, Mexican-Americans attended church infrequently, disagreed openly with church doctrines on birth control and sexual conservatism, contributed little financially to church programs, and supplied few priests and nuns to the hierarchy.

What the immigrants did support and share was a folk and cultural Catholicism, one based on mixtures of Indian and European religion and nurtured by a personalistic communalism. Every village had a patron saint and every individual his own saint's day. So whether it was the festival of the Virgin of Guadalupe or a personal saint's day, Mexicans felt constantly in touch with the spirit of Catholicism. Yet the Aztec tradition of collective security (once sought through human sacrifice) survived. Aztec religion tried to guarantee community life in the present, while Christianity sought to guarantee individual life in the future. This folk Catholicism of Mexican-Americans, though five centuries removed from the Aztecs, remained a mestizo faith emphasizing communalism in the present and individual salvation in the next world.

A family ethos also held Mexican-Americans together. In Mexico peasants had lived in clustered villages where networks of extended families assisted one another. And in the United States, as long as families moved together as migrant laborers, family unity and parental authority were maintained. Wives were expected to be obedient and sexually loyal to their husbands; children were supposed to be subservient; and husbands were expected to be sexually free but economically loyal. Even in the cities, when extended kinship ties were weakened, the family ethos survived, and all members of the family subordinated individual demands to family needs.

Finally, Mexican-Americans were bound by language and culture. Whether the border language of calo or texmex, the purer Spanish of the educated elites, or the Spanish of the foreign-born, language separated them from American society and provided a special way of interpreting life and expressing personal reactions. They shared memories or hero-worship of Pancho Villa or Emiliano Zapata, foods, *folklorico* dances, and distinctive types of dress and hairstyles. And they shared the generally Hispanic respect for machismo and personalism. In the American world of mass consumer goods and anonymous bureaucracies, these values clearly distinguish Mexican-Americans.

After 1945 Mexican-American society changed somewhat, and those changes cleared the way for the *chicanismo* spirit of the 1960s and 1970s. Once a rural, border people, they began moving to the cities in such numbers that in the late 1970s more than 90 percent were urbanites. Mexican-American barrios were worlds unto themselves, islands bound by language and culture. Ethnicity survived there, but so did problems. For the same reasons as Puerto Ricans—discrimination, language, rural backgrounds, and cultural differences—Mexican-Americans suffered from chronic poverty. If not in the fields, they usually found work only in unskilled capacities, as cooks in restaurants, porters in large buildings, maids in hotels, or laborers. By 1975 nearly two-thirds of Mexican-American families had incomes below the poverty line; few Mexican-American adults had educations above the ninth grade; and large numbers of Mexican-American high school students were functionally illiterate. And they too were caught in cities losing jobs and a national economy making the transition from a manufacturing to a service base requiring education and technical skill. Worse still, urban poverty strained family relationships, primarily because unemployed fathers were unable to fulfill their role as breadwinners.

Despite economic problems and ethnicity, signs of acculturation became more and more evident. Second- and third-generation Mexican-Americans were increasingly bilingual; Mexican-American wives, rather than acquiescing in the sexual infidelity or author-itarianism of their husbands, began to demand sexual loyalty and the sharing of child-rearing responsibilities; and young people were more independent. More important, Mexican-Americans began over-coming their cultural bias and building an institutional base to improve their status. Middle-class Mexican-Americans still relied on the League of United Latin American Citizens (LULAC) to fight discrimination, but new organizations also appeared. Nearly 350,000 Mexican-Americans served in the armed forces during World War II; but after the war, when they were denied membership in the American Legion and the Veterans of Foreign Wars, and when authorities in Three Rivers, Texas, refused to hold memorial services or bury Felix Longoria, a GI killed in the Philippines, Mexican-American soldiers formed the Ameri-can GI Forum to work for equality through legal action. The Unity Leagues of Texas and California campaigned against segregated schools, and in the 1950s Fred Ross established the Community Service Organizations in California to help Mexican-Americans meet citizen-ship requirements, adjust to American customs, obtain pension bene-fits, and enjoy full civil rights.

They soon realized that legal action was ineffective without political power, and in 1958 formed the Mexican-American Political Association (MAPA) in California, the Political Association of Spanish-Speaking Organizations (PASO) in Texas, and the American Coordinating Council on Political Education (ACCPE) in Arizona. MAPA worked for only Mexican support and the others for a coalition with white liberals, black activists, and labor unions, but all three tried to mobilize Mexican-American political power. John Kennedy's campaign in 1960 worked through MAPA, PASO, and ACCPE to form Viva Kennedy clubs, and in 1962 MAPA and PASO ran successful candidates in the Crystal City, Texas, elections. José Gutiérrez rose out of those elections and in 1970 formed La Raza Unida, a political party dedicated to community control of Mexican-American counties in south Texas.

Corky Gonzalez founded the Crusade for Justice in 1965. Schooled in local politics and Denver antipoverty programs, Gonzalez demanded reform of the criminal justice system, an end to police brutality, and good housing, schools, and jobs for Mexican-Americans. Culturally nationalistic, Gonzalez also sponsored *Chicanismo*, a pride in being Mexican-American and in mestizo roots, and a consciousness of ethnic origins which reflected an earlier Pachuco culture. A host of Chicano writers and artists—including novelists Raymond Barrio and Richard Vasquez, short-story writer Daniel Garza, playwright Luis Valdez, and

Cesar Chavez and farm laborers demonstrate during a strike against California grape growers. (George Ballis/Black Star)

painter Raul Espinoza—evoked the Chicano spirit, and Chicano studies programs swept through the schools of the Southwest in the 1970s. Near Davis, California, Mexican-American students founded Deganiwidah-Quetzalcoatl University in 1970 to promote native American and Mexican-American cultural programs. Groups like the United Mexican-American Students, the Mexican-American Student Association, and the *Movimiento Estudiantil Chicano de Aztlán* also promoted the Chicano spirit. At his annual Chicano Youth Liberation Conferences, Corky Gonzalez had delegates ratify the *Plan Espiritual de Aztlán*, a call for Mexican-American unity and pride.

Reies Tijerina was another Mexican-American activist of the 1960s and 1970s. After traveling widely in Spain and the United States, he formed the *Alianza Federal de Mercedes* (Federal Alliance of Land Grants) in 1963 and demanded the return of land taken from tejanos, californios, and nuevos mexicanos. Militant and articulate, Tijerina was a charismatic leader who denounced racism and called for ethnic solidarity. In 1966, claiming millions of acres in New Mexico and urging secession, he "occupied" Kit Carson National Forest and assaulted several forest rangers. On June 5, 1967, Tijerina and some of his supporters raided the courthouse at Tierra Amarillo, New Mexico, shot two deputies, released eleven Alianza members, and fled the town with several hostages. Sentenced to prison, Tijerina was paroled in 1971 on the condition that he dissociate himself from the Alianza, and without his leadership the movement died.

No Mexican-American leader rivaled Cesar Chavez in influence. A counterpart in time and philosophy to Martin Luther King, Jr., he too believed in nonviolence but was more committed to economic action than civil rights. Born in 1927 in Yuma, Arizona, Chavez worked as a migrant laborer after his parents lost their farm in a tax auction, but early in the 1950s, as a worker in the Community Service Organization, he saw the potential of mass action. He moved to Delano, California, in 1962 and shortly thereafter organized the National Farm Workers (later the United Farm Workers). For two years he built the union; then he struck the Delano grape growers, particularly Schenley Industries, and demanded better pay. The growers refused and Chavez turned the strike into a moral crusade, an appeal to the conscience of America. The growers used violence, strikebreakers, and anti-Communist rhetoric; and Chavez appealed to white liberals like Robert Kennedy and Hubert Humphrey, labor unions like the AFL-CIO, black leaders like Martin Luther King, Jr., and white students on college campuses. For five years Chavez led a national boycott of California grapes, fought the growers as well as the Teamsters' Union, which tried to organize a rival union, and finally, in 1970, succeeded in winning a long-term contract with the growers. Chavez had been the most successful Chicano of all.

These are the Mexican-Americans. No longer subservient and quiet, they want what American society promised to all; and fed by the continuing waves of undocumented aliens, they are the fastest growing ethnic group in the United States. And yet they are proud of their language and culture—their roots in the Old World and the New—and hope to preserve the familialism and personalism so central to their identity.

SUGGESTED READINGS

Acuña, Rodolfo. *Occupied America: The Chicano's Struggle for Liberation.* San Francisco: 1972.

Alvarez, R. S. "The Psycho-Historical and Socioeconomic Development of the Chicano Community in the United States." *Social Science Quarterly,* 53 (March 1973), 920–942.

Blawis, Patricia Bell. *Tijerina and the Land Grants.* New York: 1971.

Bradshaw, B. S., and Bean, F. D. "Intermarriage Between Persons of Spanish and Non-Spanish Surnames: Changes from the Mid-Nineteenth to the Mid-Twentieth Century." *Social Science Quarterly,* 51 (September 1970), 389–395.

Craig, Richard P. *The Bracero Program.* Austin, Texas: 1971.

Day, Mark. *Forty Acres: Cesar Chavez and the Farm Workers.* New York: 1971.

Dunne, John G. *Delano: The Story of the California Grape Strike.* New York: 1971.

Fernandez-Marina, R., Maldonado Sierra, E. D., and Trent, R. D. "Three Basic Themes in Mexican and Puerto Rican Family Values." *Journal of Social Psychology*, 48 (November 1958), 167–181.

Fitzpatrick, Joseph. *Puerto Rican Americans: The Meaning of Migration to the Mainland*. Englewood Cliffs, N.J.: 1971.

Galarza, Ernesto. *Merchants of Labor: The Mexican Bracero Story*. San Jose, Cal.: 1965.

Gamio, Manuel. *Mexican Immigration to the United States*. Chicago: 1930.

Gardner, Richard. *Grito! Reies Tijerina and the New Mexico Land Grant War of 1967*. New York: 1970.

Glazer, Nathan, and Moynihan, Daniel P. *Beyond the Melting Pot: The Negroes, Puerto Ricans, Jews, Italians, and Irish of New York City*. Cambridge, Mass.: 1963.

Handlin, Oscar. *The Newcomers: Negroes and Puerto Ricans in a Changing Metropolis*. Cambridge, Mass.: 1959.

Hauberg, Clifford A. *Puerto Rico and the Puerto Ricans*. New York: 1974.

Lewis, Oscar. *La Vida: A Puerto Rican Family in the Culture of Poverty–San Juan and New York*. New York: 1965.

Matthiesson, Peter. *Sal Si Puedes: Cesar Chavez and the New American Revolution*. New York: 1969.

McLemore, S. D. "The Origins of Mexican-American Subordination in Texas." *Social Science Quarterly*, 53 (March 1973), 656–670.

McWilliams, Carey. *North from Mexico*. New York: 1968.

Meier, Matt S., and Rivera, Feliciano. *The Chicanos: A History of the Mexican Americans*. New York: 1972.

Meinig, Donald W. *Southwest: Three Peoples in Geographical Change*. New York: 1971.

Nabokov, Peter. *Tijerina and the Courthouse Raid*. Albuquerque, N.M.: 1969.

Nelson, Eugene. *Huelga!* Delano, Cal.: 1966.

Olson, James S. "The Birth of a Discipline: An Essay on Chicano Historiography." *Social Studies*, 65 (December 1974), 300–302.

Paz, Octavio. *The Labyrinth of Solitude*. New York: 1961.

Perrigo, Lynn I. *The American Southwest*. New York: 1971.

Rendon, Armando. *Chicano Manifesto*. New York: 1971.

Romano, O. "The Anthropology and Sociology of Mexican Americans." *El Grito*, 2 (November 1968), 680–689.

Rubel, Arthur. *Across the Tracks: Mexican-Americans in a Texas City*. Austin, Texas: 1966.

Samora, Julian. *Los Mojados*. Notre Dame, Ind.: 1971.

Servin, Manuel. *The Mexican-Americans: An Awakening Minority*. Beverly Hills, Cal.: 1970.

Steiner, Stan. *La Raza: The Mexican Americans*. New York: 1969.

Stoddard, Ellwyn R. *Mexican-Americans*. New York: 1973.

Thomas, Piri. *Down These Mean Streets*. New York: 1967.

Wagner, N. W., and Haug, M. J., eds. *Chicanos: Social and Psychological Perspectives*. St. Louis, Mo.: 1971.

Chapter Twenty-Three

Asian-Americans in the Postwar World

The political and cultural perspectives of Asian-Americans changed after World War II, and most Americans no longer thought of them as "Chinks" or "Japs." Out of the rubble of the war Japan became a leading economic power, and the entrepreneurial and educational success of Japanese-Americans were just as striking. The internal cohesiveness of the Chinese-American community, as well as its economic success, won Americans' respect, and the fact that many post–1945 Chinese immigrants were refugees from Communism increased the admiration. Some discrimination continued. Asian-Americans were still absent from most social clubs and the corporate elite, but as never before in their history, Asian-Americans were enjoying access to political and educational opportunity.

It was not an unmixed blessing, however, for acceptance increased the cultural tensions already inherent in the Asian-American community. For both Chinese and Japanese, the institutional relationships that governed them before World War II began to deteriorate after 1945. Hui kuan and tong societies no longer commanded blind loyalty, and even the family associations were losing some power. Also, the postwar Chinese community was divided between native-born Chinese-Americans and new immigrants from China, Hong Kong, and Taiwan. More than 200,000 Chinese came to the United States after 1960, and because the 1960 Chinese-American population numbered only about 250,000 people, the new immigrants had an enormous impact on Chinatowns.

Japanese-Americans saw a similar breakdown in the prefectural associations. Although the Issei had found the kenjinkai valuable tools for cultural survival, the Nisei, Sansei, and Yonsei (fourth generation) considered prefectural ancestry irrelevant. And by 1978, with the Japanese-American community totaling more than 750,000 people, the native-born dwarfed the Issei in numbers and influence. Both Chinese- and Japanese-Americans had identity problems: how to move freely in American society while still feeling the pull of traditional loyalties.

At the same time more than 350,000 Filipino-Americans found themselves in ghettos or working in the fields with Mexican-Americans. They were soon to join the farm-workers' movement.

In addition to the Chinese, Japanese, and Filipinos, there were three smaller minorities: immigrants from Korea, India, and Vietnam. Korean workers migrated to the sugarcane fields of Hawaii and to railroads and commercial farms on the mainland after 1900, and by 1945 there were about 9,000 Korean-Americans. After the Korean war in 1950–1953 the Korean community grew to more than 60,000 people by 1975. Between 1820 and 1979 more than 80,000 Indians came to the United States. Those arriving before 1920 were usually farm laborers who encountered poverty and discrimination, but after World War II, and particularly after the end of the quota system in 1965, more than 60,000 Indian professionals, highly educated and Englishspeaking, immigrated and blended successfully into the American economy. And after the collapse of the Saigon regime in 1975, more than 110,000 Vietnamese refugees came to the United States and were scattered across the country in a carefully engineered government settlement program.

The Chinese

More than any other ethnic group the Chinese lived in America without becoming part of the larger society. Segregated in ghettos and overwhelmingly male, their early communities had been self-governing societies with their own justice and social welfare. The Chinese Six Companies spoke for the whole community and were the main source of employment, housing, and loans for new immigrants. Suspicious about nativism, the Six Companies and family associations urged the Chinese to work hard, save money, avoid publicity, and stay away from white America. Because the Six Companies and family associations monopolized economic opportunity, and because the immigrants felt strong loyalties to family and regional associates and distrust for the host society, the Six Companies and clans served as a conservative private government.

Social and personal goals reinforced the isolation. Because so many immigrants returned to China, the foreign-born outnumbered the native-born until 1940. Residential segregation was natural. Nearly three out of four Chinese lived in California, Hawaii, and New York in 1945, and half in San Francisco, New York City, and Honolulu. A century after the trek to the "Golden Mountain," Chinese America was still a transient, closed society.

That changed after 1945. Chinese-Americans had opposed immigration restriction since the time of the Chinese Exclusion Act of 1882, but the size of the community had decreased from nearly 300,000 in 1882 to 90,000 in 1900 to only 80,000 in 1930. Exclusion also made it difficult to establish nuclear families because Chinese men outnumbered women and new immigration was difficult. The Chinese-American Citizens Alliance campaigned to end exclusion as the only way to achieve a normal family life, and in 1924 the Citizens Committee to Repeal Chinese Exclusion joined the campaign. Chinese-Americans were no longer willing to accept discrimination quietly.

The campaign was hopeless until World War II, because labor unions, patriotic groups, and nativist organizations were still preaching about the "yellow peril." The bombing of Pearl Harbor, however, made the United States and China allies, and to counter Japanese propaganda, Congress repealed the exclusion in 1943, assigned China a quota of 105 immigrants a year, permitted foreign-born Chinese to apply for citizenship, and made special provisions for the immigration of war refugees and families of Chinese-American citizens. More than 25,000 Chinese immigrated between 1943 and 1950, most of them women and children. By 1950 there were nearly 120,000 Chinese in the United States, more than half of whom were native-born. When Mao Tse-Tung and the Communists took power in mainland China in 1949, the Chinese-American community, cut off from its homeland, finally acquired a sense of permanence in America.

Chinese-Americans continued to oppose quotas because the yearly allowance of 105 immigrants would never create a sexual balance, and when Congress eliminated quotas in 1965, Chinese immigration increased dramatically. Between 1966 and 1979 nearly 200,000 Chinese arrived, and the size of the community, from only 80,000 in 1930 and 240,000 in 1960, grew to 435,000 in 1970 and nearly 650,000 in 1979. Chinese-American life began to break out of traditional boundaries. New immigrants came from all over China—Peking, Shanghai, Hunan, and Szechwan—not just from Kwangtung and Fukien. They looked down on Cantonese traditions and felt no loyalties to the hui kuan. And because so many were poor workers employed by Chinese businessmen, they were hostile toward the well-to-do. For the first time the integrated, morally united Chinese community began to feel the centrifugal forces of American life.

Chinese-Americans began taking advantage of new opportunities. For centuries the Chinese had valued education, but in America, colleges had been closed to them. After World War II, however, they went to college in record numbers. In 1940 less than 3 percent of Chinese-Americans were professional workers, but by 1960 that number had increased to 18 percent and by 1979 to more than 25 percent. In 1960, while 16 percent of white high-school graduates went on to college, nearly 30 percent of the Chinese did. As housing discrimination eased after 1960 and many college-educated Chinese moved to integrated neighborhoods, Chinatown became a place to visit on Sunday afternoons to stock up on food or visit friends and relatives. The political, social, and economic authority of the hui kuan oligarchy was waning, just at the time new immigrants were refusing to take them seriously.

Intergenerational conflicts also contributed to the decline of hui kuan authority. Unlike their immigrant parents, the native-born had little affection for the villages and provinces of China and found their parents' territorial loyalties archaic. They felt closer to other native-born Chinese, regardless of ancestry, than to the foreign-born. And while the foreign-born always looked to the day when they would return to China—at least until 1949—the native-born were American citizens expecting to live out their lives in the United States. Instead of relying on the Six Companies or family associations for jobs or wives, they turned to American social and political institutions or simply to friends. One Chinese-American expressed those feelings:

> All the family associations, the Six Companies, any young person who wants to make some changes, they call him a communist. . . . I think the reason is, a lot of these people have a little business, they're doing pretty well, they have no ideas about how the society might change. They hold on to everything the way it was in China, in Kwangtung. Even though we're in a different society, a different era.*

As long as the native-born were a minority, the power of the traditional hierarchy had gone unchallenged; but after 1945, because of the numbers of native-born and non-Cantonese immigrants, the Six Companies ceased to be the only voice representing the Chinese in the United States.

The native-born supported the Chinese-American Citizens Alliance in its campaign for citizenship, an end to exclusion, and federal laws

* Quoted in Victor Nee and Brett De Bary, *Longtime Californin'* (New York, 1973), p. 190.

Chinese New Year festivities in New York City's Chinatown. (Rick Winsor/Woodfin Camp)

against discrimination. While the Six Companies called for isolation, submission, and a low profile, the native-born were more outspoken, more demanding in their quest for justice and equality. Through hard work, entrepreneurial skills, and education, native-born Chinese-Americans had achieved middle-class status by the 1970s and wanted political recognition and social respect for themselves as well as economic opportunity for new Chinese immigrants. They protested images of the Chinese which appeared in such TV programs as "Hawaii Five-O" and "Mission Impossible," and in such films as *The Good Earth* (1937), *The World of Suzie Wong* (1961), and *The Manchurian Candidate* (1962). The Chinese-American Citizens Alliance, the Chinese-American Democratic Clubs, the Chinese-American Chamber of Commerce, and a host of voluntary professional, business, and youth groups extolled their ethnic origins.

Chinese-Americans became more politically active. Wing F. Ong became an Arizona state legislator in 1946; Hiram Fong of Hawaii entered the United States Senate in 1959; and Wing Luke was elected to the Seattle City Council in 1962. Some Chinese-Americans were actively protesting against poverty. By 1973 Chinatown had become divided along class lines between a professional and entrepreneurial elite and the poor immigrants from China, Hong Kong, and Taiwan. The poor lived in slum housing and worked at subsistence wages. Like young leaders in the black and Chicano movements, Chinese-American youths began to demand federal action.

Still, Chinese-Americans remained outside the melting pot in the late 1970s. More visible and politically active than ever before, they maintained an ethnic perspective although some acculturation had occurred. In public schools they spoke English and behaved like other Americans; they celebrated major American holidays and joined the Boy Scouts and Girl Scouts. They watched programs on American television, drove American cars, and wore American clothes. On the other hand, most Chinese-Americans were still fluent in or at least familiar with a native language—Cantonese, Mandarin, or a regional dialect. Most were Buddhists, Taoists, or Confucians; and when they did adopt Christianity, they retained the detached, practical, and eclectic attitudes of Chinese religion. And they still took Chinese husbands and wives. Beneath all their American ways, they remained a separate people.

The Japanese

Japanese America was also changing. In the early years of the twentieth century the Issei had confronted a completely alien culture, and the rise of Japan as a Pacific power had created much fear in the United States. Many Americans doubted whether the Japanese would ever be able to assimilate. After Pearl Harbor these fears reached an emotional frenzy.

But attitudes changed by the early 1950s. Hundreds of thousands of GIs returned from the occupation of Japan impressed with the stability of Japanese society, and more than twenty thousand brought back Japanese wives. Americans were amazed at Japanese tenacity and economic skill, at their ability to rise from the ashes of World War II to economic independence. Old stereotypes of treacherous, disloyal, and depraved Japanese gave way to a new consensus about loyal, hard-working, well-educated, and law-abiding Japanese. In 1952 the McCarran-Walter Act permitted Issei to apply for citizenship, and the Immigration and Naturalization Act of 1965 ended the Japanese quota. Between 1945 and 1979 nearly 150,000 Japanese immigrated to the United States, and the Japanese-American community, composed of perhaps 280,000 people in 1941, grew to 465,000 in 1960 and nearly 750,000 in 1979. The Supreme Court ruled that California's Alien Land Laws violated the Fourteenth Amendment, and they were repealed in 1956. Japanese-Americans were living in a society that was increasingly open to them.

Tolerance gave full reign to Japanese-Americans' cultural impulses. Most Issei who came to America were educated, and they passed on to the Nisei, Sansei, and Yonsei a profound respect for learning. Now they poured into the state colleges, and by 1979 educational achievement among Japanese-Americans was second only to that of the Jews. Unskilled workers had dropped from 25 percent to only 3 percent, and the median Japanese-American income was far above the national average. Occupational and educational success did not reduce the level of community integrity; crime, delinquency, divorce, and indigence were far less likely to occur among Japanese-Americans than in the society at large. The willingness of the Japanese family to care for its sick, poor, and aged was unsurpassed in the United States.

Given their economic condition in 1945, such achievements were even more remarkable. When the army rounded them up for the relocation camps in 1942, they were permitted to take with them only what they could carry. Doctors, dentists, and medical technicians lost their professional equipment; lawyers their law libraries; fishermen their boats, nets, poles, and tackle; businessmen their inventories, buildings, and fixtures; farmers their land, leases, and implements; and families their homes, cars, and insurance policies. Congress passed the Japanese Evacuation Claims Act in 1948 to compensate them, but only $38 million was ever awarded in damages, while conservative estimates place prewar Japanese property at over $400 million. Thus after the war most Japanese-Americans had to start all over again. Despite this, they reached a prosperous middle-class status by the 1970s.

Unlike the Chinese, the Japanese did not experience cultural conflict with new immigrants after 1945. Japan was a remarkably homogeneous society, and the new Issei shared much with the older Issei. Although differences with the Nisei, Sansei, and Yonsei were substantial, the cultural gap was not nearly as great as it was between the older Cantonese settlers and the new immigrants from northern and central China. Still, Nisei did not feel close to Issei prefectural groups or the Japanese Association which represented them, and although their ties to such traditional Japanese values as family loyalty and duty were strong, they were far more acculturated than their parents. They wore shoes indoors, used knives and forks instead of chopsticks, played American sports, and selected marriage partners for romantic rather than family or economic reasons.

All this troubled Issei parents, but they were especially upset by the Nisei tendency to look upon themselves as a national rather than a prefectural group. In 1930 the Nisei had formed the Japanese-American Citizens League (JACL) to promote their interests, and prefectural origins were ignored. But while the Chinese-American Citizens Association had to compete with the Six Companies and family associations representing the foreign-born, the World War II "relocations" had destroyed Issei influence. By 1945 the Issei-dominated prefectural associations and the old Japanese Association were all but extinct. In the camps the JACL spoke for the incarcerated people, and the Issei, lacking citizenship or recognition from officials of the War Relocation Authority, could do little about their status. After the war the JACL led the campaign against the Alien Land Laws and for evacuation compensation and urged the Nisei to work hard and be "good Americans." It was the Nisei, the "quiet" Americans, who fulfilled the new stereotypes of the Japanese after 1945.

But in the 1960s and 1970s signs of Sansei and Yonsei restlessness with Nisei values appeared, just as the Nisei had tired of Issei parochialism in the 1920s and 1930s. Most Sansei and Yonsei still reflected the norms of Japanese culture as hard-working, upwardly mobile people; but, unlike the Issei and Nisei, they did not necessarily accept the wisdom of conformity, collective dependence on family and community, a high tolerance for frustration and work, a yearning for achievement, and a willingness to suppress their complaints. Most Sansei and Yonsei still adhered to some or all these values to a degree, but they were questioning them too. Juvenile crime was higher among them than it had been among the Issei or Nisei. Nor could they understand the passive way Issei and Nisei had accepted their treatment during World War II. For many Sansei and Yonsei, the Japanese-American Citizens League had sold its birthright in 1942, losing its self-respect and pride.

For the Sansei and Yonsei youth of the 1960s and 1970s, the relocation camps represented a historical event which became a distinguishing feature of ethnicity. Sensitive to discrimination and stereotyping, they protested both. Searching for their own roots, they demanded Japanese studies programs in schools and colleges, and militant Sansei talked of "yellow power" and "yellow pride," community action, and even a revolution of "Third World peoples." While liberal Sansei and Yonsei demanded cultural pluralism, radicals questioned the foundation of capitalism and liberal democracy. It was a futile line of questioning, of course, because so many Japanese-Americans were enjoying middle-class prosperity. Nevertheless, the new attitudes clearly spelled the end of Issei isolation and Nisei submission.

The Filipinos

In the 1890s the people of the United States found themselves looking abroad. Protestant missionaries were yearning to convert the "heathen millions" of Asia; businessmen were looking for raw materials and new markets; and strategists were searching for naval outposts and coaling stations in the Pacific. The Philippines met all three criteria, and in 1898 the United States offered Spain $20 million for the islands. Defeated in the Spanish-American War, Spain accepted, and after a bloody guerrilla war with Filipino nationalists, the United States took control of the islands.

In 1882 Congress had ended Chinese immigration, and the Gentlemen's Agreement of 1907 would restrict the flow of people from Japan. Asian immigration was declining just as agricultural production was booming, and American farmers needed workers to plant and harvest crops. Since the Philippines were governed by the United States, immigration restriction laws did not apply to Filipinos, and they began coming to Hawaii and California in 1900. By 1935, when the act granting the Phillipines commonwealth status subjected them to the National Origins Act, nearly 125,000 Filipinos had arrived in Hawaii and perhaps 75,000 in California. They worked as migrant farm laborers, bellboys, house servants, porters, and waiters. Between 1935 and 1946 (the Philippines became an independent republic on July 4, 1946) Filipino immigration was prohibited, and until 1965 their quota was only 100 per year, so as late as 1960 there were still only 175,000 Filipinos in the United States. After the Immigration Act of 1965, however, they became one of the fastest-growing groups in the United States, averaging nearly 25,000 new immigrants each year. By 1970 there were nearly 340,000 Filipinos in America, and that number would increase to 600,000 by 1979.

Like the Japanese and Chinese, the Filipinos lived and worked in the fields of Hawaii, the Imperial Valley, the San Joaquin Valley, the California Delta, and the Salinas Valley. Carlos Bulosan, an immigrant and writer, described his life in the 1920s:

> My first sight of the . . . land was . . . exhilarating. . . . I knew that I must find a home in this new land . . . we were sold for five dollars each to work in the fish canneries of Alaska. . . . We were forced to sign a paper which stated that each of us owed the contractor twenty dollars for bedding and another twenty for luxuries. What these luxuries were, I never found out. It was the beginning of my life in America, the beginning of a long flight that carried me down the years fighting desperately to find peace in some corner of life . . .*

Los Angeles, Stockton, San Francisco, and Seattle had large Filipino communities, but compared to the Japanese and Chinese, the Filipinos had a much more difficult time lifting themselves out of poverty. Discrimination and lack of capital prevented them from establishing a business foothold, and racist attitudes in many unions sealed off access to skilled jobs. Equally important, the Filipino community was itself

---

* Quoted in Cecyle S. Neidle, *The New Americans* (New York, 1967), pp. 303–304.

heterogeneous, and while trying to adjust to America the Filipinos also had to cope with their own differences. Immigrants from the Visaya Islands spoke Visayan; those from Manila spoke Tagalog; and those from the northern provinces of Luzon, Ilocos Norte and Ilocos Sur, spoke Ilocan. Divided internally and disliked by many Americans, they struggled for security, but most Filipinos remained unskilled workers with median incomes among the lowest in the nation.

Like so many other ethnic groups, the Filipinos became more politically active in the 1960s. The Filipino Federation of America, founded in 1925 by Hilario Camino Moncado, still offered legal aid and employment assistance, but Filipino activism took the form of a workers' movement. When white growers cut wages for asparagus workers, Filipino immigrants had organized the Filipino Agricultural Labor Association and won several strikes in the late 1930s and 1940s. In 1959, just when Cesar Chavez was forming the National Farm Workers Association for Mexican-American laborers, the AFL-CIO founded the Agricultural Workers Organizing Committee (AWOC). Led by Larry Itlion, the AWOC was primarily a Filipino union, but in 1966, after lengthy strikes against individual growers and the agribusiness corporations, the AWOC and Chavez's union merged into the United Farm Workers Organizing Committee and successfully struck the Di Giorgio Corporation in Kern County, California. Cesar Chavez remained head of the new union, but Philip Vera Cruz, a Filipino, was named vice-chairman.

Yellow Power: The Asian-American Movement

In the 1970s Asian-Americans still felt the pull of family and tradition. The Asian family had always been the basic institution of society; power flowed from a patriarchal father and loyalty was authoritarian. Individual behavior was a reflection on the family, and children were expected to be ambitious and successful. Independence was discouraged. Peace and harmony were primary values, and family members were expected to contain disruptive feelings. Throughout much of Asian America the traditional values of formal personal relations, inhibition of strong feelings, obedience to authority, loyalty to family, and high educational and occupational achievement continued to be important.

But in American society the emphasis was on individualism, freedom of expression, and equality, even though discrimination often contradicted those values. Equality for Asian-Americans seemed to require a movement against Old World values as well as against American discrimination. As a result, Asian-Americans in the 1970s underwent an identity crisis, and when some groups began demanding equality, their approach seemed more subdued than that of other ethnic groups. Though they tried to create a pan-Asian spirit that crossed cultural lines, the basic differences between Japanese, Chinese, Koreans, Filipinos, Indians, and Hawaiians were impossible to overcome. Differences in their social and economic condition also helped to prevent the growth of a unified movement for yellow power. While many native-born Chinese-Americans and nearly all Japanese-Americans had achieved middle-class prosperity, the Filipinos and Hawaiians were still poor, as were the new immigrant Chinese.

The yellow power movement, then, was handicapped from the beginning, especially by its inability to appeal to influential Japanese- and Chinese-Americans. Still, there were manifestations of Asian-American discontent. On Hawaii in the 1970s militant Polynesians in the Protect Kahoolawe Ohana occupied parts of the island of Maui, sacred homeland of their rain goddess Hina, and demanded the end of U.S. Navy test bombings there. In California Filipino farm workers continued their labor union activities. The Asian-American Political Alliance, a largely Japanese group, worked to create Asian studies programs on college campuses, as did the Intercollegiate Chinese for Social Action. And a few minor radical groups like the Red Guards and the Third World Liberation Front advocated violence to redesign society. Their appeal was hopelessly limited and their clientele small. But even if the yellow power movement had no real hope of effecting revolutionary change, Asian-Americans in general were more concerned about equality than ever before, and less willing to return to the submissive collective conformity of earlier years.

SUGGESTED READINGS

Bonacich, Edna. "Small Business and Japanese-American Ethnic Solidarity." *Amerasia Journal*, 2 (Summer 1975), 21–48.

Bulosan, Carlos. *America Is in the Heart*. New York: 1943.

Catapusan, B. T. *The Filipino Social Adjustment in the United States*. New York: 1972.

Chow, Williard T. *The Reemergence of an Inner City: The Pivot of Chinese Settlement in the East Bay Region of the San Francisco Bay Area*. Palo Alto, Cal.: 1977.

Connor, John W. *Acculturation and the Retention of an Ethnic Identity in Three Generations of Japanese-Americans*. Palo Alto, Cal.: 1977.

Conroy, Hilary, and Miyakaka, T. Scott. *East Across the Pacific: Historical and Sociological Studies of Japanese Immigration and Assimilation*. Santa Barbara, Cal.: 1972.

Gee, Emma, ed. *Counterpoint: Perspectives on Asian Americans*. Los Angeles: 1976.

Henry, Sheila E. *Cultural Persistence and Socioeconomic Mobility*. Palo Alto, Cal.: 1978.

Hirabayashi, James. "Nisei: The Quiet American? A Reevaluation." *Amerasia Journal*, 2 (Summer 1975), 1–20.

Hong, Lawrence K. "Recent Immigrants in the Chinese-American Community: Issues of Adaptations and Impacts." *International Migration Review*, 10 (Winter 1976), 509–514.

Hsu, Francis L. K. *Americans and Chinese*. Garden City, N.Y.: 1970.

———. *The Challenge of the American Dream: The Chinese in the United States*. Belmont, Cal.: 1971.

Hundley, Norris, ed. *The Asian American*. Santa Barbara, Cal.: 1977.

Kashima, Tetsuden. *Buddhism in America*. Westport, Conn.: 1977.

Kelley, Gail. *From Vietnam to America*. New York: 1977.

Kim, Hyung-Chan. *The Koreans in America*. New York: 1974.

Kitano, Harry H. L. *The Japanese-Americans*. Englewood Cliffs, N.J.: 1976.

Kung, S. W. *Chinese in American Life*. Westport, Conn.: 1962.

Lan, Dean. *Prestige with Limitations: Realities of the Chinese American Elite*. New York: 1976.

Lasker, Bruno. *Filipino Immigration to the United States*. New York: 1969.

Lee, Rose Hum. *The Chinese in the United States of America*. Hong Kong: 1960.

Li, Peter S. "Ethnic Businesses Among Chinese in the United States." *Journal of Ethnic Studies*, 4 (Fall 1976), 35–41.

Light, Ivan. "The Ethnic Vice Industry, 1880–1944." *American Sociological Review*, 42 (June 1977), 464–478.

Lyman, Stanford M. *Chinese Americans*. New York: 1974.

Melendy, J. Brett. "Filipinos in the United States." *Pacific Historical Review*, 43 (November 1974), 520–547.

———. *The Oriental Americans*. New York: 1972.

Modell, John. "The Japanese-American Family: A Perspective for Future Investigations." *Pacific Historical Review*, 37 (February 1968), 67–82.

Nee, Victor G., and De Bary, Brett. *Longtime Californin'*. New York: 1973.

Petersen, William. *Japanese-Americans*. New York: 1971.

Sung, Betty Lee. *The Chinese in America*. New York: 1972.

———. *A Survey of Chinese-American Manpower and Employment*. Los Angeles: 1976.

Chapter Twenty-Four

Native Americans in Contemporary Society

Like everyone else native Americans were trying to cope with postwar changes in political and social affairs as well as in their own circumstances. In 1945 Indians were still recovering from the wars of the nineteenth century and the Dawes Act, and although the Indian Reorganization Act of 1934 had restored tribal autonomy and tried to revive the reservation economy, poverty continued to plague them. Most still lived on the reservations, but by 1979 nearly four hundred thousand would move to urban ghettos. Native America remained a diverse collection of cultures, but important and inevitable changes were occurring. One was the decline of Indian languages. Every immigrant coming to America had watched the Old World languages weaken and disappear after the first generation, and a similar, if slower, trend was taking place in native America. By 1968, of more than three hundred languages once spoken, only forty-five—including Cherokee, Creek, Crow, and Navajo—had more than a thousand fluent adherents. The disappearance of native tongues by no means signaled the end of tribal ethnicity, but the widespread use of English indicated an increasing accommodation to white society.

Some tribes were more acculturated than others. The Hupas of California, for example, turned from traditional rites and subsistence living and adopted the tastes of white society, buying cars, television sets, appliances, and fast-food meals with money from tribal timber leases. The native language disappeared along with the old ways of hunting, fishing, dancing, and worshiping. Other tribes were hardly acculturated at all. The Hopis isolated themselves, nurtured traditional ceremonies, and kept their links to the past through reservation institutions including museums and cultural centers. Some Indians lived in cities and had no manifest ties to Indian civilization, preferring instead to function exclusively in white society. Some tribes mixed the two worlds. On the Blackfoot reservation acculturated Indians working in the white economy lived as neighbors to other tribesmen who rarely left the reservation. On the Sioux reservation at Pine Ridge, South Dakota, there were tribal murals and symbols inside the Catholic church, tribal signs on priestly vestments, and a mass with a sacred peace-pipe ceremony rather than the traditional Eucharist. No statement can describe the degree of acculturation for all native America, but it was continuing if only at the most primitive levels.

In postwar America, then, Indians too were searching out their identity in the midst of vast changes. They would join white liberals in opposing discrimination, but they would lack the political power of other minorities. While blacks numbered more than 27 million people in 1979 and Mexican-Americans more than 15 million, there were only 1 million Indians. Blacks and Mexican-Americans had some political power because of the votes they could mobilize, but native American power was much more ephemeral, highly dependent upon white opinion. Much of white liberalism in the 1960s rose from a sense of guilt about past sins. While blacks and Mexican-Americans were able to exploit the repentant attitudes of whites as well as exercise their own political power, native Americans had to rely on white help alone to generate social and political change. When ethnic activism became strong in the 1960s, other minorities broke with white liberals and took control of their own movements, but Indians could ill afford to alienate white supporters. That fact alone made the 1970s a period of confusion and stress, with Indians wondering if they could maintain the modest gains of recent years.

The Termination Program

After World War II a conservative mood blanketed America, and people yearned for more tranquil times when change had been slower and values more constant. Voices from the past sounded again. The National Council of Churches had commissioned a study of its mission system in 1944, and talk of assimilating the Indians reemerged. Anglo conformity had returned to Indian affairs. At the same time, the postwar boom in recreational camping turned the attention of white developers back to the reservations. They wanted to turn Indian land into large commercial farms or resort developments, to employ Indian land "productively." Ever since 1934 western congressmen had unsuccessfully tried to repeal the Indian Reorganization Act, dissolve the tribes, nullify their corporate authority, and remove Indian land from its trust status.

Conservative whites wanted to resolve all native American land claims against the federal government and assimilate the Indians. Some tribes had been trying for years to recover damages from the federal government for fraudulent treaty arrangements, and to settle those disputes Congress created the Indian Claims Commission in 1946. Indians immediately filed 852 claims for more than $1.2 billion, each claim arguing that the government had undervalued the land when the first treaties were negotiated. The Creeks, for example, had received $600,000 for Civil War property losses, and the Kiowas, Apaches, and Comanches a total of $2 million for undervalued real estate. Responding to a claim initiated by the Utes in the 1930s, the Indian Claims Commission awarded them $32 million in 1951. Except for the Ute settlement, however, the commission had awarded only $17.7 million by 1959. It became obvious that satisfactory settlement of all the claims would be impossible, but the attempt did pave the way for the "termination" program.

In 1950 President Truman appointed Dillon S. Myer commissioner of Indian affairs. Previously employed by the War Relocation Authority, Myer was an assimilationist who had tried to scatter Japanese-Americans among the general population in 1945. He brought that same commitment to the Bureau of Indian Affairs, hoping to dissolve the reservations and disperse native Americans throughout the country. On August 1, 1953, Congress inaugurated the termination program, passing resolutions removing federal authority over all Indian tribes, ending their status as wards of the United States, and granting them all the privileges of citizenship. State and local governments were to take legal jurisdiction over the reservations, and federal authority would be terminated.

During the Eisenhower Administration Congress "terminated" several tribes in western Oregon, the Alabama-Coushattas in Texas, the Utes and Paiutes in Utah, the Klamaths in Oregon, and the Menominis in Wisconsin. More than 1.6 million acres of reservation land fell into white hands between 1953 and 1956. Without federal funds and with tribal corporate power negated, "terminated" Indians had no means of livelihood and sold their land to support themselves. The Klamaths and Menominis suffered especially heavy losses. In 1953 about two thousand Klamaths owned more than 700,000 richly forested acres on the Oregon coast. When termination began, each Klamath could choose to leave his share of the property in a tribal trust or accept its cash value of $44,000. Most took the money and surrendered their claim in tribal property. Some of the land was sold to private interests, some reverted to the federal government, and local Oregon businessmen leased the rest. The Menominis numbered more than three thousand people and owned 234,000 acres of prime timber land in 1953. They controlled the reservation completely; produced lumber through their own logging and sawmill operations; supported their own schools and hospitals; maintained roads, plants, and buildings; and sustained their own police department. But termination created a new county for them, and a tribal corporation to manage assets; it also subjected the tribe to local and state taxes, ended federal assistance, and destroyed the reservation lumber industry. Poverty and unemployment ensued. Termination was a step backward, an assault on tribalism reflecting the values of the nineteenth rather than the twentieth century.

Native Americans and white liberals bitterly protested the program. Earl Old Person, head of the Blackfoot tribe, said:

> It is important to note that in our Indian language the only translation for termination is to "wipe out" or "kill off" . . . how can we plan our future when the Indian Bureau threatens to wipe us out as a race? It is like trying to cook a meal in your tipi when someone is standing outside trying to burn the tipi down.*

Ralph Nader denounced termination while he was editor of the *Harvard Law School Record* in 1957, and a number of liberal journals, including *Christian Century*, *Harper's*, and the *Nation*, openly criticized government policy. The National Congress of American Indians, a native American lobbying group formed in 1944, condemned termination, as did the Indian Rights Association and the Association of American Indian Affairs. By 1956 the antitermination movement had become so strong that Eisenhower called a halt to the termination program except in cases where individual tribes requested it. Once again the federal government was supporting tribal control of Indian land.

The New Indian Movement

After more than three hundred years white society still failed to grasp the essence of Indian life. Poverty stalked the reservations, and nearly three out of four Indians had incomes below the national average. Infant

* Quoted in Angie Debo, *A History of the Indians of the United States* (Norman, Okla., 1970), p. 307.

mortality rates were twice the national average; tuberculosis seven times as high; and life expectancy nearly ten years lower. By most economic indicators native Americans were far worse off than other Americans, and white liberals as well as Indians blamed the federal government for their plight. But even then, while whites looked upon reservation life in terms of the pathology of poverty, the Indians were still drawn irresistibly to the security of that environment. Whites were sympathetic about Indian poverty, but Indians had always been nonmaterialistic and noncompetitive, more concerned with the spiritual than the temporal. They had found freedom and tolerance within their communities, where they were at peace with their environment. True, they were poor by general standards, but they still nurtured a positive self-image based on a rich cultural heritage. And when white liberals proposed the same job training programs for Indians that they did for blacks—preparation for jobs which would incorporate native Americans into the white economy—many Indians objected, arguing that they were more interested in making the reservations self-sufficient than in joining white society.

But there was one major change in Indian attitudes. For the first time they began transcending tribal cultures for an "Indian" ethnicity. At the turn of the century peyotism, the Ghost Dance, the Sun Dance, and the Society of American Indians had brought some spirit of pan-Indian ethnicity. The formation of the National Congress of American Indians represented a more advanced stage of the movement, even though tribal differences were still too powerful to allow a self-conscious sense of interrelationship among all Indians. Then, as part of the termination program, the Bureau of Indian Affairs (BIA) relocated thousands of Indians to the cities where more economic opportunities supposedly existed. The BIA's goal, of course, was for Indians to acculturate into American society. Instead of assimilating, however, they congregated in ghetto colonies in Los Angeles, San Francisco, Salt Lake City, Phoenix, Denver, Chicago, and dozens of smaller cities. In the cities they also associated closely with Indians from other tribes. Facing poverty, discrimination, and the anonymity of urban life, yet detached from normal tribal relationships, they began to develop a group unity that crossed tribal lines and laid the foundation for the broad Indian organizations that would emerge in the 1960s and 1970s. Marriages outside the tribe also became common in the cities and helped generate a pan-Indian perspective.

The civil rights movement made white people more sensitive to Indian culture and society. Universities such as Stanford and Dartmouth abandoned the name "Indians" as titles for their sports teams. Stereotypical stories about native Americans, in which white successes were always "victories" and Indian successes always "massacres," appeared less frequently in the media. Films like *Little Big Man* (1970) and *A Man Called Horse* (1972) showed Indians in a sympathetic light, as did the Advertising Council's antipollution commercials featuring an Indian disappointed at civilization's rape of the land. Individual episodes of television programs like "The Waltons" and "Little House on the Prairie" presented positive images of Indian values. Books critical of white history and attitudes, including Dee Brown's *Bury My Heart at Wounded Knee* (1970) and Vine Deloria's *Custer Died for Your Sins* (1969), became best sellers. Guilty about past discriminations and prepared for change by the black rebellions of the 1960s, white Americans had become more sympathetic to Indians than ever before.

Other books and pamphlets extolling native American values appeared as Indians explained their point of view to the public. In his book *God Is Red* (1973) Vine Deloria, a Sioux, argued that the spirit of Christianity, its communal brotherhood and condemnation of materialism, had more in common with native American values than with white religions. Indians affirmed life over death, place over time, and the spiritual over the material, he argued, and offered much to the troubled psyches of industrialized society. Charles A. Eastman, a Santee Sioux and one of the founders of the Society of American Indians, had made a similar case for Indian values in *The Soul of an Indian* (1911), but it was more than sixty years before those ideas took hold in America.

The time was ripe for major changes in Indian affairs. Termination and relocation, blanketed as they were in the rhetoric of assimilation, had occurred so subtly and so closely behind the reforms of the Indian Reorganization Act, that native Americans realized they would have to keep a constant vigil against "developing" reservation land and "assimilating" the tribes. Building on the new pan-Indian spirit, white liberalism, and the renaissance of Indian values, they began organizing to promote civil rights, economic opportunity, and cultural autonomy. At the 1961 Chicago Indian Conference 420 Indians from sixty-seven tribes met to promote cultural pluralism. For years white groups like the Indian Rights Association and the American Indian Defense Association had led the struggle for native American rights, but in the 1960s Indians took control of the movement themselves.

Individual tribal organizations—such as the Iroquois League, DNA (a Navajo legal aid society), the All-Pueblo Council, the United Sioux Tribes, the United Southeast Tribes, and the Columbian Powhatan Confederacy—increased their activities. In the cities groups like the Southeast Council of Federated Eastern Indians in New York and the San Francisco Indian Cultural Center worked to keep Indians in touch with their past. And several pan-Indian associations developed in the

A native American demonstration in Washington, D.C. (Spia Press/Black Star)

1960s. Among the most moderate of them, counterparts of the NAACP and LULAC, were the American Indian Civil Rights Council, the American Indian Women's League, and Indians, Inc. More militant groups included the United Native Americans, the Young American Indian Council, the Organization of Native American Students, and the American Indian Movement (AIM).

Native American groups supported the civil rights movement and the War on Poverty, but some, such as AIM, also demanded the return of all land taken from them and complete tribal autonomy. It was an impossible crusade. By 1979, 220 million Americans depended on land once owned by native Americans, and regardless of the justice of Indian demands, the welfare of the white majority was too immediate. Surrendering the land would have thrown the economy into chaos. It would also have required a complete alteration of federal policy, as would giving Indian tribes total autonomy. Such demands pitted Indian activists against the BIA, the white community, and more moderate tribal leaders.

Whites viewed the AIM demands as hopelessly naïve, and many

Indians were afraid of AIM. Despite past abuses Indians were still the only group in the United States enjoying tax-exempt claims to a large body of land, independent tribal organizations free of state and local authority, and a cultural isolation protected by law and the social atmosphere. Moderates sympathized with the feelings of the radicals but feared they would alienate whites, destroy federal control of the reservations, and open Indian land to white interest groups, thus completing the process begun three hundred years ago.

The most pressing militant demand was the restoration of tribal lands. In western Nevada the Paiutes wanted Pyramid Lake and the land surrounding it, all of which had been guaranteed them in 1859, long before whites had seen any economic use for it. But later the Department of the Interior had constructed a dam on the Truckee River, and since then the lake had declined in size and the fish population had dwindled. In 1969 California negotiated an agreement with Nevada to divert the Truckee River, which would have destroyed Pyramid Lake. Tribal representatives fought the agreement, and in 1972 and 1973 court orders required the stabilization of Pyramid Lake at a size large enough to sustain tribal fishing needs. Paiute militance had succeeded.

The Taos Indians had similar claims on Blue Lake, an ancient tribal religious shrine in northwestern New Mexico. In 1906 the federal government had incorporated Blue Lake into the Carson National Forest, and since then the Forest Service had opened up the area to white hunters, fishermen, and campers. But for the Taos Indians the lake was the source of life and final resting place for the spirits of the dead. At a 1961 meeting of the Association on American Indian Affairs a Taos spokesman said:

> We don't have gold temples in this lake, but we have a sign of a living God to whom we pray—the living trees, the evergreen and spruce and the beautiful flowers and the beautiful rocks and the lake itself. . . . We are taking that water to give us strength so we can gain in knowledge and wisdom. . . . That is the reason this Blue Lake is so important to us.*

Late in the 1960s the Taos demanded the return of the lake. The Department of Agriculture, fearing the implications of returning land to the Indians, offered the Taos a cash payment instead, but the Indians refused. President Richard Nixon sympathized with their demands, and in 1970 Congress returned the lake and 48,000 acres of land to them.

The Pit River Indians of northern California had lost all their land in the gold rush of 1849 and in the 1950s demanded 3,368,000 acres which

*Ibid., pp. 354–355.

once had been theirs. The Indian Claims Commission decided in 1956 that the land had been taken illegally, and in 1963 the federal government awarded the Pit River Indians forty-seven cents per acre. They too refused the money, insisting on the return of the land. In June 1970 more than 150 Pit River Indians, impatient with government policy, occupied portions of Lassen National Park and Pacific Gas & Electric Company land which they claimed was Indian property. Dozens were arrested for trespassing and in early 1979 the land claim remained unsettled.

There were other examples. The Passamaquoddy Indians claimed much of the state of Maine; the Wampanoags much of central Massachusetts; and the Eklutnas of Alaska more than 378,000 acres. The Seminoles of Florida refused a congressional offer of $12 million for their land. In Littleton, Colorado, Indians occupied a BIA office to protest discrimination and corruption, and Sioux Indians camped on top of Mount Rushmore to claim it as tribal land. In 1969 a group called Indians of All Tribes occupied Alcatraz Island in San Francisco to dramatize their claims to the island, and in 1970 other Indians occupied Ellis Island in New York City and Fort Lawson in Puget Sound. In upstate New York the Iroquois fought to deny white hunting and fishing rights on their lands, and along the Puyallup River in Washington, state troopers drove Indians off fishing grounds they claimed as their own. More than 250 Chippewas occupied a lighthouse along Lake Superior in Michigan, and in 1975 Menominis took over a Roman Catholic monastery that was on former reservation land. Repossession of ancient tribal lands was the main objective of native American activism in the 1970s.

Activists were also determined to reform the Bureau of Indian Affairs and regain as much tribal autonomy as possible. Since 1824 the BIA had coordinated the reservation, allotment, termination, and relocation programs, and militant Indians felt that it had engineered the loss of tribal lands and sovereignty. To the militants, tribal leaders who cooperated with the BIA were either naïve dupes of white rhetoric or traitors to their birthright. The BIA was charged with insensitivity to tribal needs, a history of graft and corruption in shipping supplies to the reservations, a willingness to lease reservation resources at cheap rates to white interests, and a constant effort to force white education and values on Indians. In 1972 AIM members raided the BIA headquarters in Washington, D.C., to publicize their disgust for everything the bureau represented.

Then, in 1973, AIM leaders Russell Means and Dennis Banks headed for the Sioux reservation at Pine Ridge, South Dakota, took over the trading post, and expelled BIA officials. They demanded return of all

Sioux land, destruction of the BIA, removal of such tribal leaders as Richard Wilson of the Sioux Tribal Council, and a return to complete tribal sovereignty. Shots were exchanged and an FBI agent was killed. The incident alienated some whites and upset most middle-aged and older Indians who felt that destruction of the BIA would only turn Indians over to local authorities and end in another termination program. Demands for the return of tribal land and tribal sovereignty were as likely to succeed as Marcus Garvey's hope for a separate black state or Reies Tijerina's call for Mexican-American secession from the Southwest. AIM radicalism had polarized both white and native American opinion. The charges against Means and Banks were dismissed in their 1974 trial when a federal judge ruled that government prosecutors had tried to improperly influence the jury. More acculturated and yet more vocal about their plight than ever before, native Americans in the late 1970s were still a diverse and separate people in the United States.

SUGGESTED READINGS

Bahr, H. M., Chadwick, B. A., and Day, R. C., eds. *Native Americans Today: Sociological Perspectives.* New York: 1972.

Cahn, Edgar S., ed. *Our Brother's Keeper: The Indian in White America.* Washington, D. C.: 1969.

Cash, Joseph H., and Hoover, Herbert T. *To Be an Indian.* New York: 1971.

Debo, Angie. *A History of the Indians of the United States.* Norman, Oklahoma: 1970.

Deloria, Vine, Jr. *Custer Died for Your Sins: An Indian Manifesto.* New York: 1969.

———. *God Is Red.* New York: 1973.

———. *Of Utmost Good Faith.* San Francisco: 1971.

———. *We Talk, You Listen: New Tribes, New Turf.* New York: 1970.

Dozier, Edward P. *The Pueblo Indians of North America.* New York: 1970.

Hertzberg, Hazel W. *The Search for an American Indian Identity: Modern Pan-Indian Movements.* Syracuse, N.Y.: 1971.

Josephy, Alvin M. *Red Power.* New York: 1971.

Levy, Jerrold E., and Kunitz, Stephen H. *Indian Drinking: Navajo Practices and Anglo American Theories.* New York: 1974.

McNickle, D'Arcy. *Native American Tribalisms.* New York: 1973.

Price, John A. *Cultural Divergence Related to Urban Proximity on American Indian Reservations.* Minneapolis, Minn.: 1968.

———. "The Migration and Adaptation of American Indians to Los Angeles." *Human Organization*, 27 (Summer 1968), 168–175.

Reason, Charles. *Native Americans Today.* New York: 1972.

Simpson, George E., and Yinger, J. Milton, eds. *American Indians and American Life*. Philadelphia: 1957.

Sorkin, Alan C. *American Indians and Federal Aid*. Washington, D.C.: 1973.

Spindler, George, and Spindler, Louise. *Dreamers Without Power: The Menomini Indians*. New York: 1971.

Stanbury, W. T. *Success and Failure: Indians in Urban Society*. Vancouver, B.C.: 1976.

Szasz, Margaret. *Education and the American Indian: The Road to Self-Determination, 1928–1973*. Albuquerque, N.M.: 1974.

Washburn, Wilcomb E. *The Indian in America*. New York: 1975.

Wax, Murray L. *American Indians: Unity and Diversity*. New York: 1971.

Weyer, Edward, Jr. *Primitive Peoples Today*. Garden City, N.Y.: 1959.

Wissler, Clark. *Indians of the United States*. Garden City, N.Y.: 1970.

Witt, Shirley Hill, and Steiner, Stan. *The Way*. New York: 1972.

Chapter Twenty-Five

White Ethnics in Modern America

The search for community in postwar society—for equality, security, and stable neighborhoods—continued the most compelling urge in American history. But in a "nation of nations," as the ethnologist Louis Adamic called it, the quest for community seemed elusive, and its pursuit often resulted in competition and confrontation. While the headlines concentrated on blacks, Indians, and Hispanics, white ethnics were equally interested in making American values work for them. After decades of acculturation and some assimilation, several broad white ethnic groupings—Protestant, Jewish, Catholic, and Orthodox—had emerged in the United States, and their needs for security and equity would also help shape social and political life.

The White Protestants

The largest of the white subcommunities was made up of white Protestants. It is difficult to generalize about white Protestants because there has been so much conflict and competition among various groups divided by national origins, language, class, religion, occupation, and religious denomination. In 1850 a Dutch farmer in Michigan and a New England Yankee were both white Protestants but hardly members of the same ethnic group. English, Welsh, Scots, Dutch, German, and Scandinavian Americans were national, language, and religious groups rather than a single ethnic community. But throughout American history, at different stages in different places, white Protestant communities began to emerge. In New York after several generations Dutch Reformed settlers began to marry people of English descent to the point where early in the nineteenth century Dutch culture began to disappear. In the German triangle people from various German backgrounds intermarried until a larger German-American community developed, and members of that community in turn became close to people of British and Scandinavian backgrounds. In the colonial South the English, Scots, Scots-Irish, French Huguenots, and Germans slowly melted into a larger community based on race and religion.

White Protestants shared a host of values that served as the foundation for their community. Race and color were one bond. In the colonial period and early nineteenth century, race had been significant only in a negative sense. Being white brought German, English, and Scots-Irish southerners together because of the large number of blacks. The same was true of the English, Germans, and Scandinavians in the Midwest who feared the Indians, or the whites of the Southwest who disliked Mexicans and Indians. Later in the nineteenth century, when pseudo-scientific racist theories were put forward, the notion that Anglo-Saxon, Nordic, and Teutonic people were inherently superior to blacks, Indians, Asians, Jews, and Slavs became popular. All whites did not, of course articulate such ideas clearly, but the feeling that whites, especially north and west European whites, were better than other people became common.

Religious concerns similarly brought white Protestants together. Throughout American history Protestants argued incessantly over doctrine, but a common front, this time against Roman Catholicism, bound them together. From the anti-Catholic crusades of the 1840s, through the antics of the American Protective Association in the 1890s and the Ku Klux Klan in the 1920s, to the election of 1960, American Protestants have been linked by an uneasiness about, or even fear of, the Catholic church. Beyond that negative bond there were positive values shared by most Protestants. Because they had rejected centralized authority for some form of denominational or congregational autonomy, Protestants tended to be antiauthoritarian, suspicious of concentrated political or religious power. In their view religious sovereignty flowed up from the people through man-made bureaucracies rather than down to the people from a king or a pope. Out of such beliefs came the individualistic ethos of Protestantism. While the Catholic church insisted that man could be saved only through the church, the Protestants—whether in the predestination of the Calvinists, the Inner Light of the Quakers, or the "saving grace" of the evangelicals—believed people could be saved outside the church because the personal relationship with God transcended all institutions.

From that individualistic ethos came Protestant views of success and community. The development of capitalism in premodern Europe had given rise to an ambitious entrepreneurial class who resented Catholic restrictions on business enterprise. Businessmen saw in Protestantism a liberating force. Eventually Protestant theology not only liberated the entrepreneurial spirit from medieval restrictions but justified material success. Success became a sign of election and divine grace; the striving for success permeated Protestant values, not as a necessary evil but as a positive good.

Finally, Protestant individualism generated a new vision of community. While the older Catholic view of society had seen the whole as more important than any of its parts, Protestants elevated the individual and argued that the community was only a tool to promote individual goals. Once the community stopped serving individual needs, people were justified in breaking away. Protestants became, therefore, as mobile geographically as they were economically, willing to sever roots and move on to new opportunities whenever necessary, even if it meant leaving friends, relatives, and familiar places.

Most early Protestant immigrants had left peasant villages in Europe for rural America, but industrialization and urbanization had then pushed them into American cities. After World War II they moved on to the suburbs. Each time their roots and commitment to particular communities weakened, and to give themselves a sense of community the Protestants became "joiners," forming clubs and associations. Even their churches were essentially products of individual initiative, of new settlers starting their own independent congregations. In America a whole range of associational activities—YMCA, YWCA, Masons, Odd Fellows, Elks, Lions, Eagles, Moose, Kiwanis, Optimists, Rotary, Salvation Army, Gideons, Daughters of the American Revolution, country clubs, chambers of commerce, and professional groups—were overwhelmingly Protestant in composition, attempts to reconstruct community life.

Although white Protestants, because of their numbers, were scattered throughout society, they dominated elite groups during most of American history. In the largest banks, insurance companies, foundations, universities, and industrial corporations, Protestants controlled the boards of directors, and until 1945 they were dominant in the sciences, professions, and government. Even when they were not well-to-do, as in the case of farmers and skilled workers in the AFL, they often supported conservative values, especially in social, moral, and political affairs. That was an irony of white Protestant history. Extremely flexible and adventurous in economic matters, and in the vanguard of the Industrial Revolution, at the same time they favored prohibition, immigration restriction, and Sunday blue laws, and opposed gambling, prostitution, and parochial schools. In the nineteenth century most of the German, Scandinavian, and British Protestants in the North joined the Republican party, which was rural, abolitionist, and anti-Catholic. And even in the South, where white Protestants stayed in the Democratic party, they were still rural and conservative in their approach to social affairs. Individualistic, independent, democratic, ruralistic, antiauthoritarian, opportunistic economically, but conservative socially—these were the characteristics of Protestants.

It was only natural that as assimilation blurred the hard lines of national origin, language, and denomination, German, Dutch, British, and Scandinavian Americans would begin to form a more collective identity. It occurred slowly. In the second generation, as English became the main language of the communities, social relations among Protestants became easier. When industrialization and the two world wars attracted rural Protestants to the cities and disrupted kinship networks, they became more willing to associate with other Protestants from different backgrounds and did so frequently in their secular organizations. After World War II mass culture and mass consumerism gave them even more in common. And as they maintained their commitment to geographical and occupational mobility, Protestants from different national and denominational backgrounds found themselves in the same schools, neighborhoods, churches, clubs, and jobs.

More important, shared Protestant values and rapid mobility had led to ethnic and denominational intermarriage. British-Americans in Nebraska, for example, married endogamously (i.e., within the ethnic community) 49 percent of the time in 1909–1913, but only 37 percent in 1921–1925. British in-marriage rates in New Haven, Connecticut, fell from 72 percent in 1900 to 54 percent in 1950. Among Nebraska and Wisconsin Germans, endogamous marriages dropped from 81 percent in 1910 to 61 percent in 1925. In New Haven German in-marriages declined from 55 percent in 1900 to 40 percent in 1930 to 27 percent in 1950. Among Scandinavians in New York endogamous marriages declined from 61 percent in 1908 to 44 percent in 1921 to 40 percent in 1939. In New Haven Scandinavian intermarriages increased from only 17 percent in 1900 to 67 percent in 1930 to 78 percent in 1950. Nearly 60 percent of all Finnish marriages in Ohio in 1895 were endogamous, but only 25 percent were in 1935.

Those who intermarried almost always married other Protestants—the Dutch preferring Germans or Scandinavians; the Finns other Scandinavians or Germans; and the English other British Protestants, then

Scandinavians and Germans. As this occurred in generation after generation between 1840 and 1970, the descendants of mixed ethnic and denominational marriages acquired a sense of identity based on being white and Protestant. After World War II, as mass education, mass culture, and mobility became even more extensive, intermarriage rates increased and national-origin visions blurred even more.

Lutheran churches provide a good example of the blurring of national-origin perspectives. During the nineteenth century the German, Swedish, Danish, Norwegian, and Finnish Lutheran churches constantly fragmented over language and doctrinal questions. But in the twentieth century a number of mergers took place. In 1917 several Norwegian churches united into the Norwegian Lutheran Church; in 1918 the United Lutheran Church of America was formed; in 1960 the Norwegian Lutheran Church, the American Lutheran Church, and several evangelical Danish Lutheran churches merged together as the American Lutheran Church; and in 1962 the United Evangelical Danish Lutheran Church, the Finnish Apostolic Lutheran Church, the Augustana (Swedish) Lutheran Church, and a German and Norwegian Lutheran synod formed the Lutheran Church in America. People of Germanic and Scandinavian backgrounds, after generations of intermarriage, had come to look upon themselves as white Protestants and Lutherans as well as Germans or Scandinavians. Similar feelings developed among English and Welsh Methodists, Scots and Scots-Irish Presbyterians, Scandinavian and British Mormons, Episcopalians, and Congregationalists. To a lesser extent this was also true of Baptists, Disciples of Christ, Pentecostals, and Dutch and German Reformed.

Episcopalians, Methodists, Reformed, Presbyterians, and Congregationalists had high rates of intermarriage to other Protestants; and although most of them were still aware of ethnic roots, tens of millions had also acquired identities based on church, class, occupational, regional, and social loyalties as well as an increasing sense of being part of the white Protestant community. More than 900,000 Germans, 560,000 British, and 1 million Canadians immigrated after 1945 and nurtured the old ethnic cultures, but by the late 1970s nearly 110 million Americans identified with a white Protestant community, although only 70 million claimed a specific church membership.

The Jews

Although Sephardic and Chassidic Jews remained aloof, by 1945 German, Russian, Polish, Hungarian, and Rumanian Jews were all merging into a larger Jewish-American community. Many came from urban environments, and unlike some other immigrants, they were permanent residents from the beginning. Arriving with their families, they wanted economic security, and immediately after settling into the tenements, they set up businesses serving the Jewish community or found jobs as skilled tradesmen, providing a solid foundation for the Jewish business elite and the urban labor movement. While other immigrants moved slowly from unskilled to skilled and white-collar jobs, the Jewish reverence for education and the interest of parents in the success of their children lifted them quickly out of working-class life. By the 1970s more than 90 percent of college-age Jews were enrolled in colleges and universities; more than 80 percent of Jewish men were professionals, businessmen, or sales personnel; less than 10 percent were in blue-collar jobs; and Jewish family incomes were higher than those of any other ethnic group.

Out of the Jewish community came the Lehmans and Seligmans in finance; the Altmans and Gimbels in merchandising; Sidney Hillman and David Dubinsky in the labor movement; Irving Shapiro of Du Pont and William Paley of CBS; and the remarkable Jewish intellectual community, including such writers as Norman Mailer, Philip Roth, Alfred Kazin, Saul Bellow, and Bernard Malamud; the historians Oscar Handlin and Richard Hofstadter; scientists such as Jonas Salk; film producer Stanley Kubrick; and symphony conductor Leonard Bernstein. Also to be noted are Jacob Javits, Abraham Ribicoff, and Bella Abzug in politics; Fanny Brice, Sophie Tucker, Groucho Marx, Joan Rivers, Milton Berle, Jack Benny, George Burns, Lenny Bruce, Beverly Sills, and Barbra Streisand in entertainment; and Lillian Wald and Elizabeth Stern in social work. The transplanted ghetto, so close in time and spirit to the Old World, was the staging area for the most successful immigrant saga in American history.

Success and its implications, however, seemed to destroy the very communities Jews had worked so hard to build. While America offered Jews more security than any other nation, acceptance threatened Jewish ethnicity. Centuries of persecution and visions of being a chosen people had molded a sense of communality, but American prosperity weakened mutual dependence just as secularization was eroding religious ethnocentrism. As more and more successful Jews moved to the suburbs, Jewish life underwent profound changes. In the 1970s Orthodox synagogues in the urban centers seemed far away, and suburban temples, Reform or Conservative, became the focus of social life. The modern, tastefully appointed buildings staffed by American-trained rabbis, however, were more social than religious centers—secularized community headquarters for fund drives, lectures, social gatherings, and clubs. Familiarity with spoken Yiddish and older religious ceremonies lagged, as did attendance at services. Intermarriage with non-Jews climbed steadily after World War II. Most of the 6 million American Jews still valued family life, respectability, pacific conduct, philanthropy, education, and their Jewish identities in the 1970s, but many worried about whether Jewish ethnicity could survive another century in the United States.

Roman Catholic and Orthodox Americans

Two more melting pots in white America consisted of nearly 50 million Roman Catholics and 4 million Eastern Orthodox in the late 1970s. Most Catholic and Orthodox immigrants had left peasant villages, and except for temporary stays in European cities they had had only limited contact with urban life. In the United States they accepted low-paying, unskilled jobs in mines, foundries, mills, and factories. With deep ties to land, village, and family, most of them, except the Irish and German Catholics, planned to work here for a little while, save their money, and return home to pay off mortgages, buy new land, and reconstruct Old World communities. At first they were relatively unconcerned about getting ahead in America, not caring for skilled jobs or success as long as thoughts of going home dominated daily life. Crowded into wretched tenements, laboring in dead-end jobs, cut off from friends and family, they had difficult beginnings in America.

But they rose above that poverty. After a few years they realized that Old World villages were gone forever. The Slavs, Magyars, Italians, Greeks, Rumanians, Syrians, and Armenians planted permanent roots and reconstructed village perspectives in the New World. They worked hard, saved money to purchase homes, and donated money to build urban parishes. Their ghetto communities were mixed neighborhoods where other ethnic groups lived, shopped, worked, and went to school. Ethnic-language churches, parochial schools, mutual aid societies, ethnic businesses, and parish organizations circumscribed life in the Catholic and Orthodox communities. The move out of poverty was slow and uneven, depending on the group's length of time in the United States and its Old World experiences, but all improved their living standards during the twentieth century.

Advancement was especially difficult for the Irish. There were many success stories—including the Kennedys in Boston and the Buckleys in New York—but work on canals, railroads, and mills, and life in shantytowns did not leave much of an economic base for success. Instead of taking an entrepreneurial route to prosperity, the Irish often turned to politics and the church. Such Irish clerics as James Cardinal Gibbons,

John Ireland, Richard Cardinal Cushing, John Hughes, Dennis Cardinal Dougherty, Francis Cardinal Spellman, James Cardinal McIntyre, and John Cardinal Cody controlled Catholic parishes, parochial schools, hospitals, and orphanages. Irish bosses dominated politics in the Democratic wards of major American cities, and the names of colorful politicians like James Michael Curley of Boston, Tom Pendergast of Kansas City, Al Smith of New York, Richard Daley of Chicago, and of course the Kennedy brothers in Massachusetts became household words. Along with political power went jobs in the police, fire, and sanitation departments, the civil service, public schools, and public construction. From there the Irish moved rapidly into middle- and upper-class life after World War II. Except for pockets of poverty like parts of South Boston, most Irish-Americans had joined the middle class by 1975.

For the first time since the Great Famine, Irish-American concern for Ireland waned, particularly after the final separation of Ireland (except Northern Ireland) and England in 1921 and the decline of Irish immigration after 1924. The conflict in Northern Ireland during the 1960s and 1970s, as well as the visits of Bernadette Devlin to promote Catholic rights in Ulster, inspired Irish-American sympathy, but it did not compare with Irish-American nationalism in the nineteenth century.

The Irish of the 1930s, after nearly a century in America, had taken advantage of education, and by 1940 Catholic secondary schools were dominated by Irish-American faculties and students. After leaving the service in 1945, hundreds of thousands of Irish GIs went to college on the GI Bill and took up jobs in education, the professions, business, and government. The old ghettos dissolved as southern blacks moved in and Irish-Americans headed for the suburbs.

The Italian-American experience was difficult, too, as historian Alexander DeConde said, "half bitter and half sweet." Italians left the grinding poverty of the Mezzogiorno, but at first most were single males who eschewed status in America for some savings to take back to Italy. Only when their families began joining them did southern Italians look for skilled jobs and economic security. Their economic success was retarded because first-generation Italians viewed loyalty to the family as the ultimate value. They were suspicious of education because it involved alien ideas, association with strangers, and geographical and occupational mobility. The early immigrants discouraged it, urging their children instead to find a "good job."

The children of immigrants were more likely than their parents to become skilled and white-collar workers, but generational differences were narrower for Italians than for most other new immigrants. The third and fourth generations, however, responded less to old commu-

A Slovenian-American family dressed for church on Palm Sunday. The traditional costumes reflect their pride in their ethnic heritage. (Katrina Thomas/Photo Researchers, Inc.)

nity pressures and more to the American emphasis on competitive achievement. These Italian-Americans began to enter the middle class, and, represented by people like Frank Rizzo in Philadelphia, Anthony Imperiale in Newark, and Joseph Alioto and George Moscone in San Francisco, Italian-American political power became a force to be reckoned with. The tenure of Lee A. Iacocca first in the Presidency of Ford Motor Company and then at the Chrysler Corporation, and John Riccardo at Chrysler symbolized the economic arrival of Italian-Americans.

East European immigrants—Slavs, Hungarians, Rumanians, and Greeks—and Syrians and Armenians also enjoyed success and mobility in postwar America. Most had come with few industrial skills and at first no intention of staying. The Slavs and Hungarians suspected intellectuals and worried about the impact of American education. The original migrations from Europe had been socially complex affairs, often with educated professionals and intellectuals leading the way in the mid-nineteenth century, followed by peasant immigrants after 1890. German Poles preceded the Galician and Russian Poles; Bohemian intellectuals inaugurated the migration from Czechoslovakia; and Louis Kossuth's political refugees arrived ahead of the Magyar peasants. The upper classes valued education, but the peasants suspected it with a hostility bordering on antiintellectualism, for neither Catholic dogma nor the economic demands of peasant villages had rewarded educational achievement. Transplanting their suspicions to America, they destined themselves and their children to blue-collar occupations. But by the 1970s the east European communities were quite different from the earlier ones. No longer unskilled workers living in tenements and worshiping in Irish-dominated parishes, they had skilled jobs and white-collar status (more than 25 percent had become businessmen, professionals, and technicians), and had their own homes and churches.

At first the Catholic and Orthodox immigrants avoided labor unions. But when the Great Depression destroyed whatever economic security they had achieved, they flocked to the unions of the CIO: International Ladies Garment Workers, Amalgamated Clothing Workers, United Automobile Workers, United Mine Workers, United Steel Workers, and the Packinghouse Workers. They generally became loyal Democrats. After 1932 a coalition of Jewish and Catholic immigrants, workers, northern blacks, southern whites, and intellectuals put Franklin D. Roosevelt in the White House, filled Congress with Democrats, and became the foundation for the New Deal, Fair Deal, New Frontier, and Great Society—the most influential liberal reforms in American history. When John Fitzgerald Kennedy won the presidency in 1960, it seemed that the American gospel of success had fulfilled its promise to the Catholic minority. By the mid 1970s Irish, German, Italian, and Slavic Catholics had achieved educational parity with the American population in general, and the family incomes of European Catholic communities were above the national average.

Sources of Social and Economic Unrest

Successful as they were, Catholics were not far enough from their immigrant past to be complacent. Especially for those in the original settlements—Poles in Chicago, Italians in New York, Irish in Boston, Slovaks in Cleveland—the institutional ghetto was largely intact. Ethnic newspapers were declining and some ethnic associations disappearing, but ethnic consciousness and profound attachments to community and neighborhood survived. So did a certain insecurity about whether Americans were ready to accept cultural pluralism. John Kennedy's victory over Richard Nixon had been perilously narrow and the issue of religion had never gone away. Anti-Catholicism was mild compared with the paranoia surrounding Al Smith's campaign in 1928, but old epithets—"Polack," "dago," "wop," "hunkie," or "bohunk"—had not disappeared, and the popularity of "Polish" and "Italian" jokes revealed a continuing prejudice against eastern and southern Europeans. Italian-Americans were particularly irritated about tendencies to link them with organized crime. Consequently, even in the 1970s Catholics were still uneasy about their place in American society.

Nor were their economic fortunes guaranteed. Although younger Catholics in the 1970s had surpassed national averages in education and income, older Catholics were still blue-collar workers. Memories of the Great Depression were still vivid, and periodic swings in the business cycle and long stretches of unemployment, such as those resulting from lay-offs in the automobile industry in 1974 and the steel industry in 1977, made economic security fragile indeed. Changes in the American economy and in the cities were also threatening, for as the economy reached postindustrial maturity, the number of blue-collar jobs declined and white-collar jobs increased. Technological innovations were eliminating more blue collar jobs, and structural unemployment grew progressively worse. Labor unions were losing power in politics and social affairs. Businesses relocated in the suburbs, city tax bases eroded, and property owners were forced to bear the costs of education and social services. People who had struggled to buy homes for their families resented high property taxes, which threatened home ownership itself. And at the same time they had to deal with an inflationary spiral that outpaced wage increases.

Jews too worried about the future. No matter how secure they felt economically, vestiges of anti-Semitism still existed in postwar America. Social and business clubs still refused Jews membership; the great corporate board rooms were still largely without Jewish executives; and some Ivy League universities maintained anti-Jewish admission quotas as late as the 1950s. Central to postwar Jewish ethnicity was the Holocaust; it sensitize Jews to every strain of anti-Semitism, and no group in American society would become more committed to civil liberty and community security. The Holocaust also politicized American Jews, helping to offset the secularizing and assimilating forces in the United States.

Like an older Irish-American nationalism, Jewish ethnicity revolved around another country—Israel. In the late 1940s and early 1950s Israel was settled largely by survivors of the Holocaust. For most American

Jews the subtleties of international politics and diplomacy seemed irrelevant to the overwhelming question of Jewish survival, and Israel
seemed the only guarantee that world Judaism would endure. Israel
became the common ground on which American Jews united, and its
cause submerged some of the traditional differences between Jewish
businesses and Jewish unions, Jewish socialism and Zionism, and the
Reformed, Conservative, and Orthodox sects. For religious Jews Israel
represented the fulfillment of prophecy, the final stage in the dynamic
of Jewish history, and for secular Jews Israel was an alternative to
assimilation, a means of preserving ethnicity outside religion, of sustaining a secular faith in a secular American society.

Finally, Catholics and Jews were troubled about social change in
America. Most changes were inevitable transformations of Old World
customs in the New World society, but they were unnerving nonetheless. Old World families seemed doomed. When both parents worked to
make ends meet, children were naturally more independent and less
responsive to parental authority. At the same time, life in an industrialized society made children economic liabilities rather than economic
assets. In the old peasant villages children had had specific farming
chores to perform, but in American cities, with the obligations of school
and social pressure, adolescents were economically dependent on parents for many years. Parents complained about the difficulty of raising
children in the United States. After World War II hundreds of
thousands of veterans moved out of the old ethnic settlements for the
cities of the South and West, and throughout the 1960s and 1970s that
trend continued. Immigration from Europe had disrupted extended
families, but total dispersal of the extended family became com-
monplace in twentieth-century America as children and grandchildren
moved far away from home and returned only for occasional holidays
and short vacations. Parents realized that college education was important for prosperity and success, but at the same time, especially in the
1960s, colleges seemed to be giving young people strange ideas. They
became rebellious, critical of traditional values and of the church. The
two bastions of Old World culture, family and church, both changed in
the twentieth century. For Jews and the Catholic and Orthodox groups,
America still held out its promise, but beneath the dream was a troubling
reality.

The Impact of the Civil Rights Movement

Against the background of these fears and successes, the civil rights
movement during the 1960s and 1970s created a social and political
climate where white ethnicity flourished, acting as a catalyst for cultural

controversies. White ethnic groups never opposed the principle of equality; indeed, they were among the earliest supporters of egalitarianism. White Protestants in the Republican party implemented the Thirteenth, Fourteenth, and Fifteenth amendments in the 1860s and 1870s, and white ethnic groups in the CIO unions opened their doors to black workers in the 1930s, served as the power base behind Hubert Humphrey's civil rights stand at the Democratic convention of 1948, and provided the margin of victory for the Civil Rights Act of 1964. People close to discrimination themselves proved more than willing to oppose *de jure* discrimination against others. But when the black power movement gained momentum, when violence erupted in the streets, and when the federal government turned to quotas and neighborhood engineering, many whites were outraged at what they considered a perversion of liberalism. A political coalition began to emerge between white Protestant Republicans who opposed a large federal government and Jews and Catholics who felt the federal government was becoming invasive and anticommunity.

The problem was that civil rights bills could neither erase the legacy of slavery nor solve the problems of black ghettos; equality and economic security did not materialize overnight and blacks began focusing on *de facto* discrimination. A few blacks took to the streets in the 1960s to protest poverty and discrimination. Concerned about equality and the social order, the federal government began in the 1970s to enforce open housing laws, bus children across district lines to achieve racial integration, redesign electoral districts to achieve racial balances, force employers to subordinate seniority rights to those of recently hired minority workers, and impose racial quotas on the admissions and promotion policies of universities, local government, and private businesses.

But in attempting to reverse three centuries of discrimination, the government failed to understand the immigrant background and white ethnicity. Profoundly committed to homes, families, and neighborhoods as part of a peasant heritage—to houses, parishes, synagogues, schools, and playgrounds—white ethnic groups felt threatened by expanding black ghettos and the arbitrary busing of children. Insecure about their jobs in a troubled economy, they viewed union seniority rights as natural laws and were incensed at even the suggestion of modification. And in the college quotas and affirmative action programs they saw a future in which the road to affluence might be blocked by the demands of blacks, Mexican-Americans, Asian-Americans, Puerto Ricans, and native Americans. Even the Democratic party, their link to political power, had deserted them in 1972 when the delegation from Chicago, led by Mayor Richard Daley, was denied seating at the Democratic convention because it did not meet the racial, age, and sexual quotas demanded by the Democratic National Committee and liberal supporters of Senator George McGovern.

When blamed for black poverty and inequality, white ethnic groups were quick to reply that they had not been around during slavery and were not responsible for segregation or black ghettos. They argued that they had arrived in the cities at the same time as most blacks and Mexican-Americans were settling there and that they had encountered a good deal of discrimination themselves. They simply refused to be blamed, and instead of viewing the later phase of the civil rights movement as a legitimate campaign for equality, many saw it as an illegitimate attempt to destroy their neighborhoods. While blacks saw "law and order" as a euphemism for prejudice, white ethnics viewed it as a means of preserving their neighborhoods from violence. When the Catholic parents of Detroit or South Boston protested busing, or the Chassidic Jews of New York complained about federally-mandated electoral redistricting, or when labor unions sued to protect seniority rights, or when the whole Jewish community raised its voice against university quotas, or when the Irish, Polish, and Lithuanian people of Marquette Park, Illinois, opposed black civil rights marches, it was not simply prejudice. Some racism was involved because few circles in white society were free of bias, but for the most part the white ethnic groups were protesting what they saw as the imposition of reverse discrimination.

Among Jews as well as Catholics a new sense of community, and a readiness to express it, emerged in the 1960s and 1970s. Ethnic studies programs, first confined to schools and colleges attended by members of racial minorities, spread across the country in the 1970s and embraced many white ethnic groups. Meir Kahane formed the Jewish Defense League in 1968 to denounce anti-Semitism, condemn Jewish impulses to assimilate, and radicalize American support of Israel. Joseph Colombo established the Italian-American Civil Rights League, which attacked negative Italian stereotypes and the tendency to associate Italian-Americans with organized crime. Anthony Imperiale of Newark organized the North Ward Cultural and Educational Center late in the 1960s to dramatize Italians' commitment to their own neighborhoods. In 1978 Anthony Krzywicki led the Polish-American Affairs Council in demanding the resignation of Attorney General Griffin Bell for repeating "Polish" jokes. The Committee for the Defense of the Polish Name announced that although slandered,

ridiculed, and misrepresented in the media as "dumb Polacks," Polish-Americans have, for the most part, remained silent. This silence, with all its implications of ineffectuality, fear and intimidation, is the greatest

> problem facing the Polish-American community today. . . . What the
> Polish-American community needs more than anything else is an effective
> process of consciousness raising . . .*

Bumper stickers proclaiming "Polish power" or "Slovak power" or "Irish
power" began to appear around the country, as did "I'm Proud to Be
Polish" clubs and "I'm Proud to Be Irish" clubs. With the unprecedented
popularity of Alex Haley's novel *Roots* and its 1977 ABC serialization on
television, as well as NBC's 1978 presentation of "Holocaust," whites as
well as blacks turned toward personal histories in search of their origins.
The age of white ethnicity had arrived.

Beneath the rhetoric of pride and power, several concrete assumptions formed the ideological core of white ethnicity. Most important,
ethnic groups argued that pluralism was not just a racial phenomenon
but an ethnic one as well, that a large melting pot even among whites
would not emerge in the near future. They demanded respect from
society, insisting that social engineering should not destroy community
institutions and neighborhoods. Implicit in this point of view was a
conviction that all racial and ethnic groups maintain themselves voluntarily and that the government should take the approach it has traditionally assumed toward religions—doing nothing either to promote or
to destroy them. For white ethnic groups who valued community so
highly, it was not the purpose of the government to sponsor residential,
educational, or occupational dispersion programs, especially when
there was little evidence of overt discrimination.

Along with a broad view of cultural pluralism, these whites opposed
political and economic discrimination, but they also interpreted the
First, Fifth, and Fourteenth amendments on individual rather than
community lines. While working to end discrimination against individuals, the government must not accept a partnership with formally
organized ethnic groups and must never give exclusive benefits to particular groups at the expense of other groups. When Alan Bakke sued
the University of California at Davis for denying him admission to the
medical school because sixteen places had been reserved for members of
minority and disadvantaged groups, the white ethnic community rallied
to his defense. Legal briefs were filed on his behalf by the American
Jewish Committee, the American Jewish Congress, the Italian-
American Foundation, the Polish-American Affairs Council, the
Polish-American Educators Association, the Hellenic Bar Association,
and the Ukrainian Congress Committee of America.

Most white ethnic groups agreed that discrimination against individu-

---

* Quoted in Helen Z. Lopata, *Polish Americans* (Englewood Cliffs, N.J., 1976), p. 77.

als on the basis of race, religion, or national origins was wrong, but they also protested arbitrary government quotas that discriminated against individuals not included in the arrangement. They were committed to equality and pluralism, but not to a system in which the government obliterated communities, neighborhoods, and individual futures in the name of freedom. Now more vocal than ever before, they were unwilling to accept either ridicule or discrimination.

SUGGESTED READINGS

Alba, Richard. "Social Assimilation Among American Catholic National-Origins Groups." *American Sociological Review*, 41 (December 1976), 1030–1046.

Anderson, Charles. *White Protestant Americans: From National Origins to Religious Groups*. Englewood Cliffs, N.J.: 1970.

Bartley, Numan V. *The Rise of Massive Resistance: Race and Politics in the South During the 1950s*. Baton Rouge, La.: 1969.

Blau, Joseph L. *Judaism in America: From Curiosity to Third Faith*. Chicago: 1976.

Cohen, Naomi W. *American Jews and the Zionist Ideal*. New York: 1975.

Friedman, Murray. *Overcoming Middle Class Rage*. New York: 1971.

Gallo, Patrick J. *Ethnic Alienation: The Italian-Americans*. Cranbury, N.J.: 1974.

Galush, William J. "Faith and Fatherland: Dimensions of Polish-American Ethnoreligion, 1875–1975." In Randall Miller and Thomas Marzik. *Immigrants and Religion in Urban America*. Philadelphia: 1977.

Gambino, Richard. *Blood of My Blood: The Dilemma of Italian Americans*. Garden City, N.Y.: 1975.

Gans, Herbert. *The Urban Villagers: Group and Class in the Life of Italian-Americans*. New York: 1962.

Glazer, Nathan, and Moynihan, Daniel P. *Beyond the Melting Pot: The Negroes, Puerto Ricans, Jews, Italians, and Irish of New York City*. Cambridge, Mass.: 1963.

Greeley, Andrew M. *The American Catholic*. New York: 1977.

———. *The Denominational Society: A Sociological Approach to Religion in America*. Glenview, Ill.: 1972.

———. "Ethnicity and Racial Attitudes: The Case of the Jews and Poles." *American Journal of Sociology*, 80 (January 1975), 909–933.

———. *That Most Distressful Nation: The Taming of the American Irish*. Chicago: 1972.

Greene, Victor. *For God and Country: The Rise of Polish and Lithuanian Ethnic Consciousness in America*. Madison, Wisconsin: 1975.

Guttman, Allen. *The Jewish Writer in America: Assimilation and the Crisis of Identity*. New York: 1971.

Howe, Irving. *World of Our Fathers: The Journey of the East European Jews and the Life They Found and Made*. New York: 1976.

Hudson, Winthrop. *American Protestantism*. Chicago: 1961.

Krickus, Richard. *Pursuing the American Dream: White Ethnics and the New Populism*. Garden City, N.Y.: 1976.

Levine, Edward M. *The Irish and Irish Politicians*. Notre Dame, Ind.: 1966.

Lopata, Helen Z. *Polish-Americans: Status Competition in an Ethnic Community*. Englewood Cliffs, N.J.: 1976.

Marty, Martin. *Righteous Empire: The Protestant Experience in America*. New York: 1970.

McCaffrey, Lawrence J. *The Irish Diaspora in America*. Bloomington, Ind.: 1976.

Nelson, E. Clifford. *Lutheranism in North America, 1914–1970*. Minneapolis, Minn.: 1972.

Novak, Michael. *The Rise of the Unmeltable Ethnic*. New York: 1971.

Parot, Joseph. "Ethnic Versus Black Metropolis: The Origins of Polish-Black Housing Tensions in Chicago." *Polish American Studies*, 29 (Spring-Autumn 1972), 5–21.

Pienkos, Donald. "Dimensions of Ethnicity: A Preliminary Report on the Milwaukee Polish-American Population." *Polish American Studies*, 30 (Spring 1973), 5–24.

Rabinowitz, Dorothy. *New Lives: Survivors of the Holocaust Living in America*. New York: 1976.

Roland, Charles. *Improbable Era: The South Since World War II*. Lexington, Kentucky: 1975.

Rossell, Christine H. "School Desegregation and White Flight." *Political Science Quarterly*, 90 (Winter 1975–76), 675–696.

Ryan, Joseph, ed. *White Ethnics: Their Life in Working Class America*. Englewood Cliffs, N.J.: 1973.

Sandberg, Neil C. "The Changing Polish-American." *Polish American Studies*, 31 (Spring 1974), 5–16.

Schrag, Peter. *The Decline of the WASP*. New York: 1973.

Snetsinger, John. *Truman, the Jewish Vote, and the Creation of Israel*. Stanford, Cal.: 1974.

Tindall, George B. *The Ethnic Southerners*. Baton Rouge, La.: 1975.

Tomasi, Silvano M., ed. *Perspectives in Italian Immigration and Ethnicity*. New York: 1977.

Weed, Perry. *The White Ethnic Movement and Ethnic Politics*. New York: 1973.

Wenk, Michael, Tomasi, Silvano, and Baroni, Geno. *Pieces of a Dream: The Ethnic Worker's Crisis with America*. New York: 1972.

Wilhoit, Francis M. *The Politics of Massive Resistance*. New York: 1973.

Summary

Ethnic America Today

Today, more than ever before, assimilation is working against specific cultural identities based on national origins and in favor of loyalties based on income, occupation, religion, residence, and multinational heritages. More than fifty years after the National Origins Act, Old World immigrants no longer infuse new vitality into the ethnic cultures, at least not in the magnitude of earlier times. The European immigrant communities are at least two generations removed from the Old World, and the longer they remain without reinforcement from home, the more they accept American values. Some groups—like the colonial Dutch, Scots-Irish, Welsh, and French Huguenots—have largely disappeared; older immigrant Protestants are more assimilated than newer immigrant Catholics and Jews; and only the recent Puerto Rican, Cuban, Chinese, Japanese, Mexican and Vietnamese immigrants, along with blacks and native Americans, are still culturally distinct as nationality groups in the United States.

The most important step in acculturation was the loss of the Old World language, and among western European Protestants, European Catholics, Jews, Asians, and even native Americans, English has become the language of home, church, school, and commerce. Although some members of white ethnic groups are acquainted with the spoken word of their ancestors, they are rarely able to read or write it. The foreign-language press has dropped in circulation and publications by 90 percent since 1920; the nationality-parish issue no longer causes contention within the Catholic church; ethnic-language parochial schools are almost extinct; and associations based on Old World origins and dialects are disappearing. Although some recent Supreme Court decisions and federal legislation require public schools to offer bilingual education, English will no doubt continue to replace all other languages in the United States.

Other institutions have promoted acculturation. Newspapers before World War I, and also radio and films before World War II, constituted the communications media, but after 1945 television became the most potent mass medium. All over America, in practically every home, people from different backgrounds absorb a single mass-consumer culture as large corporations bombard them with slick commercials and bland programming. As parochial schools declined and public schools assumed the responsibility for mass education, Anglo-American values were further reinforced. And as junior, senior, and technical colleges mushroomed after World War II, higher education took on the aura of a natural right and a consensus of values spread throughout the country. Although Americans have by no means become homogenized, similar customs, role models, and values permeate nationality groups to one degree or another. Commercial advertisers have encouraged uniform tastes for housing, cars, clothes, and consumer goods; television and films have made actors, actresses, professional athletes, and entertainers familiar to everyone and role models for young people; American celebrations of Christmas, Thanksgiving, and the Fourth of July are observed by most Americans regardless of cultural background; and older Puritan values of material success and competitive achievement are widely accepted.

Socioeconomic and geographic mobility are also contributing to acculturation. Descendants of Catholic and Jewish immigrants have gone on to higher education in such large numbers that family income for them has reached, and for Jews and Irish Catholics surpassed, the national average. Education reshapes perspectives, challenges traditions, and creates new loyalties. Educated people tend to discard old prejudices and are more willing to move to new places. In the newer suburbs or cities of the "Sunbelt," the families, parishes, synagogues, and neighborhoods of the North and East can no longer pull on loyalties, and national origins perspectives must compete with other social divisions. Instead of revolving around questions of nationality, politics there revolves around local issues such as schools, zoning, and taxes, and federal policies, such as busing, that affect the community. Generally successful and far from their old ethnic neighborhoods, Protestants, Catholics, and Jews have lost some of the overt manifestations of national origins ethnicity.

When people move to new locales and associate with new people in church, school, and on the job, intermarriage and the subsequent dilution of national origins values is inevitable. Among racial minorities, intermarriage is still uncommon, but even there its frequency is rising. By the late 1970s Japanese-Americans were marrying exogamously half the time, Puerto Ricans in the second generation nearly 40 percent of the time, and Mexican-Americans nearly 30 percent of the time. Among whites, intermarriage is fast becoming the norm. When ethnic groups are near their primary settlements—French-Canadians in New England, Cubans in Miami, Cajuns in Louisiana, Mexican-Americans in the Southwest, native Americans on the reservations, Poles in Chicago, Jews and Italians in New York City—endogamous marriages are still common because most social relationships are confined to neighborhood, parish, synagogue, or parochial school. For the nation as a whole, however, intermarriage rates climbed rapidly in the late 1970s: nearly 70 percent for Irish and German Catholics, 50 percent for Poles, Czechs, and Italians, and 40 percent for French-Canadians. In 1940 more than 80 percent of Protestants, 84 percent of Roman Catholics, and 94 percent of Jews were marrying within those broad religious groupings, and some scholars were concluding that three melting pots—Protestant, Catholic, and Jewish—were emerging in the United States. But by the late 1970s nearly 40 percent of Jews and Roman Catholics were out-marrying. More acceptable than ever before, national origins and religious intermarriages have become a common part of American life and are the primary measure of assimilation.

And yet, four centuries into the American experience, the proverbial melting pot still seems far away. More than 60 percent of German-Americans today live in the German triangle and German belt of the North and Midwest; 75 percent of Jews are still in the Northeast; 67 percent of the Irish reside in northern cities; 80 percent of Italian-Americans remain in the northern and mid-Atlantic states; and 85 percent of the Poles and 75 percent of the other Slavic Catholics are still living in the urban neighborhoods of the mid-Atlantic and upper midwestern states. Ethnic holidays are still celebrated: St. Patrick's Day for the Irish, Columbus Day and Our Lady of Mt. Carmel for the Italians, Orange Day for Irish Protestants, Volkfest and Steuben Day for the Germans, Cinco de Mayo for the Mexicans, Midsummer for some Scandinavians, Kossuth Day for the Magyars, Pulaski Day or St. Stanislaus Day for the Poles, Mardi Gras for the Cajuns, New Year's for the Chinese and Vietnamese, Chrysanthemum Festivals or Doll Day for the Japanese, and Chanukah and Israeli Independence Day for the Jews.

Even the ethnic characteristics of certain disease patterns persist for a variety of genetic, cultural, and environmental reasons. Ashkenazic Jews have high incidences of Tay-Sachs disease, Niemann Pick disease,

Gaucher's disease, dysantonomia, and Bloom's syndrome. Sickle cell anemia most often strikes Afro-Americans. Greeks, Sicilians, and Mediterranean Arabs suffer from high rates of Cooley's anemia. Cystic fibrosis, skin cancer, and such skin disorders as psoriasis are usually confined to white Europeans. And phenylketonuria (PKU) seems to strike the Irish more frequently than other groups. Japanese-Americans have high rates of stomach cancer but very low rates of colon and rectal cancer. Jews, Poles, and Russians contract adult leukemia more frequently than most Americans, and Jewish women have inordinately high rates of breast cancer. Tuberculosis, of course, still afflicts poor people in America, especially blacks, Mexican-Americans, Puerto Ricans, Indians, and whites in Appalachia.

Ethnicity survives in America because all of its ingredients—color, nationality, religion, language, and class—persist to one degree or another. For those Americans who still experience some discrimination based on color—27 million blacks, 15 million Mexican-Americans, 2 million Asians, 3 million Puerto Ricans, 1.2 million Indians, and 1 million Cubans—ethnic identifications are strong and clear. The color line in America, so powerful throughout United States history, remains the most potent social force in the country, a fundamental means by which most Americans identify themselves and direct their community life. For blacks, Hispanics, and Asians, as well as for 175 million people of European descent, color is the critical key to social groupings.

Within these color lines, and despite the forces of assimilation, certain levels of nationality consciousness still survive. In varying degrees perhaps 34 million people claim a British heritage; 29 million a German heritage; 18 million an Irish heritage; 10 million an Italian heritage; 7 million a Scandinavian heritage; and 5 million a Cajun, French, or French-Canadian heritage. More than 6 million people are aware of their roots as American Jews; another 16 million as descendants of eastern European Catholics; and perhaps 4 million as children of Orthodox immigrants from eastern and southern Europe. In a total population of 220 million people, the United States may have more than 180 million people who are at least aware of their racial and nationality backgrounds.

The relationship between ethnicity and religion in the United States is as powerful today as it has been throughout American history. As sociologist Andrew Greeley has written, the United States is a denominationalist society for which religion has been a centrifugal rather than unifying force. The more than 6 million American Jews remain divided among the Reform, Conservative, Orthodox, Chassidic, and Sephardic traditions; more than 50 million Roman Catholics, though united in their devotion to Rome, are divided between the Latin and

Uniate traditions as well as by the folk elements of Irish, Slavic, Italian, and Hispanic culture; the 5 million people faithful to Eastern Orthodoxy are usually loyal to the Armenian, Syrian, Russian, or Greek tradition; and more than 150 million Protestants are divided by sectarian loyalties to the Baptist, Methodist, Episcopalian, Lutheran, Reformed, Presbyterian, Pentecostal, Congregational, and pietistic churches. To that group can be added several million Mormons, Seventh Day Adventists, Disciples of Christ, Jehovah's Witnesses, and Christian Scientists. Like no other society in human history, the United States is divided into hundreds of religious communities, each offering its members a sense of identity and belonging.

Though in a rapid state of decline, foreign languages still provide identity and community to many Americans. For Mexican-Americans, Puerto Ricans, and Cubans, Spanish still exists as the primary language for many and a secondary language to most. Italian is still widely spoken in New York City, Polish in Chicago, German in Milwaukee, French in Louisiana and upper New England, Chinese in San Francisco, New York, and Honolulu, and Japanese in San Francisco, Honolulu, and Los Angeles. And even where English has triumphed, distinctive accents characterize many groups and become a dimension of ethnic identity. The Irish brogue in places like New York or Boston is still clear, as is the drawl of the English and Scots-Irish in the South. Texmex and calo are powerful among Mexican-Americans, as is black English for many Afro-Americans. Distinctive phonologies still exist for the English spoken by Yankees in New England, Jews and Italians in New York City, Polynesians in Hawaii, and Cajuns in Louisiana. If not an overpowering badge of identity anymore, language still serves to unify groups of people.

Finally, class divisions divide America into distinctive communities. The upper classes with inherited wealth enjoy a sense of permanent security which liberates them from the fears and uncertainties of economic survival. Professional classes—physicians, dentists, lawyers, engineers, pharmacists, professors—enjoy unprecedented levels of material prosperity, even though inflation threatens that standard of living, and are highly committed to their occupations as part of their identities. The blue-collar Americans struggle to make ends meet and constantly worry about their economic future. And there is an underclass of chronic, ghetto poverty in urban centers and reservations where people suffer from a pathology of violence and depression bred from an environment of economic desperation. People in each of these groups feel a kinship with one another that serves to organize American society into yet another set of separate communities.

Social life in the United States revolves around these color, nationality, religious, language, and class values, creating a society of thousands of ethnic subgroups. And beneath conscious ethnicity lies the uncharted world of the unconscious; people who do not think about their roots may still exhibit behavior and values consistent with their ethnic background. These are generalizations, of course, and cannot be universally applied. Nevertheless, certain patterns persist. In Norwegian-American families husbands remain powerful and wives serve as silent supporters from whom dissent or rebellion is strongly discouraged. Italian-Americans still revere la famiglia as the only social institution to be trusted, and fathers still mete out discipline and mothers affection. In Ireland, where economic catastrophe destroyed or seriously weakened the male role as provider, mothers became dominant in family life; and although recent Irish-American progress has restored some authority to the father, the mother remains the emotional center of the family. Jewish parents still regard raising children as the purpose of marriage and family, and children are still imbued with the need to become well-educated, work hard, and succeed. And in Polish-American families fathers are still regarded with special affection by sons as well as daughters.

Other behavior patterns continue. French-Canadians in New England and Cajuns in Louisiana still nurture a powerful insularity toward outsiders, as do most Italian-Americans. Mexican-Americans and Puerto Ricans are still more attuned to the spiritual than to the material, and many are uneasy about the competitive individualism of American life. Most Indians still live in a world which moves to the rhythm of nature and tribal authority. Many Italian-Americans retain the fatalistic world view of the Mezzogiorno, and many Irish-Americans still have the pessimistic outlook of the Old World. Irish-American Catholicism retains its legalistic values while Latin Catholicism remains more cultural than institutional. Irish Catholics are still among the most politically active of American ethnic groups; and Episcopalians, Methodists, and Presbyterians are the most likely to be engaged in civil activities. German-Americans place great value on order, efficiency, and cleanliness. Scandinavian and German Lutherans tend to be more closely attached to mothers than fathers in family life. Ethnicity survives in America; and even as the forces of assimilation grow stronger in the future, ethnic family values and behavioral patterns, as well as loyalties based on color, nationality, religion, accent and language, and class, will continue to be expressed.

A multitude of overt activities in the late 1970s exposed the degree to which American life revolved around ethnic themes. One was the Wampanoag Indians' claim in 1977 to parts of Cape Cod in Massachusetts, and the Passamaquoddies' claim to most of Maine. Reminiscent of the tong wars of earlier years, San Francisco's Chinatown is divided by gang wars that have resulted in more than forty murders since 1970. Yet when police try to investigate, Chinatown folds into its cocoon of isolation. When President Jimmy Carter decided, in the name of detente, to return the crown of St. Stephen—a thousand-year-old relic symbolic of Hungarian independence—to the government of Hungary, thousands of Magyar-Americans protested. At the 1977 convention of the Orthodox Church in America, a major split appeared between the older children of immigrants who insist on retaining the Old Slavonic liturgies and younger members eager for the transition to English. The National Committee for the Freedom of Puerto Rican Nationalist Prisoners occupied the Statue of Liberty in 1977 and draped the Puerto Rican national flag from her crown; fifteen thousand Cubans marched in Miami in 1978 to protest any attempts to normalize American diplomatic relations with Fidel Castro; and the National Conference of Chicanos and Latinos called on President Carter in 1977 and 1978 to extend unconditional amnesty to all illegal aliens. The Ku Klux Klan patrolled the Mexican border in 1978 trying to capture illegal aliens, and Brown Berets from the Mexican-American community patrolled the border looking for Klansmen.

Jews are concerned about relations between the United States and Israel; Syrian-Americans are pleased about improving relations between the United States and the Arab world, but are disturbed about continued political instability in the Middle East. Croatian-American nationals are campaigning for the separation of Croatia from Yugoslavia, and French-Canadian Americans rejoice at the new political power of French separatists in Quebec. Genealogical libraries are crowded with people searching out their ancestors; family history courses are among the most popular electives in history departments across the country; and airline companies are launching vigorous advertising campaigns urging ethnic Americans to visit the Old World homes of their ancestors.

Today, more than 370 years after those first English colonists at Jamestown confronted members of the Powhatan Confederacy, ethnicity remains the dominant force in American social life; the melting pot is still a dream, not a reality; and cultural pluralism is the most realistic approach to ethnic diversity. Driven by persecution or economic decline, transported as slaves, or attracted by religious toleration, political freedom, and economic opportunity, millions of people have pursued their dreams here in the New World. And although United States history is riddled with examples of racism, discrimination, and bitter competition, most of those millions and their descendants found that dream, or at least enough of it to make the pursuit worthwhile.

SUGGESTED READINGS

Alba, Richard. "Social Assimilation Among American Catholic National-Origins Groups." *American Sociological Review*, 41 (December 1976), 1030–1046.

Anderson, Charles. *White Protestant Americans: From National Origins to Religious Groups*. Englewood Cliffs, N.J.: 1970.

Barron, Milton L. *The Blending Americans*. New York: 1972.

Calleo, David P., and Rowland, Benjamin M. *America and the World Political Economy*. New York: 1973.

Divine, Robert A. *American Immigration Policy, 1924–1952*. New York: 1957.

Galbraith, John Kenneth. *The Affluent Society*. Boston: 1952.

————. *The New Industrial State*. New York: 1967.

Gans, Herbert J. *The Levittowners*. New York: 1967.

Greeley, Andrew M. *The Denominational Society: A Sociological Approach to Religion in America*. Glenview, Ill.: 1972.

Halberstam, David. *The Best and the Brightest*. New York: 1972.

Herberg, Will. *Protestant-Catholic-Jew: An Essay in American Religious Sociology*. New York: 1955.

Horowitz, David. *The Free World Colossus*. New York: 1971.

Kendrick, Alexander. *The Wound Within: America in the Vietnam Years, 1945–1974*. Boston: 1974.

LaFeber, Walter. *America, Russia and the Cold War*. New York: 1972.

Leuchtenburg, William E. *A Troubled Feast: American Society Since 1945*. New York: 1970.

Levy, Mark R., and Kramer, Michael S. *The Ethnic Factor: How America's Minorities Decide Elections*. New York: 1972.

Litt, Edgar. *Ethnic Politics in America*. Glenview, Ill.: 1970.

Markowitz, Norman D. *The Rise and Fall of the People's Century*. New York: 1973.

Mindel, Charles H., and Habenstein, Robert W., eds. *Ethnic Families in America*. New York: 1976.

Reich, Charles. *The Greening of America*. New York: 1970.

Rosenberg, Norman, Rosenberg, Emily S., and Moore, James R. *In Our Times: America Since World War II*. Englewood Cliffs, N.J.: 1976.

Roszak, Theodore. *The Making of a Counter-Culture*. New York: 1969.

Vecoli, Rudolph J. "European Americans: From Immigrants to Ethnics." In William H. Cartwright and Richard L. Watson, Jr. *The Reinterpretation of American History and Culture*. Washington, D.C.: 1973.

White, Theodore S. *Breach of Faith: The Fall of Richard Nixon*. New York: 1976.

Index

i